Encyclopedia of Latin American Popular Music

Advisory Board

Encyclopedia of Latin American Popular Music

George Torres,
Editor

GREENWOOD

AN IMPRINT OF ABC-CLIO, LLC
Santa Barbara, California • Denver, Colorado • Oxford, England

Library of Congress Cataloging-in-Publication Data

Encyclopedia of Latin American popular music / George Torres, editor.
     pages cm
  Includes bibliographical references and index.
  ISBN 978-0-313-34031-4 (hardcopy : alk. paper)—ISBN 978-0-313-08794-3 (ebook)
  1. Popular music—Latin America—Encyclopedias. 2. Musical instruments—Latin
America—Encyclopedias. 3. Musicians—Latin America—Biography. I. Torres,
George, 1958–, editor.
  ML101.L38E53   2013
  781.64098'03—dc23   2012015166

ISBN: 978-0-313-34031-4
EISBN: 978-0-313-08794-3

17 16 15 14 13   1 2 3 4 5

This book is also available on the World Wide Web as an eBook.
Visit www.abc-clio.com for details.

Greenwood
An Imprint of ABC-CLIO, LLC

ABC-CLIO, LLC
130 Cremona Drive, P.O. Box 1911
Santa Barbara, California 93116–1911

This book is printed on acid-free paper ∞
Manufactured in the United States of America

Contents

Alphabetical List of Entries

Topical List of Entries

Countries

Argentina
Bolivia
Brazil
Chile
Colombia
Costa Rica
Cuba
Dominican Republic
Ecuador
El Salvador
French Guiana
Guatemala
Haiti
Honduras
Martinique and Guadeloupe
Mexico
Nicaragua
Panama
Paraguay
Peru
Puerto Rico
Saint Lucia
United States
Uruguay
Venezuela

Genres/Ensembles

Afro
Afro-Dominican Fusion Music
Axé Music
Bachata
Baião
Balada
Bambuco
Banda
Baquiné
Batucada
Biguine
Bloco Afro
Bolero
Bomba
Boogaloo
Bossa Nova
Calypso
Canción Romántica
Chacarera
Cha-Cha-Chá
Changüí
Charanga
Chicano Rock
Chicha
Choro
Conga
Conjunto
Conjunto Cubano
Contradanza
Corrido
Cuarteto
Cuarteto (Argentina)

Preface

This book began as a request from Greenwood Press/ABC-CLIO to edit an encyclopedia of Latin music. The publisher had recently released several successful reference works on related subjects, most notably a two-volume set entitled *Encyclopedia of Latino Popular Culture* (2004), and so on the heels of the success of that volume, this book was originally envisioned. The request was for an encyclopedia that would locate and define important concepts and achievements related to music and Latin America. In order to provide focus and make the work manageable, the publisher and I agreed that the work would be an encyclopedia of Latin American popular music that had, as its core, country profiles, concepts, genres, instruments, and themes important to Latin American music. This was in part due to the abundant coverage of Latin American folk music in current scholarship, and also due to the many studies that have examined art music in colonial and postcolonial Latin America. We also agreed to include sidebars of significant performers to highlight contributions to related subjects.

Along with the advisory board and the 57 contributors who took part in this volume, there are others who provided exceptional help in making this text possible. Kristi Ward was the original Greenwood editor who shaped this work in its genesis and early development, while George Butler took over the project from Kristi for the second phase of the enterprise. Both Kristi and George provided invaluable guidance and feedback. Thanks also to Michelle Scott and Jane Glenn at ABC-CLIO for their help with production. The project was carried out in the Music Department at Lafayette College, and I am especially thankful to Provost Wendy Hill and the Academic Research Committee for their very generous support of this project. I received much support, criticism, and feedback from colleagues at Lafayette College including J. Larry Stockton, Anthony Cummings, and Jennifer Kelly from Music, as well as Denise Galarza-Sepúlveda, Michael Jordan, and Juan Rojo from Latin American Studies. Lafayette research assistants Ray Epstein, Caitlin Lowery, and Tracy McFarlan were critical to the organization, research, typing, and editing of the work. Karalyn Enz provided important editing at a vital point in the work's development. Without them, this encyclopedia would not have seen the light of day. Special thanks are due to Paul Austerlitz, Thomas Rohde, Rebecca Stuhr, and Ramón Versage Agudelo, all of whom took a special interest in this project. Also very generous with their time and talent were Bonnie Robbins, Cindy Liparini, Gloria Tackas, and Amy Gordon, all of whom supplied much technical and administrative support. The Library at Lafayette College provided me with just about everything that was needed to complete this project, and a special thanks goes to Librarian Neil McElroy and his exemplary crew of talented staff for their assistance. Wise counsel also came from Darren Abouyon, Katherine Restuccia, Robert West, Georgina Rizk, and Maria Christensen. Raoul P. Torres and Georgina Torres, besides being supportive parents, provided help with many translations from Spanish to English. My son and daughter, Augustine and Genevieve, have been supportive in ways they could never have imagined. I offer my greatest thanks to Marguerite Nicosia Torres, who was highly influential in the realization of this work.

Introduction

For many years, the popularity of Latin American music as a topic of interest among English readers has greatly increased. This interest reflects a rise in the number of recordings and availability of Latin American music. The academic field of ethnomusicology has also produced many important texts that have done much to spark interest in Latin American music. And finally, the U.S. population has shown a great increase in the demographic fact that more and more Latinos in the United States participate in music making at various levels. Because of this level of high interest, the present work addresses the need for an English language encyclopedia of Latin American popular music. But what does it mean to say Latin American popular music? Both of the terms require a bit of qualification in order to gain an understanding of the intended scope of this encyclopedia.

Latin America

Traditionally, the term Latin America refers to both the geographical region that is south of the U.S. border and countries where the main language is Spanish and Portuguese. Geographically, this would include Mexico, Central America, the Caribbean, and South America. Variably, scholars employ a definition of Latin America that includes the Francophone West Indies where French and/or *Creole* languages are spoken. This provides a more literal interpretation of the term *Latin American*, as these are the countries whose main languages are derived from Latin. Less frequently, a more broad-minded and culturally inclusive definition refers to Latin America as all of the countries south of the United States, which includes the English-speaking countries. This is especially useful when looking at English-speaking countries like Dominica, whose colonial history shows an early occupation by France, but where a part of the population still speaks Antillean *Creole*.

One of the challenges in defining Latin America is that ultimately, we must consider the influence of the Latin American diaspora, most notably, the United States. Indeed, much of what we consider to be so-called Latin music comes from the United States, including *salsa,* Latin jazz, and Latin rock. Thus, a geographic, political, cultural, or linguistic definition will not address all of the areas that are important for the current study. Instead, this encyclopedia, by necessity, must have a broader view of Latin America in order to include the cultural contributions from United States where the Latin American population, which descended from Latin America, has influenced the subject of Latin American popular music. Therefore, for the purposes of this encyclopedia, Latin America is defined as the Spanish-, Portuguese-, and French-speaking countries of the Western Hemisphere south of the United States. Nevertheless, because of the transnational and reciprocal nature of popular music, this work also includes Latin American styles that have their origins in the United States, such as *salsa* and Latin jazz.

The English-speaking Caribbean is not included in the general working definition of Latin America in this encyclopedia for several reasons. In doing so, this text includes countries whose principal language is descended from Latin, thus staying in line with a standard definition of the region. Secondly, a recent Greenwood publication, the comprehensive encyclopedia *Caribbean Popular Music: An Encyclopedia of Reggae, Mento, Ska, Rock Steady, and Dancehall*, edited by David V. Moskowitz, allows this work to effectively complement the present encyclopedia. Lastly, some genres and performers from the English-speaking Caribbean who are important to the broader context of Latin American popular music are included to the extent that they are influential to the broader region. Thus, topics such as *calypso* and *reggae* are included because of their popularity and performance within Latin American countries.

Popular Music

The term popular music is much how Robert Cantrick referred to it as something that "Everyone talks about . . . but no one knows what it is." The handle popular music is problematic in that definitions of the term popular may bring value judgments, often dogmatic in nature, that provide little or no critical criteria in forming the definitions. This is due not only to the tacit assumptions that we may bring to the experience (discussion), but also to the ways in which we *choose* to examine popular music based on categorical declarations. Learned discussion on the distinctions between the three broad categories of folk, art (in favor of the problematic term classical), and popular music enhance our understanding of these differentiations, especially when the contexts of music making come into play. Nevertheless, even when given a set of criteria as a basis for the current discussion, there will be some contestation over whether some song or piece is indeed *popular*. In the case of Latin America, a significant challenge lies in distinguishing between folk and popular music. For example, does the *son jaliscence,* the repertoire that gave birth to the *mariachi* ensembles from Western Mexico, fall under a folk tradition or is it more of a popular music tradition? While it may be determined that it belongs to the former, its appropriation by commercial *mariachi* ensembles, which have become an international symbol for Mexican culture through mass media, place its performance by those ensembles in the realm of popular music.

Distinguishing whether a repertoire, or song from a particular repertoire, is *popular* while another may not be should not be assessed by value judgments based on how a piece sounds, or whether there are aspects of the material culture of that repertoire that make it appear folkloric. Instead, it is the degree to which they display their *popular-ness* based on more neutral criteria (e.g., what the music sounds like) that will determine their function in the culture. This last point brings to mind the idea that popular music is related to popular culture and all of the varieties of mass media that are related to popular culture. Proceeding from a methodology first introduced by Booth and Kuhn, Tracy McFarlan's entry on "Folk, Art, and Popular Music" in this encyclopedia demonstrates the importance of how musics are created, performed, and distributed. It provides a more neutral level of assessment when considering how some music might belong more to a popular music system than others. For the purposes of this encyclopedia, a popular music system shows a transmission of the repertoire leaving its home turf, through mass media dissemination to cross over other boundaries, and that economically, the repertoire is disseminated through a system of indirect patronage. The benefit of looking at the music in this way is that we will not be comparing folk sounding vs. urban sounding music. Indeed, according to the criteria that McFarlan contextualizes, the folk-inspired music of Intilli Mani will be considered popular music because of its global dissemination, while the music of the Panamanian *tamborito,* which is hugely *popular* throughout that country, might remain under the realm of folkloric music.

If transmission and economic factors play heavily in the classification of folk and popular music, then there should be some influences on the music traditionally produced by a system of direct patronage, that is, art music. For the purposes of this study, discussions of art music happen or take place only when those repertories are connected to popular musics. For example, because of its connection to popular music, the music of Argentine composer Astor Piazzolla is included in the appropriate entries on *tango* and Argentina. On the other hand, the music of Alberto Ginastera, while influenced by native music, is not covered, due to Ginastera's lack of significant ties to popular music.

The scope of the encyclopedia is limited to countries, genres, instruments, and other related nonbiographical topics. While the addition of popular artists would enhance the discussion of Latin American popular music, to do so in a one-volume encyclopedia would have limited the content of those other topics mentioned above. Additionally, the inclusion of contemporary popular artists would possibly date the relevancy of the work. It is safe to assume that the music of Tito Puente will be as relevant in 10 years as it is today, but it may not be as clear as to what the relevance of currently popular Jennifer Lopez may be in 10 years. We can certainly see what the difference of 10 years has done to the career of, for example, Ricky Martin, whose commercial successes in the late 1990s would have seemed to have cemented his longevity as a significant contributor to Latin American popular music for years to come. Nevertheless, in an effort to enrich the discussion of selected topics, the present work includes short, relevant sidebars on representative artists, both soloists and ensemble performers, in an effort to enrich the understanding of certain repertories. A further discussion on these sidebars in included in the section titled "How to Use This Encyclopedia."

The main entries in this encyclopedia are organized alphabetically by topic. Certain topics are highlighted by a sidebar on a particular performer, composer, or group, which is meant to highlight the topic by providing information on related practitioners. The sidebars are discussed below. There is also a chronology of Latin American popular music included here that is intended to give a broad sequence of significant events in their order of occurrence since the time of the Spanish encounter. The encyclopedia also includes two entry listings, one alphabetical and one topical, which provide a quick reference to the entries and sidebars.

Popular Music Resources

This encyclopedia provides a broad collection of entries in one volume for the interested student of Latin American popular music. As such, it is by design a broadly conceived work, and there is no attempt to be either exhaustive or comprehensive in its scope. Indeed, this work has relied on many authors whose research acknowledges some of the more comprehensive studies of Latin American music, broadly defined. The following will provide a short description of some of the more comprehensive and foundational studies of Latin American music that will be of use to the student of Latin American music who wishes to pursue further study on the subject.

Dale A. Olsen and Daniel E. Sheehy, editors of *The Garland Encyclopedia of World Music*, Volume 2, *South America, Mexico, Central America, and the Caribbean*, offer one of the few truly comprehensive and scholarly studies of Latin American music. The study proceeds from an ethnomusicological method, and rather than being an encyclopedia with alphabetical subject entries, the *Garland Encyclopedia* consists mostly of articles grouped by country of origin. Within each country's article are discussions of folk, popular, and art music.

Malena Kuss, Professor Emeritus of Music at the University of North Texas, is presently at work on a four-volume reference work entitled *Music in Latin America and the Caribbean: An Encyclopedic History,* to be published by University of Texas Press. Currently, only the first two volumes are available: Volume 1: *Performing Beliefs: Indigenous Peoples of South America, Central America, and Mexico* (2004) and Volume 2: *Performing the Caribbean Experience* (2007). Volume 4, *Urban Popular Musics of the New World,* will be a collection of essays that focuses on the transnational nature of Latin American popular musics. This work presents comprehensive information through its scholarly essays.

Aside from the larger more comprehensive studies of music in Latin America, there are also a handful of specialized studies that take up the subject of popular music through particular regional studies. Of special note is Kenneth M. Bilby, Michael D. Largey, and Peter Manuel's *Caribbean Currents*, which looks at the popular music in the Caribbean. Besides being a useful panorama of Caribbean popular music, there is much information on the transnational nature of Caribbean music, and the revised and expanded version in 2006 has taken into account more recent trends in the region, such as *timba* and *reggaetón.* On the subject of Brazilian popular music, curious readers would do well to consult Charles Perrone's *Brazilian Popular Music and Globalization,* which is a collection of important essays that provides a broad view of Brazilian popular music. Ned Sublette's book *Cuba and Its Music* takes on not only the importance of Cuban popular music, but also examines the transnational and cross-cultural effects of Cuban music's influence on popular musics across Latin America and the United States. On this last subject, I must mention the highly innovative and strongly influential book by John Storm Roberts, *The Latin Tinge,* as a required reading for anyone interested in the influence of Latin American music on the United States.

How to Use This Encyclopedia

For the benefit of multiple and varied forms of accessibility, the following will give some ideas as to how readers may think about using the material in this encyclopedia. In many ways, an encyclopedia brings together a collection of ideas from many different scholars and perspectives. Although the format is largely alphabetical, and seemingly linear in its presentation, the material is connected through a variety of links that make reference to other entries and resources in the text. For example, the article on *mambo* by Ramón Versage Agudelo also points (through cross-references) to related studies in locales such as Cuba and the United States, related genres such as *danzón* and *conjunto,* and related sidebars on Arsenio Rodriguez, Dámaso Pérez Prado, and Tito Puente. In the end, the reader will find many related articles that enrich one's understanding of the genre by examining the other related entries. Additionally, such an approach also allows for an exploration of Latin American popular music that goes beyond the definition of one item.

Whether beginning with the alphabetical entries, either by looking in the lists of entries by topic or by beginning with the index at the back of the work, the reader will find that this encyclopedia will serve as a preliminary reference on the most common topics in Latin American popular music. Additionally, a scholar wishing to find the essential literature on a particular area of study should consult the reading lists for important writing on the subject.

Lastly, the chronologies and sidebars, while there primarily to accent the main text, can be used as an introductory reference to some of the significant practitioners within the area of Latin American popular music.

Entries

The entries include a heading, main body, and a further reading list. Their placement in the document is alphabetical by heading, and where appropriate, in the original language, without translation, unless the translation is a common English equivalent. For example, *claves* remains in Spanish whereas guitar is listed under the English rather than the Spanish *guitarra*. Foreign words, albums, newspapers, films, TV programs, musicals, operas, and *zarzuelas* are italicized. Song titles and portions of larger works are in quotations.

The entry headings are in boldface without italics. Cross-referenced entries are also in boldface. The entries begin with a brief and clear identification of the topic that provides a quick summary for that entry. The size of the entries ranges from 200 words to about 2,500 words, depending on the content. The choice of entry size was decided in consultation with the authors and the advisory board. While it is certainly true that some entries merit more space than others, the challenge in deciding which entries would be larger is a matter of preference among those working on the encyclopedia. There were targeted entry sizes that increased or decreased in their actual length in the completed writing. That is, in some cases a projected 1,250-word entry was expanded to closer to 2,000 words, while in some cases the same projected size entry was left at only 850 words. For those entries that the reader may feel warrant a longer treatment, it is my sincere hope that the quality of the writing, rather than quantity, will prove to be more important to the reader in the end.

In general, the entries in this encyclopedia set out to convey the generally accepted viewpoints on the subjects, and there has been an effort to keep the material free of special considerations or pleading on the part of the authors, as generally, this sort of reference work is not the locus for the presentation of novel ideas or original theses.

Every entry in the encyclopedia presents at least one reference for further reading. Each of these bibliographies presents sources that would lead readers to additional information on the topics. They provide a next step for accessible investigation, and as such, they were chosen as much for their authority as for their availability. For that reason, there are few if any unpublished dissertations or theses in the bibliographies, usually only included when they represent the only significant research on the subject. Additionally, every effort was made to include, where appropriate, English language sources. In some cases, a World Wide Web resource is included. No attempt has been made to provide exhaustive or comprehensive coverage in these lists. Instead, they should be considered a starting point for further investigations. A selected, general bibliography at the end of the book directs users to broad print and electronic resources suitable for student research.

Sidebars

The sidebars that are included in this encyclopedia provide examples of significant practitioners of their art. It was never intended that the encyclopedia provide a comprehensive biographical component. Thus, there may appear to be gaps in the coverage of significant performers. Inevitably one may ask why one performer was chosen over another to represent a particular genre or musical style. There is no doubt that almost any of the chosen sidebar entries may have been replaced by another equally qualified representative. What seemed important for this study was to provide illustrative examples, by way of these sidebars, of representative practitioners. Thus they are not a declaration of the most important performers, composers, or artists. A suggestion for further reading is provided for each sidebar entry.

Chronology

In order to provide a broader context concerning popular music in Latin America, a chronology of events related to popular music in Latin America is provided before the main body of entries. There was no attempt at providing a comprehensive coverage of musical events; rather, the aim of the chronology is to place certain significant events within the context of a wider view of events in order to recognize larger relationships between related events and achievements in Latin American popular music.

Lists and Indexes

There are several lists in the front matter that will aid in the accessing of information contained in the encyclopedia. The first is an alphabetical list of the entries that form the main body of the text. There is an additional list of entries grouped under the following broad categories: Countries, Genres and Ensembles, Concepts and Terminologies, and Instruments. There is also a list of the sidebars that accompany some of the entries. Lastly, there is an index of names and subjects at the end of the text that provide references to where in the encyclopedia these terms are located.

Further Reading

Appleby, David. "Folk, Popular, and Art Music." *The Music of Brazil,* 94–115. Austin: University of Texas Press, 1989.

Behague, Gerard. "Music, c. 1920–c. 1980." In *A Cultural History of Latin America: Literature, Music and the Visual Arts in the 19th and 20th Centuries,* edited by Leslie Bethell, 311–67. New York: Cambridge University Press, 1998.

Bilby, Kenneth M, Michael D. Largey, and Peter Manuel. *Caribbean Currents: Caribbean Music from Rumba to Reggae.* Philadelphia: Temple University Press, 2006.

Booth, Gregory, and Terry Lee Kuhn. "Economic and Transmission Factors as Essential Element in the Definition of Folk, Art, and Pop Music." *The Musical Quarterly* 74 (1990): 411–38.

Colburn, Forrest D. *Latin America at the End of Politics.* Princeton: Princeton University Press, 2002.

Hamm, Charles. "Popular Music." *The New Harvard Dictionary of Music,* edited by Don Michael Randel, 646–49. Cambridge: Belknap Press, 1986.

Kuss, Malena. *Music in Latin America and the Caribbean: An Encyclopedic History.* Austin: University of Texas Press, 2004. Currently, only the first two volumes are available: Volume 1: *Performing Beliefs: Indigenous Peoples of South America, Central America, and Mexico* (2004) and Volume 2: *Performing the Caribbean Experience.*

Manuel, Peter. "Perspectives on the Study of Non-Western Popular Musics." *Popular Musics of the Non-Western World: An Introductory Survey.* New York: Oxford University Press, 1998.

Moskowitz, David V. *Caribbean Popular Music: An Encyclopedia of Reggae, Mento, Ska, Rock Steady, and Dancehall.* Westport, CT: Greenwood Press, 2006.

Nettl, Bruno. "Folk Music." *The New Harvard Dictionary of Music,* edited by Don Michael Randel, 315–19. Cambridge: Belknap Press, 1986.

Olsen, Dale A. and Daniel E. Sheehy, eds. *The Garland Encyclopedia of World Music, Volume 2: South America, Mexico, Central America, and the Caribbean.* New York and London: Garland, 1998.

Perrone, Charles A. and Christopher Dunn, eds. *Brazilian Popular Music and Globalization.* New York: Routledge, 2002.

Roberts, John Storm. *The Latin Tinge: The Impact of Latin American Music on the United States.* 2nd ed. New York: Oxford University Press, 1999.

Shaw, Lisa, and Stephanie Dennison. "Introduction: Defining the Popular in the Latin American Context." *Pop Culture Latin America!: Media, Arts, And Lifestyle,* 1–7. Santa Barbara: ABC-CLIO, 2005.

Sublette, Ned. *Cuba and Its Music: From the First Drums to the Mambo.* Chicago: Chicago Review Press, 2004.

Whitehead, Laurence. *Latin America: A New Interpretation.* New York: Palgrave Macmillan, 2006.

Chronology of Latin American Popular Music

The following chronology outlines some of the significant achievements in Latin American popular music. The chronology begins with the introduction of European culture in the Americas, and as such does not attempt to account for a chronology of music in the Americas before the arrival of the Europeans. During much of the colonial period, there is scant information regarding popular music outside of the strongly dominant European occupation. The Haitian Revolution (1794–1804) saw a mixing of classes and cultural groups, which led to a creolization of European music. This freedom allowed also for a migration of cultural groups across borders that resulted in cultural hybridizations through music. Hence, the period after the first quarter of the 19th century shows the first strong wave of popular music in Latin America. Throughout much of the chronology, the major Latin American centers (Mexico City, Havana, Rio de Janeiro, and Buenos Aires) emerge as the source for much of the popular music. Specific dates of events are provided when appropriate while references to decades and centuries may be more appropriate for historical events that occurred over a broader range of dates.

1492	Christopher Columbus arrives in Latin America, which marks the beginning of a fusion of indigenous Latin American and European cultures, a hallmark of Latin American popular music.
1550s	The African slave trade begins. Traditional African music that the slaves brought with them to the New World becomes an important underlying component of Latin American music that is still incorporated into the rhythms, style, and instrumentation of popular music today.
late 1700s	The *contredanse* and the *quadrille,* popular European styles of song and dance, are introduced to Latin America but enjoyed solely by the elites. Over time, these dances became creolized to create authentically Latin American genres of music and dance including *contradanzas, habaneras* and *danzones.*

1800s
The 1800s through the 1820s is a time period characterized by the push for freedom on the part of many Latin American colonies who achieve their independence such as Haiti (1804), Brazil (1815), and Mexico (1821). Freedom leads to the emancipation of slaves and a mixing of races, cultures, and styles of music that had historically been separated by the structure of slavery.

The *corrido* becomes a distinctly Mexican style of narrative song used to tell stories of national or local interest during the Mexican struggle for independence.

1840s
Military-style wind bands become popular across Latin America and spread traditional European song and dance styles that were previously limited to the elites to urban working classes, smaller towns, and rural areas, many of which formed their own municipal bands.

1860s
German immigration to Latin American countries such as Mexico and Argentina introduces new dance forms like the polka and instruments such as the accordion.

1870s
The Brazilian *choro* develops as musicians, long dominated by European ideas, strove to find their own artistic style strongly influenced by nationalistic sentiments. The popularity of the Brazilian *choro* continues into its golden age in the 1920s.

1880s
The *habanera* rhythm is exported from Cuba and like other Latin American dances it was originally derived from the European *contradanse.*

1897
Rosendo Mendizábal's *El entrerriano* (the man from Entre Ríos Province) becomes the first published *tango.* In the beginning of the 1900s the *tango* reaches an increasingly wider audience and, due to its growing popularity, 20 years later Carlos Gardel makes the first recording of a *tango* in 1917.

1898
Gaspar Vargas forms the musical group Mariachi Vargas. Through the use of the *son jaliciense* Mariachi Vargas demonstrates the professionalism and changes in instrumentation that would come to characterize the modern *mariachi.* In 1907 the first known phonographic recordings of *mariachi* music are made.

1917
"Pelo telephone," considered to be the first Brazilian *samba,* is recorded. *Samba* would become the most important Brazilian popular music genre, closely associated with the Brazilian Carnival even to this day. In 1928 the first *escola de samba* is formed in Brazil and in 1932 the first *samba* competition takes place during Carnival.

1927   Rita Montaner records "El Manisero" ("The Peanut Vendor") by Cuban composer Moises Simone, which becomes enormously popular leading to the *rhumba* fad in the United States and Europe.

1930s   With the advent of radio, music is spread throughout Latin America like never before. In 1930 Emilio Azcarraga establishes Radio XET in Monterrey, Mexico, and Radio XEW in Mexico City. Over time, XEW becomes the most influential radio station in Mexico.

1933   President Fanklin Delano Roosevelt establishes the Good Neighbor Policy, which initiates an era of unprecedented cultural exchange between the United States and Latin America.

1935   Narciso Martínez makes the first commercial recording of Tex-Mex music with his piece "El Huracán del Valle."

1936   *Merengue* is declared the national music of the Dominican Republic.

       Radio Nacional is established in Brazil. While it is used by Getúlio Dornelles Vargas, dictator of Estado Novo, to spread government propaganda, ample funding is also allotted to popular music. In the 1940s and 1950s *Radio Nacional* is one of the most listened to radio stations.

1940s   The 1940s marks the beginning of a widespread fusion of North American and Latin American popular music as a result of immigration and mass communication. New genres of music develop and become popular intersecting with styles of traditional music. Big Bands begin to incorporate Afro-Cuban rhythms and sounds into their arrangements and jazz musicians start to collaborate with Latin American musicians that immigrate to the United States, such as Machito.

       Brazilian *baião* achieves prominence in the popular music scene through singer-accordionist Luiz Gonzaga.

1943   "Tanga" written by Mario Bauza and performed by Machito and his orchestra is considered to be the first Latin jazz composition. Further collaborations with Dizzie Gillespie, Stan Kenton, and Charlie Parker lay the foundation for the Latin jazz movement.

1944   Trío Los Panchos has its first concert in the Teatro Hispano in New York city establishing the genre *trío romántico* and internationalizing the *bolero* as a popular song.

1947   Dizzy Gillespie and Afro-Cuban *conga* player Chano Pozo compose the influential "Manteca."

1950s   The 1950s is characterized by innovations in popular music and the rising popularity of rock 'n' roll all over the world. It was in this decade that Luiz Gonzaga develops the *trio nordestino,* Pérez Prado writes the first *mambo,* and *bossa nova* evolves in Brazil among other new musical genres.

Cumbia, a dance developed on Colombia's Atlantic coast during the colonial period, spreads throughout South and Central America and is adopted and transformed in Mexico, El Salvador, and Nicaragua in to the 1960s.

1954   Raphael Cortijo forms his group, Cortijo y su Combo, which incorporates the Puerto Rican folkloric traditions of *bomba* and *plena* into popular music.

1955   The *cha-cha-chá* is introduced in Cuba by director Enrico Jorrín. The first piece in the *cha-cha-chá* genre is "La engañadora," composed by Jorrín sometime between 1949 and 1953, but, at the time, it was registered as *mambo-rumba.*

1956   The first jam session to be known as *descarga* takes place in Cuba with singer Francisco Fellove. His recordings "Descarga Caliente" and "Cimmarron" are taken from that first session and sell over one million copies.

1958   Vinicius de Moraes and Antonio Carlos Jobim release the influential *bossa nova* recording "Chega de Saudade." A year later, the movie *Black Orpheus* is released with music composed by Jobim, which makes his music internationally popular.

1959   Fidel Castro comes to power in Cuba initiating the exodus of many artists from Cuba. The United States, in response, cuts ties with Cuba ending the long standing reciprocal popular music exchange.

1960s   As a result of the civil rights movement, a strong Latino identity consciousness develops in the United States as musicians try to reconnect with their roots in Latin America.

In response to the military dictatorships that arise in South America in the 1960s, Latin Americans begin to use music as a form of protest. *Nueva canción chilena,* for example, begins to evolve with artists like Violeta Parra and Atahualpa Yupanqui who try to popularize folkloric music in the face of oppression. Nicaraguan guerrillas organize the Sandinista National Liberation Front (FSLN) with protest music as a means of communication.

Musica Popular Brazilia (MPB) is established in Brazil to promote Brazilian popular music on a national scale. Charlie Byrd and Stan Getz organize a concert at Carnegie Hall featuring Brazilian

	musicians in 1962, which leads to the popularity of Brazilian musicians like João Gilberto and vocalist Astrid Gilberto.
1963	Antonio Carlos Jobim, João Gilberto and Stan Getz collaborate on the recording *Getz/Gilberto*. It receives four Grammy Awards in 1964 and is the best-selling jazz album of all time, a testament to the popularity of the combination of Latin American music and jazz.
1964	Johnny Pacheco and Jerry Masucci form Fania Records in New York city. Fania Records helps to circulate Latin music, especially *salsa* developed by Puerto Ricans living in New York in the 1970s.
1970s	The 1970s is marked by a widespread black consciousness movement, which results in the formation of *bloco afro* (a type of Carnival organization) and the development of *axé* music in Salvador da Bahia in northeast Brazil, the center of Afro-Brazilian culture. Hip-hop also evolves as a musical genre in the South Bronx that draws on black consciousness for inspiration to become part of the Latin American popular music scene by the 1980s.
1973	*Nueva trova* is recognized officially by the Cuban government as a political movement.
1975	Eddie Palmeri is awarded the first Best Latin Recording award at the 18th Annual Grammy Awards for his album *Sun of Latin Music,* evidence of the popularity of the integration of Latin American music into mainstream popular music.
1980s	Latin-influenced *reggae* styles (including *reggaespañol, reggae resistencia,* and *reggaetón*) begin to emerge and become popular on the international music scene. Gilberto Gil's Portuguese version of Bob Marley's "No Woman No Cry," "Não Chore Mais" ("Don't Cry Anymore"), introduces *reggae* to Brazil.
1987	*Boukman Eksperyans,* a large collective of musicians and dancers, forms in Port-au-Prince, Haiti. They play a style of music that combines elements of traditional Haitian music with rock 'n' roll.
1990s	Latin American popular music undergoes another series of transformations due to the influence of new, more modern genres such as rap, hip-hop, electronica, and techno. *Timba,* for example, emerges in Cuba as an eclectic fusion of *son* and *rumba* with elements of jazz, funk and rap. It becomes internationally popular with bands such as Los Van Van.
	Bachata, from the Dominican Republic, gains international popularity. While it actually developed in the 1960s, *bachata* was highly marginalized and virtually unknown internationally until the 1990s.

1998   The *Buena Vista Social Club* documentary and recording is made by Cuban musician Juan de Marcos González, American guitarist Ry Cooder, and film director Wim Wenders.

2000s   The Latin Academy of Recording Arts and Sciences is established and in 2000 the first Latin Grammy Awards are held, evidence of the cohesiveness of Latin American popular music.

Puerto Rican rapper Daddy Yankee combines many genres growing in popularity in the 1990s (such as rap, hip-hop, rhythm and blues, funk, and electronica) into his 2004 hit "Gasolina," which popularizes the genre *reggaetón* on an international scale.

A

Accordion

The accordion is a generic term for different varieties of a handheld, bellows-driven instrument that is central to much solo and ensemble performance in Latin America. Accordions were introduced to Latin America primarily in the 19th century by German immigrants. The instrument's sound is a result of air, set in motion by the drawing and blowing out of air from a bellows, which passes through multiple, single reeds giving the accordion its characteristic sound. Because of this double action of drawing and blowing air, there are two basic varieties of accordion: double action (produces the same note or notes on both draw and blow modes) and single action (produces different notes on either the draw or the blow). Additionally, they may employ a keyboard for the right hand and buttons to play the accompaniment for the left hand (*acordeón de tecla*), or buttons for both hands to play both the melody and the accompaniment (*acordeón de botón*). Accordion-type instruments can be found in many South American traditions including **Brazil (*sanfona*), Colombia (*vallenato*)**, and **Argentina (*bandoneón*)**. In **Mexico** and the Northern **United States**, the *acordeón de botón* (button accordion) is commonly used in *tejano* and *norteño* music. This diatonic instrument, which has the capacity to play both melody and bass simultaneously, is arranged in such a way so that when adjacent buttons are played, the result is an interval of a third. Together with the *bajo sexto* the Mexican *acordeón de botón* form the backbone of the *norteño conjunto*. Two of the early pioneers of the instrument were brothers Narciso and Raul "El Ruco" Martinez.

Further Reading

Clark, Walter Aaron. *From Tejano to Tango: Latin American Popular Music.* New York: Routledge, 2002.

García Méndez, Javier, and Arturo Penón. *Bandonion: A Tango History.* Trans. Tim Burnard. Gibsons Landing, BC: Nightwood Editions, 1988.

Tejeda, Juan. *Puro Conjunto: An Album in Words and Pictures.* San Antonio, TX: CMAS Books, 2001.

George Torres

Acordeón. *See* Accordion.

Afoxé. *See* Brazil.

Afro

A genre of Cuban popular song with lyrics often featuring black themes, *Afro* originated in the late 19th century and came out of the tradition of Cuban blackface theater. It reached its height in popularity in the 1940s and 1950s, when it was often heard within the context of sacred music and lullabies in popular ensemble situations. Within traditional Cuban popular music, it was commonly performed in the context of the ***charanga*** ensembles. The infectious rhythm of the Afro was used by American artists including Duke Ellington. Examples include "Ogguere" by Gilberto Valdez and "Bruca Manigua" by **Arsenio Rodríguez**. Its distinctive rhythm can be notated as follows.

An example of Afro rhythm. (George Torres)

An example of its use in American popular music can be heard in the Chuck Berry song "Havana Moon." It is sometimes also referred to as *Afro-Cuban*.

Further Reading

Fernandez, Raul A. *From Afro-Cuban Rhythms to Latin Jazz.* Music of the African Diaspora, 10. Berkeley: University of California Press, 2006.

Orovio, Helio. *Cuban Music from A to Z.* Durham, NC: Duke University Press, 2004.

George Torres

Montaner, Rita

Internationally renowned vocalist Rita Aurelia Montaner Fazenda (1900–1958) was also known as Rita de Cuba or Rita La Única. She was instrumental in bringing the **Afro-Cuban** salon song to prominence in **Cuba**, and throughout Latin America, North America, and Europe. As a singer, she studied Italian opera and her early professional recitals included Italian opera and music by Cuban composers. Montaner's first professional performance was at the Conciertos de Música Típica Cubana in 1922. She travelled to the United States in 1926 where she performed with Xavier Cugat at The Apollo and toured with the Shubert Follies. Returning to Cuba in 1927, Montaner appeared in black face and male drag in the ***zarzuela***, *Niña Rita, o La Habana de 1830* by Eliseo Grenet and Lecuona. She sang the *tango-congo* "Ay, Mamá Ines."

Montaner starred in many films including *Romance del Palmar* (1935) and *Sucedió en La Habana* (1938). She continued to have a successful performing career up until her untimely death in 1958. Montaner's singing was exceptional for her three-octave range and vocal stamina, versatility of style, and her wideranging repertoire.

Further Reading

Sublette, Ned. *Cuba and Its Music: From the First Drums to the Mambo*. Chicago: Chicago Review Press, 2007.

Rebecca Stuhr

Afro-Cuban

Afro-Cuban is a noun or adjective used to signify Cuban people or cultural practices of African descent in general, as well as a term that broadly describes popular Cuban music. In Spanish, it is usually not hyphenated (*Afrocubano*).

The term *Afro-Cuban* was originally introduced in 1847 by Antonio de Veitía, though it was not widely used until it was championed by Fernando Ortiz and taken up by the intellectual community during the *Afrocubanismo* movement of the early 20th century. At first, the term was used only in scholarly writings for conceptual expedience, but its vernacular usage spread to such a degree that today it is common in **Cuba** and abroad. According to some scholars, its use in marketing overextended its original meaning. At the heart of the issue is what qualifies something as *Afro-Cuban* as opposed to just Cuban.

In some sense, most Cuban music could be considered Afro-Cuban due to its instruments and rhythmic structures. Seeing this as an overuse of the term, however, some scholars refrain from using the word *Afro-Cuban* even in reference to things such as *rumba*, a Cuban creation with African antecedents. This strict approach would reserve the use of *Afro-Cuban* only to describe practices in Cuba with direct African origins, such as *batá* drumming. Generally, *Afro-Cuban* is applied to many Cuban music styles, most often in reference to pieces with a ternary beat division (6/8 or 12/8), thus evoking folkloric or religious *Afro-Cuban* drumming.

Further Reading

Fernández Robaina, Tomás. "The Term *Afro-Cuban:* A Forgotten Contribution." In *Cuban Counterpoints: The Legacy of Fernando Ortiz,* edited by Mauricio A. Font and Alfonso W. Quiroz, 171–79. Lanham, MD: Lexington Books, 2005.

Nolan Warden

Afro-Dominican Fusion Music

Afro-Dominican fusion music (*Música de fusión*) is a genre that mixes traditional music from the **Dominican Republic**, especially historically marginalized Afro-Dominican music, with more widely accepted forms of global popular music largely as an expression of racial pride and consciousness. Due to an antagonistic relationship with their Haitian neighbors and their own complex racial identity, many Dominicans have been, and often still are, resistant to accepting their African heritage. Starting in the 1970s, a movement emerged among progressive intellectuals, folklorists, and performers to recognize and promote the Dominican African heritage. This movement is currently at its strongest. Afro-Dominican fusion musicians draw from Afro-Dominican genres to create their music, some of which include *sarandunga, congo, palo, salves,* and *gagá* (for a description of these genres, see **Dominican Republic**).

Dominican Republic's Juan Luis Guerra, right, performs during the Latin Music Festival in Santo Domingo, 2010. (AP/Wide World Photos)

The point of departure in recognizing a Dominican African heritage can be traced back to the research-musical group *Convite* (communal work), a performing group of social scientists, folklorists, and musicians who were influenced by the Latin American ***nueva canción*** movement and who performed from 1974 to 1981 for the common goal of acknowledging the African heritage, which had been erased from Dominican history. *Convite*'s methodology included ethnographic study and participant observation in order to absorb the logic and way of life of rural Afro-Dominicans with the intention of creating new music with an Afro-Dominican essence. *Convite* and successive generations of fusion musicians have taken the Afro-Dominican music traditionally used to accompany voodoo-related rituals (or other forms of Dominican folk or popular religion) from its strictly rural and ceremonial settings to more urban locations, often as a form of popular music. Their music expresses and encourages political resistance, oppositional thinking, and a new racial consciousness, all of which are woven into aspects of this music. Key figures of *Convite* were sociologist Dagoberto Tejeda, singer-songwriter Luis Días, and agronomist and folklorist Iván Domínguez.

In the wake of *Convite,* a variety of groups and performers also sought to bring black consciousness to Dominicans. They range in style and preferences: for example, Luis Días performs Afro-Dominican rock and heavy metal, while Xiomara Fortuna prefers **reggae** and Brazilian music styles. Although it is difficult to generalize about such diverse musicians and projects, Afro-Dominican fusion musicians tend to be aware and make use of the tension between innovation and tradition in their music's role in constructing an African identity. Although much of its power and appeal comes from its drawing on older traditions, Afro-Dominican fusion music is clear in its emphasis on breaking old structures musically, racially, and politically. The fusion musicians' intention is to get into the Dominican consciousness through a complex set of semiotic symbols encoded in their musical sound, style, texts, performance practice, dress, and behavior. Because the white upper-classes in the Dominican Republic have always looked up to American popular music and culture, some fusion musicians strategically fuse Afro-Dominican music with rock, heavy metal, and **jazz**, while others prefer popular forms of Afro-diasporic music, all with the goal of breaking long-time prejudices against Afro-Dominican music and religion.

Some of the tools that fusion musicians employ in order to make Dominicans aware and proud of their African heritage can be found not only in their music, but also in their dress codes, CD liner notes, performance practice, and behavior. Fusion musicians invoke the leaders of black brotherhoods and voodoo deities, paint their bodies with tribal-like designs, use African phonemes in their music, and Africanize the names of their groups. Many CD liner notes include an explanation of the Afro-Dominican religious tradition associated with the music and some sort of statement of black pride as well as African art or voodoo images, or else show the musicians in African attire. Other features of fusion music include blending elements of Haitian voodoo or *rara* music with rhythms and instruments of Dominican music to show the cultural similarities between Haitians and Dominicans. Many fusion musicians also sing in Haitian *Creole* or in Spanish with a *Creole* accent.

There are about 20 fusion music groups whose roots and methodology go back to *Convite*. These musicians continue *Convite*'s goal of changing the previous self-identification of the Dominican Republic as a white Spanish country. Some currently existing groups and performers include *Kaliumbé* (Xiomara Fortuna), *Quedumbé* (Miguel Tejada), *Licuado* (Crispín Fernandez), *Drumayor* (Edis Sánchez*)*, *Marassá* (Florentino Alvarez), *Maracandé* (David Almengod), *Domini-can* (José Duluc), *Transporte Urbano* (Luis Días), *Batey 0, Son Tres,* José Roldán, Irka Mateo, Tony Vicioso, Bony Raposo, Tadeo de Marco, and Juan Luis Guerra. In New York, the groups are *Ecocumbé, Kalunga, Palomonte,* and *La 21 División.* Disbanded groups of the 1980s and 1990s included *Madora, Los guerreros del fuego, Asadifé, Paleombe,* and *Palemba.*

Further Reading

Austerlitz, Paul. *Merengue: Dominican Music and Dominican Identity.* Philadelphia, PA: Temple University Press, 1997.

Sellers, Julie A. *Merengue and Dominican Identity: Music as National Unifier.* Jefferson, NC: McFarland & Co., 2004.

Angelina Tallaj

Argentina

Argentina is a South American country bordered by **Chile, Bolivia, Paraguay, Brazil**, and **Uruguay**. Despite its location in southern South America, Argentina has been strongly influenced by European music and culture due to an influx of immigrants mostly from Spain and Italy in the late 1800s. The European presence is still reflected in the population demographics in Argentina today, which is an overwhelming 97 percent white, and just 3 percent *mestizo,* Amerindian, or other.

Argentina is not only more Westernized but also more urbanized than many other countries in South America. It has several major cities including its capital, Buenos Aires. As a result of this developed and autonomous character, it was one of the first countries in Latin America to establish copyright for composers and lyricists. Because of this musical environment, Argentina's history of popular music and its popular music industry is one of the longest, and comprises a variety of rural and urban genres and styles. Argentine musicians were recording folkloric styles from various regions of the country by the second half of the 1900s. Unique urban and mass-mediated genres were inspired by and developed out of these folk materials and have played an important role in Argentina's evolving national identities. The *tango*, perhaps the best-known Argentine musical genre internationally, has over a century of history that is both a fundamental part of the local musical and cultural imagination and is also deeply intertwined with foreign musical tastes and influences. Argentina has also been one of the leading contributors to the development of *rock en español*, outselling the rock music of every other country, except the **United States** and United Kingdom. Perhaps just as importantly, from the 1970s onward, many of the most prominent artists in each of these three major genres, folk, rock, and *tango,* have crossed or blurred these genre boundaries, creating urban popular music that reflects a distinct local identity while, nonetheless, engaging the processes and aesthetics of international rock and pop music.

While never attaining the international level of diffusion that rock or *tango* has, a number of regional or local popular genres have attained a similar degree of popularity and importance within Argentina. Most notable among these local styles are **cuarteto**, a style of tropical music influenced by Caribbean genres and especially popular in and around Córdoba province; the **polka**-influenced *chamamé* in the northeastern provinces; and several local variants on the international **cumbia**.

Folkloric Music

One of the founding figures in transforming the rural and largely oral regional traditions of Argentina into a substantial commercial music culture nationally and internationally was Andrés Chazarreta (1876–1960). An impresario and principally self-taught guitarist, Chazarreta formed a theatrical troupe in Santiago del Estero to perform the folk dances and songs of the region, and in 1921 brought it to the capital city with great success. He was also an active collector and included in the company's repertoire regional material he gathered on national tours.

Another early figure who would gain importance as a composer, singer, guitarist, and lyricist was **Atahualpa Yupanqui** (1908–1992). Born in the interior of Buenos Aires province, Yupanqui moved with his family to Tucumán province as a young boy and developed a singular musical style that drew on various rural traditions, particularly the **zamba** and **milonga**. Yupanqui's affiliation with the Communist party and particularly his anti-Peronist leanings prevented him from performing or recording for much of the decade of the 1940s, but upon renouncing his party affiliation in 1952, he regained access to these media. He established an audience for Argentine folk music abroad, living for a time in France and performing alongside Edith Piaf. His compositions have since been performed by nearly every important figure in Argentine folk music of the subsequent decades.

Beginning in the 1940s, Argentina experienced a massive internal migration, with populations from the rural areas moving toward urban centers. This population of immigrant workers, many of whom had an indigenous or *mestizo* cultural background, faced a strong degree of discrimination and racism and frequently felt alienated from the city and its musical expressions such as the *tango*. As a result, the changing demographics of the cities opened a space for a new urban and mass-mediated genre drawing on folk genres such as the *zamba*, **chacarera**, and *malambo*. Increasingly, the umbrella term *folklore* began to be used informally to describe this genre, whether describing new, commercially oriented compositions or repertoire

Yupanqui, Atahualpa

Atahualpa Yupanqui (1908–1992) was an Argentine poet, guitarist, and song-writer who assimilated his country's music and folklore into a unique musi-cal style that influenced the **nueva canción** movement. Yupanqui sought to revive traditional culture by infusing his music with the poetry, music, dance, and folklore of the *paisanos* of northwestern **Argentina** and the *Altiplano*. Al-though his poetry and songs were considered protest music, his subject mat-ter was a tribute to the indigenous people he encountered. His music uses folk rhythms like the **chacarera**, **zamba**, and **estilo**. In his **guitar** playing, he com-bined a classically refined *punteado* (plucking) style with a right hand *rasgueado* (strumming) technique influenced by folk guitarists as in the instrumental gui-tar piece "La Estancia Vieja," employing a resonant G major *scordatura*. His influence is seen in the *nueva canción* repertoire, including works by **Violeta Parra,** Victor Jara, and guitarists like **Raúl García Zárate**. Because of his early affiliations with the Communist Party, Yupanqui was forced into exile; in 1967, Yupanqui moved to Paris where he lived until his death. He was a ground-breaking artist, producing over 1,500 original poems and songs and remaining influential among successive artists.

Further Reading

Luna, Félix, and Atahualpa Yupanqui. *Atahualpa Yupanqui*. Madrid: Ediciones Júcar, 1974.

George Torres

from the oral tradition. More precisely, scholars and musicians sometimes differ-entiate between oral folk-tradition music on the one hand, and the newer urban ex-pressions based on these traditional forms on the other, calling the latter *folklore de proyección, música de proyección folklórica,* or *nativismo. Folklore* received the systematic support of the populist Peronist party, including radio distribution and government-sponsored research institutions dedicated to the documentation of musical folk culture. This support doubtless contributed to the growing commer-cial success of the genre. By the mid-1950s, popular folk singer Antonio Tormo re-corded the first album in any genre to reach one million copies in sales in Argentina.

The 1960s witnessed the greatest expansion and development in folkloric musi-cal expression, as well as its increasing politicization. This so-called *folklore* boom included important groups centered in Buenos Aires, Mendoza, and Salta. While the city of Buenos Aires itself was not the birthplace of any of the important figures in this movement, it was important as a population center and the home of the major national recording studios and radio stations. It became the adoptive home from which many musicians from the provinces could launch their careers and solidify a regional identity. Some of the best-known groups that followed this pattern during the boom were vocal quartets who would sing in parallel harmonies, accompanying themselves on three **guitars** and a *bombo*. This model was established and made most famous by the quartets Los Chalchaleros and Los Fronterizos, both originally from the province of Salta.

Simultaneously, musicians and artists in other regions of the country formed groups celebrating local musical and cultural identities. Two important groups during this time period came together with this end in mind: in Mendoza a group of writers, musicians, composers, and dancers formed the ***Nuevo Cancionero*** movement in 1963, while in Salta the group La Carpa, begun as a literary salon, later also attracted musicians and formed a nexus from which many important songs were created. The *Nuevo Cancionero* movement coalesced around the figure of poet Armando Tejada Gómez (1921–1992). Strongly influenced by the work of Atahualpa Yupanqui, the movement's best known musicians were singer **Mercedes Sosa** (b.1935) and Oscar Matus. La Carpa, a literary movement founded in 1944 and dedicated to a celebration of the culture and poetry of the northwest region, included important lyricists such as Manuel Castilla and Juan José Botelli. Its importance in the history of Argentine music is due largely to the incorporation of pianist and composer Gustavo "Cuchi" Leguizamón (1917–2000). Although Leguizamón performed infrequently and recorded even less, as a composer he remains one of the most prevalent influences on contemporary Argentine *folklore*. His compositions employ daring and dissonant harmonies, showing a familiarity with jazz and contemporary classical music. Leguizamón's music has been recorded by nearly all of the major figures in Argentine *folklore,* from Los Chalchaleros and Mercedes Sosa to contemporary figures such as Juan Falú, Liliana Herrero, and Raúl Carnota.

One of the major vehicles for the distribution and consumption of folkloric music in Argentina, and an arbiter of taste, has been the establishment of local and national folklore festivals. The most important of these is the National Folklore Festival that has taken place in Cosquín every January since 1961. It has served as a launching pad for numerous musicians' national and international careers, including Mercedes Sosa and folk-pop singer Soledad Pastorutti (b. 1980).

Tango

Tango is a dance, song, and musical form that emerged in the poor suburbs of the Uruguayan capital of Montevideo and the Argentine capital of Buenos Aires in the late 19th century. By 1913, it had gained popularity in Paris and London as a salon dance, and as a result eventually gained acceptance by middle- and upper-class

Argentine society. It was the most prominent urban popular music and dance of the Argentine capital from the 1920s through the 1940s, and is often identified as the national musical symbol of Argentina. During the 1950s and 1960s, *tango*'s popularity was eclipsed first by mass-mediated forms of folk music and later by rock. Nevertheless, newer and more experimental forms of *tango* music continued to emerge and be consumed locally and internationally, and there has been a resurgence of interest among young Argentines in *tango* music since 2000.

The *tango* as a distinct musical style began to consolidate in the last two decades of the 19th century. Demonstrating the influences of European popular song and a prevalent rhythmic pattern derived from the Cuban **habanera**, *tangos* in this period were typically written in three contrasting sections with the last marked as a *trio*. The most typical instrumental ensemble consisted of a trio of **flute**, **guitar**, and violin. It was not until the turn of the century that the instrument that would come to play the most prominent role as the sonic and visual icon of the *tango*, the German-made **bandoneón**, began to appear in *tango* ensembles. Many early *tango* musicians were not formally trained in music, and generally pieces were learned and transmitted orally. Retroactively, this generation of musicians would become known as *la guardia vieja* (the old guard), distinguishing them from the next generation and their stylistic innovations starting around 1920.

Rosendo Mendizábal's "El entrerriano" (the man from Entre Ríos province) became the first published *tango* in 1897. During the following decade, *tango* reached an increasingly wider public. No longer was it heard only in the *academias,* public dance halls in the poor outer suburbs of Buenos Aires that were closely associated with prostitution, but in other spaces as well. From 1910 to 1920, the most important musical innovations in the *tango* came in the form of new instrumentation: the piano began to replace the guitar as the most common harmonic and rhythmic instrument, and the *bandoneón* gained prominence.

Pugliese, Osvaldo

Pugliese (1905–1995) was a pioneering composer, pianist, and **orquesta típica** director who brought international attention to the **tango** through his sophisticated and innovative style. Pugliese played in a variety of ensembles until 1929 when he formed the avant garde group the Vardaro-Pugliese Sextet. He formed his first *tango* band, or *orquesta típica* in 1939, Orquesta Osvaldo Pugliese, with which he made more than 600 recordings and toured internationally.

Pugliese performed in the style of Julio Da Caro, incorporating a strong rhythmic beat that inspired dancers. This evolved into his own style, *el yumbeado,* a musical designation taken from his 1943 composition "La Yumba." It featured a heavy first beat and a very light second beat (YUM-ba). Still considered a progressive sound by contemporary *tango* artists, *el yumbeado* is the favored rhythmic pattern for today's *orquesta típcas*. Pugliese was also a Communist; he formed his band as a collective, and was banned from the radio and imprisoned multiple times for expressing his political views. Despite his conflicts with the Argentine government, he received many honors during his career.

Further Reading

Luker, Morgan James. "*Tango* Renovación: On the Uses of Music History in Post-Crisis Argentina." *Latin American Music Review* 28:1 (2007) 68–93.

Rebecca Stuhr

Bandoneonist Vicente Greco coined the term *orquesta típica criolla,* later shortened to **orquesta típica,** to describe the ensemble he formed in 1911. Greco's group included a flute, an instrument that would soon fall out of favor, but his basic configuration of sections of *bandoneones* and violins, with a piano and contrabass providing rhythmic and harmonic support, would become the standard instrumentation for the coming decades.

The year 1913 marked the explosion of the *tango* craze in Paris when a more restrained version of the dance caught on among the elites. This in turn created a greater interest in *tango* back in Argentina among the middle classes. By 1920, *tango* was being mass produced and sold on a global scale, both on record and in film.

While the earliest *tangos* may have had lyrics, few of them survive, and accounts of the period suggest that they may have been improvised and frequently were lighthearted and bawdy in character. This practice was to change radically with the introduction of *tango canción,* or *tango* song, and the worldwide success of its best-known exponent, **Carlos Gardel**. He created an emotive, dramatic style of singing that reflected the melancholy, cynical worldview of this new genre.

The period between 1920 and 1940 witnessed a proliferation in all aspects of *tango* art, and is frequently referred to as *tango*'s golden age. *Orquestas típicas* grew in size, including sometimes up to five *bandoneones* and violins. Bandleaders and arrangers worked to develop distinctive styles, and dancers would often develop strong loyalties to a particular *orquesta*'s style.

Public interest in *tango* waned in the late 1940s and 1950s due to economic crises, increasingly militarized and authoritarian governments, and other social changes. Some *tango* musicians developed smaller-ensemble sounds that were meant for the concert hall rather than for the dancer. The best known of these was **Astor Piazzolla** (1921–1992), who combined classical training and an interest in jazz with his background in *tango* to create a style he termed *tango nuevo,* or new *tango.*

Following the economic crisis of late 2001, there has been a resurgence of interest in *tango* among young Argentines. This generation of musicians often shows a strong influence from rock music, and has included electric instruments, drum sets, and other innovations into the traditional *tango* ensemble. *Electrotango* or *tango electrónico,* a subgenre of electronic music using *tango* rhythms, samples, and instruments has also become popular internationally.

Rock

By the early 1960s, Argentine musicians were producing local, Spanish-language versions of American and British-style rock 'n' roll. The Rolling Stones and the Beatles were particularly influential, and by the late 1960s *rock nacional* had produced a number of innovative bands. Los Gatos, led by Litto Nebbia, are generally recognized as producing the first original *rock nacional* hit with "La Balsa" in 1967. Two important bands emerged shortly thereafter: the blues-based Manal, and the acoustic, more experimental Almendra.

Rock music, like folklore, was severely controlled during the dictatorship (1976–1983) and musicians faced danger of imprisonment. Nonetheless, numerous bands during this period began to produce rock music influenced by jazz, Argentine folk music, and *tango,* creating a *rock nacional* defined more by a social attitude than one particular sound. Important groups included two bands led by Charly García, Sui Generis and Serú Girán, and Arco Iris.

Following Argentina's 1982 war with England over the Falkland Islands/Islas Malvinas, English-language rock was prohibited on the airwaves, providing a financial boost to local musicians. This, combined with the return of democracy in 1983, spurred an outgrowth of internationally successful bands such as Soda Stereo, Virus, and Los Fabulosos Cadillacs. Many of these show strong international influences, particularly **reggae**, ska, new wave, and punk.

Música Tropical and Regional Styles

Colombian-style popular *cumbia* came to Argentina in the late 1950s. The most important local exponents were Los Wawancó, a group formed in Argentina by Colombian and other foreign students. *Cumbia* itself continues to be a popular dance music particularly in the province of Santa Fe. In the late 1990s, a subgenre known as *cumbia villera* (shantytown *cumbia*) became popular among the urban poor. Largely synthesizer-based bands such as Damas Gratis and Pibes Chorros wrote lyrics glorifying drug use, crime, and misogyny, and were broadly vilified by the middle classes and press. Nevertheless, *cumbia* bands and DJs in large dance halls known as *bailantas*, especially in the poorer outskirts of Buenos Aires, continue to attract large audiences.

Another regional style influenced by *cumbia* and often grouped with it as música tropical is *the cuarteto* of Córdoba. A lively dance genre characterized by a distinctive rhythmic pattern called *tunga-tunga*, *cuarteto* musicians attract thousands of fans to weekly concerts in large dance halls in Córdoba province. The genre takes its name from the founding group Cuarteto Leo, which included piano, bass, accordion, and violin, but since the 1960s, influenced by *cumbia* and *merengue* ensembles, *cuarteto* groups have expanded to include large percussion and sometimes horn sections.

Further Reading

Collier, Simon, and Ken Hass. *¡Tango! The Dance, the Song, the Story.* New York: Thames and Hudson, 1995.

Florine, Jane. Cuarteto *Music and Dancing from Argentina: In Search of the* Tunga-Tunga *in Córdoba.* Gainesville: University Press of Florida, 2001.

Semán, Pablo, Pablo Vila, and Cecilia Benedetti. "Neoliberalism and Rock in the Popular Sectors of Contemporary Argentina." In *Rockin' Las Americas: The Global Politics of Rock in Latin/o America,* edited by Deborah Pacini-Hernandez, Héctor D Fernández l'Hoeste, and Eric Zolov. Pittsburgh, PA: University of Pittsburgh Press, 2004.

Vila, Pablo. "Argentina's 'Rock Nacional': The Struggle for Meaning." *Latin American Music Review* 10, no. 1 (1989): 1–28.

Michael O'Brien

Arpa (harp)

The *arpa* is a stringed instrument that has been constructed and performed in Spain since the Middle Ages. Its arrival and dissemination in Latin America can be traced back to the early decades of the Spanish invasion, when the instrument was brought to the continent by Spanish Jesuit missionaries. Like the various forms of the **guitar** derived from Spanish archetypes that are found throughout Latin America, various forms of diatonic harps with significant repertoires have flourished in **Mexico, Colombia, Paraguay, Peru**, and **Venezuela**. Within a country, there may be several varieties of harps with differences in construction, technique, and repertoire. Additionally, both indigenous and *mestizo* harp traditions exist, but for the purposes of focusing on popular music, the following remarks refer to the *mestizo* traditions encountered in these locales.

The various types of *arpa* found in Latin America show some variants in design and construction and, at the same time, have several traits in common. All of the common types are of a triangular construction, consisting of three basic parts:

The sound box, commonly referred to as the *caja de resonancia* (resonating box), or as the folkloric musicians may refer to it, the *panza* (belly), where the strings are attached at one end; a *consola* or *clavijero,* commonly referred to as the *diapason,* which holds the tuning levers; and a *columna* or *poste,* which attaches the low end of the *diapason* to the sound box. Commonly, harps have anywhere between 24 and 36 strings and are tuned diatonically. Most Latin American players get their instruments from local makers, or *lauderos.* Traditionally, the strings were gut and made from animal intestines such as goat, dog, or coyote. Today, many harp makers use available nylon, for example, from different grades and thicknesses of fishing line; some have evolved a system of using a cross-wrapping technique to produce a wound string for the thicker basses.

The *arpa jaorcha* originated in the state of Veracruz, in the southern part of the state, near the port of Veracruz. It is one of Mexico's longest standing harp traditions. This instrument has 35 or 36 strings, is tuned diatonically, and has a range of about five octaves. The *arpa jaorcha* is generally used in ensemble performances of the **son jarocho**, along with the **jarana**, and *requinto jarocho.* The role of the harp in the context of this ensemble is both melodic and harmonic, with the harpist often introducing the **son (Mexican)** with a melodic introduction after which the rest of the ensemble joins in a lively *fandango*, or instrumental introduction. After several verses, there may be an instrumental break where all of the musicians stop abruptly, leaving the harpist alone to show off his or her skill in improvisation. During the verses, the harp plays a harmony of chords or arpeggios. The repertoire for these groups consists of regional *sones.* Among the well known are "La Bamba," "El Cascabel," "La Bruja," and "El Siquirisí."

In the Peruvian Andes, the harp is a very special instrument, performed not only in ensemble settings, but also as a solo instrument with a rich repertoire. The Peruvian harp is diatonic and has between 26 and 36 strings, made of either metal or nylon. The resonator, however, is larger than most other Latin American varieties of harp. An interesting distinguishing feature to the Peruvian harp is that it is often used in outdoor ensemble processions, and the player will invert the instrument, essentially playing it upside down, and carry it in this manner while processing with the parade. The repertoire for this instrument consists of traditional *mestizo* forms such as the **huayno**, Peruvian **polka** and Peruvian **vals**. Florencio Coronado is the most well-known exponent of the solo repertoire, and he spent much of his career performing internationally with his Peruvian harp.

The Venezuelan *arpa llanera* (plains harp) is commonly part of the traditional *llanera* ensemble that includes Venezuelan **cuatro** and **maracas**. The instrument has about 32 strings, which are most often made of a combination of steel and gut. The instrument is usually played in a seated position and players use both the pads of their fingers and their fingernails to pluck the strings. The repertoire of the *arpa llanero* consists of the native **joropo** and other popular regional song forms. The *arpa llanera,* Venezuela's national ensemble instrument, in the hands of a skilled musician is also a virtuoso solo instrument.

The Paraguayan harp, also the national instrument of the country, remains one of the most vital harp traditions in Latin America. The instrument was introduced by Spanish and Irish missionaries. It usually consists of about 36 to 40 strings, which are tuned diatonically and have, approximately, a five-octave range. The instrument is played either sitting or standing, and players usually play with their fingernails. Among the popular genres played on the instrument are the *danza paraguaya* or Paraguayan polka. The instrument is used in an endless variety of ensemble situations as well as being used as a solo instrument. Throughout the country, aspiring harpists study at the many family-run harp schools, such as the *Arpa Roga* in Asuncion.

Because of its widespread use, the harp is one of the most popular instruments in Latin America. In addition to its status as a musical symbol for the region as a whole, the many varieties of regional harp traditions identify a variety of local musical traditions and repertoires. In this way, the instrument can be seen as representative of a broader Latin American musical context, while providing regional distinctiveness to local cultures.

Further Reading

Hernández Vaca, Víctor. *El arpa grande de Michoacán. Morelia, Michoacán.* Mexico: Colegio de Michoacán, 2005.

Schechter, John Mendell. *The Indispensable Harp: Historical Development, Modern Roles, Configurations, and Performance Practices in Ecuador and Latin America.* Kent, OH: Kent State University Press, 1992.

George Torres

Axé Music

Axé music is a category of Brazilian popular music from Salvador da Bahia (capital city of the state of Bahia and henceforth called Salvador) that coalesced in the 1980s and reached its commercial peak in the 1990s. Closely associated with Bahia's national and international image as the undisputed center of Afro-Brazilian culture in **Brazil**, *axé music* capitalized on the renaissance of Afro-Bahian culture and music ushered in by the ***bloco afro*** carnival groups of Salvador da Bahia to become one of Brazil's most vital entrées on the international world music scene. Notable stars and musical groups from Bahia marketed under the broad category of *axé music* include Luiz Caldas, Daniela Mercury, Carlinhos Brown, Gera Samba, and É o Tchan.

Since the early 1970s, Salvador's popular music scene unfolded in close relationship to the city's annual **Carnival** celebration and international trends in popular music. Many of Bahia's popular musicians (including those of national scope such as **Gilberto Gil, Caetano Veloso**, and Morais Moreira) have tapped into local carnival traditions (*afoxé, trio elétrico, bloco afro*) and Caribbean-associated popular music styles (***reggae, merengue, soca, salsa***) for major inspiration. *Axé music* carried this trend to a new level in the last two decades of the 20th century.

By the mid-1980s, much of Bahia's popular music was closely linked to the image of Salvador's highly participatory Carnival and to the city's reputation as Brazil's center of African cultural identity. The success of the *bloco afro* ensemble Olodum and its new musical performance style *samba-reggae* in the mid-1980s helped reinforce the reputation of Bahian carnival as a site for cultural creativity and the maintenance of Afro-Brazilian heritage. *Axé music* was a term initially used to describe (somewhat condescendingly) the new Afro-related popular music sounds coming out of Bahia in the mid-1980s. The term *axé*, derived from West African Yoruba language, is used widely in Salvador's religious Candomblé community to denote spiritual essence, power, and grace. Among the general population of Salvador, it is a common greeting and leave-taking term that marks a person's awareness of and adherence to a wide range of black cultural values. The use of *axé music* as an umbrella term for Salvador's popular music linked the city's reputation as an authentic site of African heritage to the nomenclature and exotic imagery of the global world music scene. It is not surprising that much of *axé music*'s perceived cultural authenticity was initially due to its close association with the *bloco afro* groups that paraded with thousands of costumed participants and the aural and visual impact of hundreds of drummers during Bahian carnival. Additionally, *blocos afro* organizations like Ilê Aiyê, Olodum, Muzenza, Ara Ketu, and others provided artistic training grounds for many of the percussionists, composers, singers, and dancers that would comprise *axé music*. Beginning in 1987, Bahian groups like Banda Mel and Banda Reflexus covered Carnival hits of the *bloco afro* musical repertoire in small band formats that combined vocals, percussion, electric guitars, and keyboards.

The collaborations of the *bloco afro* Ara Ketu and singer Margareth Menezes with David Byrne (1989) and of Olodum with Paul Simon (1990) were key to the marketing of the new Bahian sounds of *axé music* both nationally and internationally as authentic African diasporic global popular music. However, it was Daniela Mercury, a white Bahian singer thoroughly versed in Bahian carnival traditions, who took *axé music* to a new level of commercial popularity in Brazil with hits like "Swing da Cor" ("Swing of Color") and "O Canto da Cidade" ("Song of the City") in 1991 and 1992. These hit songs were backed up by Olodum-style *samba-reggae* rhythms and a highly percussive instrumentation. In the 1990s *axé music* became a music industry success, generating millions of dollars and further establishing Bahia's music reputation internationally. Carlinhos Brown has been one of the most enduring and creative of the artists associated with *axé music*. As a solo performer, composer, and leader of the Timbalada group (a *bloco afro*-like organization that operates out of the Candeal neighborhood of Salvador), Brown freely mixes a highly percussive sound ideal derived from the *bloco afro* tradition with many other forms of Afro-Brazilian and non-Brazilian musical traditions. Hybrid offshoots of *axé music* include the commercially successful Bahian *pagode* sounds of Gera Samba and É o Tchan.

Further Reading

Crook, Larry. *Brazilian Music: Northeastern Traditions and the Heartbeat of a Modern Nation.* Santa Barbara, CA: ABC-CLIO, 2005.

McGowan, Chris and Ricardo Pessanha. *The Brazilian Sound: Samba, Bossa Nova, and the Popular Music of Brazil.* Revised and expanded edition. Philadelphia, PA: Temple University Press, 2009.

Moura, Milton Araújo. "World of Fantasy, Fantasy of the World: Geographic Space and Representation of Identity in the Carnival of Salvador, Bahia." In *Brazilian Popular Music and Globalization,* edited by Charles A. Perrone and Christopher Dunn, 161–76. Gainesville: University Press of Florida, 2001.

Larry Crook

B

Bachata

Bachata is a popular vocal music genre from the **Dominican Republic** and is one of the most popular genres of Latin American music. This popularity is a relatively recent development since *bachata* was highly marginalized in its native country and practically unknown internationally until the early 1990s. *Bachata*'s roots have been traced to the Cuban *bolero*. The resemblance of Dominican guitar-based music to Cuban *bolero*—with moderate tempos, romantic lyrics, and sentimental vocal style—is reflected in early names for this music. Prior to the 1960s, such **guitar**-based romantic songs were called *bolero campesino* or simply *música popular*. As time went on, *bolero campesino* was influenced by other Latin American genres and began to develop a sound distinct from *bolero* and the other forms that influenced it (i.e., Mexican *rancheras* and *corridos*).

Despite the prominence of guitar accompaniment, *bachata* is essentially a vocal genre with a fairly standardized and distinctive rhythm, but a variety of chord patterns and verse forms. Its characteristic and defining timbre is due to its instrumentation and vocal style. The presence of one or two guitars, **maracas** or **güiras** (shaker or metal scraper), and **bongó** (bongo drums) is essential for *bachata*. One guitar plays lead while the other plays rhythm. The lead guitar originally played arpeggiated accompaniment patterns by plucking in classic bolero style, but later switched to playing the strings downward, with a thumb pick. The bongó and maraca (or güira) players mark a standard four-four time. The vocal style is highly emotional, sometimes almost sobbing, and it can incorporate spoken text or short exclamations such as "Mami!" *Bachata* can also be danced. Like the music, its dance bears some resemblance to that of the Cuban bolero and **son (Cuba)**, but it is quite distinct from both of them. *Bachata* dancing consists of an alternating one-two-three-kick pattern, in which the kick is a toe step or a small hop. The body movement is smooth and sinuous, but relatively reserved. In recent years, as *bachata* has gained acceptance and popularity, both the music and the dance have become more elaborate.

According to Deborah Pacini-Hernández, *bachata*'s essential characteristics are not only musical but extra-musical as well. When *bachata* crystallized as a style, it increased in tempo, became more danceable, and its lyrics became bawdy and raunchy as opposed to the quintessentially romantic and poetic bolero. The word *bachata* originally meant a rural or low-class party, or a get-together that includes music, drink, and food. The term then came to be applied to the music itself, since guitar music was the preferred music of choice for these kinds of gatherings. The music was named not by *bachata* musicians, fans, or industry entrepreneurs, but by the country's urban middle and upper classes, who intended to stigmatize and trivialize these kinds of low-class gatherings as backward and vulgar. Thus, the music's social context, the language and context of the lyrics, and the social status of the musicians were determinant factors in the very definition of *bachata*. Other names that *bachata* has received include *música de amargue*, *música de guardia*, and *cachivache*.

The first recorded example of *bachata* is "Borracho de Amor" by José Manuel Calderón in 1961. *Bachata* was born in the 1960s during a period of rural to urban migration; rural migrants lived in the poorest and most marginalized neighborhoods of the capital city, often without water, electricity, or any kind of public amenities. Between the years 1960 and 1970 the population of the capital city of the Dominican Republic, Santo Domingo, nearly doubled, and early *bachata*, whose roots were quintessentially romantic, began to reflect the hardships of the urban life especially as experienced by rural migrants. *Bachata* also reflected and helped articulate the shifting experiences of male-female relationships in this new environment. While many lyrics were romantic, many during this period consisted of macho bawdy lyrics, a male singer bitterly denouncing women as treacherous and faithless, reflecting the strains and tensions that urbanization imposed on family life and male-female relationships. Pacini-Hernández states, "Men found it increasingly difficult to fulfill their traditional roles as primary breadwinners, and women were forced to move into the workplace to supplement family income, and so *bachata* was transformed from a musical genre defined by its concern with romantic love into one concerned primarily with sexuality, specifically casual sex with no pretense to longevity or legitimacy, often mediated by money, and whose principal social context was the bar/brothel" (153).

The lyrics also conveyed a *barrio* (working-class neighborhood) humor as they manipulated words for a humorous or double entendre effect. Whereas the earlier *bolero campesino* might have been marginalized in urban contexts because of its rural nature, now *bachata* was further discriminated against because it was considered vulgar and immoral and was simultaneously disparaged as generally cheap, poorly produced, and associated with the lower classes. Nevertheless, during the 1970s and 1980s, *bachata* steadily grew in popularity among the majority of the population even though it only circulated through an informal promotion and distribution system such as inexpensive cassettes sold by sidewalk vendors, and was only heard publicly in neighborhood grocery stores (*colmados*) and bars (many of which were also brothels). Recordings of this period reflect the economic status of the music, and the *bachata* of the 1960s, 1970s, and early 1980s was primitively recorded, usually in one take and through one microphone. It was not until 1988 that *bachata* records appeared on a published hit parade, received airplay on FM radio station, were shown on TV, or were sold in commercial record stores.

While it is hard to trace exactly how *bachata* went from the margins to the mainstream, many experts agree that there were several structural changes that contributed to this shift. The sound of *bachata* bands was modernized, as they switched from acoustic to electric guitars, incorporated electric bass and synthesizers, and improved the recorded quality of the music by using multitrack recording and sound mixers. Also, *bachata* began to exhibit a more danceable nature as it adopted many features from **merengue**. Other factors that contributed to the current popularity of *bachata* included the fact that a group of liberal-minded high-profile musicians began to take an interest in *bachata*, and one of them, Juan Luis Guerra, achieved incredible international success with his album *Bachata Rosa* (1991). Guerra's *bachatas* have more polished melodies, rock harmonies, and more urbane lyrics; they are also better recorded and more elaborately arranged than traditional *bachata*. Guerra kept the basic instrumentation and double entendre-laced lyrics of the genre, and his international fame helped present the genre internationally with sweeping success.

Bachata has lost some of its significance as an urban folk genre while at the same time it now appeals to a wider and more diverse audience. In the 1990s, *bachata*'s musical and textual characteristics had become less predictable as new features were added to the previously existing forms. By the middle of the 1990s, *bachata* turned back towards romanticism as bachateros relied less on sexual double entendre and bitter lyrics in order to improve their chances of getting their records played on the radio. In the new wave of *bachata*, there has emerged a New York school, led by the South Bronx group Aventura. These groups have created a *bachata* with a transnational flavor using Spanglish lyrics and combining influences from rhythm and blues, rock, **hip-hop** and **reggaetón**. With performances in large venues such as Madison Square Garden and featuring collaborations with urban performers, Aventura's image is not typical of bachateros. *Bachata* has moved into multiple directions, while many bachateros still keep their connection to the poor by performing almost exclusively in working-class venues; others, such as Aventura, tour around the world and enjoy luxury cars and wear large gold chains. The rise from an exclusively rural tradition to an international phenomenon explains why *bachata* has been named the Dominican blues. *Bachata* today enjoys even more popularity than *merengue*, which has been celebrated as the national music of the Dominican Republic.

Further Reading

Martinez, Samuel. "Not a Cockfight: Rethinking Haitian-Dominican Relations." *Latin American Perspectives* 30, no. 3, Popular Participation against Neoliberalism (2003): 80–101.

Pacini-Hernández, Deborah. *Bachata: A Social History of a Dominican Popular Music.* Philadelphia, PA: Temple University Press, 1995.

Angelina Tallaj

Baião

The *baião* is a syncopated dance music associated with northeastern **Brazil**. It is related to several musical traditions and a cluster of rhythmic patterns commonly found in the northeast. The *baião* was crafted into a commercial popular music of national importance in the 1940s and 1950s by singer-accordionist Luiz Gonzaga (1912–1989); it became his signature genre as well as a cultural emblem of northeastern regional identity in Brazil. The emergence of the *baião* as a regional popular music challenged the supremacy of *samba* as Brazil's national music and highlighted regional contradictions embedded in the idea of Brazil's national consensus culture. The success of Gonzaga (king of the Baião) stimulated the national commercial success of northeastern musical styles and the creation of urban working-class *casas de forró*—dance-clubs where the *baião* and a cluster of other northeastern dance music genres are performed.

Regional musical traditions from the backlands and coastal areas of the northeast were first presented nationally when popular singers and instrumentalists adapted and presented northeastern musical genres such as the *toada, embolada,* and *coco* for national audiences via the broadcast and recording industries centered in Rio de Janeiro. Such regional activity was marginalized in relation to Rio-based *samba* (itself a complex set of performance styles in the process of being defined) as exemplifying fundamental qualities of Brazilian identity. Nevertheless, northeastern music became nationally popular with the rise of Luiz Gonzaga.

For the *baião,* Gonzaga used essential elements common to several musical traditions of the Northeast: a syncopated rhythmic pattern with a strong accent before beat two of a two-beat measure and modal scales with flatted sevenths, and rather static harmonic structures with ambiguous tonic/dominant/subdominant relationships. In the Northeast, a number of closely related dance rhythms (*baiano, abaianada, coco*) are performed on instruments such as *rabecas* (folk violin), *pifanos* (cane flutes), *oito baixo* (eight-bass **accordion**), ***pandeiro*** (tambourine) and ***zabumba*** (bass drum). Pre-dating Gonzaga's popularization of the term as a specific genre of popular music, *baião* was used to refer to a specific rhythmic pattern played on the *viola* (10-string **guitar**) during *desafio* song duels performed by paired singer poets in the Northeast. Gonzaga claims that he was inspired by the rhythmic patterns of the *viola* players as well as by cognate patterns played on the **zabumba** drum.

On recordings and in live and radio broadcast performances between 1946 and 1949, Gonzaga refined the rhythmic accompaniment and instrumental arrangements for the *baião*. He standardized a core instrumental trio of the **acordeón**, *zabumba* bass drum, and triangle to play the *baião* and other northeastern genres. These instruments and the musical details of the *baião* were distinct from the foreign-influenced sound of mainstream Brazilian popular music of the time and served to link the music to the cultural values of northeastern migrant worker populations flooding into Rio de Janeiro and São Paulo. Gonzaga also emphasized a distinctly northeastern pronunciation and singing style, and sang lyrics evoking nostalgia for the natural and cultural beauty of the northeast. In hit songs like "Asa Branca" (1947), "Juazeiro" (1949), and his signature song "Baião" (1949) (co-written with lyricist Humberto Texeira), Gonzaga ushered in the *baião* craze that rivaled the *samba* in popularity. During the 1950s, Gonzaga teamed with several other lyricists (notably Ze Dantas) to produce a string of hit songs. On nationally syndicated radio programs such as *No Mundo do Baião* (In the World of the Baião), Gonzaga presented the *baião,* and other northeastern genres (*coco, xote,* **forró**, *toada, xaxado, xamengo*) were presented as sprouting from the soul of the backland man to enchant the heart of Brazil. From 1946 to 1956, Gonzaga was Brazil's most frequently recorded musical star and his *baião* established regional music as a commercially viable segment of the Brazilian music industry.

By about 1960, Gonzaga and northeastern music had fallen out of national favor but remained a vibrant tradition among northeastern migrant populations in the South and among working-class audiences throughout the Northeast. Gonzaga and the *baião* would be rediscovered in the late 1960s and early 1970s by musicians **Gilberto Gil**, **Caetano Veloso** and other stars of Brazilian mainstream popular music (see **MPB** or ***música popular brasileira***).

Further Reading

Crook, Larry. *Brazilian Music: Northeastern Traditions and the Heartbeat of a Modern Nation.* Santa Barbara, CA: ABC-CLIO, 2005.

McCann, Bryan. *Hello, Hello Brazil: Popular Music in the Making of Modern Brazil.* Durham and London: Duke University Press, 2004.

McGowan, Chris and Ricardo Pessanha. *The Brazilian Sound: Samba, Bossa Nova, and the Popular Music of Brazil.* Revised and expanded edition. Philadelphia, PA: Temple University Press, 2009.

Murphy, John P. *Music in Brazil: Experiencing Music, Expressing Culture.* New York: Oxford University Press, 2006.

Larry Crook

Bajo Sexto

The *bajo sexto* is a large, 12-string, rhythm-bass instrument that is a member of the **guitar** family and is primarily played in ***tejano*** and ***conjunto*** music. The origins of the *bajo sexto* are not clear, but some believe it originated in Spain in the 13th century. Known there as the *bandolón,* it was brought to **Mexico** by Spanish settlers. Other scholars claim that it evolved from the 12-string guitar and emerged in the Bajio region of Jalisco, Mexico in the 19th century. Regardless of its origins, the *bajo sexto* did not become prominent until the late 19th century.

The *bajo sexto* looks much like the 12-string guitar, but it differs in many important ways. It has a deeper sound box, a shorter neck, and thicker strings, which are grouped in six pairs or courses. The lowest three pairs (E-e, A-a, d-d') are tuned in octaves and the highest three pairs (g-g, b-b, e'-e') are tuned in unison.

During the late 19th century, the *bajo sexto* was played at weddings and *bailes de regalos* (dances of gifts). When *conjunto* came onto the scene in the 1930s, the *bajo sexto* was used mainly as a bass instrument to complement the bass line played by the **accordion**. In the late 1930s, *bajo sexto* player Santiago Almeida established it as an important lead instrument in the *conjunto* ensemble. Bass guitar and drums were added to the *conjunto* ensemble in the late 1940s, allowing the *bajo sexto* player to move from strictly rhythmic accompaniment to more melodically driven musical lines and solos. A newer version of the *bajo sexto* called the *bajo quinto* appeared in recent years. It has five pairs of strings instead of the standard six, which allows the musician to project a clearer sound.

Further Reading

Tejeda, Juan and Avelardo Valdez. *Puro Conjunto: An Album in Words & Pictures.* San Antonio, TX: Center for Mexican and American Studies, 2001.

Erin Stapleton-Corcoran

Miguel, Luis

Multi-award-winning pop singer and heartthrob Luis Miguel (b. 1970) was born in **Puerto Rico**, but considers **Mexico** his home. At 15, he earned his first Grammy, for the duet "Me Gustas Tal Como Eres." Since then, he has recorded more than 30 albums. Miguel sings exclusively in Spanish, which has not hindered his professional career or international popularity. With his 2009 release, *No Culpes a La Noche,* he earned his 16th top 10 Top Latin Album. In the 1990s, Miguel moved from main stream pop to embrace traditional Latin American song forms when he recorded a series of four ***bolero*** albums

Romance (1991), which went gold in the United States; *Segundo Romance* (1994), which earned a Grammy; *Romances* (1997); and *Mis Romances* (2001). Miguel sang newly composed *boleros* along with traditional ballads from Mexico, **Argentina**, and **Brazil**, influencing a regional revival of *bolero*. In 2004, Miguel worked with Mariachi Vargas de Tecalitlan to record the ***mariachi***-focused *México el la Piel* album through which he celebrated the traditional Mexican *mariachi* and ***ranchera*** repertoire.

Further Reading

"Luis Miguel," *Contemporary Musicians*. Detroit: Gale Research, Inc., 1989. Vol. 34 (2002): 147–49.

Rebecca Stuhr

Balada

Balada, or the Latin American romantic ballad, began in the 1960s as a pan-Latin American musical genre with its origins in the **bolero**. *Balada* is not particular to any one country; rather, it developed simultaneously in several countries as a mix of European and Latin American styles.

Balada is a type of slow romantic song, a pop ballad, usually about love. It is typically performed by one male singer, usually accompanied by an orchestra. *Balada* singers may also be accompanied by electric **guitars**, bass guitar, and drums. Like the *bolero,* a common theme of a *balada* song is unrequited love. It reached the height of its popularity in the 1970s. *Balada* is played in a slow to moderate tempo and is smooth, typically lacking any kind of Latin American rhythm. In spite of the incorporation of rock elements like the electric guitar and drums, the emphasis is on the singer and the vocal melody.

Well-known Mexican *balada* singer José José performs during the Latin Billboard Awards. (AP/Wide World Photos)

Balada emerged in the 1960s, as rock 'n' roll was beginning to become internationally known, due to the influence of British groups like the Beatles and the Rolling Stones. *Bolero* composers and musicians like Armando Manzanero from **Mexico** modernized the *bolero* by combining soft rock elements with its sound, which eventually resulted in the creation of *balada.* Some musicologists have suggested that *balada* developed in particular from the Mexican *bolero* and the Cuban *filín. Filín* developed in the 1940s in Havana during the *trovadoresco* movement (see *trova*). *Balada* is in many ways the opposite of the **nueva canción** and other types of protest music (see **Protest Song in Latin America**) that arose in the 1960s and 1970s. Although it is often ignored by ethnomusicologists because of its commercialized and corny or *cursi* nature, *balada* is popular all over the world.

Nowadays, Latin pop has absorbed the *bolero* and become the prominent international style of music in the Spanish language. Latin pop began to be considered its own genre in the 1980s, after the widespread success of artists such as Julio Iglesias, Camilo Sesto, and Gloria Estefan. *Balada* may be considered a subcategory of *pop latino.* More recently, popular singers include Thalía from Mexico, Enrique Iglesias (Julio Iglesias's son), Ricky Martin from **Puerto Rico**, and Shakira from **Colombia**.

Balada is popular throughout the South American continent and in the Caribbean. In spite of its commercialism and elements of fantasy, *balada* remains a significant part of the Latin pop that is prevalent around the world today. In Colombia, for example, *balada* was promoted by record companies from the beginning of its formation as a genre. Julio Iglesias and Leo Dan, as well as other internationally known artists, remain popular in Colombia today.

In **Chile**, a *balada* revival occurred in the 1990s. *Balada* is considered by many listeners a guilty pleasure, as it is a sentimental, commercial genre. It is known for its romantic message and typically shies away from political or social commentary.

In the **Dominican Republic**, *balada* and the native Dominican genre **merengue** share much of the same audience, causing some to view *balada* as competition with national music. *Balada,* like *bolero* and **canción,** are sentimental love songs.

In Mexico, most of the Spanish-language music brought in from other countries may be categorized as *balada.* Traditional Mexican music consists of many romantic genres, which explains in part the success of *balada* in the country. Mexico has produced a number of popular *balada* singers. Popular *balada* singers from Mexico include José José, Luis Miguel, and Emmanuel. Artists from Spain such as Julio Iglesias and Camilo Sesto have also attained international commercial success. Roberto Carlos, from **Brazil**, is also an extremely popular *balada* singer, who records music in both Spanish and Portuguese. Well-known Spanish *baladas* include

"Lo mejor de tu vida" by Julio Iglesias, "Algo de mi" by Camilo Sesto, "Como te extraño mi amor" by the Argentine Leo Dan, "El triste" and "Lo Dudo" by José José, and "Este Terco Corazón" by Emmanuel.

Further Reading

Party, Daniel. "*Placer Culpable*: Shame and Nostalgia in the Chilean 1990s *Balada* Revival." *Latin American Music Review* 30, no.1 (2009): 69–98. Project MUSE.

Party, Daniel. "The *Miamization* of Latin-American Pop Music." In *Postnational Musical Identities: Cultural Production, Distribution, and Consumption in a Globalized Scenario,* edited by Ignacio Corona and Alejandro L. Madrid-González, 65–80. Lanham, MD: Lexington Books, 2008.

Stigberg, David. "Foreign Currents during the 60s and 70s in Mexican Popular Music: Rock and Roll, the Romantic Ballad and the *Cumbia*." *Studies in Latin American Popular Culture* 4 (1985): 170–84.

Caitlin Lowery

Bambuco

Bambuco is a musical and dance genre from **Colombia** that was distributed across **Venezuela, Cuba**, the Yucatán Peninsula, and other Caribbean regions. It is usually written in 3/4 or 6/8 meter or in an alternation of both. *Bambuco,* which is performed as a couple dance, can be either vocal or instrumental. A characteristic rhythmic feature is the persistent presence of eighth notes and a strong syncopation into the first beat of the next measure. Romantic and melancholic in character, its roots combined indigenous influences, especially from the Chibcha culture, Spanish influences, mostly from the Basque country, and African influences. Etiologically, its name could derive from Bambuck, a region in West Africa inhabited by the Carabalí people, or derive from the Bamba Indians, whose songs were called *bambucos.* Thus, Colombian *bambucos* are the most representative expression of Andean Colombian music.

Modern *bambuco* is often sung as a duet and its lyrics are often sentimental. Texts use octosyllabic *décimas* and other poetic forms. The singing is accompanied by *tiple, bandola,* **guitar**, or by *estudiantina* ensembles, composed of *bandolas, tiples,* guitars and percussion. The *bambuco característico* is the name given to the instrumental *bambucos* generally interpreted by an *estudiantina*. Currently a renaissance of Andean Colombian music has brought up numerous ensembles such as string and woodwind quartets, piano **trios**, duets, etc., that interpret *bambucos, pasillos, guabinas,* and other Andean Colombian musical styles with both traditional and contemporary approaches.

Further Reading

Varney, John. "An Introduction to the Colombian *Bambuco*." *Latin American Music Review*, 22, no. 2 (Fall/Winter 2001): 123–56.

Raquel Paraíso

Banda

Although *banda* is a generic term for a variety of ensembles consisting of brass, woodwind, and percussion instruments found throughout Spain's former colonies in Latin America, it has come to designate a specific regional band style from the state of Sinaloa on **Mexico's** northwest coast. The *banda sinaloense* (Sinaloan *banda*), or simply *banda,* which gained a reputation in the international popular music market at the close of the 20th century, typically consists of clarinets, trumpets, valve trombones, alto horns, tuba, and a drum set. It is now customary to integrate one or two vocalists into the band. Transnational *bandas* expanded the traditional **ranchera** repertory to include more internationally appealing **cumbias** and **baladas**.

The format of this ensemble dates back to the military bands of European colonists and to the brass music of German immigrants to Mexico's northern Pacific coast in the mid-19th century. The so-called *bandas populares* (popular bands or village bands) or *bandas de viento* (wind bands) were ubiquitous features of Mexico's musical life in the late 19th century and thrived in both rural and urban areas. The instrumentation of early village bands, however, was variable. The revolutionary movement of the 1910s was crucial in the development of the bands' regional characteristics because it promoted patriotism and regionalism. After the Mexican Revolution the lineup in regional bands became more and more standardized. Band membership in Sinaloa averaged from 9 to 12 musicians playing clarinets, cornets or trumpets, trombones with valves, saxhorns (commonly called *armonía* or *charcheta*), tuba, snare drum (*tarola*), and *tambora,* a double-headed bass drum with attached cymbals. Though the brass and reed instruments were imported from Europe, the drums were manufactured locally.

Bandas performed at various outdoor celebrations—bullfights, cockfights, horse races, parades, saints' days, weddings, funerals, and *fandangos* (popular dances). Like the military bands of the time, *bandas populares* played an eclectic repertory of marches, operatic selections, and popular pieces. Since their beginnings in the late 19th century, *bandas populares* have been shunned by the upper classes, labeled as vulgar and backward. Although brass band music had long served as one of the favorite pastimes of the educated classes, *banda* eventually became associated with lower-class music and was rejected by the elite as a crude imitation of their venerable military bands. Urbanization, capitalism, and eventually the culture industry altered Sinaloa society, its lifestyles, habits, and popular musical tastes, but *bandas* remained popular among the rural population and the lower-class urbanites throughout the 20th century.

In the 1920s, *orquestas* (orchestras with predominantly stringed instruments) throughout Mexico began to adjust to music from the **United States** by replacing the traditional double bass with the tuba, integrating a percussion set, and adding such instruments as saxophone and banjo. This new formation became known as the **jazz** band. Inspired by these new trends in popular music, Sinaloan *bandas* too began to play the new upper-class ballroom dances of the time, the fox-trot, the Charleston, and the *tango*.

The main appeal of the *banda* was and continues to be its danceable music, which includes a variety of rhythms, ranging from the local (Mexican) *son*, (Cuban) ***guaracha*, polka**, waltz, and schottische to fox-trot, Cuban ***danzón, bolero, cha-cha-chá, mambo***, and ***cumbia***. Unaffected by the developing radio, film, and recording industries of the early 1930s that revolutionized Mexico's musical world, *banda* musicians continued to play in their traditional surroundings; they also found ample work in the *cantinas* (bars and brothels) of the lower-class urban neighborhoods.

In the 1950s and 1960s, some of those who had moved to the cities of Mazatlán and Culiacán eventually became involved with the newer technological media—radio and recordings. To broaden their appeal, a few bandleaders began to modify the makeup of the traditional *banda* by incorporating such new elements as Cuban percussion instruments (***bongó*** drums, ***maracas***, and ***cencerros***), slide trombones, and saxophones. These commercially oriented *bandas,* known as *banda-orquestas,* performed a more cosmopolitan repertory of mainstream dance music and popular international pieces, such as big-band ***mambo***. Note-reading skills became more important for professional musicians and they aspired to achieve a more polished and precise playing style. Although the big band jazz and *mambo* era left its imprint, *banda* kept a distinct character usually referred to as *sabor sinaloense* (Sinaloan flavor). This character results from the contrast of clarinet and brass timbres, the juxtaposition of *tutti-soli* (an alternation between the whole band and the individual instrument groups of the front line: trumpets, trombones, and clarinets), and the improvisation of countermelodies on one of the frontline instruments, a technique often used while accompanying vocalists. There is a strong emphasis on volume and pulse. Dynamics are mainly generated by alternating *tutti* and *soli* sections, the latter executed on the frontline instruments.

In the mid-1980s, a *grupo* version of the acoustic *banda sinaloense* emerged in Guadalajara (the *grupo* ensemble, including synthesized instruments and a lead vocalist, plays easy-listening Mexican and international pop ballads and is one of Mexico's commercially most successful forms of popular music). This fusion became known as *tecnobanda* (also *technobanda*) or simply *banda*, although *technobanda* retained the trumpets, trombones, and percussion instruments. Saxophones were added and the characteristic *tambora* (double-headed bass drum with attached cymbals) and the clarinets were eliminated. The traditional tubas and *charchetas* (horns) were replaced with electric basses and keyboard synthesizers. Because of these changes in the instrumentation, a typical *technobanda* consists of 7 to 11 musicians only (compared to 14 to 17 musicians of a traditional, acoustic Sinaloan *banda*). Despite the profound influence of regional Mexican music, *technobanda* has been highly innovative. The integration of a vocalist allowed *technobanda* to develop a new and independent repertory. *Technobanda* and its associated *quebradita* dance style spread in the late 1980s from Guadalajara, Jalisco, to Los Angeles, California, where it gained great popularity among immigrants as well as American youths of Mexican heritage.

Accelerating processes of globalization, including mass mediaization and trans-migration, helped the growing acceptance and popularity of *technobanda* and *banda* in the United States. The early 21st century's transnational, commercially oriented Sinaloan *bandas,* such as Banda El Recodo and Banda La Costeña, have included many of *technobanda*'s innovations, in particular a lead vocalist. With an emphasis on the visual and the verbal and a shift in their musical repertory toward the more universally appealing and danceable *cumbia* and the romantic *balada,* high-profile Sinaloan *bandas* entered the circuit of commercial popular mass music. The driving force of Sinaloan *banda* music and its strength to cope with changing fashions and cultural trends can be ascribed to its versatility and adaptability. Although *banda* music became less community centered and more universally appealing when *bandas* began to record for a mass market and perform stage shows for a transnational mass audience in the late 1990s, it has not lost its regional flavor.

Further Reading

Simonett, Helena. *Banda: Mexican Musical Life across Borders.* Middletown, CT: Wesleyan University Press, 2001.

Simonett, Helena. *En Sinaloa nací: Historia de la música de banda* [Born in Sinaloa: History of Banda Music]. Mazatlán, Mexico: Asociación de Gestores del Patrimonio Histórico y Cultural de Mazatlán, 2004.

Helena Simonett

Bandola

The *bandola* is a small flat-backed chordophone found mostly in **Colombia** and **Venezuela**. Related to the Spanish *bandurria*—a 12-string chordophone—this instrument has a pear shape and a short neck. Modern Colombian or Andean *bandolas* have different numbers of strings, although the most common *bandolas* have 14 strings arranged in six triple (first and second courses) and double courses, or 12 strings arranged in six double courses. There are *bandolas* with 16 strings where the first two courses are triple and the rest are double, and some that have 18 strings and all the courses are triple. The six courses are tuned f-b-e'-a'-d''-g'' (lower to higher string) and it is played with a plectrum. As the soprano voice of the traditional ensemble called **estudiantina**—composed of *bandolas*, **tiples**, **guitar**, and percussion—*bandolas* carry most of the melodies in instrumental **bambucos, pasillos**, *guabinas*, **danzas**, and other Andean Colombian musical styles. *Bandola* also plays a chordal role when those musical genres are sung.

Bandola llanera and *bandola oriental* are the two main types of Venezuelan *bandolas*, each referring to a different geographical location where they are found within the country. Like the Colombian *bandola*, both have a pear-shaped body. The *bandola llanera*, found in the western planes, has four single strings commonly tuned b-e'-b'-f''. The *bandola oriental* from the eastern part of the country has a deeper body and eight nylon strings arranged in four double courses tuned a/a-e/e'-b'-f''.

Further Reading

Artez, Isabel. "Guitarras, bandolas y arpas españolas en América Latina." In *España en la Música de Occidente: actas del Congreso Internacional celebrado en Salamanca, 29 de octubre—5 de noviembre de 1985: "Año Europeo de la Música,"* edited by Emilio Casares, Ismael Fernández de le Cuesta, José López-Calo, and José M. Llorens. 1: 333–48. Madrid: Instituto Nacional de las Artes Escénicas y de la Música, Ministerio de Cultura, 1987.

Schechter, John Mendell. *Music in Latin American Culture: Regional Traditions.* New York: Schirmer Books, 1999.

Raquel Paraíso

Bandolím

The *bandolím* is a mandolin from **Brazil** introduced by the Portuguese in the 16th century. Unlike the bowl-back Neapolitan mandolins, the *bandolím* has a wider body and a flat back. Tops are usually made of pine spruce with backs and sides made of a variety of woods such as rosewood or maple. Its four courses, or pairs of strings, are tuned like the mandolin—G-D-A-E, from lowest to highest. The *bandolím* has long been associated with folk music, but it was not until the 20th century that it became popular in urban music, most notably the **choro**. Although chords are played on the instrument, it is used primarily as a melody instrument while other plucked chordophones take on the role of harmonic support such as **violão**, and **cavaquinho**. Its most famous practitioner was Jacob de Bandolim, born Jacob Pick Bittencourt (1918–1969). He was credited as the most influential player of the *bandolím*. His career coincides with the development of the *choro* in urban popular music, and he was considered a very skilled improviser. Among the great players, equal mention should be made of Luperce Miranda, who like Jacob de Bandolim (1907–1977) was an extraordinary talent on the instrument. He enjoyed early success in his career with his song "Pinião." Later *bandolím* notables include Hamilton Holanda (b. 1976) and Nilze Carvalho (b. 1969), both of whom belong to a more recent generation of players whose careers parallel the resurgence of the *choro* as a popular music genre.

Further Reading

Livingston-Isenhour, Tamara Elena, and Thomas George Caracas Garcia. *Choro: A Social History of a Brazilian Popular Music*. Bloomington: Indiana University Press, 2005.

Medeiros, Flavio Henrique, and Carlos Almada. *Brazilian Mandolin*. Pacific, MO: Mel Bay Publications, 2003.

George Torres

Bandoneón

The *bandoneón* is a chromatic free-reed instrument similar to the **accordeón** and *concertina*. Originally developed in the Saxony region of Germany around 1850, it is named after Heinrich Band, who first commercialized it. While it was developed as an instrument capable of playing sacred and secular Western art music and German popular music, the *bandoneón* is most closely associated today with the **tango** of **Argentina** and **Uruguay**. It also appears in the rural folk music of parts of Argentina, Uruguay, and southwestern **Brazil**.

The instrument is constructed of a square wooden frame, with button manuals for each hand, and a bellows constructed of cardboard reinforced with leather. The reeds are made of steel, and set into reed plates made of either zinc or aluminum. Early versions of the *bandoneón* had between 25 and 40 keys, but over the following century the instrument's design expanded and models exist with up to over 100 keys, resulting in 220 different notes or voices. The *bandoneón* that is standard in South America is the 72-button, 142-voice model first introduced by Alfred Arnold in 1911. Arnold, part of a family dynasty that at one time produced all of the major brands of *bandoneóns,* is the namesake of the most famous and most preferred model, the "doble A" ("double A"), which bears his initials. This model has 38 buttons in the right-hand manual, covering the treble range (a to b''') and 33 in the left covering the bass (C to b'). Each button has a separate set of octave-tuned metal reeds for when the instrument is opened and closed, effectively demanding that the performer learn two separate, unrelated keyboard layouts for each hand. The *bandoneón* is fitted with a breather valve operated by the right thumb, allowing the player to easily open or close the bellows without sounding

A man playing the *bandoneón,* an instrument that is essential to most *Tango* bands. (AP/Wide World Photos)

any of the reeds, a factor that facilitates a number of specialized playing techniques unique to *tango*.

The *bandoneón*'s precise arrival date to the Río de la Plata region has not been satisfactorily documented. Individual instances of instruments appearing in the region occur as early as 1863 in Uruguay and certainly by 1880 in Buenos Aires, but in any case the *bandoneón* was not imported and sold locally on a commercially or culturally significant scale until the turn of the 20th century.

Bandoneón production in Germany reached its peak in the 1920s and 1930s, and was already in decline by the Second World War. Production of the instrument stopped altogether when the Arnold factory, located in Carlsfeld, was expropriated by the East German government in 1948. In recent years, individual artisans have attempted to revive the practice of *bandoneón* making, but there is yet to be an operation that has taken up large-scale production.

The instrument's adoption into the *tango,* which previously had been played mostly by trios consisting of guitar, flute, and violin, significantly changed the character of that musical style. While early *tango* was often light-hearted and played at a lively tempo, the significant technical difficulties of executing melodic passages on the *bandoneón* likely contributed to the *tango*'s adoption of a slower tempo and generally more melancholy character.

In the first decade of the 20th century, the group of *tango* composers known as the *Vieja Guardia* (Old Guard) included several prominent *bandoneónists,* most notably Eduardo Arolas (1892–1924) and Vicente Greco (1888–1924), who helped establish the instrument's prominence in the genre. Generally, the instrument primarily played a melodic role, often doubling or ultimately replacing the flute in small ensembles.

The instrument's role in the genre began to expand when Pedro Laurenz (1902–1972) and Pedro Maffia (1899–1967) joined the sextet of Julio de Caro (1899–1980) in 1924. In this ensemble, the two *bandoneóns* not only played melodies, countermelodies, and accompaniment figures, but also introduced what would become one of the fixtures of later *tango* style: the virtuosic variations, contrapuntal elaborations of the original melody that showcased the *bandoneón* player or players.

As the size of the typical *tango* ensemble grew to become the **orquesta típicas** so did the size of the *bandoneón* section, which sometimes included up to five players. Undoubtedly the most respected *bandoneónist* in the *tango* tradition was Aníbal Troilo (1914–1975), also a prominent composer and bandleader. He was known for the subtle, vocal quality of his phrasing. Troilo's *orquesta* also provided the framework for another principal *bandoneónist* and composer of the second half of the 20th century, **Astor Piazzolla** (1921–1992). Piazzolla's *tango nuevo* incorporated **jazz** and nontraditional harmonies, and he was a prodigious improviser on the instrument with a very personal style of ornamentation and articulation.

Further Reading

García Méndez, Javier, and Penón, Arturo. *Bandonion: A Tango History.* Translated by Tim Burnard. Gibsons Landing, BC: Nightwood Editions, 1988.

Michael O'Brien

Baquiné (also *baquiní*)

In the **Dominican Republic** and **Puerto Rico**, *baquiné* refers to a specific variety of forms of Latin American celebrations held for the wake of an infant or child. Children's wakes have been practiced throughout most of Latin America in the 19th and early 20th centuries, though relatively few places still practice it today. In other parts of Latin America, it may go under the broader term of *velorio del angelito* (wake of the little angel), as it is believed that when an infant dies, because of its innocence, it goes to dwell among the angels.

Due to the specific nature of the event, the music for the *baquiné* consists of specific music and songs. Among the Antillean variety, where it is a custom drawn from African traditions, the music and texts may invoke African-influenced elements.

Traditionally the child is placed in the center of a room on a platform in the mother's home, surrounded by flowers and offerings from the child's life. Participants gather around the child celebrating with games, food, and music particular to the locale of the celebration.

In popular music, *salsa* artist Willie Colón composed a theme out of the *baquiné* in his album *El Baquiné de Angelitos Negros,* a 1977 Fania Records release that was also a made-for-television ballet. Colón also references the genre in the text to his song "Che Che Colé" (*A tí te gusta la bomba/y te gusta el baquiné*—You like the *bomba/*and you like the *baquiné*).

Further Reading

"The Child's Wake: A Puerto Rican Folk Tradition," by Lucy Torres. In *Conference on Minority Studies,* edited by George E. Carter, and J.R. Parker. Essays on Minority Folklore: Selected Proceedings of the 3rd Annual Conference on Minority Studies, April 1975. Selected Proceedings of the Annual Conference on Minority Studies, vol. 3. La Crosse: Institute for Minority Studies, University of Wisconsin, 1977.

Kuss, Malena. *Performing the Caribbean Experience.* Joe R. and Teresa Lozano Long Series in Latin American and Latino Art and Culture. Austin, TX: University of Texas Press, 2007.

Schechter, John M. "Corona y Baile: Music in the Child's Wake of Ecuador and Hispanic South America, Past and Present." *Latin American Music Review/Revista de Musica Latinoamericana:* 4, no. 1 (1983): 1–80.

George Torres

Batería

In Spanish- and Portuguese-speaking Latin America, the term *batería* (battery) refers to percussion, a percussion group within an ensemble, or a drum set. The combination and number of instruments that make up the *batería* vary among regions. For example, a *bolero* **trio** may consist of **bongós** and **maracas**, while the largest *schola de samba baterías* sometimes consists of several hundred participants. While these larger ensembles have many different types of instruments in their design, there is a great amount of doubling of parts among instruments. Nevertheless, most *batería* groups in Latin American popular music consist of the smaller varieties, with usually one player on a part. It is important to remember that Latin American rhythm sections commonly consist (and consisted throughout much of their history) of several different percussion instruments playing simultaneously. Each of these instruments plays an ostinato timeline pattern, and the overall effect is a composite rhythm produced by all layers of percussion. In a comparison of the surviving recordings with the many published parts for Latin American band music that appeared during the 1920s to 1950s, it is clear from the printed instrumentation roster that although a *batería* part was not provided, players were expected to know the patterns appropriate to the form or genre being performed for their individual parts. Hence, most *batería* parts in popular music are improvised percussion scores, with basic patterns given for breaks and specific rhythmic fills.

Further Reading

Torres, George. "Sources for Latin Big Band Performance: An Examination of the Latin American Stocks in the Library of Congress." *College Music Symposium*, no. 43 (2003): 25–41.

George Torres

Batucada

Batucada is a subgenre of **samba** played by the large drum ensembles of **Brazil**, most notably the *escolas de samba* (samba schools) of Rio de Janeiro. The etymology of *batucada* stems from *batuque,* a generic term referring to Afro-Brazilian drumming in general. *Batuque* has origins in the Kimbundu language of Angola and its creolized derivatives are used throughout the Portuguese-speaking world to describe various forms of music and dance of African origin. Where *batuque* is a noun, *batucar* is a verb meaning to drum that is also commonly used to describe even the simple act of tapping out a rhythm on a tabletop. *Batucada,* then, implies a drum off or drumming jam. The *samba* schools of Rio de Janeiro, with *baterías* (drum sections) that can number in the hundreds, have become eponymous of the term.

The earliest *samba* schools in the late 1920s were more like marching bands, playing *marchinhas,* or little marches. In the following decades, *samba* schools became increasingly professionalized and adapted a uniquely *carioca* (of Rio) style of drumming. As the groups grew in size, new instruments were adapted for both esthetic and practical reasons, such as keeping musicians in time. Other factors that influenced the development of the *batucada* include changing competition regulations, which set strict time limits during the **Carnival** pageant. Thus the *sambaenredo,* or themed *samba,* is today played at an incredibly fast tempo. While some critics have lamented the emphasis on speed over melody in the pageant, it is undeniable that the Brazilian *batucada* is one of the most impressive displays of syncopated rhythm on a grand scale.

A typical *samba* school consists of its *batería,* dancers, flag-bearers, and a motorized float that displays the school's allegorical theme. The float typically carries the lead singer and an accompanying musician playing the ***cavaquinho*** (a Portuguese four-stringed instrument related to the *ukulele*). The *batería* consists of numerous drums of various timbres and sizes, shakers, bells, and friction drums. To facilitate group coordination, each percussion segment has its own leader while the entire *batería* responds to calls from the main director, who uses the *apito,* a tri-tone whistle, to alert the group.

The lowest drums of the *batucada* are the **surdos** (literally meaning deaf), which are considered the heartbeat of the group and played with padded mallets. The lowest-pitched *surdo* plays the *marcação,* or the time marker on the second beat, characteristic of *samba.* A higher-pitched *surdo* responds by playing on the first beat. Other *surdos* play syncopated variations usually beginning on the second beat of the phrase. The *caixa,* or snare drum, typically plays a 16th-note pattern over the duple meter that generally drives the rhythm. The *repinique,* or tenor drum, is played with one stick and one free hand. It is the lead *repinique* player that almost always plays the various calls and pickups that mark the beginning and ending of specific musical passages. The smallest drum in the ensemble is the **tamborim**, played with a beater that is made up of multiple plastic rods bound together. The *tamborins* (plural) play chatter-like, highly syncopated phrases that punctuate certain sections of a piece.

Other percussion instruments that are essential to the *baterías* are the various idiophones and membranophones not played with mallets or sticks. The *agogô* is a double bell of Yoruban origin that has been modified in recent decades to have triple or even quadruple bells arranged in successive pitches. The **chocalho** is a type of shaker consisting of a rack of small metal plates resembling a sort of abacus. The **reco-reco** is a metallic scraper instrument with coiled springs that are rasped with a metal rod. The **cuíca** friction drum has a drumhead with a stick tied to the stretched hide. The stick is rubbed with a moist cloth, creating a high-pitched squeal that is regulated by increasing and decreasing the tension on the drumhead with the other hand. The **pandeiro**, or tambourine, is often used more for visual than musical effect in *samba* schools. A *malabarista* (juggler) dances and plays a very large *pandeiro,* throwing the instrument into the air and creating acrobatic moves while dancing. Though *malabaristas* are skilled **pandeiro** players, they serve more as dancers and are usually found in the dance sections of the *escolas de samba.*

To the untrained ear the *batucadas* of the *samba* schools may seem repetitive or even identical. However, most *baterías* have their own unique, if subtle, variations in their playing that are characteristic of each *samba* school. Today, the *batucadas* of Rio de Janeiro are famous the world over and *samba* schools can be found in many major cities throughout the world.

Further Reading

McGowan, Chris, and Ricardo Pessanha. *The Brazilian Sound: Samba, Bossa Nova, and the Popular Music of Brazil.* Philadelphia, PA: Temple University Press, 2009.

Morales, Ed. *The Latin Beat: The Rhythms and Roots of Latin Music from Bossa Nova to Salsa and Beyond.* Cambridge, MA: Da Capo Press, 2003.

Beto González

Biguine

The *biguine* is a lively *Creole* music and closed couple dance genre that originated in **Martinique**, but became very popular all over the French Antilles and in France during the 19th century. The popular history of the *biguine* goes back to the mid-19th century, just following the Martiniquan emancipation of slaves in 1848. *Biguine* reached its apex during the 1930s through the 1950s and became perhaps the most popular dance among the *Creole* population during this latter period. By the second half of the 19th century, the **mazurka** and waltz became creolized (**mazouk** and valse *creole*) and together with the *biguine,* the three were known as *mizik kwéyòl*. Through transformations and modernization, the *biguine* became one of the main progenitors to **zouk** music in the 1980s.

Like the other creolized dance genres, the *biguine* is a syncretic mix of layered African rhythms, which produce a complex composite rhythm blended with European melodies and harmony. The texts to the songs are sung in *Creole*. In the 1940s and 1950s dance hall music provided the majority of exposure to *biguine* audiences. Live orchestras were hired to provide music for social dancing. In this period, the instrumental composition of these orchestras consisted of a singer, saxophones, trumpets, a **guitar**, violins, drums, and a double bass, and occasionally, piano and *maracas*. Well-known *biguine* ensembles from this period include Roger Fanfant's Fairness Jazz and Brunel Averne's El Calderon. While these orchestras played a repertoire of *tangos*, waltzes, and other internationally popular dance music from sheet music, their creolized repertoire was written and performed in a non-literate tradition from memory.

There were two types of *biguine* practiced in this golden age (ca. 1940–1960): the *biguine classique* (in moderate tempo) and the *biguine vidé* (faster tempo). Another *biguine, biguine piqué,* is now rarely performed. The *biguine classique* was the more popular subgenre, and the following remarks refer to the more popular *bigune classique.*

The rhythm of the *biguine* went through a series of subtle transformations from the 1940s to the 1960s, which included changes in the percussion section. While earlier orchestras created their rhythm from a layering of drum set, guitar, and bass, the later versions from the late 1950s and early 1960s made more use of Afro-Cuban percussion instruments like *clave*, *maracas, bongos*, and *timbals* added to the texture. The composite rhythm is closely related to the Cuban **cinquillo** and *tresillo*.

The melody and harmony of the *biguine* is diatonic, revolving usually around tonic and dominant harmonies, with the melody playing a repetitive and syncopated rhythm. Structurally, the music consists of eight-bar periodic phrases that form alternating couplets and refrains. After a short introduction on the **guitar**, the band would play alternating refrain-couplet phrases for two passes, and then the vocal soloist would enter singing texts to the same melodic structure given previously by the instrumentalists. The lyrics of the *biguine* usually comment on daily life, or refer to the beauty of one's homeland. Into the 1960s, some of the texts became more overtly sexual, using double entendres to make pornographic allusions.

Beginning in the 1950s, the *biguine* began to be influenced by foreign repertories, including American **jazz, calypso**, Haitian popular music, and **Afro-Cuban** music. As a result, the *biguine* started to go through a period of transformation that gave the genre a more modern sound. Soon the *biguine* was becoming appropriated by other genres, which resulted in a series of hybrid forms such as *boula ka,* a cross between Guadeloupean *gwo ka* and *biguine.* By the late 1970s and 1980s, elements drawn directly from the *biguine,* along with cadence-rampa and cadence-lypso, resulted in a new hybrid genre known as *zouk.* Today, *biguine* can be heard by orchestras that play old-time repertoire to nostalgic audiences, and also among folkloric groups that see the genre as part of the repertoire of roots music.

In the **United States**, Cole Porter had a tremendous commercial success with a song entitled "Begin the Beguine," which besides being a misspelling was also originally sung to the rhythm of a *bolero*. The misnomer continued throughout the 1940s and 1950s, and *bolero* rhythm was often inappropriately labeled a beguine.

Further Reading

Benoit, Édouard, "Biguine: Popular Music of Guadeloupe, 1940 to 1960." In *Zouk: World Music in the West Indies,* edited by Jocelyne Guilbault, 53–67. Chicago: University of Chicago Press, 1993.

Desroches, Monique. "Musical Tradition in Martinique: Between the Local and the Global." *Transcultural Music Review/ Revista transcultural de musica,* 2 (1996). Online Journal. http://www.sibetrans.com/trans/a279/musical-tradition-in-martinique-between-the-local-and-the-global, accessed June 2, 2012.

Gerstin, Julian and Dominique Cyrille. Liner Notes for *Martinique: Cane Fields and City Streets,* recorded in 1962 by Alan Lomax with the assistance of Antoinette Marchand. 1 CD, Rounder Records CD 11661 1730 2, 2001 (Caribbean Voyage Series).

George Torres

Bloco Afro

The *bloco afro* is a type of **Carnival** organization that originated in the city of Salvador da Bahia in northeast **Brazil** in the 1970s as part of the widespread renaissance of black cultural forms and political consciousness. The *blocos afro* tradition rose to national and international prominence in the 1980s via an overt sociopolitical agenda of black empowerment and an influential hybrid music style known as *samba-reggae* associated with the *bloco afro* **Olodum**.

Olodum

The musical ensemble Olodum is a *bloco afro* based in the heart of Pelourinho, a historic neighborhood in **Brazil**. They are known for popularizing the rhythm *samba-reggae* and for their innovative blends of Bahian street percussion with rhythms of the African diaspora, especially those from the Caribbean. They have collaborated with Paul Simon, Michael Jackson, and Spike Lee and performed throughout the world. Olodum was founded in 1979 as a community **Carnival** association of diverse individuals continuing in the footsteps of Brazil's first *bloco afro*, *Ile Aiye*. The name Olodum is derived from the deity Olodumare (supreme god) from the Afro-Brazilian religion *candomblé*. Olodum has thousands of members but the main performing ensemble usually consists of 18 musicians and expands to 200 for Carnival. Their ensemble includes vocals, a rhythm, and brass section, and percussion consisting of **caixa**, **repique**, **surdo**, *timbals*, **timbau**, and **conga**. Olodum's songs vary between a percussion-dominated sound and a pop **axé music** style. Many songs contain intricate percussion breaks with catchy melodies and choral refrains while their lyrics address issues such as racial equality, social injustice, and black pride.

Further Reading

Crook, Larry. "Northeastern Brazil." In *Music in Latin American Culture: Regional Traditions,* edited by John Mendell Schechter, 192–235. New York: Schirmer Books, 1999.

Thomas Rohde

The rise of the *blocos afro* in the early 1970s reflected a conscious attempt among members of Salvador's black community to create a uniquely African-related cultural space for Salvador's majority black population during the city's annual carnival celebrations. Proclaiming and denouncing the history of discrimination and marginalization of the black population in the city—indeed, throughout Brazil—leaders of Ilê Aiyê (the first *bloco afro*) formed a community group in the neighborhood of Curuzu, Liberdade, and first paraded in the carnival of 1975 to, in a translation of their own words, "express the values of the black race." Influenced by the United States' civil rights movement, black nationalist movements, and the spread of African American popular music of the 1970s, Ilê Aiyê quickly became a powerful cultural mechanism for Salvador's black community, especially its youth, to reinterpret black Brazilians' contemporary and historical connections to Africa and to other African diasporic communities. A mixture of local and international Afro-related elements of music, poetry, choreography, and visual symbolism played a vital part in Ilê Aiyê's parades and performances.

Ilê Aiyê's musical dimensions drew primarily on the *samba* schools of Rio de Janeiro and the *afoxé* Carnival tradition of Salvador. A powerful drum-line with large *surdos* (bass drums), *repiques* (tenor drums), *shekere* (beaded gourd shakers), and other percussion instruments accompanied lead and chorus singers while dancers and other participants (all costumed in textiles and accessories that evoked a noble and heroic African heritage) marched in the streets of Salvador proclaiming the beauty of being black. Ilê Aiyê sang songs whose lyrics mentioned African chiefs, decried racial discrimination, and highlighted the inherent value of the black race. Through the mainstream media, Ilê Aiyê's members were accused of racial agitation. In essence, the group had touched a nerve deep in the Brazilian nationalist ideology, which proclaimed Brazil as a racial democracy. Ilê Aiyê's formation was the initial salvo in an emerging socioesthetic revolution to construct a socially engaged Afro-Brazilian identity in Salvador and in Brazil. By the early 1980s, Ilê Aiyê's grassroots success had stimulated the founding of several other *blocos afro* (Olodum, Malê Debalê, Araketu, Muzenza) and by 1983, there were 16 groups officially parading in Salvador's Carnival and perhaps another 20 or so participating unofficially. Chief among these groups was Olodum.

Olodum (founded in 1979) was particularly influential and promoted a racially inclusive ideology for the *blocos afro* and proposed a distinctly diasporic notion of African identity. The international spread of *reggae* and other contemporary Caribbean-linked musical styles (especially *merengue* and *salsa*) exerted considerable influence on members of Olodum and other *blocos afro* organizations. In the mid-1980s, Olodum musical director, drummer Antonio Luís de Souza (Neguinho do Samba), began mixing *bloco afro* drumming patterns with a variety of Afro-Caribbean rhythms. Along with his drummers, Neguinho do Samba created new drumming patterns (one dubbed *meringue* and another *reggae*) and a new performance style that became known as *samba-reggae*.

Olodum's 1987 carnival song "Faraó, Divindade do Egito" (words and melody written by Luciano Gomes dos Santos and set to the *samba-reggae* performance style by Neguinho do Samba) became a national hit and catapulted Olodum and its musical group to unprecedented success. By the late 1980s, Olodum and other *blocos afro* from Salvador da Bahia were establishing themselves in the national and international music industry. Olodum went on to record with Paul Simon and Michael Jackson in the 1990s. Simultaneously, a number of Bahian musicians tapped into the street-level energy of the *bloco afro* tradition and translated it into a world music format that was marketed as *axé music* in the 1990s.

Toña La Negra

Afro-Mexican singer Toña La Negra (Maria Antonia del Carmen Peregrino Alvarez), (1912–1982) is chiefly remembered for her interpretation of **boleros**, although she originally trained as an opera singer. She first became famous for her rendition of Agustin Lara's "Enamorada." Lara wrote "Lamento Jarocho" especially for her and she received seven encores when she first performed it at the Esperanza Iris Theater. She performed throughout her career with her brother, **tres** guitar player Pablo "El Negro" Peregrino, and his band Son Clave de Oro. Toña toured the United States and **Cuba**, had a successful film career, and was heard regularly on station XEW, which made her one of the earliest stars of bolero. In 1938, Toña had her first film appearance in Auguila o sol. She went on to sing "Alma de Veracruz" in the film Maria Eugenia, and "Eternamente" in Konga Roja. She contracted with RCA Victor and recorded with Orquesta Gigante de Chucho Zarzosa, Juan Garcia Esquivel, and her brother Pablo Peregrino.

Further Reading

Strongman, Roberto. "The Latin American Queer Aesthetics of El Bolereo." *Canadian Journal of Latin American & Caribbean Studies* 32, no. 64 (Nov. 2007): 39–78.

Rebecca Stuhr

Further Reading

Crook, Larry. *Brazilian Music: Northeastern Traditions and the Heartbeat of a Modern Nation.* Santa Barbara, CA: ABC-CLIO, 2005.

Crowley, Daniel J. *African Myth and Black Reality in Bahian Carnival.* Los Angeles, CA: Museum of Cultural History, UCLA, 1984.

Moura, Milton Araújo. "World of Fantasy, Fantasy of the World: Geographic Space and Representation of Identity in the Carnival of Salvador, Bahia." In *Brazilian Popular Music and Globalization,* edited by Charles A. Perrone and Christopher Dunn, 161–76. Gainesville: University Press of Florida, 2001.

Larry Crook

Bolero

The Latin American *bolero* is a song and dance form that originated in **Cuba** in the 19th century. Its name originates from the Spanish *bolero,* though few surface similarities exist between the two. Having migrated to the broader part of Latin America in the early 20th century, the *bolero* eventually became the dominant genre for romantic ***baladas*** in Latin America from the 1930s to the 1950s. Since the 1980s the *bolero* has enjoyed a new popularity of old repertoire among younger listeners, thus continuing to serve as a dominant genre of Latin American popular music.

The early history of the *bolero* goes back to the migration of the Spanish *bolero*, a song and dance form that flourished in the 18th and 19th centuries. This Spanish version is typically in 3/4 with musical characteristics similar to the *seguidilla* and *fandango*. One of the more noticeable features is the rhythm of an eighth note followed by two-16ths and four-eighths.

In Latin America, the *bolero* originated in Cuba as a duple-meter song and dance form during the last half of the 19th century in Santiago de Cuba, most likely from musical characteristics drawn from the early Spanish *bolero*. Nevertheless, on the surface, early Cuban *boleros* would appear to have more in common with the Cuban ***contradanza*** and ***danzón*** than with the Spanish *bolero*. The *bolero* then became part of the evolving family of 19th-century Cuban genres whose lineage includes the ***habanera***, *contradanza,* and *danzón.* The first *bolero* in Cuba is credited to Jose "Pepe" Sanchez, whose "Tristezas" was written in 1885, though some could point to the term *bolero* being applied to other non-Spanish examples as early as 1830. The genre at this time remained in the provinces and outside of Havana until around the 1920s. At this time, traveling orchestras as well as advances in the media, including radio and sound recording, helped bring the *bolero* not only into Havana, but also into a wider audience throughout Latin America via **Mexico**.

Throughout much of Latin America, there was a strongly felt part of colonialism that continued to favor European tastes of more indigenous styles. During the period between Mexican independence (1821) and the Mexican Revolution (1910–1920), there was very little appreciation for indigenous Mexican music among the upper classes. Because of this, the *canción mexicana* would play an important role in urbanizing the *bolero* in Latin America, and thus lend an important hand in extending its appeal beyond rural audiences.

An example of bolero rhythm. (George Torres)

The *canción mexicana* had two basic styles: one that is part of a *mestizo* tradition and one that belongs to a more European *bel canto* style of singing. It is this latter type of song that had the greater affect on the *bolero,* with musical traits that include tonal harmonies, a melodic style that emphasizes a strong and clear technique, and a strong emphasis on vocal tone production. Influential songs that employed this style include "La Paloma," "La golondrina," and "Estrellita" by Manuel Ponce.

The first signs of the *bolero* in Mexico come from the period just after the Revolution when songs such as "Estrellita" were most popular among their listeners. Through a musical connection between Cuba and the Yucatan Peninsula in Mexico, traveling Cuban troupes did much to introduce regional Mexican audiences to emerging genres such as the *bolero*. The most important exponent of this Yucatan school of *bolero* composition was Guty Cardenas from Mérida. Using Yucatan as an entry point, the *bolero* spread throughout the rest of Mexico.

The period from the 1930s to about 1960 marks the era known as the *"epoca de oro"* (golden age) of the *bolero*. Beginning with the works of **Agustín Lara** and ending with the performances and recording of ***trios románticos*** like **Trio Los Panchos**, the *bolero* in this era went through a kind of urbanization and crystallization that changed it from a rural sound to a more urban popular style. This was largely due to the influence of Agustin Lara, whose style of writing, using modern melodic and harmonic formulas as well as smoothing out rhythmic features, made an everlasting change in *bolero* style.

After Lara, the most strongly felt changes in *bolero* performance lie in the hands of the Mexican *trios románticos,* which were a product of the Cuban and Mexican **duos** and trios that had existed in the period just prior, including Los Hermanos Martinez

---

Trio Los Panchos

Trio Los Panchos was comprised of singer-guitarists from **Mexico** who from 1944 to 1981 were the foremost exponents of the *trío romántico* and its musical speciality, *bolero*. The original group consisted of Alfredo Gil (1915–1999), Chucho Navarro (1913–1993), and Hernando Aviles (1914–1986), the latter performing the role of lead vocalist.

At their peak, Los Panchos were the most popular musical ensemble in Latin America, but they also toured successfully in Europe, Asia, North Africa, and North America. In Japan they sold records by the thousands, eventually recording six records in Japanese. Los Panchos recorded some 2,500 songs on 250 albums. They also collaborated with solo singers such as Javier Solis and American pop chanteuse Edyie Gormé. The latter collaboration, *Canta en Español* yielded Los Panchos one of their biggest selling albums, and the recording of "Sabor a mi" became a favorite among Hispanic Americans in the **United States**. Los Panchos performed with different lead vocalists until 1981 when Gil officially retired. Navarro continued to perform until his death in 1993.

Further Reading

Torres, George. "The *Bolero Romántico:* From Cuban Dance to International Popular Song." In *From Tejano to Tango: Essays on Latin American Popular Music,* edited by Walter A. Clark, 151–71. New York: Garland, 2002.

George Torres

Gil and Trio Calaveras. But it was Trio Los Panchos who had the greatest influence on the *tríos romantíco.* Los Panchos, whose debut was at the Teatro Hispano in New York in 1944, consisted of three singers, all who accompanied themselves on **guitar** and sang in a high, sweet sounding, three-part harmony. By 1945, Alfredo Gil added a new sound to the group by incorporating his newly invented *requinto* (a small soprano guitar) with which he played florid introductions and interludes between the verses giving the trio its characteristic instrumental sound. Coupled with a rhythm section on recording and live performances, the sound of Trio Los Panchos was at once melodically and harmonically sophisticated, with a subtle, underlying Afro-Cuban rhythm. Los Panchos's unique blend of instruments, rhythms, and harmonies would be emulated by other trios for the next 15 years, and their special sound would become popular all over the world. Alfredo Gil, Chucho Navarro, and Hernando Avilés formed Los Panchos in New York City after coming to the **United States** to complete a radio contract. In their long career, the group toured extensively throughout the world in the years that followed, eventually recording songs in Greek and Japanese.

The themes in *bolero* poetry often deal with themes of bittersweet, unrequited, betrayed, or eternal love. Although often categorized as sentimental or corny, *bolero* poetry has earned the respect of poets and musicians in Latin America. Indeed, Latin American authors such as Manuel Puig have used the *bolero* as a basis for their own novels. One of the techniques of *bolero* poets is the use of extremes in the texts. *Bolero* scholar Iris Zavala has shown that these words of affirmation, which are discretely negated, appear as at once positive and negative extremes: to die/to live, to love/ to abhor, presence/absence.

In performance, the texts are often set as verse/refrain structures with the verses repeating in the form of two double periods in *bolero* rhythm, and with a formal structure of AABA, ABAB, or AABB. After 1955 and the emergence of the *cha cha chá*, it was not uncommon within an AABA structure to have the B section set as a *cha cha chá,* resulting in a *bolero-chá.* Vocally, the singers would sing in either unison or three-part harmony, with a vocal variation of some kind at the repeat. For example, a section of a song with texted harmony might be repeated with the accompanying harmony being hummed underneath the lead vocal.

Guitars are the distinguishing instrumental feature to this sound, and the combination of two guitars and a *requinto* balanced nicely with the voices. Transposition was done by use of the *capo,* which also provided alternatives to harmonic inversions on the guitars, thus avoiding the sound of the two standard guitars playing in the same tessitura. The *requinto* would play the majority of the passagework, including rapid melodic introductions, while the other guitars played a syncopated *bolero* rhythm underneath. The rhythm section usually consisted of two or three instruments, usually maracas and bongos, the latter sometimes being replaced by the **congas**. Other instruments might include **güiro,** *timbals*, and **clave**. The rhythm section served as an anonymous backup, with the focus always being the trio.

The trio format became standard and many groups followed in the path of Los Panchos, including, Los Tres Aces, Los Tres Diamantes, and Los Tres Reyes. Another stream of performance practice comes from the solo singer/interpreter, which came from the tradition set forth by Agustin Lara. Solo song allowed more freedom for individual expression and remained popular in Latin America with interpreters such as Maria Grever, Toña La Negra, and Daniel Santos. The solo *bolero* was important in the development of *salsa* as ballad song, and it continues to hold an important place in that genre.

In the 1980s, a younger generation of singers began to perform older *epoca de oro* repertoire as parts of their performances and recordings. Many of these younger artists, such as Gloria Estefan, **Luis Miguel**, and Linda Rondstadt incorporated it into their songs as a tribute to the music of their parents and grandparents. Most of these performances are in the form of a solo singer, though one group from **Colombia**, Los Trio, had great success in the late 1990s recreating the trio sound of three voices accompanied by three guitars. In spite of the rise and fall in popularity of the *bolero* throughout its history, the genre continues to be performed throughout the world.

Further Reading

Aparicio, Frances R. "Woman as Absence: Hetero(homo)sexual Desire in the Bolero." In *Listening to Salsa: Gender, Latin Popular Music, and Puerto Rican Culture,* 125–41. Hanover, NH: Wesleyan University Press, 1998.

Campos, Rene Alberto, and Robert Baum. "The Poetics of the Bolero in the Novels of Manuel Puig." *World Literature Today* 65, no. 4 (1991): 637–42.

Pedelty, Mark. "The Bolero: The Birth, Life, and Decline of Mexican Modernity." *Latin American Music Review/Revista de musica latinoamericana* 20, no.1 (Spring–Summer 1999): 30–58.

Torres, George. "The *Bolero Romántico:* From Cuban Dance to International Popular Song." In *From Tejano to Tango: Essays on Latin American Popular Music,* edited by Walter A. Clark, 151–71. New York: Garland, 2002.

Zavala, Iris M. *El Bolero: Historia De Un Amor.* Madrid: Alianza Editorial, 1991.

George Torres

Bolivia

Bolivia is one of only two landlocked countries in South America, and as a result has been strongly influenced by the musics and cultures of its neighboring nations of **Brazil, Peru, Paraguay, Argentina**, and **Chile**. Bolivia has also drawn on its folk traditions for musical inspiration because it has a large indigenous population (30% *mestizo,* 30% Quechua and 25% Aymara) and three official languages, Spanish, Quechua and Aymara.

The first Bolivian popular music superstars were the La Paz female **duos** Las Kantutas (named after the national flower) and Las Hermanas Tejada (The Tejada Sisters). Similar in style to Mexican female vocal duos, Las Kantutas and Las Hermanas Tejada became famous in 1940s Bolivia through their live performances on nationally broadcast Radio Illimani. Both duos traveled to Argentina to record because Bolivia lacked its own recording company until 1949. Las Kantutas, known for their interpretations of the *taquirari* and *carnival,* helped popularize both Eastern lowland genres throughout the country. Bolivian *orquestas de jazz* (swing bands) and *orquestas típicas* (Argentine *tango* ensembles) that played national and international genres were fashionable as well in the 1940s.

The Cuban-derived *bolero* was popular in Bolivia in the 1950s. La Paz singer Raúl Shaw Moreno, an ex-member of Mexico's famous *bolero* **Trio Los Panchos**, toured the Americas and recorded for major international labels with his Mexican-style, Bolivian *bolero* **trío romantíco** Los Peregrinos (The Pilgrims). Arturo Sobenes y Los Cambas was another popular Bolivian *bolero* group. In addition to their mainly international repertory, these tuxedo-clad groups also played local *mestizo* genres, such as *huaynos*, and were often accompanied with an Andean *charango*.

Bolivian rock groups appeared in the 1960s. Benefiting from the local recording industry's expansion, middle- and upper-class youths formed these bands inspired by popular Latin American *Nueva Ola* (New Wave) ensembles such as Uruguay's Los Shakers. The earliest Bolivian rock groups, dedicated at first to Spanish language covers of international hits, include Los Bonny Boy Hots, Los Crickets (later named Los Grillos), Los Black Byrds, and Los Loving Darks. Since the 1990s Octavia has been one of Bolivia's most popular rock groups.

The mid-1960s saw the rise of a new Andean musical style that quickly became the main Bolivian national popular music. The superstar La Paz group Los Jairas (The Lazy Guys) initiated this trend. *Quena* (end-notched bamboo flute) soloist Gilbert Favre of Switzerland founded Los Jairas in 1966 with three Bolivian musicians: guitarist Julio Godoy, singer and *bombo* player Edgar Yayo Joffré and *charango* soloist Ernesto Cavour. The group's novel instrumental line-up became the model for countless Bolivian *conjuntos*. Played by groups wearing colorful *ponchos*, this musical style has usually been labeled *folkloric* music on recordings and at *peñas* (folk music venues), but it actually pertains to the realm of urban popular music. The national and international mass media played a key role in the creation of this new tradition, which was only loosely based on rural indigenous music. Like *folkloric*-popular music groups worldwide, Los Jairas and other Bolivian *conjuntos,* such as Savia Andina, stylized rural folk traditions to appeal to urban audiences. For example, *conjuntos* mainly used the *kena* and *zampoña* (pan-pipe) as solo and duo instruments—not as part of community-based wind ensembles (*tropas* or consorts) as in typical highland villages.

In the late 1960s, Los Ruphay of urban La Paz performed somewhat more faithful interpretations of rural indigenous music on recordings such as the tourist-oriented folk music of Bolivia. Grupo Aymara, Kollamarka, and the Paris-based Boliviamanta followed this trend in the 1970s and 1980s. The fusion group Wara played this nativist repertory too, as well as rock and heavy metal numbers.

Since the 1980s Los Kjarkas have been Bolivia's most popular *conjunto.* From Cochabamba, Los Kjarkas added the *ronroco* (a large *charango*) and the *wankara* (a type of drum) to the standard *conjunto* line-up. The group's recordings present *mestizo* genres from different regions, especially from the Andean highlands and valleys. Many of their hits are *caporales* and *chuntunquis.* Los Kjarkas helped popularize both *mestizo* genres throughout Bolivia and beyond. The danceable *caporal,* often confused with the Afro-Bolivian **saya**, is much enjoyed by young people. The triple-meter *chuntunqui* resembles the Latin American **balada** (ballad) when interpreted in Los Kjarkas's characteristic romantic style. Proyección and Amaru are among the numerous groups in this mold.

Latin American *música tropical* (tropical music) has dominated Bolivia's airwaves since the 1990s. Bolivian *música tropical* groups (who primarily hail from La Paz and Cochabamba rather than the tropics) mainly perform the Colombian *cumbia* genre, whose duple-meter pulse resembles that of the Andean *huayno.* Bolivian groups like Maroyu and Climax, whose Peruvian-influenced style is known as *cumbia chicha,* often adapt local *huayños* into **cumbias**, as well as play their own compositions. More popular among the middle- and upper-class are *música tropical* ensembles modeled after Argentine and Uruguayan groups.

Further Reading

Céspedes, Gilka Wara. "Huayño, Saya, and Chuntunqui: Bolivian Identity in the Music of Los Kjarkas." *Latin American Music Review* 14, no. 1 (1993): 52–101.

Forero, Juan. "Young Bolivians Adopt Urban U.S. Pose, Hip-Hop and All." *New York Times,* May 26, 2005 (sec. A; Foreign Desk; El Alto Journal: 4).

Solomon, Thomas. "Dueling Landscapes: Singing Places and Identities in Highland Bolivia." *Ethnomusicology* 44, no. 2 (2000): 257–80.

Fernando Rios

Bomba

Bomba is an African-related tradition consisting primarily of dance and drumming styles that were developed by black slaves in **Puerto Rico** during the Spanish colonial period (1508–1898). *Bomba* is based on a call-and-response structure with linguistic interjections in Spanish, *Creole,* or an African language. For every style, a group of dancers do one among eight dance forms while the choir replicates or responds in unison to a leading voice accompanied by barrel-shaped membranophones (or *bulá* drums) and two idiophones.

It is estimated that there are between 27 and 52 different genres and substyles that fit under the umbrella of *bomba.* To European-trained listeners, most *bomba* styles may be categorized in two groups according to their time signature. The first is in the simple duple meter of 2/4 and includes the **congo**, for example. The second group includes *bomba* styles that are in simple 3/4 or compounded 6/8 meter, such as the *holandé, leró,* and *yubá.*

Community-based gatherings known as *bombazos* feature a dance form of *bomba* that is known as *piquetes. Piquetes* consist of duel exchange between a solo dance performer and a drum. Other *bomba* dances consist mainly of creolized versions of European forms, namely the *leró, tumba, kokobalé,* and *congo.*

During the Spanish colonial administration, *bomba* was restricted to plantations, *haciendas,* and religious holidays when *bomba* practitioners could do public performances in town squares and open spaces. The earliest known scores that had the specifically *bomba*-related **cinquillo** pattern were by visiting New Orleans pianist Louis Moreau Gottschalk. In subsequent years, *cinquillo* was notably featured in *danzas* by Manuel G. Tavárez and **Juan Morel Campos**.

In 1898, when Puerto Rico became a territory of the **United States**, *bomba* was confined to coastal Afro-Puerto Rican communities and academic circles. It was not until the early 1900s that visiting commercial producers, Columbia and Victor, recorded the first *bombas.* The early 1900s was also when **plena**, whose defining rhythms are said to draw on the *bomba* style, emerged to become Puerto Rico's most representative Afro-Caribbean music and dance.

In two distinct ways, the tides for *bomba* surged even further after 1950 with the help of government-run cultural programs and through local commercial recordings. Initiatives by two local government agencies, the Puerto Rico Division of Community Education and the Institute of Puerto Rican Culture, conspired with independent producers to render commercial *bomba* as a true counterpart to the 1940s and 1950s *mambo* craze. A recording by Armando Castro in the early 1950s is presumed to be the earliest *bomba* recording and was followed by **Rafael Cortijo**'s widespread radio and television broadcasts in 1954.

It was Cortijo's orchestral arrangements that combined locally flavored brass and saxophone sounds with a *mambo*-oriented Afro-Cuban percussion format entailing

Cortijo, Rafael

Cortijo (born Rafael Cortijo Verdejo, 1928–1982) was a Puerto Rican composer, singer, and bandleader who modernized the **bomba** and **plena** while reestablishing the African and working-class roots into Puerto Rican music. Cortijo was born and raised in the barrio of Santurce, San Juan, and it was there that he met his lifelong friend and collaborator, singer and percussionist, Ismael Rivera (1931–1987). By 1954 he had formed his own group, Cortijo y su Combo, which gave Rivera much exposure as a *sonero*. The makeup of the group was almost completely Afro-Puerto Rican, and along with the preference for African-derived genres, as well as black references and heavy alliterations in the texts, his music greatly challenged, and even threatened, the Eurocentric beliefs regarding black Puerto Rican music. In the 1960s and 1970s, Cortijo's music, which brought the traditions of *bomba, plena,* and Cuban **son** together, infused a strong Puerto Rican element into **salsa**, for which he is considered one of the genre's influential pioneers. He died of pancreatic cancer in 1982, in San Juan, and he was buried in his hometown of Santurce.

Further Reading

Rodríguez, Juliá E. *Cortijo's Wake: El Entierro De Cortijo*. Durham: Duke University Press, 2004.

George Torres

the fusion of compounded 6/8 *yubá* songs with *bambulaé* or *sicá* rhythms. Perhaps aware of *bomba*'s past cumulative cycle in the hands of slaves, Cortijo's formulaic blends set in stories of everyday life restarted a similar cumulative cycle for what later came to be known as *salsa*.

In 1970, Cortijo and *timbalero* Kako Bastar released the album *Ritmos y Cantos Callejeros,* which tested the possibility of introducing an innovative dual bandleader-and-lead-singer image for **salsa**: instead of featuring a *sonero* as the bandleader's companion, this album showcased Cortijo and a percussion soloist in a display of various *bomba* rhythms, like *bambulé.*

Other attempts to diversify the Afro-Caribbean **salsa** repertoire by introducing *bomba* are evident with efforts by Willie Colón, Hector Lavoe, and other *salsa* artists. But, due to the marked emphasis on Cuban-*conjunto* styles (as proposed by moguls of the U.S.-centered music industry), *bomba* rhythms barely acquired a comparable prominence. Still, festivals and indigenous commercial venues helped *bomba* styles maintain their substantial presence in Puerto Rico alongside *plena*. Roberto Anglero's "Si Dios Fuera Negro" (1979) exemplified the ongoing vitality of *bomba* among Puerto Ricans of all socioeconomic groups well into the 1980s.

Beyond the New York– and Puerto Rico–based circuits, *bomba* had its resonance in Colombian bands like Fruko y Sus Tesos (1971) and La Verdad (1986–1988) alongside Joe Arroyo's skillful tongue-twisting lyrics in the song "Las Cajas" and his evocations of Puerto Rican peasant songs in "Sentencia China." Subsequent performances by Arroyo with *bomba* patterns included songs such as "Oriza," "El muerto vivo," and "Canto a Panama." A true landmark in global *salsa* was the novelty of Orquesta de la Luz, a Japanese ensemble, whose song "Flores y Tambores" also acknowledged *bomba* practitioners with the initial remark, "Gracias, Borinquen" and the accompaniment of *bomba* drumming. *Bomba* was also prominent in Gloria Estefan's 1993 song, "Mi Tierra," which became a worldwide hit.

Some of *bomba*'s most ardent followers are a host of grassroots individuals and institutions that organize dance and music schools, festivals, and conferences to foster the understanding of its roots in the African diaspora. In the United States, this enthusiasm is found in various cities like Chicago, which was the host of the First *Bomba* Research Conference in 2005. New York City has also attracted well-established *bomba* and *plena* groups like Pleneros de la 21 and Viento de Agua, and is home to personalities like Mickey Sierra, Angel Luis Torruellas, and Obanilú Gutiérrez.

The emergence of *bomba* adherents among the younger population is remarkable for the influence it has left on music genres such as **hip-hop** and **reggaetón**. The Welfare Poets, an ensemble of African American and Puerto Rican activists, incorporated *bomba* into their rap performances and La Bruja, a *Santería*-inspired singer, became known for mixing poetry recitals with *bomba* rhythms. Female-directed *bomba* ensembles such as Alma Moyó have even put into question male-oriented hierarchies that have been a traditional part of *bomba*. But perhaps the ensemble most actively engaged in performing *bombas* is Yerbabuena whose public presentations include the use of *bulá* drums in various styles.

In various other ways, *bomba* has acquired considerable validity and acceptance both within and outside of Puerto Rico. The arrangements by artists such as Tego Calderón, Vico C, and La Sista attest to the popularity of call-and-response speeches and rhythmic styles in *reggaetón* as a method to address matters of youth and cultural identity. Calderón is credited for bringing *reggaetón* to the forefront in 2002 with his album, El Abayarde, which featured distinctive *bomba* styles.

Further Reading

Álvarez Nazario, Manuel. "Historia de las Denominaciones de los Bailes de Bomba. Número Especial del Caribe." *Revista de Ciencias Sociales* 4, no. 1, Marzo (1960): 59–63.

Álvarez Nazario, Manuel. "Notas Sobre el Habla del Negro en Puerto Rico Durante el Siglo XIX." *Revista Instituto de Cultura Puertorriqueña* 1, no. 2 (1959): 43–48.

Conrad, Tato. 2005. "Historia—El Bambula Boricua," *Puertoritmo,* http://www.puertoritmo.com.

Díaz Díaz, Edgardo. "La Gomba Paraguaya: un Documento para el Estudio de la Bomba Puertorriqueña." *La Canción Popular* (January–June 1986): 8–14.

Ferreras, Salvador E. "Solo Drumming in the Puerto Rican Bomba: an Analysis of Musical Processes and Improvisational Strategies." Ph.D. diss., The University of British Columbia, Canada, 2005. Available at www.salferreras.com/writings/Sal-Ferreras-Thesis.pdf.

Torres, Tato "Tato Brujo." "¡Cuando la bomba ñama . . . !" http://www.puertorico.com/forums/music-arts/10205-what-bomba-y-plena.html, 2002.

Edgardo Díaz Díaz

Bombo

In Spanish, the term *bombo* can refer generally to any large, low-pitched drum from the concert bass drum or kick drum on a drum set to various folkloric drums found from the Caribbean to the Southern Cone. In the context of Latin American popular music, *bombo* most frequently refers to the cylindrical, double-headed drum from the northwest region of **Argentina**.

Bombos are traditionally constructed by hollowing out a tree trunk by hand and attaching thick animal hide skins (typically cow, sheep, or goat) with the fur still intact to each end. These heads are connected by interlaced rawhide cords, which can be adjusted to change their tension. The heads are held in place by tall wooden rims, or *aros*.

Musicians typically play the instrument seated, either balancing it horizontally on the lap or under one arm or supporting it in a stand. The drum is typically played with both hands, using wooden sticks or cloth-covered beaters. In folkloric styles from the Southern Cone such as *chacarera*, *cueca*, and *zamba,* the *bombo* typically underlines the bi-metric nature of the rhythm, playing higher-pitched notes on the wooden rim of the drum that emphasize the 6/8 meter and lower-pitched notes in the center of the head that emphasize the 3/4 meter.

The *bombo* rose to national and international prominence in the 1960s with its inclusion in widely popular Argentine folkloric groups such as Los Chalchaleros and Los Fronterizos, Pan-Andean groups such as Inti Illimani and Quilapayún of Chile, and, later Los Kjarkas of **Bolivia**.

Further Reading

Baumann, Max Peter. "The Kantu Ensemble of the Kallawaya at Charazani (Bolivia)." *Yearbook for Traditional Music* 17 (1985): 146–66.

Michael O'Brien

Bongó

The *bongó* is a coupled set of two drums, usually held between the player's knees while seated and struck with the hands. Its two drums, the smaller called *macho* (male) and the larger known as *hembra* (female), usually measure around 7.25 inches and 8.5 inches. Most are constructed from wooden staves, but fiberglass is also common. The drumheads are usually made of animal skin, though synthetic heads are becoming increasingly popular. The *bongó* is usually not tuned to specific pitches. Instead, it is tuned to a general range preferred by the player, usually in an interval of at least a fourth. Today, almost all types of *bongós* are tuned by means of metal tensioning rods. Musically, the *bongocero* (or *bongosero* meaning the *bongó* player) usually plays a specific rhythm known as *martillo* (hammer) and switches to *cencerro* (handheld cowbell) during the **montuno** sections of Cuban music.

It is more common in English to hear the word bongos, though the plural is needless since the drums are never separated. In Spanish, *el bongó* refers to the coupled set, while *los bongoes* (also *bongós* or *bongoses*) would refer to multiple sets. The origin of this name is not clear but some believe it came from the *bonkó enchemiyá* of the Afro-Cuban Abakuá society. Fernando Ortiz, the first Cuban scholar to document Afro-Cuban instruments, convincingly suggested that the name also could have come from an archaic Bantu word for certain types of drums, and it was that word that instead influenced the Abakuá language.

The *bongó* has both African and European influences but it was created in **Cuba**. It originated in the eastern provinces of Cuba in the music called ***son***, and its predecessor ***changüí***. In both styles, it was the main percussion instrument and the only drum. Precursors to the modern *bongó* were developed at least by the late 1800s and commonly had a head that was tacked on and tuned by heat, though a number of regional tuning mechanisms existed depending on particular African influences in a given area. Early versions were often a single small drum held between the knees. Early coupled sets used straps that hung one drum on each side of a player's leg. They later were joined by a piece of wood, as with the modern *bongó*.

The *bongó* spread throughout Cuba in the early 1900s along with *son*. It was brought from the eastern provinces to Havana by military troops in 1912, according to Ortiz, and had become the most popular Cuban drum by the 1930s. At that time, it was also being popularized worldwide by bandleaders such as Don Azpiazú. The *bongó* probably reached its height of worldwide fame with the ***mambo*** in the 1940s and 1950s, and was then surpassed in popularity by the ***tumbadora*** and ***timbal***.

Over the years, the construction of the *bongó* has varied. Its tacked-on heads were replaced by metal tensioning mechanisms, commonly known as lugs. This began by the 1940s and spread steadily until it became the norm by the end of the 1960s. This tuning method allowed the *bongó* to achieve much higher pitches than before, a fact that was also aided by its decreasing size. Modern groups that interpret *changüí* music often use a larger *bongó* to signify an older sound. Animal skins (such as goat and cow) and wooden drum shells (traditionally of cedar) are still the most common materials for the *bongó,* though fiberglass shells are common and synthetic heads are gaining popularity.

Performers such as Armando Peraza, José Mangual, Jack Costanzo, Candido Camero, Ray Romero, Chino Pozo, Manny Oquendo, among others, have aided the worldwide popularity of the *bongó.* Today, it is a relatively common instrument and has been incorporated extensively into popular music styles of non-Cuban origin, especially Dominican **bachata**.

Further Reading

Fernandez, Raul A. *From Afro-Cuban Rhythms to Latin Jazz.* Berkeley, CA: University of California Press, 2006.

Nodal, Roberto. "The Social Evolution of the Afro-Cuban Drum." *Black Perspective in Music* 11, no. 2 (1983): 157.

Nolan Warden

Boogaloo

Boogaloo, or *bugalú,* is a genre of Latin American music that achieved mass popularity from 1966 to 1969. It arose after the fading **charanga** and **pachanga** crazes of the early and mid-1960s and preceded the rise of **salsa** in the 1970s. A product of young Latin musicians living in New York City, boogaloo combined **Afro-Cuban** and African American elements to become a subgenre of Latin Soul. It is sometimes called the first Nuyorican music because its practitioners were the first generation of Puerto Ricans born and raised in Harlem.

Both Latin and African American musical idioms should be present for music to be considered boogaloo. This leads to a flexible range of stylistic influences from the Latin **mambo, son montuno, guajira**, and **guaracha**, to the more African American rhythm and blues, soul, rock 'n' roll, funk, and doo-wop. Also found in boogaloos are improvised Spanish lyrics in the style of the **son montuno**, English lyrics with African American references such as "sock it to me," and "hog maws and chitlin," hand clapping, vocal outbursts, crowd choruses, and short, repetitive, rhythmic piano motifs. Boogaloo's bawdy lyrics tend to give the music a party-like atmosphere.

The mixing of Latin and African American music can be traced to the 1940s with **Machito** and Dizzy Gillespie's **cubop** experiments. By the mid-1960s, the shows at the famous Palladium Ballroom in Manhattan were only attracting Latin audiences while primarily playing *mambos.* Second generation Puerto Ricans in Harlem grew up influenced by the established Latin bandleaders such as Machito,

Tito Rodríguez, and Tito Puente as well as doo-wop, rhythm and blues, and rock 'n' roll. This led to the desire for a fusion-based music that blacks would dance to. Ray Barretto's 1963 hit "El Watusi," Mongo Santamaria's 1963 hit "Watermelon Man," and Cal Tjader's "Soul Sauce" in 1964 all foreshadow the popularity of boogaloo. These feature a Latinized rhythm and blues mixed with typical *conga* rhythms. Barretto's hit reached number three on the top 20 chart, making it the first hit from a Latin band to reach that spot. "El Watusi" contained spontaneous and conversational vocals, a rowdy atmosphere, and hand clapping paving way for the typical boogaloo sounds. "Watermelon Man" has a funk rhythm but is fused with *timbals* providing a backbeat.

Joe Cuba's sextet 1966 hit, "Bang Bang" from the album *Wanted Dead or Alive,* coincided with the closing of the Palladium Ballroom. The album sold over a million copies and initiated the mass popularity of boogaloo music. The success of "Bang Bang" sent Joe Cuba on tours with the leading funk, soul, and Motown artists of the time such as James Brown and The Supremes. The song contains a short repeated piano vamp, chanting, *timbals,* and the repeating chorus singing the track's title. Cheo Feliciano improvised Spanish lyrics and Willie Torres interjected with African American phrases in English. Other quintessential boogaloo songs were "I Like It Like That" by the Pete Rodríguez Orchestra, "Pete's Boogaloo" by Tony Pabon, which was the first boogaloo played on the radio, and "Jala Jala y Boogaloo," by Ricardo Ray who coined the term boogaloo.

The boogaloo craze was long lasting compared to other fads but ended abruptly due to problems between artists and their record companies. As a result of overbooking and little pay, teenage boogaloo bands like The Lat-Teens and The Latin Souls began to disappear. The rise of Fania Records, a monopoly that would come to define the Latin sound of the 1970s, also contributed to the demise of boogaloo. A 1997 remake of "I Like It Like That" featuring a **hip-hop**, house, and Latin fusion by Nito Nieve testified to the enduring influence of Latin and African American fusion.

Further Reading

Salazar, Max. "Afro-American Latinized Rhythms." In *Salsiology: Afro-Cuban Music and the Evolution of Salsa in New York City,* edited by Vernon Boggs, 237–48. Westport, CT: Greenwood Press, 1992.

Raymond Epstein

Bossa Nova

Bossa nova, a form of **jazz** influenced by Brazilian musical rhythms and styles, conquered audiences with its beautiful melodies, sophisticated harmonies, and subtle and original rhythm. It gained international prestige in the 1960s after being embraced by North American jazz musicians. Among countless hits are "Chega de Saudade," "Desafinado," "Garota de Ipanema," "Samba de Uma Nota Só," "Meditação," "Corcovado," "O Amor em Paz," "Samba do Avião," "Inútil Paisagem," "Dindi," "Triste," "A Felicidade," "Lígia," "Vivo Sonhando," "Águas de Março," "Se Todos Fossem Iguais a Você," "Só Danço Samba," and "Insensatez" (Antonio Carlos Jobim); "Influência do Jazz," "Primavera," "Minha Namorada," "Maria Ninguém," "Se É Tarde Me Perdoa," "Lobo Bobo," and "Você e Eu" (Carlos Lyra), "Barquinho," "Rio," "Você," and "Vagamente" (Roberto Menescal), "Batida Diferente," "Chuva," and "Estamos Aí" (Maurício Einhorn).

Bossa nova's precursors in the 1940s included the music of acoustic guitarist Garoto (Aníbal Augusto Sardinha), who used altered and dissonant harmonizations, pianist Dick Farney, and composer Custódio Mesquita, whose biggest hits were two foxtrot songs, "Mulher" and "Nada Além," which were American in style. Vocal group Os Cariocas contributed to the development of *bossa nova* with their innovative and daring harmonies that were soon assimilated by American vocal groups.

During the 1950s, several jazz-influenced Brazilian musicians and composers introduced harmonic and melodic innovations that became fundamental for the development of *bossa nova*. Among these, the most important was the pioneering pianist-composer Johnny Alf. His performances at the Hotel Plaza bar in Rio de Janeiro in 1953 and 1954 attracted the attention of young musicians and singers who, captivated by his innovations, went to listen to him night after night. Among these young musicians was João Gilberto who was a singer and acoustic guitar player who later started the *bossa nova* movement, Candinho (José Candido de Mello Mattos Sobrinho—an acoustic guitarist), Luiz Bonfá (an acoustic guitarist and composer), Aurino Ferreira (a saxophonist), João Donato (a pianist, accordionist and composer), Bebeto Castilho and Manuel Gusmão (both bassists), Sylvia Telles, Claudete Soares and Alaíde Costa (singers), Luiz Eça (a pianist), and Lúcio Alves (a singer). Alf changed the direction of Brazilian popular music with his elaborate, harmonically daring compositions, whose melodic sense was of unique beauty. It was a giant step for the renovation of language, which germinated the seed of *bossa nova*. Some of his masterpieces include "Rapaz de Bem," "Ilusão à Toa," "Céu e Mar," "Fim de Semana em Eldorado," "Disa," "O Que é Amar," and the seminal "Eu e a Brisa," With the recording of the classic "Rapaz de Bem," Alf became the spiritual father of *bossa nova* and set the direction for future musicians to follow, such as **Antonio Carlos Jobim** who even received informal lessons from Alf.

Another decisive influence came from the 1953 album *Brazilliance* created by acoustic guitarist Laurindo Almeida and saxophonist Bud Shank. Accomplishing a groundbreaking fusion of jazz and Brazilian music, the album provoked a thrill with Shank's audacious improvisations and proved that it was possible to improvise over Brazilian themes, something that had been unthinkable until then.

Jobim, Antônio Carlos

Antônio Carlos Brasileiro de Almeida Jobim (1927–1994), popularly known as "Tom" Jobim, was an important composer of the latter 20th century because of his contributions to the development of *bossa nova* through his brilliantly crafted melodies and the popular success of his numerous songs. Jobim contributed as composer, arranger, and pianist to the Grammy-winning recording *Getz/Gilberto* (1964). Several of his recordings have also been inducted into the Latin Grammy Hall of Fame. Besides Getz, Jobim has recorded with Sinatra, João Gilberto, Astrud Gilberto, and Elis Regina.

Jobim worked as an arranger, transcriber, and conductor for radio, television, and recording companies in Rio. In 1956 he composed music for the play *Orfeu da Conceição* by Moraes, and in 1958 contributed songs and arrangements for Elizete Cardoso's recording *Canção do Amor Demais*. Jobim's popularity increased in 1959 with his musical contributions to João Gilberto's recording *Chega de Saudade* and the film *Black Orpheus*. In 1962 he achieved success in the United States with the song "Desafinado." His early popular compositions are primarily *bossa novas*, but later in his career he experimented with *choro*.

Further Reading

Reily, Suzel Ana. "Tom Jobim and the Bossa Nova Era." *Popular Music* 15, no.1 (1996): 1–16.

Thomas Rohde

Acoustic guitarist-composer Luiz Bonfá won international fame for his contribution, "Manhã de Carnaval," the theme of the film *Black Orpheus* and "Samba de Orfeu," Other highlights from his repertoire are "Menina Flor," "Gentle Rain," "Saudade Vem Correndo," and "Mania de Maria."

Throughout 1956 and 1957, João Gilberto was exhaustively listening to the *Chet Baker Sings* album. Impressed by Baker's colloquial style, Gilberto radically changed his way of singing, abandoning his previous model, Orlando Silva, to adopt Baker's vocal style. Gilberto became, together with Antonio Carlos Jobim, *bossa nova*'s biggest icon. His **guitar** beat originated the essential rhythmic characteristic of *bossa nova*. Gilberto continues to perform with great success.

Another notable talent was João Donato, whose original jazz-influenced style is evident in "Minha Saudade," "Silk Stop," "Até Quem Sabe," and "A Rã." Donato settled in Los Angeles in 1959, where he lived until 1973, recording and playing with jazz and Latin music musicians. Donato remains active and in high demand for tours throughout the **United States**, Europe, and Japan.

Historically, the recording of the first *bossa nova* record in 1958 is credited to singer Elizeth Cardoso: *Canção do Amor Demais,* featuring João Gilberto at the acoustic guitar. At that point, the prolific partnership of Antonio Carlos Jobim and Vinicius de Moraes had already begun. Moraes, a poet in the strict sense, had an international reputation as a lyricist. It was because of Moraes's influence on and contribution to Brazilian popular music, that the Brazilian elites began to take notice.

A group of youngsters excited by the new musical tendencies of Jobim and Moraes would gather at singer Nara Leão's home to explore the new repertoire. Among the participants at these meetings were Roberto Menescal, Ronaldo Bôscoli, Carlos Lyra, Chico Feitosa, Durval Ferreira, and Oscar Castro Neves, all of whom would contribute to the success of the *bossa nova* movement.

At the time, the music was seething in the four clubs of legendary Beco das Garrafas, Rio de Janeiro's 52th Street. Every night someone would bring in a new composition, a new idea, a new arrangement. Those clubs revealed Luiz Carlos Vinhas, Luiz Eça, Sérgio Mendes, Toninho Oliveira, Dom Salvador, and Tenório Junior (piano); Baden Powell, Neco, Rosinha de Valença, Waltel Branco, and Oscar Castro-Neves (acoustic guitar); Claudete Soares, Leny Andrade, Alaíde Costa, and Sylvia Telles (voice); Raul de Souza and Edson Maciel (trombone); Sérgio Barrozo, Tião Neto, and Manuel Gusmão (bass); Jorge Ferreira da Silva, J. T. Meirelles, and Aurino Ferreira (sax); Edison Machado, Victor Manga, Milton Banana, and Dom Um Romão (drums); and Maurício Einhorn (harmonica). Inspired by Laurindo Almeida and Bud Schank's recorded improvisations, those instrumentalists began to develop the samba-jazz genre, and the small combos Tamba Trio, Bossa Três, Salvador Trio, Trio 3-D, and Rio 65 Trio blossomed.

Brazilian youth became enraptured by *bossa nova* with João Gilberto's *Chega de Saudade* album, which defined the new idiom with radical innovations in melody, harmony, and rhythm. This album would be worshipped by musicians, singers, and listeners. After 1959, the new music started to win international acclaim, with four events decisive to its success abroad. First, acoustic guitarist Charlie Byrd did a Brazilian tour and, enchanted with what he heard there, he recorded several albums with Brazilian repertoire. Second, the groups American Jazz Festival and Dizzy Gillespie's Quintet came to Brazil in 1961. Upon their return, Gillespie, Lalo Schifrin (piano), Zoot Sims and Coleman Hawkins (sax), Herbie Mann (flute), and Curtis Fuller (trombone) recorded *bossa nova* albums. Third, in 1962 Charlie Byrd and saxophonist Stan Getz recorded the *Jazz Samba* LP and "Desafinado" became a big hit overnight. Its success led to the organization of a *bossa nova* concert at Carnegie Hall with Brazilian musicians, opening an international work market for national artists.

In the following year, Stan Getz recorded with João Gilberto and Antonio Carlos Jobim, the album that transformed "Garota de Ipanema" into Jobim and *bossa nova*'s trademark. It was also the album in which Astrud Gilberto had her opening as a singer. At that point, Jobim was *bossa nova*'s most popular artist; world famous, his prestige became increasingly higher, and his inspired compositions became megahits in most Western countries.

With the success of **rock** and the Beatles, *bossa nova* ceased to be the music of Brazilian youth, despite continuing to be prestigious abroad. After a long period of stagnation, a rebirth of *bossa nova* in Brazil has taken place, with concerts, festivals, recordings, and re-releases of albums from its golden period, one of the most creative eras of Brazilian popular music.

Further Reading

Castro, Ruy. *Bossa Nova: The Story of the Brazilian Music That Seduced the World.* Chicago: A. Cappella, 2000.

McGowan, Chris, and Ricardo Pessanha. *The Brazilian Sound: Samba, Bossa Nova, and the Popular Music of Brazil.* Revised and expanded edition. Philadelphia, PA: Temple University Press, 2009.

Alvaro Neder and José Raffaelli

Brazil

Popular music in Brazil reflects the origins of its population: Africa and Europe (specifically Portugal). Early Portuguese settlers unsuccessfully tried to enslave Brazilian Natives. As a result they resorted to importing large numbers of slaves from Africa. Later waves of immigration brought a large number of people from other parts of Europe, all contributing to the makeup of the current Brazilian population, which is now 53.7 percent white, 38.5 percent mulatto, and 6.2 percent black. In order to understand the origins and evolution of Brazilian music, one must understand some of the social, racial, political and musical forces that shaped it.

The single most important feature that separates Brazilian music from that of other New World traditions is its African-derived rhythm, a reflection of both a large slave population and the differences in slavery in Brazil as compared to the rest of the Americas. The most significant difference was in sheer numbers: 250,000–350,000 slaves were taken from Africa to the **United States**, but well over two million slaves were forced to go to Brazil. This difference can be largely attributed to Brazil's relative proximity to Africa. Slavery in Brazil lasted two more generations than in the United States (universal emancipation was not granted until 1888 in Brazil) and more slaves were imported to Brazil during the 19th century than the rest of the Americas combined (less than 3% to the United States, over 60% to Brazil). Treatment of slaves was also greatly different, most notably because in the United States and elsewhere, slave family groups and tribes were separated, but in Brazil they were kept together to a large extent. As a result of the fact that slaves tended to be kept in family and language groups, a great deal more of their culture was preserved. They stayed closer to their roots and were able to maintain their religious practices and musical traditions that were based on percussion instruments and complex rhythms.

Portuguese immigrants and African slaves mixed from the very beginning of the colony; Brazilian music as a result reflects the racial blending of the population. Whereas in the United States miscegenation was generally discouraged and even illegal in many states, it was encouraged in Brazil. This said, there was great resistance by the intellectual elite to the emergence of black culture and black music, an indication of the prevalent racism in Brazil. The elite turned to the idea of miscegenation, which was understood not only as a process by which all the different races would be joined together, but also as a means of tempering, and eventually eradicating the "undesirable" races under the influence of white European blood. The process was known as *branqueamento,* literally, whitening. Indeed, few Brazilians before the great European immigration of the early 20th century could claim a total lack of African blood, and as much as 75 percent of Brazil's current population has some black ancestry; people of color were also worse off economically and socially. The range of skin colors found in Brazil from very dark to light, and the intersecting and interdependence of the concepts of race and class in Brazilian society necessitate a consideration of both race and class in discussions of musical traditions.

Afro-Brazilian Music: *Samba*

The most important single genre of popular music in Brazil is the **samba**. Over time, it has evolved into a number of dance and song forms, the most important of which was the *samba de roda,* the ring *samba,* in which participants form a circle, one participant at a time dancing while others keep time rhythmically. This dance tradition developed among slaves in the northeast state of Bahia, and was in common practice by the early 19th century. The word *samba* came to represent many things, including the gathering at which the *samba* was danced. With emancipation in 1888, many former slaves took the *samba* with them as they migrated to the southeastern cities of Rio de Janeiro and São Paulo. In Rio, former slaves developed a new form of *samba* based on the *samba de roda* called the s*amba do morro,* or the hill samba, reflecting the fact that most former slaves lived in the hillside *favelas,* or slums, that dot the city.

Samba continues to be danced today in a variety of forms. One of the most important is the *Carnaval samba,* performed in Rio de Janeiro by groups called *escolas de samba,* or s*amba* schools, that compete during **Carnaval**. This tradition goes back to the 1930s and features the *samba-enredo,* the theme *samba,* which is meant to convey the themes represented in the presentation. The *samba* schools of Rio have become the most popular and visible aspect of contemporary *Carnaval* celebrations, but are by no means the only one. Throughout the rest of Brazil other types of *Carnaval* celebrations take place, including São Paulo's version of *Escolas* *de Samba,* and in the northeastern state of Bahia, *Carnaval* revolves around street parties featuring a *Trio Elétrico,* a band playing on a truck with a high-powered sound system.

Samba continued to evolve during the 20th century, and led to several other genres, one of which is the *samba-canção,* or *samba* song. This slower version of the *samba* became popular in the 1930s and was performed and recorded primarily by white singers such as Noel Rosa and **Carmen Miranda**, one of Hollywood's biggest stars in the 1940s, and one of the first Brazilian musicians to introduce Americans to Brazilian popular musical culture. Another development was the ***bossa nova***, or new style of *samba,* that developed in the late 1950s with composers and performers such as **Antônio Carlos Jobim**, João Gilberto, and Venícius de Morais. This genre blended the *samba* with the harmonic sophistication of American **jazz**, brought to Brazil by American servicemen in World War II and by Brazilian musicians who performed in the United States, most notably Garoto, the guitarist in Carmen Miranda's band. *Bossa nova* became

Miranda, Carmen

Carmen Miranda (1909–1955) was one of Hollywood's biggest stars in the 1940s, and introduced Americans to Brazilian popular music culture. Known as the Brazilian bombshell, Miranda was actually born in Portugal. In the late 1920s, Miranda got her first recording contract and became one of **Brazil's** most popular singers. She made seven movies in Brazil before she was discovered by the American Lee Schubert, who brought her to the United States to star on Broadway.

Miranda's success in New York led to her starring in Technicolor productions, at first without speaking parts and later as an exotic, tropical pan-Latina woman. She was the most popular woman in film in the 1940s, and for a time one of the highest paid women in America. She lost some of her luster by the end of the 1940s, and was cast in a series of black-and-white B-movies with the likes of Groucho Marx, Jerry Lewis, and Dean Martin. As her career progressed, she moved away from her Brazilian musical roots.

Further Reading

Garcia, Thomas George Caracas. "American Views of Brazilian Musical Culture: Villa-Lobos's Magdalena and Brazilian Popular Music." *The Journal of Popular Culture* 37, no. 4 (May 2004): 634–47.

Thomas George Caracas Garcia

very popular among the cultural elite, and became an important part of jazz repertoire outside of Brazil; many *bossa nova* hits became jazz standards and are still popular today.

African influences—the use of percussion and complex rhythms—are strongly present in other northeastern musical traditions as well. One of these traditions is the Afro-Brazilian religion called *Candomblé.* Originally the product of African slaves, it developed in the state of Bahia into a pan-tribal religious tradition that includes possession rituals in which music, exclusively provided by singing and percussion, is vital. Another African-derived music is that of *capoeira,* a dance and martial art. Slaves were not allowed to practice fighting, which was disguised as a dance form, accompanied by percussion and a musical bow, the *berimbau.* It is very popular in Bahia, where it originated, as well as the rest of Brazil, and has even generated a strong international following. Other Afro-Brazilian music of note includes *afoxé,* a music associated with the *Candomblé* tradition and important in Bahian *Carnaval, maracatú,* a *samba* derivative popular in the state of Pernambuco during *Carnaval,* and a more recent hybrid, *samba-reggae,* which fuses Jamaican reggae and ska with *samba.*

Instrumental Music

In terms of instrumental music, **choro** is the most important Brazilian popular genre. Developed in the 1870s in Rio de Janeiro, *choro* originally was an improvisatory style of playing popular European dances popular by amateurs, as well as the gatherings at which it was played. Musicians of the day, moving toward a national popular music, adapted the **polka**, waltz, *schotische* and other European dances to their tastes. This adaptation included influences from African-derived music, most notably rhythm. The polka, for example, assimilated African rhythms to a large degree; this dance was adapted to the point that it became distinct from the European polka and was known simply as *choro.* The typical ensemble for *choro* performance included a wind instrument, **guitars** of various sizes, and percussion. The heart and soul of the tradition was the *roda de choro,* or *choro* circle, a social and musical gathering in which amateur musicians would play for sheer pleasure. *Choro* later evolved into a professional genre, filling the need for music in the nascent entertainment industry by the early 20th century. The professional *choro* diminished in popularity through the 1940s, but it never disappeared. Other Brazilian genres, most notably *samba,* surpassed *choro* in popularity. It saw a series of revivals, first in the 1960s and later in the 1980s. More recently, *choro* has enjoyed a tremendous wave of popularity; musicians playing in *choro* ensembles throughout Brazil, and in major cities *choro* once again can be heard regularly, both in public performance and in the more intimate *roda de choro.*

Regional Music

There are many regional genres in Brazil, some of which have assumed national importance. Among this regional music is *música nordestina,* or music from the Northeast, a large geographic region with economic, cultural, and social realities much different than in Rio and the Southeast. This region is one of the poorest in Brazil, and the many *Nordestinos* migrated to the Southeast in search of a better standard of living, taking with them their musical traditions; music from the Northeast can be heard today throughout Brazil. Although *samba* was originally from the northeast state of Bahia, where it continues to be the most important genre, there are other northeastern genres that are not derived from *samba,* and that have a different rhythmic and instrumental makeup. Although *samba* is dominated by the **batucada**, or drums, other northeastern genres use the **accordion** and **guitars**, with a different style of percussion and rhythmic component than *samba.* A dance music that developed in the northeastern state of Pernambuco, *forró*, is one of the most important of these genres. This music combines Portuguese and African influences, is danced by couples, and remains very popular throughout Brazil. Other regional genres include the **baião**, the development of which mirrored that of *forró* in the state of Bahia, *frevo*, a northeastern *Carnaval* music, and *de repente,* an improvised blues-like music that most often takes the form of a competition in which two performers try to best each other within a strongly defined stylistic framework. Many dance forms, popular both in Brazil and abroad, are also from the Northeast, notably **lambada**, which enjoyed a boom in Brazil and internationally in the 1980s.

Another popular music tradition that has regional roots and has become important throughout the country is *música sertaneja*, Brazil's version of American country music, and often referred to as truck driver or cowboy music. Its name comes from the *sertão,* the backlands in Brazil away from the Atlantic coast, today associated with the interior of the Northeast and Central Brazil. This music is part of a larger movement that embraced the American cowboy lifestyle, and performers (usually singing in duets) dress in American West influenced clothing and sing about themes similar to country music in the United States, often including rodeo. Just as American country music became important nationally, *sertanejo* is popular throughout Brazil, in both urban and rural settings.

MPB, Rock, Funk, and Rap

Among the most important popular music in Brazil is **Música Popular Brasileira** (MPB). This music developed from **tropicália**, an artistic movement from the 1960s that encompassed poetry, theater, and music, and that often reflected a degree of political protest during the military dictatorship (1964–1985). The music of MPB reflects the many influences on Brazilian music: Portuguese melodic style, *bossa nova, samba,* and *samba-canção,* as well as American rock 'n' roll, and jazz. MPB is not a distinct genre, but rather a name given to a wide range of musical styles that reflect the same esthetic, generally built around a voice and a **guitar**. Among the most popular and important performers of MPB are **Gilberto Gil, Caetano Veloso**, Elis Regina, and Milton Nascimento, among many others.

Rock 'n' roll is another important Brazilian genre, again with roots outside of Brazil. Although American **rock** reached Brazil in the 1950s, there was no significant Brazilian rock movement until the 1960s, and this usually included a mixing of rock, jazz, MPB, and other Brazilian music with the American sound and instrumentation. Among the first bands to enjoy success in rock were Jovem Guarda (The Young Guard) and Os Mutantes (The Mutants), whose lead singer, Rita Lee, was a leading force in the 1970s and continues to be one of the biggest names in Brazilian rock. The 1980s saw rock's biggest commercial success, with bands such as Barão Vermelho (The Red Baron) and Legião Urbana (Urban Legion) attaining

Regina, Elis

Elis Regina Carvalho Costa (1945–1982) was an important figure in the **MPB** (Brazilian popular music) movement. During her 1965 televised performance at the first Festival of Brazilian Popular Music, Elis won over the audience with her unique interpretation of "Arrastão" and became much sought after by MPB composers, many of whom achieved recognition because of Elis's interpretation of their songs. She signed her first recording contract at 14, and released her first album the next year. Following a 1965 performance, Elis released the album *Dois na Bossa* with Jair Rodrigues. In the same year, Elis and Rodrigues co-hosted the important *O Fino da Bossa,* a television program that brought attention to new musicians. Elis toured internationally in 1969, and in 1974 released with Antonio Carlos Jobim her most popular album, *Elis e Tom.* As a performer, Elis was known for her range and spirituous delivery; her perfectionism and intensity earned her the nicknames of Hurricane and Little Pepper. Although Elis died tragically in 1982 following a cocaine overdose, her popularity and reputation as Brazil's greatest female singer continue to the present.

Further Reading

McGowan, Chris and Ricardo Pessanha. *The Brazilian Sound: Samba, Bossa Nova, and the Popular Music of Brazil.* Philadelphia: Temple University Press, 2009.

Rebecca Stuhr

national and international acclaim. The 1990s saw continued commercial success with the Mamonas Assassinas (Killer Breasts), who sold millions of CDs before a tragic plane crash killed all five members of the band. The rock scene in Brazil expanded to include derivatives such as heavy metal, punk, and others, and many rock bands started their own record labels.

Rap and **hip-hop** also occupy an important place in Brazilian popular music, reflecting many of the same cultural forces that led to the development of these genres in the United States. An important music tradition with a similar esthetic is funk, or *funk carioca* (the name coming from the nickname of Rio natives, *cariocas*), a dance music that is very popular among the youth of Rio de Janeiro. It is usually heard in a dance party setting known as *baile funk,* or funk dance. *Funk carioca* blends Brazilian and Afro-Brazilian rhythm and percussion with sampling and other electronic technologies to create a new, driving sound. It is sung, rapped, or instrumental, often blending all of these. The dance parties at which this music is popular tend to be violent and sexual, reflecting the lyrics of a great deal of this music. *Funk carioca* has become popular outside of Brazil as well, particularly in Europe, where many recordings were made since the year 2000.

Whereas *baile funk* and *funk carioca* are part of the contemporary popular music scene in Rio de Janeiro, in other urban areas rap and hip-hop are important, most importantly in São Paulo. As is the case with funk, young people at the lower part of the socioeconomic spectrum are the primary practitioners of rap. Most participants are of color, and much rap is associated with *favela,* or slum, culture. As is the case with rap in Europe, Brazilian rappers initially copied American models, later adapting the music to their own tastes, including local ideas of rhythm and percussion. This copying included dress, mannerism, and performance style. A large underground movement developed in the 1980s, which included a number of independent labels, using new recording technologies and allowing rappers to establish themselves. Both rap and funk have also been influenced by a drug culture and the drug trade, since drug lords control the *favelas* that are the origins of most of this music and the live events at which they are performed. As was the case with rock artists in Brazil, many rappers started their own labels, leading to the strong indie label scene in Brazil today.

Further Reading

Béhague, Gerard. "Rap, Reggae, Rock, or Samba: The Local and the Global in Brazilian Popular Music (1985–95)." *Latin American Music Review* 27, no. 1 (Spring/Summer 2006): 79–90.

Crook, Larry N. "Black Consciousness, Samba Reggae, and the Re-Africanization of Carnival Music in Brazil." *World of Music* 35, no. 2 (1993): 90–106.

Livingston-Isenhour, Tamara Elena, and Thomas George Caracas Garcia. *Choro: A Social History of a Brazilian Popular Music.* Bloomington: Indiana University Press, 2005.

McGowan, Chris and Ricardo Pessanha. *The Brazilian Sound: Samba, Bossa Nova and the Popular Music of Brazil.* Revised and expanded edition. Philadelphia, PA: Temple University Press, 2009.

Perrone, Charles. *Masters of Contemporary Brazilian Song: MPB 1965–1985.* Austin: University of Texas Press, 1989.

Perrone, Charles A. and Christopher Dunn, editors. *Brazilian Popular Music and Globalization.* New York: Routledge, 2002.

Tinhorão, José Ramos. *História social da música popular brasileira.* Lisbon: Caminho, 1990.

Thomas George Caracas Garcia

Bugalu. *See* Boogaloo.

C

Cajón

The *cajón* is an idiophone or percussive wooden box of Afro-Peruvian origin. The sides and the back of the box use half- to three-quarter-inch thick wood while a thinner sheet of plywood is used for the head or *tapa*. A 10- or 12-millimeter sound hole is cut in the back. The top edges of the front wooden piece are nailed loosely to the sides of the box to allow the wood to vibrate as the player, who sits on top of the box, hits it with the palm of his hands or his fingers. The *cajón* has many different sonorities and percussive pitches and timbers, although two basic sounds are key to the Afro-Peruvian rhythms that accompanies: a deep bass sound that is obtained by hitting the center of the drum's head, and a more high-pitch tone obtained by slapping its top corners. Sometimes the *cajón* is played by hitting its sides and back as well.

The *cajón* is said to have originated in the port of Lima as slaves sat and played on wooden crates used to transport merchandise. Others believe that this

A street procession of cajón players during the Fifth International Festival of the Peruvian Cajón in Lima, Peru, 2012. (AP/Wide World Photos)

drum is a descendant of box drums found in some parts of Africa and the Caribbean. It is very much used in Afro-Peruvian musical styles such as *tondero, marinera, landó, festejo,* etc. Its popularity has spread throughout the Americas, especially in **Cuba**, where it is associated with the *rumba*. While Peruvian *cajón* generally has a rectangular shape, Cuban *cajón* has an octagonal shape and is smaller in size. Introduced to Spanish *flamenco* by guitarist Paco de Lucía in the 1790s, it is very much used in contemporary arrangements and settings of *flamenco* musical styles.

Further Reading

Feldman, Heidi Carolyn. *Black Rhythms of Peru: Reviving African Musical Heritage in the Black Pacific.* Middletown: CT: Wesleyan University Press, 2006.

Raquel Paraíso

Calypso

Calypso is a music and dance genre popular throughout the Caribbean and the Americas, with a musical approach that is comparable, in terms of its influence, to the blues. While its development began in the 1920s, it gained a wide audience in Trinidad in the mid-1930s and remained unique to the island until 1944 when the Andrews Sisters covered Lord Invader's "Rum and Coca Cola." *Calypso*'s success stems from its adaptability, cosmopolitanism, and its international marketability. Still a popular genre, *calypso*'s contemporary form is known in Trinidad as **soca**.

Calypso's precursor is the West African song-boast, through which opponents boast of their strength and prowess, juicing up for combat known as *kalinda* or stick fighting, a focal point in the **Carnival** celebration in Trinidad. By 1900, song-leaders, or *chantwells,* were singing in English and their songs were called *calypsos*. The direct challenges and violence of stick fighting and song-boasts evolved into a form of improvisational, rhetorical play. *Calypsonians* often had aggressive personas. Growling Tiger (Neville Marcano), for instance, began his public career as a boxer. The suggestive violence lingered as the genre developed.

As *calypso* evolved, *calypsonians* targeted public officials and addressed political issues. In this regard, *calypso* is comparable to the blues. Its lyrics express resistance and probe power struggles between men and women or rich and poor through double-entendre, allegory and exotic, comic images. It provides emotional purgation through text and form, and catharsis through the subtlety and wit of its texts and the improvisatory nature of its musical form.

Trinidad's population comes from throughout the Caribbean and the Americas and many of *calypso*'s melodic ideas come from Tobago, the Grenadines, Barbados, **Martinique**, and Jamaica. The sense of motion, instrumentation, and texture draws on **Venezuela's** *paseos* and *aguinaldos,* Martinique's *bel airs* and *biguines*, and the **jazz** of New Orleans. Though most *calypso* lyrics are in Caribbean English, a *calypsonian* typically turns to *patois* drawn from Caribbean French *Creole* when he wishes to emphasize a particular idea. But, the most important impact of the French presence is an aristocratic and cosmopolitan self-consciousness that remains a key element in *calypso.*

The cosmopolitan air of *calypso* was crucial to its success. The *calypsonian* wanted to demonstrate his familiarity with the urban world and this pleased producers anxious to market a product across ethnic and national lines. Unfortunately, artists and producers operated from unequal positions of power and profited unequally in turn. A reciprocal relationship had existed between the **United States** and Trinidad since the late 1800s, which gave the United States ready access to Trinidad's resources and provided Trinidad with increased revenue, a way to resist British colonialism and to express a new sense of nationalism. *Calypso* proved to be an ideal commodity for both Trinidad and the United States. By the time Decca Records traveled to Trinidad to record *calypsos* in 1938, Trinidadian entrepreneurs had established a profitable relationship with New York City's recording studios. By the early 1940s, calypsonians enjoyed popularity among West Indians living in New York, Trinidad, the Caribbean, and Latin America through radio broadcasts and recordings. As *calypso* spread, it influenced other genres and traditions.

Calypso's wit, political commentary, and topicality have influenced Jamaican *mento,* Haitian *compas,* Dominican *bélé,* Martinique's *kassav* and *zouk*, and Central American genres. In **Panama**, it is sung in Spanish, but provides a bridge between Spanish and English ideas and images. In **Guatemala**, it enables Garífuna musicians of Caribbean, Arawak, African descent, to carve a national presence. In **Guyana**, it connects those of French, Spanish, East Indian, and African heritage. In the United States, *calypso* thrives as an exotic aperitif from the Andrews Sisters' cover of Lord Invader's "Rum and Coca Cola" in 1945, to Harry Belafonte's "Banana Boat Song" of 1956, to Harry Nilsson's 1971 hit, "Coconut." In the 21st century, contemporary artists such as Zap Mama continue to draw from the sound and aesthetics of *calypso.*

The instrumentation heard on early recorded *calypsos* included **guitar, *cuatro*,** violin, bass, **flute**, and/or clarinet. The violin, often doubled by the flute or clarinet, lays out the melody in the opening verse and then alternates as foreground with the *calypsonian.* The *cuatro* serves as the engine, lifting the rhythmic feel by means of syncopated chords, lightly articulated around the patterns that follow. The guitar emphasizes the *cuatro*'s accents in chords and provides a single-note, inner or bass voice. During vocal verses, the rhythmic accompaniment becomes simpler and quieter. Occasionally, the violin or winds fills between vocal phrases. As *calypso* spread, guitars and piano replaced the *cuatro* layer. Leads and fills were played by clarinet and C-melody saxophone. The inner, lower voice was doubled by piano and cello. A successful *calypso* performance presents a sense of motion that is light and upbeat, a voice that explores multiple rhythms, inflections, and colors with fluidity and poise combined with topical and often subversive verses.

Further Reading

Best, Curwen. *Culture @ the Cutting Edge Tracking Caribbean Popular Music.* Kingston, Jamaica: University of the West Indies Press, 2004.

Guilbault, Jocelyne. *Governing Sound: The Cultural Politics of Trinidad*'s *Carnival Musics.* Chicago studies in ethnomusicology. Chicago: University of Chicago Press, 2007.

Regis, Louis. *The Political Calypso: True Opposition in Trinidad and Tobago, 1962–1987.* Barbados: Press University of the West Indies, 1999.

Michael Farley

Campana. *See* Cencerro.

Canción. *See* Canción Romántica.

Canción Ranchera. *See* Ranchera.

Canción Romántica

There are two basic kinds of *canción* in **Mexico:** simple songs of Spanish origin and romantic songs inspired by Italian opera. *Canción romántica* is the latter genre. It is a sentimental song genre found primarily in Mexico and often cited as a precursor to **bolero**. *Canción romántica* is generally not for dancing, but for listening.

Italian opera was enormously popular in Mexico in the 19th century. Mexico saw its first opera production in 1711 with *La Parténope,* Paisiello's *Il barbiere di Siviglia,* and Cimarosa's *El filósofo burlado,* which were performed at the Coliseo Nuevo in Mexico City in 1806. Following the triumph of Rossini's *Il barbiere di Siviglia* in Mexico City in 1824, Mexico City, Havana, and other major Latin American cities enjoyed increasingly frequent performances by touring Italian opera troupes, who visited in 1831, 1835, 1839, 1840, 1841, and 1842. Operas that had been successful in Italy proved very popular on the Mexican stage, including *Il barbiere, La gazza ladra, Tancredi,* and *Otello* by Rossini, *Norma* and *La Sonnambula* by Bellini, and *Lucia di Lammermoor* by Donizetti; their arias (vocal solos) were often sung in parlors. Furthermore, the royal order restricting performances to the Spanish language was lifted with Mexico's independence, allowing Italian opera to be performed in its original language. By the mid-1800s, Italian operas were so much in vogue that Italian troupes were premiering Verdi's works in Latin America as quickly as three years after their European premieres. Italian opera not only dominated the concert hall but also Mexican conservatories, where curricula and student recitals were focused on Italian opera.

Opera also transcended elite salons to be heard in the city soundscape; as recounted by Madame Calderón de la Barca in her mid-19th-century memoir *Life in Mexico,* melodies from operas by Bellini and Donizetti were quoted in liturgical music, included in the repertory of military bands, and whistled in the streets as the popular music of the day. Mexico City was not the only city seeing operatic performances: the troupes also visited regional cities and towns in Jalisco, Puebla, and Veracruz, sometimes performing in open air for a nominal entrance fee. The arias from these operas were also taken up by country musicians, particularly in the Bajío (parts of Michoacán, Guanajuato, and Jalisco), which became a center of the *canción* in the 19th century; they imitated the melodic and harmonic patterns on their guitars and harps.

A second influence on the *canción romántica* was Mexican literary romanticism, including poets such as Fernando Calderón, Igancio Rodríguez Galván, and Guillermo Prieto. Literary romanticism featured a variety of meters and rhythms, containing 8, 10, 11, or 12 syllables. Texts centered on expressing ideas or sentiments rather than on narrating a story, as was the case with **corridos**.

By the 1830s, a style of romantic song had begun to circulate in musical salons of the middle-to-upper classes in Mexico City that drew from the *cantabiles* (slow sections) of arias and *cavatinas* (arias introducing a character) of Italian opera. This influence was most easily detected through ornamental aspects of the melody, such as melismas, trills, mordents, portamentos, appoggiaturas, large leaps, and *fermatas* (held notes), which were common in Italian arias and were technically challenging to the singer. Songs of the early to mid-19th century such as "El susurro del viento" (1850), "La dormida" (Mexico City, mid-19th century), and "La mirada" contained the melismas, leaps, cadenzas (improvised flourishes just prior to a final cadence), and voices in parallel thirds common in such arias, while "A tí te amo, no más, no más a tí" (Dolores Guerrero, Durango, 1840) featured many chromatic appogiaturas.

In addition to this surface ornamentation, these songs resembled Italian opera in the structure of the melodies. Most melodies by Italian operatic composers, such as Bellini and Verdi, followed the lyric form. In this form, the first four measures carry a melody A; the next four feature a variation of melody A (A'), in an antecedent-consequent form, ending in a perfect authentic cadence (cadence of predominant-dominant-tonic, noted as PAC); the next four measures provide a contrasting middle B, often based on a fragmentation of A; and the last four measures is either a repeat of the consequent (A') or a new cadential phrase (C). Note that the following typical format for a Mexican *cancíon* (e.g., "Marchita el alma," Zacatecas, 1885, arranged by Manuel Ponce, 1916) has the same structure as the lyric form:

Melody	A	A'	/ B	A'''				
Melody (detail)	a	b	a'	c	/ b	b	a''	c
Harmony	I-V	V-I	I-ii	V-I	/V-I	V-I	I-ii	V-I
PAC	PAC							

Furthermore, the harmonies of these songs were typically more complex than Spanish-inspired genres, including applied dominants (e.g., V/V), modulations or tonicizations of other keys, mixtures of minor and major modes (particularly for vi), harmonic shifts of a third, deceptive cadence, and other chromatic harmonies often encountered in Italian opera of the Romantic Era; songs with such features included "La mirada," "Ella gime" (Cholula, 1870), "Tu nombre, María" (Guanajuato, 1900), "Tan dulces son tus ojos" (Morelia, 1898), and "No me mires ni me escuches" (Tlaxcala, 1896). Finally, direct quotes of operas could be heard in such songs as "Pálida estoy" (Jalisco, 1885), which referenced Gilda's aria "Tutte le feste al tempio" from Act II of Verdi's *Rigoletto.*

From the 1890s to about 1940, another style of *canciones* flourished in Mérida in the Yucatán. This style also recalled Italian references in its frequent fermatas, applied dominants, and modal mixture (e.g., Guty Cárdenas' "Flor"). In addition, many songs had the 6/8 meter of the Colombian *bambuco,* while others contained habanera-type rhythms reminiscent of the Cuban *bolero.* Of the 447 songs in Juan Ausucua's compilation *El Ruiseñor yucateco: coleccioñ de canciones de todos los generos,* 147 were Cuban, 119 were from central Mexico, 9 were *coplas* from Spanish *zarzuelas,* and 132 were Yucatecan. The *cancíon yucateca* was also noted for its literary merit, with poets such as Luis Rosas Vega ("La peregrina"), José Esquivel Pren, Felipe Ibarra y de Regil, and Ricardo López Méndez noted for song lyrics, which often contained references to Mayan culture. The most famous composer was Guty Cárdenas; others included Juan Manuel Vargas and Filiberto Romero ("Canciones del Mayab").

According to Garrido, a more Mexican style of *cancíon romántica* began with the song "Perjura" composed by Miguel Lerdo de Tejada in 1901. As with earlier *canciones,* it contained tonicizations of other keys, but its second section had a lively triplet-duplet rhythm. This style continued to be cultivated until about 1950 by Mexico City–based composers, including Alfonso Esparza Oteo ("Te he de querer," "Rondalla"), Mario Talavera ("Gracia plena," "La cancíon flor de mayo"), and Ignacio Fernández Esperón ("Tata Nacho"), who continued the practice of modal mixture. This stage of the *cancíon romántica,* along with the Cuban *bolero,* was considered the immediate precursor to Mexican *bolero.*

Perhaps the most noted composer of *canciones románticas* was Manuel M. Ponce (1882–1948), whose "Estrellita" (1912) has been recorded in a variety of styles by **Trio Los Panchos, Pérez Prado**, Charlie Parker, and many others. While he was credited as the father of Mexican musical nationalism for his lecture "La musica y la canción mexicana" (1913), some of his songs still showed the influence of European Romanticism, with "Estrellita" resembling Schumann's "Traumerei" in its melodic contour and prominent harmonies. Ponce also wrote many arrangements of Mexican folksongs, such as "Acuérdate de mí," "Adiós mi bien," and "Trigueña hermosa."

Similar songs in the style of Romantic art song were heard in **Cuba** in the 19th century, where Italian opera was also popular. Among those cited by Carpentier include "La Corina" (1820), inspired by Madame de Staël's novel *Corinne;* "La Isabela" by Ramón Montalvo, inspired by Lord Byron's "To Jenny" and "Dulce Chactas." Songs such as "Canción de la rosa" and "Recuerdos de Bellini" were printed in the music magazine *Apolo Habanero* (1835).

Further Reading

Carpentier, Alejo. 2001. *Music in Cuba.* Cultural studies of the Americas, v. 5. Minneapolis: University of Minnesota Press. First printed in 1946 as *La música en Cuba.*

Geijerstam, Claesaf. 1976. *Popular Music in Mexico.* Albuquerque: University of New Mexico Press.

Huebner, Steven. "Lyric Form in Ottocento Opera." *Journal of the Royal Music Association* 117 (1992): 123–47.

Mendoza, Vicente T. *La canción mexicana ensayo de clasificación y antología.* Tezontle, México: Fondo de Cultura Económica, 1982. First printed 1961.

Olavarría y Ferrari, Enrique de, and Salvador Novo. *Reseña histórica del teatro en México, 1538–1911.* México: Editorial Porrúa, 1961.

Noriko Manabe

Carnival

Carnival (*Carnaval* in Portuguese) is the pre-Lenten festive celebration that takes place throughout the Christian world over several days, ending on Ash Wednesday. Although it is most strongly associated with the Catholic Church, Eastern Orthodox churches and some Protestant denominations also practice versions. It is European in origin, but has been embraced throughout the New World and exists today in various manifestations. What distinguishes New World Carnival celebrations is the use of local dances, many of which have African roots, reflecting the importance of the legacy of slavery in the Americas. The most famous Latin American Carnival celebration is in **Brazil**, where it has become an important part of national identity. The Brazilian version of Carnival celebrations features many African-derived music and dance forms, most notably samba, the most important popular music genre in Brazil.

Carnival came to the rest of Europe from Italy, but its roots go as far back as Greek and Roman festivals to Dionysius and Bacchus. These celebrations were characterized by the temporary subversion of civil order, and included processions of masked dancers. Later Christian festivals were devoted to patron saints or St. Mary, still following the old traditions of masquerades, processions, floats and flowers. The etymology for the word is unclear, but it may be from *carne vale,* Latin for put away the meat, referring to the Lenten fast. Another interpretation is farewell to the flesh, with both culinary and carnal implications.

Carnival was at first tolerated by the Church; it was incorporated into the Church calendar after the Counter-Reformation. As Catholic Europe took control of the Americas and other parts of the world, they brought with them their Carnival traditions. New World Carnival celebrations commonly represent a blending of European with African and Native American traditions. The Portuguese took Carnival to its colonies, including parts of Africa, India, and China (for example, in the former Portuguese colony of Goa in India, there is a long tradition of Carnival), but Portuguese Carnival celebrations lacked the finesse of the French and Italian varieties. It was, in fact, violent. The most famous example of Carnival today is in Brazil, where Portuguese influences mixed with African-derived culture to form a complex Carnival celebration in various traditions, some directly from Portuguese models, and others exclusively Brazilian. Several traditions eventually evolved into to the most recognized face of Carnival today, the *samba* school competitions of Rio de Janeiro.

Carnival in Rio until the middle of 19th century was based on the Portuguese model of *entrudo,* a brutal costumed revelry chiefly consisting of a vulgar battle where water, flour, and paint were thrown about indiscriminately at people on the streets. The participation of slaves and people of all classes allowed it to attain even more elaborate forms, still thumbing its collective nose at social norms. *Entrudo* was followed by what came to be known as the *Grande Sociedades,* or Great Societies, which included parades and masquerades. Great Societies modeled their masked balls on the Parisian Carnival model, mostly dancing the **polka** and its spin-off, the *maxixe*. These societies were inherently bourgeois, exclusively for the rich, white elite; the poor could only observe their betters.

Another Carnival tradition was *Zé Pereiras,* groups that would march while making lots of noise, led by percussion. They were distinguished by their lack of dancing. By the 1890s these *Zé Pereiras* were mixing with black Carnival revelers who paraded in groups called Cucumbis, which featured feathered Indian costumes leading the procession. A tradition that followed was the Corso, a parade of middle-class merrymakers in carriages and later open cars, copying from Spanish and French models of processions with flowers.

A Carnival tradition that appeared early in the 20th century includes the *cordão* and the *bloco,* scattered bands of street dancing masqueraders with bands of percussion. *Bloco* came to designate any informal group of *carnavelescos,* but they were generally from lower classes. Although they were often loosely organized and less ambitious than the *cordão,* they nonetheless represent an expansion of street dancing exclusively to percussion. Contemporary with the *bloco* and *cordão* is the *rancho,* which were formed mostly in working-class neighborhoods. They included men and women, mulattos and blacks, who paraded with percussion instruments in costumes that represented a theme, or *enredo.* They appeared at a time when a great number of Afro-Brazilian were seeking a means by which to participate in Carnival that represented their own neighborhoods and tastes, as they had been rejected from the existing forms of street Carnival. Although **choros** and **maxixes** were their original music of choice, *ranchos* later embraced the Afro-Brazilian *samba,* which represented a deliberate reaction to the exclusion of black and mulatto Brazilians from Carnival.

In the 1920s, the chic Carnival of *corsos* and Great Societies continued to dominate the scene for the upper classes. *Blocos* and *cordões* were seen throughout the city, but *ranchos* made up of poorer people began gathering at Praça Onze, in the less desirable neighborhood of Estácio. This was a time in social, political, and economic flux that saw wholesale societal changes, many of which were reflected in the newest Carnival organizations, the *escola de samba* or samba school. In search of their own means of expression and participation, poor blacks took elements from both *ranchos* and **blocos** to form these new, highly organized groups that were associated with the neighborhoods from which they came.

The first *samba* schools were founded in 1928. They were associated with the *favelas,* or slums, many of which sprouted up around 1900 throughout the city, filling the needed for access to work for lower class blacks, many of whom had migrated to Rio de Janeiro from the Northeast in the wake of emancipation in 1888. With this migration came the *samba,* and with the invention of the new *escolas,* *samba* took its place as the preeminent Carnival music. The *escolas* represented the desire of these *favela* dwellers to participate in Carnival in their own fashion with their own music—*samba*—that quickly became universally recognized cultural symbol of Brazilian identity. *Samba* became the most popular music genre, heard on the radio and recordings, but mostly recorded by white performers such as Noel Rosa and Carmen Miranda. In the *samba* of the *escola,* however, was not this commercial version, but rather the *samba-enredo,* the theme *samba,* used as part of the combined forces of the escolas to espouse a theme. *Escolas* competed in all aspects of the parade—costumes, percussion section, floats, root, dancing, etc.— for fame and status, at first sponsored by newspapers and later by the municipal government. The first competition was in 1932, with Estação Primeira, a former *bloco,* winning. Competitions increased in ferocity and scope, and at the same time became increasingly a means of escape.

Samba schools grew in number from the 1930s onward, and schools grew in size from several hundred participants to several thousand. These competitions were held on the streets of Rio, but there was little space for the growing groups of observers, which meant an increasingly foreign audience with increased air travel. With nationwide color television in the 1960s, a need developed to improve the venues of *samba* school competitions. In an attempt to cash in on both large crowds and television angles, in 1984 the city built the Sambódromo, a *samba* stadium. Capable of holding in excess of 150,000 fans, this construction changed the nature of the *Escolas de Samba.*

Samba school competitions represent the most visible aspect of contemporary Carnival celebrations in Rio, but are by no means the only one. Older traditions such as *blocos* and the cordão continue, and there are numerous Carnival balls and parties. Throughout the rest of Brazil other types of Carnival celebrations take place, including São Paulo's version of *samba* schools, and in northeastern Brazil, Carnival revolves around street parties featuring the Trio Elétrico, a band playing on a truck with a high-powered sound system. Similar festivities can be found throughout the Americas, and Carnival continues to be one of the most important holidays in the region.

Further Reading

Chasteen, John. "The Prehistory of Samba: Carnival Dancing in Rio de Janeiro, 1840–1917." *Journal of Latin American Studies* 28, no. 1 (Feb. 1996): 29–47.

Gardel, Luis D. *Escolas de Samba: An Affectionate Descriptive Account of the Carnival Guilds of Rio de Janeiro.* Rio de Janeiro, 1967.

Raphael, Alison. "From Popular Culture to Microenterprise: The History of Brazilian Samba Schools." *Latin American Music Review* 11, no. 1 (Spring–Summer, 1990): 73–83.

Sheriff, Robin E. "The Theft of Carnival: National Spectacle and Racial Politics in Rio de Janeiro." *Cultural Anthropology* 14, no. 1 (Feb. 1999): 3–28.

Thomas George Caracas Garcia

Cavaquinho

The *cavaquinho* is a Brazilian instrument of the lute family with four steel strings that is used in a wide variety of popular and folk music traditions throughout the country. Derived from the slightly larger *cavaco* (essentially the same instrument known as *ukelele* in Hawaii), the *cavaquinho* is also related to the older Portuguese stringed instrument known as the *machete.* In most musical contexts, the *cavaquinho* functions primarily as a strummed rhythmic and harmonic accompaniment to a vocal or instrumental melody. It is generally played with a plastic plectrum and its four strings are most commonly tuned (from lower to higher pitches) to D-G-B-D.

The *cavaquinho* is used to accompany many of Brazil's dramatic folk dances and is an essential instrument in many forms of rural and urban **samba**, including the highly percussive style of the *samba* schools (see **batucada**) performed during **Carnival** presentations, on modern recordings of *samba,* and in the back-to-the-roots style of *samba* known as *pagode*. It is also one of the primary instruments of the **choro** ensemble.

In the 1880s, the **flute, guitar**, and the *cavaquinho* formed an early style of *choro* ensemble known as a *terno* that performed popular European dances for parties in Rio de Janeiro. In the 1920s, the influential Oito Batutas group led by **Pixinguinha** and other ensembles regularly used the *cavaquinho*. During the 1930s and 1940s, the *cavaquinho* was also an indispensable instrument used by the professional *choro* ensembles known as *conjuntos regionais* (regional combos) that were hired by radio stations and recording studios from the 1930s through to the 1950s to accompany singers and to play instrumental numbers. Recordings and radio broadcasts spread the modern sound of the *conjunto regional* and the *cavaquinho* throughout **Brazil** and increased the demand for stylistic versatility and virtuosic performance practices. Nelson Cavaquinho, Waldir Azevedo, and Henrique Cazes are three outstanding musicians who have explored the virtuosic solo possibilities of the *cavaquinho*.

Further Reading

Livingston-Isenhour, Tamara Elena, and Thomas George Caracas Garcia. *Choro: A Social History of a Brazilian Popular Music.* Bloomington: Indiana University Press, 2005.

Larry Crook

Cencerro

The *cencerro* is an **Afro-Cuban** percussion instrument played in popular music ensembles. It is essentially a cowbell that has had its clapper removed. It is generally played with a wooden or metal stick, and depending on how and where it is held and struck will determine the tone of the instrument. It can either be handheld or mounted on a drum like a **conga** or **timbal**. The *cencerro* has a rural origin, and its early history is related to another type of time-keeping bell called the *guataca* or hoe blade. The latter is believed to be the first cowbell, and it is still used in some types of folkloric Cuban music today. The *cencerro* may come in a variety of sizes, usually depending on the function of the bell within the music. The largest of these bells is the *campana grande*. Next in size is the *mambo* or *timbal* bell, because it is commonly mounted on the *timbals*. Next in size is the *cha-cha* bell used in the performance of **cha cha chá**. The smallest bell is the **charanga** bell, which is used in the *charanga* orchestras. When held, the sound of the bell can either be open or closed (muted with the index finger), and it may either be struck on the mouth (wide, open end), the middle of the bell, or the neck of the bell (the narrower, closed end), the latter producing a higher pitched sound. The *cencerro* plays an ostinato timeline pattern that becomes part of a composite rhythm when combined with the rest of the percussion instruments.

Further Reading

Uribe, Ed. *The Essence of Afro-Cuban Percussion and Drum Set.* New York: Warner Brothers, 1996.

George Torres

Chacarera

The *chacarera* is a musical style from the northwest region of **Argentina** that is danced by nonembracing couples (*parejas sueltas*). Like the Argentine *zamba* and the Peruvian *zamacueca* and its derivatives, the *chacarera* is a *criollo* genre; that is, original to the New World but derived from European antecedents.

The *chacarera* shares the characteristic **sesquialtera** with many *criollo* genres from the region, a form of bimetricality that superimposes 6/8 and 3/4 meters simultaneously. Traditionally, *chacareras* employ one or more **guitars** that play rhythmic strumming patterns (*rasgueos, see* **rasgueado**) including characteristic accented notes on muted strings (*chasguidos*) as well as melodies. *Chacareras* can be vocal or instrumental, and in the latter case may include a violin or **bandoneón** as well as the guitar. Both vocal and instrumental *chacareras* frequently use the **bombo** for rhythmic accompaniment. Lyrics are typically written in *coplas*, a Spanish poetic form consisting of rhyming octosyllabic couplets.

The choreography of the *chacarera* consists of a fixed set of approaches, turns, and retreats, interspersed with sections where men perform a more free *zapateo* (athletic toe- and heel-tapping) while women perform a *zarandeo* (flourishes with a long skirt).

Although originally a regional style, the folklore boom of the 1960s brought the style to national prominence through vocal quartets such as Los Fronterizos and Los Chalchaleros, and composers such as **Atahualpa Yupanqui** and Eduardo Falú. *Chacarera* remains one of the most common styles used by contemporary Argentine folklore composers such as Jorge Fandermole and Raúl Carnota, who have adapted it by adding complex, **jazz**-influenced harmonies, and **rock** and pop instrumentation and production values.

Further Reading

Abecasis, Alberto. *La chacarera bien mensurada.* Rio Cuarto, Argentina: Universidad Nacional de Rio Cuarto, 2004.

Hodel, Brian. "The Guitar: Alive and Well in Argentina." *Guitar Review* 60 (1985): 1.

Michael O'Brien

Cha-Cha-Chá

Cha-cha-chá is a Cuban music and dance music genre introduced in the 1950s by composer, violinist, and orchestra director Enrique Jorrín. Its name is derived from the onomatopoeic sounds produced by the ***güiro*** and the cowbell, which is in turn is imitated by the shuffling of the dancers' steps.

The *cha-cha-chá* is in 4/4 rhythmic pattern with distinctive ***conga*** and bass patterns and also makes use of the *güiro* and cowbell, and the drums. Its structure varies, although it most commonly consists of an introduction, a main section in binary form, which may be repeated, and a final section similar to the ***montuno***, which usually repeats only one line of the chorus. The rhythms evolved out of the *nuevo ritmo* or new rhythm section of the ***danzón***. The choreography for the *cha-cha-chá* features open and closed couples dancing. The steps are marked by the rhythm of *güiro* and cowbell. The texts, humorous and narrative, are based on well-known topics, stories, and daily events. Many different personalities and characters exist within the *cha-cha-chá* repertoire.

"La engañadora" is considered to be the first piece in the genre. Enrique Jorrín published this song in 1953 while a member of Orquesta América, and he originally designated it as *mambo-rumba.* Other evidence points to composer Ninón Mondejar, who designated his compositions, "Yo no camino más" and "La verde palma real" as *cha-cha-chá.* All these compositions are milestones in the process of the *cha-cha-chá*'s evolution, but Jorrín was the most consistent contributor to the genre. *Cha-cha-chá* was created and refined by the ***charanga*** orchestras, which played primarily in recreation society halls, and later in ballrooms. Through the musical arrangements and orchestration of director Rafael Lay Apesteguia and flutist Richard Egües, the Orquesta Aragón enriched the *cha-cha-chá* and achieved unparalleled popularity during the 1950s as they brought the genre to its stylistic climax. Two of the most outstanding composers of *cha-cha-chá* in these same years were flutist Jose Antonio Fajardo and composer director Felix Reyna. Cuban *charangas* influential to the development of the *cha-cha-chá* include the aforementioned

Orquesta Aragón, Fajardo y sus Estrellas, and the Orchesta Sensación and Orchesta Sublime.

As it evolved, *cha-cha-chá* interacted with other national and international music styles and it has contributed to several hybrid genres such as *bolero-cha, el danzon-cha, mambo-cha,* and *son-cha,* which were developed and performed by Cuban and Latin American groups. Its continual adaptation has assured *cha-cha-chá*'s musical relevancy to the present time. *Cha-cha-chá* has also been performed by other types of bands like **jazz** bands, folkloric music groups, **rock**, pop, and **hip-hop** groups, as well as orchestras with an open instrumental format. After its *época de oro* (golden age), Cuban composers continue to flavor their music with elements of *cha-cha-chá* and ensembles have adapted it to fit their particular style. As an instrumental genre, the *cha-cha-chá* has become part of the Cuban musical identity. Composers in **Cuba** and abroad combine *cha-cha-chá* with other musical forms as an identifying feature. As a dance genre, *cha-cha-chá* thrives especially in Europe, where it is a stylized ballroom couples dance performed in international dance competitions.

Cha-cha-chá is a highly significant musical genre that has had a major impact on the world's popular music. Since its introduction in the 1950s, *cha-cha-chá* has remained central to the Cuban national musical identity. Musicians have adapted the sound and rhythm of the *cha-cha-chá* to fit diverse musical expressions and settings. Through the wide distribution and dissemination made possible by the recording and media industry, it has become ubiquitous in contemporary popular music.

Further Reading

Manuel, Peter. *Essays on Cuban Music: North American and Cuban Perspectives.* Lanham, MD: University Press of America, 1991.

Marrero, Gaspar. *La orquesta Aragón.* Havana: José Martí. 2001.

Morales, Ed. *The Latin Beat: The Rhythms and Roots of Latin Music from Bossa Nova to Salsa and Beyond.* Cambridge, MA: Da Capo Press, 2003.

Steward, Sue. *Musica!: Salsa, Rumba, Merengue, and More: The Rhythm of Latin America.* San Francisco: Chronicle Books, 1999.

Sublette, Ned. *Cuba and Its Music.* Chicago: Chicago Press Review, 2008.

Grizel Hernández and Liliana Casanella

Changüí

Changüí is a music and dance genre deeply rooted in the customs and lifestyles of **Cuba**. *Changüí* originated in Guantanamo, the eastern province of the country, and can refer to the music, the dance, or the instrumental ensemble.

The *changüí* began to develop at the end of the 19th century, evolving from specific transitional forms of song styles, and dance. The earliest recorded evidence of its existence is a reference from 1868, in the context of the Latin American wars of independence. Its form demonstrates the influence of diverse sociocultural elements of Canary, Bantu, and Franco-Haitian origin. Its musical syntax is defined, in terms of instrumentation, by the presence of the *tres*, the *bongó*, and the **marímbula**. The metallic **güiro** and the **maracas**, which the lead singer plays, are added to these instruments.

The *tres* is the main instrument, and its performance centers on the articulation of melodic-rhythmic patterns of various divisions and the distribution of accents, which establishes a syncopated timeline pattern that breaks up and reappears in a distinct way. The *tres* introduces, accompanies, creates melody and establishes motives or additional phrases as a response, to finish each one of the lines. This makes the performance of the *changüí* incompatible with the typical **son**.

The *bongó* performs segmented rhythmic phrases that are emphasized at climactic moments. It creates a pattern of short sounds called *picaos,* into which the *marímbula* inserts symmetric accents. These can be abrupt, in simple or double time, and determine the climax heard in the drum, both supporting and interrupting the *tres* pattern. The *marímbula,* apart from providing the bass, supports the rhythm and timbre, integrating specified and improvised accents. Between it and the *bongó,* a kind of call is established that serves as an interrelational cue. The *güiro* and the *maracas* act as rhythmic stabilizers.

The structure of the pieces consists of an introduction, provided by the *tres;* the body of the musical number, stated by the chorus in unison or by a lead singer; and lastly, the **montuno**, where the climactic improvisations are performed over a repeated chorus. The texts are structured in various ways, from the quatrain or *regina,* to a combination of improvised or memorized couplets or **décimas**. Compositions vary significantly in structure as they may contain long or short lines, free verse or stanzas of four lines (quatrains) with assonant or consonant rhymes.

The dominating presence of a single chorus, with short, inserted interjections, contrasts with the exposition; place names refer to regions where the genre is frequently performed; texts reflect everyday actions, occasionally satirical or humorous but chiefly rural in nature. Notable metatexts refer to the genre itself, as well as its developers and the *changüí*'s social function. The vocabulary of the genre belongs to the rural areas, and is characterized by common phrases such as *cumbanchar* (to have a good time, to go out dancing) and *parrandear* (to go out on the town, to party), which primarily allude to revelry. The dance is a closed couple dance, related to the *masón* of the *tumba francesa,* with steps more distinctive than the *son.* Its short drags, tilts and passes are related to the syncopation of the *tres* and the *picao* of the *bongó.*

The *changüí* appears in important national and international performances, according to the tradition maintained by old families such as the Latamblets and the Valera-Mirandas, and historically important individuals such as Chito Latamblet, Pedrito Speck, and Carlos Borromeo y Olivares who were members of the group Changüi de Guantanamo. Other performers include the Grupo Estrellas Campesinas, the Changüi Tradicional, and the Septeto Tradicional Guantanamero.

At present, the *changüí* has spread beyond its rural festival origins to join the realm of popular music. Musicians such as Lilí Martínez, Elio Revé and Juan Formell have introduced elements of the *changüí* to diverse musical forms and *sonero-salsero* contexts. Guitarist, composer, and orchestra director Leo Brouwer has also brought *changüí* into art music.

Musicological studies have placed the *changüi* within the so-called **son (Cuba)** complex, however, Danilo Orozco, musicologist, demonstrates that it constitutes an independent genre, born in a parallel process to the development of the *sones,* although it is clearly connected with the *son* in terms of instrumentation, native rural festival context, and diverse forms of lyric structure.

Further Reading

Font, Mauricio A., and Alfonso W. Quiroz. *Cuban Counterpoints: The Legacy of Fernando Ortiz.* Western Hemisphere Studies. Lanham, MD: Lexington Books, 2005.

Lapidus, Benjamin L. *Origins of Cuban Music and Dance: Changüí.* Lanham, MD: Scarecrow Press, 2008.

Neris González and Liliana Casanella

Charanga

The *charanga* is an instrumental ensemble that embodies the evolution of Cuban music. It has flourished as a distinct type of ensemble since the 19th century and has significantly influenced the development of several national and international music genres. Its earliest roots can be found in the French instrumental **trio** comprising piano, violin, and **flute**, which was brought to **Cuba** by immigrants from **Haiti**. This trio subsequently included Cuban percussion instruments and then gradually replaced the traditional *orquesta típica* or wind orchestras, which had been performing in Cuba since the 18th century.

The wind orchestra was made up of two clarinets, a cornet, a key trombone, a figle, two violins, a double-bass, a *timpani* (*timbals* or *pailas*), and a **güiro**. It reached the height of its popularity during the 19th century when *charanga* orchestras became the quintessential performers of **danzón** and, later, newer Cuban genres, as well as foreign styles such as waltz, **polka**, minuet and rigodon. The most famous *charanga* orchestras include those directed by Enrique Peña or José Belén Puig.

The transition from the wind orchestra to the *charanga francesa* began in the early 20th century, as the result of expanding expressive needs, which required the use of more instruments. Thus up to three additional violins were added, as well as the flute and the piano. These additions have been essential to the *charanga*'s definitive sound. The rest of the wind instruments were gradually excluded, while the percussion instruments remained (*güiro* and *timbal*), and the **congas** were added. The most common *charanga* form includes one flute, two or three violins, a double-bass, a piano, *pailas,* the *güiro, congas,* and two or three singers. Another variant of the form may include two flutes, one or two trumpets, a cello, and a **guitar**.

During the 1930s and 1940s, the *charangas* declined due to the rise in popularity of the **son cubano**. The *charanga* would evolve in response to this popularity, and years later, after violinist Enrique Jorrin of the *charanga* Orquesta América, created the **cha-cha-chá**. Jorrin created his own orchestra, evolving the *charanga* sound further by adding the trumpet, amplified bass, and violins to balance the sound. By about 1959, the name of *charanga francesa* was simplified to *charanga*. The singers were added and the repertoire was modified to accommodate dance music genres such as *cha-cha-chá, son, guajira,* and **mambo**. The most popular *charangas* of this time were that of Cheo Belén Puig, and the groups Orquesta Gris, Aragón, Sensación, Sublime, Arcaño y sus Maravillas, Americá, Ideal, Las Melodías del 40 and Fajardo y sus Estrellas.

This process of adding and removing instruments within the *charanga* came in response to musical performances of contemporaneous ensembles such as those performing *son.* These changes generated structural change that led to the development of new genres such as **danzonete***,* and to the performance of **danzón** in combination with popular genres such as *cha-cha-chá* and the *mambo.* In the late 1960s and the 1970s, the ascension of *son* as the prevalent genre meant that the *charanga* adapted its playlists to suit the preferred dance styles. It combined *cha-cha-chá* with other genres, to create new forms and steadily evolve of the *charanga*'s instrumentation.

The ensemble of Los Van Van best exemplifies *charanga*'s renewal with modified instrumentation. Its director Juan Formell combined electronic instruments such as the electric bass and guitar, synthesizers, drums, amplified violins, and violoncello for the first time in the same orchestra, and replaced the five-key flute for the new system flute. At the same time, Formell broke all the established rules of orchestration to create a different treatment of the choruses, presenting them as vocal quartets with the strings performing in a rhythmic style rather than in the typical melodic style.

Today, *charanga* is considered part of the Cuban musical environment. Some *charangas* remain closely linked to the traditional style, not only in their playlists but also in their stage performances. Such *orquesta* tipica ensembles include Sensación, Jorrín, and Charanga Típica de Rubalcaba. Other ensembles, such as Manolito Simonet y su Trabuco and Los Van Van, try new sounds taken from contemporary styles. Orchestras such as Original de Manzanillo and Aragón attempt to follow both tendencies at once by experimenting with current mixes along with their classical repertoire.

The *charanga* proves once again that it is the format of the ensemble that best embodies the history and evolution of Cuban popular music.

Further Reading

Gerard, Charley. *Music from Cuba: Mongo Santamaria, Chocolate Armenteros, and Cuban Musicians in the United States.* Westport, CT: Praeger, 2001.

Leymarie, Isabelle. *Cuban Fire: The Story of Salsa and Latin Jazz.* New York: Continuum, 2003.

Manuel, Peter. *Essays on Cuban Music: North American and Cuban Perspectives.* Lanham, MD: University Press of America, 1991.

Grizel Hernández and Liliana Casanella

Charango

The *charango* is a small, fretted lute originating in Andean South America. Found most prominently in the indigenous and *mestizo* musical traditions of highland **Peru, Bolivia**, and northern **Argentina**, the instrument also figures significantly in newer urban folk music styles popularized since the mid-20th century.

Unlike other chordophones introduced to South America during the colonial era, such as the **harp**, violin, and **guitar**, the *charango* is widely regarded as a hybrid invention, combining the form of a Spanish guitar or *vihuela* with an Andean aesthetic preference for high-pitched, thin musical textures. In existence by the early 18th century, the instrument's original distribution also suggests that it was a favored instrument of native *arrieros,* or muleteers, who likely influenced and appreciated its small size and portability.

Charango construction varies widely by region, musical tradition, and individual taste. Most instruments resemble a small guitar, roughly two feet in length (approximately 65 cm), with a waisted body and either a flat back or, most commonly today, a rounded wooden soundbox. Historically, armadillo shells or large gourds were also often used to make the soundbox, though these instruments are increasingly rare; armadillo shell versions of the instrument are also known as *quirquinchos* (*quechua* is Spanish for armadillo). Strings are set in four or five single, double, or triple courses, with exact tuning, string material, and number of frets depending on the tradition, location, and even season for which the instrument is used. The most common style of *charango,* played and sold in urban areas throughout the Andes today, uses five double courses of nylon strings, tuned G/G—C'/C'—E'/E" (split octave)—A'/A'—E"/E", with 15 to 18 frets. Larger versions of the instrument, such as the *ronroco,* maintain this A-minor tuning an octave lower, while smaller versions such as the *walaycho* or *chillador* may transpose it up a fourth or a fifth.

At least three different major styles of *charango* performance may be distinguished today. Among indigenous communities, especially in Bolivia and southern Peru, the instrument is typically strummed to accompany vocal performance. In this context, the *charango* primarily provides percussive and melodic, rather than harmonic, accompaniment; the melodic line played on the uppermost strings is strummed along with the remaining open strings, producing a dense, droning effect. This technique influences the variety of tunings used by indigenous players, who alter tunings based on the type of music and time of year of a given performance, as well as to match the preferred range of any singers. In these indigenous contexts, the *charango* is primarily a courting instrument played by young men to woo women, and is thus associated with beliefs in the seductive powers of the Andean *sirena* or mermaid.

A second style of *charango* playing emerged in the early 20th century among *mestizo* residents of southern Peru. Divorced from its courtship context, and fitted with gut, and later nylon, strings, which produced a deeper and more resonant sound, *mestizo* performers developed a playing style that alternates sections of plucking and strumming. Plucking is accomplished with the thumb and forefinger of the right hand, producing the melody and an accompanying harmonic line in thirds, while full chords are strummed in the introduction, conclusion, and at transition points. Closely tied to the intellectual and artistic movement known as *indigenismo* (Indian-ism), this new modernized form of playing brought the *charango* into urban forms of popular entertainment, even as it projected the instrument as a symbol of Andean culture. This style of playing is featured prominently in many recordings from the golden era of the Peruvian **huayno** (the most prominent genre of Andean music and dance) from the 1950s to the 1970s, particularly those by Ayacuchan folklorist Jaime Guardia.

A third, even more virtuosic style of playing the *charango* developed in the mid-20th century in the larger cities of Bolivia, Argentina, and **Chile**. The *charango* was one of several instruments incorporated into the urban Andean music ensemble that developed at this time, which also featured the guitar, *zampoña,* or **sikus** (panpipes), *kena* (end-notch flute), and **bombo** (bass drum). Building on elements of the *mestizo* style, musicians such as Bolivia's Mauro Nuñez, Ernesto Cavour, and others adopted elements of classical guitar technique and their own innovations, including faster strumming patterns, right-hand tremolos, and lightning-fast finger-picking, to transform the *charango* into a solo concert instrument. Renowned Chilean folklorist **Violetta Parra** also adopted the instrument at this time, setting her own compositions to *charango* accompaniment and influencing a later generation of Chilean **nueva canción** (new song) musicians to take up the instrument, who would popularize it around the world during their tours in the 1970s and 1980s.

In recent years, the *charango* has continued to grow in popularity, and is now commonly played in urban folk and popular musics throughout Andean South America. It has also been featured in a number of high-profile popular music recordings internationally, including songs by Shakira and by the Argentine producer and Oscar-winning film composer Gustavo Santaolalla.

Further Reading

Rios, Fernando. "Music in Urban La Paz, Bolivian Nationalism, and the Early History of Cosmopolitan Andean Music: 1936–1970." Ph.D. diss., University of Illinois, Urbana-Champaign, 2005.

Stobart, Henry. *Music and the Poetics of Production in the Bolivian Andes.* London: Ashgate, 2006.

Turino, Thomas. "The Charango and the 'Sirena': Music, Magic, and the Power of Love." *Latin American Music Review* 4, no. 1 (1983): 81–119.

Turino, Thomas. "The Urban-Mestizo Charango Tradition in Southern Peru: A Statement of Shifting Identity." *Ethnomusicology* 28, no. 2 (1984): 253–70.

Jonathan Ritter

Chicano Rock

Chicano rock refers to rock music played by Mexican Americans. The term does not imply a specific unifying style because Chicano artists have approached rock music in diverse ways, reflecting their regional experiences with Anglo and African American communities. Its roots began around 1950 when Chicano artists in south Texas and southern California modeled themselves after African American rhythm and blues artists. In the 1970s, Chicano artists openly celebrated their ethnic identity, which produced a unique hybrid style of rock music. By the 1990s, Chicano rock continued to diversify into many styles.

While **conjunto** and **orquesta** ensembles were popular in the 1950s in Texas, many Chicanos also liked **jazz** and rhythm and blues. In 1954 members of San Antonio's *Conjunto* Mexico formed the band Mando & the Chili Peppers. The band had its own show on local television and in 1957 released the album *On the Road with Rock 'n' Roll*. From San Benito, Freddy Fender recorded his first rock 'n' roll songs in 1957, including a cover of Elvis Presley's "Don't be Cruel" sung in Spanish. In 1959 Fender's song "Holy One" became a regional hit. By the mid-1960s, a unique style known as the "West Side Sound" emerged in San

Antonio, which combined elements of rhythm and blues, rock 'n' roll, doo-wop, soul, and *tejano* music. Two popular bands were The Royal Jesters and Sunny & the Sunliners. From Dallas, Sam the Sham & the Pharaohs hit the charts in 1965 with "Wooly Bully," a song that introduced **Tex-Mex** flavored rock 'n' roll to mainstream audiences.

In the 1950s in Los Angeles a number of Chicano musicians honed their skills playing jazz and rhythm & blues before switching to rock 'n' roll. Artists include The Armenta Brothers, Bobby Rey, Gil Bernal, The Rhythm Rockers, and the beloved Ritchie Valens. In the early 1960s a scene known as the Eastside Sound emerged in Los Angeles. Many of these bands such as The Romancers, The Blendells, and The Premiers recorded under Eddie Davis and Billy Cardenas. The two most popular bands were Cannibal & the Headhunters, well-known for their version of "Land of a Thousand Dances," and Thee Midniters, whose 1965 release "Whittier Boulevard" unified soul, gospel, surf rock, jazz, and Latin elements into a new sound that future bands followed.

Mexican Americans' efforts to improve their position in American society, termed the "Chicano Movement," marked a new consciousness in the 1960s that later emerged in Chicano rock in Los Angeles and the San Francisco Bay Area. Unlike previous artists, bands of the 1970s drew attention to their Mexican heritage by using imagery from Mexican culture, singing in Spanish, and celebrating Chicano life through their lyrics. The music drew heavily from jazz, rhythm and blues, Mexican music, and Latin dance music, all mixed with a rock approach. In Los Angeles, two of the most popular bands, El Chicano and Tierra, grew out of earlier Eastside Sound bands. El Chicano achieved national recognition in 1970 with their song "Viva Tirado." The same year, Rudy and Steve Salas founded Tierra, a band that achieved commercial success in 1980 with their cover song "Together." Other important bands include Macondo, *Tango*, Yaqui, Redbone, and Ruben & the Jets.

In the San Francisco Bay Area, Carlos Santana help create **Latin rock** when the band named after him combined Latin, blues, rock, African drumming, and psychedelic jams at their monumental 1969 performance at Woodstock. Other multiethnic bands followed Santana's lead while adding more Chicano references to their music. Malo, whose song "Suavecito" was a hit in 1972, included Carlos Santana's brother Jorge and Willie G. of Thee Midniters. Former member Coke Escovedo later formed Azteca and Richard Bean formed Sapo.

As younger Chicano artists wanted to be more directly political, they turned to punk rock. By the 1980s, Club Vex in Los Angeles was a hub for Chicano bands like The Zeros, The Brat, The Bags, Los Illegals, and The Plugz. Other Chicano punk scenes emerged in the 1990s in Chicago and Texas. Presently, Chicano rock bands like Los Lobos, Quetzal, Girl in a Coma, and Los Lonely Boys represent a wide range of styles and innovative mixtures.

Further Reading

Molina, Ruben. *Chicano Soul: Recordings and History of an American Culture.* La Puente, CA: Mictlan, 2007.

Reyes, David, and Tom Waldman. *Land of a Thousand Dances: Chicano Rock'n'Roll from Southern California.* Albuquerque: University of New Mexico Press, 1998.

Francisco Orozco

Chicha

Chicha, also known as *cumbia andina,* is a Peruvian popular music genre that fuses influences from the Colombian *cumbia*, the Andean *huayno*, and transnational pop/rock instrumentation. *Chicha* emerged as a distinctive genre in **Peru** in the late 1960s, and reached the height of its popularity in the 1980s. Associated primarily with the poorer marginal neighborhoods founded by highland migrants to the capital city, Lima, *chicha* nonetheless had a significant following in most of the country's major cities. Though its popularity waned in the 1990s, *chicha* groups continue to attract large audiences today, within Peru as well as beyond the country's borders in neighboring South American countries.

Cumbia first established a following in Peru in the 1960s, appealing to an unusually broad cross-section of the population in terms of both class and ethnic identity and geographic dispersion. Covers of Colombian *cumbias* were performed by diverse ensembles, from vocal soloists in the country's capital to brass bands in rural parts of the Andean highlands, and eventually gave birth to Peruvian variations on the genre. Los Destellos, founded in Lima by guitarist Enrique Delgado in 1968, is widely regarded as one of the most influential early bands. Their instrumental line-up—including two electric **guitars**, electric bass, and *timbals,* later expanded to incorporate **congas, bongos**, and keyboard—as well as Delgado's melodic, riff-based style of guitar playing established an instrumental model and characteristic sound that continues to define the genre to this date.

Rapid urbanization in Peru during the mid-20th century led to tremendous economic and cultural changes in cities such as Lima and Arequipa, where the particular form of Peruvian *cumbia* known as *chicha* developed. First-generation migrants in the 1950s and 1960s had established a thriving recording industry and performance circuit for commercial versions of the highland *huayno,* a double-meter music and dance genre widespread throughout the Andean highlands of **Peru** and **Bolivia**. By the early 1980s, children of those migrants began incorporating melodic influences—and at times, entire songs—from the *huayno* repertoire into the rhythms and tropical instrumentation of the Peruvian *cumbia*. Though coastal and jungle versions of the *cumbia* persisted in different parts (and demographics) of the country, *chicha,* or *cumbia andina* (Andean *cumbia*), dominated the listening habits of urban *provincianos* (provincial migrants). *Chicha,* referring to a type of homemade corn beer drunk throughout the Andes, also cemented the highland associations of the subgenre; the word's association with this music reportedly began with one of its early hits, "La Chichera" ("The Chicha Seller"), by the group Los Demonios del Mantaro, from Peru's central Mantaro Valley. Today, the word's association with this music has also made it synonymous, in a derogatory way, with anything deemed cheap or low class in Peru.

Shunned by more traditional media outlets such as television and radio in the 1980s, *chicha* musicians carved out an alternate media space among working-class migrant audiences through live performances in outdoor venues in poorer neighborhoods, sometimes called *chichodromos,* as well as through widespread distribution of their music via pirated cassettes. The genre's biggest and most enduring success in these realms was the band Los Shapis, founded by guitarist Jayme Moreyra and singer Julio Edmundo "Chapulín" Simeon in Lima in 1981. They had their first hit with "El Aguajal," an adaptation of a popular *huayno,* which was followed by a long string of hits in the following decade that reflected the lives and concerns of their predominantly urban, *provinciano* audience. Indeed, one characteristic feature of the genre, and of Los Shapis in particular, was an emphasis on simple and direct lyric messages, in contrast with the poetic flourishes of other Peruvian genres such as the *huayno* and the *Creole vals.* The singer "Chacalón" (Lorenzo Palacios) was also a major star of the decade. His unexpected death in 1992 drew more than 20,000 people into the streets to follow his casket through the working-class migrant neighborhoods where he had made his name.

Chicha's popularity faded to some extent in the 1990s, as its novelty waned and the genre faced heightened competition for urban audiences' attention in the country's increasingly diverse media market. By the end of the decade, *chicha* was overshadowed by *techno-cumbia,* another local variation on the *cumbia* which dropped *chicha*'s Andean influences, updated its sound, and featured primarily female singers and dancers. Nonetheless, *chicha* has endured into the new millennium. Many of the popular bands of the 1980s continue to perform and record regularly, and their earlier hits remain widely available. Television miniseries based on the lives of iconic singers Chacalón and Chapulín were major hits in recent years, appealing to audiences far beyond their prior core fan base, and point to the genre's continued longevity.

Further Reading

Bullen, Margaret. "Chicha in the Shanty Towns of Arequipa, Peru." *Popular Music* 12, no. 3 (1993): 229–44.

Hurtado Suárez, Wilfredo. *Chicha Peruana: Música de los Nuevos Migrantes.* Lima: Grupo de Investigaciones Económicas, 1995.

Montoya, Rodrigo. "Música *Chicha:* Cambios de la Canción Andina Quechua en el Perú." In *Cosmología y Música en los Andes,* edited by Max Peter Baumann, 483–95. Vervuert: Iberoamericana, 1996.

Romero, Raul. 2002. "Popular Music and the Global City: Huayno, Chicha, and Techno-*Cumbia* in Lima." In *From Tejano to Tango,* edited by Walter Aaron Clark, 217–39. New York: Routledge, 2002.

Turino, Thomas. "Somos el Perú [We are Peru]: *Cumbia Andina* and the Children of Andean Migrants in Lima." *Studies in Latin American Popular Culture* 9 (1990): 15–38.

Jonathan Ritter

Chile

Chile is situated on the Pacific coast of South America, bordered by **Argentina, Bolivia**, and **Peru**. The population of Chile is over 95 percent white and *mestizo,* while 4 percent of the people are Mapuche Indians. As a result, Chilean popular music has been largely influenced by traditional and as well as foreign styles.

In the 19th century, the most popular genres were associated with *Creole* dances or *bailes de tierra,* of which there are three types: *bailes serios* such as *rin, contradanza, churré,* ***vals,*** *gavota,* and *cuadrillas,* which were mainly performed in aristocratic gatherings; *bailes de chicoteo* such as ***zamba,*** *fandango,* and *cachucha;* and finally a third type including the genres *cielito, pericón, sajuriana, perdiz,* and *campana,* which mixes the characters of the two former categories. *Bailes serios* and *bailes de chicoteo* were introduced in Chile in approximately 1817 by the Army of the Andes.

In the 20th century, traditional genres such as ***cueca, tonada,*** and ***vals*** were widely distributed in the 1920s and 1930s through *música típica* ensembles such as Los Cuatro Huasos, Los Huasos Quincheros, and Los Provincianos. These groups evoked the folklore of central Chile by dressing such as *huasos* (Chilean cowboys). *Cueca, tonada, vals,* and other traditional Chilean genres like *canción, mapuchina, pericona, sirilla, refalosa, cachimbo,* and *trote* circulated in the 1960s and 1970s, and developed in various movements such as *neofolklore,* ***nueva canción,*** and *canto nuevo.* Music from other Latin American countries, especially Argentina, **Mexico**, and **Cuba**, was widely circulated in Chile during the 1930s. Urban and rural styles such as ***tango,*** Peruvian *vals,* ***maxixe, samba, rumba, conga, guaracha, balada, corrido, boleros, cumbia, marcha***, and ***ranchera*** were broadcasted via radio, films and recordings. Styles originated in the **United States**, particularly foxtrot, **jazz, rock**, pop and fusion, exerted a strong influence in Chilean popular music beginning in the 1950s.

Parra, Violeta

Violeta Parra (1917–1967) was a Chilean songwriter, performer, folk music compiler, and graphic artist. She played a key role in the resurgence of folk music in Latin America in the 1950s and in the subsequent development of the *nueva canción* movement. Her work was inspired by diverse folk music traditions, achieving a great popularity through mass distribution.

Parra became popular in the 1950s, particularly with her songs "Casamiento de negros" and "Qué pena siente el alma." In 1954, she traveled to the Soviet Union, Germany, and Italy before moving to France, where she lived for two years. In 1957 she worked for the University of Concepción in **Chile**, whereupon she founded and managed the *Museo de Arte Popular*. Back in Paris in 1961, Parra continued recording and preparing art exhibitions. She performed at the United Nations and at UNESCO. Her paintings, *arpilleras* (tapestries), and wire sculptures were displayed at the Louvre's *Musée des Arts Decoratifs*. Upon her return to Chile in 1965, she set up a circus tent in *La Reina* (a neighborhood in Santiago) to promote Chilean popular culture. Parra committed suicide at the age of 49.

Further Reading

Morales T., Leonidas. *Violeta Parra: la última canción.* Santiago de Chile: Editorial Cuarto Propio, 2003.

Katia Chornik

Nueva canción Chilena (Chilean New Song) came to light in the 1960s during a period of political struggle across Latin America, becoming associated with left-wing political activism (see **Protest Song in Latin America**). The roots of *nueva canción* are found in the work of artists such as **Violeta Parra** and **Atahualpa Yupanqui**, who revitalized Latin American folk music. In 1965, Angel and Isabel Parra (Violeta Parra's children) founded "La Peña de los Parra," a nightclub that established the sound of *nueva canción* and found an audience for future luminaries such as Patricio Manns and Víctor Jara. Augusto Pinochet's 1973 coup badly affected *nueva canción* artists, who were forced to go underground. Víctor Jara was tortured and killed, and well-known ensembles such as Inti-Illimani and Quilapayún were exiled. An urban movement called *canto nuevo* emerged after the military government banned traditional Andean instruments. The subjects of *canto nuevo*'s songs were largely about the city, and electronic musical instruments began to be used. Well-known groups belonging to this tendency are Barroco Andino, Ortiga, Aquelarre, and Santiago del Nuevo Extremo.

Nueva Ola Chilena (Chilean New Wave) materialized in the early 1960s in response to the international boom of rock 'n' roll. It was the first big phenomenon of music sales, tightly linked with mass media, radio, and especially television. Young Chilean artists performed rock and pop songs mostly from the English-speaking world. Well-known artists included Los Ramblers (their single "El rock del mundial" inaugurated the Nueva Ola movement), Peter Rock, Los Carr Twins, Buddy Richard, Los Red Junior, Luis Dimas, José Alfredo Fuentes, Fresia Soto, Cecilia, Gloria Aguirre, Pat Henry, Alan y sus Bates, and Los Rockets. *Nueva Ola Chilena* received harsh criticism because it was regarded as a commercial movement that did not represent the Chilean tradition.

The development of Chilean rock began in the 1960s, notably with the bands Los Jocker's, Aguaturbia, Los Mac's, Los Jaivas, and Congreso. The military coup badly affected rock musicians because assemblies and night shows were banned and the local recording industry was in recession. In the 1980s, musicians became overtly involved with politics, Los Prisioneros being the most influential band of this period. During the last two decades, Chile has had a thriving rock music scene, with many groups performing and recording in the country and abroad. Well-known contemporary bands include Los Tres, La Ley, Fulano, Lucybell, Tiro de Gracia, Sinergia, Difuntos Correa, Los Bunkers, Dracma, Santo Barrio, Javiera y Los Imposibles, Mamma Soul, Gondwana, Chancho en Piedra, and Los Tetas.

Further Reading

Advis, Luis, and Juan Pablo González. *Clásicos de la música popular chilena.* 2 vols. Santiago: Ediciones Universidad Católica de Chile, 1999–2000.

González, Juan Pablo. "Hegemony and Counter-Hegemony of Musician Latin-Americans: The Chilean Pop." *Popular Music and Society* 15, no. 2 (1991): 63.

González, Juan Pablo. "The Making of a Social History of Popular Music in Chile: Problems, Methods, and Results." *Latin American Music Review/Revista de música latino-americana* 26, no. 2 (2005): 248.

Katia Chornik

Chocalho

The *chocalho* is a Brazilian shaker or rattle used in a broad range of settings and genres. It can be made of metal, wood or plastic, filled with shells, stones, seeds, or rice, and varies in shape and size. *Chocalho* and *ganzá* are interchangeable terms whose selection varies depending on region and musical style. The instrument typically maintains a steady rhythmic pulse with accents placed on the first and fourth agitations, creating a swing-like feel. African Brazilians have used *chocalhos* in folkloric and religious music throughout Brazilian history. During the 1920s the group Os Oito Batutas integrated the instrument into Brazilian popular music and since then it has been used frequently in ***samba, choro, bossa nova***, and many others styles.

Four types of large *chocalhos* may be used in an *escola de samba* in support of the snare drums: *chocalho, ganzá, chocalho de platinela,* and *rocar.* Many *chocalhos* are cone-shaped, metal shakers with handles while *ganzás* may have one to three separate large, metal cylinders set in a row. The *chocalho de platinela* has multiple sets of tambourine-style jingles mounted on an aluminum frame and the *rocar* is similar but mounted on wood. These instruments produce loud, crisp sounds capable of cutting through an enormous ***bateria***. Most are held at shoulder level with two hands and are played by shaking the entire instrument back and forth. They are physically demanding to play and their use is sometimes limited to particular sections of songs.

Further Reading

Sabanovich, Daniel. *Brazilian Percussion Manual: Rhythms and Techniques with Application for the Drum Set.* Van Nuys, CA: Alfred, 1994.

Thomas Rohde

Choro

The Brazilian music genre known as *choro* originated in Rio de Janeiro, and was the most popular style of instrumental music in **Brazil** from the 1870s to the 1920s. The *choro* developed at a time when nationalism was an important artistic and intellectual force in Brazil. Long dominated by European ideas, Brazilian musicians, artists, and writers strove to establish their own artistic identities. Their search for a new artistic voice led to experimentation with established European traditions, which they modified to reflect what they perceived as new and uniquely Brazilian. In the 20th century, *choro* evolved into a genre on its own having fewer associations with European styles and representing a nationalistic reaction to European cultural dominance.

When it first appeared, *choro* was not only an improvisatory style of playing popular European dances, but also the name for the gatherings at which it was played. Musicians of the day adapted the **polka**, waltz, *schottische,* and other European dances to their tastes. This adaptation was influenced by African-derived rhythms such as ***lundu***, a dance that blended African and European features, *música* *de barbeiros,* literally barber's music, and *fazenda* or plantation bands whose members were slaves who entertained the owners. Musicians assimilated African rhythms into their playing style to the point that it became so distinct from the European dances that it became known by a different name, *choro.*

There are several etymological theories as to the word's origin, the most common suggests that it comes from the Portuguese verb *chorar,* to cry. *Choro* musicians are often described in the literature as weepers. A more convincing theory is that the name comes from an earlier instrumental tradition called *choromeleiro,* which featured the same instruments as the *choro* ensemble: **flutes** or other wind instruments, guitars of differing sizes, and percussion. The name *choromeleiro* actually comes from the *choromela,* a folk oboe used in wind bands both in colonial Brazil and originally on the Iberian Peninsula. A *choromeleiro* was a musician who played *choromela* in an ensemble, and over time the term came to designate any musician, regardless of his or her instrument, who played in an ensemble including *choromelas.*

The *choro* style emerged around 1870 and was the dominant instrumental style of playing for 50 years. The *choro* genre was not fully developed until the 1920s, and its move from style to genre paralleled the move from amateur to professional performance. The listeners of *choro* shifted over time as it lost its popularity among its early audience, the lower class, but became more popular with the middle and upper classes due to radio and recordings. As a result of its new position in society, the radio, and availability recordings, the *choro* style developed into a distinct genre and it was performed by musicians who had increasing professional opportunities.

Pixinguinha

Composer, arranger, flutist, saxophonist, and bandleader, Pixinguinha (1897–1973) had an enormous influence on the development of Brazilian popular music. Pixinguinha, a black Brazilian, was a pivotal figure in the process of cultural mediation between racially defined segments of the population at a time when the **samba**, the **choro**, and the Brazilian music industry were in formative stages. Equally proficient in written and improvised forms of music making, Pixinguinha's early activities as a virtuoso flutist in Rio de Janeiro put him in contact with *choro* musicians, **Carnival** bands, and top orchestras of the city. In 1919 he formed the popular group Oito Batutas, which performed throughout **Brazil** and then traveled to Paris and **Argentina**. In the 1920s, Pixinguinha freely incorporated genres, instruments, and performance styles influenced by American jazz bands into his music.

By the end of the 1920s, Pixinguinha emerged as a major artistic figure in the recording industry. Over the next 30 or so years, he worked with virtually all of Brazil's top singers, instrumentalists, and recording orchestras.

Further Reading

Livingston-Isenhour, Tamara Elena and Thomas George Caracas Garcia. *Choro: A Social History of a Brazilian Popular Music.* Bloomington: Indiana University Press, 2005.

Larry Crook

These changes both in the style-genre and social function are demonstrated by examining the most important musicians in the early *choro* tradition. Antônio Calado was one of the first well-trained, famous musicians to embrace the style. The music he composed demonstrated many of the characteristics of the style of playing and was copied by the amateurs of the early *choro*. Military bandleader Anacleto de Medeiros composed for amateurs, and his music on the surface was little removed from the European models. In the early 1900s, four musicians—Ernesto Nazaré, João Pernambuco, **Pixinguinha**, and Garoto—represented both the transition of *choro* into a distinct genre and shift from an amateur style to a professional one. Ernesto Nazaré was one of the first musicians to perform the *choro* style professionally, and he set the precedent for others. His compositions, although relatively sophisticated, demonstrated the characteristics of the evolving genre. João Pernambuco was an amateur who turned professional. He was one of the first to incorporate these characteristics of *choro* in solo **guitar** as well as ensemble music. By the time Pixinguinha was composing most of his music, the genre was well established, and his music represents the fully mature *choro* style as a unique genre completely distinct from European models. Garoto, who played with **Carmen Miranda** in the **United States**, fused the harmonic sophistication of American **jazz** with the *choro*.

As *choro* music became more accepted by upper class society, there were more and more opportunities for *choro* musicians to make a living with their music. The *choro* became part of the military band repertoire, and as such *choros* were formally composed, notated, and arranged. Musicians in these bands were expected to read music and audiences demanded a higher standard of technical ability, making the amateurs less inclined to become involved with this aspect of *choro*. The budding film industry required music both to accompany films and to entertain the audience between reels and popular musicians often filled that role. With the establishment of the recording and radio industries, new demands were placed on the *choro,* which had to adapt in order to find a new place in society.

Still, the heart and soul of the *choro* tradition was the *roda de choro,* or *choro* circle, a social and musical gathering in which musicians would play for sheer pleasure. This entirely amateur event was governed by specific rules of behavior and as a result it was difficult for a newcomer to join. Throughout the *choro*'s history, the *roda* remained the most constant and unchanging part of the tradition. The social element of the *choro* changed, and although musicians have never stopped gathering to play the *roda de choro,* the *choro* otherwise disappeared from the social scene in the capital. As the amateurism that so characterized the *choro* in its first 50 years of existence started to diminish, the **samba** took over its role as a largely amateur pursuit. The *roda de choro* tradition continued uninterrupted since its inception, but because of the fact that the tradition for the most part was transmitted orally, much of the technique and performance practice of the early *choro* has been lost.

The professional *choro* diminished in popularity through the 1940s and into the 1950s, but it never disappeared. Other Brazilian genres, most notably **samba**, surpassed *choro* in popularity. It became in a sense marginalized, played by older musicians in the *roda.* In the late 1950s and early 1960s, the *choro* enjoyed a brief revival, and, although there were still some amateur *choro* musicians playing in Rio de Janeiro and elsewhere, this revival was for the most part by professionals producing polished, clean performances far removed from the traditional *choro* performance practice. The 1980s saw a strong revival of *choro,* in part due to state sponsorship as a response to intense feelings of dissatisfaction among a number of social groups because of shifting social, political, and economic circumstances. The military dictatorship recognized *choro* as a means by which to reinstill a feeling of nationalism in the Brazilian populace.

More recently, *choro* has enjoyed a tremendous wave of popularity. More and more musicians of younger generations are playing in *choro* ensembles throughout Brazil, and in major cities *choro* once again can be heard regularly, both in public performance and in the more intimate *roda de choro.*

Further Reading

Béhague, Gerard. "Popular Musical Currents in the Art Music of the Early Nationalistic Period in Brazil, Circa 1870–1920." Ph.D. diss., Tulane University, 1966.

Garcia, Thomas George Caracas. "The Brazilian Choro: Music, Politics and Performance." Ph.D. diss., Duke University, 1997.

Garcia, Thomas George Caracas. "The *Choro,* the Guitar and Villa-Lobos." *Luso-Brazilian Review,* 34, no. 1 (Summer 1997): 57–66.

Livingston, Tamara. "Choro and Music Revivalism in Rio de Janeiro, 1973–1995." Ph.D. diss., University of Illinois at Urbana-Champaign, 1999.

Livingston-Isenhour, Tamara Elena, and Thomas George Caracas Garcia. *Choro: A Social History of a Brazilian Popular Music.* Bloomington: Indiana University Press, 2005.

Thomas George Caracas Garcia

Cinquillo

One-measure *cinquillo* rhythm. (George Torres)

The *cinquillo* is a five-pulse, rhythmic cell that is used as an *ostinato* timeline pattern in **Cuban** popular music. The rhythmic figure (2-1-2-1-2) is usually part of an asymmetrical, two-measure cell that alternates between a syncopated five-pulse measure (*cinquillo*) and a nonsyncopated, four-pulse measure (2-1-2-1-2 | 2-2-2-2). The syncopated side is called the strong side, while the nonsyncopated side is the weak side. Compositions may begin the pattern on either the strong or the weak side. Like the *clave* and *tresillo,* the *cinquillo* has its origins in timeline patterns from Sub-Saharan Africa that eventually found its way to Cuba via Haitians who migrated there in the 19th century. Within the fabric of an ensemble, the *cinquillo* is essential to the rhythm section, which layers various *ostinato* parts to provide an overall composite rhythm. Instruments responsible for playing the *cinquillo* may include the *claves*, the *güiro*, the *timbals*, and the piano. Besides providing a framework for the rhythm, the *cinquillo* rhythm is often present in the melody of a piece. The *cinquillo* is an essential rhythmic figure in the Cuban *contardanza* and the *danzón*, and it also appears in Puerto Rican *bomba* and the Haitian *meringue.* Because of its strong association with the *danzón* genre, the two-measure *cinquillo* figure is also known as *danzón clave.* The rhythm has also become prominent in American popular music genres including jazz and rock 'n' roll.

Further Reading

Floyd, Samuel A. Jr. "Black Music in the Circum-Caribbean." *American Music* 17, no. 1 (Spring 1999): 1–38.

George Torres

Clave

Clave is an Afro-Cuban timeline pattern used in Cuban folkloric and popular music, though its effect has extended far beyond Cuba by influencing American musics from Argentina to the United States. The term *clave* is a Spanish noun derived from the Latin *clavis,* which means key. This word was originally applied to the Cuban instrument known as **claves**, but it eventually came to define a rhythmic pattern that is beat on a hardwood or iron idiophone or clapped. The *clave* may be plainly defined as a timeline, sometimes called a cycle length or just a cycle, made up of four equidistant basic pulses. It may be broken up into an equal number of segments, either into two or multiples of two (a binary time span) corresponding to a 4/4 measure, or three and multiples of three (a ternary time span) corresponding to a 12/8 measure. But most frequently, *claves* are formed in asymmetrical patterns where not all of the time values coincide with basic pulses. As a result, more often than not, there is a rhythmic clash, or cross-rhythm, between divisive (symmetrical) rhythms and additive (asymmetrical) rhythms. *Claves* are usually five-stroke or seven-stroke patterns; for example, the *son clave,* which is the most widespread and universally known rhythmic pattern, is a five-stroke pattern whose time values are unevenly distributed within the time span. It consists of three short (S) strokes and two long (L) ones arranged the following way: S-S-L-S-L. It is mainly the specific phrasing of vocal and instrumental parts that determines the manner the clave is to be performed, that is, either in its straight form, as S-S-L / S-L called a 3–2 clave, or in its reversed form, as S-L / S-S-L called a 2–3 clave. It should be emphasized that melodic designs corresponding to the S-S-L segment are prone to containing additive rhythmic motifs, while the S-L segment is more likely to exhibit divisive rhythmic motifs.

The origin of *clave* rhythms is undeniably African, but not all *claves* arrived in Latin America as readymade patterns. The *son clave* does not seem to have existed in traditional African music, though it does exist in some African popular genres owing to the pervasive influence of Cuban music. On the other hand, the structural similarity of the *clave* to an extremely widespread time line in West and Central Africa (the standard pattern, especially in its five-stroke version) suggests a genetic link between the former and the latter. Thus, it also suggests a Latin American transformation of the ultimate African ternary model.

There are various ways of notating the *claves* using the standard music notation. Nevertheless, a variant of the Box Notation Method, also called TUBS (Time Unit Box System), is especially apropriate for the transcription of time lines. In that variant, one symbol for the strike and another for the pause are used. One may, thus, notate the *son clave* as follows: (16) [x . . x . . x . . . x . x . . .]. Another important clave rhythm played with the *claves* is that of the ***rumba,*** whose notation is: (16) [x . . x . . . x . . x . x . . .]. The number in parentheses, or cycle number (16), indicates the total number of strikes and rests in both binary time spans. It is worthwhile noting that both *claves* are used in secular contexts. Moreover, there are ternary *claves* as well, having 12 as their cycle number, like the five-stroke *abakuá clave,* used in the rituals of a male secret society in western provinces of **Cuba** and played with a clapperless bell: (12) [x . x . . x . x . x . . .], as well as the very widespread seven-stroke *bembé clave,* generally used in Cuban cult music and played with any iron idiophone. Its notation is: (12) [x . x . x x . x . x . x]. Still, there exist *clave* rhythms, which are performed with the *claves* in an utterly different context, like some patterns used for the *punto,* a secular rural Cuban genre, which owes a great deal to the Spanish legacy, but has, nonetheless, borrowed some African musical traits, like, the use of a timeline. Here is one of the main *clave* rhythms in the *punto,* which are often subject to variations, as are seven-stroke other ternary *claves:*

(12) [x . x x . xx . x . x .]. It should be pointed out that this *clave* is a reversed version of an African timeline from the Guinea Coast known among the Arará (Ewe-Fon) descendants in Matanzas Province in Cuba that goes: (12) [x . x . x . x. x x . x].

The reversal of the *clave* is a significant aspect of this topic, which, as shown above, is not exclusive to the *son clave*. In order to discuss this, the concept rhythmic density will prove helpful. Rhythmic density is related to the relative length of time values within the time span. The shorter the time values, the higher the rhythmic density; the longer the time values, the lower the rhythmic density. Arguably, when the greater rhythmic density of the melodic design fits the structure of the usually additive structure of the first three strokes of the *clave,* the 3–2 modality is used; but if that greater rhythmic density accommodates the usually divisive structure of the last two strokes of the *clave* rhythm, the 2–3 *clave* modality will be suitable for use. Very often, the melodic phrases corresponding to the 2–3 *clave* are acephalous ones, that is, they do not start on beat 3 of a 4/4 measure, but off-beat.

In Cuban genres such as *rumba* and **conga**, the 3–2 *clave* prevails; however, the 2–3 *clave* is more frequent in more melodic genres such as **bolero** and urban traditional song. The *son* and **salsa** use both, and sometimes switch from one modality to another within the same musical item, according to the specific phrasing in each section of the piece. But according to experienced Cuban composer and conductor Ricardo Leyva, the 3–2 *clave* is more Cuban than the 2–3 *clave,* the latter being more characteristic for *salsa* music.

The apparent similarity between the ternary African standard pattern (which may also be notated as 22323) and the binary *son clave* (accordingly 33424) is outstanding, as is the resemblance between the ternary *abakuá clave,* another version of the standard pattern, and the binary *rumba clave*. The standard pattern (1) and the *son clave* (2), which partition the space in a very similar fashion (S-S-L-S-L, regardless the mathematical ratios of their respective time values), can be more accurately compared "by expressing duration in units of 1/48th of a cycle," the lowest common denominator, as Jeff Pressing does:

(1) 8+8+12+8+12/48

(2) 9+9+12+6+12/48

Pressing has identified five rules of rhythmic transformation, among them there is one rule that refers to "maximally similar analogue aproximation, as for example the ratio of 22323 to 33424." He concludes that "[t]hose transformations are more common and basic which preserve the pattern in a holistic sense," as with the *clave*.

Rolando Pérez Fernández poses the following hypothesis that due to psychological and social variables, African ternary rhythms in Latin America, including *claves,* have undergone a generalized process of binarization resulting in an overwhelming predominance of binary rhythms in secular music, while religious and ritual music have mostly maintained the African preference for ternary rhythms.

Further Reading

Loza, Steven. "Review—essay La binarización de los ritmos ternarios africanos en América Latina." *Latin American Music Review,* 11(2): 296–310, Autumn-Winter 1990.

Nketia, J.H. Kwabena. 1974. *The Music of Africa.* New York/London: Norton & Company.

Pérez Fernández, Rolando A. *La binarización de los ritmos ternarios africanos en América Latina.* Havana: Casa de las Américas, 1986.

Pressing, Jeff. "Cognitive Isomorphisms in Pitch and Rhythm in World Music: West Africa, the Balkans and Western Tonality." *Studies in Music,* 17 (1983): 38–61.

Rolando Antonio Pérez Fernández

Claves

Musical duo Machito and Graciella Grillo perform at Glen Island Casino, New York, NY, in 1947. Graciella is seen here playing the *claves*. (William P. Gottlieb/Ira and Leonore S. Gershwin Fund Collection, Music Division, Library of Congress)

Claves are a percussion musical instrument, known in more formal terms as a struck idiophone. *Claves* consist of two cylindrical dowels made of wood, plastic, or fiberglass, measuring about 8–10 inches (20–25 centimeters) in length and 1 inch (2.5–3 centimeters) in diameter. They may be solid or hollow in the center, which amplifies their clear, high-pitched, penetrating sound. One stick serves as the striker while the other stick acts as the resonator. To play *claves,* the resonator stick is held by the fingertips of the nondominant hand with the palm facing up. The other stick, which acts as the striker, is held in the dominant hand by the thumb, pointer, and middle finger. The player then uses the striker to hit the resonator *clave* in the center.

Claves originated in **Cuba**, emerging from contact between African slaves and Spanish indentured servants several centuries ago. Similar percussive instruments can be found in Europe, North America, Africa, East Asia, Southeast Asia, and Polynesia. *Claves* are also used throughout Latin America and the Caribbean, particularly in countries whose music has a strong African influence. Nevertheless, *claves* are most commonly found in **Afro-Cuban** musical genres, such as the *son cubano* and *salsa*.

Claves are used to play repeating rhythmic patterns or ostinatos in Cuban music, which are known as *clave* rhythms. There are several different *clave* rhythms, including the *son clave, rumba clave,* and 6/8 *clave*.

Further Reading

Sublette, Ned. *Cuba and Its Music: From the First Drums to the Mambo.* Chicago: Chicago Review Press, 2004.

Erin Stapleton-Corcoran

Colombia

Colombia, the northernmost country in South America, was a Spanish colony from the founding of the city of Santa Marta in 1526 until gaining independence in 1819. Nearly 300 years of Spanish rule left a strong social hierarchy influenced by ancestry, education, skin color, and geography that exists to some extent to the present day. Colombia's population is primarily of mixed heritage *mestizo, mulatto,* and zambo (African and Indian ancestry), and of European, Indian, and African descent. The country is one of the most biologically diverse in the world and features abundant geographical variety including three separate chains of the Andes Mountains, Amazonian rainforest, grasslands, and, unique to South America, both Atlantic and Pacific coasts that define its five main regions. In spite of the fact that a majority of the country's over 43 million inhabitants live in the Andean region, Colombia has distinct regional cultures as opposed to a dominant national culture. Colombia's popular music traditions emanate from four of these regions (save the Amazonian region), reflecting this regional diversity that has typified the country's political, social, and cultural history.

By the early 19th century, established European dances such as minuets, quadrilles, waltzes, and *contradanzas* were popular in the salons of the elite classes in Colombia's urban areas and were usually played on piano or string instruments. Eventually, this repertoire expanded to include newer European styles including **polkas** and *mazurkas* as well as creolized versions of European styles such as the *pasillo*, based on the waltz, and urbanized versions of indigenous folk genres such as the *bambuco*. Beginning in the 1840s, military-style wind bands became popular and helped spread these styles of music to urban working classes, smaller towns, and rural areas, many of which formed their own municipal bands.

Música andina, the music of the Andean highland region is a style altogether distinct from the panpipe-based *música andina* of the rest of South America. It consists of vocal **duos** or **trios** accompanied by **guitar**, the mandolin-like ***bandola***, and the ***tiple***, a native guitar-like instrument with 12 strings in four courses. Representative genres include *bambuco, pasillo, guabina,* and *torbellino.* As music became integrated into discussions of Colombian nationhood toward the end of the 19th century, *bambuco* in particular was given a preeminent role as an emblem of national identity. Emilio Murillo, Jorge Añez, and the duo Wills and Escobar were among the important second generation musicians who cemented the popularity of *música andina* through national and international tours and recordings produced mainly in New York during the 1910s and 1920s.

Municipal wind bands of the early 20th century in *La Costa,* Colombia's northern Caribbean coast, began to incorporate into their repertoire adaptations of regional folk genres of **flute** and drum-based *conjunto de gaita* ensembles such as **porro,** *cumbia, gaita, mapalé,* and *bullerengue.* **Jazz** bands specializing in North American and Cuban music in the 1920s continued this adaptation as well as orchestras that adapted folk genres to a dance orchestra format in the late 1930s. Bandleaders such as Lucho Bermúdez, Pacho Galán, composer and singer José Barros, and later Edmundo Arias were the innovators of this style, alternately known as *música tropical, música costeña,* or simply *porro.* The popularity and spread of *música tropical* was greatly aided by the radio and recording industries, both of which began in *La Costa.* The recording industry remained centered in *La Costa* through the end of the 1940s, by which time the style had become the preeminent national and international music. By the 1960s, as a result of the waning popularity of dance orchestras and a recording industry shift to Medellín, a simplified version of *música tropical* had become popular and was marketed internationally as *cumbia.* It was derided within Colombia as a degraded representation of *música tropical* and referred to as *chucu-chucu* or *raspa. Cumbia* would become the basis for local variations in countries such as **Mexico** and **Peru**.

Vallenato was another important musical genre from the Colombian coast. It originated from the sung oral poetry tradition of *La Costa* that included ***baladas,*** *coplas,* and ***décimas*** (10-line stanzas). Songwriters such as Rafael Escalona, Emiliano Zulueta, Tobías Enrique Pumarejo, and Freddy Molina who were all from the elite classes in *La Provincia,* the area around the city of Valledupar, began composing songs in these styles. They were recorded by guitar-based groups led by Guillermo Buitrago and Julio Boveo beginning in the 1940s and later by accordionist-singers including Chico Bolaños, Alejo Durán, and Leandro Díaz. Aided by folklorists and journalists such as Gabriel García Márquez, and the initiation of the *Festival de la*

Leyenda Vallenata (The Festival of the *Vallenato* Legend) in 1968, *vallenato* began to find a significant audience in the 1970s. It vaulted to national popularity in 1978 when *El Binomino de Oro* (the Golden Pair) combined *vallenato* with romantic pop. This *vallenato romántico* (romantic vallenato) continued its popularity into the 21st century with recording artists such as Jorge Celedón and Pipe Peláez.

El Litoral Pacifico, the tropical rainforest region on the Pacific Coast, is predominantly Afro-Colombian with a strong Afro-Colombian culture. It has been largely isolated for much of the nation's history in spite of the fact that the city of Buenaventura has long been Colombia's most important Pacific port. The region's two most prominent musical expressions are *chirimía* and *música de marimba.* *Chirimía,* from the northwestern province of Chocó, is a fusion of the European wind band with African styles and esthetics, similar to the blends of tradition that transpired in *costeño* genres. *Música de marimba,* from the southern Pacific region, is a style played by **marimba** and hand drum-based ensembles, typified by polyrhythmic rhythm *currulao.*

In the 1950s and 1960s, there was an effort in Buenaventura to adapt *currulao* to the dance orchestra format. While the trend achieved only regional success, it did launch some artists, most notably singer Leonor González Mina and composer Petronio Álvarez, to widespread prominence. Multiple factors led to increased visibility for the Pacific culture beyond the region during the 1980s and 1990s. Some of these factors included mass urbanization especially to Cali in the 1980s and the official recognition of Afro-Colombian territorial rights in 1991. The inauguration in 1997 of Cali's Petronio Álvarez Festival, an annual festival of music from the Pacific that features both traditional and urbanized versions of *música de marimba, chirimía,* and related genres also broadened awareness of Pacific culture as did the release of albums of urbanized versions of Pacific genres by Grupo Saboreo, singer Markitos, and others, in the late 1990s. By 2009, the "Petronio" was being broadcast nationally, reflecting an emerging national presence for Pacific musics.

Los Llanos, Colombia's eastern Orinoco Plains region, is more closely tied to the southern grasslands of **Venezuela** than to the rest of Colombia, both in terms of geography and culture. The two nations share a cowboy-based culture and the string-based *conjunto llanera, Los Llanos*'s most representative ensemble. The *música llanera* of the **conjuntos** includes genres such as **joropo**, the polyrhythmic courtship dance, as well as the *galerón* and the **corrido**. Never having achieved national status, *música llanera* nevertheless remains an important regional style.

A number of different styles of international music have developed significant regional followings within Colombia, which have been instrumental as markers of regional and subcultural identity and have led to locally produced varieties. In Medellín, genres such as Mexican **ranchera** and especially Argentinean **tango** have long enjoyed great popularity because they are said to resonate with the local existential sense of *despecho* (tragic anger and despair). Singer **Carlos Gardel**'s 1935 death in a plane crash in Medellín has been a significant factor in the enduring popularity of *tango* and of Gardel himself in the city. Local musicians have distilled these genres into the **accordion**-based *música de carrilera* (railroad music) named for the railroad workers who disseminated it to the surrounding areas of Antioquia province.

Since the 1950s, **rock** has come to represent cosmopolitanism and rebellion for many middle-class youth. While this is a countrywide trend, rock-based culture has largely centered around Bogotá and, to a lesser extent, Medellín. After a number of groups experimented with adding rock elements to *música costeña,* the first Colombian rock bands, including Los Flippers, Los Speakers, and Los Yetis, appeared in the mid-1960s. The nation's rock movement has branched off into the subgenres of punk with bands including La Pestilencia and I.R.A., heavy metal including bands such as Kraken and Masacre, and ska with 1.280 Almas and Dr. Krapula. The Bogotá-based group Aterciopelados has also attained international popularity and acclaim.

Salsa became an important symbol of local identity in Cali beginning in the 1970s. The genre's antecedents, particularly Cuban *son,* were popular among working classes in Cali and in the coastal regions of the nation, and the first Colombian *salsa* orchestras, such as Fruko y Sus Tesos and Joe Arroyo y La Verdad, emerged elsewhere. Despite this, it was Cali that became most associated with the genre, as it reflected the local image of carefree dancing, partying, and drinking. What began as a grassroots movement in the 1970s blossomed into the city's emergence as a center for *salsa* consumption and production during the 1980s and 1990s with groups such as Grupo Niche, Orquesta Guayacán, and La Misma Gente all based in the city.

In Cartagena, African genres such as highlife and *soukous,* and Afro-Caribbean genres such as ***reggae***, ***zouk***, and ***soca*** became popular among working class Afro-Colombians beginning in the 1970s. This popularity expanded to other areas of *La Costa,* and, in the 1980s, musicians developed a local style called *chapmeta* or *terápia* (therapy). This regionally derived variant has been viewed as a vehicle for Afro-*costeños* to reassert their blackness after the national appropriation of other Afro-derived *Costeño* genres.

While some Colombian artists and groups such as Bermúdez, Galán, Arroyo, Grupo Niche, and the *cumbia* group La Sonora Dinomita had achieved some international success, the breakthrough for Colombian artists in the international market occurred in 1993 with Carlos Vives's album *Clásicos de La Provincia.* Vives's music was a unique fusion of *vallenatos* from the 1950s and 1960s with musical and esthetic elements borrowed from rock, jazz, ***merengue,*** and folkloric *costeño* styles. His success had two major ramifications for Colombian popular music. It paved the way for Colombian artists to enter international markets including musicians of traditional *costeño* folkloric music such as Totó La Momposina and Los Gaiteros de San Jacinto as well as singer-songwriters such as Shakira and Juanes. Additionally, Vives's successful use of fusion styles encouraged other artists to create hybrids of Colombian and North American genres. This was first evidenced by the *pop tropical* trend of the 1990s and then in the 2000s by fusions of folkloric rhythms from various regions—but predominantly the Caribbean and Pacific coasts—with rap (Bomba Estéreo, Choc Quib Town), funk (Mojarra Eléctrica), *salsa* (La Republica), electronica (Sidestepper), jazz (Puerto Candelaria, Grupo Bahía), and rock (Tumbacatre, La Revuelta).

Further Reading

Wade, Peter. 2000. *Music, Race, and Nation: Música Tropical in Colombia.* Chicago: University of Chicago Press.

Waxer, Lise. 2002. *The City of Musical Memory: Salsa, Record Grooves and Popular Culture in Cali, Colombia.* Middletown, CT: Wesleyan University Press.

Ramón Versage Agudelo

Comparsa. *See* Conga.

Conga

The words *conga* and *comparsa* are used interchangeably to refer to an **Afro-Cuban Carnival** band as well as a stylized type of street music and dance. Some of the musical rhythms and dance movements used in *conga* performance have become simplified into a novelty dance that was incorporated into depictions of Afro-Cuban culture and Hollywood movies. One of the most significant names associated with this dance style is Desi Arnaz, Jr., who many inaccurately believe created the *conga* line.

Congas were street processions with roots in African slave processions. They were originally part of a pre-Lenten Carnival celebration or a Christmas time celebration performed by Afro-Cuban *cabildos,* or social associations. As a result of the raucous singing, dancing, and requisite revelry characteristic of the *conga,* the processions were considered vulgar by polite white Cuban society and were banned from 1900 to 1937. After its reintroduction in the late 1930s the *conga was* enjoyed by both blacks and whites alike who invested time and resources into clubs and social groups.

At around the same time, a nightclub or dancehall *conga* gained international popularity. Initially it spread with performances abroad by Eliseo Grenet, Xavier Cugat, and Desi Arnaz, Jr., to American and European ballrooms. These *conga* performances relied on a highly stylized yet simplified version of the music and dance. International publishers and record companies released many commercial recordings of popular *conga* tunes. Many popular composers responded to the demand for the *conga* with their own compositions. Eventually, the ballroom conga made it to Hollywood where it was used in motion pictures, most notably with Cugat and Arnaz. Famous examples of *congas* from the late 1930s and 1940s include "Bim Bam Bum" by Rafael Hernadez, "Uno, dos, y tres" by Rafael Ortiz (which was later, and more famously known as "1, 2, 3, Kick"), and "Se Fue La Comparsa" by Ernesto Lecuona.

As a dance, the urbanized *conga* became more of a simplified version of its street procession forerunner. Because of its rhythmic simplicity, the *conga* is relatively easy to learn and participate in. Though it could be danced alone, it is most commonly performed in a *conga* line as an imitation of the Carnival trenes (trains). Holding the person in front of them by the waist or the shoulders, dancers step to a four-pulse rhythmic pattern that coincides with a 2–3 **clave**. The train of dancers moves either forward or backward to the syncopated rhythm, alternating left-right steps on the beat of the first three pulses, and kicking in anticipation of the fourth pulse, hence the mnemonic directive or "1–2-3-Kick" (where the English translation of the conga "Uno, dos, y tres," comes from). As quickly as the conga rose to popularity, it was replaced in the 1950s by the more modern ***mambo*** and ***cha cha chá***.

The *conga* has been referenced in popular music. Chuck Berry mentioned it in his 1957 hit "Rock 'n' Roll Music" where Berry uses the line "It's way too early for the congo (sic)" in order to set up his preference for rock 'n' roll music in the chorus. His use of the word congo is a phonetic corruption of *conga*. Gloria Estefan and the Miami Sound Machine also had great success with their 1985 song "Conga," which invited listeners to surrender to the allure of the *conga* rhythm. But it is perhaps Desi Arnaz, Jr. who was most closely associated with the *conga*.

Further Reading

Moore, Robin D. *Nationalizing Blackness: Afrocubanismo and Artistic Revolution in Havana, 1920–1940.* Pitt Latin America series, edited by Billie R. DeWalt. Pittsburgh: University of Pittsburgh Press, 1997.

Roberts, John Storm. *The Latin Tinge: The Impact of Latin American Music on the United States* Rev. ed. Oxford: Oxford University Press, 1999.

Sublette, Ned. *Cuba and Its Music: From the First Drums to the Mambo.* Chicago: Chicago Review Press, 2004.

George Torres

Conga Drum. *See* Tumbadora.

Conjunto

Conjunto in Spanish-speaking regions of Latin America is a generic word for a musical ensemble or group. Within this broad classification, several prominent genres of Latin American popular music have used the term *conjunto* as a referential designation that goes beyond the generic to connote specific musical styles and instrumentations. There are two popular genres known specifically as *conjunto*. The first is the Cuban ***conjunto cubano***, a genre credited to **Arsenio Rodríguez**, who added piano and several trumpets to the traditional ***son cubano*** instrumentation. The other is *conjunto tejano* or tex-mex *conjunto,* which refers to the style of music and instrumentation of southern Texas that was influenced by the northern style of Mexican music, or *música norteña.* The core of these ensembles consists of a button ***accordion***, and a ***bajo sexto*** (six-course bass **guitar**), to which the electric bass and drum set have later been added. The mainstays of this genre's repertoire include the **polka**, *canción,* and ***vals***. Early pioneers in this genre, such as Raul "El Ruco" Martinez's "Dueto Alegre," were responsible for influencing later generations of *norteño* superstars such as Los Tigres del Norte and Flaco Jimenez.

Further Reading

Peña, Manuel. *The Texas-Mexican Conjunto: History of a Working-Class Music.* Austin: University of Texas Press, 1985.

George Torres

Conjunto Cubano

Conjunto is a type of Cuban popular music ensemble characterized by the performance of ***son*** as its central musical genre. As early as the 1920s there is evidence of the occasional presence of the *conga* drum, piano, and trumpet in recordings of groups that regularly performed the *son* (***sextetos*** and ***septetos***), but the *conjunto* was not established as a fixed form until the 1940s. The Cuban ***tres*** and composer **Arsenio Rodríguez**, helped found the *conjunto* by incorporating these instruments into the Sexteto Bellamar, later to become the Conjunto de Arsenio Rodríguez.

The classic *son conjunto* added the double bass, the ***bongó***, the ***tumbadora***, two to four trumpets, and a **guitar** to the traditional sextet. The *tres* remained the primary instrument along with the piano. The vocal parts consisted of one to three singers who performed as soloistis or as a chorus and who also played the ***güiro***, ***maracas***, and ***claves***. In terms of timbre, the function of each instrument in this configuration is clear; the *tres* plays a melodic function, free or improvised, together with the piano and the trumpets. At the same time, the latter two serve as harmonic support while the bass plays a harmonic foundation, a part that can also be played by the piano. In turn, the *bongó* and the *tumbadora* play free rhythmic patterns while the *maracas* and the *claves* maintain rhythmic stability.

Because of its popularity, the *conjunto* became an important vehicle within the *son* genre as a source of the subsequent **salsa** movement. Along with the *son,* the *conjunto* repertoire contains a number of genres, especially the **guaracha** and the **bolero**.

The inclination toward the *son* or *guaracha* in the repertoire of the *conjunto* and the *tres* or the guitar as its lead instruments demonstrates a performance complexity that has contributed to the popular classification of performance styles as *macho* (masculine) and *hembra* (feminine). These distinctions, in turn, reflect complex sociocultural processes, which have to do with race and musical references. Based on these distinctions, three groups emerged that typified the two styles: the Conjunto de Arsenio Rodríguez that is characterized by the robust performance of *son* with elements of Afro-Cuban traditions, and the Casino Conjunto and the Sonero Matancera whose playlists prioritized the *guaracha* and the *conga de salón* with musical arrangements characterized by **jazz**-like harmonies and **Afro-Cuban** song influences.

Audiences that gathered for these groups were different in terms of ethnic and social composition and the context or locations in which they worked. In the same way, the treatment of the *contratiempo* (back beat or counter-rhythm) generated certain preferences for dancers. Black and *mestizo* audiences would attend the music and dance work of the groups considered masculine. Noteworthy followers of Arsenio Rodríguez include the Conjunto Chapottín, the Bolero, Modelo, or Los Astros de René Álvarez; representatives of the Casino style include the conjunto de Luis Santí and Jóvenes del Cayo.

The style and format generated by the Sonora Matancera have reached great popularity in the Latin American and Caribbean regions. This *conjunto* is notable for its orchestration for two trumpets performing passages in unison, or at simultaneous intervals of thirds, sixths, and eighths. The singers' parts show a prevalence of a *timbre agudo brillante*. The piano, the bass, and the percussion play the rhythmic-harmonic base, providing a steady accompaniment of a singularly simple and brilliant tone color. The individual style of its performers produced certain expectations that set the standard for later groups such as the Gloria Matancera, the Conjunto Caney, Laíto y su sonora, or the Muso y su sonora.

Although all the leading groups are characterized by distinct, high-quality performances, the *bolero* constitutes the common element of the *conjuntos'* repertoire. The use of this genre made for unique combination pieces in *conjuntos* like that of Robert Faz known as Mosaicos. The introduction of electro-acoustic instruments, which began in the 1960s, strengthened the evolution of this form, as it demonstrated the modernization of its sound. Nevertheless, the core of the basic model persists, as demonstrated by the performances of Adalberto Álvarez in his groups Son 14 (with added trombone) and Adalberto Álvarez y su Son, who introduced a keyboard, *hi-hat,* electronic *tom-toms,* a bass drum and cymbal, and another trombone, with which he has incorporated, at different times, the *tres,* and the guitar. Another of his contributions lies in the orchestrations and complexity of harmonic progression.

Further Reading

Fernandez, Raul A. *From Afro-Cuban Rhythms to Latin Jazz.* Music of the African Diaspora, 10. Berkeley: University of California Press, 2006.

González Bello, Neris, *Liliana Casanella y Grizel Hernández. La Encuesta del Siglo XX. Música Cubana.* Multimedia. (Inédito).

Sublette, Ned. *Cuba and Its Music: From the First Drums to the Mambo.* Chicago: Chicago Press Review, 2004.

Waxer, Lise. "Of Mambo Kings and Songs of Love: Dance Music in Havana and New York from the 1930s to the 1950s." *Latin American Music Review / Revista de Música Latinoamericana,* 15, no. 2 (1994): 139–76.

Liliana Casanella and Grizel Hernández

Contradance. *See* Contradanza.

Contradanza

The *contradanza* is an instrumental form and dance of European origin that during the 18th century was transplanted into Caribbean colonies, which, in its creolized Cuban version, in the late 19th century made a wide impact throughout the Americas and Europe. Its name derives from *contredanse,* a French corruption of English country dance. A popular court genre in France in the 18th century, *contredanse* was taken by the Bourbons to Spain, where it acquired the name of *contradanza,* and then to the American colonies. In 1798 in Havana there were some 50 daily public balls, starting with a minuet and featuring several *contradanzas.* The *contradanz*a was danced by men and women facing each other in two opposite rows and led by a dance-leader. Meanwhile *contredanse* became popular in the French Caribbean, where it was danced as well by blacks.

The 1791 slave rebellion in St. Domingue (**Haiti**) produced a massive migration of Europeans, who resettled with black and *mulatto* servants in New Orleans and in the Cuban eastern province of Santiago. Such migration reinforced the novelty of the *contradanza* and established its mass popularity in **Cuba**, but was not solely responsible for its introduction in Cuba.

The early decades of the 19th century in Cuba saw the *contradanza* lose its stiff, aristocratic character and acquire new musical and choreographic traits. Musically, it presented two sections and had its most recognizable feature in the accompaniment, with the presence of an *ostinato* (related to the *cinquillo* pattern common in Latin American music) that provided rhythmic drive and a steady syncopated foundation.

contradanza accompanying ostinato   *cinquillo* isorhythm

Contradanza accompanying *ostinato* and a *cinquillo* isorhythm.
(George Torres)

Originally an instrumental style, the Cuban *contradanza (*also known as **danza** or *contradanza criolla)* would later also become a vocal form, under the name of *contradanza habanera* or simply **habanera**. It existed in sophisticated and popular forms practiced by both the white elite and blacks, with variable instrumental formats. In Havana, both bourgeois salons and poorer ballrooms provided work for pianists and composers of *contradanza*. In its salon version, the genre became a quintessential type of piano music incorporating European Romantic influences.

The first published *contradanza* appeared in Cuba as a score for piano in 1803. Popular short *contradanzas* for piano, together with *habaneras* and *danzones,* were written by Manuel Saumell (1817–1870), the initiator of Cuban musical nationalism and a friend of American virtuoso and composer Louis Moreau Gottschalk (1829–1869), the champion of romantic *Creole* piano and himself the author of various *contradanza. Contradanza* were composed by other important Cuban authors such as Nicolás Ruíz Espadero (1832–1890), Ignacio Cervantes (1847–1905), and Ernesto Lecuona (1895–1963).

The daring adoption of couple dancing and the fusion of Romantic harmony with African syncopation in the *contradanza* provided a symbol of emerging Cuban nationalism, and was attacked by reactionaries because of its scandalous black character. It is perhaps ironic that the lascivious African nature detected by contemporaries in the *contradanza,* and in related Cuban forms such as **danzón** today sound rather bland when compared to a genre such as the Cuban **son**, which eventually became the national musical symbol. As a dance, the *contradanza* provided the basic step subsequently found in other Cuban dances such as *son,* **cha cha chá** and **salsa**.

During the mid-late 19th century, the instrumental *contradanza* and *habanera* spread throughout Latin America, playing a role in the genesis of seminal forms such as Argentinian *milonga* and ***tango***, Brazilian ***maxixe***, and Mexican and Puerto Rican *danza*. The *contradanza* reached the **United States** and Europe in the form of *habaneras* and eventually found its way into operas such as Georges Bizet's *Carmen* and in the work of French and Spanish composers Camille Saint-Saëns, Emmanuel Chabrier, Claude Debussy, Maurice Ravel, Isaac Albéniz, and Manuel de Falla. Following the oft-quoted reference about the Spanish tinge by early **jazz** pianist Jelly Roll Morton, various writers have also convincingly argued that the Cuban *contradanza,* especially via the work of Gottschalk, has played an important role in the genesis of American ragtime and then jazz.

Further Reading

Carpentier, Alejo. *Music in Cuba.* Minneapolis: University of Minnesota Press, 2001 [originally published as *La música en Cuba.* Habana, 1946].

Fernández, Nohema. "La Contradanza Cubana y Manuel Saumell." *Latin American Music Review* 10, no. 1 (June 1989), 116–34.

Lapique, Zoila. "Aportes Franco-Haitianos a la contradanza cubana: mitos y realidades." In *Panorama de la música popular cubana,* edited by R. Giro, 153–72. Havana: Letras Cubanas, 1995.

Roberts, John Storm. *Latin Jazz. The First of the Fusions, 1880s to Today.* New York: Schirmer, 1999.

Vincenzo Perna

Coro

Coro is both the Spanish and Portuguese word for chorus. Within the sphere of popular music it refers to two or more singers singing together, often in alternation with a soloist or another *coro.* The *coro* is especially popular in genres that have their origins in West African traditions of leader–group alternations, sometimes referred to as call and response. In such a fabric, the leader improvises verses while the *coro* sings a recurring response. The *coro* is a common feature in the Cuban ***son montuno*** and in the Brazilian ***samba***. In the case of the *son monutuno,* the text sung by the *coro* provides a refrain that is in contrast to the preceding *son* section where the vocalist sings complete or extended verses, often functioning as the narrative to the song. In this case, the *coro* provides a contrast of static action when compared to the verse's more kinetic action. A *coro* was also used in the *montuno* sections to **Latin jazz** numbers, as in the **Machito** and Charlie Parker combination, "Mango Mangue." In this example the *coro* alternates with Parker's instrumental improvisations in the place where the lead singer would normally be improvising.

Further Reading

Robbins, James. "The Cuban 'Son' as Form, Genre, and Symbol."*Latin American Music Review / Revista de Música Latinoamericana* 11 (Autumn–Winter) 1990: 182–200.

Rosa, José and Hector Neciosup. *The History of Music From Cuba, The Caribbean, South America and the United States.* World Music Survey. Casselberry, FL: Contemporary Latin Music Educators, 2008.

George Torres

Corrido

The *corrido* is a narrative song or folk ballad accompanied by one or more **guitars** or, more recently, **accordion**-driven *norteño* groups or *bandas* (brass bands from **Mexico's** northern Pacific coast). The *corrido* is a folk song type not primarily associated with dance, though people may dance to *corridos* when performed by dance bands, in **polka**, or waltz rhythm. The genre has evolved as a *mestizo* cultural form associated with the rise of a national consciousness especially during the early decades of the 20th century and in the context of border conflicts with the United States. *Corridos* handed down on leaflets are considered an important source for the documentation of Mexico's unofficial history. They comment not only on political events, national affairs, and natural disasters, but also on crimes, family feuds, horse races, romantic entanglements, immigration, and more recently drug trafficking.

Historically, the *corrido* is a Mexican folk ballad that stems from the Spanish *balada*, a ballad tradition that flourished in Renaissance Spain. In its poetic forms and narrative subjects, the Mexican *corrido* is essentially true to its roots in Iberian narrative poetry, although there are some non-narrative examples, such as simple love songs or political commentaries that are also referred to as *corridos*. The term *corrido* itself is probably a shortening of the term *romance corrido,* a through-sung ballad. Its transformation into a distinct Mexican form occurred during Mexico's struggle for independence in the early 1800s although the formative period in the rise of the *corrido* remains a matter of speculation—mainly because both the Spanish ballad and the Mexican *corrido* were essentially oral traditions that only occasionally manifested themselves in print. Contradicting other *corrido* scholars who believe that the *corrido* emerged and evolved within Mexican territory, the Texan folklorist Américo Paredes posited the Texas-Mexican border as the birthplace of the ballad tradition itself. In fact, in the 1850s a number of *corridos* began to surface in south Texas. These early ballads depicted the cultural conflict between the encroaching Americans who took possession of the Mexican territory in 1848 after the Mexican-American war and the Mexican farmers who had been living there since the early 1700s. The lyrics of these early *corridos* addressed the deeds of Texas-Mexican folk heroes. One of the best examples of the border *corrido* is "El Corrido de Gregorio Cortéz," which narrates the bloody encounter between the Mexican farmer Cortéz and an American sheriff. Cortéz's heroic actions became an important element in the emerging group consciousness of Texas-Mexicans.

Because the *corrido*'s central function is to relate a story or event of local or national interest, *corrido* scholars focused mainly on the genre's evolution and its importance as a social and literary document. The *corrido* is a song with a rather declamatory melody in either duple or triple time (polka or waltz rhythm). The melodic phrases are repeated for each stanza; occasionally, the *corrido* has a refrain, which may be in a different rhythm. The melodies frequently have a range of less than an octave. The short range allows the *corrido* to be sung at the top of the singer's voice, which is an essential part of the *corrido* style. There is a preference for the major key; the harmony is based on the tonic, dominant, and subdominant chords. Whereas in earlier times the *corridista* (balladeer) used to accompany himself simply on guitar, singers are nowadays accompanied by **norteño** groups or full-size **bandas**. The *corrido* usually follows the literary structure of the *copla*, consisting of eight-syllable quatrains (or less frequently stanzas of six lines). Rhyme, meter, and strophe structure of the *corrido* are quite flexible and many compositions break away from the established patterns. This flexibility contributed in no small part to the genre's popularity and survival.

In oral tradition, folk tunes exist in an array of versions or variants. Yet, folk tunes are essentially combinations of prefabricated elementary forms such as scheme, motif, theme, and formula. The creation of new tunes is largely based on permutations of more or less readymade elements. The *corridos*' literary devices are: an opening statement of date and place; an introductory reference to the singing of the *corrido;* a reference to the singer, the audience, or the song; dramatic speech events; journeys; certain words, exclamations, proverbial expressions, metaphors, and allegories; a bird messenger; a farewell, and so forth.

Although the *corrido* text is extremely detailed and abounds in dates and names, its purpose is not to convey news, as often believed. Rather, the *corrido* depends on a prior transmission of news. Its goal is to interpret, celebrate, and ultimately dignify events already thoroughly familiar to the *corrido* audience or community. In many ways, the corridos were the history book of the illiterate, providing an intriguing folk counterpoint to Mexico's official history. In contrast to the emotional and *bel canto* style of **ranchera** (Mexican country song) singers, the *corridista* uses a deadpan language and performance style. Even the most melodramatic incidents are described in this matter-of-fact style. Although the language employed in *corridos* is mostly simple and direct, the meanings of the texts are difficult for outsiders to understand. Not only do they feature the everyday language of the local *rancheros* (farmers, country people) or, in the more recent *corridos,* the drug traffickers, they are also full of double entendres and allusions to local events, places, and individuals.

Corrido narratives are usually in third-person discourse (with commercial *corridos* related to the world of drug traffickers being an exception). Because Mexican ballads are commonly written by male authors, they display mostly masculine-oriented themes and a strongly patriarchal ideology. Like the epic *romancero* of 16th-century Spain, which depicted bold and reckless young men, the Mexican *corrido* extols the heroic deeds of male protagonists. Women usually play secondary roles in the narratives.

Some *corrido* scholars limit the production of the true *corrido* to the period from 1880 to 1930. According to the Mexican musicologist Vicente Mendoza, after that period, the *corrido* lost its authentic folk character, its freshness, and "spontaneity that emanated from the pen of mediocre writers," and it became "cultured, artificial, and often false." Thus, he concluded that everything points to the decadence and the near death of this genuine folk genre. Contemporary *corrido* scholars disagree with this view as many newly composed *corridos* still fit the classic heroic *corrido* style, using the traditional *corrido* language, the typical speech event dialogues, a stylized vocabulary of preset formulas, and plenty of references to local men and places. Moreover, throughout northern Mexico and along the Pacific coast, the *corrido* remains a vital component of rural culture with an intimate connection to people's daily lives. Here, like in earlier times, the primary medium for disseminating *corridos* is live performance.

The alleged demise of the *corrido,* in fact, has much to do with the changing process of transmission that began after the revolution and that turned a face-to-face transmitted folk genre into a product of popular culture. When the emerging recording industry began to take an interest in the *corrido* in the late 1920s, the long story ballads had to fit on the 78-rpm disk (*corridos* often started on side A and continued on side B). The massive commercial exploitation of the *corrido* reduced the narratives to the three-minute format of popular songs. However, with the spread of industrialization and urbanization, the recorded radio performance has become a major factor in keeping this musical tradition alive. In northern Mexico and along the Mexican-American border and the American Southwest, the long-story ballad tradition still goes strong, although, as some *corrido* scholars argue, not as much as a living tradition but as a preservation of the old repertory.

Further Reading

Herrera-Sobek, María. "The Theme of Drug Smuggling in the Mexican Corrido." *Revista Chicano-Riqueña* 7, no. 4 (1979): 49–61.

McDowell, John H. *Poetry and Violence: The Ballad Tradition of Mexico*'s *Costa Chica.* Urbana: University of Illinois Press, 2000.

Mendoza, Vicente T. *El Corrido Mexicano: Antología, Introducción y Notas.* Mexico City: Fondo de Cultura Económica, 1954.

Nicolopulos, James. "The Heroic Corrido: A Premature Obituary?" *Aztlán* 22, no. 1 (1997): 115–38.

Paredes, Américo. *"With His Pistol in His Hand": A Border Ballad and Its Hero.* Austin: University of Texas Press, 1958.

Helena Simonett

Costa Rica

Costa Rica is a Central American country with a population comprised largely of the descendants of European immigrants. The largest ethnic minorities in Costa Rica are African (2% of the four million inhabitants) and American Indian (1% of the total population). While the Hispanic influence on Costa Rican music is demonstrated through parallels, thirds, melodies, and Western harmonies, the rhythmic structures and many of the instruments are derived from African traditions.

Costa Rican music has much in common with **romances** or ballads, and *coplas*, from Spain, generating related styles such as *retahila* and **bomba**, popular in the Guanacaste area, as well as the rest of the country. The Guanacaste province is widely considered to have produced the most influential folk music in the country. The African population is concentrated in the Limón area, in southeastern Costa Rica along the Atlantic coast, while in the Valle Central area, containing the capital of San José, *romances* remains popular.

Two types of the **marimba** are commonly found in Costa Rica, the chromatic and the diatonic *marimba*. The *marimba grande* is considered a national symbol associated with the Guanacaste region. The diatonic *marimba simple,* which has 30–42 wooden keys, was brought into Costa Rica in the 18th century, while the chromatic *marimba grande,* a national symbol of Costa Rica, has 78 keys. Other important instruments include the Spanish **guitar** and the *mandolina* in **rondalla** ensembles.

In music from Guanacaste, singers frequently insert *coplas* into a song or dance after exclaiming *bomba* to indicate the need for a musical break for the *copla.* The quatrains themselves became known as *bombas,* which are interspersed within the *punto guanacasteco,* a couple dance.

Two of the most well-known traditional music styles include the *parrandera* and the **pasillo**. *Parrandera* comes from the word *parranda,* meaning party music, of a fast and joyful nature, which can be instrumental or dance music and is sometimes called *punto* or **son**. Different types of ensembles may play *parrandera,* varying from a *marimba,* guitars, and bass drum and cymbals, to small brass wind bands called *cimarronas.* The *pasillo* is a type of waltz comparable to the Colombian form of the same name, whose treatment differs significantly by region.

In the center of Costa Rica, slow vocal and instrumental forms are popular, played in 3/4 meter accompanied by guitars, but in the Guanacaste province, in the northwestern region, fast instrumental versions are more prevalent. The *tambito* rhythm remains popular in the Valle Central area, in 6/8 and sharing the hemiola characteristics of *parrandera.*

Among the Afro-Caribbean population, **calypso** and **Carnival** music remain influential traditions. *Calypso,* originally imported from Trinidad and popular in the 1950s and 1960s, currently enjoys renewed interest due to the popularity of **reggae** and other Caribbean sounds. The *cuadrilla,* an English square dance, was brought to Limón, but declined in popularity until recently, as folklore revival groups now perform the dance. The Carnaval de Limón is based on Panama's carnaval de Colón (Christopher Columbus's Carnival), and centers on a major parade of **comparsas** (dancing groups and percussion ensembles).

Costa Rican music has been heavily influenced by European genres such as the *fandango, jota* (Aragon), *paso doble,* **polka**, as well as other styles including the **tango**, **bolero**, **mariachi**, and guitar *trío*. Popular music in the first half of the 20th century was dominated by the *bolero* and *tango,* as well as other international styles. Local bands began to emulate international styles such as **rock**, rap, and **jazz**, which are popular among the younger generation. Caribbean and Latin American genres focused on dance such as **salsa**, **merengue**, **cumbia**, **reggae**, **calypso**, and **soca** also remain popular in Costa Rica with a somewhat older audience. Many working-class individuals also enjoy Mexican genres like *rancheros, corridos*, and **norteños**, as well as Colombian **vallenatos** and *cumbias,* while the upper and middle class tend to prefer the Spanish *pasodoble.*

Dance clubs, or *salones de baile,* in Costa Rica frequently host live bands that play *bolero pirateado* and *merengue,* in addition to other popular styles, although many young people go to *discotecas* playing rock and techno. Revival groups have been gaining support since the 1980s, bringing back *criollo* and *mestizo* music, to combine it with popular dance rhythms like *bolero, cumbia,* and *salsa.*

Further Reading

Cervantes Gamboa, Laura. "Información básica acerca de la música tradicional indígena de Costa Rica." *Kañina* 19, no. 1 (1995): 155–73.

Garfias, Robert. "The Marimba of Mexico and Central America." *Latin American Music Review / Revista de Música Latinoamericana* 4, no. 2 (1983): 203–28.

Zeller, Bernal Flores, and Laura Cervantes Gamboa: "Costa Rica." In *The New Grove Dictionary of Music and Musicians,* edited by S. Sadie and J. Tyrrell. London: Macmillan, 2001, volume 6, pp. 528–33.

Caitlin Lowery

Cowbell. *See* Cencerro.

Cuarteto (Argentina)

Cuarteto is a popular dance music style from Córdoba, **Argentina**. Its most distinguishing musical feature is a characteristic rhythmic pattern played on the piano or electronic keyboard and bass, which is onomatopoetically called *tunga-tunga.*

Cuarteto lyrics are frequently about romantic love, or about the pleasures of *cuarteto* music and dancing itself. *Cuarteto* has enjoyed several decades of enormous popularity in Córdoba and the surrounding provinces, but has yet to achieve widespread diffusion or acceptance in the capital or internationally. *Cuarteto* fans are generally in the working class and even in Córdoba the music and its audience remain quite stigmatized among the middle and upper classes.

Cuarteto, which means quartet in Spanish, gets its name from the Cuarteto Leo, the group that established the style in 1943. The group was named after its pianist, Leonor Marzano, who is credited with inventing the characteristic *tunga-tunga* pattern of accompaniment. He also included double bass, **accordion**, and violin, accompanying a singer. The group rose to prominence in Córdoba during a period in which that city experienced a massive internal migration of workers drawn by the burgeoning automobile industry. This new population of marginalized, working-class residents began to frequent dance halls on the outskirts of the city, and *cuarteto* music became the musical style most closely associated with them.

Cuarteto musicians have been strongly influenced by foreign dance music styles such as ***cumbia*** and ***merengue***, starting in the 1960s. This influence is visible in changing instrumentation; since the mid-1980s the violin has been an increasingly rare presence in *cuarteto* ensembles, while percussion sections have expanded to include ***congas,*** the Dominican *tambora*, and metal ***güira***, as well as *timbals*, and drum sets. Some groups have included brass sections or other wind instruments such as saxophone, while others have made use of digital samplers to allow keyboard players to imitate these timbres.

This increasing diversity of stylistic influences has led some *cuarteto* artists to divide their sets into two different subgenres: *tropical,* up-tempo tunes showing a stronger *cumbia* and *merengue* influence, and *moderno,* which are slower, and more influenced by **jazz** and **rock** as well as international romantic Latin American styles such as pop ***bolero***. *Moderno* settings typically use drum set rather than the battery of Latin percussion instruments. Some artists have resisted these stylistic changes, and promote a more traditional style called *cuarteto cuarteto.*

Cuarteto groups are frequently contracted to perform for special occasions such as patron saint days and political rallies, but most *cuarteto* groups maintain a very active performing schedule in and around Córdoba at a regular set of large dance halls dedicated exclusively to this activity. Groups must also maintain a rigorous recording schedule if they are to reach and retain popularity; many groups record an average of two CDs each year. Groups will borrow from each others' repertoire in live performance but only record their own original material, or original adaptations of tunes drawn from an international repertoire of non-*cuarteto* styles.

The best-known *cuarteto* artist is singer, bandleader and composer Carlos "La Mona" Jiménez, who has been performing and recording as a solo artist since leaving the Cuarteto de Oro in 1984. He remains enormously popular with *cuarteto* audiences not only for continuing to innovate musically (he has at times included in his act such rarities as the piccolo and African dance) but for writing socially conscious lyrics and reaching out to the economically disadvantaged by collecting clothing and food and donating cars and houses to his fans. *Cuarteto* fans in Córdoba see Jiménez as the personification of a quintessentially local popular identity. His performances are peppered with references to specific neighborhoods, both through lyrics and through an elaborate series of hand signals that are traded back and forth with audience members.

Other important performers have included the band Chébere, also founded in 1984 and characterized by a particular emphasis on a more elaborate *tropical* style, and the solo singer Rodrigo Bueno, who is most often known only by his first name or his nickname, "El Potro" ("The colt"). Rodrigo rose to popularity in the late 1990s, attaining a degree of success among middle-class audiences, even in the national capital, that remains unique among *cuarteto* artists. His career was cut short when he died in a car crash in June 2000 when he was 27.

Further Reading

Florine, Jane. "*Cuarteto:* Dance-Hall Entertainment or People's Music?" *Latin American Music Review* 19, no. 1 (Spring/Summer 1998): 31–46.

Florine, Jane. Cuarteto *Music and Dancing from Argentina: In Search of the* Tunga-Tunga *in Córdoba.* Gainesville: University Press of Florida, 2001.

Michael O'Brien

Cuatro

The term *cuatro* is used for any of the several varieties of Latin American **guitar**-type instruments. The word *cuatro* means four in Spanish, and while it may refer to the number of strings or courses (sets of doubled strings to be stopped by the player simultaneously), some *cuatros* have more than four courses. The two most common types are the four-string Venezuelan *cuatro* and the five-course Puerto Rican *cuatro*.

The Venezuelan *cuatro* is the national instrument of **Venezuela**, and played throughout the country in both rural and urban areas. It uses a reentrant tuning for its four nylon strings; from the fourth to the first string, it is tuned A-D-F#-B, with the B sounding an octave lower than usual. It is used mostly as an accompanying instrument in ensemble music, playing simple chords and using a sophisticated *rasgueado* technique for the right hand. Since the 1930s, a concert tradition, led by Fredy Reyna (1917–2001), has emerged that uses a more sophisticated right-hand technique to pluck individual notes as well as strum chords. Variants of the Venezuelan *cuatro* can be found in other parts of the Caribbean.

The Puerto Rican *cuatro* is the national instrument of **Puerto Rico** as well. It appears to have derived from the 16th century, Renaissance *vihuela* or four-course Spanish guitar, as it originally had four courses, with a fifth course added later. The tuning of the instrument's steel-strung courses, from lowest to highest is B-E-A-D-G, with the two lowest courses (B and E) tuned in octaves. The *cuatro* was originally played as an accompanying instrument in *jibaro* music, playing mostly a melodic function. Since the 1920s a virtuoso tradition began to emerge through the efforts of players such as Ladislao Martínez (1898–1979), Tomas "Maso" Rivera, and Yomo Toro (b. 1933). Nowadays, the Puerto Rican *cuatro* comes in an electrified model that one hears in more urban contemporary genres such as *salsa*.

Further Reading

Kuss, Malena. "Puerto Rico." In *Music in Latin America and the Caribbean: An Encyclopedic History,* 151–88. Austin: University of Texas Press, 2004.

George Torres

Fernandez, Joseito

José "Joseito" Fernández Diaz (1908–1975) was a Cuban composer, singer, and bandleader. He is remembered for his song "Guantanamera," which became internationally famous after its performance by groups such as The Sandpipers and Pete Seeger. Fernandez was raised in Havana, **Cuba**, and, as a teen, performed as a singer in several groups, including Juventud Habanera and Los Dioses de Amor. In 1928 he wrote the song "Guantanamera" based on a preexisting melody by **tres** player Herminio "El Diablo" Wilson. The song was a vehicle for Fernandez's poetic extemporization, although the song today is known through the words of Jose Marti, which were added to the song in the 1950s by the Spanish composer Julián Orbón. The newly texted version became a worldwide success, and in spite of the improvisatory origins of the song, the Fernandez-Martí interpretation remains the unofficial version of the song in recordings as well as the published sheet music. According to Fernandez's daughter, the composer was so proud of his song being an emblem of Cuban nationality, that he never wanted to receive compensation for the song.

Further Reading

Leymarie, Isabel. *Cuban Fire: The Story of Salsa and Latin Jazz.* New York: Continuum, 2002.

George Torres

Cuba

The Republic of Cuba is the largest country in the Caribbean with an estimated population of more than 11 million. The total area of Cuba is 110,860 sq km and it is comprised of more than 1,600 keys, islands, and islets. The main island, Cuba, is the largest (105,007 sq km) and most westerly in the Antilles. Cuba is situated at the entrance to the Gulf of Mexico, which is to the north and northwest; to the north and northeast is the Atlantic Ocean; to the south and southeast is the Caribbean Sea. Cuba's immediate neighbors include: **Mexico** to the west; Jamaica and the Cayman Islands (UK) to the south; **Haiti** to the east; the Florida Keys, the Bahamas, and the Turks and Caicos Islands (UK) to the north and northeast. Like many of these other nations in the Caribbean, the popular music of Cuba has been influenced by African, indigenous, and European musics.

Cultural Contact

Prior to the arrival of Columbus (October 28, 1492), the island of Cuba was inhabited by the Guanahatabey and Arawak Amerindian groups. The Arawak subgroups, Siboney and Taino, subsisted in close proximity on the island, having displaced the Guanahatabey to the western portion of the island, though colonial accounts indicate that the Taino were predominant. Little is actually known of these indigenous groups in Cuba beyond the accounts of Spanish colonial agents. The island of Cuba was claimed for the Spanish crown in 1511 when Diego Velázquez disembarked at Baracoa, Cuba (on the northeast coast), with 300 men, and though the invasion force met with resistance from the Arawak (first led by Hatuey), the Spanish force soon established itself as a presence on the island. Though the collective demise of the indigenous groups was rather swift in the years following the first invasion, succumbing to disease, slaughter, and often suicide as an alternative to Spanish oppression, the vestiges of Cuba's Amerindian people were neither short-lived, nor insignificant to the historical record.

The rapid decline of the indigenous populations did, however, lead to the importation of African slaves, beginning in 1526, as the new labor force in the relatively unsuccessful mining efforts on the island. Due to its geography, Cuba came to be most valued as a port for the Spanish fleet, providing repairs and food. It was the latter that led to the earliest developments in Spanish agriculture on the island. Cuba's plantation economy was established relatively late in its colonial period, and farming was, up to the economic transformations of the late 18th century, essentially a subsistence activity, often with European/*Creole* landowners working alongside African slave labor. Though a 10-month British occupation (1762–1763) of Havana brought with it the introduction of a vigorous international trade culture, it was not until the economic reforms of the Bourbon monarchy after 1789 that shipbuilding in Havana and the expansion of the sugar industry were permitted, the latter necessitating the liberalization of earlier restrictions on the trans-Atlantic slave trade. It was, however, the slave uprisings in St. Domingue (later named Haiti), beginning in 1791 and eventually leading to Haitian independence (1804) that markedly transformed the island economy.

The Colony in Transition: Sugar, Labor, and Independence

The social unrest that ensued from the slave uprisings in St. Domingue, and the attendant decline of the sugar production, effected a rise in sugar prices worldwide and an exodus of sugar-growing expertise into Cuba, particularly the landowning and administrative elite. Given that the financial success of the sugar industry in St. Domingue had been predicated on an enormous African slave labor force, these conditions were replicated in the designs of the newly established sugar industry sector in Cuba. The early years of the 19th century were marked by an astounding increase in the flow of slaves from West Africa to meet the demands of Cuba's burgeoning sugar-based economy. As early as the 1820s, there were already an estimated 1,000 *ingenios* (sugar plantation-processing complexes) in Cuba. Despite the 1817 agreement to the cessation of the trans-Atlantic slave trade between England and Spain, the economic dividends of Cuba's plantation economy proved too lucrative for Spain: the arrival of enslaved Africans increased.

Cuba in the 19th century remained a region marked by racial tensions. The continuing condition of slavery juxtaposed with a growing population of free blacks, the legacy of Haitian independence, and continuing fears among the white Cuban minority of a slave revolt like that of Haiti, produced a climate of racial severance that remained unaddressed until well into the 20th century. This climate of fear gave rise to an increase in the establishment of *cabildos* or *cofradías:* mutual-aid assemblies based on regional Iberian guild-fraternities. These councils were legislated in Spanish colonies, under the name of a patron Catholic saint and the auspices of a diocesan Catholic priest, allowing persons of African heritage to congregate for social events. Though the endorsement of these organizations by the Catholic Church and the colonial elite was directed simultaneously at quelling the social tensions inherent in Cuba's slave-labor economy and facilitating the development of Catholic orthodoxy in the regions, the *cabildos* proved to be as likely to facilitate organized dissention as they were to foster the preservation of African-derived religious and musical practices. Additionally, these Afro-American congregations attended to many of their community needs (such as amalgamating resources for legal defenses, financing manumissions and funeral costs), much in the same way that the *palenques* (clandestine settlements of escaped slaves) acted as sites of cultural preservation and social welfare. The persistence of **Afro-Cuban** sacred traditions (such as *Santería, Palo Monte, Arará, Abakuá*) and their rich musical heritages owe much to the power of these early assemblies.

With larger numbers of African Cubans manumitted under Spanish law, the immigration of thousands of Chinese indentured laborers began in 1847 to counter the attrition of plantation labor. Often working side by side with black slaves, Chinese laborers became a crucial part of the Cuban economy, and like their Afro-Cuban counterparts, they distinguished themselves as soldiers and officers in the struggles for independence from Spain. After various attempts at a graduated emancipation of Afro-Cubans, slavery was officially abolished in 1886. Ironically, sugar remains Cuba's principal crop and largest export commodity today.

Music and Cultures in Contact

Cuba, particularly the capital Havana, in the 19th century exhibited a vibrant artistic life infused with European concert musics that superceded the artistic output of North American centers. At the same time, a *Creole* musical culture was taking shape as the European and West African musical traditions on the island became fused into uniquely Cuban musical sensibilities and expressive genres. The musical adaptations, for example, visited upon the vestiges of Spanish *contradanza* in Cuba's 19th-century salons, led to uniquely Cuban popular musical genres such as the *danza cubana* (the **habanera**), which would go on to exert its influence in the colonial courts of **Mexico**, European opera, Argentinean *tango*, and proto-**jazz** of the **United States**. The international appeal of Cuban music has been long-standing.

The 19th century also marked the emergence of the *Creole* drum, song, and dance complex known as **rumba** (not to be confused with **rhumba,** one of the earlier and more prominent examples of authentic African and European musical hybridity). Though the dance and rhythmic vocabulary of *rumba* is predominantly of Afro-Cuban origin (e.g., *Yuka, Abakuá*), European musical practices are nonetheless as prevalent in the genre: Spanish lyrics, Iberian harmonic progressions, *bel canto* style, and tertiary harmonization. Certainly, the prioritization of the highest-pitched drum in the ensemble indicates a uniquely Cuban transformation because West African drumming styles normatively designate the lowest drum as the principal one. With the exception of the street parades of the Epiphany and other pre-Lenten **Carnivals**, which were multifaceted events exhibiting unpredictable mixtures of cultural repertoires, no other popular forms of musical entertainment in the 19th century (e.g., *coro de clave,* salon dancing, **bolero**, comic theater) approached the symmetry of sociomusical elements found in *rumba*.

Salvador Repilado, one of the sons of late Cuban singer Compay Segundo, participates in a rehearsal of Compay Segundo's band a few hours prior to the live performance in 2010 at La Cigale concert hall in Paris. (Miguel Medina/AFP/Getty Images)

The Republic: The First 60 Years

The first two decades of the republic were fraught with discord as Cuba struggled to construct its own estimable nationhood amid the lurking interests of the United States and racial enmity on the island. It was not until the spread of *son* that Cuban popular music embodied a sonic ideal of racial conciliation, though the dance genre met with consternation in its early years from many Cuban elite for its lascivious nature and association with colored Cubans. It was in 1922 that Cuba became the first Caribbean nation to broadcast its music on radio waves and Cuba's international status as a hub of musical and entertainment activity gradually escalated, as did its musical influence. A gradual migration ensued, bringing Cuban musicians to Havana in search of musical opportunities, and *son,* along with other musical genres such as the *danzón* of the *charanga* orchestras, soon captured wider public attention. The musical migration, however, was not only internal: the growing flow of American tourists to the island nation effected both an appetite for Cuban music abroad and a fluency among Cuban musicians in jazz and swing band styles. By the 1940s and 1950s, the artistic and commercial cross-pollination between Cuban and American dance music had become so entrenched that it is nearly impossible to estimate the multifaceted ways in which the mobility of musical repertoires (and musicians) took effect, though *cubop* as well as the popularity of *mambo* and *salsa* are conspicuous examples.

Musical Innovation Post-1959

On January 1, 1959, the rebels led by Fidel Castro successfully overthrew the regime of Fulgencio Batista, for many on the island an icon of the continued American interference in Cuban affairs. The numerous social and culture shifts set in motion by the revolution brought about sweeping changes to U.S. foreign policy concerning Cuba. As a result of the escalating acrimony and political brinkmanship between the two nations (e.g., Bay of Pigs, Cuban Missile Crisis, trade embargo, assassination attempts), the extraordinary musical dialogue of the preceding 30-odd years was effectively ended. Nonetheless, the first 15 years of the revolution were marked by arresting artistic innovation, evocative of the nationalistic fervor of the time, and numerous dance rhythms appeared on the scene, captivating Cuban popular culture: *dengue*, *mozambique*, *pilon*, and *songo*.

The years immediately following the revolution were also typified by the introduction of numerous musical hybrids, in no small part influenced by the innovative music of 1960s and 1970s United States and Britain (e.g., jazz, soul, funk, rock). Though the fascination with foreign musical forms met with some anxiety and at times outright repression on the part of the Cuban government, many of these ensembles were at the vanguard of Cuba's post-revolutionary artistic innovations: the Orquesta Cubana de Música Moderna (1967), which included many early members of Irakere; the Quinteto Cubano de Música Moderna (1959); the Grupo de Experimentación Sonora de ICAIC, including many influential composers of *nueva trova*. The establishment of a Cuban national recording company, EGREM (Empresa de Grabaciones y Ediciones Musicales, 1964), gave unprecedented recording opportunities to the many musical innovators of the period.

The institution of various state performing arts ensembles moved Afro-Cuban music and dance closer to the center of the national identity, most notably in the Conjunto Folklórico Nacional de Cuba (1962) and Danza Contemporanea de Cuba (1959). The period was also marked by the rise of independent folklore ensembles such as Los Muñequitos de Matanzas (1956) and Guaguancó Marítimo Portuario

(1961, later Yoruba Andabo). The social history of Afro-Cuban and Cuban popular dance music soon came to be established in the national school curricula, and their study was also included in the main state-run musical institutions—Escuela Nacional de Arte (ENA), Instituto Superior de Artes (ISA), and various divisions of the Escuela de Superación Profesional.

Recent Trends

With the dissolution of the Soviet Union and the end of its foreign aid to Cuba, the Castro government was forced to open its borders to outside financial interests in order to minimize the effects of the economic crisis that necessarily followed. Today, Cuba is arguably more connected to the outside world than it has been since the revolution, which has had profound effects on the course of Cuban popular music since 1990. Perhaps no music better captures the contradictions of Cuban society in the post-Soviet era better than *timba*. *Timba* is arguably one of the most eclectic and virtuosic popular music genres in the world today, in no small part due to Cuba's many well-trained musicians, also well-versed in the numerous musical styles shaping the genre: *son, songo,* funk, rap, dancehall, and 1980s jazz fusion.

Though the appeal of *timba* is both cross-generational and widespread (also influencing contemporary *salsa*), several other Cuban musics enjoy prominence at home and abroad. Spanish-language rap and *reggaetón* groups in Cuba are a conspicuous presence, indicative of the degree to which American **hip-hop** culture has informed contemporary youth sensibilities. And since the late 1990s, Cuba has seen a decided resurgence in traditional *son* ensembles, popularly known as the Buena Vista Social Club phenomenon, after the musical collaboration between American guitarist Ry Cooder and a near-forgotten generation of Cuban *son* artists. The international success of this endeavor created a foreign familiarity with Cuba's musical heritage and effected an upsurge of *son* ensembles among musicians seeking economic opportunities in Cuba's tourism industry.

Further Reading

Beardsley, Theodore. "Rumba-Rhumba: Problema internacional músico-lexico." *Revista/Review Interamericana* 10, no. 4 (1980–81): 527–33.

Fernandes, Sujatha. "Fear of a Black Nation: Local Rappers, Transnational Crossings, and State Power in Contemporary Cuba." *Anthropological Quarterly* 76, no. 4 (2003): 575–608.

Hagedorn, Katherine J. *Divine Utterances: The Performance of Afro-Cuban Santería.* Washington, DC: Smithsonian Institution Press, 2001.

Manuel, Peter, ed. *Essays on Cuban Music: North American and Cuban Perspectives.* Lanham, MD: University Press of America, 1991.

Moore, Robin. *Music and Revolution: Cultural Change in Socialist Cuba.* Berkeley, CA: University of California Press, 2006.

Moore, Robin. *Nationalizing Blackness: Afrocubanismo and Artistic Revolution in Havana, 1920–1940.* Pittsburgh: University of Pittsburgh Press, 1997.

Perna, Vincenzo. *Timba: The Sound of the Cuban Crisis.* Burlington, VT: Ashgate, 2004.

Robbins, James. "The Cuban Son as Form, Genre, and Symbol." *Latin American Music Review* 11, no. 2 (1990): 182–210.

Rodriguez, Olavo Alén. "Cuba." In *South America, Mexico, Central America and the Caribbean.* Vol. 2 of *The Garland Encyclopedia of World Music,* edited by Dale Olsen and Daniel Sheehy. New York: Garland, 1998.

Rondón, César Miguel. *El libro de la salsa: Crónica de la música del Caribe.* Caracas: Ediciones B, 2007.

Sublette, Ned. *Cuba and Its Music: From the First Drums to the Mambo.* Chicago: Chicago Review Press, 2004.

Waxer, Lise. "Of Mambo Kings and Songs of Love: Dance Music in Havana and New York from the 1930s to the 1950s." *Latin American Music Review* 15, no. 2 (1994): 139–76.

Michael D. Marcuzzi

La Lupe

Cuban singer La Lupe (1939–1992), called "The Queen of Latin Soul," was known for her vibrant and flamboyant performing style. Her music is recognizable through her trademark "*ahí namá*" and "*ay yi yi yi.*" She sang with the trio Los Tropicuba until 1958 after which she went solo. She released her first album, *Con el Diablo en el Cuerpo,* in 1961 and in 1962 she left **Cuba** and began singing at La Barraca, a nightclub in Manhattan. After releasing the single "Que Te Pedi" with **Tito Puente**, Lupe recorded and toured the Latin music circuit in the **United States**, **Venezuela**, **Mexico**, **Puerto Rico**, **Panama**, and Spain. In 1969 La Lupe became the first Latin female artist to sell out Carnegie Hall and the first Latin female artist to appear at Madison Square Garden. La Lupe's popularity started to wane by the late 1970s; however, the inclusion of her song "Puro teatro" in the 1988 film *Women on the Verge of a Nervous Breakdown* rekindled an interest in her music.

Further Reading

Aparicio, Frances R. and Valentín-Escobar, Wilson A. "Memorializing La Lupe and Lavoe: Singing Vulgarity, Transnationalism, and Gender." *Centro: Journal of the Center for Puerto Rican Studies* 16 (2) (2004): 78–101.

Erin Stapleton-Corcoran

Cubop. *See* Latin Jazz.

Cueca

Cueca is the most popular traditional music genre and dance of **Chile**. It is also played in **Peru, Bolivia, Argentina**, and **Mexico**, where it is called *marinera* or *chilena*. *Cueca* is a mixed partner dance with no body contact. The man follows the woman persistently, imitating a cock courting a hen. The couple pursues and retreats, passes, and circles one another in an imaginary ring, twirling handkerchiefs as they dance.

Cueca is played in most regions of Chile with some variations. The *cueca nortina,* from the north of Chile, has no lyrics. Instruments such as the panpipe or brass bands and percussion are often used. In the folk-urban tradition of Santiago and Valparaíso, *cuecas chilenera* and *porteña* are performed, both usually sung and accompanied by **guitars**, piano, **accordion**, and tambourine. In southern Chile, *cueca chilota* is sung by men and accompanied by accordions, guitars, and ***bombo***.

The music, usually in the major mode, has a unitary formal scheme with a repeated section that forms a period of 52 bars called *pie* (couples generally dance three *pies*). The subjects of the lyrics are varied. Themes are often historical, romantic, related to local customs or to the cities. The latter is known as *cueca urbana, brava,* or *chora.* The lyrics are divided into three parts called *cuarteta, segudilla,* and *remate.* The *cuarteta* is a four-line stanza of eight syllables in ballad-stanza rhyme (abcb pattern). The *segudilla* is a seven-line stanza of five and seven syllables, with the fourth line repeated and lengthened with the syllable *sí* or *ay sí.* The *remate* (also known as *pareado* or *cerrojo*) closes the form with two rhyming verses of seven and five syllables.

Sources suggest that *cueca* was first performed in Chile in the 1820s. Researchers have proposed four different origins: *Creole,* Arab-Andalusian, indigenous, and African but the first two are most commonly accepted. The *Creole* theory suggests that *cueca* derived from the Peruvian *zamacueca* via piano scores, which were performed in Chilean aristocratic ballrooms. Later on, *zamacueca* would have reached the countryside and been adapted by the masses. Toward the second half of the 19th century, this dance would have evolved in such a way as to become a dance of distinct form and character. The second theory proposes that *cueca* is primarily a musical form rather than a dance, rooted in the Arab-Andalusian musical tradition, which developed in Spain between the 9th and 16th centuries, particularly the vocal production, the use of instruments such as the hexagonal tambourine and the style of singing in a round.

Up to the early 20th century, *cueca* was primarily performed in inns called *chinganas* or *fondas*. Later on, it reached a far wider audience through broadcasts and recordings by *música típica* ensembles such as Los Cuatro Huasos and Los Quincheros, becoming identified with the image of the *huaso* (Chilean cowboy). During the late 20th and early 21st centuries, the overall popularity of *cueca* has declined and is danced primarily during the celebrations of the National Day (September 18) and at official ceremonies. Nevertheless, during the last few years, there have been signs of a comeback of this genre seen through a number of young urban groups. In the 1990s, the well-known rock/pop group Los Tres played *cuecas* in "La Yein Fonda" during the National Day celebrations in a suburb of Santiago called Ñuñoa, and later performed *cuecas* on MTV international music television channel.

Famous *cueca* musicians include Los Chileneros, Los Hermanos Campos, Violeta, Roberto, Isabel and Ángel Parra, Segundo Zamora, Nano Nuñez, Margot Loyola, Pepe Fuentes, Los Afuerinos, Luis Araneda, Los Truqueros, Los Santiaguinos, Las Capitalinas, Las Torcazas, Los Tricolores, Chamullentos, and Los Porfiados de la Cueca. Some of the most popular cuecas are "La rosa y el clavel," "Adiós Santiago querido," "La consentida," "Chicha de Curacaví," "Los lagos de Chile," "El guatón Loyola," "Los lagos de Chile," and "El chute Alberto."

Further Reading

Claro Valdés, Samuel. *Chilena o cueca tradicional.* Santiago: Ediciones Universidad Católica de Chile, 1994.

Feldman, Heidi Carolyn. *Black Rhythms of Peru: Reviving African Musical Heritage in the Black Pacific.* Music/culture. Middletown, CT: Wesleyan University Press, 2006.

Knudsen, Jan Sverre. "Dancing Cueca 'With Your Coat On': The Role of Traditional Chilean Dance in an Immigrant Community." *British Journal of Ethnomusicology* 10, no. 2 (2001): 61.

Katia Chornik

Cuíca

A *cuíca* is a Brazilian friction drum with a thin bamboo stick embedded into a single goat-skin head. It is known by a variety of names including puíta, tambor onça, and roncador. *Cuíca* is found throughout **Brazil** where it is used primarily in small musical ensembles to accompany dance. The model for the instrument derives from the Bantu regions of Central Africa and was introduced into Brazil by enslaved Africans from that area as early as the 16th century. A wet cloth is used to rub the stick back and forth, producing vibrations that are transferred to the skin, resulting in vocal-like tones that can be low or high in pitch. By pressing on the skin while rubbing the stick, the pitch of the tone can be altered. The *cuíca* was incorporated into the percussion section of the escolas de samba from Rio de Janeiro in the mid-20th century and now occupies an important position in those organizations. While the *cuíca*'s primary function remains as tonal/rhythmic accompaniment, the instrument's technical possibilities have achieved virtuosic dimensions and the most expert players perform simple melodies on the instrument.

Further Reading

Bolão, Oscar. *Batuque é um privilégio: A percussão da música do Rio de Janeiro (Batuque is a privilege: Percussion in Rio de Janeiro's Music)*. Rio de Janeiro, Brazil: Lumiar Editora, 2003.

Larry Crook

Cultural Imperialism

Cultural imperialism is a theoretical approach to forms of public culture such as film, television, radio, the news media, and music. It must be understood as a historically localized practice and incitement. In Latin America, the doctrine emerged from a body of 1960s and 1970s era scholarship critical of the economic and political dependency of Latin American nations on the **United States** and Europe. Despite radical reformulations of the idea in the late 20th century, the intensification of linear progress narratives associated with neoliberalism has given cultural imperialism new vigor in the early 21st century, particularly in the news media, but also in academic circles. In many countries in Latin America, post-authoritarian uses of cultural imperialism frame national identity by separating broadly acceptable public-cultural practices from those thought to be culturally intimate. These intimate ways of being, deemed both central to national character and simultaneously extremely embarrassing, are relegated to an ostensibly lower class position by virtue of their dominated and subservient nature.

Music is an important site at which to explore such acts of categorization because of the way it is often conceived of as mixing philosophical argument with embodiment. This mixture is frequently thought to grant music considerable power; the argument is that music enters bodies and minds at the same moment. For this reason, throughout Latin America, music provides a zone in which the regional, the national, and the pan-national are defined and renegotiated. Proponents of cultural imperialism frequently view musical practice as the frontline of the battle for self-determination.

Cultural imperialism involves a series of nested concepts. First, within the context of the world system, its supporters argue that locations deemed central shore up their economic and political control over locations referred to as peripheral by cultural means. Note that culture, here, is defined more as expressive practice than in the more ample social and cognitive sense elaborated within anthropology. This notion of cultural control, in turn, relies upon the assumption that the dynamic interplay of global and local is best understood by way of nation-states. Countries such as the United States (the target these days) and Europe (the oppressor before the Second World War) populate airwaves, television stations, movie theaters, record stores, and book and magazine stands with texts aimed at fashioning subservience. In the news media and on street corners, where theorizing about the subject occurs, the discussion often stops here. In scholarly corners, however, the analyst making use of cultural imperialism as an explicative framework frequently points to the way each individual is recruited to a project of foreign power in the act of listening, singing, and/or dancing. In such cases, the subservience in such an interpolation is often thought to have been manufactured through the enactment of cultural material deemed foreign, which, it is believed, quashes local specificity. Then, in time, when that which is deemed folkloric is gone and an ostensibly incumbent sense of real identity has disappeared, the theory is that the central power will have a much easier time manipulating Third World masses. These masses play along with the endeavor by failing to educate themselves about their traditions.

Interpretations of music that make use of the notion of cultural imperialism separate what is under analysis into two categories: co-opted or resistant. This oversimplifies the richness of empirical reality, separating folkloric genres, high-artistic forms of rock (*música popular Brasileira*, for instance), **jazz**, and classical music from genres with larger sales figures, such as pop, country, romantic and evangelical music, and **hip-hop**. Scholars who fail to toe the line by elevating musical texts produced along folkloric or artistic lines while debasing widely circulating ones are described as alienated if they are Latin American, and oppressors if they are from elsewhere. In this way, manifestations of public culture are permitted to signify only along strictly demarcated lines given by a functionalism of imperial power.

The notion of cultural imperialism justifiably incites inquiry into the complexities of domination in Latin America. It is no coincidence that the dependency theory on which cultural imperialism rests was often formulated during foreign-supported military dictatorships that spearheaded economic miracles. These miracles frequently expanded industrialized production while diminishing workers' rights and widening the gap between rich and poor. Such regimes, which roughly held sway between the early 1960s and the early 1990s, also made use of censorship of the press, with cyclical festivals such as **Carnival** and soccer matches to mollify mass unease. It is, therefore, the case that during this period, many nations experienced new forms of social control, some of it understandable in light of the imperialism of foreign powers.

Nevertheless, it is worth inquiring into the underlying assumptions that the doctrine of cultural imperialism requires as a way of analyzing the musicality of Latin American history and culture. First, for cultural imperialism to function, one must assume a certain coherence on the part of central efforts and interests. Drawing upon selective readings of the critical theory of Theodore Adorno, Max Horkheimer, and Walter Benjamin, one may posit a monolithic culture industry as a unified body of actors, institutions, and practices aiming, consciously or not, at the subjugation of the masses. Supplemented with postmodern doses of Foucauldian capillary power, such theories frequently fashion an ever-present and menacing First World, or perhaps a local elite, which, frighteningly, does not simply dominate from the top, but also, from the bottom-up.

Second, for cultural imperialism to function as an explicative paradigm, one must assume that the production of public culture dictates its consumption. For example, one must assume that because American rock 'n' roll is an industrial product promulgated by large record companies in order to make money, its money-making capacity therefore shapes the way in which listeners will be able to hear it. Acts of listening, singing, dancing, and playing thus may be reduced to a musical text's ostensibly original profit goal. In short, since cash circulates back to a foreign-owned company responsible for producing a text, this means that the *users* of said text can only reinforce that company's global domination in listening to it.

But a host of empirical and theoretical problems attend such analyses, as a brief test case demonstrates. In **Brazil**, few musical genres are more subject to criticism as an artifact of cultural imperialism than commercial rural *música sertaneja*. Proponents of cultural imperialism point to this electric and electronic country music and the fact that, sometimes, famous *duplas* perform versions of Nashville hits, as evidence that Brazilian musical tastes are being co-opted by a foreign-owned culture industry.

But what goes unnoticed here are the terms in which Brazilians are actually hearing these Nashville songs. First, the lyrics are often profoundly different in their Portuguese versions, pointing to the utter desperation that the *música sertaneja* genre requires instead of an often comic North American distance from powerful emotions. But even more important, the brother (*dupla*) form of *música sertaneja* keeps the focus quite squarely on a type of social production with roots in colonial land-tenure and rural-to-urban migration patterns organized by brotherhood. North American country is largely a solo affair. In fact, a detailed analysis of the way in which even these ostensibly most derivative Brazilian musical texts are performed reveals a far more complex set of localized conventions than the doctrine of cultural imperialism could explain. The tremendous irony of arguments espousing cultural imperialism is that they become a mechanism for policing the tenets of taste, which, in turn, assist in maintaining class boundaries.

What is required instead is a way to continue to acknowledge the effects of imperial power while simultaneously allowing for local agency and complexity. Anthropologist Marshall Sahlins, long-time critic of what he calls the despondency theory upon which dependency theory was based, suggests looking at structures of conjuncture. According to this approach, one must first understand the logics at the root of cross-cultural encounters. Other approaches have been presented by a series of Latin American theorists. Most famously, Garcia Canclini suggests reframing the debate by thinking of processes of cultural reconversion whereby local actors put cultural texts to multiple uses. Renato Ortiz recommends rethinking a new and highly mediated Brazilian tradition that simultaneously preserves and elides long-standing Brazilian patterns. Roberto Schwarz seeks to reveal the ways in which readings of public-cultural texts must be embedded in their incumbent forms of economic production, such as neoliberalism. And Claudio Lomnitz problematizes the notion of an overwhelmingly powerful imperial presence by asking us to focus on more manageable contact zones. Together, such perspectives promise to provide more empirically rich and theoretically rigorous approaches to musicality in Latin American contexts. Such perspectives help to grapple with domination without reducing its effects to functionalist polarities, thereby preserving the richness of musical dispositions.

Further Reading

Appadurai, A., and C. Breckenridge. "Why Public Culture?" *Public Culture* 1, no. 1 (1988): 7–9.

Canclini, N. G. Cultural Reconversion. *On Edge: The Crisis of Contemporary Latin American Culture,* edited by G. Yúdice, J. Franco and J. Flores, 29–43. Minneapolis: University of Minnesota Press, 1992.

Dent, A. S. "Country Brothers: Kinship and Chronotope in Brazilian Rural Public Culture." *Anthropological Quarterly* (Spring 2007): 455–95.

Dent, A. S. "Cross-Cultural 'Countries': Covers, Conjuncture, and the Whiff of Nashville in Brazilian Country Music (Música sertaneja)." *Popular Music and Society* 28, no. 2 (2005): 207–29.

Herzfeld, M. *Cultural Intimacy: Social Poetics in the Nation State.* London: Routledge, 1996.

Lomnitz, C. Deep *Mexico, Silent Mexico.* Minneapolis: University of Minnesota Press, 2001.

Ortiz, R. *A Moderna Tradição Brasileira: Cultura Brasileira e Indústria Cultural.* São Paulo: Editora Brasiliense, 1999.

Sahlins, M. "What Is Anthropological Enlightenment? Some Lessons from the Twentieth Century." In *Culture in Practice: Selected Essays,* edited by M. Sahlins, 501–26. New York: Zone Books, 2000.

Schwarz, R. "Brazilian Culture: Nationalism by Elimination." In *Misplaced Ideas,* 1–19. London: Verso, 1992.

Alexander Sebastian Dent

Cumbia

Cumbia is a dance music with roots in **Colombia's** Caribbean coast, but has become popular throughout Latin America in various stylized forms. The earliest usage of the term dates to the late 19th century in reference to the music and dance of Afro-descendant and indigenous people, who by that point had been living in close proximity for centuries in the areas around Cartagena, a key port in the colonial slave trade. Lack of documentation makes it difficult to know more about *cumbia*'s origins, although in its folkloric form *cumbia* is symbolically depicted as having a triethnic heritage: African percussion and call-and-response, indigenous **flutes**, and Spanish lyrics. *Cumbiambas,* nighttime parties attended by black and indigenous workers, were the site of a courting dance between men and women, adding a gendered layer to this origin myth. Folkloric *cumbia* is in duple meter, and usually performed at a slow-to-medium tempo by a small ensemble featuring several drums (***bombo**, llamador, alegre*), a wooden scraper (*guacharaca*) and shakers (*guaches* or ***maracas***) playing a characteristic three-strike pattern, and flutes, either the vertical *gaitas* or the transverse *caña de millo*. The diatonic **accordion**, imported from Germany at the end of the 19th century, also found its way into *cumbia* repertoire.

Beginning in the late 1940s, stylized big-band arrangements of *cumbia* such as those of Lucho Bermúdez gained popularity in Colombia's larger cities among increasingly urbanized, middle- and upper-class, and often lighter-skinned audiences. Simultaneously, groups such as Los Corraleros de Majagual blended some of the elements of folkloric *cumbia* with those of military wind bands from coastal savanna towns, appealing to a darker-skinned, working-class audience. The repertoire of all these groups fell under the umbrella term *música tropical,* which also included ***porro**, fandango, bullerengue,* and *paseos,* to name a few, and was promoted abroad through an active touring circuit that brought *música tropical* to other Latin American countries, just as it brought Cuban ***son***, Mexican ***rancheras***, and Argentine ***tango*** to Colombia. Also important in the diffusion of *cumbia* was a nascent recording industry, led by labels like Discos Fuentes. It was not long before locally accented *cumbias* sprouted throughout Latin America, making it ubiquitous yet uniquely local.

In **Mexico**, *cumbia* found several interpreters, from Mike Laure's guitar-infused covers of Colombian standards to Beto Villa's *orquesta tejana*. **Conjunto** musicians from the border, long familiar with the accordion, added *cumbia* to their repertoire of waltzes, **polkas**, and ***corridos***. In all these different settings *cumbia* became a marker of class, the music of marginalized urban poor and U.S.-bound migrants. It also continued a process that had begun in Colombia of stripping down *cumbia* to a more rhythmically straightforward music, emphasizing the three-strike pattern usually played by the *maraca* or the scraper, and adding drum kit, keyboards, and electric bass. Artists such as **Selena**, Los Tigres del Norte, Banda El Recodo, and Celso Piña represent the variety of *cumbia* styles found just along the border.

In **Peru**, *cumbia* was taken up in the late 1960s by indigenous migrants from the highlands bound for the rapidly urbanizing poor neighborhoods of Lima and other cities. Combining *música tropical* with the quintessentially Andean **huayno** rhythm, and adding garage-band style guitars with effect pedals and organs proved to be a successful formula that captured people's indigenous roots and urbane aspirations. Called *cumbia amazónica* or *chicha,* it became a symbol of cultural hybridity and the working class. Similarly in **Argentina**, *cumbia,* which first arrived in the 1940s and 1950s and had long been popular with the working class, developed a local flavor of synthesized low-fidelity sounds. As the Argentine economy collapsed in 2002, *cumbia villera,* a style that fermented in the Buenos Aires slums, became an antiestablishment voice critical of the government.

Paradoxically, while *cumbia* was finding success abroad, its popularity in Colombia was waning. The **salsa** boom of the 1970s hit Colombia hard and replaced *cumbia* as the preferred dance genre. In the 1980s and 1990s, **vallenato**, a related accordion-based genre from the coast made inroads in the interior of the country, crossing race and class boundaries, leaving *cumbia* as a style from a bygone era. However, the nationwide popularity of *vallenato* allowed the coast to become a symbol of the nation, leaving open the door for a 21st-century *cumbia* resurgence. DJs and musicians in Colombia and other major cities around the world are remixing the many different sounds of *música tropical* with **hip-hop** and other electronic dance genres, referencing both the traditional and modern, the local and global, and creating a new, cosmopolitan *cumbia* sound.

Further Reading

L'Hoeste, Héctor Férnandez. "All *Cumbias*, the *Cumbia*." In *Imagining Our Americas,* edited by Sandhya Shukla and Heidi Tinsman, 338–64. Durham, NC: Duke University Press, 2007.

Wade, Peter. *Music, Race and Nation.* Chicago: University of Chicago Press, 2000.

Juan C. Agudelo

D

Danza

Danza is an urban 19th-century Caribbean derivative of *contra* dances introduced from Europe in the late 18th century. The family of *contra* dances included *quadrilles, rigaudons,* and *lancers,* as well as Spanish **contradanzas** that were rooted on the longways style of the English country dance. This latter type, reported in Spain around 1711, is the one considered to be the most common (albeit not exclusive) tableau for the emergence of *danza* in the Caribbean. The early longways style consisted of two duple-metered eight-bar sections of melodies played to a similar recurring dance format of men and women in two lines, initially facing each other and later evolving into figures prescribed by a dance caller, or *bastonero.*

Urban dance orchestras in the Caribbean consisted primarily of lower-class military-band members, or musicians of African ancestry who slowly, but surely, converted *contradanzas* into a *Creole* genre known as *contradanza del país.* As local white upper-class patrons entered the dance arena to the stately and dignified melodies of the opening bars, they were exposed, or ambushed, in the latter section to voluptuous Afro-Caribbean rhythms. The first reported example of local *contradanzas* took place in San Pascual Bailón, **Cuba**, in 1803, containing elements like the so-called **habanera** (as a rhythmic pattern) in march-like melodies common in military repertoires.

Frequently, composers drew their melodic styles from the Italian arias performed in opera productions, sponsored mainly by local merchants and the buoyant sugarcane industry. With the influence of European Romanticism, *contradanza del país* emerged in the 1840s as a way for dancers to reject the authoritarian caller and the longways system in favor of the independent couple, a modality observed today in slow, moderate, and fast dances of urban contemporary societies. Events like the Paris Revolt of 1848 inspired local writers to adopt *Creole contradanza* as an emblem of an antimonarchic Caribbean, free from the chains imposed by Spain and Roman Catholicism. Perhaps not coincidentally, these *danzas* seldom featured the Andalusian cadences associated with peninsular Spanish music.

Variants of *contra* dance existed with similar or different names in countries like danza, **Puerto Rico**, the Lesser Antilles, **Venezuela, Colombia**, the **Dominican Republic, Haiti, Mexico**, Curazao, **Brazil, Argentina**, and **Uruguay**. Whenever these distinctive versions were performed in Europe, peninsular Spaniards referred to them indistinctly as *danza antillana* (Antillean *danza*). The popularity and significance of the Antillean *danza* is documented in "La Borinquena," a suave and romantic *danza* that became Puerto Rico's national anthem.

The Puerto Rican *Danza*

In order of relevance, the versions of *danza* from Puerto Rico and Cuba are considered to be the most representative, yet they are dissimilar to each other due to factors such as demography and migration. In Cuba, the *contradanza* featured the binary patterns of the *habanera* and was renamed *danza,* and later called *danza cubana*. In Puerto Rico, by the 1840s, *contradanza* was known as **merengue** and it consistently combined the binary rhythms associated with the Cuban *danza* with a 2/4 time signature embracing triplets more suitable to 6/8 or 3/4 measures, a likely contribution of immigrants from Venezuela. Another way in which Cuban *danza* is distinct from the *danza* of Puerto Rico is that Cuban *danza* is invariably comprised of only two parts: the *prima* and the *segunda,* which are repeated ad infinitum in the dance context, perhaps with ornaments or improvised variations. Puerto Rican *danzas* similarly display a two-part structure with a different analytic nomenclature, that is, a first part called *paseo* followed by a section called *merengue*. But by contrast to the Cuban *segunda, merengue* evolved into a multipart form generally consisting of three 16-bar melodic sections, concluding with the theme of the introduction. This expansion helps explains why the entire genre was also known as *merengue*.

In 1849, Governor Juan de la Pezuela issued a decree banning *merengue* in Puerto Rico. Dance organizers, musicians, and the public responded by camouflaging the expression under the name *upa* and later as *danza*. By the mid-1850s, Spanish military bands included *danzas* in regular nightly outdoor concerts known as *retretas,* occasions for bandleaders to show their instrumental expertise through *obbligato* arrangements of popular arias and *cavatinas*. The mid-low register of euphonium *obbligato* (known popularly as *contracanto de bombardino*) along the entire *merengue* section is among the most characteristic elements of Puerto Rican *danzas*. This subordinate line was adopted as left-hand countermelodies in *petit salon danzas* that became popular among local elite dilettante ladies. "Un viaje a Bayamón" ("A trip to Bayamón," 1867) by Manuel G. Tavárez reveals the use of low-register melodies much like euphonium-third-section solos.

San Juan and Ponce: Two Schools of *Danza*

By 1870, two schools of *danza* were discernible through differences that arose out of formal, rhythmic, and stylistic developments. In San Juan, *danza* kept its ties with the old Spanish *contradanzas* while maintaining the prominence of accompanying *habanera* rhythms in short and equidistant phrases with boisterous and lighter themes reflected from suggestive titles, such as "Zabaleta, Rabo de puerco" and "Ay, yo quiero comer mondongo."

After moving from his native San Juan to the southern city of Ponce, Manuel Tavárez (1843–1882) set the foundations for a freer cosmopolitan, romantic *danza* that reaffirmed its Afro-Caribbean profile. Tavárez, who was educated in Paris, is credited for strengthening this French piano tradition. His *danzas* consisted of enlarged melodic phrases, with triplet and quintuplet figures evenly inscribed in scores like his *danza,* "Margarita" (1870). Local performers transformed these left-hand *obbligato* figures into alternating African-related uneven patterns of 3-3-2 and 2-1-2-1-2, resulting in the voluptuous languidness characteristic of the slow *danza romántica* for piano. Another of Tavarez's contributions is the occasional use of distant tonalities, as in his *danza* "Un recuerdito" ("A little souvenir," ca. 1877). This style of playing that developed in Ponce is best represented by Tavarez' pupil, **Juan Morel Campos**.

Morel Campos, Juan

Juan Morel Campos (1857–1896) is considered one of the most prolific **danza** composers in the Caribbean. Most of his estimated 300 *danzas* were written for dance ensembles that combined military-band and string-ensemble formats. But Campos extended his resume to include roles as conductor and arranger for a traveling Cuban minstrel, an Italian opera, and several Spanish **zarzuela** companies.

He was a protege who could play various musical instruments and improvise when some of his instruments were unavailable in remote cities. Campos was able to endow *danza* with melodic and harmonic sophistication, while still maintaining "that austere, provincial, sober and defiant" character of the music from his native city of Ponce. Traces of Italian cantabile are also clear in the *danzas* he composed in the 1880s, such as "Alma Sublime" ("Sublime Soul"), "Tormento" ("Torment"), and "Influencia del Arte" ("Influence of Art").

Piano reductions of Campos's *danzas* became widely acclaimed in world concert halls and were played along side petit piano compositions by Chopin, Schumman, Liszt, and others. These danzas were later recorded in the 1940s by Jesús María Sanromá.

Further Reading

Thompson, Donald. *Music in Puerto Rico: A Reader's Anthology.* Lanham, MD: Scarecrow Press, 2002.

Edgardo Díaz Díaz

The Prodigy of Juan Morel Campos

Danza is said to have reached its highest musical level with Juan Morel Campos (1857–1896), who was also the most prolific composer in the region. Most of his estimated 300 *danzas* were written for dance ensembles combining military-band and string-ensemble formats. Eventually, orchestras in Puerto Rico drew on Morel Campos's classical (*danza*) ensemble to standardize a format consisting of **flutes**, clarinets, violins, euphonium, trumpets, a bass, a *güiro*, and *timbal*. An euphonium player (or *bombardinista*), Morel Campos established the tradition of double-euphonium *contracanto* (in thirds and sixths) along with *bombardinista* Domingo Cruz ("Cocolía"), whose malabarisms and speeches on this instrument predated, by decades, the era of **jazz** improvisations. Morel Campos was also a noted orchestra conductor, working in South America and the Caribbean, and arranged music for traveling Cuban minstrel, Italian opera, and Spanish *zarzuela* companies. He played multiple instruments, had significant improvisational skills, and readily rearranged music for ensembles lacking the full complement of instruments required, in particular for opera scores. Morel Campos was trained by French-educated Tavárez, and by Spanish-trained Antonio Egipciaco but his work adapting Giusseppe Verdi's latest opera scores for local performances provided him with a unique foundation and understanding of orchestration. Morel Campos, with this fluidity, flourished as a composer. He gave more freedom to the standard *paseo-merengue* structure of the *danza,* and endowed it with melodic and harmonic sophistication even as it maintained the austere, provincial, sober, and defiant character of his native city of Ponce. Traces of Italian cantabile are clear in Morel Campos' *danzas* composed in the 1880s, like "Alma Sublime" ("Sublime Soul"), "Tormento" ("Torment"), and "Influencia del Arte" ("Influence of Art"). His *danza* "Felices Días" ("Merry Days," 1894) is considered a masterpiece and still popularly played today. While these works also show marked contrasts in tonal harmony, the influence of chromaticism is observed especially in *danzas* like "Noche deliciosa" ("Delicious Night"). In the hands of pianists like Julio Arteaga, Gonzalo Nuñez, Anita Otero, and Elisa Tavárez, piano reductions of *danzas* by Morel Campos became widely acclaimed in world concert halls, along with similar salon piano compositions by Chopin, Schumman, Liszt, and others. Pianist Jesús María Sanromá recorded these *danzas* in the 1940s under RCA Red Seal, a label then exclusively reserved for classical music.

Danza in the 20th Century

Despite the increasing presence of the Cuban *danzón* in Puerto Rico, the early years of the 20th century saw *danza* maintaining its standing as the most popular genre in all aspects of socioartistic life in Puerto Rico. In Ponce, the legacy of

Morel Campos was continued by Juan Ríos Ovalle, Jaime Pericás, and Arturo Pasarell, while in the capital, this expression inspired compositions by Braulio Dueño Colón and Julián Andino. In between these two schools was Angel Mislán, whose *danza* "Tú y Yo" (1882) is considered to predate the modern one-tile **bolero**. While these composers are said to have merely recreated the form that was at its peak during Morel Campos's career, it is José Ignacio Quintón (1881–1925) who maintained—and closed—Danza's creative cycle by enlivening it with *jíbaro* (peasant) music in French-Impressionist chord progressions. By the mid-1930s, the introduction of the *bolero* and other Cuban forms in the main social venues led to the decline of *danza* as a living symbol of collective Puerto Rican aspirations, but in the 1970s, a period of renaissance in local mass culture, the *danza* regained luster as a popular and patriotic genre. The most representative is Antonio Cabán Vale's "Verde Luz," a piece that is required as a part of family parties and social gatherings.

Danza as Merengue in the Dominican Republic

In the Dominican Republic, newspapers, chronicles, and other documents report early *contradanza* derivates such as the *tumba dominicana* overlapping with the intrusive **merengue** first introduced by itinerant musicians and military bands from Puerto Rico in 1854. In the Dominican Republic, then, the terms *danza* and *merengue* have always been terms that indicated a single musical expression introduced by military bands from Puerto Rico. Between 1869 and 1892, several Puerto Rican musicians abandoned their regiments and remained in Santo Domingo, adding their names to the list of Dominican composers who promoted the *danza* in urban dance halls. Peasant musicians joined the military bands and brought band instruments and *danza*-related styles, like the *contracanto de bombardino*, to typical **conjuntos**. This *contracanto* was later adopted by saxophonists among Dominican rural *perico ripiao* (*merengue típico*) ensembles. Related euphonium solos, or *cantos de bombardino* in the third section of the *danza,* may well be seen in saxophone *jaleo* sections of the Dominican *merengue* and the Haitian *meringue*. Versions of double-saxophone counterpoint reminiscent of Morel Campos's style for euphonium, are heard through 1950s recordings of Haitian *meringues* by orchestras like the one directed by Nemours Jean-Baptiste. In favor of the urban *danza* in vogue since the 1870s, high-class Dominicans rejected the musical contributions of local peasants, but during the American occupation of the Dominican Republic (1916–1924), the resulting identity crisis for Dominicans compelled writers and composers to embrace a nationalist stance that closed their world to external influences, to the extreme of denying linkages between *merengue* and *danza*. Eventually, a form described as *jaleo* (referring to the unique rhythmic qualities of the second sections) is appended to the *danza* much like the rural **son** became attached to the urban *danzón* in Cuba around 1910. In this way, *danza* came to be presented to the world, by official decree, as the Dominican *danza*. After 1940, composers in Santo Domingo systematically displaced the original *merengue* multipart section by expanding the *jaleo* to the point that *merengue*, as it is known today, is a quite distinct and unique reaffirmation reminiscent of the long-postponed autochthonous legacy.

Further Reading

Díaz Díaz, Edgardo. "*Danza* antillana, conjuntos militares, nacionalismo musical e identidad dominicana: Retomando los pasos perdidos del merengue." *Latin American Music Review* 29, no. 2 (2008): 232–62.

Díaz Díaz, Edgardo. "El merengue dominicano: una prehistoria musical en diez pasos." In *El merengue en la cultura dominicana y del Caribe: Memorias del Primer Congreso de Música, Cultura e Identidad en el Caribe,* edited by Dario Tejeda, 178–209. Santiago de los Caballeros: Centro León, 2006.

Díaz Díaz, Edgardo. "La musica bailable de los carnets: forma y significado de su repertorio en Puerto Rico (1877–1930)." *Revista Musical Puertorriqueña* 5 (1990): 2–21.

Díaz Díaz, Edgardo and Peter Manuel. "Puerto Rico: The Rise and Fall of the Danza as National Music." In *Creolizing Contradance in the Caribbean,* edited by Peter Manuel. Philadelphia: Temple University Press, 2009.

Veray, Amaury. "The Danza: A Traditional View." Translation by Donald Thompson of "La Misión Social de la Danza Puertorriqueña de Juan Morel Campos." In *Music in Puerto Rico: A Reader's Anthology,* edited and translated by Donald Thompson, 64–71. Lanham, MD: Scarecrow Press, 2002.

Veray, Amaury. "Vida y desarrollo de la Danza Puertorriqueña." In *Ensayos sobre la Danza Puertorriqueña,* edited by Marisa Rosado 23–37. San Juan: Instituto de Cultural Puertorriqueño, 1977.

Edgardo Díaz Díaz

Danzón

The Cuban *danzón* is a music-and-dance genre that first took hold in the latter part of the 19th century and was derived from the European *contradanza* (Fr., *contredanse*), which was already well established as a shared medium of popular social dance in Latin America and the Caribbean, particularly in the circum-Caribbean area. The *contradanza* served as an alternative to the gentrified and highly intricate continental minuet, allowing for widespread social participation. The shared nature of regional practices also facilitated the easy mobility, adaptation, and transformation of musical and choreographic repertories, which readily transgressed linguistic, ethnic, cultural, and class divisions between circum-Caribbean sites, as well as within them. This *contradanza-contredanse* tradition is in effect an intricate complex of related forms that share a basis of structured suites of steps, figures or danceable episodes. These music-and-dance genres, such as the *danza,* the (*danza*) *habanera, quadrilles/kwadrils,* lancers, the *tumba francesa,* and *merengue* among others, have also incorporated, or are often structured in combination with, other social dances of European extraction, such as the polka, waltz, or the mazurka. The Cuban *danzón* is but one outstanding expression in the arresting *Creole* mélange that characterizes much of the music of Latin America and the Caribbean region evolving from the contradanza.

The *contradanza* in Cuba took on a rather unique rendering within the nation's 19th-century social and musical milieu, and though the lines of demarcation are anything but absolute, by the early decades of the nineteenth century, a new *creole* genre known as the *danza* became discernible in Cuba. This *creole* style, which came to be known on the international scene as the *danza habanera,* or simply the *habanera,* gained currency in Europe and the Americas for its unique rhythmic flavor and iconic bass line (see Musical Example 1). Though the effects of the *danza* continued to take hold outside of the island nation, its gradual transformation into the *danzón* was already afoot in the last quarter of the 19th century in Cuba. The Cuban composer Miguel Faílde is credited with composing the first *danzón,* "Las Alturas de Simpson," performed on January 17, 1879, at the Lyceum of Matanzas, Cuba. Though Faílde's place in the historical record is not likely to change, many earlier shifts to the performance practice of the *danza,* both in terms of its choreography and its musical form, presaged the stylistic features of the *danzón* and antedated Faílde's composition.

Musical Example 1: A *habanera* bass line

(George Torres)

Publications of *danzón* compositions for piano flourished in late 19th- and early 20th-century Cuba, directed at a more socially mobile class with pianos in their homes; however, this music, as a dance music, was still performed by one of two distinct instrumental ensembles: the *orquesta típica,* which had been the characteristic salon wind orchestra of 19th-century Cuba, and the *charanga francesa,* featuring the piano, violin(s), and the Cuban five-keyed, wooden flute as the main melodic instruments. The *charanga francesa* gained in popularity beginning in the 1890s and gradually came to supplant the former as the preferred salon ensemble over the course of the next two decades. Common to both ensembles was the *paila* (*timbals*), a Cuban percussion instrument derivative of the orchestral timpani. The timpani, used in the earlier Cuban orquesta típicas of the 19th century, were eventually replaced with the paila, which was responsible for producing the underlying rhythmic drive of the *danzón,* the *baqueteo* (see Musical Example 2a). The rhythm was performed on the two drums of the paila using cross-stick, rim shot, and direct strokes to accentuate the genre's emblematic isorhythm (2+1+2+1+2 | 2+2+2+2), which subsumed the Cuban *clave* rhythm (see Musical Example 2b).

Musical Example 2a: The *baqueteo*

Paila

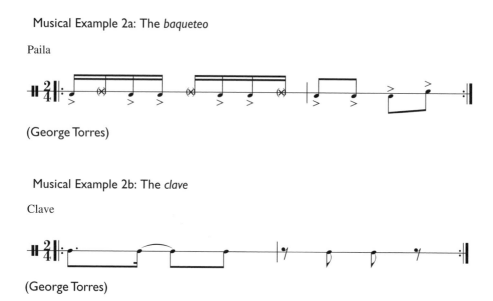

(George Torres)

Musical Example 2b: The *clave*

Clave

(George Torres)

The choreography of the earlier *contradanza* and *danza* was primarily based on the longway figure—two opposing lines of dancing pairs—that formed the basic position from which dance figures would be executed, and to which the dancers would return. *Contradanzas* and related forms throughout the circum-Caribbean region were based on a shared familiarity with set figures, and at times the interchanging of partners in the execution of the same. However, what above all else characterized the *danzón* was a departure from the longway formation, and other collective figures, in favor of couples dancing. As such, the *danzón* was a decidedly different spectacle to take in visually, and it afforded greater variation and liberty on the dance floor as the importance of set figures was eroded over time, as was the need for a caller to mark changes to the collectively danced figures.

Unlike the *contradanza-danza* musical structure, which featured a binary form of two eight-measure phrases, each repeated for a total 32 measures (AA[1] BB[1] or 8+8+8+8), the *danzón* featured additional musical materials set to a modified rondo form (e.g., AA[1] BB[1] AA[1] CC[1] AA[1]). By all indications, before the establishment of the *danzón,* the orchestra típicas performing *danzas* were already accommodating requests for longer musical forms (a feature that would later come to define the *danzón*), in effect extending the dance time and allowing the dancers to demonstrate the latest figures of the day. Most often these orchestras were performing the binary-form *danzas* multiple times as the readymade solution to extending the musical pieces and as a means of soliciting gratuities from the dancing public wanting to keep the music going; however, to the same end, these orchestras were also finding ways to segue from one composition to the next, developing impromptu suites of pieces.

The emergence of the modified rondo form of the *danzón* was then a somewhat expected solution to the requests from the dancers for more musical material while still remaining assonant of the earlier binary form of the *danza*: the *danzón* maintained the repeating eight-measure phrases and a recurring initial A section. It is an excellent reminder of the fact that musical change has often been the result of responses to social tastes (such as those of the dancers), as opposed to the oft-held notion that it emerges from the inspiration of a single musician (such as Miguel Faílde). The *danzón* was music (and dance) with a high level of social integration and interaction, and the genre remained the preferred dance music of Cuba into the 1920s, when its popularity was rivaled and eventually eclipsed by the Cuban *son,* which came to redefine the Cuban musical landscape after the advent of radio on the island in 1922.

Further Reading

Arcaño, Antonio. *Arcaño y sus Maravillas.* Havana: EGREM 918 (compact disc). Schloss, Andrew, prod. 1982. *The Cuban* Danzón*: Its Ancestors and Descendants.* Washington, DC: Folkways Records FE 4066 (LP), 2008.

León, Argeliers. *Del canto y el tiempo.* Havana: Editorial Pueblo y Educación, 1974.

Manuel, Peter, editor. *Creolizing Contradance in the Caribbean.* Studies in Latin American and Caribbean Music. Philadelphia, PA: Temple University Press, 2009.

Michael D. Marcuzzi

Danzonete

Danzonete is a sung ***danzón***, a Cuban musical style that developed from the French ***contredance*** that arrived in **Cuba** around 1798 with the first migratory wave of French refugees fleeing the Haitian Revolution. The first known *danzonete,* "Rompiendo la rutina," dates from 1929. It was flutist Aniceto Díaz (1887–1964) who innovated the *danzón* by introducing a vocal part to the composition. For some authors, the *danzonete* marks the evolution of the *danzón* while this musical style was losing popularity against the growing popularity of the Cuban *son*. The *danzonete* assumes most of the musical characteristics of the *danzón*. It uses a 2/4 meter and it has four parts: an introduction of eight measures, two 32 measures played by the violins and the other instruments, the sung section and the bridge that precedes the refrain that leads to the coda. It is a bit faster than its predecessor due to inclusion of some of the rhythmic features of the *son*.

The *danzonete* is associated with the so-called French ***charanga*** or *charanga típica,* an ensemble that included violin, **flute**, piano, string bass, ***güiro*** (a scraped gourd) and ***timbal***, and that superceded the *orquesta típica,* which instead of the flute, piano, violins, and string bass included clarinet, cornet, trombone, bassoon, and tuba.

Great singers of *danzonete* included Merceditas Valdés, Paulina Álvarez, **Celia Cruz, Rita Montaner**, Celina González, Elena Burke, and Maria Teresa Vera, as well as Fernando Collazo, Pablo Quevedo, and Barbarito Díez.

Further Reading

Évora, Tony. *Orígenes de la música cubana: los amores de las cuerdas y el tambor.* Madrid: Alianza Editorial, 1997.

Linares, Maria Teresa. *La música y el pueblo.* Havana, Cuba: Editorial Pueblo y Educación, 1974.

Raquel Paraíso

Décima

The *décima* is a commonly sung poetic form characterized by stanzas comprising 10 lines of verse typically of eight syllables each, arranged to produce a conventional rhyme scheme, the most popular being the espinela form of AB BA AC CD DC. As a form celebrated in the literature of Iberia's Siglo de Oro (the Golden Century of 1550–1650) and rooted in practices dating centuries before that, the *décima*, even in folkloric and popular music, carries a legacy of distinction that persists today. In the Americas, the song structure, popularized in part by the importation of Spanish theatrical music, became associated with a wide range of popular songs, dance rhythms, and contexts. For contemporary folkloric and popular singers throughout Central and Latin America, the tradition of presenting verse in *décima* structure provides an opportunity to offer social commentary, display wit and inventive skill, as well as assert heritage and social status.

Song types employing the structure are called *décimas* in **Cuba, Puerto Rico, Panama**, and **Venezuela**, as well as in communities where migrants from these countries live, including the **United States**. Nevertheless, the structure also appears in other guises and is a characteristic of many genres, such as some *aguinaldos*, and ***corridos*** as well as various ***sones*** of **Mexico**. The ***son jarocho*** and the ***son huasteco*** of Mexico employ *décima* poetic structure, as do the ***puntos*** of Cuba, the **payadas** and tonos of **Chile** and **Argentina**, and the desafio of **Brazil**. The latter are often improvised in public duels or competitions between singers who must invent appropriate verse on the spot, often addressing a theme suggested by the audience. In other contexts, singers perform memorized, precomposed verses. In

Hawaii, singers of *seis* typically mix and match prelearned *décima* verses, rather than exchange lines of newly composed verse as is more common among singers of *seis* in Puerto Rico.

The common association of *décima* with Iberian or white racial lines did not prevent it from being integrated into Afro-Latin music genres, as in certain examples of Cuban *rumba*. Nor has the structure been employed only in music of rural provenance, although association of the *décima* with *campesino* practice remains strong.

Further Reading

Armistead, Samuel. *The Spanish Tradition in Louisiana: Isleño Folk Literature.* Newark, NJ: Juan De Cuesta, 1992.

Behague, Gerard. "Improvisation in Latin American Music." *Music Educators Journal* 66, no. 5 (1980): 118–25.

Paredes, Américo and George Foss. "The Décima Cantada on the Texas-Mexican Border: Four Examples." *Journal of the Folklore Institute* 3, no. 2 (1966): 91–115.

Pasmanick, Philip "Felipe." "Décima and Rumba: Iberian Formalism in the Heart of Afro-Cuban Form." *Latin American Music Review* 18 (1997): 252–77.

Pasmanick, Philip "Felipe." Deciman (a collection of articles, anthologies, videos, photos and online sound files), Online, September 2007, www.deciman.blogspot.com

Solis, Ted. "'You Shake Your Hips Too Much:' Diasporic Values and Hawai'i Puerto Rican Dance Culture." *Ethnomusicology* 49 (2005): 75–119.

Janet L. Sturman

Descarga

Descarga, literally meaning unloading, is a Cuban performance practice that began in the 1940s whereby musicians create pieces spontaneously. Also known as a discharge or jam session, these improvised pieces give instrumentalists the freedom to showcase their musical talents. *Descargas* usually features a *tumbao* bass line with a repeating piano melody (*guajeo*) that could be found in a *son montuno*. This strong rhythm section, coupled with simple chord changes, provides the foundation for the soloist. Trumpets, saxophones, and percussion instruments like the *conga*, *bongós*, and *timbals* are commonly improvised on in these musical events. *Descarga* falls in between *salsa* and **Latin jazz** in terms of the amount of Cuban structure preserved when combined with **jazz** soloing. The first Cuban *descargas* were highly influential in the development of improvisation in Cuban popular music.

The first sessions to be called *descargas* were produced in **Cuba** in the 1950s but recordings of improvised pieces can be found with the emergence of Latin jazz in New York in the early 1940s. On May 29, 1943, in the Park Palace Ballroom, **Machito** and his orchestra played "Tanga," a piano vamp based on broken chords. His players would take turns soloing using jazz phrasings resulting in a different version of the song at each show. Later in the decade, *descargas* appeared at famous New York clubs like Royal-Roots, Bop City, and Birdland. Dizzy Gillespie and Charlie Parker's pieces with the Machito Orchestra in 1948 and 1949 produced tracks that were 10 to 15 minutes long, unheard of at the time. Tito Puente's live sets featured extended jazz improvisations, one famous tune being "Picadillo."

The first organized *descarga* in Cuba was witnessed by jazz sponsor Norman Grantz in 1952. His amazement led to the cross-fertilization of Cuban improvisation. Pianist Bebo Valdés's 1952 seven-minute **guajeo** piece titled "Con Poco Poco" would become successful not only in Cuba, but in the **United States** upon its 1953 release. "Con Poco Poco" featured Gustavo Mas on tenor saxophone, *conguero* Rolando Alfonso, and bassist Quique Hernández. Valdés and Mas would influence Les Brown and tenor saxophonist Dave Pell whose orchestra in 1953 played "Montoona Clipper" at the Palladium Ballroom in Hollywood, based on "Con Poco Poco." In 1955, Valdés and Mas produced Cuba's second *descarga* entitled "Mambo Caliente." In 1956 the word *descarga* was first used to describe the music with vocalist Francisco Fellove's 17-minute "Descarga Caliente." Fellove innovated **Afro-Cuban** scat singing in the same session with the track "Cimmarron." Both were released in 1957 worldwide under Panart Records, selling over one million copies. Chico O'Farill organized *descargas* as well, notably "Descarga 1" and "Descarga 2," the latter of which featured trombone, *conga, timbals,* and bass solos, yet only three minutes of it was recorded.

Bassist Israel "Cachao" Lopez became famous for his Cuban *descarga. Cuban Jam Sessions in Miniature* was recorded after gigs were over in the early hours of the morning. Released by Panart in 1957, this record established Cachao as a premiere Afro-Cuban bassist. In 1961 and 1962 he recorded *Descarga Con Cacbao* and *Jam Session with a Feeling* respectively for Maype Records. New York radio DJ Dick "Ricardo" Sugar aired Cachao's 1957 LP furthering his international status and influencing many New York musicians such as Hector Rivera and Ray Baretto with their respective hits "Tumba Que Tumba" and "Cocinando Sauce."

The *descarga* tradition continued into the 1960s and into the **salsa** era. The Alegre All Stars released their first LP in 1963 featuring *descarga* influenced by Valdés and Cachao. Tito Rodriguez's 1968 *descarga* was also dedicated to Cachao. Fania Records recorded *descargas* featuring Johnny Pacheco in 1965 with the *descarga* "Azucare." In 1972, Fania produced the movie *Our Latin Thing*, the first picture featuring the Cuban *descarga.* Two years later, the Tico-Alegre All Stars played the *descarga* "La Cosa Alegre" at Carnegie Hall. Ricardo Ray, Joe Cuba, Ray Mantilla, Charlie Palmieri, and Paquito D'Rivera are just a few of the Latin jazz musicians that have recorded their *descargas.*

Further Reading

Salazar, Max. "La descarga cubana: The History of Afro-Cuban Music and Improvisation." *Latin Beat Magazine,* February 1997.

Raymond Epstein

Dominica

Dominica is an island between the Caribbean Sea and the North Atlantic Ocean that is about halfway between **Puerto Rico** and Trinidad and Tobago. As a result of being occupied by both France and England, people in Dominica speak both English and French *Creole.* Despite the fact that a majority of its population (86.8%) is black, for more than two centuries Dominicans were taught to believe that their African-derived traditions were uncultured and evil. It was not until the late 1950s that efforts began to be made to promote an authentically Dominican culture and, as a result, sense of pride in the music of Dominica.

Historically, the principal musical genres in Dominica included *bélé* and the quadrille. *Bélé* is a traditional Dominican type of song and dance accompanied by a drum, triangle, and **maracas** that is performed on major holidays and is often associated with the working class. The quadrille is a more formal style of music and dance that, like many other popular genres in the Caribbean, was adopted from Europe.

Dominica first developed a modern popular music scene with the introduction of *calypso* in the 1960s, which became integrated into the Dominican **Carnival** celebration. In the 1970s, a new musical form developed in Dominica derived from *calypso* known as *cadence-lypso.* But, in the 1980s, musics from neighboring islands such as *zouk* from **Martinique** and *soca* from Trinidad eclipsed the popularity of *cadence-lypso.*

Today Dominica, like many other countries in the Caribbean, enjoys a wide range of popular music that draws on its unique historical roots as well as styles introduced from other nations such as **jazz,** *reggae*, soul, and rhythm and blues.

Further Reading

Guilbault, Jocelyne. "Dominica." In *The Garland Encyclopedia of World Music,* edited by Dale A. Olsen and Daniel E. Sheehy, 840–44. New York: Garland Publishing, 1998.

Tracy McFarlan

Dominican Republic

The Dominican Republic is a Caribbean country that shares the island of Hispaniola with **Haiti**. The two major genres of Dominican popular music are *bachata* and *merengue*. A third distinctively Dominican genre, although it enjoys less mass-mediated popularity, is **Afro-Dominican fusion music**. Current Dominican artists are also producing popular music within genres such as **rock,** *nueva canción*, **Protest Song in Latin America,** *reggaetón, son*, pop, *salsa*, and, primarily in the New York Dominican community, rap and rhythm and blues. As early as 1936, *merengue* was declared the national music of the Dominican Republic, and until the mid-1990s, *orquesta merengue* was the most popular mainstream genre; however, since the 1990s, *bachata* has surpassed it in popularity. During the 1960s, 1970s, and 1980s, these two musical genres articulated the class struggles that characterized Dominican society, each representing the interests and values of distinct social and economic groups. *Bachata* was primarily working class music, especially for migrants from the countryside, and it contrasted with the images of glamour and sophistication associated with *orquesta merengue* and the upper classes. Afro-Dominican fusion music, although marginalized for most of its existence, emerged in the 1970s and is currently at the peak of its popularity.

Early *merengue,* dating back to the 1850s, can be described as a pan-Caribbean ballroom dance that evolved from the European *contradanza* and was infused with Afro-Caribbean rhythmic inflections. While there are still forms of *merengue* performed in Haiti, **Venezuela**, and **Colombia**, it was in the Dominican Republic that a particular type of Dominican *merengue—merengue típico cibaeño*—achieved the status of national music. *Merengue típico* is a genre of music that flourished in the *Cibao* region of the Dominican Republic, a region known for its lighter skinned population. It was commonly performed by an ensemble of **accordion,** *güira* (metal scraper), double-headed *tambora* drum, and a bass instrument called *marimba*. Later in the 20th century, saxophones were added, and the *marimba* was replaced by an electric bass. Because of its association with a lighter skinned and more European population, *merengue* played an important role in the formation of Dominican national identity and exaltation of Spanish values during the dictatorship of Rafael Leonidas Trujillo (1930–1961), when an orchestrated version of *merengue típico cibaeño,* played by a big-band-like ensemble featuring trumpets and saxophones, became the national symbol of the Dominican Republic. Yet, even after Trujillo was assassinated in 1961, *merengue* remained the music that represented Dominicanness, as 31 years of imposition had been internalized by many Dominicans. This orchestrated version of *merengue,* popular in the Dominican Republic and abroad, stands in contrast to the more folk-derived and rural *merengue* *típico,* which was often considered backwards. However, *merengue típico* was not replaced entirely as it continued to exist in rural communities in the Dominican Republic. In urban areas of the *Cibao* region, a *merengue típico moderno* developed through the adding of **conga** drums and electric bass to the traditional instrumentation. In recent decades, *merengue típico* has been mixed with **hip-hop**, creating a new urban style. *Orquesta merengue,* while enjoying extreme local and international popularity up to the 1990s, is also changing, often drawing from Afro-Dominican music to remain fresh and popular.

Bachata is a vocal popular music that has become one of the most popular genres of Latin American music today. This popularity is a relatively recent development since *bachata* began as a highly marginalized genre and was practically unknown internationally until the early 1990s. Despite the prominence of **guitar** accompaniment, *bachata* is essentially a vocal genre with a highly emotional vocal style appropriate for the character of its lyrics, which articulate issues of a hard working-class life. The instrumentation of *bachata* consists of one or two guitars, **maracas** or *güiras* (shaker or metal scraper), and **bongó** drums. The word *bachata* originally meant a rural party or get-together that included music, drink, and food. The term then came to be applied to the music itself, since guitar music was the preferred music of choice for these kinds of gatherings. The music was named not by *bachata* musicians, fans, or industry entrepreneurs, but by the country's urban middle and upper classes, who intended to stigmatize and trivialize these kinds of low-class gatherings as backward and vulgar.

Bachata was born in the 1960s during a period of rural to urban migration; rural migrants lived in the poorest and most marginalized neighborhoods of the capital city, often without water, electricity, or any kind of public amenities. Between the years 1960 and 1970, the population of the capital city of the Dominican Republic, Santo Domingo, nearly doubled, and early *bachata,* whose roots were quintessentially romantic, began to reflect the hardships of the urban life as experienced especially by rural migrants. *Bachata* also reflected and helped articulate the shifting experiences of male-female relationships in this new environment. Many *bachatas* composed during this period consisted of macho bawdy lyrics; a male singer bitterly denouncing women as treacherous and faithless, reflecting the strains and tensions which urbanization imposed on family life. By the 1990s, *bachata* lost some of its significance as an urban folk genre while, at the same time, it now appeals to a wider and more diverse audience. It is also being mixed with rhythm and blues, **reggaetón**, and hip-hop.

Afro-Dominican fusion music (*Música de fusión*) is a genre that combines traditional Dominican music—especially historically marginalized Afro-Dominican music—with accepted forms of global popular music largely as an expression of racial pride and consciousness. Starting in the 1970s, a movement emerged among progressive intellectuals, folklorists, and performers to recognize and promote the African heritage of the Dominican Republic, a movement that led to the promotion and creation of forms of Afro-Dominican-influenced music.

Many forms of sacred drumming traditions from the Dominican Republic have found their way into Afro-Dominican fusion and *merengues* as well as other forms of popular music. All originally ritualistic, these forms have been increasingly showing up in music and dance clubs. Until the 1970s, these genres were left out from historical accounts of Dominican music due to the racist policies of the Trujillo regime. These genres include *congo, sarandunga, palo,* and *gagá. Congo* and *sarandunga* are associated with specific Afro-Dominican brotherhoods or *cofradías,* which are traditional Afro-Caribbean societies created as mutual aid and ritualistic social structures among disenfranchised populations. *Palo* is the most widespread music and dance of the country. Many current scholars claim that it should have been, instead of *merengue,* the national music of the Dominican Republic; however, because of its African features and religious association, it has been repressed. *Palos* are one-headed drums, although there is no standardized type throughout the country. There are also different types of ensemble sizes and rhythmic patterns. *Palo,* like *congo* and *sarandunga,* is also associated with Afro-Dominican religious brotherhoods as well as used in rituals of Dominican Vodou. *Gagá* is a Haitian-Dominican magic-based carnavalesque society of the Lenten season, introduced into the many Dominican sugarcane settlements in recent decades by Haitian seasonal workers. In recent decades, *gagá* has been Dominicanized by second- and third-generation Haitian-Dominicans, as songs are being sung in Spanish in addition to those in Haitian *Creole.* The name itself is a Dominican transliteration of *rara,* the name it receives in Haiti. Despite its carnavalesque appearance, there is a ritualistic aspect to *gagá* as well.

Dominican forms of popular music, which could previously be defined as either rural or urban, are now experiencing a rich period of cross fertilization and influence. Although Dominican popular music began in an effort to claim Spanish tradition through *orquesta merengue,* current movements point away from Europe toward Africa. These African-influenced genres have steadily increased in visibility and popularity in the early 21st century.

Further Reading

Austerlitz, Paul. "The Jazz Tinge in Dominican Music: A Black Atlantic Perspective." *Black Music Journal* 18 (1998): 1–19.

Hernandez, Deborah Pacini. "'La lucha sonora': Dominican Popular Music in the Post-Trujillo Era." *Latin American Music Review / Revista de Música Latinoamerican* 12 (1991) 2: 105–23.

Angelina Tallaj

Dúo

A *dúo* is an ensemble of two players, either vocal or purely instrumental, and usually accompanied by **guitars** or some other type of plucked strings. The *dúo* is the simplest of ensembles in Latin America, and for that reason it is seen throughout Latin America with each country or region having its own type of *dúos*. In **Cuba**, the *dúo* may consist of one or two guitars and a *tres*, with the two instrumentalists singing a harmony, the first or top voice known as *primero* and the second or bottom voice known as *segundo*. The celebrated singer from Buena Vista Social Club, Compay Segundo, got his name for his ability and reputation to provide this lower harmony. The repertoire for the Cuban *dúo* consists mainly of *boleros* and *canciones trovadorescas, claves, criollas* and *guajiras*. In **Mexico**, a similar *dúo* might consist of guitar and *requinto romantico*, as in the repertoire for *sones istmeños* from Oaxaca. In **Colombia**, the *dúo banbuquero* performs music for two voices accompanied by a guitar and a *tiple*. A typical *dúo* performance will have an instrumental introduction where one of the players performs a melodic lead, either memorized or improvised, to an accompanying harmony from the other instrument. In between the verses, there may be an extended solo by the lead instrument, and the melodic instrument may also play instrumental tags at the ends of vocal phrases. The vocalists will usually sing a parallel harmony together or they may sing a simple alternation, or call and response. Sometimes an urban *dúo* is accompanied by a rhythm section, but in spite of the addition of the percussion instrumentalists, the identity of the ensemble remains a *dúo*.

Cuban artists Omara Portuondo (left) and Compay Segundo perform a *dúo* in Mexico City, 2002. (Hector Guerrero/AFP/Getty Images)

Further Reading

Llerenas, Eduardo, Enrique Ramírez de Arellano and Baruj Lieberman, producers. "The *son*," in liner notes to *Antología del Son de Mexico*. 3 Compact Discs, 5–7. Mexico City: Corason, 1985.

Rodríguez, Olava Alén. "Cuba." *The Garland Encyclopedia of World Music, Volume 2: South America, Mexico, Central America, and the Caribbean,* 822–44. New York: Garland Publishing, 1998.

George Torres

Dupla. *See* Dupla Caipira.

Dupla Caipira

The *caipira **duo*** (*dupla*) practices a largely melancholic rural music that emerges from the Central-Southern region of **Brazil** (the states of São Paulo, Minas Gerais, Goiás, Mato Grosso do Sul, Paraná, and Mato Grosso). The term *caipira,* roughly translatable as hick or hillbilly, was once an epithet for the ostensibly lazy and antimodern resident of the backcountry. Now, however, the term and its associated music are enjoying a renaissance as the backbone of a distinctly local identity in the Central-Southern region of Brazil.

The *dupla,* often a pair of brothers, sings the entire *caipira* song harmonized in parallel thirds or sixths. Traditional instrumentation has one performer on a six-string nylon **guitar**, and the other playing the consummate instrument of Central-Southern rurality, the *viola caipira* (a small 10-string, steel-string guitar with a strident tone). Instrumentation reveals a division of labor within the *dupla,* which extends into other aspects of performance. One singer takes the higher, *primeiro* voice for the life of the *dupla* (singers do not alternate), while the other sings the lower *segundo.* The melody may rest in either the higher or lower register, and the singer who carries the melody most often also writes songs, tells stories on stage, organizes the order of performance, and manages scheduling and finances. This hierarchical aspect of *dupla* performance alternates with an egalitarian pose in which hierarchy is neutralized; the quality of a *dupla* is measured by the blending of its two voices. It is said that a truly superb *dupla* will stay in tune at all times, so that, if one performer slips out of tune by accident, the other will simply follow. The frequently melancholy lyrics treat the importance of tears, the grief that accompanies betrayal in love, and the sadness of having to leave the countryside for the city. Perhaps the most important song form is the *moda de viola* (or *viola* song) a recitative in which the voices double the *viola,* though other significant forms include the *cururû, toada, batuque,* and *pagode de viola.* The Central-Southern region from which this music springs draws a sense of identity from its agriculture, particularly cattle production centered on a large refrigeration plant built in the São Paulo town of Barretos in the early 20th century, and its folklore (especially *música caipira*) and Portuguese dialect, which are at the forefront a mixture of Portuguese and Indigenous elements.

The history of the *dupla* form is difficult to trace, but it is certainly tied up with the informal Catholicism of the region. Dual harmony singing characterizes important rituals such as the *Folia de Reis,* or Three Magi Parades, as well as the animation of secular backcountry parties. In these contexts, songs often last 10 minutes or longer, contain some improvised lyrics, and may also be accompanied by dancing. *Música caipira* began its dialogue with urban forms of public culture in 1910, when amateur folkloricist, poet, physical-education teacher, brick-factory owner, and circus-tent master, Cornélio Pires, brought *duplas* to São Paulo's MacKenzie University. Pires was also the first to record *música caipira* in 1929, marshalling his considerable rhetorical, fund-raising, and entrepreneurial skills to persuade Columbia Records of the wisdom of the undertaking. In the 1930s and 1940s, the genre accounted for as much as 40 percent of national music sales, by one scholar's estimate.

Some academics suggest that commercial recording marked the end of the legitimate *dupla caipira.* They claim that the transformation of *música caipira* in the late 1950s and early 1960s into *música sertaneja,* with its increasing use of electric guitar and bass, drum kits, and treatment of romantic themes, furthered the disappearance of *caipira;* however, practitioners in the early 20th century do not agree. Alongside a late 20th- and early 21st-century growth of popularity of commercial Central-Southern rural music, called *música sertaneja,* the *dupla caipira* is enjoying a renaissance led by brothers Pena Branca and the now late Xavatinho, and Zé Mulato and Cassiano. These duos draw upon the work of Zé Carreiro and Carreir-inho, Alvarenga and Ranchinho, and Tião Carreiro and Pardinho, as well as Liu and Leu, Zico and Zeca, Zilo and Zalo, and Tonico and Tinoco. A recent group of musicians using the solo *viola caipira* as a means of exploring Central-Southern tradition includes Ivan Vilela, Paulo Freire, and Roberto Corrêa.

Further Reading

Dent, Alexander Sebastian. "Country Brothers: Kinship and Chronotope in Brazilian Rural Public Culture." *Anthropological Quarterly* 80, no. 2 (2007): 455–95.

Dent, Alexander Sebastian. "Country Critics: Mu´sica Caipira and the Production of Locality in Brazil." Ph.D. diss., University of Chicago, Department of Anthropology, August 2003.

Dent, Alexander Sebastian. *River of Tears: Country Music, Memory, and Modernity in Brazil.* Durham, NC: Duke University Press, 2009.

Alexander Sebastian Dent

E

Ecuador

Ecuador is located on the western side of South America, bordered by **Colombia** and **Peru**. The equator passes through the country, which is geographically diverse, as it has both a mountainous Andean region and Amazonian rainforest. The population is 65 percent *mestizo,* while 25 percent is Native American, 7 percent white, and 3 percent of the people are of African descent. Spanish is the official language, although several Amerindian languages are also spoken, especially Quechua. The traditional music of Ecuador, often played by groups of *mestizo* musicians, includes *albazos, pasacalles,* and ***pasillos***, all of which are considered part of the *música nacional. Pasacalles* and *albazos* typically highlight a particularly valued aspect of its region of origin, such as its women, instruments, or landscape. The *pasacalle* is a kind of *pasodoble* with some elements unique to Ecuador. The *albazo* is a kind of rhythmic dance music, like the famous traditional piece "Aires de mi tierra."

Pasillos, which began as indigenous music, became the most popular Ecuadorian genre in the early 20th century. In the 1950s, *pasillo* faced competition in Ecuador from international styles like ***bolero***, ***tango***, ***vals***, as well as *ritmos tropicales* like ***guaracha*** and ***cumbia***. The *pasillo* incorporated elements of the European waltz and is also found in Colombia, **Panama**, and **Venezuela**. The instrumental *pasillo* is usually performed as quickly as the instrumentalists are able to play it, in contrast to the *pasillo lento,* which is sung slowly to communicate the emotion of the piece, and accompanies the **guitar**, mandolin, and other stringed instruments. Julio Jaramillo (1935–1978) was one of the most well-known *pasillo* performers as he toured Latin America, playing *boleros, tangos, valses* and ***rancheras***, in addition to *pasillos.*

The *sanjuán* is danced in Quechua-speaking communities in the Andes Mountains. The *sanjuanito,* similar to the *sanjuán,* is associated with the Imbabura province, in the northern mountains of the country. *Sanjuanitos* may have a traditional, historical theme (such as the death of Atahualpa, the last Incan emperor) or be autobiographical in nature. The main instrument in the genre is the ***rondador***, a traditional Ecuadorian instrument known in English as a panpipe, consisting of 8 to 34 tubes, which are not placed in order by length. The *rondador* is usually made of cane, and like the **harp**, it is sometimes played on street corners.

Bomba is popular in the Chota river valley in northern Ecuador among people of African descent. The dance-song *bomba* is traditionally accompanied by guitars, *güiros,* and *maracas*. *Bombas* originally were written on the subject of love, but in the 1980s and 1990s, some composers created songs of political significance. *Bomba* has moved to larger cities like Quito and may be heard in *discotecas* and street performances. The *marimba* dance, called *curralao,* is also performed in the Chota River Valley region, but has lost ground to popular styles like *cumbia* and *bolero* in recent years, and is now played mainly for tourists.

Rock music, which gained worldwide recognition in the 1950s, became popular with Ecuadorian young people, perhaps due to its association with rebellion. In the 1970s, bands such as Sueños de Brama, Mozzarella, and Luna Llena popularized hard rock, while in the 1980s, groups such as Spectrum, Blaze, and Post Mortem impacted the development of heavy metal in Ecuador. Carlos Sanchéz Montoya directed the first rock program on Radio Pichincha. More recently, the band The Four Horsemen has gained fame for their covers of Metallica and Megadeath.

Juan Fernando Velasco has emerged as a significant singer of Latin pop, as he performed in Madison Square Garden in 2006, and in 2008, at the Paz sin Fronteras (Peace without Borders) concert, along with internationally acclaimed performers Juanes, Alejandro Sanz, and Juan Luis Guerra.

Further Reading

Alberto, Carlos, and Coba Andrade. *"Danzas Y Bailes En El Ecuador."* Latin American *Music Review / Revista de Música Latinoamericana* 6, no. 2 (1985): 166–200.

Arroyo Avilés, Alexandra. "El rock en el Ecuador." LANIC. University of Texas. Web. January 2, 2010.

Godoy Aguirre, Mario. "La música en el Ecuador." LANIC. University of Texas. Web. January 3, 2010.

Handelsman, Michael. *Culture and Customs of Ecuador.* Westport, CT: Greenwood Press, 2000.

Riedel, Johannes. "The Ecuadorean *'Pasillo': 'Musica Popular,' 'Musica Nacional,'* Or *'Musica Folklorica'*?" *Latin American Music Review (Revista de Música Latinoamericana)* 7, no. 1 (1986): 1–25.

Schechter, John Mendell. *Music in Latin American Culture: Regional Traditions.* New York: Schirmer Books, 1999.

Caitlin Lowery

El Salvador

El Salvador, the smallest country on the American continent, is situated to the southwest of **Honduras**, just below **Guatemala**. The population is 90 percent *mestizo,* as the majority of Salvadorans are of American Indian, European, and African descent, with a minority of whites (9%) and Amerindians (1%). As a result of the mixing of different races and ethnicities, the popular music of El Salvador is a fusion of African, European, and indigenous influences.

African slaves introduced two variations of the **marimba**, the *marimba de arco* (with a bow) and the *marimba criolla* to El Salvador. The most well-known modern version is a three-octave *marimba de arco* and the music is always instrumental. In the 1920s and 1930s, *marimba* ensembles played internationally, touring Europe and the United States. In 1932, however, there was a coup d'état that resulted in a *matanza* (massacre) of the indigenous population in which 30,000 people were killed. The indigenous population, along with its traditional instruments like *marimba de arco,* virtually disappeared. Because they could be adapted to play new styles, *marimba* ensembles remained popular until the 1950s and 1960s, when **rock** came on the world music scene. A gradual revival of the indigenous Salvadoran culture began in the 1990s.

The first third of the 20th century is considered the golden age of Salvadoran popular music, as the *Marimba Centroamericana* became popular both in El Salvador and abroad. In the 1920s, the first radio station in El Salvador, owned by the government, played waltzes, foxtrots, ***rancheras, sones***, and ***songos***. These genres, along with the ***tango*** from **Argentina**, formed the basis of Salvadoran popular music, as musicians from El Salvador created their own versions of these styles. Pancho Lara was the well-known Salvadoran composer of "El Carbonero," which he wrote in the 1930s and is considered a national hymn. In the 1940s and 1950s, *marimba* ensembles made the ***bolero, cha-cha-chá, mambo***, and swing popular.

The ***nueva canción*** movement developed in the 1970s, but the Salvadoran Civil War in the 1980s forced some musical groups into exile in the **United States** as the violence escalated. The musical group Cutumay Camones, founded in 1982, helped define the *nueva canción* of the national liberation struggle of El Salvador, or Frente Farabundo Martí para la Liberación Nacional (FMLN), as did the band Yolacamba Ita. They performed popular protest music which connected and mobilized the working classes and boosted morale. The Cutumay Camones played rhythms popular with the lower classes, such as *boleros, **corridos, cumbias***, and *rancheras*. The title of their first recording, Vamos Ganando la Paz ("We Are Winning the Peace") became a slogan of the FMLN.

Today the majority of the music played for entertainment, particularly in urban areas, comes from the United States. Young people also frequently listen to ***rock en español*** as well as disco music. Mexican music remains popular in rural regions. For example, Mexican *rancheras* are commonly heard throughout the country. Rafael Barrientos founded the Orquesta Internacional de Lito Barrientos, which produced the famous *cumbia* "Cumbia en do menor." Concerts showcasing national music were popularized in the 1990s. They were promoted by the Instituto Salvadeano de Turismo and performed by the Ballet Folklórico, both within El Salvador and abroad.

Popular music within El Salvador is influenced to a great degree by North American trends, with the incorporation of electric **guitars**, bass guitars, synthesizers, and amplifiers. The Salvadoran band Ayutush has a unique **rock** sound, sometimes called Guanarock. Popular genres from other areas of Latin America include Dominican *bachata* and *merengue*, as well as **hip-hop** (as demonstrated by groups like Pescozada) and *reggaetón*. Rap groups like Mecate and *reggae* band Anastasio y los del Monte are also popular. The impact of foreign music, especially from the United States, is evident throughout the country, although it is particularly dominant in cities.

Further Reading

Alegría, Claribel. "The Two Cultures of El Salvador." *The Massachusetts Review* 27, no. 3/4, Latin America (1986): 493–502.

Almeida, Paul, and Ruben Urbizagastegui. "Cutumay Camones: Popular Music in El Salvador's National Liberation Movement." *Latin American Perspectives* 26, no. 2, Reassessing Central America's Revolutions (1999): 13–42.

Scruggs, T.M. "Música y el legado de la violencia a finales del siglo XX en Centro América." *Revista Transcultural de Música* 10 (2006).

Caitlin Lowery

Estribillo

The *estribillo* is the refrain of a musical piece, which may be repeated exactly or with modifications throughout the number. It may be purely instrumental or comprised of a stanza or several lines. Frequently used in several genres of folk and popular music (both song and dance), it originated from the broad traditions of popular song.

The *estribillo* may appear at the beginning or the end of each stanza of a piece. It is essential to the piece's musical structure, as its primary function is to emphasize, repeat, and summarize the action of the piece for the listener. In dance music, it provides the thematic center that shapes the song's narrative, and contains the textual climax that conveys the meaning of the story. Generally, the refrain is related to the song's title, although it can sometimes replace the title if it gains significant recognition. Historically, the gradual increase of its structural complexity shows the evolution of the thought processes of composers and audiences.

In **Venezuela**, the *estribillo* is a polyphonic traditional chant sung as a duet. It is performed at wakes, prayer services, and Christmas festivities, and can be of a secular or religious nature. The chorus is performed in a lively 6/8 meter. The typical stanza is a quatrain, comprised of four six-syllable lines. It is also a type of *joropo* in the eastern region of the country. It is accompanied by the *cuatro, maracas,* *bandola oriental,* mandolin or **accordion**, *caja,* **guitar**, or ***marimba***. It also has a 6/8 meter, with a fixed harmonic pattern in a major key. Melodies are improvised on the main instrument in a rhythmic pattern of two groups of three-quarter notes in the form of an *ostinato.* The singing is characterized by *cotorriao* (a phonetic corruption of *cotorrear,* to chatter) and is sometimes performed in competition.

Further Reading

Miró-Cortez, Carlos. "The Nativity in Iquique, Chile. The Christmas Carols of the Fraternities of Las Cuyacas and Pastoras." *Studia Musicologica Academiae Scientiarum Hungaricae,* T. 18, Fasc. 1/4 (1976): 81–152.

Riedel, Johannes. "The Ecuadorean 'Pasillo': 'Musica Popular,' 'Musica Nacional,' or 'Musica Folklorica'?" *Latin American Music Review / Revista de Música Latinoamericana,* 7, no. 1 (1986): 1–25.

Liliana Casanella

Estudiantina. *See* Rondalla.

F

Filín

Filín is a musical genre that developed in Havana, **Cuba**, in the 1940s. It is characterized by its melodic and harmonic style, literary content, and use of the Cuban song. By the 1970s it had gained widespread popularity surpassing the intermediate period of the Cuban *trovadoresco* movement. It was preceded by the **trova tradicional** movement and was followed by the **nueva trova** movement. The *trovador* Luis Yañéz reputedly popularized the use of the term *filín* within the movement, which stood for good taste in music, style, depth, and singing with feeling. The word *filín* is derived from the English word feeling.

Filín developed in informal musical gatherings in the houses of young people from the more modest sectors of society. They would meet to listen to and play popular songs and dance music. They derived their musical styles from genres such as **jazz**, blues, swing, **tango**, *trova tradicional,* and Cuban dance music. Through their improvisations and fusions of styles, the older forms gave way to new creations, which went on to become standards. In this way the *filín* established new groups or studios and *trovadores.* The musicians would play "Rosa Mústia" by Angelito Díaz at the start of the musical gatherings, as it was the *filineros'* anthem, and they ended the evening with "Hasta Mañana Vida Mía" by Rosendo Ruiz.

The most common meeting places included the Callejón de Hammel (where *trovador* Angelito Díaz lived) and Jorge Mazón's house. It is here that several authors and performers flourished, such as José Antonio Méndez, César Portillo de la Luz, Ñico Rojas, *"El Niño"* Rivera, Rosendo Ruiz, Justo Fuentes, Leonardo Morales, Aida Diestro, Rolando Gómez, Tania Castellanos, Elena Burke, Omara Portuondo, and Moraima Secada. Other notable artists included Martha Valdés, Piloto y Vera, Frank Domínguez, Ela O Farril, and Meme Solís. In their frequent rehearsals, they relied on *"El Niño"* Rivera and occasionally Bebo Valdés and Pedro Justiz for the instrumental arrangement of the repertoire.

In the 1960s, Pablo Milanes merits mention, as do accompanying guitarists Froilán Amézaga, Elena Burke, Martín Rojas, all of whom made *filín* a specialty. Other important musicians in the movement included guitarist-composers César Portillo and José Antonio Méndez, pianists Adolfo Guzmán, Frank Domínguez, and Frank Emilio Flyn; vocal quartets included Orlando de la Rosa, las D'Aida, Meme Solís, and Los Bucaneros y el Rey; and ensembles included Conjunto Casino. Recordings and performances of the *filín* repertoire by musicans in other genres helped to spread the movement to a wide audience.

The nightclubs Sherezada in the Fosca and El Pico Blanco in the Hotel St. John (the *filín* corner) were places that, after 1959, offered a professional-commercial venue for the movement. El Gato Tuerto and Dos Gardenias also contributed to the success of *filín* and its repertoire was published by the Asociación Editorial Musicahabana and affiliated with the Partido Socialista Popular (PSP). The radio station Mil Diez provided programming time to César Portillo de la Luz. Some characteristic songs include "La Gloria eres tu" (José Antonio Méndez), "Contigo en la distancia" (César Portillo de la Luz), "Fiesta en el cielo" ("*El Niño*" Rivera), "Mi ayer" (Ñico Rojas), "En nosotros" (Tania Castellanos), "Oh, vida" (Luis Yañez y Goméz), "Tú me acostumbraste" (Frank Domínguez), "Duele" (Piloto y Vera), and "Con tus palabras" (Martha Valdés).

The performance style associated with *filín* is intimate and familiar, reflective, and hopeful. It does not draw attention to technical or vocal virtuosity. The lyrics are a kind of poetic discourse full of amorous sentiment that uses a colloquial language. It is written fundamentally in the first person with a structured form. The musical accompaniment is consistent with this style. The stylistic range of interpretations present in versions of the same song can be heard in the various melodic elaborations and the idiosyncratic accents between the singer and accompaniment. A constant rubato is prevalent, which leads to a semideclamatory style, with use of phrase breaks and *portamentos* and sections of intense chromaticism. Instrumental sections serve as introductions and interludes and have a certain air of harmonic sophistication that highlights the performers' competence. It compensates for the successive leaps of fifths, sixths, sevenths, and octaves with alternation of conjunct intervals, many times in a graceful flowing form. The harmonic sequences make use of ninths, elevenths, and other higher numbered chords.

The *filín* is popular throughout Latin America. Its prevalence in **Mexico** is due to the influence of Vicente Garrido, Mario Ruiz Armegol, Álvaro Carillo, Luis Demetrio, and Armando Manzanero; in **Costa Rica**, Ray Tico has helped to popularize the style. More recently, the repertoire gained international recognition through covers done by Grammy-winning Mexican singer Luis Miguel.

Further Reading

Moore, Robin. *Music and Revolution: Cultural Change in Socialist Cuba.* Music of the African Diaspora, 9. Berkeley: University of California Press, 2006.

Morales, Ed. *The Latin Beat: The Rhythms and Roots of Latin Music from Bossa Nova to Salsa and Beyond.* Cambridge, MA: Da Capo Press, 2003.

Sublette, Ned. *Cuba and Its Music.* Chicago: Chicago Review Press, 2004.

Liliana González and Grizel Hernández

Flauta. *See* Flute.

Flute

The European transverse flute began as single-piece, six-holed, cylindrical-shaped wooden instruments made from different varieties of wood. The model for the contemporary flute, the Boehm flute, was developed in the 19th century and gradually standardized in terms of its dimensions and length. It was not until well into the 20th century that metal (primarily silver, but also gold, and platinum), most evident in the performance of Cuban flute music, became the standard material used to make the body of the flute.

There are two popular types of flutes, the transverse or side-blown flute and the vertical or duct flute. In the transverse or side-blown flute, sound is created when the flutist presses the mouthpiece just under his or her lower lip and blows across the embouchure. Depending on style, the tone can be pure, warm, and buzzy, or high-pitched. The duct flute is played vertically with the mouthpiece in the player's mouth. The flute, both vertical and transverse, is prevalent throughout Latin America. Different types of Latin American flutes include the European metal flute, a five-keyed, wooden Cuban flute, a variety of end-blown Andean flutes and pipes, the Colombian *gaita,* a duct flute used in *cumbia* ensembles, and the Brazilian *pife,* which is a small, high-pitched, open-holed instrument.

The flute is particularly important in the Brazilian ***choro***. The *choro* evolved out of the *terno,* a trio consisting of a transverse flute, **guitar**, and **cavaquinho**. This ensemble played both European dance music for parties and social occasions and informally, improvising melodies and accompaniments. This spirit of improvisation became an important part of *choro.* The flute would take an often familiar melody and improvise with it in counterpoint to the accompaniment. As the *choro* evolved other instruments took the melodic line but the flute remained an important part of the genre. Joaquim Antônio da Silva Callado was one of the first *choro* composer-flute players. He was a highly acclaimed classical flutist and his playing featured chromaticisms and octave leaps and created one of the first ensembles, Choro Carioco, in 1870. **Pixinguinha** (Alfredo da Rocha Viana, Jr.) was another popular *choro* flutist in the first half of the 20th century. Like Callado, Pixinguinha was also a composer and virtuoso performer. He spread *choro* to Paris and added a saxophone and elements of **jazz** to the genre. Other important *choro* flutists included Benedito Lacerda, Patápio Silva, and Mário Séve (a flutist/saxophonist who performed progressive *choro* with the ensemble Nó em Pingo D'Água in the late 1970s).

The flute is also an important part of the Cuban **charanga** tipica. *Charanga* ensembles feature transverse flutes and violins as primary melodic instruments and use the piano, acoustic bass, *timbals, güiro, congas*, and vocals as accompaniment. The traditional Cuban flute is wooden and derived from the 18th-century French-style flute, which made its way from **Haiti** to **Cuba** and ultimately evolved into a distinctly Cuban-style, five-keyed flute. In *charanga* style ensembles the flutist plays rapid improvised passages on the upper registers of the instrument, an octave above the violins. This technique requires great skill and stamina, especially when played with the five-keyed wooden flute. *Charanga* flute playing features arpeggios, repeated riffs and phrases that interact with the rhythm section of the ensemble. Like *choro,* the repertoire is derived from European dance forms and the music is composed, arranged, and written down and as a result it has classical elements but with a strong improvisatory character. Johnny Pacheco (b. 1930) is one well-known Dominican *charanga* flutist. He learned the high-trilling Cuban style of flute playing from Cuban flutist and bandleader Gilbert Valdés as used in the traditional wooden instrument throughout his career. He received many honors as a composer, bandleader, producer, and versatile musician. With his orchestra, Pacheco y Su Charanga, he introduced a popular new dance known as "Pachanga." One of his most notable accomplishments was the creation of Fania Records, which helped to start the careers of many Latin musicians. Other well-known *charanga* flutists include Melquiades Fundora, Jose Fajardo, Nestor Torresm Richard Egües, Orlando "Maraca" Valle, and Eduardo Rubio.

Further Reading

Leymarie, Isabelle. *Cuban Fire: The Story of Salsa and Latin Jazz.* New York: Continuum, 2002.

Livingston-Isenhour, Tamara Elena Garcia, and Thomas George Caracas. *Choro: A Social History of a Brazilian Popular Music.* Bloomington: Indiana University Press, 2005.

Miller, Susan. "The Charanga Flute Players of Cuba." *PAN* 2 (2008): 2.

Rebecca Stuhr

Folk, Art, and Popular Music

Folk, art, and popular are terms that describe three broad categories of music. These labels are applied for a variety of reasons including style, marketing, and academic taxonomy. They create areas of reference for understanding some of music's intrinsic processes such as issues of transmission, economics, audience, content, and musical training. But while these terms can be useful for organization and categorization, they can also be restrictive, and as stylistic identifiers they are at times misleading and inconsistent. For the labels folk, art, and popular to be applicable to the music of Latin America, the distinctions between them must remain broad and their boundaries, by necessity, fluid since the blending between them is an inevitable part of the hybridization and intercultural contact that has occurred in Latin America, especially as a result of the urbanization and industrialization characteristic of the 1900s.

Folk music is preserved through collective and cooperative action in societies where no one individual has the time or money to spare for the creation of music as their livelihood. Where self-sufficiency is rarely taken for granted, individuals, small groups, or whole communities take part in performing a shared repertoire of songs frequently labeled functional music because of its connection with nonmusical activity. Even though a piece of folk music may be claimed by an entire community, it is usually composed by a single individual or small group and then transmitted to a larger population through incidental learning at special occasions or sociocultural events. Folk music is, as a result, usually vocal and instrumental with predictable rhythmic patterns, and carried out by nonprofessionals with minimal or incidental musical training on instruments that are not labor-intensive. While folk music is often considered the music of the rural, native, or indigenous people, this is not always the case. In the **United States**, for example, the songs "Take Me Out to the Ball Game" or "Happy Birthday" could be considered folk music because they are approved by the group, learned incidentally after prolonged exposure, and are usually tied to special occasions or events. In Latin America, the music performed in Haitian *Vodou* rituals or at *Herranza,* a Peruvian animal branding ceremony, are forms of regional folk music that were created locally, passed down over generations, and exist independently of any popular or art music traditions.

Within the Latin American context, art music is commonly associated with the ideals of European classical music and operates through a system of direct patronage whereby musicians are supported by a single source (whether it be, for instance, an individual, university, or governmental body). Art musicians are professionals who perform their music, usually for elite groups, after years of formal training and apprenticeship. Latin American art music first developed during European colonization from the 1500s to the 1800s. It had its antecedents in the European classical tradition as Latin American social groups sought to differentiate themselves from the lower classes and aspire to the tastes and ideals of the Europeans. From the 1920s to the 1950s, following the Latin American wars of independence, there was a period of strong nationalistic sentiment in art, literature, and music. This nationalism was expressed in Latin American art music as composers began to include creolized European dance forms in their compositions as a way to honor the authenticity of the music of the *mestizo,* African, and Amerindian groups. Composers such as Carlos Chavez and Heitor Villa-Lobos sought to incorporate uniquely Latin American elements of music into their compositions, integrating European art music with Latin American folk instruments and rhythms. Chavez, for example, based his *Sinfonia India* on Mexican Amerindian melodies, and Villa-Lobos was well known for incorporating Brazilian popular genres into his compositions as seen in his *Choros #1* for guitar. Beginning in the 1960s, art music in Latin America became increasingly more innovative with composers experimenting with serial music, indeterminacy, and electronic music composition.

Popular music is often seen as the music of the people and, as a result, it is sometimes dismissed by critics as lowbrow or common. As the focus of this encyclopedia, the definition of popular music, though potentially debatable, is an important one to establish. Despite contextual variation, popular music is mass-disseminated music of the post-industrial age. Beginning in the 19th century, popular music developed at a time of profound change due to modernization, industrialization, and urbanization. The musical processes that accompanied these societal developments shared distinct characteristics different from that of the art and folk music systems and together these characteristics evolved into what became known as popular music. One of the most important of these characteristics was the creation of a system of indirect patronage whereby popular music became dependant on not only a technological means of collecting an audience and disseminating the music (radios, phonographs, computers, etc.), but also on a merchandiser to act as an intermediary between the artist and the audience (music publishers, record companies, concert venues, the film industry, etc.). As a result, the evolution of popular music would have been impossible without the innovations that developed due to modernization, urbanization, and industrialization, such as printed sheet music, player piano roles, phonograph recordings, and the radio.

Because popular music developed as a result of urbanization it is fitting that in Latin America its evolution took place predominantly in the major city centers of Mexico City, Havana, Buenos Aires, and Rio de Janeiro. The following examples provide instances of hallmarks in popular music from these regions. Mexican composer Juventino Rosas won recognition as one of the first Latin American popular musicians when his waltz, "Sobre las olas" was published and performed internationally in the late 1800s. In the early 1900s popular music began to gain momentum in major cities. The Cuban **habanera** exterted a strong influence in the Caribbean and also formed the rhythmic basis of *tango* music, which has continued to be a noteworthy popular music genre. In the hands of Mexican singer and songwriter **Agustin Lara**, the Cuban **bolero** fused with *cancion mexicana* to create a new style of internationally recognized Mexican *bolero*. Carnival also exerted an influence on the development of popular music in Latin America. In Brazil, for example, urban *samba,* which developed out of the *sambas* of **Carnival** celebrations, originated in Rio de Janeiro in the 1920s and 1930s. This new urban *samba* was then exported internationally through the popular music system to become an intrinsic part of Carnival celebrations all over Latin America. More recently, genres such as **jazz**, rock 'n' roll, rap, *reggae*, and **hip-hop** have fused with the folk and art music traditions that already existed in Latin America to create dynamic new genres such as *reggaetón* and *rock en español*. The ultimate outcome of the modernization of the 1900s has been a gradual homogenization of popular music in Latin America and all over the world as musicians and merchandisers are forced to respond to the tastes of the mass audience in order to ensure their continued popularity and success. The limit to creativity caused by this mass listenership is a characteristic unique to popular music and has shaped the development of the sound and style of many genres that fit within its label, such as *balada*.

Despite their inherent differences, there are not always clear delineations between the systems of folk, art, and popular music. There is often a blurring of boundaries as genres of music either change systems and adapt to match the new modes of transmission, or alternatively, are appropriated by other artists and styles of music both within and outside of their original system. In Latin America, the Colombian *vallenato* is an example of the affect that a change in systems has on a musical genre; the music of **Astor Piazzolla** shows the ways music has been appropriated across different systems. *Vallenato* began as a folk music tradition in northern **Colombia**. The earliest *vallenato* ensembles consisted of an **accordion**, *caja* (small drum), and *guaracha* (stick scraper). But, after it spread to city centers and gained a popular following, an electric bass, a **guitar**, and **Afro-Cuban** percussion (such as the *conga* and **cowbell**) were added to the original **trio** instrumentation. These new instruments gave the *vallenato* a distinctly modern sound, which reflected urban tastes, a testament to the effect of the shift from a folk to a popular music system. The work of Astor Piazzolla, an Argentinean composer and *bandoneón* player, is an example of the appropriation of music across different systems. Piazzolla developed what became known as the new *tango* by infusing his art music compositions with *tango* rhythms, appropriating elements of urban popular music. The affect of changing music systems and appropriation of styles by different artists and genres shows that even armed with the labels folk, art, and popular, music evades classification, which is what makes music in Latin America such a fluid and dynamic field of study.

Further Reading

Appleby, David. "Folk, Popular, and Art Music." *The Music of Brazil,* 94–115. Austin: University of Texas Press, 1989.

Behague, Gerard. "Music, c. 1920–c. 1980." In *A Cultural History of Latin America: Literature, Music and the Visual Arts in the 19th and 20th Centuries,* edited by Leslie Bethell, 311–67. New York: Cambridge University Press, 1998.

Booth, Gregory, and Terry Lee Kuhn. "Economic and Transmission Factors as Essential Element in the Definition of Folk, Art, and Pop Music." *Musical Quarterly* 74 (1990): 411–38.

Hamm, Charles. "Popular Music." *The New Harvard Dictionary of Music,* edited by Don Michael Randel, 646–49. Cambridge: Belknap Press, 1986.

Manuel, Peter. "Perspectives on the Study of Non-Western Popular Musics." *Popular Musics of the Non-Western World: An Introductory Survey.* New York: Oxford University Press, 1998.

Nettl, Bruno. "Folk Music." *The New Harvard Dictionary of Music,* edited by Don Michael Randel, 315–19. Cambridge: Belknap Press, 1986.

Shaw, Lisa, and Stephanie Dennison. "Introduction: Defining the Popular in the Latin American Context." *Pop Culture Latin America!: Media, Arts, And Lifestyle,* 1–7. Santa Barbara: ABC-CLIO, 2005.

Tracy McFarlan

Forró

Forró is the name of a type of social gathering in **Brazil** where, most commonly, music is played live and couples dance. The word is probably short for *forrobodó,* which was a style of dance accompanied by live music that appeared around the 19th century among the lower, working class. *Forró* has its roots in a kind of entertainment practiced as a backyard pastime after a hard day's labor in the dry hinterland of northeast Brazil known as the *sertão,* which is a very poor area with a high rate of illiteracy. It is also related to the Catholic June feasts that are widely celebrated in rural areas commemorating the days of Saint Anthony (June 13), Saint John (June 24), and Saint Peter (June 29). Beginning in the 1930s, migrants moved in large numbers from the northeast to the south. They began to hold *forró* events in the big cities. By the 1960s, these migrants were creating what came to be called *forró* houses. As a result, the word *forró* began to refer to a place, such as a nightclub, that offers music and dancing. The first important and longest operating *forró* house in São Paulo was Forró do Pedro Sertanejo, which remained opened for 27 years, from 1965 to 1992. During the 1950s and 1960s *forró* developed into a specific genre of dance music by Jackson do Pandeiro (José Gomes Filho, 1919–1982).

In the musical realm, *forró* is an umbrella term for a variety of genres related to the northeastern Brazil and its culture. The main musical genres played at a *forró* event are **baião**, *xote, arrasta-pé,* and *forró* itself. *Baião* and *forró* have the same dance but *forró* is the faster of the two. *Xote* and *arrasta-pé* feature different dance steps. *Xote* is considered the *bolero* of the Northeast while the *arrasta-pé* style of dancing is closely related with *quadrille* and *pas-de-quatre.*

Forró as a backyard entertainment used to be instrumental, without singing or lyrics. It was played on a variety of instruments such as the button accordion, cane-like transverse **flutes** (called *pifes* or *pífanos*), *rabeca* (a sort of rural violin), or *viola* (a 6- or 10-string guitar). It was not until the 1940s that *forró* became popular with the music of Luiz Gonzaga (1912–1989), who was a musician, singer, and **accordion** player. He was called the king of *baião* (one of his first hits is called "Baião," 1946) and through *baião*'s success he also introduced *xote* and *arrasta-pé.* It

Joquinha Gonzaga plays accordion at New York's Lincoln Center in 1999 during a tribute to his uncle, Brazilian folk musician Luiz Gonzaga. (AP/Wide World Photos)

was Gonzaga who created the northeastern trio (*trio nordestino*) of the *zabumba* (a medium-size double-headed drum), piano-accordion and triangle. He also introduced lyrics to the music he recorded. His lyrics usually were written with other people such as Humberto Teixeira (1915–1979) and Zédantas (José de Souza Dantas Filho, 1921–1962). The lyrics that they wrote featured aspects of northeastern culture and reinforced the character of this regional music. They created an image of Northeasterners as violent and dangerous. Gonzaga was popular until the 1960s, when he was superceded by **bossa nova**.

In the 1970s and 1980s, there were some isolated hits by Genival Lacerda ("Severina Xique Xique" in 1975) and Clemilda ("Prenda o Tadeu" in 1985). These *forró* recordings were noted for the double entendre in their lyrics and as a result were classified as pornographic *forró,* or *porno-forró.* In São Paulo in the 1990s there was a discovery of *forró* music by university students who began to play what became known as university *forró* (*forró universitário*) that was marketed as a middle-class, polite, well-educated *forró.* The students hired trios usually formed by northeastern migrants such as Trio Virgulino and Trio Sabiá, to play at their parties and soon opened university *forró* houses. The students also began to have their own *forró* bands. Falamansa and Rastapé were the first of these groups to be successful playing and recording university *forró.* Although they began as trios, these university *forró* bands began to add other instruments to their music including electric guitar, bass, and traps as well as lyrics that represented their own tastes and worldview but they still claimed to be performing traditional *forró*.

The year 2000 was the peak of the *forró* revival with the release of the film *Eu, Eu, Eles* (*Me, You, Them*). Directed by Andrucha Waddington and with musical direction provided by **Gilberto Gil**, *Eu, Eu, Eles* was an Oscar candidate in the category of best foreign film. The movie provides an accurate representation of *forró* because it combines the old style of *forró* music with more modern versions of it.

Some of the most important performers of *forró* music besides Gonzaga are Jackson do Pandeiro, Dominguinhos (José Domingos de Moraes), Marinês (Inês Caetano de Oliveira), Abdias do Acordeon, Trio Nordestino, Genival Lacerda, Carmélia Alves, Luís Vieira (Luis Rattes Vieira Filho), Pedro Sertanejo (Pedro de Almeida e Silva), Oswaldinho do Acordeon, Clemilda (Clemilda Ferreira da Silva), Sandro Becker, Zé Duarte, Mastruz com Leite, Frank Aguiar (Francineto Luz de Aguiar), Flávio José, Trio Sabiá, Trio Chamego, Trio Virgulino, Waldonys, Arlindo dos Oito Baixos, Falamansa, and Rastapé.

Further Reading

Crook, Larry. *Brazilian Music: Northeastern Tradition and the Heartbeat of a Modern Nation.* Santa Barbara, CA: ABC-CLIO, 2005.

Fernandes, Adriana. "Music, Migrancy, and Modernity: A Study of Brazilian Forró." Ph.D. diss., University of Illinois at Urbana-Champaign, 2005.

Ramalho, Elba Braga. "Luiz Gonzaga: His Career and His Music." Ph.D. diss., University of Liverpool, 1997.

Adriana Fernandes

French Guiana

French Guiana is a South American country bordering the North Atlantic Ocean, between **Brazil** and Suriname. *Creoles,* who are descendants of freed slaves, make up the largest percentage of its total population, which is about 220,000 people. Nevertheless, the Maroon and Amerindian population represent a significant cultural demographic that has influenced French Guiana's popular music. The middle-class *Creole* population has, since the 19th century, imitated European musical models with the significant genres being music for ballroom orchestras and outdoor bands. Maroon-influenced music such as the drum-based Aleke has grown from a regional style of folkloric music to a popular music style that has gone beyond the borders of French Guiana to festivals of Aleke music in Suriname and the Netherlands. Kaseko music from Suriname is popular in French Guyana and is believed to have first evolved out of *Bigi Pokoe,* which was a style from the 1930s played by large brass bands during festivals and strongly influenced by Dixieland **jazz**. Nowadays the ensembles include electric **guitars** and keyboards with influences from abroad such as **calypso** and rock 'n' roll.

Further Reading

Bilby, Kenneth. "'Aleke': New Music and New Identities in the Guianas." *Latin American Music Review / Revista de Música Latinoamericana* 22, no. 1 (2001): 31–47.

George Torres

Frevo

Frevo is a syncopated genre of music and an improvisatory style of dance closely associated with marching band participation in **Carnival** celebrations from Pernambuco, **Brazil**. An expressive form of urban vernacular culture, its roots lie in the second half of the 19th century among multiracial walking clubs (*clubes pedestres*) comprising working-class Carnival revelers in Pernambuco's capital city of Recife. In the early 20th century, the *frevo* became Pernambuco's premiere Carnival music and a regional cultural marker of the multiracial mixture in the northeastern state. During the 1930s, the *frevo* entered national consciousness in Brazil via the country's nascent recording and broadcast industry centered in Rio de Janeiro. It reached its peak of national popularity in the 1940s and 1950s.

Early History of *Frevo*

The first written record of the term *frevo* (likely a slang expression derived from *ferver,* meaning to boil over) appeared in the Recife newspaper *Jornal Pequeno* (1907) in a Carnival club's advertisement that announced a march titled "O frevo." The term quickly captured local imagination regarding the social exuberance of Carnival in Recife and the effervescence of its music and dance. Journalist Osvaldo de Almeida—writing under the pen name "Pierrot"—helped popularize the term through his Carnival column in the *Jornal Pequeno.*

During the late 19th century, a hybrid musical repertoire was developing among military bands in Pernambuco that was used to accompany Carnival celebrations, including the parading of working-class clubs. Band repertoire drew from cosmopolitan social dances (***tango***, waltz, **polka**), military marches, and from a common inventory of songs that revelers sang in the streets during Carnival. Mixtures of polkas and marches led to the hybrid designation *marcha-frevo.* This was a syncopated march in fast tempo featuring two short sections of 8-16 measures in length, each repeated. By the early 20th century, wind, brass, and percussion ensembles called *fanfarras* (fanfares) featuring *requintas* (small b-flat clarinets), trumpets, trombones, and a percussion core of *tarol* (snare), **surdo** (bass drum), and **pandeiro** (tambourine) became the standard accompaniment for the Carnival *frevo*. Bandleaders composed and arranged the two-part form for the brass and wind instruments of their fanfares over which experienced *requinta* players improvised melodic variations. The percussion accompaniment developed syncopated cadences and performance styles that were passed on in oral tradition. These musical dimensions of *frevo* developed in close relation to the participatory esthetics of parading revelers and interactions with *capoeira* (Afro-Brazilian martial-arts dance) groups that accompanied marching band parades. *Fanfarras* also played lyrical selections called *marchas carnavalescas* (Carnival marches), which mixed instrumental sections with songs sung by adoring Carnival crowds. Like the instrumental *frevo,* the *marcha carnavalesca* developed syncopated rhythmic elements in conjunction with dancing participants.

By the 1920s, middle-class revelers in Recife began forming Carnival associations known as *blocos carnavalescos* (Carnival Blocs). The musical repertoire of these groups mixed popular genres such as **samba**, *tango,* and Carnival marches with local traditions of lyrical serenading and Christmas-time *pastoril* tradition typically sung by young girls. In contrast to the loud and rhythmically hard-hitting nature of the fanfares, *blocos carnavalescos* favored softer ensembles called *orquestras de pau e corda* (orchestras of wood and string) that included guitars, **flutes**, mandolins, violins, banjos, and *pandeiros.* The male-oriented *pau e corda* ensembles provided accompaniment to female singing groups (*corais feminos*) that were intergenerational in nature comprising relatives and close friends. Several nationally known popular music composers (Raul and Edgard Moraes, Nelson Ferreira) from Recife participated in the *blocos carnavalescos* and wrote marches, *sambas,* and *tangos* for the *blocos,* which were published in sheet music form and later recorded. The *marcha de bloco* (*bloco* march) became the favored genre among these groups. Its characteristics included a slow tempo, a mildly syncopated rhythmic accompaniment, use of minor keys and simple modulations, and highly sentimental lyrics. The *marcha de bloco* included a verse/refrain format with a recurring instrumental interlude before each subsequent verse. During the late 1950s, this form of composition would acquire the label *frevo de bloco,* after the national commercial success of Nelson Ferreira's "Evocação No. 1."

Nationalizing the *Frevo*

In the 1930s, the *frevo* entered Brazil's national recording and broadcast industry located in Rio de Janeiro with songs and instrumental pieces composed by musicians from Pernambuco. These were published under a variety of genre designations:

marcha nortista (northern march), *marcha pernambucana* (Pernambuco march), and *frevo pernambucano* (Pernambuco *frevo*). By the end of the 1930s, two distinct subgenres of recorded *frevo* were: *frevo* (an orchestrated instrumental *frevo* following the basic two-part plan of Pernambuco's Carnival *frevo*) and the *frevo-canção* (an orchestrated *frevo* with an instrumental section followed by a solo song). From 1933 to 1938, Os Diabos do Ceu led by **Pixinguinha** (Alfredo da Rocha Viana Filho) recorded eight instrumental *frevos* while the *frevo-canção* was being recorded by some of Brazil's most popular vocalists of the time, including Mário Reis, Aracy de Almeida, and Francisco Alves. While the composers were largely from Recife, the recording arrangements and performances were by Rio de Janeiro-based musicians. Major *frevo* composers included Capiba (Lourenço da Fonseca Barbosa) and the Irmãos Valença (João Vítor do Rego Valença and Raul do Rego Valença).

Rio de Janeiro's dominant position in the production of *frevos* prompted calls in Recife for a musical infrastructure to support the local production of *frevos*. Officially sponsored competitions for *frevo* songs and instrumental pieces in the Recife area stimulated new compositions that were arranged by the bandleaders of local radio orchestras. From 1931 through the mid-1960s, Nelson Ferreira led the PRA-8 orchestra of the Rádio Club de Pernambuco and, in 1952, Discos Rozenblit opened its doors in Recife and established the local record label Mocambo where *frevos* and other local musical genres were prioritized. The first recording released by Mocambo (1953) featured a *frevo* by Nelson Ferreira titled "Come e Dorme" on side one and a *frevo-canção* by José Menezes and Ademar Paiva titled "Boneca" on side two. Both recordings featured the PRA-8 orchestra under the direction of Nelson Ferreira.

The 1950s and 1960s witnessed the codification of the *frevo* into three main commercial subgenres: *frevo-de-rua* (instrumental *frevo*), *frevo-canção* (song *frevo*), and the *frevo de bloco* (marcha carnavalesca). A new generation of composer-bandleaders of *frevo* included José Menezes, Duda (José Ursino da Silva), Guedes Peixoto, and Clovis Perreira. Claudionor Germano and Expedito Baracho were important *frevo* singers from Recife.

In the 1970s, several failed attempts to market *frevo* to younger generations resulted in the decline of Discos Rozenblit and its eventual closing in 1980. New efforts were undertaken to revitalize the tradition by bringing the music in line with modern recording and production values associated with Brazilian rock and **MPB**. Some of Brazil's most popular singers of the era including **Gilberto Gil**, Caetano Veloso, and Alceu Valença were contracted to cover *frevos canções* for the Asas da America recording series launched by CBS/Sony Music. Rejected by *frevo* traditionalists and not widely popular among rock and MPB audiences, such endeavors were short lived.

Most recently, some post Mangue Beat musicians in Recife have drawn on the *frevo* for continued inspiration. Chief among the latest developments is the group Spok Frevo Orquestra led by saxophonist Spok (Inaldo Cavalcanti). This group has infused new life into the *frevo* tradition by emphasizing tight formal arrangements, expanded harmonic resources, and improvisatory performance practices reminiscent of the role of the *requinta* players of an earlier era.

Further Reading

Crook, Larry. *Brazilian Music: Northeastern Traditions and the Heartbeat of a Modern Nation*. Santa Barbara, CA: ABC-CLIO, 2005.

McGowan, Chris, and Ricardo Pessanha. *The Brazilian Sound: Samba, Bossa Nova, ad the Popular Music of Brazil.* Revised and expanded edition. Philadelphia, PA: Temple University Press, 2009.

Larry Crook

G

Gaga. *See* Afro-Dominican Fusion Music.

Grever, María

María Grever (1885–1951) was a prolific composer and singer. Accomplished as a pianist, violinist, and singer, she published her first song, "A una ola," when she was 18. It sold three million copies. Grever, **Mexico's** first famous female composer, wrote between 200 and 500 romantic songs into which she incorporated folk rhythms and elements of Mexican and Spanish style *tango*. She worked with American lyricists to translate her songs into English. Enrico Caruso helped bring her songs international popularity. Grever's songs were broadcast frequently on the radio, and she wrote music for many films and Broadway musicals including the 1944 film *Bathing Beauty* and the 1941 musical *Viva O'Brien*. Her popularity peaked in the 1930s and 1940s. Her most popular songs include "Bésame," "Make Love with a Guitar," "My First, My Last, My Only," and her biggest hits, "Ti-pi-tin" (performed by Benny Goodman) and "Cuando Vuelva a Tu Lado," or "What a Difference a Day Made" (performed by Vikki Carr, Trios Los Panchos, Frank Sinatra, Dinah Washington, and many others).

Further Reading

Malspina, Ann. "Maria Grever." In Diane Telgen, and Jim Kamp, eds., *Notable Hispanic American Women,* 184–86. Detroit: Gale Research, 1993.

Rebecca Stuhr

Gender in Latin American Popular Music

The study of gender within the context of Latin American popular music considers the ways in which the people of Latin America interpret their roles as men and women using music as one form of expression. Gender, the cultural, social, and historical interpretation of the biological and physiological state of being male or female, is undoubtedly an important part of the construction of both personal and cultural identity along with other factors such as age, race, and sexuality. Recent studies have pointed to gender as a learned phenomenon that is socially and culturally imposed, which makes it difficult to define in concrete terms. As a result, gender is a variable field of study that has altered over time and taken on different meanings in different cultural contexts. In studying the importance of gender in the context of Latin American popular music, scholars have used a variety of methodological approaches including textual analysis, evaluations of the production, consumption, and reception of popular songs, and studies of the separate gender roles for men and women musicians.

Gender, in Latin America, is derived in part using two important concepts: *machismo* and *marianismo*. In Spanish, the word *machismo* is used broadly to define masculine traits, cutting through class lines to describe the generosity, dignity, and honor expected of men from all social positions. But *machismo* also has wide-ranging connotations, and has even been interpreted as dominating and chauvinistic. *Marianismo* is the female counterpart to *machismo* that is used to describe the ideal of femininity and a veneration of female virtues such as purity and moral strength. Because many Latin American countries are deeply immersed in Catholicism, the role of women, termed *marianismo,* is often linked to the maternal figure of the Virgin Mary. Traditionally, domesticity is highly respected in Latin America and while men are concerned with the public sphere, women dominate the private sphere of the household. Even though urbanization, modernity, and political revolutions have challenged traditional sex roles, the gendered expectations represented by *machismo* and *maranismo* are so inherent in Latin American culture that their vestiges still remain an important part of understanding gender in both the Latin American and popular music contexts.

As a central means of expression, music is one of the many ways that Latin Americans have wrestled with issues relating to traditional and modern gender roles. With music, Latin Americans have reinforced the social constructions of gender and sexuality that they cannot discuss directly due to social taboos and mores. But music does not just passively reflect society, it also provides a public forum for models of gender organization to be affirmed, tested, or challenged. Popular music, often found as an outgrowth of mass culture in large urban centers, is especially susceptible to volatile changes as the boundaries between traditional and modern sex roles clash. By examining different aspects of Latin American popular music including its texts, reception, and sex roles, scholars have gained a better understanding of the role that music plays in the critical analysis of gender identity in Latin America.

Textual analysis is one important way that musicologists conceptualize the role that gender plays in Latin American popular music. Scholars are especially concerned with the ways in which gendered language in song texts create stereotypes that intersect with other social and historical factors. For example, Frances Aparicio discusses women as absence through the lens of the texts of **boleros**. The image of the lost, or fallen woman, known as *perdida* in Spanish, is prevalent in *boleros* and alludes to the abandonment of the domestic sphere as women began to work outside the home a result of the industrialization and urbanization of the turn of the century. To Aparicio, *boleros* are an alternative discourse on masculinity that have allowed men to be open, raw, and emotional while still attempting to retain their dominance and control over women. María Herrera-Sobek considers the Mexican **corrido** in order to make larger claims about Latin American popular music. Through literary analysis of the lyrics of the *corrido,* Herrera-Sobek identifies five types of recurring images, or archetypes, of women: the good mother, the terrible mother, the mother goddess, the lover, and the soldier. She sees these archetypes, which tie the role of women to motherhood, as a product of not only the patriarchal system inherent in the Latin American notions of *machismo* and *marianismo,* but also the class consciousness and widespread worldviews found in Mexican society. John Murphy links his textual analysis of **samba** lyrics with issues of work and money that appear prominently in *samba* songs from the 1920s to the 1950s. While these musicologists primarily consider song texts, other scholars have approached gender issues in popular music by considering its reception or by examining the sex roles of male and female musicians.

The reception of songs and the opinions of the consumers who actively use and enjoy the music is a telling and often overlooked aspect of popular music. Peter Manuel studies the ways in which Latina women help to produce meaning through the plurality of their responses to popular songs, specifically those that are overtly misogynistic. He describes how some of these women find misogynistic lyrics to be offensive, while others feel that even sexually explicit songs give women the opportunity to express their sexuality on their own terms on the dance floor. Brenda Berrian considers the different ways in which male and female performers are marketed in the French Caribbean. She finds that as a result of the struggling recording industry, women feel more intense pressure than men to conform to preset molds that often exploit their female sexuality to sell their music. In addition, Berrian studies how French Caribbean musical groups such as Kassav and Zouk Machine perform for and market themselves differently at home than they do abroad by changing the lyrics and length of their songs. These reception studies of Latin American popular music coupled with close textual analysis lead other scholars to consider the fixed gender roles that are found in Latin American popular music.

Scholars have begun to highlight the often clearly delineated gender boundaries for the roles of women and men as musicians performing Latin American popular music. While there are exceptions, the different roads for inclusion taken by male and female musicians are often clearly marked. Susan Thomas raises questions about these gender barriers in her study on the Cuban *nueva trova* movement, which she found to be dominated almost entirely by men. Through interviews with both male and female *trovadores,* Thomas uncovered the stigmas associated with including women in the genre. For example, female *trovadoras* were often thought to be lesbian, they could rarely perform outside of Cuba, and their music was often dismissed as children's music. Thomas linked these stigmas to historical factors especially the extreme homophobia, institutionalized repression of sexual deviance, and strong emphasis placed on the ideals of *machismo* found in Cuba after the 1959 Cuban Revolution. The Mexican *ranchera* is another example of a genre that has been long associated with men. Women performing within this genre are limited to singing and even such a well-known female *ranchera* as Lucero has chosen to adopt the *traje de chorro,* the cowboy outfit of a man. Through analysis of the constrained worlds of male and female performers, some scholars have come to understand gender roles within the Latin American popular music context.

Gender is no less complex when applied to Latin American popular music than it is in any other field of study. The approaches to its study touched on here, while representative of the methodologies used by musicologists and scholars within the broader academic study of gender, are by no means an exhaustive sampling. Nevertheless, influential scholars have illuminated aspects of gender within Latin American popular music through the methods of textual analysis, reception, and gender role studies.

Further Reading

Aparicio, Frances R. *Listening To Salsa: Gender, Latin Popular Music, And Puerto Rican Cultures.* Hanover, NH: University Press of New England, 1998.

Berrian, Brenda F. *Awakening Spaces: French Caribbean Popular Songs, Music, And Culture.* Chicago: University of Chicago Press, 2000.

Herrera-Sobek, María. *The Mexican Corrido: A Feminist Analysis.* Bloomington: Indiana University Press, 1990.

Manuel, Peter. "Gender Politics in Caribbean Popular Music: Consumer Perspectives And Academic Interpretation." *Popular Music and Society* 22, no. 2 (1998): 11–29.

Manuel, Peter, Kenneth M. Bilby, and Michael Largey. *Caribbean Currents: Caribbean Music From Rumba To Reggae.* Philadelphia: Temple University Press, 2006.

Murphy, John P. *Music in Brazil: Experiencing Music, Expressing Culture.* New York: Oxford University Press, 2006.

Thomas, Susan. "Did Nobody Pass The Girls The Guitar? Queer Appropriations in Contemporary Cuban Popular Song." *Journal of Popular Music Studies* 18, no. 2 (2006): 124–42.

Whiteley, Sheila. *Women and Popular Music: Sexuality, Identity, and Subjectivity.* London: Routledge, 2000.

Tracy McFarlan

Gran orquesta. *See* Orquesta.

Guadeloupe. *See* Martinique and Guadeloupe.

Guaguancó

Guaguancó is the most common form of ***rumba*** and often synonymous with the word *rumba* itself. *Guaguancó* appeared in Matanzas and Havana, **Cuba**, during the final decades of the 19th century. Some say it was born from the *rumba yambú*, played on ***cajónes*** (box drums), though it is now usually played on ***tumbadoras***.

As a dance, *guaguancó* is a pantomimic sexual pursuit between a man and woman. As they dance, tension builds since the man will inevitably attempt a *vacunao* (a pelvic thrust) or other sexually symbolic movement that the woman playfully rejects.

The musical form of a *guaguancó* is characterized by an introduction of nonsense syllables called the *diana*. It is sung by a soloist and explores the scale tones before transitioning to the *inspiración* (canto), often with Spanish ***décima*** poetic structure and simple harmonization. The final section (known as ***estribillo, montuno***, or ***coro***) is usually done in a faster tempo, uses leader group alternation singing, and features the dancers along with quinto drum improvisation.

Popular music often references *guaguancó* by using the characteristic melody of the *tumbadoras* and the ***clave*** or *guagua* pattern. The drum melody does not usually align with *clave* in traditional ***rumba***, but in some popular versions it does. Examples include "Quimbara" by **Celia Cruz** or "Mi Guaguanco" by Mongo Santamaria. Los Van Van regularly uses *guaguancó,* as in the piece "Consuelate Como Yo."

Further Reading

Sublette, Ned. *Cuba and Its Music: From the First Drums to the Mambo*. Chicago: Chicago Review Press, 2004.

Nolan Warden

Guajeo

In Cuban popular music, a *guajeo* is a repeated, often syncopated, two-bar or four-bar phrase played by a melodic instrument and it functions as an accompanimental ostinato, which interlocks with the ***clave***. The musical function of the *guajeo* is twofold: it both punctuates the rhythm by lining up with the *clave* and outlines the harmony by emphasizing the chord note members through a temporal distribution over the said measures. The earliest *guajeos* originated from patterns played on plucked string instruments, like the *tres*, but over time they were incorporated into the holding patterns of other instruments, most notably the piano, where the latter adopted patterns that were derived directly from the *tres*. The term is thus synonymous with the term **montuno**. Within different instrumental combinations, different instruments or groups of instruments may be assigned the *guajeo*. In the early **son** recordings by *sextetos* and **septetos** *de son,* the *guajeo* is played by the *tres*. In the context of **charanga** orchestras, the violins will play the repeated pattern, and in the fabric of the **gran orquesta**, the pattern may be given to the saxophones in harmony. The *guajeo* originated in folkloric styles like the **guajira**, but through its appropriation into more popular styles, it has become the backbone of harmonic patterns used in piano styles for **salsa** and **Latin jazz**.

Further Reading

Mauleon, Rebecca. *The Salsa Guidebook.* New York: Sher Music Co., 1993.

George Torres

Guajira

The *guajira* is a genre of **Cuban** popular song whose stylistic roots originated from the broader complex of *musica guajira* or country or peasant music, which was cultivated among the *campesinos* (farmers or rural peasants) in the Cuban countryside. Early *guajiras* were written in a 6/8 and 3/4 meter that resulted in a **sesquiáltera** rhythm. The sung texts were frequently about the rural countryside and sung in rhymed **décima** stanzas. By the late 19th century a newer style of Urban theater or salon *guajira* was developed by Jorge Anckermann. The texts, written by urban composers, provided a romanticized view of country life, and this newer style of *guajira* used a bipartite structure (minor-key first half, followed by a major-key second half) that would influence subsequent *guajira* composers. By the 1930s the *guajira* was merged with the dance-oriented, duple-meter **son** to create a hybrid known as the *guajira-son*. This style, sometimes known as *guajira de salón,* was made extremely popular by artists such Guillermo Portabales and Ramón Veloz. The most iconic of Cuban popular songs, *Guantanamera*, is a *guajira-son*. Most *guajira-sons* revolve around one chord progression, often I-IV-V in major, or a variation around descending Phrygian tetrachord in the minor, i-bVII-VI-V.

Further Reading

Manuel, Peter. "The 'Guajira' between Cuba and Spain: A Study in Continuity and Change." *Latin American Music Review* 25, no. 2 (2004): 137–62.

George Torres

Guaracha

The *guaracha* is a Cuban musical genre of singing and dancing loosely associated with the origins of dancism (esthetics related to dance and its derivations) of the 19th century, with some types of songs and with an intergeneric character, due to the mixture of genres and styles.

A large part of the bibliography on *guaracha* recognizes its Hispanic roots and attributed qualities to be sung and danced. Some sources suggest its presence in **Cuba** since the 16th or 18th century, in the brothels and bars of the Havana harbor. Another hypothesis sets its origin in Spain during the 18th century under the form of Andalusian tap dancing, but the most well-recognized dates go back to the early 19th century and some suggest it emerged in the blackface theater of the 19th century.

Guarachas were originally performed in urban festivities including serenades, krewes, and routes. In ballrooms, pieces of *guaracha* were sung over the melody of the **contradanza**, which were composed from old *guarachas*. Diaries from the independent wars of the 19th century referred to the existence of camp *guaracha* and *guaracha* is also found in the **trova** anthology of the country. It was an essential element of comedy and blackface theater, where it replaced the *jacaras* or picaresque songs inserted in *tonadillas, sainetes,* and *entremeses* from the golden century of Spanish theater represented in Cuba.

Up until the 19th century, some *guarachas* could be very close to dancism or song depending on the lyrical performance approach. The strong presence of basic rhythmic-accented patterns (**cinquillo, tresillo**, or the *habaneroso* model) defined the stage *guaracha* as the synthesis of some species converging in Cuba during the age of blackface theater, especially **son, danzon**, and **bolero**. Theater *guaracha* was originally conceived in 6/8 meter and later the binary meter was regularized and standardized. Other times, rhythmic combinations took place (6/8 or 3/4, with 2/4 beat measures) in an unregulated order, which resulted in more dynamic contrasts of rhythm. Its height of popularity came after the second half of the 19th century, when *guaracha* brought together a number of elements already present in the genre including its popular character, humorous and ironic language, and song. The *guaracha* was performed by popular characters of blackface theater such as the *negrito* or little black boy, the *mulatta,* or the Galician. The lyrics of the *guaracha* usually had a humorous, ironic, or satirical tone, with the use of stylistic devices such as mispronounced words, wordplays, allegories, personification, and double entendre to mask topics such as sex and politics that were historically censored.

As *son* became popular in the first decades of the 20th century, *trova* became a second branch of *guaracha* perpetuating a pattern of *guaracha-son* with the addition of **montuno**. *Guaracha* was performed by septets and groups and favored a dancing *guaracha*. The generic type of *guaracha-son* assumes a faster tempo and the lyrics are more humorous and picaresque than in *son*, while the **rasgueado** of the accompanying guitar seems closer to tanguillo style performed by trios and other string-based ensembles. Miguel Matamoros, Ñico Saquito, and the duet Los Compadres established new styles of *guarachas* in the 20th century as did Faustino Oramas, also known as "El guayabero," and Pedro Luis Ferrer.

Further Reading

Robbins, James. "The Cuban 'Son' as Form, Genre, and Symbol." *Latin American Music Review/Revista de Música Latinoamericana* 11, no. 2 (1990): 182–200.

Roy, Maya. *Cuban Music: From Son and Rumba to the Buena Vista Social Club and Timba Cubana.* Princeton: Markus Wiener Publishers, 2002.

Sublette, Ned. *Cuba and Its Music: From the First Drums to the Mambo.* Chicago: Chicago Review Press, 2004.

Neris González and Liliana Casanella

Guataca. *See* Cencerro.

Guatemala

Guatemala is a Central American country with an indigenous community of Mayan peoples that comprises more than half of the native population. The traditional music of Guatemala derives from the two distinct cultures of the country: the *Ladino* tradition and the Mayan culture.

The *Ladino,* or Spanish-speaking population (*Creole*), is mainly concentrated in urban areas along the southern coast and the eastern lowlands. Their music demonstrates a strong Hispanic influence and incorporates Latin American and American styles. The main instrument of Guatemala is the **marimba**, a popular folk instrument of African origin. The *marimba* is used for festive dancing, procession, and dance drums. The *marimba sencilla* was formed with the addition of *cajones armonicos,* or wooden box resonators. The keyboard of the *marimba* was enlarged to reach six-and-a-half octaves on the chromatic *marimba grande.* The *marimba de tecomates,* although less widely used than previously, is still sometimes played as a solo instrument, and together with the *chirimía,* the *xul,* and the *tamborón.*

The most popular musical style is the **son guatemalteco** (*son chapín*), which is the national dance of Guatemala. *Son guatemalteco* is played by *marimba* ensembles of 6- to 12-string instruments, *guitarillas* (**tiples**), and **maracas**. The music is comprised of a **son** rhythm with **zapateado**, or stamping, like the Spanish *flamenco.* The stanzas contain four octosyllabic lines, and the music is characterized by triadic harmony and 6/8 meter. *Son guatemalteco* and popular music form part of the *marimba* repertoire. **Corridos** are also enjoyed in many parts of Guatemala, played by 6- to 12-string **guitars**, *guitarilla*, **arpa**, and *marimba*. The songs are similar to the *corridos* of **Mexico**, and the subject matter is often topical and narrative in nature. Other frequently played styles include *canciones* **rancheras** and **huapangos**, in addition to **vals**, **marcha**, and international genres.

Garífuna musicians, part of the black Caribbean population who are descended from the Arawak and Carib Indians and African slaves, live mainly on the Caribbean coast. Their traditional music ensemble consists of the *garaón*, a wooden membranophone, *sísira*, the spiked gourd rattle, and occasionally the *weiwintu*, a conch-shell trumpet, but many variations exist, which include the electric guitar, electric bass, **batería, congas**, and sometimes a trumpet. Ensembles frequently perform *puntas, parrandas,* and **calypsos**. Additionally, *Garífuna* musicians play **reggae** and **rock** music, and combine rock with traditional rhythms to form *punta rock*.

Popular genres with elements of local or traditional styles such as *corridos,* **pasillos, son, vals**, along with other Spanish American genres may be heard in upper-class homes in Guatemala. Other popular styles today include the fox-trot, *mazurka* (or *ranchera*), the *pasodoble,* the **polka**, and the **schottische**. Since the 1920s, African rhythms like **danza (habanera), merengue**, and **samba** have also been enjoyed in the country. International styles are currently popular in urban areas, as they are played in nightclubs, restaurants, and hotels for tourists and city-dwelling *Ladinos*.

The Guatemalan rock group Alux Nahual created a different type of music than the typical Latin American band, one that was not based on Afro-Caribbean rhythmic patterns. After the advent of *disco-móviles* in the 1970s, music from the **United States** was widely available, prompting many Guatemalan groups to stop copying American styles and find a niche playing tropical music, notably the *merengue*. Social unrest in the 1970s and 1980s made it difficult for bands to survive, as concerts were sometimes interrupted by the police who searched and sometimes arrested members of the audience. Alux Nahual was sometimes criticized because the group did not play tropical music nor fall neatly into the category of **rock en español**, but the band provided an important link between pop and rock in Central America. The highpoint of the group's international recognition came in 1995 when they played a sold-out show in the Los Angeles Palace. Ricardo Arjona, a Guatemalan pop singer, has also gained popularity in recent years, as well as two Grammy Awards, the 2006 Latin Grammy for Best Male Pop Vocal Album and Best Latin Pop Album in 2007.

Further Reading

Cortes, Alfonso Arrivillaga. "La Musica Tradicional Garifuna En Guatemala." *Latin American Music Review (Revista de Música Latinoamericana)* 11, no. 2 (1990): 251–80.

Garfias, Robert. "The Marimba of Mexico and Central America." *Latin American Music Review (Revista de Música Latinoamericana)* 4, no. 2 (1983): 203–28.

O'Brien, Linda L. "Marimbas of Guatemala: the African Connection." *World of Music* 25, no. 2 (1982): 99–104.

Pacini Hernandez, Deborah, Héctor D. Fernández l'Hoeste, and Eric Zolov. *Rockin' Las Américas: The Global Politics of Rock in Latino America.* Pittsburgh: University of Pittsburgh Press, 2004.

Schechter, John Mendell. *Music in Latin American Culture: Regional Traditions.* New York: Schirmer Books, 1999.

Caitlin Lowery

Güira. *See* Güiro.

Güiro

The *güira* and *güiro* are the names given to a range of Latin American percussion instruments of the scraper variety. *Güiros* are cylindrical notched idiophones that are made in many different sizes, but most are roughly about a foot in length and about four to five inches in diameter. Notches or perforations run along one side of the instrument, and these indentations are scraped with either a wooden stick (*pua*) or a small metal comb.

Güiros come in several varieties found in many parts of Latin America, with distinctive types coming most notably from **Cuba, Puerto Rico**, and the **Dominican Republic**. The Cuban and Puerto Rican types are made from a gourd (*güiro*) and have notched ridges. Both of these types have two holes on the nonridged side of the instrument that the player uses to hold the instrument. The Dominican type is traditionally made from a sheet of metal, which is perforated using a small nail with small indentations. There may be hundreds of these indentations in one *güiro*. The sheet is rolled outward so that the perforations protrude from the instrument's surface, and it is then finally rolled into a cylinder.

The *güiro* is found throughout Latin America and is used in both rural and urban popular music. It is also known as *calabazo, guayo, güícharo ralladera, rascador,* and *rayo.*

Further Reading
Mauleón, Rebeca. *Salsa Guidebook for Piano and Ensemble.* Petaluma, CA: Sher Music Co., 1993.

Orovio, Helio. *Cuban Music from A to Z.* Durham, NC: Duke University Press, 2004.

George Torres

Guitar

The guitar and guitar-type instruments in Latin America consist of many regional varieties, which are based on European models that came to the Americas during the colonial period. Many forms of popular music rely on the traditional European guitar of Spanish origin, but many other forms make extensive use of regional varieties that have retained their unique folk-like quality within the realm of popular music. After some 500 years of development, and with the addition of electronic instruments, the sound of guitar-type instruments remains the heart and soul of Latin American popular music.

The early history of the guitar in Latin America begins with the cultural encounter that occurred when Spaniards invaded Mesoamerica in the early 16th century. Early chronicles in the 16th century attest to the popularity of *vihuela* (an early forerunner to the guitar), and the guitar in **Mexico**. By the end of the 16th century, accounts of guitars in South America document the widespread appropriation of plucked stringed instruments from Spain and Portugal. While the standard guitar of its day was favored by elites among the more urban centers, in the provinces and rural areas guitars were being adopted by the native population and refashioned to suit the tastes, needs, and resources of each region. As a result, many variants of guitars were adapted by the local cultures. The continued developments in instrument construction, technique, and repertoire have left us a legacy of rich and varied traditions.

Because of the many varieties of instruments, the following will only discuss a few of the most popular in order to give a sense of the variety of types found in Latin America. These local instruments may be either single strung or they can have sets of strings, or courses, which are intended to be fingered and plucked simultaneously.

The *charango* comes from the mountainous regions of **Ecuador, Bolivia**, and **Peru**. It is one of the most characteristically Latin American-looking instruments. Traditionally the body (the back and sides of a guitar) is made from the shell of an armadillo, and so the size of the instrument will depend on the size of the animal shell. The instrument consists of five nylon-string courses tuned reentrantly from lowest to highest, g-c-e-a-e. The instrument is used in ensembles, but has also developed a solo tradition for the performance of traditional Andean repertoire. The *charango* is played with the fingers of the right hand and has a developed system of *rasgueado* strumming.

The *tiple* is the national instrument of **Colombia**. It is also played in some parts of **Venezuela** and **Argentina**. Its design resembles that of a standard Spanish guitar, but with a slightly shorter string length. There are four sets of steel, tripled strings tuned from lowest to highest d-g-b-d, as in the top four strings of the guitar. Along with the *bandola*, the *tiple* is often used to accompany the *bambuco*. The instrument is played with a pick.

The Mexican *mariachi vihuela* is a five-stringed guitar used in the *mariachi* ensembles, which originated in the western part of Mexico. Prior to the spread of *mariachi* music as Mexico's national music, the *vihuela* did not leave the region. From the front view, the instrument resembles a smaller Spanish guitar. From the side, the instrument has a slightly rounded back that has a curved spine. The instrument is tuned from lowest to highest a-d-g-b-e, with a reentrant tuning in the first and second strings. It is normally strummed and thus serves a harmonic function in the ensemble, utilizing a sophisticated lexicon of *rasgueados,* or *redobles.*

The standard Spanish guitar has remained a common instrument for popular music, and it is found all over Latin America in ensembles. It is almost always played with the fingers of the right hand in both harmonic and melodic contexts. The guitar was very important in the *bolero romántico, bossa nova, vieja trova, nueva trova,* and *nueva canción.* The early *tango* repertoire used the guitar as the primary accompanying instrument. Many Latin American composers who write or have written in the classical idiom have employed the performance practice techniques from the regional variety of guitars to the standard classical repertoire. Composers and performers such as Agustín Barrios and **Raul Garcia Zarate** gave the music in their performances a regional sound by incorporating regionally derived techniques and sounds into their repertoire.

The examples of guitar construction, technique, and repertoire show the great diversity of the use of plucked strings in Latin America. The parallel developments of the standard guitar and the regional varieties that were drawn from the Iberian prototypes show a kind of musical odyssey that instruments make take when leaving the hands of one culture and are then left to the local genius of the adopting culture. This has happened once again, following the advent of rock 'n' roll and rhythm and blues in the 1950s, with the electric guitar, which has found a place in Latin American popular music. The electric guitar has already had an influence on the performance of traditional instruments, as can be seen in the development of electric versions of *tres*, *charango,* and *tiple.*

Further Reading

Evans, Tom and Mary Anne Evans. "The Guitar in Latin America." *Guitars: Music, History, Construction and Players From the Renaissance to Rock,* 208–17. New York: Paddington Press, 1977.

Sheehy, Daniel, "Popular Mexican Musical Traditions." *Music in Latin American Culture: Regional Traditions,* edited by John Schechter, 34–79. New York: Schirmer Books, 1999.

Stover, Rico. *Latin American Guitar Guide.* Pacific: MO, Mel Bay Publications, 1995.

George Torres

Guitarra. *See* Guitar.

Guitarrón

The *guitarrón* is a very large, fretless, six-string acoustic bass played in Mexican *mariachi* music. It has a figure eight-shaped soundbox that has a convex back panel. The back and sides of the *guitarrón* are constructed of a lightweight wood like cedar, while the soundboard may be made of spruce, *tacote,* or *granadillo* wood. Although the *guitarrón* resembles a **guitar**, it evolved from the 16th-century Spanish *bajo de uña.* Versions of the *guitarrón* in the 19th century usually had four or five strings instead of six.

The *guitarrón* produces a low, sonorous sound that does not require electronic amplification. It is tuned A′–D–G–c–e–a, which keeps the pitch of the instrument in a lower range. The *guitarrón* strings are of a heavy gauge and are usually made of plastic or metal. To further increase volume and depth of sound, the musician uses a technique in which two strings are plucked simultaneously, either in octaves or unison.

Modern Mexican *mariachi* groups usually consist of at least two violins, one or two trumpets, occasionally a diatonic **harp**, a Spanish **guitar**, a *vihuela*, and a *guitarrón.* The guitar, *vihuela,* and *guitarrón* function collaboratively as the *armonia,* meaning rhythm section. Playing together in an interlocking style, these three instruments provide the rhythmic and harmonic backbone for the rest of the instruments. Although the *guitarrón* may play parts of the melody, it usually does so to support the harmony and rhythmic structure of the piece, rather than to play a complete melodic line.

Further Reading

Aparicio, Frances R. and Candida Frances Jáquez. *Musical Migrations: Transnationalism and Cultural Hybridity in Latin/o America.* New York: Palgrave Macmillan, 2003.

Erin Stapleton-Corcoran

Gwo ka (Gwoka)

Gwo ka refers to a kind of folkloric drum music from **Guadeloupe**, which was originally associated with *léwòz* performance, but later found itself appropriated by popular musicians as an emblem of national identity in the 1970s. The *léwòz* was an outdoor social celebration with music and dance that was originally performed after workers had received their pay. The music consisted of a leader group alternation style of singing accompanied by *gwo ka* drums and other percussion instruments. These hand drums normally consist of two different-sized drums: a low-pitched *boula,* and a higher-pitched *makyé.* In performance, one *makyé* improvises over a steady holding pattern supplied by any number of *boulas.* There are seven essential *gwo ka* rhythms, six of which are in binary rhythm. After having spent most of its history as an object of scorn by the dominant social groups (largely because of the low social status of the practitioners and the nonliterate tradition from which it originated), *gwo ka* drumming became an emblem for an emerging national identity. During the late 1960s, Guy Conquette was one of the first popular musicians to use *gwo ka* as a symbol of national pride. Gérard Locquel, a **jazz** musician whose group Gwo Ka Moden recorded several albums, incorporated a method of using *gwo ka* rhythms for other instruments. The arrival of *gwo ka* on the international level was completed with the work of the super group Kassav, whose first two albums made use of *gwo ka* drums and their rhythms, thus bringing this African derived, indigenous Antillean music to worldwide recognition.

Further Reading

Guilbault, Jocelyne. *Zouk: World Music in the West Indies.* Chicago: University of Chicago Press, 1993.

George Torres

Habanera

Originally a dance called *danza habanera,* it later became a style of music simply known as *habanera* that appeared in **Cuba** at the beginning of the 19th century. Written in a 2/4 meter like the *contradanza*, the *habanera* has an introduction that precedes a couple of sections of 16 measures and 4 phrases (AABB) each. The first section is minor and the second one is major. The most characteristic musical features of the *habanera* are these two contrasting sections and the persistent rhythmic pattern, which the *habanera* took from the *contradanza,* the so-called *tango* rhythm (dotted 8 note–16th note–two 8 notes), a rhythmic unit that became well-known outside of Cuba as a *habanera* rhythm. The syncopated rhythm of the Cuban *habanera* was later incorporated into the various American and European musical styles that were appearing at the moment such as ragtime, *Creole* songs in Cuba, the Argentinean *tango,* and the *flamenco tango.*

The *habanera* derived from the European *contredance* or **contradanza**, which was brought to Cuba by numerous Frenchmen immigrating from Louisiana and Haiti. Cubans then adapted the *contradanza* to match their musical taste and sensitivity. From the *contradanza* emerged a variety of danceable musical genres that flourished in the American salons including the *habanera.* By 1868, *contradanza* was already being incorporated into pieces by important composers such as Manuel Saumell (1817–1870) and Ignacio Cervantes (1847–1905). Records indicate that the first printed *habaneras*, then called *danzas habaneras*, appeared in Cuba in 1825. "El amor en el baile" is considered one of the first *habaneras* published in Cuba. Out of the *contradanza* and the *habanera*, several Cuban proper musical styles were born such as **danzón**, **danzonete**, *danzón mambo*, **cha-cha-chá**, and **pachanga**. While the *habanera* as a dance disappeared from Cuba in the second half of the 19th century, it still remains popular as a type of music.

The *habanera* was also brought to **Argentina** by sailors traveling between the Río de la Plata and the Caribbean. It took root during the 1860s and it was gradually transformed into the musical style called *milonga*, which is present in the Argentinean *tango*. As the *habanera* and the *milonga* were absorbed by the *tango* the combination was given a range of different names such as *habanera tangueada*. One of the most well-known *habaneras*, "Tú," by Sánchez de Fuentes appeared in Paris as a *tango-habanera*. It was the Cuban composer Sánchez Fuentes who, through his own *habaneras*, gave the genre an autonomy from the *tango* and a much more expressive freedom to the singing. Other well-known *habanera* composers include Sebastián Yradier y Salaverry (1809–1865), who was the author of the famous *habaneras* "La paloma" and "El arreglito" as well as Saint-Saen, Falla, Fauré, Sarasate, and Chabrier.

Further Reading

Betancur Álvarez, Fabio. *Sin clave y bongo no hay son: música afrocubana y confluencias musicales de Colombia y Cuba.* 2nd ed. Medellín, Colombia: Editorial Universal de Antioquia. Colección Interés General, 1999 (1st ed. 1993).

Gómez García, Zoila and Victoria Eli Rodríguez. *Música latinoamericana y caribeña.* La Habana: Editorial Pueblo y Educación, 1995.

Rivera, Jorge B. *Historia del tango. Sus orígenes.* Buenos Aires: Corregidor, 1976.

Salinas Rodríguez, and José Luis. *Jazz, flamenco, tango: las orillas de un ancho río.* Madrid: Editorial Catriel S.A., 1994.

Raquel Paraíso

Boukman Eksperyans

Boukman Eksperyans is a collective of musicians and dancers who play music that combines elements of traditional Haitian music with rock 'n' roll. The group's numerous members include six members of the *Beaubrun Lakou* (extended family group living communally). The first name of the group comes from a *Vodou* priest who was a catalyst of the revolution of 1804. The group's second name is the Haitian *Creole* equivalent of experience. The group emerged in the 1980s when *Vodou Adjae,* or *mizik rasin,* overtook the popular Haitian style *com pas.* The *rasin* style is a combination of *Vodou* ceremonial music, folk and rock 'n' roll elements. The Boukman Eksperyans sound incorporates dance music with elements of *Vodou,* **reggae**, **rock**, and Caribbean sounds. They gained popularity through the island's annual **Carnival** celebration. The group's message is one of political resistance and, as such, they have suffered censorship on their island home. The group's 1991 debut album, *Vodou Adjae,* was nominated for a Grammy. Throughout the 1990s the group released several more critically acclaimed albums and toured the world, producing music that supports and uplifts the Haitian people.

Further Reading

Largey, Michael D. *Vodou Nation: Haitian Art Music and Cultural Nationalism.* Chicago: University of Chicago Press, 2006.

David Moskowitz

Haiti

The popular music from the Republic of Haiti, which forms the western portion of the Caribbean Island of Hispaniola, has played a unique and influential role in popular music from the Caribbean. Its music, like its culture, comes from a mixture of African and European influences. From 1492, it was a Spanish colony, until it was ceded to the French in 1697, which governed the country until Haitian independence in 1804. Because of the large sugar industry established by the French, most of the island's inhabitants were slaves imported from Africa, which resulted in a social hierarchy of European, mixed race, and black populations. Even after independence, this sort of social stratification guided cultural tastes, which influenced the course of popular music in Haiti. Another important factor in Haiti's musical diversity is the creolization that developed among European and indigenous cultures, resulting in syncretic manifestations within cultural forms of expression such as Kreyol (the French *Creole* language) and Vodou (the syncretic religion of Haiti that mixes West Africana and Catholic practices). Musical hybrids that developed through the mixing of styles define much of Haiti's popular music evolution, as well as reciprocal transmissions with other countries in the Caribbean.

After Haitian independence, there began a mixing of social groups and classes, for which musically, resulted in a creolization of African and European musical styles. The earliest of these was the *contradanse,* which was originally an English dance imported to Haiti via France. The *contradanse* flourished, in variant forms, throughout the Caribbean, eventually establishing strong traditions in **Cuba** and **Puerto Rico**, as well as Haiti. A five-note musical figure called *quintolet* (*cinquillo* in the Spanish-speaking Caribbean) became a chief feature to the *contradanse* and would figure prominently in the *méringue*. From the mid-19th century to the mid-20th century, the *méringue* became a music and dance symbol of Haiti. The *méringue* was enjoyed equally among the working classes as well as refined social groups among Haiti's elite. Related to the *méringue* is the Martiniquan *biguine,* which was very popular in Haiti from the 1930s to the 1950s. While several variants of *biguine* were popular, the moderate tempo *biguine calssique* was most widespread. The *biguine* was popular among its supporters for its use of *Creole* French in its sung texts.

During the 1950s, *biguine* came under the influence of foreign repertories, including **jazz, calypso**, Haitian popular music, and Afro-Cuban music, and the *biguine* would eventually become appropriated by other genres that held significant influence in Haiti, most notably, **konpa**. *Konpa* is a style of Haitian music that developed in the 1950s and evolved into the 1980s through different manifestations, which include the genres of *konpa direk, kadans rampa,* and *mini djaz.* The genre would eventually become influential in the creation of **zouk** music. The genre derived from a type of Dominican *méringue* called *perico ripiao* or *Cibaeño*-style, which had become extremely popular in Haiti. Very important in the development of *konpa* was Nemours Jean-Baptiste. Nemours's altered *merengue* beat, which also included songs with *Creole* texts, helped to identify the new sound as utterly Haitian. Nemours's ensemble instrumentation consisted of vocals, accordion, bass, guitar, saxophones, trumpets, *tanbou* (a Haitian barrel drum), and a percussion section. Nemours's *konpa* was eventually dubbed *konpa direk* (direct or straight ahead rhythm). At roughly the same time, Weber Sicot developed his own variant of *konpa,* which he dubbed *kadans rampa* or rampart rhythm.

With the arrival of small-group rock bands that began to emerge in the 1960s, *konpa*-style ensembles began to favor a smaller guitar-based instrumentation. The new instrumentation (electric guitars, drum set, and one saxophone), combined with a new interpretation of *konpa,* provided a more relevant form of jazz-influenced dance music for 1960s Haitian youth. Tabou Combo was perhaps the most successful group to come out of this movement, not only in Haiti, but also among the Haitian diaspora in the United States and Paris, where in the latter, the group's hit "New York City" became a top seller for the band in 1975.

Mizik twoubadou is a different type of smaller, guitar-based genre that originated from the influences of Cuban *son* ensembles from the 1920s. With the influx of the newly developed transportable music medium of phonograph recordings, Haitian musicians began experimenting with Cuban song styles that used two **guitars, maracas**, and hand drums. The texts, sung in *Creole,* generally have romantic love and relationships as their theme. The contexts for music *twoubadou* are flexible, but they are most commonly heard in places where tourists gather (hotels, beaches, etc.), where the musicians may approach a small group who becomes the temporary audience, and who will provide a gratuity for the group's musical attention.

Influenced by the Jamaican roots rock movement ***reggae***, in the late 1970s and early 1980s there developed a genre of roots music called ***mizik rasin***, which borrowed elements from traditional Afro-Haitian music, including *rara* and Vodou, and incorporated them within popular music styles. The texts of the songs were also sung in *Creole,* and musicians would often incorporate instruments used in Vodou and *rara* celebrations. Important contributors of *mizik rasin* artists include **Boukman Eksperyans**, Foula, and Sanba-yo.

Haitian **hip-hop**, or *Kreyól* hip-hop, has developed in Haiti and abroad since the 1980s and mixes American-style hip-hop beats with Haitian popular styles, such as *konpa,* and uses lyrics sung in *Creole*. Artists such as Papa Jube and Original Rap Staff have enjoyed successful careers in Haiti and abroad. The most internationally successful Haitian artist to emerge from hip-hop is Wyclef Jean, who after enjoying success in the American group The Fugees, went on to be an influential solo artist whose career in the United States has had a strong influence on Haitian youth, and who has developed his musical style beyond hip-hop to include diverse styles and musical influences.

Further Reading

Averill, Gage. *A Day for the Hunter, a Day for the Prey: Popular Music and Power in Haiti.* Chicago studies in ethnomusicology. Chicago: University of Chicago Press, 1997.

Bilby, Kenneth M, Michael D. Largey, and Peter Manuel. *Caribbean Currents: Caribbean Music from Rumba to Reggae.* Philadelphia, PA: Temple University Press, 2006.

Fleurant, Gerdès. "Haiti." In *Music in Latin America and the Caribbean: An Encyclopedic History,* edited by Malena Kuss, 251–64. Austin: University of Texas Press, 2004.

Largey, Michael. "Haiti: Tracing the Steps of the Meringue and Contredanse." *Creolizing Contradance in the Caribbean,* 209–30. Philadelphia, PA: Temple University Press, 2009.

George Torres

Harp. *See* Arpa.

Hip-Hop

Latin American hip-hop, a recent addition to transnational Latin popular music (e.g., *salsa*, *merengue*, *samba*), has been influential as a subculture since the early 1980s, predominantly among dispossessed youth. Rapping has been incorporated into Cuban *salsa* and *timba*, and gave rise to fusions such as *reggaetón*, Dominican *merenrap,* Colombian *cumbia-rap,* and Brazilian *embolada-rap* and *samba-rap.*

Although hip-hop has come to be regarded as a black music, its Latin roots are too frequently overlooked. Born in New York's South Bronx neighborhood in the early 1970s, hip-hop's early vanguard—poorer African American and Puerto Rican youths—put aside gang enmity to initiate the artistic elements that have come to be associated with the world of hip-hop: spray-painted graffiti murals on subway trains and the fascia of overpasses, breakdancing (b-boying/b-girling, popping), MC-ing (rapping), and DJ-ing (scratching or sampling). Puerto rocks, Nuyorican youth involved in hip-hop's nascence, were innovators of the iconic graffiti and breakdancing of early hip-hop culture. Crazy Legs and the Rock Steady Crew, but one example of Latin hip-hoppers who rose to international prominence, were featured in hip-hop films *Wild-Style* (2002), *Breakin'* (2003) and *Beat Street* (2003).

Hip-hop vocabulary, attitudes, and fashions serve as important identity markers for many Latin American youth, especially in locales such as **Cuba** where the scarcity of spray cans and sound systems severely prevented the development of graffiti and DJ-ing. Similar to the **rock**, heavy metal and folk music genres that permeated Latin America markets, certain features of North American rap music and hip-hop culture have been adopted by Latin American *raperos/as* (rappers), while others have found little favor. Rap-recording labels are found in most metropolitan areas, where rap is also featured on radio stations and television shows. Vibrant Latin hip-hop scenes—Latin rap, chicano rap, or urban regional—can be found in Miami, New York, Los Angeles, and cities in the southwestern **United States**, and have led to the inclusion of Latin hip-hop as a category of the Latin Grammy Awards.

Stylistic Influences

The regional distinctiveness of the various forms of rap music in Latin America are often circumscribed by the use of local vernacular and popular genres as well as resident musical traditions and their instruments (e.g., *trés*, *guitarrón*, *conga*, and *batá*). Some Chilean rappers, for example, recycle *nueva canción* lyrics and samples and *rap cubano* cites nationalist poetry over samples of *timba, nueva trova*, *son*, and *rumba*. The first mainstream Spanish-language rapper, the Puerto Rican Vico C who was known for his 1989 hit "La Recta Final," incorporated Dominican *merengue* into New York hip-hop beats in the early 1990s. Brazilian, Venezuelan and Cuban rap artists are as likely to reference African-derived religious traditions such as *Candomblé* and *Santería* as they are Christianity.

Rap music has been effectively available in Latin America through the sale of commercial and pirated CDs since the 1990s. Major influences for early Latin American rappers include: Cypress Hill, a U.S. rap group featuring Spanish-speaking members Sen Dog and B-Real, Cuban American Mellow Man Ace (brother of Sen Dog), **Puerto Rico**'s Latin Empire and Vico C, Public Enemy, Salt n' Pepa and TLC (for Latina *raperas*), various North American political and Latino rappers, and *reggaetón* artists. Molotov and Caló, two early Mexican rap groups, were influenced by Chicano-American rapper Kid "El Jefe" Frost, whose 1990 album *Hispanic Causing Panic* promoted nationalist Chicano pride, the Caló dialect (Hispanicized American English), Pachuco esthetics, and the return of Aztlán.

The Advance of Hip-Hop in Latin America

As early as 1982, hip-hop emerged in the urban *barrios* (neighborhoods) of **Argentina, Brazil, Chile**, Cuba, **Colombia**, and **Venezuela**, which were often overcrowded and impoverished. North American hip-hop films and rap music, such as Sugarhill Gang's 1979 hit "Rapper's Delight," inspired small communities of Latin American youth to embrace hip-hop's new forms of artistic production. In Caracas, Perucho Conde remixed Sugarhill Gang's "Rapper's Delight" into "La Cotorra Criolla," while Kid "El Jefe" Frost spearheaded the *Sindicato Argentino del* Hip Hop (Argentine Hip Hop Syndicate) in Moron, a city west of Buenos Aires. In 1984, a lively hip-hop scene exploded in the *barrio* Las Cruces of Bogota, Colombia, with rap group La Etnnia and breakdancing-graffiti group, New Rapper Breaker. Colombian hip-hop then migrated to Cali, Medellín, and Baranquilla. By 1984, De Kiruza released the first Chilean rap album, and within four years, hip-hop was flourishing with rap groups such as Panteras Negras and Los Marginales.

By 1988, Cuban rap groups appeared in Alamar, a marginalized Havana suburb, after a popular breakdancing movement was formed in underground gatherings (*bonches*) in the earlier part of the decade. Brazil's hip-hop movement, born in São Paulo *favelas* (slums), emerged in the early 1980s, coinciding with the end of Brazil's brutal military dictatorship (1964–1985). Hip-hop had reached Rio de Janeiro by 1992 with Gabriel o Pensador's "Tô Feliz, Matei o Presidente" ("I'm Glad, I've Killed the President"), a rap song addressing the corruption scandals, resignation, and impeachment of former president Fernando Collor de Melo.

Both Havana and Caracas hosted their first rap festivals in 1995, the same year that hip-hop culture ostensibly materialized in **Uruguay** and Mexico City (before spreading to Guadalajara, Durango, and **Guadeloupe**). The presence of hip-hop could be felt throughout South and Central America by the late 1990s.

Hip-Hop Themes in Latin America

Latin American hip-hop culture and regional rap subgenres are often delineated on a continuum of commercial and underground styles and social themes. Rap lyrics are likely to address issues of identity, violence, racism, gang warfare, drug trade, social inequality, political marginalization, imperialism, globalization, poverty, marginalization, and homelessness, though with varying objectives. In Cuba, Argentina, Chile, and Brazil, *raperas* (female rappers) such as Mágia and Las Krudas (Cuba), and Cris (Somos Nós A Justiça, Brazil) use the medium to denounce sexism, machismo, and biological determinism. The rap lyrics of Tina, a São Paulo hip-hop, funk and R'n'B artist, promote an inspiring Christian message popular among young, Afro-Brazilian women.

Irrespective of stylistic distinctions, this music has empowered marginalized youth, providing a medium to address their disaffection. For this reason, Latin American hip-hop has been compared to the ***nueva canción*** movement of the 1960s. This is especially true in Chile, as well as Cuba. And, some Latin American hip-hop movements have gone on to attain state and nongovernmental support for their social activism. Near Calí, Colombia, the Aguablanca Cultural Network has provided a neutral space for 25 rap and breakdancing groups since 1994. In Cuba, *rap cubano* was formerly acknowledged by the State in 1998, constituting an unofficial dialogue with the government to address issues of racism, sexism, prostitution, and police violence (Fernandes and Stanyek 2007). In 2002, the Cuban government founded the Agencia Cubana de Rap (Cuban Rap Agency), a state-run recording studio, label and magazine devoted to hip-hop.

Many Latin American youth afflicted by urban decay and gun violence are drawn to North American gangsta rap music, in spite of its superficial and commercial character. The hit song "Diário de um Detento" ("A Convict's Diary"), by São Paulo rappers Racionais MC's, details a convict's daily routine in prison and sold the most copies of any independently released record in Brazil. The video, featuring clips from inside São Paulo's infamous Candiru prison, won MTV Brazil's Video of the Year award (1998). In countries like Cuba, however, gangsta rap is criticized for its violence and explicit American content.

Rap, like commercial *salsa,* tends to hypersexualize both men and women. Latin Rap's early mega-hits, "Rico-Suave" (1991) and "Mentirosa" (1989), explicitly detailed themes of womanizing and the stereotype of the scornful, lying woman, while early ***reggaetón*** delivered even more explicitly sexist lyrics: El General's "Tu Pum Pum" (1991), a notable example, made unambiguous references to women's buttocks. While some female rappers accept this sexualized image, other Latin American *raperas* demand an end to such treatment.

Due to the association between rap and African American culture, Latin American hip-hop has undoubtedly provided many Afro-Latins with a means to proudly endorse their African heritage. Like the Brazil's ***samba*** schools and ***blocos afros***, São Paulo's *Movimiento Hip-hop Organizado* (Hip-Hop Movement Organization) acts as an Afro-Brazilian community and educational center (Fernandes and Stanyek 2007). Since 1998, *rap cubano* has been involved with the annual Black August concerts. Inspired by North America's black power movement and icons such as Malcolm X, these concerts have encouraged an Africanized identity, which many rappers endorse through their lyrics or Africanesque sartorial flair. Conversely, numerous North American Latin rappers contest such overt African pronouncements, defending their own brown pride and tackling exclusion from the increasing dominance of African Americans in the hip-hop arena.

Further Reading

Chalfant, Henry, director. *From Mambo to Hip Hop: A South Bronx Tale.* 58 mins. DVD. 2006.

Diccionario de Hip-Hop y Rap Afrolatinos. Coordinated by Zona de Obras. Madrid: SGAE, 2002.

Fernandes, Sujatha and Jason Stanyek. "Hip-Hop and the Black Public Spheres in Cuba, Venezuela and Brazil." In *Beyond Slavery: The Multilayered Legacy of Africans in Latin America and the Caribbean,* edited by Darién J. Davis, 199–222. Lanham, MD: Rowman and Littlefield, 2007.

Forman, Murray and Mark Anthony Neal, eds. *That's the Joint: The Hip-Hop Studies Reader.* New York: Routledge, 2004.

Perkins, William Eric, ed. *Droppin' Science: Critical Essays on Rap Music and Hip Hop Culture.* Philadelphia: Temple University Press, 1996.

Talia Wooldridge

Honduras

Honduras is a Central American country with a population of about 8 million. Of the population, 90 percent is *mestizo* and 7 percent Amerindian. One of the more significant contributions to Honduras's music culture comes from this Amerindian population, out of the coastal culture of the Garifuna peoples who speak the Arawakan language.

In the realm of popular music, older traditions like the **marimba** ensembles found in **Guatemala, Nicaragua**, and southern **Mexico** are popular within the country, as are **guitar**-based performances of traditional styles such as the *corrido*. Honduran *punta* emerged in the late 1970s from a type of Garifuna music with strong Caribbean influences. Through the modernization of *punta* instrumentation and performance practice, many *punta bandas* emerged and acquired much success throughout Honduras. Most notable among these is Banda Blanca whose 1991 hit "Sopa de Caracol" ("Snail Soup") became an international success and earned the group an international following. The song is sung to a bilingual text with the verses in Arawakan and the chorus in Spanish. The group's instrumentation has modern *banda* influences consisting of several horns, keyboard and rhythm sections of electric bass, electric guitar, and drums.

Other significant forms of popular music demonstrate contemporary influences from popular music from other western influences such as the **United States**. Singer-songwriter Guillermo Anderson has become a popular singer abroad, yet many of his biggest successes reference his native homeland such as "En mi País" and "Mi Carguito," the former becoming a type of unofficial alternative national anthem for Hondurans. **Rock** bands have also become very popular in Honduras and several have gained an international reputation among Spanish-speaking audiences with groups like Diablos Negros and Khaoticos. Currently *reggaetón* enjoys popularity among younger audiences with artists like Ragamoffin Killas experiencing an international reputation.

Further Reading

Greene, Oliver N., Jr. "Ethnicity, Modernity, and Retention in the Garifuna Punta." *Black Music Research Journal* 22, no. 2 (2002): 189–216.

George Torres

Huapango

The *huapango* is a *son*-based, traditional Mexican family of related musics from Northeast Mexico, blending elements of folk and indigenous musical practice, and developing into distinct regional varieties, including the highland *arribeño* trio style and the *norteño* dance. All musical forms of the *huapango* feature falsetto singing alternating with violin passagework, improvisation, and complex **sesquial-tera** rhythmic patterns alternating patterns of 3/4 and 6/8, and sometimes inserting phrases in 2/4. This regional style is unique for the number of verses sung (often improvised) and the large repertory of songs in minor keys.

1. The *huapango típico* or *huapango mariachi* is more commonly known as the *son huasteco.* This is one of the seven principal kinds of *son,* from the north-eastern subtropical region of Mexico known as the Huasteca, near the Gulf of Mexico (see: **son huasteco**).

2. The folk or classic *huapango* can be found in northern Veracruz and Puebla, southern Tamaulipas, and eastern San Luis Potosí, Hildalgo, and Queretaro. It is associated with festivals of indigenous peoples such as the Totonacs and displays indigenous styles (most notably, the use of falsetto vocals). The Huastecan language, still spoken today, belongs to the Yaxu branch of the Totonac-Mayan family.

The *huapango* dance is performed on a wooden platform, accompanied by a trio of musicians (*trio huasteca*). *Huapango* couples dance is saturated with complicated foot stomping called *zapateado* (from *zapato,* meaning shoe), which softens during sung verses. Except for modern Tamaulipas, Huastecan female dancers wear the pre-Columbian garments called the *cueitl* (Nahautl for wrapped skirt, sometimes covered with an apron), *petob* (headpiece), and *quetchquémitl* (top covering, pronounced keskemet, called *dhayem* in Tenek, the modern language of Huastecos). In states where the indigenous element is stronger, the *cueitl* is embroidered to match the *quetchquémitl.* Theatrical dance costuming for men consists of a *guaya-bera* and palm hat, carried in the right hand.

The name developed from the Náhuatl *huapali* (wood) and the locative fragment *–co* (in or on); many trios still perform in indigenous languages. A common Nahautl *huapango,* sung at traditional ceremonies (including weddings) is "Xochipizáhuatl," which praises both the Virgin of Guadalupe (Mexico's patron saint) and the Aztec goddess Tonantzin. Spanish huapangos, such as in "*El querreque,*" are improvised both at festivals and in bars traditionally restricted to men.

The music for this is called *huapango huasteco,* and it is usually performed on a violin, a *jarana huasteca* (small five-stringed Mexican guitar tuned in a ninth chord), and a *huapanguera* (*guitarra quinta*), a deep-bodied Mexican guitar with a larger resonator and eight strings (five courses of two single and three double strings); this trio ensemble is sometimes preserved within larger ensembles, such as *mariachi* groups, when they choose to reference the *huapango* style. *Huapanguera* bass parts can include drones, melodic counterpoint to the violin, and glissandos. Two singers alternate humorous semi-improvised *coplas.*

3. Three indigenous groups known collectively as the Otopame occupy the east-central part of Mexico: the Pame, Chichimec, and Otomí. String music is played throughout this whole region, and they share the most complex of the *mestizo* chordophone musics: the *haupango arribeño.*

Highland *huapango* (*huapango arribeño*) is an indigenous form: texts range from current events to bravura displays of improvised folk poetry lasting up to six hours.

The Pame preserve the traditional ensemble: two violins and a standard six-stringed guitar (*guitarra sexta*). The Chichimec have a more recent and *mestizo*-influenced arrangement of instruments: *guitarra huapanguera,* two violins, and a Jalisco-style *vihuela* (a small round-backed guitar). These usually accompany Spanish literary genres (secular and sacred), such as poems in couplets (*coplas*) and 10-line stanzas (*décimas,* performed only by the Pame), and songs and instrumental music for deceased infants and children (*angelitos,* little angels).

Décimas are performed in two ways: as recited poetry or as a *valona,* a quatrain glossed by four stanzas, each of which ends with the respective line of the quatrain, and the whole is sung in a recitative, like a *salmodia.* This style relates to Otopame ritual practices documented during the colonial period. Contemporary *huapango arribeño* practitioners call themselves *compañeros del destino* and have expanded across the U.S.-Mexico border, enhancing the folk repertory of *tejano* communities. *Décimas* are performed during folk dances called *topadas* (buttings), musical duels that can last all night while listeners dance to the rhythms of the *jarabe,* the *poésia,* the *son,* and the *valona.*

4. *Huapango tamaulipeco (haupango norteño)* is a fast dance in 6/8. This dance style and rhythm is typical of prerevolutionary *conjunto norteño* ensembles, consisting of accordian, bajo sexto, double bass, drums, and saxophone, with violinists sometimes improvising between verses. It is also one of the main indigenous Mexican forms to be incorporated into *música tejana* (Texas-Mexican music): although the repertoire of the *tejano conjunto* consisted principally of salon music dances like the polka, schottishe, and mazurka, the incorporation of the regional *huapango tamaulipeco* strengthened the music's ethnic identity and balanced the repertoire.

Further Reading

Carter Muñoz, K. "Que siga el huapango! Reclaiming the Décima and Political Commentary in Son Huasteca and Arribeño and 'La-Leva's' Re-signification in Mexican Rock." Thesis, University of Washington, 2006.

Chávez-Esqiuvel, A. "Compañeros del destino: Transborder Social Lives and Huapango Arribeño at the Interstices of Postmodernity." Thesis, University of Texas at Austin, 2010.

Haynes, N. "The Huapango of the Huasteca Tamaulipeca." Thesis, University of Texas at Austin, 1983.

Hernández Ochoa, Arturo. *20 Años de la Fiesta Annual del Huapango: Amatlán, una Fiesta que nunca Termina: Encuentro de las Huastecas.* Amatlán, Veracruz: Patronato Pro Huapango y Cultura Huasteca, 2009.

Lozano, M. "Usos politicos y sociales del huapango: Pánuco, Veracruz, 1940–1964: incluye un CD con huapangos." Thesis, San Luis Ptosí, 2003.

Martínez Hernández, Rosendo. *Fiesta en la Huasteca: una Mirada a la Huapangueada, los Sones, la Poesía y las Danzes Tradicionales de mi Tierra.* México: R. Martínez Hernández, 2005.

Strachwitz, Chris. *Music of Mexico, Vol. 3: La Huasteca; Huapangos y Sones Huastecos Los Caimanes y Los Caporales de Panuco.* El Cerrito, CA: Arhoolie Records CD431, 1995.

Laura Stanfield Prichard

Huayno

The *huayno* is a popular song and dance form indigenous to the Andean region of **Peru**. It features a fast and upbeat duple meter. Traditional ensembles involve Western and native instruments such as violin, trombone, **charango**, and **quena**. *Huayno* compositions combine instrumental sections with strophes sung in Spanish or Quechua (Peruvian native language). Lyrics encompass themes of love, economic struggle, and bucolic remembrance of the highlands landscape. Melodic phrases utilize pentatonic scales and are usually fluid and embellished, with a preference for high pitches and brilliant timbres. Forms frequently emphasize binary structures, presenting a harmonic movement from a major section to a relative minor section or vice versa. Occasionally, a faster and celebratory coda—also known as *fuga*—is introduced to provide closure. As a dance, *huayno* comprises the interaction between male and female couples. Such couple-centered choreography relates to the ancient indigenous notion of *yanantin,* or complementary duality, which has played a preponderant role in shaping Andean social values and cultural milieus through history.

The *huayno* emerged in Peru as a manifestation of an ongoing process of *mestizaje.* This process compounds a syncretism of ethnic and cultural elements that derive from Amerindian and western cultures. Contrary to an exoticist view of *huayno* as living patrimony of the Incan Empire, the genre is in actuality not more than 400 years old. Even though scholars have argued that *huayno* was originally a funeral dance with little popularity among pre-Hispanic communities, its most salient characteristics were crystallized during colonial times and henceforth.

A Peruvian ensemble plays a traditional *huayno*. (AP/Wide World Photos)

Historically, *huayno* has experienced multiple changes in standard instrumentation and compositional procedures as well as other areas; much of this change has resulted from the use and adaptation of European instruments and esthetic priorities. String instruments such as the ***charango*** and the *arpa indigena* were derived from the **guitar** and **harp**, becoming extremely popular. The Spanish language was incorporated into song lyrics and the use of raised sevenths, or leading tones. These alterations led to an expansion of the genre's expressive capabilities. In that sense, the performance of *huayno* served as a vehicle for an increasing participation of indigenous and *mestizo* groups at a national level, enfolding a survival strategy for the Andean community within the ongoing process of cultural amalgamation.

After 1950, the genre started to grow in popularity. Several commercial recordings were made and distributed via radio and eventually other mass media. Artists such as Pastorcita Huaracina and Jilguero del Huascaran became icons of Andean nationhood, bringing working-class audiences music that reflected the sharp consciousness of the social and economic issues that oppressed indigenous groups. Peruvian upper classes—which previously had rejected Andean music as boisterous and primitive—slowly started to accept *huayno* as one tangible voice within the nation's multifaceted identity. In light of its power to attract rural and indigenous listeners, the genre also became popular in **Bolivia, Argentina**, and

Chile. Groups such as Inti-Illimani and Quilapayun from Chile proposed a fusion of *huayno* with popular Latin American rhythms, promoting, in this way, a pan-Latino consciousness. In Argentina, songwriter **Atahualpa Yupanqui** and singer Mercedes Sosa borrowed *huayno* instrumentation and sonorities to develop a contemporary language that appealed to the local sensibility. Their goal was to reformulate *huayno* in order to spread a message against the inequalities afflicting indigenous communities.

In the 1970s and 1980s, *huayno* served as a point of departure for the creation of styles that reflected Peruvian movement toward integration. While the process of *mestizaje* was still painful, indigenous populations managed to solidify their cultural presence through the development of a genre that merged *huayno*'s traditional elements with more contemporary styles such as **cumbia** and rock. The emergence of a *Peruvian tropicalism*—rooted both in a rich indigenous past and in the flow of transnational influences—was a key element in the reinforcement of the Andean identity. Born in the context of migratory movements that took entire communities from the highlands to the coastal city of Lima, *Peruvian tropicalism* included styles such as Andean *cumbia* and **chicha**, which rapidly captivated the masses.

The popularity of the *chicha* surpassed all other native musical forms in Peru. It combined *huayno* elements—e.g., melodic phrases, inner pulse, preference for brilliant tonality—with *cumbia*'s danceable duple syncopations. Part of *chicha*'s success relied on the use of Afro-Caribbean percussion instruments, the electric guitar, and the bass. These instruments conferred a sense of pride and modernity to the *mestizo* and disenfranchised audiences. Ensembles such as Chacalon y La Nueva Crema and Los Shapis appeared in massive concerts at which Lima's immigrant working-class had the chance to dance and socialize. *Chicha* concerts led thereafter to the formation of a new type of sociocultural dynamic in the country.

In the 1990s and 2000s, a new incarnation of *huayno* once again achieved popularity without precedent. Techno-*cumbia,* a hybrid form that fuses electronic dance music, *cumbia,* and *huayno,* took the country by surprise when singer Rossy War's single "Nunca pense llorar" broke records for sales across the nation. This time, however, the popularity reached the middle and upper classes. From that point on, *huayno* and its multiple intersections have remained an expression that embodies central aspects of the Amerindian and Peruvian *mestizo* population.

Further Reading

Romero, Raul R. *Debating the Past: Music, Memory, and Identity in the Andes.* New York: Oxford University Press, 2001.

Turino, Thomas. *Music in the Andes: Experiencing Music, Expressing Culture.* New York: Oxford University Press, 2008.

Carlos Odria

Hybridity and Cultural Syncretism

The enormous diversity and complexity of Latin American music is derived from cultural processes that in many cases have endured for half a millennium. Key among these is syncretism, a process of mutual influence and adaptation among different cultural traditions. In a syncretic fusion, two or more cultures meld and combine to form a new culture, drawing from—but wholly distinct from—its sources. This process is naturally smoother when the source cultures hold common facets. Most Latin American cultures typically draw from a combination of three distinct sources: European, African and Native American, with occasional less-pronounced influences from India, the Middle East, China, Japan, and others. The extent and nature of these combinations differed dramatically throughout the Americas and were affected by myriad factors such as climate, language, religion, geographical terrain, socioeconomic factors, and historical developments, as well as any number of unique localized factors.

The three principal root cultures were themselves not monolithic and homogenous. The South and Central American continents prior to 1492 were home to thousands of different groups whose diversity was as widespread as its geographical landscape, with levels of development that ranged from hunter-gatherer tribes to agrarian societies and to powerful civilizations, including prominently the Aztecs, Maya, and Incas. These civilizations drew freely from conquered lands and trading partners, and represented the syncretic fusion of hundreds of civilizations that emerged on the American continent starting around 3000 BCE. Knowledge acquired over millennia—of an agricultural technique or the construction of a particular instrument, for example—was seldom lost but instead passed on to succeeding cultures. As a result, pre-Columbian cultures often shared similar traditions including healing ceremonies, relationships with nature and animals, worship of totems and deities, rituals dedicated to the agricultural cycle, and contact with—or protection from—the supernatural.

The European source cultures were also enormously varied, with contributions not only from Spain but also Portugal, England, France, the Netherlands, and other countries. Moreover, each country often had various internal factors that made up its cultural influence. Notably, Spain at the time of the Conquest had inherited a syncretic mixture of Moorish, Gypsy, and Sephardic Jewish influences, as well as elements from the various regions of the Iberian peninsula such as Galicia, Castile, and Andalusia. Each of these, and many others, affected in varying degrees the emergence of Latin American culture and music.

African cultures were also not homogenous, and their influence on New World culture reflected this diversity. African slaves originated from both West Africa (in modern Senegal, Guinea, Ivory Coast, Ghana, Togo, Benin, and Nigeria) and

Central Africa (in modern Gabon, Congo, Angola, Zambia, Zimbabwe, and Mozambique). They seldom spoke the same language, and belonged to various—often enemy—ethnic and cultural groups, including prominently the Bantu, Ewe, Ashanti, Fon, Ibo, Yoruba, and Mandinga. Moreover, Africans faced different challenges in different places, as colonial powers differed greatly in their tolerance of African culture, religion, instruments, and musical practices. These differences combined with the various cultural characteristics of the Africans themselves, resulting in cultural traditions that were extremely diverse.

Perhaps the most important factor in the development of Latin American society was that the predominantly male European colonists seldom brought their families with them, which very quickly led to a forced mixing of European, African, and American populations. In time, *mestizo* (a mixture of European and Native) and *Creole* (European and African) cultures came to dominate many regions of Latin America, though they too developed in profoundly diverse ways. Other important factors were the economic potential of a particular territory and the availability of a workforce, which in turn was affected by the relative prevalence of European diseases. In **Mexico** and **Peru**, disease decimated but did not completely annihilate the Native populations, negating the necessity to bring large numbers of African slaves to these areas. Conversely, many Caribbean islands saw the complete extinction of the Native inhabitants. African and Native cultures were thus not felt uniformly across the continent, greatly affecting the syncretic dynamic.

Yet another factor was the religious syncretism that permeated the continent. Catholicism (and to a lesser extent Protestant denominations) provided the overarching blueprint for the continent's religious identity, which then absorbed, to varying degrees, elements from African and Native beliefs, as well as scattered elements of Islam, Judaism, Hinduism, and other faiths.

Colonial church and civil authorities realized early on that the most efficient way of achieving their goals was to incorporate existing Native elements into the transplanted European culture, creating a completely new entity. One strategy was to build churches and cathedrals on the same sites as the old temples, to provide a sense of religious continuity. Since music had been an important part of Native religious ceremonies, the Church emphasized it in Catholic services, to make the new converts feel at home in the new religion. Soon, much of the Native population accepted the new faith, though the priests were less successful in eradicating the old system of beliefs. Native celebrations, feasts, and processions were surreptitiously adapted to the Christian faith and held away from the watchful eyes of priests and church officials. Idols would find their way onto altars, hidden under crosses or stashed away in church walls. As a result, Native religions endured, at first alongside (but separate from) Christianity, and increasingly in a mixture of interconnected Christian and Native beliefs that adapted to the specific needs of the populace.

Meanwhile, African religions were emerging wherever African slaves were present in the Americas, providing them with a sense of identity and spiritual continuity. These included Cuban *Santeria,* Haitian Vodou, Jamaican Obeah, and Kumina (as well as the more recent Rastafarian movement), Brazilian Candomblé, and hundreds of other less-famous traditions throughout the continent. Most of these religions are a combination of Christian and African (and sometimes Native) beliefs, and were often based on communications with ancestral spirits (e.g., *orishas* in *Santeria, lwas* in Vodou) that dwelled in the African continent and that provided spiritual help and practical advice. To shield these activities from the disapproving eyes of the authorities, the ancestral spirits were merged with Catholic saints and hidden under a Christian veneer. Over time, the two deities—and the two faiths—came to be intermingled and fused together to produce hybrid religions and cultures.

The fusion of European, Native, African, *mestizo,* and *Creole* characteristics quickly distinguished Latin American cultures from its sources, and in time the continent became less of a European cultural outpost and acquired its own character and identity. From these syncretic cultures emerged most of the classical, folk, and popular music of Latin America (as well as the art, architecture, literature, etc.). European ballroom dances (such as the *minuete, jota, malagueña, seguidilla,* **contradanza**, *waltz,* **polka**, and *mazurka*) emerged from high-society salons and became popular dances, performed in rural settings, now infused with Native or African rhythms and instrumentation, but also retaining European dance steps such as the **zapateado** and the *zarandeo.* Thus, the Martinican *quadrille* was a dance of the 18th century French salons, typically accompanied by small orchestras made up of slaves or former slaves. After the ball, the musicians would perform the music at their own get-togethers, melding it with their Afro-Caribbean drumming traditions. In time, this *kwadril* became one of the source components of the popular **zouk** of recent years.

European instruments such as the **guitar** and the **harp** became prevalent throughout the continent, embraced by various ethnic groups. Many soon became hybridized, yielding new variations that had been unknown in Europe (e.g., the Peruvian **charango** and the **jarana** from Veracruz), with corresponding tuning systems, performance techniques and composition ideals. The harp, brought to the Americas by Jesuit missionaries, took hold in many *mestizo* and Native cultures, most prominently the Mexican *arpa jarocha,* the Venezuelan *arpa llanera* and the *arpa paraguaya.*

Similarly, African instruments (drums, **marimbas**, and thumb-pianos) and practices (complex syncopated rhythms, call-and-response singing, ritual dancing) were often adopted by other ethnic groups, while African Americans almost invariably embraced European and Native instruments, forms and styles, and combined them with their own. Yet mixing African and European music did not automatically yield a generic result, as can be attested by the marked differences between Brazilian *samba*, Cuban *rumba*, Jamaican *reggae*, and Dixieland **jazz**. Some syncretic processes derive from unusual sources, the result of unique historical factors. Thus, Trinidadian chutney combines African rhythms with East Indian melodies and instruments, while the music of the Central American Garífuna combines African and Native elements with virtually no European contributions.

Syncretism manifested itself in the continent's art music as well, including prominently in the colonial **villancico** *guineo* and *mestizo e indio,* which purported to represent African and Native culture. While 19th-century art music (particularly opera) often attempted to include ethnic elements, these were usually stylized versions of European trends. Conversely, the nationalist movements in the 20th century did successfully combine European art music with Native, African, *mestizo,* and *Creole* folk music, including prominently in the works of Chávez, Ginastera, and Villa-Lobos. One began finding in the concert hall the **tangos**, *sambas*, **sones**, and rumbas that had previously been the domain of the village, the *barrio,* the nightclub or the Carnival parade.

The syncretic process redoubled in the second half of the 20th century, with continuous cross-pollination aided by increased migration, recording and transmission technology, and mass commercialization. British and American rock influenced styles such as Brazilian **tropicália** and Argentine *rock nacional*. The Colombian **cumbia** was adopted and transformed by numerous traditions, from the Mexican borderlands to Argentina. Styles such as **salsa**, **soca**, *reggae, samba,* and dozens of others emerged from local and national contexts to become hemispheric and even global phenomena. In the process, they continually influenced each other, producing limitless combinations of syncretic styles. Yet paradoxically, the same period also saw the increased homogenization of Latin America's music. The forces of globalization and modernization transformed and re-created countless styles outside of their original context, usually in some commercial venue. As Latin American music became an important contributor to the so-called world music phenomenon, it often adopted a pop orientation, colored by aural uniformity, mass media dissemination, Western influences and essentially the same rock 'n' roll instrumentation: electric guitars, bass, synthesizers, and drum sets. The meaning of the music in terms of its function and social representation was altered by this transformation, and in the process, much of the individuality that engendered it was lost.

Further Reading

Clark, Walter A. "Preface: What Makes Latin American Music 'Latin'? Some Personal Reflections." *Musical Quarterly* 92, no. 3/4, Latin American Music (Fall–Winter 2009): 167–76.

Davis, Martha Ellen. " 'Bi-Musicality' in the Cultural Configurations of the Caribbean," *Black Music Research Journal* 14, no. 2 (Autumn 1994): 145–60.

Floyd Jr., Samuel A. "Black Music in the Circum-Caribbean," *American Music*, 17, no. 1 (Spring 1999): 1–38.

Guilbault, Jocelyne. "Créolité and the New Cultural Politics of Difference in Popular Music of the French West Indies," *Black Music Research Journal*, 14, no. 2 (Autumn 1994): 161–78.

Hill, Donald R. "West African and Haitian Influences on the Ritual and Popular Music of Carriacou, Trinidad, and Cuba," *Black Music Research Journal*, 18, no. 1/2 (Spring–Autumn 1998): pp. 183–201.

Jong, Nanette de. "An Anatomy of Creolization: Curaçao and the Antillean Waltz," *Latin American Music Review*, 24, no. 2 (Autumn–Winter 2003): 233–51.

Martin, Denis-Constant. "Filiation of Innovation? Some Hypotheses to Overcome the Dilemma of Afro-American Music's Origins," *Black Music Research Journal*, 11, no. 1 (Spring 1991): 19–38.

Quintero, Angel G., and Roberto Márquez Rivera. "Migration and Worldview in Salsa Music," *Latin American Music Review*, 24, no. 2 (Autumn–Winter 2003): 210–32.

Shepherd, John A. "A Theoretical Model for the Sociomusicological Analysis of Popular Music," *Popular Music*, 2 (1982): 145–47.

Wade, Peter. "African Diaspora and Colombian Popular Music in the Twentieth Century," *Black Music Research Journal*, 28, no. 2 (Fall 2008): 41–56.

Waterman, R. A. " 'Hot' Rhythm in Negro Music," *Journal of the American Musicological Society* 1 (1948): 24–37.

Mark Brill

Immigrant Music

The number of first-generation immigrants and their descendants living in the **United States** has burgeoned since the liberal American immigration reform of 1965. In 2010, an estimated 55 million people (or 17 percent of the total national population) classified themselves in one of the specific Hispanic or Latino categories (Mexican, Puerto Rican, or Cuban). Destinations for immigrants broadened in recent decades and sizeable Latino immigrant communities have now settled in virtually every American state. A United States Census Bureau report foresees the national Hispanic and Latino population rising to 30 percent by 2050. Accordingly, Latin American and Latin music will increase their already significant impact on the American soundscape in the 21st century.

Americanized interpretations of Cuban dance music from ***danzón*** and ***rumba*** to ***mambo*** and ***cha-cha-chá*** filled American dance halls from the 1930s to the 1950s. Argentine ***tango*** and Brazilian ***bossa nova*** gained popularity among mainstream audiences while Mexican ***mariachi*** and other *folklórico* ensembles are widely known to a national public. But Latin American music has also been a considerable outside influence on popular music styles of the United States such as **jazz** (or more recently rap), and numerous bandleaders and musicians of Caribbean and Latin American heritage have shaped various musical scenes, particularly in the larger urban centers. While immigrants brought their regional music genres with them to the United States such as ***bachata***, ***vallenato***, or ***banda***, for example, some genres developed as a result of collaborations among musicians of different national origins. ***Salsa***, for instance, is considered one of the most dynamic and significant pan-American musical phenomena of the 1970s and 1980s. Incorporating multiple styles nurtured by Cuban and Puerto Rican immigrant musicians to New York City, it quickly became a favorite dance music among all Latino communities in the United States as well as in the Caribbean and Latin America. ***Reggaetón***, which emerged in the late 1990s as a blend of Jamaican music influences of ***reggae*** and dancehall with Puerto Rican genres and the Boricua/Latino-centric rap scene in New York City, took the younger Latino generations by storm.

The large metropolitan areas on both the East and West Coast, but increasingly also in the Midwest, constitute a fertile ground for musical innovation. Immigration-heavy cities have given birth to numerous transnational popular music phenomena. *Technobanda* and its associated *quebradita* dance style, for example, spread in the late 1980s from Guadalajara, Jalisco, to Los Angeles, California, where it gained great popularity among immigrants as well as American youths of Mexican heritage. In the early 21st century, *pasito duranguense* ("the little step from Durango," a state in northwestern **Mexico**) originated in Chicago as a fusion of Mexican *banda, norteño* and *grupero* music, while the dance steps were borrowed from the Mexican American *quebradita* and Dominican **merengue**. *Duranguense*'s phenomenal rise of popularity reflects the growing importance of Latino immigrants and their own music styles. Despite the fact that the American news media tends to advertise Latin pop stars who sing in English rather than immigrant music, regional Mexican music accounted for more than half of all Latin music sales in the United States, according to a 2001 report of the Recording Industry Association of America. In the summer of 2004, various *duranguense* groups claimed almost one-half of the spots on Billboard's Top 25 Latin Albums chart.

Visibility through National Awards and the Media

Although many genres performed, listened, and danced to by Caribbean and Latin American immigrants stay within the confines of their own communities, the more commercially oriented music styles are made accessible to a national audience through the media. The music industry has contributed to an increased awareness by creating awards such as the Billboard Latin Music Awards that grew out of the Billboard Music Awards program from *Billboard Magazine*, an industry publication charting the sales and radio airplay success of musical recordings. Nine years after the awards' inauguration in 1990, the awards ceremony was broadcast on the television network Telemundo, the second largest Spanish-language media company in the United States, and it since has become the network's highest-rated music special. Recognizing the most popular Latin music on the charts, the Billboard Latin Music Awards features top solo performers and Latin groups vying for honors in such categories as pop, **rock**, tropical, Mexican regional music, and *reggaetón*. In 2000, the National Academy of Recording Arts and Sciences designated seven categories of the Grammy Awards for Latin music performance: Latin pop, **Latin rock**/alternative, traditional tropical Latin, *salsa, merengue,* Mexican American, and *tejano*. Meanwhile, all major recording labels have Latin divisions. Among the most successful Latin labels in the United States are Disa, Fonovisa, Sony Music Latin, and Universal Music Latino.

Assimilation versus Multiculturalism

Latin Americans, like other groups of immigrants, assimilated in varying degrees to the American way of life. The 1960s to 1970s Mexican American rhythm and blues and **rock** bands from East Los Angeles adapted musical styles representative of the American mainstream rather than developing any particular, regional musical style as, for example, the Texan Mexican musicians did with *conjunto* and *orquesta*. While the musical replenishment from south of the border has had a major impact on Mexican American musical production and consumption, several Latin American music genres were brought to the United States via **Mexico**: the *mambo* was introduced by Mexico City–based bandleader **Pérez Prado** and a Mexican version of the *bolero* was popularized by Los Panchos and other *bolero* trios in the 1940s and 1950s. Mexicans, not Colombians, brought *cumbia* to the United States and when Colombian immigration began to surge in the 1990s, it was *vallenato,* not *cumbia* that enjoyed the status as a quintessential symbol of Colombian identity. Today it is Mexican immigrants, not Colombians, who numerically constitute the largest proportion of *cumbia* fans in the United States. While some of the *cumbia* listened to by Mexicans is still produced in **Colombia**, most of it is produced by Mexican *norteño* bands in Mexico as well as in the United States.

The rapid growth and popularity of Latin immigrant music since the 1990s has been spurred by a change in American immigration policy: while assimilation had been its main goal before the 1980s, the celebration of multiculturalism in the 1990s has encouraged people of different heritage to reaffirm and bolster their ethnicity and to express their cultural loyalty with their home country. Moreover, improvements in technology, communications, transportation, as well as interpretations of citizenship by governments have created a new form of transnationalism. Modern technologies such as electronic and digital communication are now readily accessible for a larger part of the population of the Western hemisphere. As a result, immigrants are more intensely involved in the social, economic, political, and cultural life of both home and host societies. Transnational circulation of music genres between Latin America and the United States has increased and many Latin genres today are products of this cultural exchange.

Further Reading

Aparicio, Frances and Cándida Jáquez. *Musical Migrations: Transnationalism and Cultural Hybridity in Latina/o America.* New York: Palgrave Macmillan, 2003.

Loza, Steven. *Barrio Rhythm: Mexican American Music in Los Angeles.* Urbana: University of Illinois Press, 1993.

Pacini Hernandez, Deborah. *Oye Como Va! Hybridity and Identity in Latino Popular Music.* Philadelphia, PA: Temple University Press, 2010.

Ragland, Cathy. *Música Norteña: Mexican Migrants Creating a Nation between Nations.* Philadelphia, PA: Temple University Press, 2009.

Rivera, Raquel Z., Wayne Marshall, and Deborah Pacini Hernandez. *Reggaetón.* Durham, NC: Duke University Press, 2009.

Roberts, John Storm. *The Latin Tinge: The Influence of Latin American Music in the United States.* New York: Oxford University Press, 1979.

Simonett, Helena. *Banda: Mexican Musical Life across Borders.* Middletown, CT: Wesleyan University Press, 2001.

Washburne, Christopher. *Sounding Salsa: Performing Latin Music in New York City.* Philadelphia, PA: Temple University Press, 2008.

Helena Simonett

J

Jarabe

Jarabe is the national dance of **Mexico**, with several sections in contrasting meters. Several regional variations exist and are named after. It began as one element of a *son*-based traditional Mexican musical genre, and by 1900 had expanded into a series of regional *sones* or *canciones* linked together in one composition.

The Spanish word *jarabe* (meaning syrup) referred to a Mexican dance as early as 1789, when "El *Jarabe* Gatuno" was condemned by Inquisition authorities on moral grounds. On July 9, 1790, a *jarabe* performance took place at the Mexico City Coliseum and the dance was banned by the Viceroy soon after. In the early 1800s, the *jarabe* was still a single, short dance, often included in *sones*. Scholar R. Stevenson documented that all allusions to the *jarabe* were "clearly disparaging" prior to the period of independence (1810–21). Its identity as part of an oppressed *mestizo* culture catapulted it to prominence as Mexican insurgents won independence from Spain in 1821: *jarabes* were honored as symbols of mexicanidad. Alfred Robinson described alta california society in 1829 in his *Life in California before the Conquest* (San Francisco, 1925): he emphasized the *jarabe* and the recently introduced waltz as symbols of the weakening hegemony of the Spanish.

By 1900, the *jarabe* developed into one multisection composition; this was most prevalent in the west-central states of Colima, Durango, Jalisco, Michocán, and Nyarit. Typically, a *jarabe* will begin in 6/8, be followed by other sections in 3/4 or 2/4, return to 6/8, and end in another meter. The 6/8 meter is a constant pattern with no contratiempos or sesquialtera (6/8, 3/4) juxtaposition of accents as in the *son jaliscience*. They were played by brass bands (bandas del pueblo) in bandstands (quioscos) set up in town plazas. Over the course of the century, a *jarabe* became purely instrumental accompaniment for dancers, and in its traditional form constituted a highly improvised choreographic tradition.

With the Mexican Revolution, beginning in 1910, came a nationalist movement in cultural thought and policy. Representations of folkloric traditions that had been banned became key elements in education, tourism, and public welfare programs sponsored by the Seguro Social. Many sectors of government, including the armed forces and police, began to subsidize folk forms over classical music and dance. By the latter half of the 19th century, "El Jarabe Tapatío" was celebrated not only in

Jalisco (a tapatío is something or someone from the city of Guadalajara, Jalisco) but throughout much of Mexico. The Russian ballerina Anna Pavlova danced on pointe to this *jarabe* in Mexico City (1918), popularizing choreographic innovations that further standardized the piece.

Originally, the *jarabe* was danced by female couples in order to avoid the wrath of the church. As ecclesiastical influence waned during the revolutionary period, that gave way to mixed couples. José Vasconcelos, secretary of public education from 1921 to 1924, directed his agency (through its Aesthetic Cultural Department) to encourage traditional music and dance; on the 100th anniversary of the founding of the Republic (1921), thousands watched as dozens of couples danced "El Jarabe Tapatío" in a Mexico City ceremony unveiling the version to be taught throughout the country ("Jarabe Nacional"). This established the piece as an archetype, though at the expense of losing much of its dynamic quality as a social dance.

The "Jarabe Nacional" is composed of excerpts from six regional tunes. The "Jarabe de Jalisco" begins the story of courtship: a charro, dressed in the traditional three-piece suit composed of a vest, jacket, and silver buttons down the seam, makes initial courtship gestures to la china (wearing a traditional Pueblan china poblana outfit). The man attempts to woo the woman through machismo and zapateado stamping and foot tapping to the "Jarabe del Atole" (from the early 1800s) and the popular "Son del Paloma," in which the courting birds of the lyrics (commonly sung until the 1920s and well-known to most audiences) are interpreted through dance. After the charro impresses the woman, the tune changes to the "Jarana Yucateca" (a typical dance melody from the Yucatan peninsula): he becomes drunk with glory and is dismissed as a borracho (an inebriate). Ultimately, he succeeds in conquering the china during the "Jarabe Moreliano" (from the state of Michoacán), throwing his hat to the ground and kicking his leg over his partner's head as she bends down to pick it up. The couple concludes with a triumphant march to a military tune called "La Diana," and feigns a kiss behind the man's sombrero.

Further Readings

Cashion, Susan Valerie. "The Son and Jarabe: Mestizo Dance Forms of Jalisco, Mexico." *Journal of the Association of Graduate Dance Ethnologists* 3 (Fall–Winter 1979–1980): 28–50.

Olaso, Irma. "El jarabe—prototipo de todos los jarabes mexicanos." M.A. thesis, CSU-Sacramento, 1977.

Saldívar, Gabriel. *El Jarabe, Baile Popular Mexicano.* 2nd ed. Guadalajara: Gobierno del Estado de Jalisco, 1989.

Stevenson, Robert. *Music in Mexico: A Historical Survey.* New York: Crowell, 1971.

Laura Stanfield Prichard

Jarana

The *jarana* is a musical instrument used in the ***huasteco*** and the ***jarocho*** Mexican *son* traditions. The *jarana* from the Huasteca region (a territory that crosses over the states of Hidalgo, San Luis Potosí, Tamaulipas, Puebla, Querétaro, and northern Veracruz) is a small five-stringed **guitar** used in the traditional ensemble along with a deep-bodied guitar called *huapanguera* and a violin. The *jarana* and *huapanguera* establish the chordal and rhythmic drive of the music. The *jarana* from the *jarocho* tradition in the southern region of the state of Veracruz is a fretted narrow-bodied guitar that has eight strings arranged in five courses, usually arranged in two single outer strings and three double courses in between. This instrument comes in at least four sizes, the smallest being called *mosquito*. The *jarana* is often used in the *jarocho* ensemble, which traditionally consists of a diatonic **harp**, a *jarana,* which provides rhythmic and chordal accompaniment, and a *requinto* (a four-stringed, shallow-bodied guitar that is plucked with a plectrum commonly made of cow-horn).

The *jarana* is also the main dance in Mexico's Yucatan state. Etymologically, the term means *alboroto* or uproar, *fiesta. Jaranas* are played by orchestras comprised of clarinets, trombons, saxophons, timpani, and *güiro* (a scraped gourd). Traditionally, *jaranas* are danced by couples properly attired: women wear the typical and colorful Yucatecan *huipil,* dancing shoes and hand-knitted shawls, and men dressed with a typical silk or linen *guayabera* (white shirt) with a woven palm hat and colorful bandanna in the front pocket.

In the Afro-Peruvian tradition, *jarana* refers to the context of competition in which the *Creole marinera* musical style takes place. When sung in competition or *contrapunto,* the *marinera* is performed by two or more singers accompanied by two guitars, **cajón** and handclapping. *Jarana* is also the name given to the three strophes that the *marinera* uses in this competition: *primera de jarana, segunda de jrana,* and *tercera de jarana,* each having to follow certain poetic strophic and rhyming rules.

Further Reading

Sheehy, Daniel E. "Mexico." In *The Garland Encyclopedia of World Music.* Volume 2*: South America, Mexico, Central America, and the Caribbean*, edited by Dale A. Olsen and Daniel E. Sheehy, 600–25. New York and London: Garland Publishing, 1998.

Tompkins, William. "The Musical Traditions of the Blacks of Coastal Peru." Ph.D. diss., Ethnomusicology, University of California at Los Angeles, 1981.

Raquel Paraíso

Jazz

Jazz first emerged in the early 1900s and is arguably the most significant and influential musical contribution of the **United States** in the 20th century. As a musical style, the earliest jazz combined a number of African American styles and practices with European, Latin American, Caribbean, and newly formed American musics. Key to this stylistic mix was the unique cultural climate of 19th-century New Orleans, which was set apart from the rest of the United States due to its Caribbean flavor and its alternating French and Spanish governance. This cosmopolitan and multicultural setting from which many of the early innovators of jazz emerged, such as Louis Armstrong, Sidney Bechet, and Jelly Roll Morton, marked the music as transcultural in its stylistic scope. However, the diversity of cultures that contributed to early jazz are rarely acknowledged due in part to the black/white racial dynamics of the United States that provide no space for people who do not belong to such racial classifications, such as *Creole*, Latin American and Caribbean peoples. In fact, it was not until the late 1930s when jazz musicians first began acknowledging their intercultural past. The most famous testament was made by *Creole* pianist Jelly Roll Morton who commented that "If you can't manage to put tinges of Spanish (meaning Caribbean and Latin American) in your tunes, you will never be able to get the right seasoning, I call it, for jazz." Duke Ellington also made similar comments. In particular they were referring to a number of rhythm influences from various Caribbean traditions that played a significant role in the rhythmic foundations of early jazz.

What sets jazz apart from other music is the open-ended system of production that it employs, in and of itself reflective of an esthetic, which was inherited by African American culture, whereby jazz performers are free to incorporate a wide range of traits from diverse influences without sacrificing the music's fundamental identity. Some writers, like Amiri Baraka, have preferred to view jazz as a verb, rather than a descriptive noun, in the sense that it is more a way of making music, which has at its core an esthetic of individual expression through improvisation and an openness to outside influence.

Though the music is most often associated with African American culture, its worldwide popular appeal, facilitated by the newly emergent phonograph recording and radio broadcasting industries in the 1920s, quickly spawned numerous localized scenes throughout the United States and Europe establishing the music as a truly global phenomenon. By the 1930s, swing, as jazz was known at the time, was synonymous with popular music and musicians such as Duke Ellington, Count Basie, and Benny Goodman led highly successful big bands (large ensembles of fifteen or more musicians that feature highly sophisticated dance music arrangements). In the 1940s, a new form of jazz, known as bebop, was developed by musicians, such as Charlie Parker and Dizzy Gillespie. This newer style featured small groups and emphasized highly technical and virtuosic improvisations that began to move the music away from the popular realm and more toward art music, a direction that would continue throughout the last half of the 20th century. Along with bebop came a renewed interest in cross-cultural and cross-stylistic experimentation, often fueled by political concerns that captured the fervor of the burgeoning civil rights movement in the United States. One example is Gillespie's collaborative work with Cuban percussionist Chano Pozo, which not only popularized Latin music and jazz mixings, or **Latin jazz**, but also served to acknowledge common cultural roots of African Americans and other descendants of African peoples in the postcolonial Americas.

Numerous other substyles emerged in the years to follow. In the 1950s, Horace Silver and Ray Charles explored soul, rhythm and blues, and jazz mixings, called soul jazz. In the 1960s, Stan Getz and Charlie Byrd experimented with Brazilian music, collaborating with guitarist João Gilberto and vocalist Astrid Gilberto and Ornette Coleman, John Coltrane, and Cecil Taylor established a vibrant jazz avant garde scene. In the 1970s, groups such as the Mahavishnu Orchestra and groups led by Miles Davis incorporated **rock** and funk into the mix, spawning a style known as fusion. In the 1980s, Wynton Marsalis led a neoclassical movement, which reinvigorated interest in pre-1960s jazz styles. He successfully lobbied for jazz to be on par with classical music, establishing the prestigious jazz at Lincoln Center program. At the turn of the century, we have experienced even further internationalization of jazz with growing scenes in Asia, Latin America, and in parts of Africa; however, jazz remains mostly aligned with art music performance, often subsidized through state funding or private philanthropic organizations. This is especially the case with the European jazz scene. Numerous jazz stars from outside of the United States have emerged as influential innovators in recent years. Examples for Latin America and the Caribbean include Cuban clarinetist and saxophonist Paquito D'Rivera, Panamanian pianist Danilo Perez, and Brazilian woodwind specialist and composer Hermeto Pascoal.

Further Reading

Baraka, Imamu Amiri. *Blues People: Negro Music in White America*. New York: W. Morrow, 1963.

Berliner, Paul. *Thinking in Jazz: The Infinite Art of Improvisation*. Chicago: University of Chicago Press, 1994.

DeVeaux, Scott. *The Birth of Bebop: A Social and Musical History*. Berkeley: University of California Press, 1997.

Fiehrer, Thomas. "From Quadrille to Stomp: The Creole Origins of Jazz." *Popular Music* 10, no. 1 (January 1991): 21–38.

Monson, Ingrid. *Saying Something: Jazz Improvisation and Interaction*. Chicago: University of Chicago Press, 1996.

Schuller, Gunther. *Early Jazz: Its Roots and Musical Development*. New York: Oxford University Press, 1968.

Schuller, Gunther. *The Swing Era: 1930–1945*. New York: Oxford University Press, 1989.

Washburne, Christopher. "The Clave of Jazz: A Caribbean Contribution to the Rhythmic Foundation of an African-American Music." *Black Music Research Journal*, no. 1 (Spring 1997): 59–80.

Williams, Martin T. *The Jazz Tradition*. New York: Oxford University Press, 1970.

Chris Washburne

Joropo

Joropo is a popular folkloric dance and its accompanying music is representative of the plains culture of **Venezuela** and **Colombia**. Its adoption as a symbol of Venezuelan national identity throughout the first half of the 1900s contributed to ensuring its place within present-day Venezuelan and Colombian popular music. *Joropo's* contemporary significance is evidenced by its media presence and substantial music sales, by the ongoing demand for live performances, as well as by its impact on the region's art music, **rock**, pop, and contemporary **jazz** styles.

Several historical processes converged in the evolution of *joropo* as an autonomous cultural activity. The unsuccessful search for *el Dorado* (the legendary city of gold) brought about the predominance of agriculture, particularly cattle ranching, and the slave trade as the area's principal economic activities. The presence of Catholic missionaries also played an important role in setting the stage for the development of *joropo*. From this socioeconomic backdrop emerged the way of life of the transient *Creole* horsemen, workers of the large *haciendas*. *Joropo* was their principal form of cultural expression, identity, and entertainment.

Joropo is no exception to the tricultural character of most Latin American folk music, with traits drawn from European (predominantly Spanish), African, and Amerindian cultures. Examples of its direct lineage to Spain can be observed in various ways: the musical and choreographic gestures shared with the Spanish *fandango*; the various styles of *bandurrias* and **guitars** that were introduced by the Spanish colonists (which in time evolved into the present-day **bandolas** and the **cuatro**); and the introduction of the **copla** and **décima** poetic forms. Other European characteristics are represented by the creolized waltzes and the adoption of various French classical dance-form terms. Its African character manifests itself in the multilayered polyrhythmic nature of the rich metric framework and rhythmic phrasing. The principal indigenous inheritance is the obligatory presence of **maracas** in the traditional *joropo* ensemble.

Traditional *joropo* ensembles include the **harp** or **bandola** as the principal melodic instrument. In many areas, the *bandola* was the more common of the two, but progressively, the harp has taken over as *joropo's* principal iconic instrument. The other instruments utilized in *joropo* are the **maracas**, the **cuatro**, and the comparatively recent addition of the electric bass.

Colombian *joropo* dancers take part in festivities for the 468th anniversary of the city of Bogota in 2006. (AFP/Getty Images)

Traditional *joropo* is made up of three regional styles: *joropo llanero* (of the plains), *joropo oriental*, and *joropo central*. Of the three regional styles, *joropo llanero* is the most popular and can be further divided into two substyles: the *pasaje* and the *golpe*. *Pasajes* are characteristically romantic and lyrical. Their tempos are relaxed and their forms more rigid. These qualities favored the *pasaje's* more vigorous commercialization during the emergence of radio and the recording industry in the region, and thus, the *pasaje* gained more popularity among the general population than the *golpe*. In contrast, the *golpe* is characterized by faster tempos, a more percussive texture, and high degrees of improvisation, resulting in a more intense and aggressive character. There are presently over 30 *golpe* song forms, identified principally by their harmonic structure and cyclical forms. Examples include the *zumba que zumba*, the *periquera, quitapesares*, and *el carnaval*. A parallel can be drawn between *golpe* performance and the jazz idiom regarding the relationship between harmonic form and improvisation, and its relevance within both genres: as a blues progression provides a framework and point of departure for jazz performers to improvise over, so do *golpe* forms provide a framework for *joropo* players. The *golpe* is a favorite choice of performers during competitions and festivals. Musicians can showcase their skills through *joropo's* inherent dramatic virtuosity.

Fundamental to *joropo's* stylistic identity is a polymetric pulse of 3/4 and 6/8. This interlocking rhythmic duality dominates all aspects of *joropo* and is sometimes referred to as its *clave* (key): the upper accents fall on the third and sixth eighth notes of the 6/8 note groupings while the lower accents fall on the first and third quarter notes of the bar of 3/4. A variation of this *clave* shifts the pattern backwards (in relation to the downbeats) by one beat. Additional superimpositions of binary sequences over the *clave* produce an infinite range of rhythmic variations and relationships vital to *joropo's* dynamic and infectious character.

Some of the most important *joropo* artists and groups (past and present) from both Colombia and Venezuela include: Reynaldo Armas, Fulgencio Aquino, Hugo Blanco, Arnulfo Briseño, Los Hermanos Chirinos, Juan Farfan, el Indio Figueredo, Raúl Gonzalez, Anselmo Lopez, Lila Morillo, Eneas Perdomo, Luis Ariel Rey, Luis Silva, Isaac Tacha, Juan Vicente Torrealba, Orlando Valderrama, and Aries Vigoth.

Further Reading

Calderón, Claudia. "Estudio analítico y comparativo sobre la música del joropo, expresión tradicional de Venezuela y Colombia." *Revista Musical de Venezuela* 39 (1999): 219–58.

Gerard Béhague, et al. "Venezuela." *Grove Music Online*. Online, November 2010. Oxford Music Online website, www.oxfordmusiconline.com.

Bernardo Padrón

K

Konpa

Konpa refers to a style of Haitian music that developed in the 1950s and evolved into the 1980s through different manifestations, which include the genres of *konpa direk, kadans ranpa*, and *mini djaz*, to eventually become influential in the creation of *zouk* music.

During the 1950s, a style of Dominican **merengue** called *perico ripiao* or *Cibaeño*-style became extremely popular in **Haiti**. Many bands and personalities traveled to play in Haiti and the music was prominent on Haitian radio. At the height of the popularity *merengue* in Haiti, a local variation on the Dominican archetype emerged through the work of Nemours Jean-Baptiste, who altered the *merengue* beat. Nemours's ensemble instrumentation consisted of vocals, **accordion**, bass, **guitar**, saxophones, trumpets, *tanbou* (a Haitian barrel drum), and a percussion section. This new variation on the Dominican *merengue* became known as *konpa direk* (later *konpa* for short). The term means direct rhythm or straight ahead rhythm, and was so dubbed by Nemours's guitarist, Raymond Gaspard. Nemours's altered *merengue* beat along with *Creole* texts distinguished the new sound, which Haitians claimed as their own creation. His *konpa* was slower than its Domincan prototype, and the ensembles that played *konpa* in the late 1950s and early 1960s resembled the American big band instrumentation. Around the same time that Nemours's newly created music sensation was becoming popular among Haitians, a former member of Nemours's orchestra, Weber Sicot, came up with his own variation of the *merengue* very similar to Nemours's *konpa*. Sicot called his new dance *kandans rampa*, which is roughly translated as rampart rhythm. While the differences between these two styles of *konpa* are slight, there was enough of a distinction for the creators and their ardent supporters to create a dual fan base, which was fueled by a fiercely competitive rivalry between the two artists. Even after a reconciliation between Nemours and Sicot in the 1960s, this rivalry remained apparent.

With the advent of small group rock 'n' roll from the United States and Great Britain in the 1960s, the instrumentation of *konpa* ensembles began to reflect a bias towards a smaller, guitar-based sound. As the name of the big band dance orchestras in Haiti were known as *djaz*, these smaller ensembles became known as *mini djaz*, a term that was believed to have been coined by Haitian DJ, Rico Jena Baptiste. The make-up of these smaller ensembles did away with the larger horn sections, but continued to maintain a trumpet, saxophone, or accordion as one of the lead instruments, a leftover from the earlier style of *konpa* instrumentation. Notable artists associated with two distinct styles in *mini djaz* included Shleu-Shleu and Tabou Combo. The popularity of *mini djaz* continued until the mid 1970s, when dynamic foreign influences from the *Creole*-speaking Antilles outside of Haiti began to dominate trends in popular music that eventually would shape the sounds of Haitian *konpa* in the late 1970s and early 1980s.

The music of the other *Creole*-speaking nations in the Caribbean began to influence the sounds of popular music in places where *konpa* and *kadans* had previously dominated. The genre of *cadence-lypso*, with origins in **Dominica**, was especially influential on *konpa* music of the late 1970s. The sound of bands such as Exile One and Gramacks, both from Dominica, began to achieve great popularity among Haitian youth at this time. Exile One's use of horn sections in their arrangements was especially influential, and many Haitian *mini djaz* bands began to reintroduce the fuller horn sections into their ensembles in an effort to emulate the sounds of the foreign bands.

By the 1980s, the genres and musical styles of *konpa* and *mini djaz* had given way to emerging musics such as *nouvelle jenerasyon* (new generation) and ***mizik rasin***, both of which sought to find a closer connection to Haiti's folk roots, and an emphasis on *Creole* references, if not explicitly in the sung texts, then at least in the titles of the songs themselves. Nevertheless, the legacy of *konpa* was great on the emerging sounds in the late 1970s and early 1980s, and, is evident as one of the main ingredients in ***zouk*** music, which through the works of bands like Kassav, became the most internationally famous music to come from the *Creole*-speaking Caribbean.

Further Reading

Averill, Gage. *A Day for the Hunter, a Day for the Prey: Popular Music and Power in Haiti*. Chicago studies in ethnomusicology. Chicago: University of Chicago Press, 1997.

Averill, Gage. " 'Toujou sou konpa': Issues of Change and Interchange in Haitian Popular Dance Music." In *Zouk: World Music in the West Indies*, edited by Jocelyne Guilbault. Chicago: University of Chicago Press, 1993.

Bilby, Kenneth M., Michael D. Largey, and Peter Manuel. *Caribbean Currents: Caribbean Music from Rumba to Reggae*. Philadelphia, PA: Temple University Press, 2006.

George Torres

L

Lambada

Lambada is a couple dance of Brazilian origin that enjoyed international popularity during the late 1980s and early 1990s. The *lambada's* modern origins are from the 1970s in the city of Belém in the northern Brazilian state of Pará at a time when **salsa, merengue**, and electrified *carimbó* were in heavy rotation over northeastern Brazilian radio stations. Journalists began to refer to such music as *lambada*, which in Brazilian Portuguese means lash, whip, or slap. The style consisted of a syncopated 2/4 rhythm in a fast tempo with repeated motives on **guitars** or horns accompanied by a rhythm section. As a dance, the *lambada* also was the result of a mixture of styles including *merengue,* **maxixe**, **samba**, and **forró**. Characteristics of the dance include a tight body contact, inserting the right leg between the partner's legs, spinning, turning, and dips. The dance is very sensual and the female partners wear short skirts making the spins and the turns very provocative. By the late 1980s, the dance had spread well beyond the region and *lambaterias*, clubs where enthusiasts went to dance *lambada*, opened up throughout the country's urban centers. International success of the *lambada* occurred when the band Kaoma, under the influence of French impresario Olivier Lamotte d'Incamps, took *lambada* music and dance from a visit he made to Puerto Seguro back to France. Through a successful media blitz, Kaoma popularized *lambada* internationally. Kaoma's success was thanks to their hit "Chorando se foi," which later turned out to be an unauthorized translation and reinterpretation of a Bolivian song "Llorando se fue" by Los Kjarkas. Previous to Los K'jarkas interpretation it had been made popular by Márcia Ferreira, a successful *lambada* chanteuse from Pará. Kaoma's version of the song sold over five million copies worldwide. As a result, Los K'jarkas sued Kamoa. Since the early 1990s, the *lambada* dance broadened out to be performed over other more current styles of music, including the *flamenco rumba* styles of groups like the Gypsy Kings as well as other more modern Arab-Andalusian styles. Eventually the dance became associated with Caribbean styles such as **soca**, *merengue, salsa,* **konpa**, and **zouk**, the latter becoming a hybrid form that still enjoys popularity among dancers: *lambazouk*, Rio style *zouk* or Carioca *zouk*.

Further Reading

McGowan, Chris, and Ricardo Pessanha. *The Brazilian Sound: Samba, Bossa Nova, and the Popular Music of Brazil*. Revised and expanded edition. Philadelphia, PA: Temple University Press, 2008.

George Torres

Latin Jazz

Latin jazz is a musical style that integrates rhythms derived from various Latin American dances with the harmonic practice and improvisation of **jazz**. A mixture of instrumental timbres can also be a factor where most frequently standard jazz instruments are combined with Latin percussion. Two important rhythmic characteristics that distinguish Latin jazz from straight jazz are the former's use of even rather than swung eighth notes and its foundation in the *son **clave*** and *rumba clave* rhythmic patterns.

Latin American influence in jazz has traditionally been undervalued by historians, but it has been present since the music's inception. W. C. Handy's use of ***habanera*** rhythm in "St. Louis Blues" and Jelly Roll Morton's reference to the "Spanish tinge" in jazz are the two most frequently cited early examples. The association of jazz with dancing meant that many early jazz bands were also playing Latin repertoire to accommodate popular Latin dances in the **United States** such as the *tango* in the 1920s and the *rhumba* in the 1930s. The latter was popularized by the Don Azpiazú's Havana Casino Orchestra's hit "The Peanut Vendor," which was also recorded by Louis Armstrong and Duke Ellington.

The birth of true Latin jazz, as opposed to Latin influence in jazz, is generally traced to New York City in the 1940s. Trumpeter Mario Bauzá, a veteran of several jazz groups, teamed with bandleader Frank "Machito" Grillo to form the Afro-Cubans in 1942, a group that featured jazz soloists in Latin Big Band settings. The Afro-Cubans' "Tanga" has been described as the first work of what came to be called Afro-Cuban Jazz. Dizzy Gillespie, who had played with Bauzá in Cab Calloway's band, began an important and lifelong role in Latin jazz by hiring Cuban *conga* player Chano Pozo. The Gillespie/Pozo collaboration, including a 1947 recording of their "Manteca," inaugurated a style known as *cubop*, a fusion of bebop and Cuban music. The later 1940s witnessed the participation of many other prominent jazz musicians in Latin jazz styles, including Charlie Parker, Fats Navarro, and Stan Kenton. Cuban-born Chico O'Farrill, who moved to New York in 1948, drew on his formal training and knowledge of both jazz and Cuban music to become a significant Latin jazz arranger and composer with works such as *Afro-Cuban Jazz Suite*.

The most popular Latin dance of the late 1940s and 1950s was the *mambo*, which was of Cuban origin. The popularity of the *mambo* helped to bring Latin jazz into the jazz mainstream in the 1950s. One of the most important musicians in this regard was bandleader/percussionist **Tito Puente**, whose group played both Latin dance numbers and Latin versions of jazz tunes. Pianist George Shearing and vibraphonist Cal Tjader formed Latin jazz combos, and by the end of the 1950s, most jazz musicians were including Latin jazz in their repertoire.

Machito (Francisco Raúl Gutiérrez Grillo)

Machito (1908–1984) was a Cuban bandleader, baritone singer, and *maraquero* famous for his lead role in the influential **Latin jazz** band The Afro-Cubans. The Afro-Cubans fused the melodic and improvisatory aspects of **jazz** with **Afro-Cuban** rhythms. Machito left **Cuba** in 1937 for New York where The Afro-Cubans were founded by his brother-in-law Mario Bauzá. By 1940 The Afro-Cubans consisted of Machito singing with an ensemble of two trumpets, two saxophones, piano, bass, *timbals, bongos,* and *conga*. Bauzá's interest in bebop along with Machito's grounding in *clave* formed the Latin Jazz style cubop. "Tanga" became The Afro-Cubans's theme song and is an example of jazz improvisation featured over a *clave* rhythm. Chords played for an extended duration, common with The Afro-Cubans, would influence the modal jazz movement of the 1950s. Machito collaborated with bandleader Stan Kenton, with whom he recorded a version of "El Manicero" ("The Peanut Vendor"), a Cuban staple. He also recorded "Mango Mangué" with Charlie Parker, and collaborated with Dexter Gordon and Stan Getz. Machito influenced many Latin jazz and *salsa* artists including Tito Rodriguez and Larry Harlow.

Further Reading

Austerlitz, Paul. *Jazz Consciousness: Music, Race, and Humanity.* Middletown, CT: Wesleyan University Press, 2005.

Raymond Epstein

One characteristic of Latin jazz in the 1960s was the importance of Brazilian sources to the style (it is worth noting that some scholars object to the inclusion of Brazilian-influenced music under the label Latin jazz as well as the overly general nature of the label itself). Jazz musicians touring **Brazil** discovered the *bossa nova* and the *samba*; one of these was guitarist Charlie Byrd, who recorded **Antonio Carlos Jobim's** "Desafinado" with saxophonist Stan Getz in 1962. This recording contributed significantly to the rise of Brazilian-influenced Latin jazz. Gerry Mulligan, Herbie Mann, and Mongo Santamaria (an important figure in many types of Latin jazz) were among the other musicians to play in the style.

Fusion with other styles of music, especially rock and funk, was a significant trend in Latin jazz (and jazz in general) in the 1970s. Rock guitarist Carlos Santana's version of Puente's "Oye Como Va" is a notable example, but the most important group of the era in this respect was Irakere, formed by pianist Chucho Valdes and including trumpeter Arturo Sandoval and saxophonist Paquito D'Rivera. The Fort Apache Band was one of the most prominent Latin jazz ensembles of the 1980s; their album *Rumba para Monk* reinterprets the music of Thelonious Monk from an Afro-Cuban perspective. Among the highly regarded Latin jazz artists to emerge since the 1980s are pianist Gonzalo Rubalcaba, pianist Danilo Perez, and saxophonist David Sanchez.

Further Reading

Fernandez, Raul. *Latin Jazz: The Perfect Combination*. San Francisco: Chronicle Books, 2002.

Kernfeld, Barry. "Latin Jazz." In *Grove Music Online*, edited by Laura Macy. www.grovemusic.com.

Roberts, John Storm. *Latin Jazz: The First of the Fusions, 1880s to Today*. New York: Schirmer Books, 1999.

Santoro, Gene. "Latin Jazz." In *The Oxford Companion to Jazz*, edited by Bill Kirchner, 522–33. New York: Oxford University Press, 2000.

Washburn, Christopher. "Latin Jazz: The Other Jazz." *Current Musicology* 71–73 (Spring 2001– Spring 2002): 409–26.

Lars Helgert

Latin Rock

The term Latin rock refers to a Latin American-infused style of **rock** that was developed during the 1960s and 1970s. The genre incorporates Latin American rhythms and structures into a rock style and songs are often sung in Spanish. Prior to the emergence of rock 'n' roll, Latin rock was influenced by different music styles in an indirect way with cultural connections such as clothing, slang words in Spanish, and Latin American musical styles such as ***son, mambo, mariachi, rumba, tango, tejano***, and ***norteño***. While Elvis Presley represents the most iconic artist of the rock 'n' roll era, the Chicano rocker Ritchie Valens became an early figure for Latin rock with his recording of the Mexican song "La Bamba," as his most well-known song. During the 1960s, attempts at integrating Mexican Americans into political, social, and cultural aspects of the United States, as well as the intention of preserving their own ethnicity, identity, and language, helped to create a strong Latin Rock presence in popular music, with artists such as Carlos Santana, Tierra, Malo, El Chicano, War, and Los Lobos among others.

Latin rock is a mixture of both North American and Latin American influences that have developed over time. The wave of Mexican immigrants to the **United**

States from the 1920s to 1940s created fertile ground for musical confluences between North America and Latin America. As early as the 1930s, for example, Mexican Americans from Texas and California combined the boogie-woogie with Cuban *son* in an effort to assimilate to the American lifestyle while still preserving their Mexican traditions. In the 1950s rock 'n' roll helped to intensify the interactions of ethnic groups from Latin America and the United States to create the beginnings of the Latin Rock music scene. This intercultural exchange had diverse influences including blues, country, **jazz**, and swing, as well as the rhythms of Latin America such as ***Tex-Mex***, *tejano, norteño,* ***samba***, and *tango*. By combining a myriad of different sources, Latin rock expanded the possibilities of composition with Latin American rhythms and syncopation including *sesquiáltera* (two against three) and Cuban *clave*, the latter borrowed from *son* and *rumba*.

One of the most well-known musicians during the late 1950s and 1960s was Mexican guitarist Javier Bátiz, who became a mentor figure for Carlos Santana. Santana, who became famous at Woodstock, brought Latin Rock into the mainstream by combining African American and Latin American with rock 'n' roll. It was with the exposure of Santana's music that Latino-American bands gained increased popularity in the 1970s. Bands such as Malo, El Chicano, and Redbone all had top-selling songs including "Suavecito," "Tell Her She's Lovely," and "Come and Get Your Love." The success of these groups was due to their biculturalism, multilingualism, and intercultural competence, which became standard aspects of performers in the genre. Most notable among these groups from the 1970s was Los Lobos, who became successful by balancing their sound between rhythm and blues, rock 'n' roll, and Latin-infused rock. In the 1980s, groups such as Cruzados and Los Illegals strengthened the Latin American market within the broader context of American rock.

Further Reading

Avant-Mier, Roberto. *Rock the Nation: Latin/o Identities and the Latin Rock*. New York: the Continuum, 2010.

McCarthy, Jim and Sansoe, Ron. *Voices of Latin Rock: The People and Events That Shaped the Sound*. Milwaukee, WI: Hal Leonard Corporation, 2004.

McFarland, Pancho. *Chicano Rap: Gender and Violence in the Postindustrial Barrio*. Austin: University of Texas Press, 2008.

Pacini Hernández, Deborah. *Oye como va!: Hybridity and Identity in Latin Popular Music*. Philadelphia: Temple University Press, 2010.

Reyes, David and Waldman, Tom. *Land of a Thousand Dances: Chicano Rock 'n' Roll from Southern California*. Albuquerque: University of New Mexico Press, 2009.

Strom Roberts, John. *The Latin Tinge: The Impact of Latin American Music on the United States*. New York: Oxford University Press, 1999.

Tatiana Flórez-Pérez

Laúd

The *laúd* or lute is a pear-shaped body plucked chordophone of variable number of strings. It is a direct descent of the Arabic *'ud*, a fretless chordophone with a bigger resonance box than its European counterpart. It generally has four double courses and one lower bass string. It is used in both classical and popular music throughout the Arabic countries as well as in Turkey, Iran, Pakistan, Armenia, and Greece.

The old version of the Spanish *laúd* was commonly used in Spain between the 14th and the 18th centuries. This instrument experienced a rebirth with a renovated interest for Renaissance and Baroque music around 1930 and throughout the 20th century. Presently, the Spanish *laúd* used in folkloric traditions consists of a pear-shaped body with 12 metallic strings arranged in six double courses. Traditionally it is played in the **estudiantina** ensembles, which are comprised of *laúdes, bandurrias*, and **guitars**. Both the *bandurria*—smaller than the *laúd*—and the *laúd* are tuned in fourths (a-e-b-f#-c#-g#), the latter being an octave lower a-e-b-f#-c#-g#.

The Cuban *laúd* is very similar to the Spanish one, although the tuning is different, the Cuban being d-a-e-b-f#-c#. It has a pear-shaped body and a fretted fingerboard. Like the Spanish *laúd*, the instrument is plucked with a plectrum. It is played in musical styles such as **son** cubano, where it plays composed and improvised melodies. This instrument was brought to **Cuba** by Spanish immigrants during the colonial period and in the early 20th century.

Further Reading

Cano Tamayo, Manuel. *La guitarra: historia, estudios y aportaciones al arte flamenco.* Granada: Ediciones ANEL, 1986.

Sublette, Ned. *Cuba and Its Music: From the First Drums to the Mambo.* Chicago: Chicago Review Press, 2004.

Raquel Paraíso

Lundu

The *lundu* is a Brazilian music and dance genre that arose in the early 18th century from the music of Bantu slaves. As it developed in **Brazil**, it became the earliest Brazilian popular music genre to combine African rhythm with European harmony, melody, and instrumentation. Over time, *lundu* came to signify three separate phenomena: a dance, a song type, and an instrumental genre.

The *lundu* dance shares its roots with **samba**; in its earliest form it was a dance accompanied exclusively by drums and voices. It was a courtship dance involving a man and a woman, with movements suggesting advance and retreat, and included stamping and snapping of the fingers above the head, gestures common in the Spanish-influenced *fandango*. Accounts by foreigners traveling in Brazil in the 19th century describe the dance as lascivious, citing undulating body movements and sexually suggestive gestures such as the *umbigada*, the touching of one dancer's navel to another's. The *lundu* dance was at first popular among blacks and mulattos in Salvador (Northeast Brazil) and Rio de Janeiro. The *lundu* was soon adopted first by the poorest among the white population and then moved steadily and quite rapidly up the social scale, so that by the early 19th century, foreign visitors regarded it as the national dance of Brazil. The longevity of the dance is striking; long after the vocal and instrumental forms had disappeared, the *lundu* dance continued to be cultivated throughout the 19th and into the 20th century. Although not very popular today, *lundu* still has a presence in Brazil's musical scene.

The vocal *lundu* took on two forms: one popular among the lower classes, and the other suitable for the salon of the upper and middle classes. The popular lower-class *lundu* song was generally accompanied by the **guitar**, at times with the addition of a melodic instrument such as a **flute**. These vocal *lundu* shared many style characteristics with other Brazilian genres, including the use of African-derived rhythm and syncopation. One account described these songs as "bantering, disorderly, stunning, as often as not with a sting of coarse irony." These songs were rarely published, but rather were transmitted orally among practitioners and as a result few examples of this version of the *lundu* survive. Domingos Caldas Barbosa, the Brazilian mulatto singer who introduced the Brazilian songs to the court at Lisbon in the late 1770s, was known for singing the *lundu-canção*, or *lundu* song, and was responsible for elevating this popular song to the concert stage. When the *lundu* song reached Portugal, it became a respected salon genre known as the *doce lundu chorado*. Throughout the early part of the 19th century, the *lundu* sung with piano accompaniment enjoyed increasing popularity among the upper classes of Rio de Janeiro. The exotic origins of the *lundu* song came to interest composers and theater musicians, and by the 1820s it had become popular in the theaters of Rio de Janeiro. Upper-class vocal *lundus* began to be published as sheet music in the late 18th and early 19th centuries. By the late 19th century, this version of the *lundu* had lost rhythmic complexity, and the acceptance of the *lundu* by the upper classes was an important step in the assimilation of black music into colonial and imperial society.

In addition to the dance and song forms, there was an instrumental form of *lundu* popular in the late 19th century. It was most often a rendition of a popular *lundu* song with the melody played by a flute or clarinet accompanied by a small, five-course guitar called the *viola* and later by the larger, six-string guitar. Although it did not demonstrate the melodic tendencies of a true instrumental genre, the instrumental *lundu* was a precursor of other representative popular instrumental genres of the 20th century, including the ***maxixe*** and ***choro.***

Further Reading

Araújo, Mozart de. *A modinha e o lundu no século XVIII: uma pesquisa histórica e bibliográfica*. São Paulo: Ricordi Brasileira, 1963.

Béhague, Gerard. "Popular Musical Currents in the Art Music of the Early Nationalistic period in Brazil, Circa 1870–1920." Ph.D. diss., Tulane University, 1966.

Garcia, Thomas George Caracas. "The Brazilian Choro: Music, Politics and Performance." Ph.D. diss., Duke University, 1997.

Kiefer, Bruno. *A Modinha e o Lundu: Duas Raizes da Música Popular Brasileira*. Porto Alegre: Editora Movimento, 1977.

Livingston-Isenhour, Tamara Elena, and Thomas George Caracas Garcia. *Choro: A Social History of a Brazilian Popular Music*. Bloomington: Indiana University Press, 2005.

Thomas George Caracas Garcia

Lute. *See* Laúd.

M

Mambo

Mambo is an **Afro-Cuban**-derived song and dance genre that enjoyed widespread popularity among both Latino and mainstream audiences in the **United States** during the 1950s. *Mambo* emerged from the genres *danzón* and Cuban *son* and is typified by a musical texture that features several melodic lines layered on top of one another and a formal structure that often consists of multiple variations on a single, repeated section. As with many Latin American genres, *mambo's* origins are somewhat disputed and subject to a certain amount of speculation, which can be seen in discussions of the word's etymology. While alternately said to be of Kongo, Bantu, or Yoruba derivation, it is universally acknowledged to be West African in origin and to have been used by Afro-Cubans to refer to musical practices associated with religious events and further defined as conversation, message, or chant. More recently, the term has been used to refer to a repeated instrumental line in the improvisation-based montuno section of Cuban genres such as *son* and *danzón*. *Mambo* was also the title of a 1938 *danzón* composed by cellist Orestes López, who along with his brother, bassist and arranger Israel, "Cachao," were members of flutist Antonio Arcaño's *charanga* Orquesta Arcaño y sus Maravillas, in which the *montuno* was extended and featured melodic and harmonic ostinatos. This innovation, along with the enhancement of the *charanga's* percussion section, led to the new style being called *danzones de nuevo ritmo* (*danzones* in a new rhythm). It is not clear, however, that the López brothers invented this practice. Others had been conducting similar experiments in expanding the *son* ensemble—as well as the genre's structure, harmonic texture, and use of driving syncopation—simultaneously. The new ensemble and the musical sound resulting from these changes both came to be called *conjunto*. These innovations have generally been attributed to *tres* player, arranger, and composer **Arsenio Rodríguez**, based on his group's popularity in the 1940s.

In New York, musicians with backgrounds in both Cuban genres and **jazz**, such as Frank "**Machito**" Grillo and his musical director and lead trumpet player Mario Bauzá, a veteran of Chick Webb and Cab Calloway's big bands, built on the innovations of the *conjuntos,* combining the rhythms, formal structure, and percussion section of *son* with the harmonic textures and instrumentation of swing bands to create a distinct New York sound. This distinction was furthered by the lindy-influenced dancing style developed by young Latinos at dance clubs like the Palladium

Mambo dancers at the Savoy Ballroom in the Harlem neighorhood of New York City in 1953. (AP/Wide World Photos)

Ballroom, which began featuring Latin music in 1947 and became the center of the *mambo* culture in the early 1950s hosting the bands of Machito, Julliard-trained *timbalero* (see *timbal*) and arranger **Tito Puente**, and singer Tito Rodríguez. The Palladium attracted a cross-section of New York's multiethnic populations including African Americans, Jews, Italians, and Irish in addition to Latinos as well as literary and Hollywood elite, and jazz musicians playing at nearby clubs, such as Birdland. What was now being called the *mambo* craze reached such levels that clubs like the Savoy Ballroom and the Apollo Theater implemented *mambo* nights, and The Palladium began programming *mambo* exclusively beginning in 1952. That same year, Arsenio Rodríguez moved to New York permanently. Recognizing that popularity of *mambo* far exceeded that of the *conjunto* style that he was playing, he would begin both insisting and lamenting that he had invented the genre.

While the Big Three—Machito, Puente, and Tito Rodríguez—were the genre's biggest names in New York, for much of the rest of the country, *mambo* became nearly synonymous with **Pérez Prado**, who developed a separate and distinct variety of the genre and was also the first to use the term *mambo*. The Cuban-born pianist Prado, who had begun his experimentations with *mambo* as early as 1942 while playing with the Orquesta Casino de la Playa, moved to **Mexico** in 1948 where he made a series of records for RCA Victor with his own band beginning the following year. These recordings included "Mambo No. 5," "Que Rico El Mambo," and "Cerazo Rosa (Cherry Pink and Apple Blossom)," all of which became mainstream hits in the United States. Prado's success caused RCA Victor to switch his records from its international catalog to its pop listing (the only Latino artist to receive this distinction at the time) and led to his highly successful tour of the West Coast. As a result of Prado's tour, a number of American bands imitated Prado's style, which was typified by moderate tempos, sparse arrangements, saxophone ostinatos punctuated by brash staccato brass interjections, and Prado's own trademark grunts.

Although Prado's style proved unpopular with New Yorkers and many Latino audiences, critiqued by some as overly simplified, showy, and commercial, his band produced several musicians who would become highly influential in Latin music, including Mongo Santamaría, Johnny Pacheco, and Beny Moré, whose Banda Gigante would borrow heavily from *mambo*. The *mambo* craze, which would hit its peak in 1954, resulted in a number of *mambo* novelty songs recorded by non-Latino

Pérez Prado, Dámaso

Dámaso Pérez Prado (1916–1989) was a composer, music arranger and orchestrator, pianist, and director. His musical background was predominantly folkloric and *rumbero* (see **rumba**). Although the originator of the **mambo** may be debated (see also **Arsenio Rodríguez**), many believe that it was Pérez Prado who synthesized, refined, and advanced *mambo*.

In 1944, Pérez Prado began to incorporate features of North American music into Cuban rhythms and melodies. Later he moved to **Mexico**, and in 1949, he formed the group known as the Orquesta de Pérez Prado. There he recorded his universally popular piece "Mambo no. 5," which was followed by "Qué rico el mambo" and "Mambo no. 8."

Pérez Prado arrived in New York in 1952 for his *época de oro* (golden age), a period of approximately 10 years, during which time he earned the title of *El rey del mambo* (the mambo king). Among his numerous achievements were his best-selling record *Patricia,* his composition *Exotic Suite of the Americas,* his creation of *dengue,* and his work with eleven films from the Mexican cinema as an actor, musical arranger, and choreographer.

Further Reading

Sierra, Carlos J. *Pérez Prado y el mambo.* México: Ediciones de la Muralla, 1995.

Neris González

artists, such as Perry Como's "Papa Loves Mambo," Rosemary Clooney's "Mambo Italiano," Ruth Brown's "Mambo Baby," and Bill Haley and The Comets' "Mambo Rock." In addition, recordings by artists and groups specializing in exotica, such as Yma Sumac and The Martin Denny Orchestra, as well as by serious jazz musicians, such as Stan Kenton, George Shearing, and Cal Tjader, helped fuel the mainstream clamor for *mambo.*

Another factor in the spread of *mambo* was the popularity of the TV series *I Love Lucy,* which ran from 1951 to 1957 and was the highest rated show for four of the six years of its run (and in the others ranked no lower than third). The run of the series, which featured Cuban-born singer and bandleader Desi Arnáz playing a caricaturized version of himself and occasionally included Arnáz singing with his orchestra at his fictional Tropicana Club, coincided with *mambo's* greatest years of popularity. While Arnáz's style owed more to his former mentor Xavier Cugat than to the New York *mambo* orchestras, or even Prado and could not properly be called *mambo,* the distinction was surely lost on the majority of viewers. The effect of millions of Americans being exposed to Latin music and rhythms weekly cannot be overlooked in providing a context in which *mambo* became more acceptable to non-Latino audiences. By the late 1950s the *mambo* craze waned. It was supplanted in popularity by—and according to some as a direct result of—both **cha-cha-chá**, a genre also adapted from **danzón** by Cuban **charangas** that featured slower, more danceable tempos and simpler rhythms relative to *mambo,* and by the rise of rock 'n' roll. In spite of its decline in popularity, *mambo* became a fixture in the professional ballroom dance arena, and Puente and other bandleaders continued playing their Latin jazz–informed style bearing whatever label was in vogue at any given moment.

Mambo experienced a resurgence of sorts beginning in the 1980s. Machito & His Salsa Big Band won the Grammy Award for Best Latin Recording in 1983. Despite the group's name, its music was much closer stylistically to what Machito had been playing 30 years previously than to music being produced at Fania Records, the New York-based label that gave birth to the term *salsa* in the late 1960s and a driving force in the genre throughout the 1970s. Puente began enjoying increased exposure in mainstream media beginning in the middle of the decade and continuing into the 1990s, with appearances on TV shows such as *The Cosby Show, The Simpsons, Sesame Street,* and *Late Night with David Letterman* and in the 1992 movie *The Mambo Kings* in which Puente has a cameo as himself at The Palladium circa 1950. The movie spurred renewed interest in *mambo* and the artists who had popularized it, resulting in a proliferation of reissues and repackaging of material, many bestowing the title *mambo* king on everyone from Prado to Puente to Arnáz. Also appearing in the wake of the film were a series of highly acclaimed albums by Mario Bauzá, and by ¡Cubanísmo!, a Cuban *mambo*-tinged group led by veteran trumpeter Jesús Alemañy, whose 1996 debut album featured two Arsenio Rodríguez compositions and another entitled "Homenaje a Arcaño." *Mambo* was also among the hodgepodge of musical genres and images serving as representations of 1950s exotica and mainstream suburban chic reappropriated as alternative urban kitsch for the retro lounge culture of the 1990s. The genre, and especially Prado, experienced yet another brief surge in interest in the wake of Lou Bega's 2003 novelty hit "Mambo No. 5 (A Little Bit Of)," based on the Prado song of the same name.

Further Reading

Garcia, Davíd F. *Arsenio Rodríguez and the Transnational Flows of Latin Popular Music.* Philadephia: Temple University Press, 2006.

Loza, Steven. *Tito Puente and the Making of Latin Music.* Urbana and Chicago: University of Illinois Press, 1999.

Roberts, John Storm. *The Latin Tinge: The Impact of Latin Music on the United States,* 2nd ed. New York: Oxford University Press, 1999.

Waxer, Lise. "Of Mambo Kings and Songs of Love: Dance Music in Havana and New York from the 1930s to the 1950s." *Latin American Music Review (Revista de Música Latinoamericana)* 15, no. 2 (1994): 139–76.

Ramón Versage Agudelo

Maracas

The *maracas* are a variety of Latin American handheld percussion instruments used in both folk and popular music. Classified as idiophones they are a type of seed-filled canister rattle with handles and are most commonly played in pairs. The instrument obtains its sound by being shaken from the handle, which sets the beads inside of the canister in motion, striking the walls of the canister to give it its distinctive sound. *Maracas* are made from a variety of materials, with the handles normally made of wood, while the canister may be made from materials such as calabash, wood, shellacked rawhide, or plastic. The canister is filled either with seeds or with plastic beads. The instrument is commonly shaken in the air with accents created by the forward and backward motion of the hands. They also may be played against the performer's body, which can help give another type of accent. The instrument is a vital part of many Latin American musics, especially in the Caribbean, Colombia, Venezuela, and Brazil, where it is played within the fabric of an ensemble's rhythm section. Famous performers include Machito, Ismael Rivera, and Glen Velez. *Maracas* have been incorporated into Western art music as part of the orchestral percussion battery, and they have been used frequently in European and North American popular music as an auxiliary percussion instrument.

Further Reading

Uribe, Ed. *The Essence of Afro-Cuban Percussion and Drum Set.* New York: Warner Brothers, 1996.

George Torres

Marcha

Marcha is the Spanish and Portuguese word for march, a musical genre that has its origins in the music for military bands. European military bands brought to the Americas were responsible for a military band culture that transplanted itself in cities throughout all of Latin America. Military bands and municipal bands modeled on the military type provided entertainment in the town squares on weekends and selected holidays. As part of their repertoire, the bands would perform regional marches associated and identified with a particular region. In **Mexico**, for example, marches that are identified with a particular state are known and performed outside of the region, as in the Marcha de Zacatecas, one of Mexico's most celebrated marches. As a result of these pieces leaving the region and enjoying a transcultural popularity, military marches became a mainstay of the *banda* repertoire. In **Brazil**, the march became an important genre in popular music. This incorporation of *marcha* eventually led to the formation of important hybrid forms in Brazil's popular music as in the mixture of the two genres, **polka** and *marcha,* which eventually became the *marcha-polka* and then the *frevo.* The *marcha carnavalesca* is a **Carnival** song using a syncopated *marcha* rhythm. The *marcha de bloco* (also called the *frevo de bloco*) is a slower tempo *marcha* with moderately syncopated rhythms in a minor key. The *marcha de rancho* with smoother rhythms than the traditional *marcha* is another Carnival march with ironic texts and influenced by the older *rancho* tradition, with "As pastorinhas" by Noel Rosa being a classic example.

Further Reading

Crook, Larry. *Brazilian Music: Northeastern Traditions and the Heartbeat of a Modern Nation.* Santa Barbara, CA: ABC-CLIO, 2005.

George Torres

Mariachi

Mariachi is a traditional music originating from a wide region of western **Mexico**, which includes the states of Jalisco, Nayarit, Colima, Aguascalientes, Zacatecas, Sinaloa, Michoacán, Guanajuato, and Guerrero. The macro-regional manifestation

Mariachi Vargas

Mariachi Vargas is a **mariachi** musical group founded in 1898 by Gaspar Vargas (1880–1969) in southern Jalisco. Now the prototype of modern *mariachi*, it changed the rural music of Jalisco to the urban commercial style *mariachi*. From 1898 to 1930, Mariachi Vargas was a traditional *mariachi* consisting of four self-taught musicians from Tecalitlán, who played chordophone instruments and a repertoire consisting mainly of **sones** and some **jarabes**, **valonas**, songs, **corridos**, **valses**, and **polkas**.

Silvestre Vargas assumed the directorship in 1933, outfitting seven regional musicians with a rustic *traje de charro*. They incorporated the trumpet in 1940 and Ruben Fuentes joined in 1944; Fuentes became codirector and initiated a modernization process of learned musical technique.

From 1954 to 1975, Mariachi Vargas took the form of the modern *mariachi* to interpret a new repertoire with arrangements of **huapangos**, **rancheras**, **boleros**, and **valses**. Jesus Rodriguez joined as codirector in 1955, experimenting with rhythmic combinations and complex harmonies for **baladas**. Since 1975, Mariachi Vargas has become a spectacular *mariachi* of 12 talented musicians and begun to perform medley pieces that showcase different regions of Mexico and the world.

Further Reading

Jáuregui, Jesús. "De la comarca a la fama mundial." In *El Mariachi. Símbolo musical de México*, 320–51. México: Taurus, 2007.

J. Jesús Jáuregui Jimenez

of *mariachi* was formed through a long process that combined indigenous cultural elements with those brought over from Mediterranean Europe and from sub-Saharan Africa, which resulted in a unique mixture, within which local variations with different instrumental personnel, performance, and singing practices, as well as special features regarding lyrics and how to dance.

The traditional *mariachi* was linked to festive and ritual life of rural communities, played generally by stringed instruments and had a reduced number of players: at least two but not more than five. It was a variant of an ensemble from New Spain and America consisting of **harp**, violin (rabel), and **vihuela**, and its manifestation corresponds to an oral tradition, which did not base its transmission on systems of written notation, so its musical and textual tradition now constitutes a marginalized collective heritage, still seen in remote populations of western Mexico, particularly where the Huichol, Cora, and mountain *mestizos* live.

Today the term *mariachi* refers to a musical ensemble, but in the 19th century it was used to refer to a popular open-air festival (*fandango*), the group of musicians, the songs that they performed, the platform on which the dancers performed **zapateado**, and to various ranches in the Nayarit-Sinaloa region. The etymology of the word is unknown, although the historical-linguistic analysis supports an indigenous origin in various languages of the Yutoazteca family, and has been traced back to 1832 to a toponymy reference for the name of a ranch called *mariachi/che* in Santiago Ixcuintla, Nayarit, rejecting the possible association with the French term for marriage (*mariage*).

Since the end of the 18th century, the **son** and the **jarabe** constituted the principal genres of the *mariachi* tradition in the secular sphere, while the minuet was the typical musical prayer for religious occasions. The **corrido** was the epic genre par excellence, and during the 19th century incorporated in its repertoire were **valses**, **polkas**, *chotes* (see **schottische**), *mazurkas, jotas,* and *costillas*. Those *mariachis* eventually included some aerophone instruments, like the transverse **flute**, but with the arrival of the military bands that spread throughout all of Mexico, and municipal wind bands at the end of the 19th century, *mariachi* groups appeared that included valve aerophones as an added instrument, which did not alter the chordophone balance of the group.

In the year 1907, for the first time, a *mariachi* orchestra from Jalisco wore the *traje de charro* (cowboy suit), imitating the *orquestas típicas* of the period. Since 1908, the music of one *mariachi* called Quartet Coculense was disseminated by North American record companies and in 1925, the first concert of *mariachi* music was broadcast over the radio in Mexico City. Since then, the *mariachi* has been rooted in the country's capital, where in the 1930's music for a new *estilo bravío*, which was advocated as *jaliscience* (Jalisco style) began to be composed, and was presented as rustic style, having as one of its original interpreters Lucha Reyes, a native of Guadalajara with a penetrating voice. The emergence and formation of modern *mariachi* in Mexico City led to a transformation of the elements of traditional *mariachi:* increased number of ensemble musicians, the use of the *charro* uniform, an alteration of the musical balance to enthrone the trumpet as an essential instrument, and the incorporation of songs with themes and urban texts like "Guadalajara," "Cocula," and "El Mexicano." Some time later, Jose Alfredo Jimenez added a spoken text to address internal conflict and frustrations of the Mexican male.

In 1940, *mariachi* music was integrated into classical music worldwide as a representative of Mexico. *Sones de mariachi,* arranged by Blas Galindo, is a work that surpassed exposition of rural issues and promoted these works to the rank of national airs. This step was a decisive move for the *orquesta typica* and the *mariachi trio ranchero* with trumpet, which dominated the national Mexican scenery.

The development of modern *mariachi* is linked to the course of development of singers in the **ranchero** style, most notably Pedro Vargas and Miguel Aceves and idols Jorge Negrete, Pedro Infante, and Javier Solis, who helped in its dissemination at the international level. Among composers, Tomas Mendez, Cuco Sanchez, and Chava Flores excelled, and among arrangers, Manuel Esperon and Ruben Fuentes. In the second half of the 20th century, the cowboy singers Cornelio Reyna and Vicente Fernandez came to the scene as well as popular singers Maria de Lourdes and Aida Cuevas, and the composer Juan Gabriel, who introduced playful or amorous themes with gender-neutral lyrics. Over time, idols and songs are replaced regularly, and *mariachi* music adjusts to hybrid interpretations distanced from its classic sound.

Few *mariachi* groups, considered among the elite, succeeded exhibiting themselves as soloists, among those Mariachi Mexico de Pepe Villa and Mariachi Vargas de Tecalitlan, whose musicians are performers, singers, and dancers/choreographers. Some of these ensembles introduced the genre *mariachístico,* and had steady development of their careers, but the majority of these acts were of variable significance. An egalitarian complaint has been made for the inclusion of women and the formation of female *mariachi* ensembles has been accepted. The majority of popular *mariachis,* however, remain without proper social recognition, and as ephemeral groups lacking in economic resources to compete.

The modern *mariachi* emerged as a product of mass communication media, those in America and disseminated by Latin America in the **United States** through radio, records, and movies. In fact, it was the golden age of Mexican cinema that forged the visual and sonic stereotype of the *mariachi* as a rustic jalisciense ensemble composed of *mestizos* with an image closer to Europeans and distanced from the indigenous and the black.

Although it is the musical symbol of Mexico, the special fusion of rhythmic, musical, and textual elements of various cultural branches has risen the *mariachi* to a universal rank having popularity not only in **Colombia, Venezuela, Costa Rica, Guatemala**, Aruba, and the United States, but also in Spain, Italy, France, Holland, Belgium, the Balkans, and even in Japan. In a non-Spanish-speaking context, the *mariachi* first circulated as an exotic music, but was soon adopted as worthy representative of a Latin American cultural amalgam. It is paradoxical to observe that while in Mexico the diffusion of the music has fallen, in the United States the *mariachi* entered the university in 1962, from when it began its academic study and the schooling of its profession. At the same time, festivals and conferences of *mariachi* began to emerge, among them the Tucson Mariachi Conference in 1983 whose success later prompted the International Mariachi Conference in Guadalajara in 1994.

In current-day, modern Mexico, among the *mariachi* elite, espectaculaers or and monumentales are perhaps a new version of the *orquesta típica porfiriana,* with whom they share the following characteristics: they are composed of musicians of note, they dress in the cowboy suit, they interpret the vernacular music of different regions in Mexico, they exhibit themselves as representatives of the national music, they have the medley as one of their principal genres, and their presentations are delivered on stage for an audience gathered to listen. From the traditional *mariachi,* they maintain the habit of playing while standing and have a conductor/performer, but the instrumental contribution is the unique style of trumpets that is not originally from Jalisco, but Mexico City.

Further Reading

Jáuregui, Jesús. *El Mariachi. Símbolo musical de México.* Mexico: Taurus, 2007.

Moreno, Yolanda. *Historia de la música popular mexicana (los noventa)*, Mexico: Alianza Editorial, 1989.

Sheehy, Daniel. *Mariachi Music in America.* New York: Oxford University Press, 2006.

J. Jesús Jáuregui Jimenez

Marimba

The *marimba* is a type of xylophone consisting of wooden bars suspended over a set of resonators and struck with mallets, the *marimba* first emerged in Latin America during the colonial period. Recreated from diverse African models brought to the Americas by slaves, evidence suggests that use of the instrument was once widespread throughout Latin America, including in **Brazil, Cuba**, and **Peru**, though extant *marimba* traditions today are found in only two regions: Central America, including southern **Mexico**; and northwestern South America, along the Pacific coast of **Colombia** and **Ecuador**.

In the Meso-American region, the *marimba* is found in urban areas of all countries in Central America except Belize and **Panama**, and is especially prominent in the indigenous and *mestizo/ladino* musical traditions of **Guatemala**, where it is considered the national instrument, and the southern Mexican states of Oaxaca and Chiapas. The near-disappearance of Afro-descendant communities in this region by the 19th century, as well as the instrument's early acceptance by the indigenous Mayan population, have largely obscured the *marimba's* African origins in Central America, and led to the instrument being primarily associated with indigenous and nationalist musical traditions. Nonetheless, aspects of African musical influence remain, particularly in the *charleo* or buzzing sound of the instrument, which is created by a thin membrane stretched across a small hole in each resonator.

Several types of *marimba* are played in the Guatemalan/Mexican region. The *marimba de tecomates* is a single-rank, diatonic instrument with gourd resonators. Typically played by a single musician in indigenous communities, it is performed for both sacred and secular occasions, and may be accompanied by a small drum or cane **flute**. The *marimba sencilla,* or simple *marimba,* is a larger diatonic instrument with suspended wooden box resonators, which emerged in urban areas in the 19th century and allows multiple players to perform on a single, freestanding instrument. Finally, the *marimba doble,* or double *marimba,* is a chromatic, double-rank instrument with box resonators, typically suspended from an ornately carved wooden frame, and played by three to four people simultaneously. This instrument was invented in the late 19th century to allow for more complex arrangements of popular music and became the favored instrument of urban, *mestizo marimba* ensembles. Often performed in pairs of a *marimba grande* (large *marimba*) and *marimba cuache* (tenor *marimba*), and accompanied by a rhythm section including drumset and bass, the *marimba doble* remains the dominant version of the instrument found throughout Central America today, and was the prototype for the North American orchestral marimba earlier in the 20th century.

The exception to this characterization is the Nicaraguan *marimba de arco* (arc or hoop *marimba*), found in the Pacific coastal area of southern **Nicaragua** and most prominently associated with the city of Masaya. Retaining the arc found on the northern *marimba de tecomates* but substituting tubular resonators carved from cedar wood, the *marimba de arco* is performed in a **trio** that also includes **guitar** and *guitarilla,* a small four-stringed lute. Unlike the *marimba sencilla* or *marimba doble,* in which melody, harmony, and bass lines are divided between multiple players, the *marimba de arco* is a solo instrument, with the bass line and harmony/melody divided between the performer's left and right hands, respectively.

The South American *marimba* tradition differs substantially from its Central American counterpart. Played almost exclusively by Afro-descendant populations in Ecuador and Colombia, the musical ensemble and esthetic bear a much closer relationship with African musics, including leader–group alternation, drum ensemble accompaniment, and cyclical, improvisatory forms, though without the characteristic buzzing sound of Central American and most African *marimbas.* The *marimba* itself in this region is traditionally a single-rank, diatonic instrument of roughly three-and-a-half octaves, with bamboo resonators, though chromatic double-rank instruments have recently become popular. The instrument is played by two performers, one of whom plays an ostinato-like bass figure called the *bordón,* the second of which plays the more improvisatory treble line called the ***tiple***. They are accompanied by an ensemble including two *cununos* (wedge-tuned hand drums, similar to a Cuban **conga**), one or two ***bombos*** (bass drums played with sticks), several *guasás* (bamboo shakers), and vocalists, including a *glosador* (lead singer) and several *respondadoras* (female choir). The *marimba* ensemble typically plays to accompany folk dances that correspond to the different *temas* or themes played by the *marimba* itself. Since the 1990s, the *marimba* has become an important symbol of Afro-Ecuadorian and Afro-Colombian identity and is celebrated in numerous festivals every year throughout the region.

Further Reading

Navarrete Pellicer, Sergio. *Maya Achi Marimba Music in Guatemala.* Philadelphia, PA: Temple University Press, 2005.

Scruggs, T.M. "Central America: Marimba and Other Musics of Guatemala and Nicaragua." In *Musics in Latin American Culture: Regional Traditions,* edited by John Schechter, 80–125. New York: Schirmer Books, 1999.

Jonathan Ritter

Marímbula

The *marímbula* is a Cuban thumb piano used by early ***changüí*** and ***son*** groups primarily as a bass function within an ensemble. The instrument consists of a large wooden resonating box with one to several holes in the front. Across the front of the box is fastened a rod that acts as a bridge to hold a series of metal tongues of different sizes, which are fastened by a pressure rod that is fitted over the bridge. The keys are tuned by adjusting the length of the free or long ends of the tongue, which are then plucked by the player. Normally players pluck the metal tongues while straddling the instrument for a seated performance position. The instrument originated in the Oriente province of **Cuba**, and eventually spread to other parts of the Caribbean where it was used in regional folk musics of **Haiti**, the **Dominican Republic, Puerto Rico**, and Jamaica. The instrument was cultivated by African slaves who used whatever material was available to them, including crates for the resonator, and bamboo, or premanufactured steel items, such as hack-saw blades, for the tongues. While the *marímbula* is still used today in Cuban *changüí* ensembles, its use in the Cuban *son* was eventually superseded by the double bass.

Further Reading

Thompson, Donald. "The Marímbula: An Afro-Caribbean *Sanza.*" *Yearbook of the Inter-American Institute for Musical Research* 7 (1971): 103–16.

George Torres

Martinique and Guadeloupe

Martinique and Guadeloupe are islands in the eastern Caribbean Sea. Former French colonies, they were incorporated into the Republic of France as overseas *départements* in 1946. Due to their history of plantation slavery, the population of the two islands is predominately Afro-*Creole.* Although French is the official language, most Martinicans and Guadeloupeans speak *Creole* in daily conversation, and *Creole* is the language most commonly used in the folk and popular music of the French Antilles.

The folk music of Martinique and Guadeloupe is based on African antecedents, with influences from European dance music, particularly the French *contredanse* and quadrille. In Martinique, these dances developed into the *bèlè* (of which there are several varieties), the *kalenda*, and the *haute taille*. Musical accompaniment is exclusively song and percussion instruments including a drum called the *tanbou bèlè* and a metal rattle called the *chacha*. In Guadaloupe similar dances known collectively as *bamboula* or *gwotambou* developed, with accompaniment of call and response vocals and percussion. In recent years these dances have become emblematic of the region's Afro-*Creole* heritage and are featured in folkloric presentations at festivals and tourist shows at local hotels.

In the 19th century, Afro-*Creole* musicians blended the Afro-*Creole* music with European dances such as the **waltz** and the **polka** to create various styles of urban dance music known collectively as ***Musique Créole***. The three main song types of *Musique Créole* are ***biguine, mazouk*** *(mazurka),* and *valse Créole*. Instrumentation is not standard, but generally features clarinet, saxophone, trumpet, and bamboo flute as solo instruments, a rhythm section made up of drum set, piano, bass, and banjo or guitar, along with Afro-*Creole* percussion such as the *tibwa* (Fr. *petit bois,* "little sticks") and *chacha*. *Biguine* musicians found success in mainland France in the 1920s and 1930s, and were popular there until newer styles emerged in the 1970s.

Carnival has been part of the festival calendar in both Martinique and Guadeloupe since colonial times. While "foreign" music such as ***calypso*** and ***soca*** enjoy great popularity in contemporary Carnival celebrations, there have been important local developments in recent decades. Among the changes in *Vaval*, the name for Carnival in Martinique, is the introduction of *groups à pied:* neighborhood-based marching bands featuring brass instruments, *tanbou, chacha,* as well as homemade percussion made of various types of containers and PVC pipe. In Guadeloupe in the 1960s, urban youth revitalized Afro-*Creole* drumming traditions in a new style and ensemble called ***gwoka*** (Fr. *Creole gros ka,* "big drum"). Seven traditional rhythms associated with *gwoka* accompany improvisatory dancing by male and female soloists. As in Martinique, this new style has become associated with Carnival as well as other celebrations.

In the 1980s, ***zouk*** emerged as the dominant form of urban dance music in the region, combining various styles of French Antillian music with ***reggae*** and ***salsa***. As with *biguine* in earlier decades, performers of *zouk*, such as the super-group Kassav, have enjoyed considerable success in mainland France. From the 1990s to the present, Jamaican dance hall has been very influential throughout the Caribbean. French Antillean youth have created a style called *ragga* in response, rapping in French *Creole* about local issues, and blending dance hall music with the *tibwa* rhythm of other genres.

Further Reading

Guilbault, Jocelyne. *Zouk: World Music in the West Indies*. Chicago, IL: University of Chicago Press, 1993.

Manuel, Peter Lamarche, Kenneth M. Bilby, and Michael D. Largey. *Caribbean Currents: Caribbean Music from Rumba to Reggae*. Revised and expanded. Philadelphia, PA: Temple University Press, 2006.

Hope Smith

Maxixe

From its emergence in the late 1870s to its decline in the 1920s, few genres of popular music were as wildly popular, and as controversial, as the Brazilian *maxixe,* a fast-paced couples dance in which bodies are pressed together and the legs are often intertwined, similar to the contemporary *lambada.* A mainstay of **choro** ensembles, the *maxixe* was associated for many years of **Carnival** celebrations until it was supplanted permanently by the *samba*. The *maxixe's* impact on popular music led it to be the first great contribution of the lower classes of Rio de Janeiro to the popular music of **Brazil**.

The *maxixe* dance was related to the **polka**, which arrived in Rio de Janeiro in the 1840s and quickly became popular among all social classes. When danced by the lower strata of society, the Brazilian version of the polka involved a tightly embracing couple, with exaggerated movements of both legs and torso. Brazilian musicians accompanying the dance naturally adapted the rhythms of the polka to better support the movements of the dancers, and the *maxixe* was born.

The etymology of the word *maxixe* to refer to the dance is uncertain. One popular belief is that the dance was invented by a popular dancer whose nickname was Maxixe (a bitter fruit popular in many Brazilian dishes) who added quick improvised steps to the polka, and musicians played the polka at a faster tempo to accommodate his fancy new steps. Another commonly held belief is that the name comes from the macho nature of the dance itself, in which the male is clearly the dominant partner. From *dança do macho* comes *machice* or *machiche,* which over time adopted the orthography of the fruit.

Few popular dances caused as much moral outrage among the self-proclaimed guardians of culture as the *maxixe*. Shortly after it took Rio de Janeiro by storm, the *maxixe* was publicly condemned as low-class, vulgar, and lascivious, danced in halls frequented by loose women and unscrupulous men. The *maxixe,* together with other genres exhibiting overt African rhythmic influences such as *lundu* and *samba,* was seen as the cause of the moral decline of Brazilian society, actively moving it away from the genteel nature of European models into decadence. Even more disturbing to the upper class was the fact that young white women could and did dance the *maxixe* with black partners. At times, cultured society became so morally outraged by the *maxixe* that they insisted the police close down the dance halls where it was practiced. In 1907 the Minister of War even banned the *maxixe* from performance by military bands because of the character it encouraged.

Despite the attitudes of the elite, or perhaps in part because of its notoriety, the dance was quickly adopted by instrumental ensembles of the day, and it was assimilated and stylized by the middle sectors and high society. One such stylized form was the *maxixe de salão,* a more restrained version of the dance than was practiced in the dance halls and bars. In 1895 the *maxixe* attained a degree of social respectability with the opening of an operetta called *Zizinha maxixe* that included popular *maxixes* with lyrics added. By 1901 the *maxixe* had gained enough respect to support the publication of a newspaper in Rio de Janeiro called *O Maxixe,* and in 1906, a theatrical revue called *O Maxixe* opened at the prestigious Teatro Carlos Gomes. Although the *maxixe* dance was eventually accepted in the salon (albeit in a somewhat tamed version), and had become popular in theater productions, the term *maxixe* was avoided. Instead the more acceptable euphemism **tango** or *tango brasileiro* was often used in its place. By the 1910s however, the terms *maxixe* and *tango* were often used interchangeably.

At the time of the *maxixe*'s greatest popularity, French culture dominated artistic and intellectual thought in Brazil. It was not uncommon for Brazilians of sufficient means to go France for their education, and just as they eagerly adopted French culture, Parisians eagerly embraced Brazilian culture. The *maxixe* was quickly adopted in Paris for its exoticism and sensuality. Known as the *matchitche,* the dance spawned derivatives including the *Apaché* (Apache dance), named after the American Indian tribe because of its savage imagery, and which remained popular in Parisian bohemian society for some time.

By the 1930s the *maxixe* dance had declined in popularity, supplanted by the urban *samba* and new imports such as the foxtrot and Charleston introduced by American **jazz** bands that were becoming popular in Rio de Janeiro. The *maxixe,* however, remained in the *choro* repertory as an instrumental genre, and *maxixes* continue to be composed today.

Further Reading

Béhague, Gerard. "Popular Musical Currents in the Art Music of the Early Nationalistic period in Brazil, Circa 1870–1920." Ph.D. diss., Tulane University, 1966.

Efegê, Jota. *Maxixe—a dança excomungada.* Rio de Janeiro: Conquista, 1974.

Garcia, Thomas George Caracas. "The Brazilian Choro: Music, Politics and Performance." Ph.D. diss., Duke University, 1997.

Livingston-Isenhour, Tamara Elena, and Thomas George Caracas Garcia. *Choro: A Social History of a Brazilian Popular Music.* Bloomington: Indiana University Press, 2005.

Tinhorão, José Ramos. *Pequena história da Música Popular.* São Paulo: Circulo do Livro, 1980.

Thomas George Caracas Garcia

Mazouk

The *mazouk* is the Creolized version of the European ***mazurka***, a 19th-century European social dance of Polish origin, which reached its height of popularity in Europe during the 1830s and 1840s. It was during this time that a mulatto elite in the French Caribbean began cultivating creolized versions of genres imported from Europe. These included a trio of Africanized dances—the ***biguine***, *mazouk,* and ***vals creole,*** together known as *mizi kwéyòl.* The *mazouk,* like the Polish *mazurka,* is in a simple triple meter with an accented second beat. Like the *biguine,* the *mazouk* uses a typical rhythm derived from the ***cinquillo*** pattern called *tibwa mazouk.* Part of the creolization of the *mazouk* was the addition of the African-influenced layered percussion rhythms with individual parts playing an *ostinato* timeline pattern, a complex, composite rhythm, to the European styled melody and harmony. *Mazouks* are sectional in their musical structure with repetitions of each strain before continuing to the next, the repetition having some sort of variation. A standard *mazouk* might also have a contrasting section known as *la nuit* with a contrasting rhythmic structure. The popularity of the *mazouk* lasted through the French Antilles's golden age of ballroom dance music into the 1950s.

Further Reading

Cyrille, Dominique, Malena Kuss, and Julian Gerstin. "Martinique." *Music in Latin America and the Caribbean: An Encyclopedic History.* Austin: University of Texas Press, 2004.

George Torres

Merengue (Dominican Republic)

Emerging as a pan-Caribbean genre in the 19th century, *merengue* gained prominence in the **Dominican Republic**, where it was embraced as a national symbol in the middle of the 20th century and was then spread throughout Latin American as a transnational commodified form. The musical and choreographic style of Dominican *merengue* reflects a marriage of African and European elements: interlocking, responsorial relationships of musical instruments and dance steps express a basically African-derived esthetic, while melodies and ballroom dance influences reflect European influences. Dating to the 1840s, the earliest references to *merengue* are found in **Puerto Rico**, where it was considered a variant of the ***danza***. Local

Merengue dancers wearing traditional dresses perform during the opening ceremony of the XIV Pan American Games at the Olympic Stadium Juan Pablo Duarte in Santo Domingo in 2003. (Antonio Scorza/AFP/Getty Images)

variants of *merengue* developed in **Haiti, Venezuela, Colombia**, and the Dominican Republic, where it was first documented in1854. In all these countries, *merengue* was danced by independent couples (instead of in groups) and was marked by Afro-Caribbean rhythmic tinges.

Eurocentric Dominican elites rejected *merengue* in the late 19th century for its suggestive dance style and African influences. The Afro-Dominican rural population, however, adopted *merengue,* infusing it with even more African influences, and rural variants developed in several regions of the country; some are still performed today (especially *pri-prí,* also known as *merengue palo echao,* which is played in Villa Mella). Only the Cibao region's variant, however, gained prominence. During the mid-19th century, *merengue típico cibaeño* (Cibao-style folk *merengue*) was performed on the *tambora* (a double-headed drum), the **güira** (a metal scraper), and string instruments. By the 1870s, the button **accordion** had supplanted the string instruments, and by the early 20th century an alto saxophone was occasionally added.

American President Woodrow Wilson ordered an invasion of the Dominican Republic on May 5, 1916, and the **United States** established a military government that ruled the country until 1924. When the occupation began, most upper-class

Dominicans rejected both rural Afro-Caribbean genres and modernistic North American imports in favor of European-influenced forms such as the waltz, **polka**, and *danza*. The patriotic mood that arose in the face of the American presence, however, encouraged composers to take interest in local rural music; Cibao natives Juan Francisco García and Julio Alberto Hernández composed concert pieces based on *merengue*. Influenced by this trend, Cibao bandleader Juan Espínola made a mark by performing refined *danza*-tinged *merengue* arrangements for ballroom dancing. By the 1920s and 1930s, salon dance bands were influenced by North American popular music introduced by the occupying Marines. The **jazz** vogue, however, did not meet a wholly favorable reaction in the face of anti-American sentiment that reigned during and after the occupation. In 1933, the Cibao bandleader Luis Alberti diffused these sentiments by fusing *merengue* with big-band jazz. This new jazz-tinged *merengue* style soon found a permanent, though small, place in the Cibao dance band repertories.

The Dominican dictator Rafael Trujillo rose to power in 1930. Despite the fact that he himself was of partial African and Haitian descent, Trujillo espoused a racist idea of Dominicanness that excluded explicit links to Africa and Haiti from officially sanctioned national culture. Like the Nazis, he understood that folklore can be a potent symbol of the nation, and in 1936 brought Luis Alberti's band, renamed Orquesta Presidente Trujillo, to the capital city to play jazz-influenced big-band arrangements of *merengue* at high-society balls. All of the country's dance bands were required to perform newly composed *merengues* praising the dictator, and *merengue* became a significant national symbol. Trujillo's embrace of *merengue* issued from the music's syncretic nature: in spite of its distinctly African-based esthetic, *merengue's* European elements set it apart from African-influenced Dominican ritual drumming such as *palos,* making it compatible with the dictator's Eurocentric and anti-Haitian brand of Dominicanness. Under Trujillo, *merengue* was often performed on live radio broadcasts, but it was rarely recorded in the Dominican Republic. Ex-patriot Dominican bandleader Angel Viloria, however, recorded many merengue LPs in New York City in the 1950s, gaining fame not only among Latinos in the United States, but also in Haiti and **Cuba**. Ironically, in spite of the anti-Haitianness of Trujillo's nationalism, which played such an important role in the development of the genre, Dominican *merengue* gained popularity in Haiti during this period, even exerting a major influence on the preeminent Haitian popular music, **konpa** (which, interestingly, was also influenced by Haitian *méringue*).

Despite *merengue's* close association with Trujillo, the music remained popular after the dictator's fall; an anti-Trujillo *merengue* entitled "La muerte del chivo" ("The Death of the Goat") made a big hit immediately following his assassination in 1961. Bandleader Johnny Ventura incorporated *salsa* elements and rock 'n' roll performance style into his style of *merengue,* which abandoned big-band instrumentation in favor of a smaller *conjunto* (combo) format. Significantly, during the 1965 Dominican civil war, Ventura sang to troops that resisted North American forces, which had invaded the Republic in support of neo-Trujilloist elements. The country opened to outside influences as never before in the post-Trujillo era, and under the influence of bandleaders such as Wilfrido Vargas and Juan Luis Guerra, *merengue* incorporated outside elements ranging from romantic *baladas* to Colombian and Haitian *konpa,* to **hip-hop**. During this period, a coterie of young Dominicans began to challenge the Eurocentrism that had long characterized Dominicanness. While this trend never reached the prominence of negritude movements elsewhere in the Caribbean, it is significant that several high-profile *merengue* musicians invoked Afro-Dominican culture in their music in the 1990s; bandleader Kinito Méndez, for example, incorporated Afro-Dominican ritual *palos* and *slave* influences into his music, gaining fame with his version of a traditional rural song dedicated to the Afro-Dominican *Vodú luá* (or spirit) Ogun Balenyó.

Despite *merengue's* phenomenal popularity, a new Dominican music called *bachata* became increasingly popular beginning in the 1970s. As a genre, *bachata* is distinguished by its **guitar**-based instrumentation and texts whose street language ironically comments on working-class life, often employing bawdy double meanings. Several musical types, including *merengue,* are performed within the rubric of *bachata.* But *merengue* still gained a high profile in the growing Dominican diaspora in the late 20th century, where it fomented social cohesion and served as a symbolic counterforce to Anglo hegemony. Gaining access to the transnational music industry, *merengue* became diffused throughout Latin America and beyond, even challenging *salsa's* position as the preeminent Latin Caribbean dance music. Dominican *merengue* became so popular in Puerto Rico that many musicians and fans there came to consider it their own. This embrace is all the more significant when one considers the fact that *merengue* was first documented in Puerto Rico. In spite of this transnationalization, traditional accordion-based *merengue* remained popular, incorporating new influences, even from **hip-hop**. Hip-hop also influenced the development of a new *merengue* variant, sometimes called *merengue de mambo,* which, like earlier forms of the music, was criticized for lewdness in lyric and dance style.

Further Reading

Alberti, Luis. *De música y orquestas bailables dominicanas, 1910–1959.* Santo Domingo: Taller, 1975.

Austerlitz, Paul. *Merengue: Dominican Music and Dominican Identity.* Philadelphia: Temple University Press, 1997.

Davis, Martha Ellen.1976. "Afro-Dominican Religious Brotherhoods: Structure, Ritual, Music." Ph.D. diss., University of Illinois, 1976.

Jorge, Bernarda. *La música dominicana, siglos XIX–XX.* Santo Domingo: Editora Universitaria—UASD, 1982.

Pacini Hernandez, Deborah. *Bachata: A Social History of a Dominican Popular Music.* Philadephia: Temple University Press, 1995.

Pérez de Cuello, Catana and Rafael Solano. *El merengue: música y baile de la República Dominicana.* Santo Domingo: Verizon, 2005.

Tallaj, Angelina. Forthcoming. "Performing Blackness, Resisting Whiteness: Dominican Music and Identity." Ph.D. diss., City University of New York.

Paul Austerlitz

Méringue (Haiti)

Méringue is a creolized genre of Haitian music and dance that emerged in the 19th century that descended from the *contredanse* via the *carabinier*. Indeed, by the beginning of the 20th century, the *méringue* superseded the *contredanse* in popularity. From the mid-19th century to the mid-20th century, the *méringue* became a music and dance symbol of **Haiti**. The *méringue* was developed at a time in Haiti's history when European social dances were being mixed with African-derived music. Examples of *méringue* performance were enjoyed equally from among the working classes to refined social groups among Haiti's elite. As a distinct genre, the term *méringue* is problematic in that it may be used to refer to a variety of different Haitian song and dance forms. Among the more elite groups, it was donned as a kind of elite parlor music known as *méringue lente* or *méringue de salon*. Among lower social groups, *méringues* were also performed during **Carnival** in a procession known as *méringue de carnaval*. Among bourgeois society, the term may refer to a type of social dance that was accompanied by dance bands of the period. The term also designates music performed by itinerant musicians, usually of a lower social station, performed in tourist areas such as hotels, restaurants, and airports.

In spite of the apparently close association between the *méringue* and the Dominican *merengue*, there is a considerable amount of disagreement regarding the African origins and Haitian influence of *méringue* on the Dominican *merengue*. Gage Averill points to the considerable amount of political tension between these two countries as a reason for the disagreement about the genre's origins.

As a dance, the *méringue* was performed in a variety of contexts depending on the venues. In the ballroom among the middle and upper classes, the *méringue* was a couple dance, which was expected to be learned among the well-bred members of Haitian society. It was thus the favorite dance among the Haitian elite. Averill points to a well known statement that attested to the importance of the dance at social gatherings: "*Mereng ouvri bal, Mereng fenmen bal. . .*" ("The *méringue* opens the ball, The *méringue* closes the ball. . ."). At the other end of the social spectrum, the *méringue de carnaval* was danced as a street procession and adapted to the exuberant spirit of Carnival.

The chief musical characteristic associated with *méringue* is a five-pulse rhythm, which was appropriated from the *contredanse,* and this rhythm is known in Haiti as the *quintolet,* and in **Cuba** as the *cinquillo*, with the rhythm approximating a long-short-long-short-long subdivision. This rhythm, with strong associations to many types of Caribbean musics, appears to have reached Cuba via Haiti, after the 1804 revolution, with a close Cuban relative being the *danzón*. Depending on the context of performance, the *quintolet* could either be performed as a syncopated rhythm, or as a more rubato-like interpretation where the five pulses are played more or less evenly across the measure, the former interpretation more common in dance band interpretations, while the latter was more common in solo salon music for piano.

The *méringue* provides an interesting example of a crossover genre that was capable of interclass contact among different social strata in Haiti. This can be seen in examples of composers of art music, who would compose *méringues* for the various social groups mentioned above. For art music composers, the *méringue* served as a vehicle for infusing African elements into the art music of Haiti. Composers such as Ludovic Lamothe, Justin Elie, Werner Anton Jagerhuber, and Frantz Casséus all used *méringue*-influenced rhythms in some of their classically derived music, which resulted in their maintaining a strong connection to the popular. Lamothe's output consisted of compositions in the style of *méringue de salon,* such as "La Dangerouse" for solo piano, as well as a *méringue de carnaval* entitled "Nibo," which won the prize for best song competition in 1934. Additionally, Casseus's "Coumbite" (Kreyol: *konbit*), which is cast in a *quintolet* rhythm, became a pop hit for Harry Belafonte under the title "Merci Bon Dieu."

Further Reading

Averill, Gage. *A Day for the Hunter, a Day for the Prey: Popular Music and Power in Haiti.* Chicago studies in ethnomusicology. Chicago: University of Chicago Press, 1997.

Bilby, Kenneth M., Michael D. Largey, and Peter Manuel. *Caribbean Currents: Caribbean Music from Rumba to Reggae.* Philadelphia, PA: Temple University Press, 2006.

Largey, Michael. "Haiti: Tracing the Steps of the Meringue and Contredanse." *Creolizing Contradance in the Caribbean,* 209–30. Philadelphia, PA: Temple University Press, 2009.

George Torres

Mexico

Mexico is bordered by the **United States** to the north and Belize and **Guatemala** to the south. The population is 60 percent *mestizo,* 30 percent Amerindian, 9 percent white, and 1 percent other. Mexico was ruled by Spain for nearly three centuries, after the conquest of the Aztec (Mexica) Empire. Music in Mexico is a combination of traits from different musical traditions. Like its racially mixed peoples, the *mestizos*, musical traditions have an essential *mestizo* character. Iberian music and dance brought to Mexico have been kept alive and have blended with native traditions. *Afro-mestizo* traditions are mainly found along the Gulf coast and in the Pacific coastal area. Most Amerindian musical events coincide with the Catholic liturgical calendar and feature a syncretic mixture of European and Amerindian elements. Indigenous music, dance, and ritual are still thriving throughout Mexico but are essentially incompatible with the popular musical world.

Except for the African-derived **marimba** (xylophone), found throughout southern Mexico, all folk instruments are adopted and adapted from European instruments. The violin, the diatonic **harp**, and the **guitar** were all introduced early during the colonial period. The import of brass and wind instruments from Europe in the second half of the 19th century led to the formation of municipal and community bands. The diatonic button **accordion** was brought to Mexico's Northeast by German and Czech immigrants in the late 1800s.

The Iberian folk and popular religious repertories diffused by missionaries during the colonial period had a significant influence on music and dance in New Spain, still evident in the many folk religious plays associated with Christian holidays. As Spanish dominance deteriorated in the late 18th century, music and dance with a more local character began to emerge. Transformations of Spanish folk expressions into local genres and styles gained in popularity after 1810, when Mexico achieved independence from Spain and when the ecclesiastical control of social and cultural life diminished. At the same time Mexicans' interest in European fine-art music grew stronger. Although the country's upper classes enjoyed a musical life dominated by Italian opera and lighter musical theater derived from the Spanish *zarzuela*, local tunes and dances (*sones* and *jarabes*) found their way into the musical comedies featured at the cities' theaters. Upper-middle-class parlors resounded with song and romantic piano music. During the last decades of the 19th century, a definable Mexican national style emerged. Mexicans' struggle during the 19th century to affirm their own cultural and political identity eventually led them to turn to their folk and folklore in order to differentiate their national heritage from other nation-states. *Mestizo* folk music came to be considered the most representative and most consistent expression of Mexican music.

Mexico's repertory of popular music, from its very beginnings in the 19th century, cannot always be sharply distinguished from those of folk music traditions and art music as these categories overlap substantially (see **Folk, Art, and Popular Music**). In fact, popular music genres in Mexico were often urban renditions of folk genres, whereas the most popular folk songs were influenced by 19th-century European salon music. This ambiguity is reflected in the common use of the term popular music: in the Spanish language the term *música popular* actually means music of the people, encompassing what ethnomusicologists call folk and traditional as well as popular urban music. Outside academia, mass-mediated popular music is commonly referred to as *música pop* (pop music) or *música comercial* (commercial music).

National and Regional Musics

The urban *orquesta* (a small orchestra dominated by string instruments), favored by the upper and expanding middle classes for serenades and private events, played selections of the popular and semiclassical repertories. During the first decades of the 20th century, the music of composers like Miguel Lerdo de Tejada, the director of Mexico City's Orquesta Típica (an ensemble formed in 1884 consisting of an array of string instruments, wind instruments, and marimba, with musicians dressed in folkloric garb), acquired an intensely Mexican flavor. In the mid-1920s, Los Trovadores Tamaulipecos, a string band from northeast Mexico, spearheaded the creation of the new *ranchera* style, which would become Mexico's quintessential popular music genre.

From the numerous regional folk string ensembles, it was the *mariachi* from the state of Jalisco that in the 1930s developed into Mexico's national music ensemble. Part of the state's efforts to produce a more integrated society was the creation of an official folklore that would help blur regional differences. Cultural missionaries were sent out by the government to study and collect folk songs and dances throughout Mexico. Existing traditional practices were modified and institutionalized for the new nationalism. The *mariachi* originally consisted of **harp**, *guitarra de golpe* (guitar type), and one or two violins. The urbanized *mariachi* replaced the harp with the more practical **guitarrón** (bass guitar). The developing radio, film, and recording industries of the early 1930s were influential in forming the typical *mariachi* ensemble with added trumpets. Nationalistic radio laws issued by the Mexican government privileged certain popular cultural forms in order to ensure that the medium would disseminate a uniquely Mexican culture and thereby promote a sense of national solidarity.

The *mariachi* fit the kind of national ideology propagated by the postrevolutionary government, but many other distinctive local ensemble types remained virtually unknown outside their regions of origin. Some of these marginalized styles survived the century, though mostly in modernized versions, and were ultimately embraced by the national and international popular music industries. Among those were the brass band traditions. As one of Europe's most significant cultural exports of the 19th century, the brass band was introduced to every colony overseas. Facilitated by the mass production of brass instruments and new valve mechanisms, *bandas populares* (popular bands) became a ubiquitous feature of Mexico's musical life in the late 19th century and thrived in both rural and urban areas. **Bandas** were performed at various outdoor celebrations such as bullfights, cockfights, horse races, parades, saint days, weddings, and funerals. Like the military bands at that time, popular bands played an eclectic repertory of **marchas** (marches), operatic selections, and popular dances such as waltz, **polka**, and *schottische*. In the early 20th century, specific combinations of brass, woodwind, and percussion instruments consolidated in different regions of Mexico. It was the revolutionary movement of the first two decades of the 20th century, however, that played a crucial role in the development of bands' regional characteristics, inasmuch as it was a major impetus to both patriotism and regionalism.

Another of those peripheral music styles was the accordion-driven *conjunto norteño*, a small ensemble from rural northern Mexico. Introduced by German and Czech settlers in the late 19th century, the button accordion appealed to the local musicians who developed a mixed repertory of popular dances such as *schottisches, redowas,* polkas, **canciónes** (songs), and **corridos** (folk ballads descended from the Spanish romance). This music migrated with the peasants to the cities, where *norteño,* due to the modernization of the instrumentation in the 1950s (most notably the addition of an electric guitar and a drum set), eventually spread from the

---

Velázquez, Consuelo

Composer and lyrist Consuelo Velázquez (1916–2005) wrote "Bésame mucho." It was the only song to top the U.S. charts for 12 weeks running, and it had two million radio and television performances, according to BMI, at the time of Velázquez's death. Velázquez's music career began at an early age, and she gave her first performance at the age six. She graduated from the national conservatory in Mexico City as a classical pianist at age 20. As a composer of songs, Velázquez wrote about suffering lovers, claiming to rely on her imagination for her subject matter. She wrote "Bésame mucho" when she was 25, and, as she claimed, "had never been kissed." She worked at radio station XEQ, planning their classical music programming and was featured on her own program under a male pseudonym since radio was considered immodest for women. Many well-known performers covered Velázquez's songs, including Frank Sinatra, the Beatles, Elvis Presley, Diana Krall, Cesaria Evora, and Placido Domingo. Her popular songs include "Anoche," "No me pidas nunca," "Déjame quererte," "Pensará en mí," "Yo no fui," "Que seas feliz," and "Cachito."

Further Reading

Fox, Margalit. "Consuelo Velázquez Dies; Wrote 'Bésame Mucho.'" *New York Times* Obituary, January 30, 2005.

Rebecca Stuhr

working-class neighborhoods to the dancehalls of the middle classes. Nowadays, *norteño* figures among Mexico's commercially most popular music styles.

Throughout most of the 20th century, the Mexican media industries were controlled and centered in Mexico City, which largely determined trends and fashions in popular music. Emerging in the 1930s, the *comedia ranchera* (ranch comedy), the most enduring genre of Mexican cinema, helped to establish the *canción **ranchera***, a kind of romantic pseudo-folk song performed by famous singing actors with *mariachi* accompaniment. After World War II, the ***canción romántica***, a more refined and sentimental version of the *canción ranchera,* arose and gained in popularity, in particular among middle-class urbanites. During the golden age of Mexican romantic music in the 1940s and 1950s the ***bolero***, originally a Cuban form that was adapted by Mexican composers and performers in the 1930s, enjoyed great popularity in the capital and other cities. A slow and soft musical style emphasizing vocal melody, the *bolero* was able to give authentic voice to the new cosmopolitan

Lara, Agustín

Agustín Lara (1897–1970) is considered **Mexico's** greatest songwriter. His song output is believed to have reached about 700 songs, though only about 420 survive in documented sources. Lara's early reputation was as a member of Mexico's cabaret culture, where he worked as a pianist and singer. Many of his songs from this period pay homage to the fallen woman archetype. Lara brought the Mexican urban popular song to national prominence. He assimilated national and international styles in his music, such as the Mexican **son**, Argentine **tango**, waltz, fox trot, and most importantly, Cuban **bolero**. The *bolero,* in the hands of Lara, was transformed from a lively 2/4 song to a slower and more rhythmically refined 4/4 version. Much of Lara's success was gained through the performances of some of his famous interpreters which included, among Mexican interpreters, Maria Felix, Toña la Negra, Pedro Vargas, Chavela Vargas and many other trios like Los Panchos, whose repertoire consisted mainly of *boleros*. Among international performers, his interpreters include Bing Crosby, Frank Sinatra, Jan Pearce, Mario Lanza, and Julio Iglesias.

Further Reading

Franco, Adela Pineda. "The Cuban Bolero and Its Transculturation in Mexico: The Case of Agustin Lara." *Studies in Latin American Popular Culture* 15 (1996): 119–30.

George Torres

sentiments of the displaced urban masses. The *boleros* of the prolific composer-pianist **Agustín Lara** (1897–1970) are nowadays considered Mexico's classic popular music style. This romantic genre gained international fame through the interpretations of the guitar-based **trios** like Los Panchos and Los Ases in the 1940s and 1950s. The *bolero* and the hybrid *canción-bolero* flourished until they gave way to new musical developments, which enraptured Mexico's youth in the early 1960s: rock 'n' roll and an international ballad type popularized by the famous crooners Frank Sinatra and Julio Iglesias. In order to compete with the modern trends, Mexican *bolero* composers modernized the genre by incorporating elements of rock 'n' roll. This new pop ballad genre came to be known as ***balada***. Singers such as José José and Juan Gabriel defined *balada's* golden era in the 1970s. In the following decade, the Mexican *balada* was largely absorbed into the international Latin pop category. Throughout the 1980s and 1990s most composers and songwriters drew from previously popular styles. Luis Miguel, a young Mexican pop star, was instrumental in reintroducing the romantic *bolero* to a new, transnational generation in the 1990s.

The Rock 'n' Roll Era

During the early 1960s rock 'n' roll became a major influence on Mexican politics, society, and culture. Derived from an imported commodity, ***rock en español*** quickly established itself as an authentic local form of music in Mexico City. The rise of a massive student-led resistance, which revolted against authoritarian rule in 1968, linked rock 'n' roll with protest against the government. This countercultural movement, *La Onda* (The Wave, also known as *La Onda Chicana*), emerged as a vehicle for resistance politics and as an outlet for alternative articulations of self and national identity among middle-class Mexican youths. Like elsewhere in Latin America, **rock** music was considered subversive and threatening by both the nationalist establishment on the right and the intellectual critics on the left. While critics condemned Mexican rock music as a bourgeois imitation of an imperialist cultural expression, rock artists and fans alike suffered harassment and abuse at the hands of the Mexican government and its police force. After the countercultural movement had lost momentum and most native rock bands had broken up, the genre was absorbed by the disempowered lower-class youths of the marginalized zones of urban Mexico. In the early 1980s, the punk-rock youth from the *barrios* (*los chavos banda*) made themselves heard with a music that addressed their needs and concerns. The 1980s also produced two other trends of native rock: the rock-fusion carried by the middle classes and the other rock, a commercialized and sanitized teenybopper rock movement. With the 1986 student protests, rock music (both foreign and national) experienced a revival.

Música Grupera

The *onda grupera* (literally the group wave) is a hybrid as well as transnational phenomenon. Inspired by the 1960s Mexican pop ballad/rock groups that imitated English and American rock music and the Colombian **cumbia** craze that swept Mexico in the early 1960s, the *grupo* (group) ensemble with its synthesized instruments, electric guitar, and lead vocalist emerged as one of Mexico's commercially most successful forms of popular music in the 1980s. *Grupos* play easy-listening Mexican and international pop ballads as well as tropical *cumbias* (a typical Mexican style not to be confused with its Afro-Colombian source) and are characterized by a common-denominator bubblegum sound rather than a distinctive Mexican regional style or flavor. Due to a lack of access to the mainstream media as well as for economic survival in the local music market, the first generation of *gruperos* (*grupo* musicians) in the 1970s developed a hybrid music style and mixed repertoire that borrowed from the *balada* pop tradition, *cumbia tropical* (tropical *cumbia*), rock, and *ranchera* (Mexican country music) and that would mainly appeal to the lower classes. The pioneer groups hailed from anywhere between the southeastern peninsula of Yucatán to Acapulco on the Pacific coast, but eventually Mexico's northeast became the hub for the *grupo* movement. The phenomenon peaked in the early 1990s when it became part of massive, Woodstock-style marathon dance concerts in major cities such as Monterrey, Nuevo León, and Guadalajara, Jalisco.

Other Transnational Music Phenomena

In the mid-1980s, a *grupo* version of the acoustic *banda sinaloense* appeared in Guadalajara. This fusion became known as *tecnobanda* (*technobanda*) or simply *banda* (consisting of electric bass, keyboard synthesizer, saxophone, trumpets, drums, and vocalist). In the early 1990s, southern California was swept by the *banda* movement, carried and supported by large numbers of recent immigrants from Mexico and Central America. *Tecnobanda's* accelerated tempo and powerful amplification set off a dance craze that spread to other parts of the United States and back to Mexico. After the Mexican media mogul Televisa discovered *tecnobanda* as a transnational marketable commodity, it soon entered the Mexican mainstream and opened the doors for other regional popular music forms. A decade after *tecnobanda's* international breakthrough, a local group that, like *tecnobanda,* fused Mexican rural-rooted music with synthesizers and drum sets, busted out of Chicago and made headlines in the United States when peaking the Billboard Latin charts in 2003. The novelty sound became known as *pasito duranguense* (little step from Durango). Although the Durango groups mainly reinterpret Mexican standards such as *rancheras* and *baladas, el pasito duranguense* is a distinctly Chicago invention, and in the Mexican home state of Durango, it is consequently called Chicago sound.

Both the *tecnobanda* and the *pasito duranguense* phenomena owe much to the *onda grupera,* which paved the way in the music industry for keyboard-driven, eclectic youth music, yet rooted in Mexican sensibilities.

Mexicanized Foreign Dance Music

Various dance music imported from the Caribbean were popularized and Mexicanized throughout the 20th century such as the Cuban **danzón** and the **mambo**. Cuban bandleader **Pérez Prado's** work in Mexico in the 1950s made the *mambo* even more fashionable and local dance bands quickly integrated the new trend into their own repertories. This dance music is known in Mexico as *música tropical* (tropical music) or *música bailable* (danceable music), which also encompasses the *cumbia,* a genre that has been popular among Mexico's dancing audiences since the 1960s. Mexican regional ensembles, from accordion-based groups to brass bands, joined the **cumbia** craze, popularizing the genre in urban and rural areas alike. Over time, *cumbia* music became more associated with Mexico's lower and working classes. Instrumental in the development and dissemination of *cumbia* has been Monterrey, the center of a potent cultural industry promoting predominantly *música norteña* and *música grupera.* During the 1980s, Monterrey's increasingly more professional recording and entertainment industries propelled the pop-influenced *grupera* music and *grupo/norteño* fusions out of their regional confines. By the early 1990s, commercial *cumbias* enjoyed prominence in the whole of Mexico as well as in parts of the United States. Apart from this heavily commercialized music, there exists a lesser-known regional style of *cumbia,* the Monterrey *colombiana,* which has remained more closely connected to the original musical style from the Caribbean coastal region of Colombia, in sound as well as in instrumentation (Olvera Gudiño 2005). Apart from *cumbias, colombianos* (Colombians) also reinterpreted other popular Colombian genres like **porro** and **vallenato** as an expression of their own rural origins and marginalization. In spite of the indifference and even open hostility of the local mass media, the music was able to transcend its marginal confines, and within two decades, it had spread to other cities of the Mexican northeast. The late 1990s saw an increasing acceptance of the *Monterrey colombiana* after the popular culture industry had discovered it as a potentially lucrative new musical style. Due to the increasing decentralization of Mexico's culture industry and the proliferation of new channels of communication in the 1990s, popular genres such as the tropical *cumbia* began to be recorded outside of the established recording centers, both south and north of the border.

Electronica

In the beginning of the the 21st century, the nor-tec phenomenon emerged from the border city of Tijuana and, through the Internet, it quickly conquered a global audience. Marketed as a kind of ethnic electronic dance music, nor-tec samples sounds of traditional music from northern Mexico and transforms them through computer technology used in European and American techno music and electronica.

Further Reading

Carrizosa, Toño. *La Onda Grupera: Historia del Movimiento Grupero* [The Grupo Wave: A History of the Grupo Movement]. Mexico City: EDAMEX, 1997.

Madrid, Alejandro L. *Nor-tec Rifa! Electronic Dance Music from Tijuana to the World.* New York: Oxford University Press, 2008.

Olvera Gudiño, José Juan. *Colombianos en Monterrey: Origen de un gusto musical y su papel en la construcción de una identidad social.* Monterrey, NL: Fondo Estatal para la Cultura y las Artes de Nuevo León, 2005.

Pedelty, Mark. *Musical Ritual in Mexico City: From the Aztec to NAFTA.* Austin: University of Texas Press, 2004.

Simonett, Helena. *Banda: Mexican Musical Life across Borders.* Middletown, CT: Wesleyan University Press, 2001.

Zolov, Eric. *Refried Elvis: The Rise of the Mexican Counterculture.* Berkeley: University of California Press, 1999.

Helena Simonett

Milonga

An African-derived word native to the Río de la Plata region of **Argentina** and **Uruguay**, *milonga* can refer to a number of interrelated concepts: an improvisatory song form, of which exist distinct rural and urban versions; a lively couples dance played by *tango* ensembles; a social event where dancers gather to dance *tango*, *vals*, and *milonga;* and the location where such an event takes place.

The precise etymology of the term *milonga* is unclear, although it is undoubtedly Afro-Argentine in origin. Scholars have identified possible cognates in Kimbundu and Ki-Kongo meaning word, argument, and moving lines of dancers. In any case, it is clear that the term came into use in River Plate Spanish in the mid-19th century; one of its first appearances in print is in José Hernández's classic *gauchesco* poem "Martín Fierro" in 1872. In this early period, the *milonga* in question was a song form for solo voice and **guitar** accompaniment, and was based on texts consisting of octosyllabic lines, frequently in the ten-line *décima* stanzas derived from popular Spanish poetry. These texts could be either pre-composed or improvised, and the *milonga* formed the rhythmic and musical basis for improvised song duels known as *payadas* or *contrapuntos*. Musically, these *milongas* were distinguished by a rhythmic base related to the *habanera*, sometimes simplified to the pattern known as *tresillo* in **Cuba**, known locally as a 3–3–2 rhythm, referring to the number of eighth note subdivisions in each of the three notes of the pattern.

In the 20th century, the *milonga* was given new prominence by the urban folklore boom, becoming a vehicle for populist folk poetry by musicians such as **Atahualpa Yupanqui** (1908–1992). A distinctly urban *milonga* emerged in both instrumental and vocal versions among *tango* musicians starting in the 1930s with important *milongas* by composer Sebastian Piana (1903–1994) such as "*Milonga triste*" and "*Milonga* sentimental." Frequently these pieces were in livelier tempos than the folkloric versions, and were danced, like the *tango,* by embracing couples. Many important *tango* composers also wrote *milongas,* including notable contributions by Anibal Troilo (1914–1975; "La tablada," "La trampera"), Pedro Laurenz (1902–1972; "Milonga de mis amores"), and Julián Plaza (1928–2003; "Nocturna"). Among the proponents of urban sung *milongas,* guitarist and singer Edmundo Rivero (1911–1986) was particularly well-known for an oeuvre rich in a nearly archaic version of *lunfardo,* the underworld slang of Buenos Aires, which frequently deals with criminal themes. *Tango nuevo* composer Astor Piazzolla (1921–1992) also wrote both instrumental and sung *milongas,* including the well-known "Milonga del angel" in the former case, and "Jacinto chiclana" in the latter, to a text by Jorge Luis Borges (1899–1986).

Milonga as a specific dance form, rather than a general term for a social gathering involving dance, was strongly influenced by the choreography of the *Afrorioplatense candombe.* In fact, early commentators suggested that *milonga* prior to the turn of the 20th century was nothing other than *compadritos* (European-descended lower-class urban men) copying the steps they had witnessed in the *candombe.* Over the course of the 20th century, the *milonga* became a lively, playful dance where dancers maintain a more constant motion than in *tango,* occasionally dancing in rhythmic counterpoint to the musical phrase rather than in rhythmic unison with it.

The term *milonga* as referring to the event or locale for such dancing also generated two related terms: *milonguero,* a person who dances *tango* and *milonga* in such locales, and *milonguita,* a working-class woman whose skill in dancing made her a popular partner for bourgeois men and an object of their desires. The *milonguita* becomes a literary trope in *tango* lyrics; she is typically originally naïve, but the limited options offered by her station in life lead her into whirlwind, inevitably fatalistic romances with the playboys who romance her. Usually in these narratives the only true freedom the *milonguita* is afforded is to betray and abandon these men.

Further Reading

Collier, Simon. "The Tango is Born: 1880s–1920s." In *Tango! The Dance, The Song, The Story,* edited by Simon Collier. London: Thames and Hudson, 1995.

Savigliano, Marta. *Tango and the Political Economy of Passion.* Boulder, CO: Westview Press, 1995.

Thompson, Robert Farris. *Tango: The Art History of Love*. New York: Pantheon Books. 2005.

Michael O'Brien

Mizik Rasin

Mizik rasin is a roots music that emerged in the 1980s, which brought traditional Afro-Haitian music, especially the music of *rara* (Haitian **Carnival** music) and Vodou, together with popular music. The movement was influenced, in large part, by *reggae*. Besides having its texts in *Creole* the music was heavily influenced by Haitian Vodou, to the point where musicians would incorporate instruments and rhythms of Vodou ceremonies, often going directly to the practitioners of Vodou ceremonies to receive legitimate instruction. Because roots music that is Vodou-influenced was suppressed during the reigns of the two Duvaliers, Papa Doc and Baby Doc, the movement did not surface until after 1987, though the formations of the movement date from before then.

Early attempts at unifying traditional music and popular music in **Haiti** existed prior to *mizik rasin*. Groups such as Jazz de Jeunes either attempted a stylistic interpretation of Vodou rhythms and themes, or would entitle their songs with names or deities from Vodou. Prior to the end of the Duvalier regime, Afro-Haitian music (i.e., Vodou and *rara*) was seen by the much of the dominant population (Haitian government, elites, and the Catholic church) as an undesirable cultural element, and so allusions and references to Haitian Vodou were frowned upon by the these civic and social groups. During this *kilti libete* (freedom culture) movement of the 1970s, much of which existed in exile as a result of the Haitian brain drain when many intellectuals left Haiti because of the repressive Duvalier era, many artists influenced by the works of groups like Jazz de Jeunes began to experiment with a more serious and methodical appropriation of Afro-Haitian music and dance. It was on the heels of this period that *misik rasin* came about, and, within **Haiti**, musicians followed their inspiration to the *lakou* (ceremonial Vodou compounds or communities), where musicians learned the authentic practices of Vodou music and dance. When the Duvalier regime finally imploded, the musicians were free to come out of artistic exile, both at home and abroad, with their musical style. What resulted was what Gerdès Fleurent has called a bi-musicality where musicians were trained in both Western and Afro-Haitian styles of music composition and performance.

Notable examples of *mizik rasin* artists include **Boukman Eksperyans**, Foula, Sanba-yo, and RAM. Boukman Experyans, formed out of a collective of early *samba*, or roots groups in Haiti, in 1985, is credited with being the first group to successfully meld electric **guitar**, bass, and synthesizer with traditional

Afro-Haitian percussion. True to the pro-peasant ideals, as well as an honoring of indigenous Haitian culture, Boukman Experyans had a successful hit in Haiti with the song "Se Kreyòl, nou ye," a song that pushes the pride of an African cultural heritage, as well as indigenous Haitian mentality. Foulah, formed from Group Sa, played a mixture of avant garde and Vodou-**Jazz**. RAM, a group popular since the early 1990s, makes use of current events to provide social commentary on political situations, often through poetic allusion and metaphor. Their Carnival *rara* song, "Anbago," provides a commentary on the then current OAS/U.S. embargo in Haiti.

Misik rasin was the first urban middle class genre of Haitian popular music to embrace the Afro-centric roots of Haiti's music and successfully integrate it into popular music in a convincing and significant way, not just as a cultural accent, but also as a basis for a spiritual understanding that would lead to practical applications in everyday life.

Further Reading

Averill, Gage. *A Day for the Hunter, a Day for the Prey: Popular Music and Power in Haiti.* Chicago studies in ethnomusicology. Chicago: University of Chicago Press, 1997.

Bilby, Kenneth M., Michael D. Largey, and Peter Manuel. *Caribbean Currents: Caribbean Music from Rumba to Reggae.* Philadelphia: Temple University Press, 2006.

Fleurent, Gerdès. "The Song of Freedom: Vodou, Conscientization, and Popular Culture in Haiti." In *Vodou in Haitian Life and Culture: Invisible Powers,* edited by Michel, Claudine, and Patrick Bellegarde-Smith, 51–64. New York: Palgrave Macmillan, 2006.

George Torres

Modinha

The Brazilian *modinha* is a sentimental and romantic style of song, derived from the Portuguese *modas, arias,* and *cantigas,* that emerged from late colonial-era Brazil (1700–1822) and became one of the first internationally recognized musical styles of Latin America. The Portuguese word *moda,* meaning fashion or a generic song, together with the suffix *inha* (a diminutive) means endearing song. The development and popularization of the *modinha* was achieved through a process of social and cultural exchange between Brazil, West Africa, and Europe along the Portuguese Atlantic slave trade routes. The frequent use of West African influenced pattern-based syncopation in the melody and accompaniment, and Brazilian vernacular in the text, distinguish it from the Portuguese *modinha* and similar European song styles. The Brazilian *modinha* was initially popular in the court and aristocratic salons of Portugal during the late 18th century and subsequently throughout Brazil until the early 20th century.

A typical *modinha* has a lyrical melody that conveys a melancholy mood, is slowly paced, emotionally expressive, and generally utilizes a poetic style that maintains a perspective of distance between the subject and narrative voice. *Modinhas* have undulating melodies with wide intervallic leaps, are often in minor keys with shifts to major, and are usually written in two-part strophic form. Historically, they were composed for single voice or two harmonized voices often with figured bass accompaniment and were frequently accompanied by the *viola* (five-course steel-string, guitar) and other instruments such as the flute, although the piano or harpsichord were favored in salon performances and in printed music. Two types of *modinha* developed over time: the salon *modinha*, a composed work influenced by the Italian opera and popular among the elite class; and the *modinha da rua*, or street *modinha*, an improvised work orally transmitted and popular with the middle and poor classes.

The Brazilian *modinha* was brought to Portugal in the late 1700s by the Brazilian mulatto priest and poet-musician Domingos Caldas Barbosa (1740–1800) and it was during this time that the use of the term *modinha* became common. The European obsession with exoticism and the prevalence of African culture throughout Brazil led to the gradual integration of these elements into Brazilian music. The rise of the middle class population in Brazil beginning in the 1700s facilitated the proliferation of popular music styles; chief among them was the *modinha*. The move of the Portuguese royal court to Brazil in 1808 to avoid the invasion of Napoleon, in concert with the established popularity of the *modinha* in Portugal, then further amplified the popularity of this musical style throughout Brazil and by the mid-1800s it was one of the most commonly published styles of music in Brazil.

During the middle to late 1800s, the *modinha* became more sophisticated due to the incorporation of aria influences as Italian opera grew in popularity and performances at this time often included improvised ornamentation of the melody, a trait of the *bel canto* style. *Modinhas* were usually written in 2/4 meter, but pieces in 3/4, 4/4, and 6/8 were increasingly common during this period as a result of the influence of the aria and waltz. Once the *modinha* was adopted by the poorer classes throughout Brazil it began to decline in popularity eventually falling out of fashion in the elite salons. It was replaced by the **lundu**, which had more pronounced African influences.

Since the early 20th century, the *modinha* has been referenced by composers of all genres of Brazilian music to evoke a traditional and national identity in their works. Brazilian classical composers such as Villa-Lobos, Gnattali, and Ovalle frequently incorporated the *modinha, seresta, cantiga,* and *canção,* all closely related song styles, into their compositions and cited them in texts. Two prominent pieces that utilize the *modinha* song form are the "Modinha" by Villa-Lobos and Manuel Bandeira from the cycle of *14 Serestas* (1925); and the "Modinha" from the play

Orfeo da Conceição (1956) by **bossa nova** innovators Jobim and Moraes. Since its inception, the *modinha* has influenced the entire lineage of popular Brazilian sentimental song styles including: *lundu-canção, choro-canção, **samba**-canção, **bolero**,* ballad, *bossa nova, **música popular brasileira*** or **MPB**, and more recently the genre *musica romántica* as popularized by Roberto Carlos.

Further Reading

Araújo, M. de. *A Modinha e o Lundu no Século XVIII.* São Paulo: Ricordi Brasileira, 1963.

Behague. G. "Biblioteca da Ajuda MSS 1595/1596: Two Eighteenth Century Anonymous Collections of Modinhas." *Yearbook.* IV. Inter-American Institute for Musical Research, 1968.

Fryer, P. *Rhythms of Resistance.* Hanover: University Press of New England, 2000.

Livingston-Isenhour, T. and Garcia, T. *Choro: A Social History of a Brazilian Popular Music.* Bloomington: Indiana University Press, 2005.

Thomas Rohde

Moña

Moña is a type of instrumental interlude often found in **salsa**, customarily appearing after the **mambo** (the primary instrumental interlude) has been already stated, and like the *mambo,* the *moña* is typically inserted between two **montuno** sections. Irrespective of subtle differences over the years in implementation, the functional constant of the *moña* has been to increase the rhythmic and contrapuntal intricacy for dancing pleasure. Originally consisting of short improvised figures over the harmonic-rhythmic ostinato of the *montuno,* since the 1970s many arrangers have taken to formally devising greater harmonic, melodic, and rhythmic complexity in the *moña*—often achieved by splitting horn choirs (e.g., trumpets or trombones) into multiple parts (divisi).

The writing team of Eddie Palmieri and Barry Rogers (in Palmieri's band, La Perfecta) effectively propelled this device into the language of 1960s *salsa,* though the technique was established as early as the post-1946, three-trumpet **conjunto** of **Arsenio Rodríguez**. Cuban trumpeter, Felix Chapottín, was famous for the improvised lines he played against the set parts of the other two trumpets, a feature of Rodriguez' *diablo* sections (García 2006). Today, the technique of writing or improvising a first trumpet line above the arranged horn parts, called a *champola,* is commonly found in Cuban **timba.**

Further Reading

Carp, David. "Salsa Symbiosis: Barry Rogers, Eddie Palmieri's Chief Collaborator in the Making of La Perfecta." *Centro Journal* 16, no. 2 (2004): 42–61.

García, David. *Arsenio Rodríguez and the Transnational Flows of Latin Popular Music.* Philadelphia: Temple University Press, 2006.

Michael D. Marcuzzi

Montuno

The musical term *montuno* is applied to Cuban music in a variety of ways. Loosely translated as "from the mountains," *montuno* refers to the rustic, mountainous region of Oriente, the eastern province of **Cuba** and birthplace of **son**. Hence, **son montuno** would literally denote the traditional (*típico*) *son* style associated with the eastern region of Cuba.

On its own, however, *montuno* is most commonly used as a structural marker, namely the repeating call-and-response sections delivered by the lead voice (*sonero*) and the chorus (**coro**) that are found in *son*, **salsa**, **guaracha**, and other related genres. The *sonero* ideally renders improvised melodies with text (called *guías, inspiraciónes,* or *pregónes*) that relate to the subject of the set text of the *coro,* which is usually harmonized. Though the *montuno* is typically a repeating alternation between the lead singer and the chorus, in some cases the role of the lead singer can be substituted with improvised horn solos or spontaneous horn riffs (short melodic-rhythmic figures; see **moña**).

The normative structure of a *son* or *salsa* is comprised of two parts. The song-like first part, referred to as *canto, tema,* or *largo* (somewhat archaic), was originally a melodic setting of Iberian poetic forms (e.g., **décima**, **coplas**), though today the song is usually a strophic form (i.e., several verses set to the same melody) or standard Euro-American song form (e.g., AABA). The second part is characterized by the *montuno,* which is typically set to a simple two- or four-measure harmonic progression and repeated like a loop. This second section of the *son-salsa* structure marks the beginning of a more forceful rhythmic drive in the ensemble arrangement (conspicuously heard in the **cowbells** taken up by both the *timbals* and **bongó**) and also comprises various instrumental interludes (e.g., **mambo**, moña, instrumental solos), each inserted between two *montuno* sections. Experienced listeners and dancers are well attuned to this fundamental partition in the *son-salsa* form. The rhythmic upsurge of the second section, marked by the cowbells that accompany the *montuno* and various instrumental interludes, make it the most compelling in terms of activity on the dance floor.

So important is the *montuno* to these Cuban and Cuban-derived dance forms that many songs effectively endure as memorable choruses or are remembered for a single innovative improvisation by the *sonero,* rather than as songs per se. The best of these short phrases—quips, puns, cutting observations—are readily adopted by listeners as part of colloquial speech, a type of vernacular reproduction that is not without clear historical precedent. *Montunos* have historically been popular vehicles for competitions between singers wishing to demonstrate their musical and linguistic prowess, often at the expense of another. These informal contests, or *controversias,* had much in common with the cutting session among **jazz** musicians insofar as they helped to hone musical skills, to establish a pecking order among musicians, and provide engaging entertainment for the listening public. The widespread imitation or quotation of the rhythmic, melodic, or verbal savvy of a *sonero* or a *coro* is built into the internal structure of the *montuno* itself: the need for a chorus to perform the *montuno* always ensures the *soneros* of an audience, and an attentive one at that since many *soneros* learned their art form singing in the chorus behind great performers. Furthermore, the repetitive nature of the *montuno* makes it a superlative mnemonic device for a receptive audience.

Finally, *montuno* can also refer to the syncopated harmonic outline played on the piano that has become so emblematic of Latin dance music. This piano technique, also called a **guajeo**, is invariably played during the *montuno* sections of an arrangement, making the rhythmic drive all the more compelling.

Further Reading

Orovio, Helio. *Cuban Music from A to Z.* Durham, NC: Duke University Press, 2004.

Robbins, James. "The Cuban *son* as Form, Genre, and Symbol." *Latin American Music Review* 11, no. 2 (1990): 182–210.

Michael D. Marcuzzi

Mozambique

The *mozambique* was arguably the most popular rhythm of 1960s in **Cuba**, part of a series of dance trends that swept the island nation beginning with the **pachanga** (1959) and including the *dengue, pacá, simale, guachipupa, upa-upa,* and *pilon,* among others. The *mozambique,* which refers to both the music and the attendant dance style, is near synonymous with its creator, the legendary Cuban percussionist, Pedro Izquierdo Padrón (1933–2000), more popularly known by the stage name Pello el Afrokán. The *mozambique,* like many of the music-and-dance innovations of 1960s Cuba, was part of a surge in musical creativity that seemed to distill the social excitement and enthusiasm of the first decade after the Cuban Revolution (1959). The *mozambique* conveyed the carefree, celebratory nature of its times, and Pello's band was undoubtedly one of the most dynamic in Cuba's musical history.

There are numerous musical influences in the composition of the *mozambique*—before his rise to public prominence with the *mozambique,* Izquierdo was well established as a drummer of folkloric and popular dance musics (particularly **rumba**), as was his father before him. At its core, however, the *mozambique* is a rhythm derived from the *comparsa,* Cuba's **Carnival** rhythm. Izquierdo later went on to record an LP in 1988 of Carnival songs and performance styles of *comparsas* from the most famous neighborhoods in Havana, Cuba (historically, each neighborhood would mount their own musical repertory, ensemble, dancers, and entourage as part of the annual street parades).

Pello's *mozambique* in the 1960s was almost always performed with a large band, which included sections of trumpets, trombones, vocalists, coiffured female dancers ("Las Afrokanas"), and numerous percussionists—at times Pello insisted on as many as twelve **tumbadoras**. (He would later add electric bass and piano to the mix.) Nonetheless, Cuban percussionist Ángel Chang, who performed with Pello's band in the 1960s, insists that the core rhythm of the *mozambique* is derived from six percussion parts: *clave*, two **cowbells**, two *bombos* (bass drums), and *tumbadoras* (two *conga* drums played by one player). The additional people, a signature feature of Pello's ensemble, were simply part of the musical extravaganza that was the *mozambique.*

The song repertory of the *mozambique* was largely composed of short phrases or couplets that were ideal for a music made for dancing. Pello's compositions, such as "Maria Caracoles," "Ileana quiere chocolate," and "Digan lo que digan," were easily remembered by listeners for their short, incessant, call-and-response choruses: the tune was the chorus. Pello also constructed some explicit connections between the *mozambique* and **Afro-Cuban** sacred music: the floor show productions "Senseribó" and "Baroko" were overt references to Afro-Cuban Abakuá rites (not well received by all of its membership), and many of the melodies on Pello's LP, *Un Sabor Que Canta,* are borrowed from Afro-Cuban religious chants, to which Pello added his own lyrics.

The *mozambique* was first catapulted into the limelight on July 6, 1963, on the Cuban television program, *Ritmos de Juventud.* (Pello would appear regularly on the show in the 1970s.) After the television spot, the ensemble went on to perform as part of Carnival festivities in February 1964, helping to extend the ensemble's popularity throughout the island (Moore 2006, 182). And, Pello's ensemble was one of the first, and very few, to travel abroad in the years soon after 1959: a 1965 tour took his ensemble and the *mozambique* to Europe, which included a performance at the Olympia Theater in Paris.

The *mozambique* also took hold in the **United States** and **Puerto Rico**. Artists such as **El Gran Combo**, Richie Ray, Carlos Santana, Batacumbele, and Bobby Valentin all recorded original *mozambiques* or covers of Pello's tunes, though no other musician outside of Cuba was more aligned with the rhythm than pianist Eddie Palmieri (1965). The most prolific in his use and adaptation of the rhythm, Palmieri's connection to the *mozambique* was ultimately controversial. Though at one point Palmieri actually laid claim to having invented the *mozambique,* what was in the end more contentious was the saber rattling directed at Palmieri's label

Tico by the Cuban government over royalties that were never paid to Izquierdo. Tico also faced the ire of extremists in the Cuban exile community for promoting music associated with Castro's Cuba. Some of these responses included bomb threats.

By the 1970s, Pello had pared down his ensemble's size. The *mozambique's* popularity had been somewhat diminished by the numerous dance trends and the emergence of popular dance bands like Los Van Van. Pello nonetheless continued to appear in various clubs and cabarets in Havana, and in 1979 his ensemble played New York's Carnegie Hall as well as toured Japan. Though Pello continued to promote the *mozambique* and find engagements for his ensemble, because of his stature in Havana's musical community, he eventually became most utilized as the musical director and/or contractor for high-profile events and important rooms, such as the Capri Hotel's Salon Rojo in the 1990s. After Izquierdo's passing in 2000, his grandson Omar Merencio Izquierdo (Pello Jr.) released a recording of mozambiques titled *La Explosion De Mi Ritmo* (2001).

Further Reading

Moore, Robin D. 2006. *Music and Revolution: Cultural Change in Socialist Cuba.* Berkeley: University of California Press.

Discography

Palmieri, Eddie. 1965. *Mambo con Conga is Mozambique.* Tico, LPTICO1126.

Pello el Afrokán. 1989. *Un Sabor Que Canta.* Vitral, VCD 4122 (Re-issue of Areito LD-4122).

Michael D. Marcuzzi

MPB. *See* Música Popular Brasileira.

Música Popular Brasileira (MPB)

MPB (an acronym for Música Popular Brasileira or Brazilian popular music) is the generic denomination for a plurality of genres and hybrid musical practices that have prevailed in Brazilian popular music since the 1960s. MPB is an important part of Brazilian popular culture, so ubiquitous that its overarching ramifications are confusing to the noninitiated. Not all Brazilian popular music is considered MPB: some music styles stand by themselves without being considered MPB, such as the traditional *samba* (even if there is much traditional *samba* in MPB). This acronym was embraced by both audiences and music marketers in the 1980s, 1990s, and 2000s, and, like *axé* music or Brazilian **rock**, has little to do with the music originally made in the 1960s.

Influenced by *bossa nova's* musical and literary sophistication, MPB in the 1960s also embraced the rich and diverse traditional subaltern Brazilian musical heritage, offering multiple kinds of music and lyrics and appealing to virtually all tastes. As a result of the combined efforts of *bossa nova* and MPB, Brazilian popular music after the 1950s is regarded as a legitimate art form by the élites while remaining highly pertinent to the subaltern classes. Chronicling and intervening in every aspect of social reality since the 1960s and combining bourgeois sophistication with grassroots appeal, MPB became one of the most relevant forms of Brazilian art and culture.

MPB is very important with regard to media studies. Its popularization was linked to the music festivals that rose in the 1960s (mainly from 1965 to 1968). For their part, these festivals were the first highly successful product to be sold by the then incipient Brazilian television industry to the Brazilian masses. An MPB frenzy developed in these years, as this music became central to Brazilian life and influenced other media. MPB, then, was the first mass-media phenomenon in **Brazil**.

MPB's motley character has offered a problem regarding classification. Not being a genre, and escaping traditional musicological definitions, MPB encouraged critics and historians to utilize sociological considerations in discussing it, ignoring its musical esthetics: critics associated MPB with leftist middle-class university students engaged in the promotion of authentic Brazilian music in opposition to the right-wing military dictatorship that reigned from 1964 to 1985. This interpretation is not entirely wrong, since it accurately portrays the discourse of many MPB followers in the 1960s. But it fails to account for the music of MBP artists such as the black singer/songwriter Jorge Ben, who released the album *Samba esquema novo* in 1963. This MPB production merges *bossa nova, maracatu* and *samba* with **jazz** and black-tinged American pop music elements. Ben was also the creator of the *samba*-rock hybrid style in the 1960s. His music was clearly not protest music; his main objective was to get people out on the dance floor, and while his utilization of Afro-Brazilian esthetics relates to political debates about race, it supersedes the traditional left–right dichotomy suggested by traditional MPB critics. The first Brazilian artist to use American soul music, Ben inspired other MPB artists who would later follow the same route, including Wilson Simonal, Tim Maia, Cassiano, Gerson King Combo, and Ed Motta. MPB's sound was central to its practitioners, and what made its cultural, political, and social commentary possible; attention to musical style must be at the center of any discussion of MPB.

Critics also failed to attend to the gender discussion implied in the choice of diverse musical elements in the work of MPB artists such as Nara Leão and Maria Bethânia. Leão, an upper-class white singer from Rio de Janeiro who was cherished by some of the most important male composers of *bossa nova* as the inoffensive muse of the movement, broke with this group to record modern arrangements of traditional *samba* songs by composers of Rio de Janeiro's slums like Cartola and

Nelson Cavaquinho, who were, until then, ignored by the middle classes. Approximately at the same time, Bethânia (a dark-skinned, lower middle-class singer from upstate Bahia) was doing the same with then forgotten composer Noel Rosa. Leão's musical eclecticism, which is tied to the artistic and personal freedom she pursued, combined Brazilian traditional genres with jazz elements like blue note inflections as in "Nanã" (Moacyr Santos) in her first album *Nara* (1964). Bethânia and Leão's renovated approach to Brazilian music was considered regressive at the time, but after some years, such modernization of older classics became tacitly accepted as one of MPB's trademarks. Their musical commentaries, derived from the meanings of different styles, equate to a dialogical gendered discourse.

Both Leão and Bethânia acted in the protest musical *Opinião* (Rio de Janeiro, 1964), which also gathered composers João do Vale and Zé Kéti, representing respectively the impoverished northeastern migrant and the urban slum dweller, to create an allegory of Brazil. The immense success of this antidictatorship manifestation among university students helped form the reductionist idea that MPB is all about traditional political binaries. Suddenly Bethânia saw herself defined and limited by the protest tag, and she struggled hard until she succeeded in affirming her independent artistic and personal styles. Other composers and/or interpreters who helped define MPB during the 1960s are Elis, Edu Lobo, Geraldo Vandré, Quarteto em Cy, Nana Caymmi, Chico Buarque, MPB-4, Milton Nascimento, and Paulinho da Viola, not to mention the artists linked to *tropicália*, which appeared after 1967: **Caetano Veloso**, Torquato Neto, **Gilberto Gil**, Tom Zé, Gal Costa, Mutantes, and Rogério Duprat, among others.

After the rise of *tropicália* in 1967–1968, **rock**, soul, funk, and American pop music overcame the marginal condition to which they had been relegated by the intelligentsia and became mainstream. These styles continued to have a strong impact over MPB. Rock, *reggae*, and virtually all transnational or international styles also came to be considered MPB, even if sung in another language.

In the 1970s, the high level of musical and literary creativity in MPB continued with another talented new generation formed by Raul Seixas, Djavan, Belchior, Fagner, Ednardo, Novos Baianos, Ivan Lins, Gonzaguinha, João Bosco, Aldir Blanc, Jorge Mautner, Walter Franco, Ney Matogrosso, Alceu Valença, Elba Ramalho, Zé Ramalho, Luiz Melodia, Itamar Assumpção, Rumo, Premeditando o Breque, Ná Ozzetti, Vânia Bastos, Leila Pinheiro, Eduardo Gudin, the Clube da Esquina collective (Milton Nascimento's collaborators: Lô Borges, Márcio Borges, Fernando Brant, Beto Guedes, Ronaldo Bastos, Tavito, Wagner Tiso), among many others. In the political realm, violent repression subsided after 1972, following a gradual distension.

The next decade saw the end of the communal utopianism of the 1960s (which had been kept alive by the struggle against the dictatorship ending in 1985) and the rise of a pragmatic Brazilian rock. Disenchantment with direct political activism,

Veloso, Caetano

Caetano Veloso (b. 1942) is an **MPB** (Brazilian popular music) artist, a co-founder of the **Tropicália** movement and composer of many famous Brazilian **Carnival** anthems. His music is characterized by lyrical melodies, an original and masterful poetic style, and, in his **guitar** playing and vocals, a dominance of **bossa nova**.

Veloso began his musical career as a composer for films, television, and theater. In the mid-1960s, Veloso, **Gilberto Gil**, and others founded the *Tropicália* movement. The controversial productions of the *tropicalistas* challenged Brazilian musical traditions and criticized the Brazilian military dictatorship (1964–1985), resulting in Veloso and Gil's exile to London from 1969 to 1972. Veloso's innovative blending of **rock**, pop, Brazilian, and Latin American music styles into MPB subsequently redefined the genre. He has been strongly influenced by the Brazilian concrete poets and issues of Brazilian life. As a result, his compositions represent both popular and intellectual Brazilian thought filled with inventive wordplay and modern urban images. Veloso reached the height of his popularity during the 1980s and continues to record and tour internationally.

Further Reading

Veloso, Caetano, and Barbara Einzig. *Tropical Truth: A Story of Music and Revolution in Brazil.* New York: A.A. Knopf, 2002.

Thomas Rohde

however, did not prevent Brock artists, who claimed to be part of MPB, from protesting against government and politicians' corruption and commenting on other Brazilian social problems, even if they resorted to sarcasm rather than exhortation. Some of the groups that appeared in this period were Blitz, Titãs, Barão Vermelho, Os Paralamas do Sucesso, and Ultraje a Rigor e Legião Urbana.

The 1990s had as one of its greatest musical movements the so-called *Mangue beat,* innovated by Chico Science & Nação Zumbi and Mundo Livre S/A, who were followed by Mestre Ambrósio, Cascabulho, and others. This movement fused contemporary international pop tendencies with traditional music such as *maracatu, coco, ciranda* from the impoverished northeastern Pernambuco state. New MPB names continue to appear every day; the style entered the 21st century as strong as ever, assimilating diverse musical subcultures, while keeping their differences within the same denomination. In this sense, musical and cultural plurality, diversity, and respect for difference continue to be the best characteristics to define MPB.

Further Reading

Crook, Larry. *Brazilian Music: Northeastern Traditions and the Heartbeat of a Modern Nation.* ABC-CLIO world music series. Santa Barbara, CA: ABC-CLIO, 2005.

Dunn, Christopher. *Brutality Garden: Tropicalia and the Emergence of a Brazilian Counterculture.* Chapel Hill, NC: University of North Carolina Press, 2001.

Stroud, Sean. *The Defence of Tradition in Brazilian Popular Music: Politics, Culture, and the Creation of Musica Popular Brasileira.* Ashgate popular and folk music series. Aldershot, Hants, England: Ashgate, 2008.

Larry Crook

Música Sertaneja

Música sertaneja is commercial rural music from **Brazil**'s Central-Southern region (see also *dupla caipira*). It is highly produced, instrumentally electric and electronic (electric **guitar** and bass, drum-kit, and keyboards) and is sung by male **duos** that are usually two brothers. Its lyrics exhaustively explore loss and sadness. More specifically, they reflect on a bygone time of wholeness that is no longer accessible because the singer's true love has left, and/or the singer has had to leave the countryside for the city. The longing for a country past filled with love results in the split-subjectivity of the singing voice in the present. In *música sertaneja,* right now can only ever be partial. Singers obsessively mull over the intensity of their emotions and the impossibility of controlling them. This inverts conventional expectations for masculine behavior by putting raw male sentiment on show. Whereas other Brazilian musical genres such as *samba* postulate an empowered male who finds a new love quickly, the singing voice of *música sertaneja* wails. This earns the genre a host of epithets from its detractors, most of which focus on the absurdity of masculine vulnerability. Such slurs reveal the music's cultural intimacy (see **Cultural Imperialism**), in part resulting in its erroneous classification as lower class in much scholarship.

The term *sertaneja* means of the *sertão,* or of the backlands, but this is not the northeastern *sertão* made famous by Euclides DaCunha in his classic work of nonfiction, *Rebellion in the Backlands,* which describes the destruction of a late 19th-century religious movement in the state of Bahia. Instead, the musical use of the term here refers to a more amorphous rurality, and, musically, dates from famous producer and performer, Palmeira, in his attempt to describe modernizing *música caipira* in the early 1960s. The updated *caipira* sound incorporated electric **guitar**, bass, and drum-kit, and increasingly treated the theme of romantic love.

"It's no longer just *caipira*," Palmeira is reported to have said; "these days, it's all *sertaneja*."

Despite its regionally focused base of production, *música sertaneja* is one of the largest selling genres in the nation, accounting for somewhere between 10 and 15 percent of national sales in the late 20th and early 21st centuries The growth in popularity of this music is tied up with an increasing turn to the rural in the sphere of public culture, indexed by the popularity of rurally themed soap operas, and the explosion of a form of rodeo that mingles long-standing Brazilian traditions with American-style bull riding at locations such as Barretos, Americana, and Jaguariuna, in the state of São Paulo. All of this is taking place as the region becomes increasingly urbanized. *Música sertaneja,* which provides the sonic accompaniment to this turn to the rural, is most closely associated with the careers of three brother *duplas*: Chitãozinho & Xororó, the late Leandro & his brother Leonardo (currently enjoying a solo career), and Zezé di Camargo & Luciano (the subject of one of the highest grossing films in Brazilian history, *Francisco's Two Sons*). Recently, *dupla* Cezar Menotti & Fabiano have also enjoyed considerable success.

The current popularity of *música sertaneja* within the context of an augmented rurality in the urbanizing Central-South may be read as a means of responding to, and shaping neoliberal reform in social, economic, and political domains. The longing for the past evidenced in this genre flies in the face of the linear progress narratives on which the economic miracles of the dictatorship years were based (1964–1985), and also critiques the continuation of such modernizing notions under redemocratization. *Música sertaneja,* once thought to be the province of poor migrant workers, now spans social classes and educational levels, and provides its users with a way to reflect upon Brazil's hunger for progress. The new Brazilian rurality proposes that change has been too quick, too violent, and too permanent. In place of the developmentalist logic that characterizes neoliberalism, *música sertaneja* proposes a country cosmopolitanism that seeks the universality of a longing for the rural past across national borders, particularly in places such as Canada, Australia, Mexico, and the United States. In this way, musically instantiated rurality seeks to supplant a universal hunger for change with the desire for stability, wholeness, and love.

Further Reading

Carvalho, M. d. U. "Musical Style, Migration, and Urbanization: Some Consideration on Brazilian 'Musica Sertaneja'[Country Music]." *Studies in Latin American Popular Culture* 12 (1993): 75–94.

DaCunha, E. *Rebellion in the Backlands.* Chicago: University of Chicago Press, 1944.

Dent, A. S. "Country Brothers: Kinship and Chronotope in Brazilian Rural Public Culture." *Anthropological Quarterly* (Spring): 455–95, 2007.

Freire, P. d. O. *Eu Nasci Naquela Serra: A história de Angelino de Oliveira, Raul Torres e Serrinha.* São Paulo: Paulicéia, 1996.

Reily, S. A. " 'Música Sertaneja' and Migrant Identity: The Stylistic Development of a Brazilian Genre." *Popular Music* 11(3): 337–58.

Alexander Sebastian Dent

Música Típica

Panamanian *música típica* is a violin or **accordion**-based dance music genre, derived from the country's folkloric musical traditions, such as the *mejorana* and *tamborito*. *Música típica* is **Panama's** most popular music genre. While its contemporary form maintains traditional musical elements, it is heavily influenced by transnational musics such as *vallenato, cumbia, salsa*, and *merengue*. To avoid confusion, Panamanians have adopted other informal terms to distinguish commercialized *música típica* from its more traditional counterpart *música típica popular* or *píndin*.

Música típica is a rural-identified musical tradition from Panama's interior provinces of Coclé, Herrera, Los Santos, Veraguas, and Chiriquí. In the early 20th century, a *música típica conjunto* featured the violin as the principal melodic instrument and was supported by a Spanish **guitar**, triangle, and a variety of percussion instruments endemic to Panama, such as one or two *tambores* (*repicador, pujador*), and a *caja* (double-headed drum played with a hand and a stick). These **conjuntos** performed regularly at *bailes populares,* which were commonly held at cantinas, bars, open-air plazas, or private homes. Although the *música típica* repertoire from the late 19th and early 20th century was primarily instrumental, *conjuntos* sometimes included a vocalist in their lineup. It was not uncommon for a female vocalist to perform *salomas,* high-pitched vocal ululations that often require abrupt changes in vocal register akin to yodeling.

The primary rhythms employed in the *música típica* genre include the *atravesao, la cumbia* (similar to *paseo vallenato* and not to be confused with the Colombian *cumbia*), the *danzo´n-cumbia,* and the *pasillo*.

Panama's exposure to transnational music genres, facilitated by the advent of radio in the 1930s, as well as a growing demand for imported commercial recordings and touring musicians from the **United States** and Latin American, inspired *música típica* musicians to experiment with outside musical influences. In the 1940s, the accordion replaced the violin as the principal melodic instrument. The construction of larger dance venues (*jardines, toldos*), especially in Panama City where a burgeoning population of rural migrants was settling, and the introduction of electronic amplification, may partly explain the decision made by Rogelio "Gelo" Córdoba, Dorindo Cárdenas, Ceferino Nieto, and other *música típica* violinists to transition to the sonically more powerful accordion.

In the late 1960s, *música típica* composers and musicians, experimenting with **Afro-Cuban** music, sparked significant innovations in style and instrumentation.

The earliest changes impacted the percussion section; Cuban-derived instruments, such as the *timbals* and ***conga*** drums (identified in Panama as *tumbas* or tumbadoras), replaced the Panamanian tambores. Another noted development was the inclusion of a bass instrument. While Roberto "Papi Brandao" was the first *música típica* artist to introduce the stand-up bass into his *conjunto,* Ceferino Nieto's experimentation with the electric bass launched the trend for other *música típica* conjuntos.

Acclaimed accordionist Osvaldo Ayala introduced additional innovations to the *música típica* genre in the 1970s and 1980s. Ayala, who was significantly influenced by Colombian ***vallenato***, is credited as the first *música típica* artist to record songs with narrative complexity, singing lyrics that explored the emotional nuances of romantic relationships and estrangement. In the early 1980s, Ayala experimented with the latest advances in music technology, namely the Musical Instrument Digital Interface (MIDI), and was the first to incorporate electronic keyboard and percussion into his *conjunto* and sound recordings.

Today, *música típica* uses the standard ensemble of a diatonic button accordion; one or two vocalists; *timbals*, *congas,* ***güiro***, drum synthesizers, an electric bass, and an electric guitar. If the *conjunto* features one male and one female vocalist, the former serves as the lead vocalist, while the latter functions as the *salomadora.* The lead vocalist in a *música típica conjunto* is almost invariably male and the *salomadora* vocalist is a female.

In the 1990s, *música típica* experienced an unprecedented commercial boom partly due to the experimentation and innovation of several recording artists, most notably Samy and Sandra Sandoval. In the early 1990s, this brother–sister duo was relatively new to the *música típica* scene. Vocalist Sandra Sandoval and accordionist Samy Sandoval, backed by their *conjunto* Ritmo Montañero, collaborated with Panamanian composers and musicians with backgrounds in rock, **hip-hop**, *reggae*, and other popular music genres, to help redefine their style and image. While the Sandovals' new recordings were stylistically more transnational, the duo was also steadfast in their observance of *música típica's* more traditional elements. Their artistic efforts proved successful, attracting a noticeably younger and more ethnically diverse fan base throughout Panama. Their national success launched them into the global music market and they are one of the few *música típica* artists to perform extensively throughout the world, particularly in the United States, the **Dominican Republic**, Belgium, and the Netherlands.

The increasingly favorable national response to *música típica* in the 1990s also benefitted other long-established, *música típica* Panamanian accordionists. For example, Victorio Vergara experienced a sudden surge in popularity, achieving a level of commercial success unprecedented in his 30-year musical career.

Since the 1990s, the Panamanian government has honored numerous *música típica* artists, including Dorindo Cárdenas, Ulpiano Vergara, and Alfredo Escudero, for their artistic contributions to Panamanian folklore and popular culture. Nina Campines and Osvaldo Ayala have served as Panama's Ambassadors of culture. In 1995, Osvaldo Ayala became the first *música típica* artist to perform and record with the country's National Symphony Orchestra, a feat that he repeated in 2010.

Further Reading

Buckley, Francisco. *La música salsa en Panamá y algo más.* Panama: Editorial Universitaria Carlos Manuel, 2004.

Reyes Monrroy, Julio C. *Victorio Vergara Batista: El tigre de la Candelaria; el mandamás de la taquilla y el acordeón.* Panama: Editora Azul, 1998.

Saavedra, Sergio P. *Samy y Sandra: La historia.* Panama: Sergio Pérez Saavedra, 2003.

Sáenz, Eráclides A. "El violín en la música vernacular panameña." *Lotería* 415 (1997): 49–57.

Schara, Julio C. *Un estudio sobre el pindín.* Panama: Direccion Nacional de Patrimonio Historico, 1985.

Zárate, Dora P. *Sobre nuestra música típica.* Panama: Editorial Universitaria, 1996.

Melissa González

Musique Créole

Musique Créole is an umbrella term for several styles of urban dance music that emerged in the French-speaking islands of the Caribbean, particularly **Martinique** and **Guadeloupe**. In the 19th century, the most popular dances in French society were the **polka**, the **mazurka**, and the waltz. Their equivalents in the French Antilles are, respectively, *biguine*, *mazouk*, and the *valse créole*. These are the three main song types of *musique Créole,* with several variants on these forms emerging over the course of the 20th century.

As in most of the Caribbean, French Antillean dance styles are a blend of African and European musical characteristics. In the second half of the 19th century, an elite class made up of locally born whites and Afro-*Creoles* revered and sought to emulate French culture. However, the musicians who provided music for upper class ballroom dances were from the Afro-*Creole* working class, who reinterpreted fashionable dances by blending aspects of African-based polyrhythm with European-based melodies and harmonies. The *biguine* is a syncopated dance in simple duple meter, based on an eight-bar binary structure. Both the *valse créole* and *mazouk* are in simple triple meter with alternating sections (A B). The contrasting section of the *valse créole* is often in compound duple meter. In the *mazouk,* there may be a contrasting section called *la nuit* that has a different rhythmic pattern than the first section.

The typical ensemble for accompanying these dance styles in the early part of the 20th century included a clarinet, violin, cello, or trombone, and a military style bass drum. The melodies usually accompanied lyrics that expressed aspects of daily life, particularly love and romance, and the beauty of the Caribbean. In the 1920s, a number of Antillean musicians emigrated, finding employment in Paris playing various styles then popular, such as New Orleans style **jazz** and various Latin American dances such as the *tango*, *bolero*, and *rumba*. Martinican clarinetist Alexandre Stellio was the first musician to introduce traditional *biguines* and *mazouks* to Parisian audiences. Influenced by playing with various jazz bands in Paris, Stellio changed the sound of the traditional ensemble by adding piano and drum set. Stellio's Orchestre Antillais performed at the 1931 Exposition Coloniale International de Paris, and their success with Parisian audiences created a demand for the *biguine* and related styles with ballroom dancers throughout the city.

Cole Porter's "Begin the Beguine," which was written in 1935 while the composer was living in Paris, is based on the rhythms of the Antillean *biguine:* Porter uses the Spanish rather than French *Creole* spelling of the dance. The popularity of Porter's tune, despite the fact that it lacks the rhythmic vitality of a true Antillean *biguine,* did help draw attention to Caribbean music in Europe and North America. Meanwhile, Antillean dance orchestras both in Paris and back in the Caribbean continued to perform a wide repertoire of genres, and gradually changed the orchestration of their ensembles to a big band format. Famous Martinican musicians of the 1930s and 1940s include the singer Léona Gabriel and bandleaders Sam Castendet and Pierre Rassin.

In the 1950s and 1960s, bandleaders continued to diversify the sound of *musique Créole*. During this time, there were strong influences from the surrounding Caribbean, particularly Cuban **mambos**, *rumbas, boleros,* and **calypso** from Trinidad and Tobago. There were, however, composers who sought to find a local sound. One example is Martinican composer Frantz Denis "Francisco" Charles. Francisco had studied **Afro-Cuban** and African dance and drumming in Paris, and when he returned to Martinique he learned *bèlè* drumming from rural musicians. He then opened his own nightclub with a house band comprised of *bèlè* drum, *tibwa* (little sticks played on bamboo), piano, **guitar**, and *congas*, inviting local songwriters to debut their latest works with the band. He also hosted a daily radio show that featured both established artists and new talent. Thus by tapping into Martinique's Afro-*Creole* traditions, Francisco helped to modernize *musique Créole.*

During the 1960s and 1970s, Haitian styles such as mini-jazz and kadans came to dominate the popular music scene in the region. It is the blending of these styles with *musique Créole,* along with other French Antillean music such as Dominican cadence, which resulted in *zouk* in the 1980s. However, new variants of *musique Créole,* particularly *biguine,* continued to emerge during this time. These include *biguine vidé* (or just *videé*), a type of *biguine* played on the road during **Carnival** in Guadeloupe and Martinique. This style features large percussion based ensembles that accompany call-and-response singing. In the 1970s and 1980s the singer and bamboo flutist Eugene Mona blended *biguine* with **gwo ka** drumming, **rock**, and **reggae** to accompany his songs that made powerful commentaries on life in contemporary Martinique. The continued relationship between *musique Créole* and jazz is represented in the music of groups such as Malavoi, Falfrett, Difé, and Pakatak, as well as the annual Festival Jazz Biguine in Martinique. While *musique Créole* may be less popular as social dance music, it continues to be an influential part of the region's cultural heritage.

Further Reading

Cyrille, Dominique. "Sa Ki Ta Nou (This Belongs to Us): Creole Dances of the French Caribbean." 2002. In *Caribbean Dance: From Abakuá to Zouk,* edited by Susanna Sloat, 221–44. Gainesville: University Press of Florida.

Cyrille, Dominique, with Malena Kuss and Julian Gerstin. "Martinique." 2007. In *Music in Latin America and the Caribbean: An Encyclopedic History. Volume 2: Performing the Caribbean Experience,* edited by Malena Kuss, 281–320. Austin: University Press of Texas.

Guilbault, Jocelyne, with Gage Averill, Édouard Benoit, and Gregory Rabes. *Zouk: World Music in the West Indies.* Chicago: University of Chicago Press, 1993.

Hope Smith

N

Nicaragua

Nicaragua is the largest country in Central America, bordered by **Honduras** and **Costa Rica**. The majority of Nicaraguans are *mestizo* (69%), although 17 percent of the population is white, 9 percent black, and 5 percent Amerindian. The culture of Nicaragua has been significantly influenced by both the **United States** and **Mexico**. For example, Mexican music styles like *canción ranchera* are popular in the western region of the country, as are musical **trios** like the famous group Los Girasoles. *Mariachi* bands are also common on the Pacific coast. The Mexican influence is often attributed to the prosperity of the Mexican film industry, beginning in the 1930s.

Since the 1940s, **Afro-Cuban** styles like *rumba*, *mambo,* and *cha-cha-chá* have enjoyed considerable popularity in Nicaragua. Cuban genres such as *guaracha* and *bolero* also became popular around the same time. Mexican and Colombian *cumbia* is danced in the country and gaining widespread acceptance. Also, the *son nica* achieved recognition in the same decade, as it was promoted to combat Mexican dominance of Nicaraguan music. Camilo Zapata is credited with the invention of the style, as he borrowed from the repertoire of the *marimba de arco* trio comprised of the *marimba*, **guitar**, and *guitarilla*. The *baile de la marimba,* a traditional Indian dance performed in Amerindian communities on the western coast of **Guatemala**, accompanied by Spanish music styles, reflects the influence of European cultures on indigenous music. The *baile de la marimba* is now considered the national dance of Nicaragua. The music is generally performed in 6/8 meter and the harmonic support in a major key. The main instrument is the *marimba de arco,* accompanied by the guitar and *guitarilla.* With the advent of the radio and record players, the *marimba* declined in importance until the 1950s, when *música nacional* consisting mainly of folkloric genres played by *marimba de arco* trios, gained popularity.

Other popular styles included *corridos*, which were linked to the legendary figure Augusto Sandino, consisting of four line *coplas*, with a simple melody. *Corridos* are closely connected to the Spanish *romances*. These songs were used to spread Sandino's revolutionary messages to the largely illiterate lower classes.

In the 1960s and 1970s, Nicaraguan bands began playing **rock** music, which was especially celebrated by the rebellious youth. The *nueva canción*, or new song movement associated with the Sandinista struggle (*Frente Sandinista de Liberación Nacional*), became popular in the 1970s as *música de protesta* (see **Protest**

Nicaraguan musicians in the back of a truck during a funeral march. (Dreamstime)

Music in Latin America) or *música testimonial*. The *nueva canción* movement, popularized in part by Carlos Mejía Godoy, was connected with the popular classes, and the lyrics often contained political and social satire. His song "El zenzontle pregunta por Arlen" ("The mockingbird asks about Arlen") refers to the assassination of Arlen Sui, a Nicaraguan singer-songwriter and Marxist who was assassinated by Anastasio Somoza Debayle. Giocanda Belli's poem *"Cuando venga la paz,"* recorded by Carlos Mejía Godoy, emphasizes the reason for the internal struggle within Nicaragua, which is a more peaceful future.

In 1979, the Sandinista Popular Revolution succeeded in ending the Somoza dictatorship that had long dominated Nicaraguan politics, in an event known as the *triunfo* or *victoria* (triumph or victory). The 1980s was marred by political instability caused by U.S. opposition to the leftist policies of the Sandinista government. In 1990, the first woman was elected president of Nicaragua, Violeta Barrios Torres de Chamorro, defeating Sandinista candidate Daniel Ortega, the incumbent. A wave of Nicaraguans migrated to the United States in the 1980s, as a result of the difficult economic situation and continued internal political struggle, but many moved back in the 1990s in the so-called return of the Miami boys.

Further Reading

Clark, Walter Aaron. *From Tejano to Tango: Latin American Popular Music.* New York: Routledge, 2002.

Pring-Mill, Robert. "The Roles of Revolutionary Song—a Nicaraguan Assessment." *Popular Music* 6, no. 2, Latin America (1987): 179–89.

Schechter, John Mendell. *Music in Latin American Culture: Regional Traditions.* New York: Schirmer Books, 1999.

Scruggs, T.M. "Cultural Capital, Appropriate Transformations, and Transfer by Appropriation in Western Nicaragua: 'El Baile De La Marimba.'" *Latin American Music Review / Revista de Música Latinoamericana* 19, no. 1 (1998): 1–30.

Scruggs, T.M. "'Let's Enjoy as Nicaraguans': The Use of Music in the Construction of a Nicaraguan National Consciousness." *Ethnomusicology* 43, no. 2 (1999): 297–321.

Scruggs, T.M. "Música y el legado de la violencia a finales del siglo XX en Centro América." *Transcultural music review/Revista transcultural de musica,* 10 (2006).

Caitlin Lowery

Norteño

Música norteña (music or the north) or simply *norteño* is a popular music genre originally from **Mexico's** northern states. It shares many similarities with the Texas-based *conjunto* (ensemble), its counterpart across the U.S.-Mexico border. Both *norteño* and *conjunto* have folk-based rural origins and feature a core instrumentation of button **accordion** and *bajo sexto* (a type of **guitar** with six double courses of strings). This duo has grown to include other instruments such as *tololoche* (double bass), which has largely been replaced by the electric bass since the mid-1950s, *tambora de rancho,* a homemade drum later replaced by the drum set, and saxophone, but the two core instruments still characterize the sound of the ensemble. Both traditions have mutually influenced each other, as they have become the favorite music styles in the area and a strong marker of northern Mexican identity. Although *norteño* bands such as Los Tigres del Norte have had a large following among mostly blue-collar Mexican immigrants in the United States for decades, it was not until the 1990s, however, that rural-rooted, regional music from northern Mexico turned into a hot commodity on both sides of the border.

Música norteña emerged as a truly intercultural practice when Spanish colonial, Mexican national, and 19th-century immigrant traditions were blended to create a cheerful musical style with new instrumental sounds. Although it is impossible to reconstruct the exact origins of *norteño* music for it was a specific expression of a common people, learned and passed down from generation to generation by ear, the beginnings of *norteño* as a distinct genre can be traced to the arrival of the button accordion in the U.S.-Mexico border area in the 1860s and 1870s. Introduced by European settlers, notably of German and Czech origin, Mexican people not only adopted the loud, sturdy, and relatively inexpensive instrument but also the popular European dances of the time: **polka**, waltz (see *vals*), *mazurka,* quadrille, and *schottische*. *Norteño's* history becomes more tangible with the interest of the nascent recording industry in regional music expression. North of the border, several companies began to record native Texas-Mexican and Mexican musicians and singers in the 1930s. South of the border, the industrial capital Monterrey became a leading force in the development of a potent media industry, which was not only decisive in the shaping of regional popular music, but also furthered transregional expressions by disseminating them to other parts of Mexico via powerful radio stations. By the 1940s, the typical *norteño* ensemble consolidated, featuring the three-row diatonic button accordion, *bajo sexto,* saxophone, contrabass, and drum set. Vocal genres were performed in a characteristic Hispanic type of folk polyphony, two high-pitched voices singing in parallel thirds and sixths (usually the accordion and *bajo sexto* players), in a fast tempo, and with a strongly tonal harmonic support. The repertory consisted of a combination of instrumental polkas, schottisches, and *redowas* with the lyric-oriented *canciones mexicanas* (Mexican songs) or ***rancheras***, ***huapangos***, and ***corridos*** (folk ballads). The latter had become the main narrative expression of the *norteño* tradition in the early 20th century.

The crystallization of a distinct northern music style was stimulated by musical interrelations between south Texas and northern Mexico. Mexican musicians such as Los Alegres de Terán, Antonio Tanguma, and Lalo García gained popularity on both sides of the border. New popular dance rhythms such as the ***bolero*** and the ***cumbia*** were incorporated into the *norteña* repertory by Pedro Yerena and Juan Montoya in the 1940s and by Beto Villa and Ramón Ayala in the 1960s, respectively. Changes in the instrumentation consolidated the modern *conjunto* sound in the 1950s when most groups added a modern drum, substituted an electric bass guitar for the contrabass, and introduced amplification for the accordion and the *bajo sexto* as well as microphones for the singers.

Norteño is one of the most thriving types of popular Mexican music nowadays. Many of the famous Mexican bands such as Ramón Ayala y sus Bravos del Norte, Los Tigres del Norte, and Los Rieleros del Norte are based in the United States, and their music is recorded and produced within the United States. Although *norteña* music has kept its working (or lower) class image to a certain degree, it has been able to transcend its geographic and social confines. In the United States, it continues to play a significant role as a vehicle of expression of the migrant experience and cultural heritage of many Mexicans.

Further Reading

Bensusan, Guy. "A Consideration of Norteña and Chicano Music." *Studies of Latin American Popular Culture* 4 (1985): 158–69.

Burr, Ramiro. *The Billboard Guide to Tejano and Regional Mexican Music.* New York: Billboard Books, 1999.

Peña, Manuel. *The Texas-Mexican Conjunto: History of a Working-Class Music.* Austin: University of Texas Press, 1985.

Helena Simonett

Nueva Canción

Nueva canción (new song) refers to a socially conscious folkloric-popular music movement that originated in the Southern Cone in the 1960s and spread throughout Latin America in the 1970s and 1980s. It is closely related to **Cuba's *nueva trova*** (new Troubadours) and **Argentina's** *movimiento nuevo cancionero* (new song movement). In 1967, leftist Latin American musicians attending Cuba's First International Meeting of Protest Music first considered using the name *nueva canción* for a progressive Latin American music movement, however, the term primarily caught on in **Chile** following 1969's First Festival of Chilean Nueva Canción. *Nueva canción* later became mainly a generational category for socially conscious Chilean artists and songs from the 1960s and 1970s.

Nueva canción is difficult to define stylistically because of its international scope and eclectic nature. *Nueva canción* musicians generally view themselves as socially committed artists who interpret the folk music of the common people. Like most folk revivalists worldwide, *nueva canción* artists typically adapt rural musical traditions in a manner that is esthetically pleasing to middle- and upper-class urban audiences. *Nueva canción* compositions are intended mainly for listening rather than dancing (unlike most rural genres) and frequently exhibit carefully written lyrics with progressive (sometimes explicitly political) messages. Strongly associated with leftist pan-Latin Americanism, *nueva canción* artists usually play instruments and/or genres from various Latin American countries (e.g., Andean *kena* **flute** accompanied with Venezuelan *cuatro* and Argentine *bombo* drum).

Chilean singer/songwriter/guitarist **Violeta Parra** (1917–1967) laid much of the groundwork for the *nueva canción* movement (although she died before the movement acquired its name). Parra patterned many of her songs on rural *mestizo* genres that she had learned during frequent travels to the Chilean countryside. Before becoming well-known, Parra lived in Europe from 1955 to 1956. In Paris, Argentine musicians from Buenos Aires introduced her to the highland Andean *charango* (ukulele-size string instrument) and *kena* (end-notched bamboo flute), instruments later highly identified with *nueva canción*. During Parra's second stay in Europe (1962–1965) the political content of her song lyrics notably increased. She wrote future *nueva canción* classics such as *La Carta* ("The Letter") and performed at Paris's L'Escale and La Candelaria, Left Bank venues where Latin American musicians including her son Ángel and daughter Isabel also played. The Parra family returned to Chile in 1965 and founded Santiago's La Peña de los Parra and La Carpa de la Reina, which like Paris's L'Escale and La Candelaria presented rural Latin American musical traditions to cosmopolitan urban audiences. In contrast to Paris's largely apolitical scene, however, in the Chilean capital overtly leftist sentiments were front and center at the pioneering Parra venues, where folkloric-popular music became closely linked to leftism and pan-Latin Americanism. These sentiments inspired Violeta Parra's song "Los Pueblos Americanos" ("The American Peoples/Nations") and Patricio Manns's "Si Somos Americanos" ("If We Are Americans"). For the emerging *nueva canción* movement La Peña de los Parra and La Carpa de la Reina functioned as the main center of activity. La Peña de los Parra's house ensemble, named Los de la Peña (later known as Los Curacas), was among the first urban Chilean groups to specialize in highland Andean repertory.

After Violeta Parra's suicide in 1967, her friend Victor Jara and her children Ángel and Isabel Parra became the movement's key figures. In 1969 Jara's "Plegaria a un Labrador" ("Prayer to a Worker") earned the top prize at the First Festival of Chilean *nueva canción*. Another famous song by Jara, "Preguntas por Puerto Montt" ("Questions about Puerto Montt"), boldly denounced the Chilean military's massacre of striking workers, naming government official Pérez Zujovic as the main culprit. Jara, like Violeta Parra and the Parra siblings, fit into the folk music protest singer/songwriter/guitarist mold (as did Argentine folklorist Atahualpa Yupanqui, an important influence on many *nueva canción* musicians). Also very popular in Chile were 4–5-member ensembles that sang in 2–4-part harmony, accompanied with guitars and *bombo*. Dressed in rural garb (e.g., ponchos), these urban groups modeled themselves after superstar Argentine folkloric-popular ensembles (e.g., Los Chalchaleros, Los Fronterizos). This was the case with *Quilapayún* (Mapuche for "Three Bearded Men"), directed at first by Ángel Parra and later by Jara. Inti-Illimani, whose Bolivian name (Illimani is a La Paz mountain) reflected the group's early repertory of Andean instrumental pieces, was another Chilean university student ensemble active in the late 1960s.

The *nueva canción* movement lent its support to leftist presidential candidate Salvador Allende and his Popular Unity coalition. In the run-up to Allende's 1970 electoral victory, the Popular Unity anthem *Venceremos* ("We Will Triumph") was standard *nueva canción* repertoire. After the election, *nueva canción* artists continued to back Allende. Amid escalating polarization across political and class lines, *nueva canción* musicians performed on a regular basis at Popular Unity rallies and wrote numerous compositions in support of the Allende administration and its initiatives (e.g., nationalization of resources, agrarian reform). "El Pueblo Unido Jamás Sera Vencido" ("A United People Will Never Be Defeated"), perhaps the most famous *nueva canción* song, dates from this period. During the Allende years (1970–1973), Chilean *nueva canción* artists forged closer relationships with socially conscious musicians from other Latin American countries, such as Daniel

Rodríguez Dominguez, Silvio

Cuban singer Silvio Rodríguez (b. 1946) is a founder of the ***nueva trova*** movement. He was suspended from radio and television by the Cuban government for acknowledging the Beatles as an influence on his style, but after the institutionalization of *nueva trova* in the 1970s, he was promoted by the Cuban government and become the first *nueva trovador* to record an album. He performed in **Argentina**, **Nicaragua**, Spain, and other countries as **Cuba's** cultural ambassador. He was elected to the Cuban National Assembly in 1992.

Rodríguez's songs cover a range of topics. Several early songs appear critical of censorship, while "Reino de todavía," among others, addresses the socioeconomic difficulties of Cuba following the fall of the U.S.S.R. His pro-socialist sentiments are expressed in "El necio" and his anti-imperialist stance in "Canción urgente para Nicaragua." He has also written several elegies to Che Guevara. Stylistically, many of his songs feature a folk-rock style reminiscent of early Bob Dylan or Victor Jara, while others feature chromatic harmonies recalling traditional Cuban styles.

Further Reading

Manabe, Noriko. 2006. "Lovers and Rulers, the Real and the Surreal: Harmonic Metaphors in Silvio Rodríguez's Songs." *Transcultural Music Review* 10 http://www.sibetrans.com/trans/a154/lovers-and-rulers-the-real-and-the-surreal-harmonic-metaphors-in-silvio-rodriguezs-songs

Noriko Manabe

Viglietti of Uruguay, Mercedes Sosa of Argentina, and **Silvio Rodríguez**, and Pablo Milanés of Cuba.

General Augusto Pinochet's 1973 coup violently ended the Allende era, sending many *nueva canción* musicians into exile, sometimes after they had endured imprisonment (e.g., Ángel Parra). Victor Jara was executed by the military. In Chile, *nueva canción* was forced underground, gradually reemerging in the form of the less-politicized *canto nuevo*. *Quilapayún* and *Inti-Illimani* had been representing the Allende administration (as its cultural ambassadors) in France and Italy, respectively, at the time of the coup. Exiled for the next 15 years, like many other *nueva canción* artists they settled in Europe, where the music of the Andes had been growing in popularity since the late 1960s, mainly due to the efforts of the Paris-based Argentine-led groups Los Incas and Los Calchakis. This prior interest in Andean folkloric-popular music set the stage for Chilean *nueva canción*'s enthusiastic reception in post-1973 Europe, the site of many leftist solidarity-themed *nueva canción* concerts for the next decade. These events not only showcased Chilean ensembles—including ones formed in exile such as Patricio Manns' Karaxú—but also socially committed musicians from Argentina (e.g., Mercedes Sosa) and other South American countries, many of whom had likewise fled from U.S.-supported right-wing military dictatorships. The *nueva canción* movement also gained a following in the Caribbean and Central America, especially in Mexico City. *Nueva canción* festivals held in Mexico (1982), Nicaragua (1983), Ecuador (1984), Argentina (1985), and other countries added to the movement's internationalization. In 1988, Chilean *nueva canción*'s exile status ended with the restoration of democracy. Today, *nueva canción* musicians freely perform in Chile as well as continue to tour worldwide.

Further Reading

Fairley, Jan. "La Nueva Canción Latinoamericana." *Bulletin of Latin American Research* 3/2 (1984): 107–15.

Morris, Nancy. "Canto Porque es Necesario Cantar: The New Song Movement in Chile, 1973–1983." *Latin American Research Review* 21, no. 2 (1986): 117–36.

Rios, Fernando. "*La Flûte Indienne:* The Early History of Andean Folkloric-Popular Music in France and its Impact on *Nueva Canción*." *Latin American Music Review* 29, no. 2 (2008): 145–81.

Fernando Rios

Nueva Trova

Nueva trova is a musical movement that emerged in the mid-1960s in **Cuba**. Starting as a frankly worded, grassroots scene, it came to be supported by the Cuban government from the 1970s onwards. *Nueva trova* drew from diverse musics. The music of Pablo Milanés, who started his career as a *filín* musician, showed the influence of *trova tradicional* and *son* (e.g., "Son para despertar a una negrita"). **Silvio Rodríguez** was initially more influenced by North American folk and folk-rock, particularly Bob Dylan and Woodie Guthrie, with songs featuring acoustic **guitar** accompaniments that alternated between picking (e.g., "Historia de las sillas") and *rock*-like strumming (e.g., "Te doy una canción"); nonetheless, the style of "*Canción de la trova*" also shows homage to the *trova tradicional*. The lyrics cover a wide range of topics from the personal to the philosophical to the political. Many songs address love, but the sexual double-entendre or machismo that peppers other popular genres are uncommon.

In spirit, *nueva trova* had much in common with ***nueva canción***, which had taken hold in South America a few years earlier as a socially and politically conscious song movement. These artists visited Cuba through pan-Latin American song festivals arranged through the Consejo Nacional de Cultura (1965), as well as the Encuentro Internacional de la Canción Protesta (July 1967) and the Festival de la Canción Popular in Varadero (December 1967) arranged by Haydée Santamaría, a member of Castro's inner circle.

As founder and director of the Casa de las Américas, Santamaría was instrumental in bringing the *nueva trovadores* into the public. A group of youths, including Rodríguez, had begun gathering at the ice cream parlor Coppelia in Havana to exchange poetry and music, discuss works by Cuban and international writers, and give occasional concerts; Rodríguez had also appeared on the television show *Música y estrellas* in June 1967. In February 1968, Santamaría arranged for Rodríguez, Milanés, Noel Nicola, and others to appear in monthly concerts at the Casa de las Américas, of which she was the founder and director; many of these concerts were televised. Also in the early months of 1968, *Mientras tanto,* a half-hour Sunday evening show centered on Rodríguez, was broadcast on national television.

It was not long before these artists began to run into difficulties with the authorities, as the ideological atmosphere had become particularly intolerant following the nationalization of economic activities. Popular music and fashions associated with the **United States**, such as long hair and rock, were viewed as decadent and were censored by the Cuban government. Accordingly, *Mientras tanto* was taken off the air, and Rodríguez was suspended from radio and television broadcasts. He and Milanés were rumored to have spent time at re-education or work camps, and Rodríguez eventually left Cuba to sail on a fishing boat in 1969. Some songs of this period, such as Rodríguez's "Debo partirme en dos" or "Resumen de noticias," addressed controversial subjects such as censorship.

Their fortunes were to change. In 1969, the Grupo de Experimentación Sonora (GESI) was formed at the film institute ICAIC, under the direction of the composer Leo Brouwer, with Rodríguez, Milanés, Nicola, Sara González, Sergio Vitier, and Pablo Menéndez among its members. This organization gave the group legitimacy as film composers and offered them an opportunity to make recordings, take classes in music, and collaborate with other musicians.

Furthermore, official attitudes toward *nueva trovadores* softened as the authorities observed Chilean *nueva canción* artists such as Victor Jara making goodwill trips for the socialist government of Salvador Allende in 1971; meanwhile, *nueva trovadores* were increasingly invited to international festivals in Latin America. By 1973, the Movimiento de la Nueva Trova (MNT) was officially institutionalized, and *nueva trovadores* began to receive sponsorship from the government with wide media exposure and many opportunities to perform and record. Song lyrics during this period became less critical of Cuba itself, but more anti-imperialistic (e.g., Rodríguez's "Canción urgente para Nicaragua"), nationalistic (e.g., "El Mayor"), and metaphorical (e.g., "Sueño con serpientes"). Although more socially critical texts have increased following the fall of the Soviet Union, first-wave artists such as Rodríguez and Milanés are considered to be working with the government rather than expressing oppositional views; nonetheless, they remain very popular throughout Latin America and Spain.

Since the 1980s and beyond, several artists, who call themselves *novísima trova,* have emerged, airing the difficulties of Cuban life. Carlos Varela, who plays in a rock style, addresses themes such as the death of rafters (such as "Círculo de tiza") and families split between Cuba and the United States (such as "Foto de familia"). Particularly allegorical is "Guillermo Tell," where Tell's son asks his father to put the apple on his own head. Other prominent names include Pedro Luis Ferrer, with his allegory of an authoritarian grandfather ("Abuelo Paco"), Gerardo Alfonso, and Gema y Pavel.

Further Reading

Díaz Pérez, Clara. *Sobre la guitarra, la voz: Una historia de la nueva trova cubana.* Havana: Editorial Letras Cubanas, 1994.

Manabe, Noriko. "Lovers and Rulers, the Real and the Surreal: Harmonic Metaphors in Silvio Rodríguez's Songs." *Trans* 10, http://www.sibetrans.com/trans/trans10/noriko. htm, 2006.

Moore, Robin. 2006. "Transformations in Nueva Trova." In *Music and Revolution: Cultural Change in Socialist Cuba,* 135–69. Berkeley: University of California Press.

Noriko Manabe

Orquesta

Orquesta is a generic Spanish term for the word orchestra. In Latin American popular music, it is often used to describe small to medium instrumental ensembles, which may or may not necessarily have more than one instrument on a part. Modifiers may refine the usage of the term, such as *gran orquesta* or *orquesta típica*, though the latter is used for so many different ensembles throughout Latin America that its usage defies any particular definition. The following are some of the more popular uses of the term *orquesta* in Latin American popular music.

Within the genre of *tango* the *orquesta tipica* became the standard instrumentation for *tango* ensembles consisting of two **bandoneón**, two violins, a piano, and a string bass, which may or may not have a solo singer added to the orchestra.

Within Cuban popular music, there are several uses of the term *orquesta.* The earliest examples are the predominantly wind-based *orquesta típicas,* who from the early 19th to the early 20th centuries, formed the main type of popular music format. Numbering anywhere from about eight to twelve players, their repertoire consisted of **contradanzas**, minuets, *rigadoons,* and *quadrilles.* Well-known *orquesta típicas* include Orquesta Flor de Cuba, Orquesta Faílde, and Orquesta de Enrique Peña.

Another type of orchestra that was popular in Cuba during the first half of the 20th century were the *orquestas* known as **charangas**. The *charanga francesa,* which derived from the *orquesta típica,* normally consisted of piano, bass, *timbals,* and other percussion, two violins, and a Cuban **flute**. Notable ensembles include Orquesta Torroella and Orquesta Romeu.

One of the more internationally popular *orquestas* is the *gran orquesta* or Cuban big band that flourished during the 1940s and 1950s. The standard orchestration for big band or *gran orquesta* consists of five saxophones (two altos, two tenors, and a baritone), four trumpets, two trombones, piano, bass and *ad lib* percussion. This instrumentation reflects a strong American **jazz** influence and its creation was credited to **Machito** in the early 1940s, who wanted to give Cuban ensembles a more American sound. Representative groups include Machito and his Afro-Cubans, Beny More's Orquesta Aragón, and Orquesta **Pérez Prado**.

Further Reading

Torres, George. "Sources for Latin Big Band Performance: An Examination of the Latin American Stocks in the Library of Congress." *College Music Symposium,* 43 (2003): 25–41.

George Torres

Orquesta Típica (Cuba)

The *orquesta típica* (typical orchestra, also known as folkloric orchestra) is a music ensemble that emerged in **Cuba** in the 19th century. The oldest European-derived ensemble in Cuba, the *orquesta típica* was an adaptation of military marching bands for entertainment purposes. Instrumentation varied, but the ensemble often consisted of two clarinets, two violins, a cornet or trumpet, a trombone, an ophicleide (a type of bass bugle), *timbals* (a military-style drum), and later, **Afro-Cuban** instruments such as the *pailas* and *güiro*.

The *orquesta típica* performed in ballrooms of Colonial houses throughout Cuba, playing a number of different styles of dance music. The favored style was the *contradanse*, an English country dance that was brought to Cuba by French aristocrats who had fled from **Haiti** during the Haitian Revolution of the 1790s. The *contradanse* was adapted for performance by *orquesta típica* ensembles, and by the 1800s the *contradanse* had evolved into the ***contradanza***, which featured African-derived instruments such as the *paila* and *güiro*. The *contradanza* became the first genre of Cuban music that was popular abroad. In 1879, Miguel Failde performed—with an *orquesta típica* ensemble—the first ***danzón*** piece, a statelier, more improvisatory version of the *contradanza* that featured a five-beat, one-bar rhythmic pattern known as the ***cinquillo***.

Although the *orquesta típica* began to fall out of popularity by the early 20th century—due in part to its replacement by the *charanga* ensemble—the *orquesta típica* played a great hand in the creation of several Cuban musical genres, including the ***danzonette*** in the late 1920s, the ***mambo*** in the 1940s, and the ***cha-cha-chá*** in the 1950s.

Further Reading

Sublette, Ned. *Cuba and Its Music: From the First Drums to the Mambo.* 1st ed. Chicago: Chicago Review Press, 2004.

Erin Stapleton-Corcoran

P

Pachanga

Pachanga is a rhythm associated with popular dance music. It originated in **Cuba** and was popular at the time of the Cuban Revolution in 1959. It developed further in the **United States**, where its popularity peaked in the 1960s. *Pachanga* spread throughout Latin America, particularly to **Colombia** and **Argentina**. Eduardo Davidson, the creator of *pachanga,* wrote "La pachanga," one of his most frequently covered songs. Excerpts of the song demonstrate the simplicity of the lyrics, which were usually comprised of an invitation to dance: "*Señores que pachanga, me voy con la pachanga. Ay mamita qué pachanga, me voy con la pachanga.*" The most typical steps of the dance were to take two steps forward and then to shake a foot in both directions in a sort of small hop.

The Orquesta Sublime, also known as la pachanguera de Cuba, introduced *pachanga* to dancers at the Jardines de La Tropical in Havana. Their *pachanga* recording reached Number 1 on the National Hit Parade. The Orquesta Fajardo y sus Estrellas took *pachanga* to the Caribbean and New York, performing it at the Palladium in New York. After Eduardo Davidson immigrated to the United States, the *pachanga* was no longer danced in Cuba. From that moment on, a new style developed, the New York variant of the *pachanga* or *Pachanga newyorkina*. It became popular in the city as some considered this new style a freer form of the **cha-cha-chá**. Others perceived it as a rhythm closer to **merengue**. The New York variant is usually defined as more rhythmic. Rafael Lam referred to it as "a mixture of **son montuno** with Cuban **zapateo** and something of *merengue.*"

Some of the most outstanding performers of *pachanga* include Santiago de Cuba–born singer Rubén Ríos, who was one of the first artists to record the *pachanga;* Argentina's Luisito Aguile and Carlos Argentino, who shared the title of "*El rey de la pachanga*" with Tito Rodríguez; Graciela Pérez of the Orquesta Machito y sus Afrocubana; and Tito Puente. Notable **charangas** performing *pachanga* include Charlie Palmieri's Duboney and Johnny Pacheco y su charanga, Sexteto de Joe Cuba, Conjunto Casino, and Rolando Laserie. Pacheco claimed to be the creator of *pachanga* as did the Sexteto de Joe Cuba.

Further Reading

Baker, Geoffrey, and David F. García. "Arsenio Rodríguez and the Transnational Flows of Latin Popular Music. By David F. García." *Music and Letters* 89, no. 2 (2008): 290–92.

Díaz Ayala, Cristóbal. *Música cubana: Del Areyto al Rap Cubano*. Fourth edition. San Juan: Fundación Musicalia, 2003.

Dorsey, Margaret E. *Pachangas: Borderlands Music, U.S. Politics, and Transnational Marketing*. Austin: University of Texas Press, 2006.

Orejuela Martínez, Adriana. *El son no se fue de Cuba. Claves para una historia 1959–1973*. Letras cubanas, 2006.

Liliana González

Pambiche

Pambiche is a Latin American dance form that is derived from the complex of dances that evolved out of the **merengue tipico**. It is thought to have originated

---

Blades, Rubén

Rubén Blades (b. 1946) has performed and composed traditional Afro-Cuban *salsa*, and *salsa* fused with **jazz**, **rock**, pan-Latin, and world music, since the 1960s. Blades combines dancability with socially conscious lyrics. His political awareness began to develop following the violent U.S. suppression of a 1964 Panamanian student uprising. He later worked at Fania Records, which led to his collaboration with Willy Colón with whom he released *Siembra* (1978) and *Maestra Vida* (1980).

Blades formed Seis del Solar in the early 1980s, eschewing the traditional *salsa* horn section and incorporating rock and jazz elements. He continued to experiment with lyrics and collaborations but returned to his *salsa* roots and released another album, *Antecedentes* (1988). Blades won seven Grammy's, including a World Music Grammy for *Mundo,* featuring a fusion of Irish, Arabic, and Afro-Cuban musical traditions.

Blades has won many awards for political activism, including the United Nation's World Ambassador against Racism. He also ran for president of Panama and became Panama's Minister of Tourism.

Further Reading

Balaguer, Alejandro. "Ruben Blades: Minister of Salsa: Better Known Outside His Country as a Singer-Songwriter and Actor, This Renaissance Man Today Speaks from a Political Stage, as Panama's Minister of Tourism." *Americas* 60 (Jan.–Feb. 2008): 14–21.

Rebecca Stuhr

during the American occupation of the **Dominican Republic** (1916–1924); the name *pambiche* is derived from a phonetic corruption of Palm Beach, which was the fabric worn by American soldiers during the occupation. As the legend goes, the *merengue estilo yanqui* (Yankee style) became known as *pambiche* (Palm Beach style) because the Americans were neither capable of dancing well, nor with the nuance appropriate for the rhythm. While it is possible that the name *pambiche* originated during the U.S. occupation, it is more likely that the form existed long before the name *pambiche* was given to the dance. It is performed at a slower tempo than the *merengue* and utilizes a ***cinquillo***-based *tambora* rhythm.

Further Reading

Austerlitz, Paul. *Merengue: Dominican Music and Dominican Identity.* Philadelphia, PA: Temple University Press, 1997.

George Torres

Panama

As a passageway between the Atlantic and Pacific Oceans as well as the North and South American continents, Panama is largely defined by its geographical identity as the crossroads of the world. Panama's history as a former Spanish colony, Colombian province, and **United States** protectorate have created inextricably interwoven cultural pathways that contribute to its rich tapestry of popular expressive cultures.

Though identified as a Central American country, Panama is culturally more akin to its South American and Caribbean neighbors. Colombian ***vallenato*** and ***cumbia***, for example, have significantly influenced Panama's folk music traditions, known collectively as ***música típica***. Throughout the 20th century, the rise of radio and television media, along with the importation of commercial recordings and touring musicians from **Cuba**, **Puerto Rico**, and other Caribbean countries, have played a pivotal role in the commercialization of *música típica* today considered to be Panama's most popular music.

Caribbean music genres such as ***calypso***, ***soca***, and ***reggae*** are very popular. Although *calypso* groups were emerging as early as the 1930s, the genre's golden age of commercial development occurred in the 1960s and 1970s when artists such as Lord Cobra and Lord Panama achieved considerable fame in Panama and abroad. Panama has also played a pivotal role in the development and popularization of *reggae* throughout Latin America. Starting in the late 1970s, artists cultivated a musical sound that intertwined Jamaican *reggae* rhythms with Spanish lyrics, consequently spawning the *reggae en español* movement. In the early 1990s, Edgardo Franco Low, otherwise known as El General, popularized a dancehall music style sung or rapped in Spanish (often recording English and Spanish versions of the same song) now known as ***reggaetón***. Today, *reggae en español* and *reggaetón* continue to enjoy immense popularity throughout Panama, especially with the country's young population.

Panamanian *salsero* and songwriter **Ruben Blades** is the country's most prominent exponent of ***salsa***. Blades's collaboration with Puerto Rican composer and trombonist Willie Colon led to the production of several albums under the Fania label. Their 1978 album *Siembra* continues to be the best selling *salsa* album ever at over 25 million copies. Other Panamanian musicians who have established international careers in *salsa* include trumpetist and member of the Fania All-Stars Vitín Paz. From 1968 until 1990, the *salsa* group Bush y sus magnificos, fronted by percussionist Francisco "Bush" Buckley, was a dominating force in the salsa scene, having recorded multiple albums of original material and touring internationally.

Panama's contributions to **jazz**, while manifold, are not well known beyond the country's borders. One of the earliest figures to emerge, Luis Russell, relocated to New Orleans where he began a career as a jazz pianist and bandleader. Flutist and saxophonist Mauricio also became an important jazz musician working with major figures such as **Machito**, Mongo Santamaria, Tito Puente, Charlie Mingus, and Dizzy Gillespie, among many others. In recent years, Panama has experienced a renewed interest in jazz. Grammy award–winning jazz pianist and composer Danilo Perez, who has served as cultural ambassador to Panama, founded the Panama Jazz Festival in 2003.

Panama's complex political, economic, and military relationship with the United States, spanning most of the 20th century, has left an indelible mark on the nation's popular cultural landscape. Just as rock music was gaining ground as a popular music genre in the United States and Britain during the 1960s, a similar music scene was also flourishing in Panama. While many of the first Panamanian-based rock groups were cover bands, others such as Woodstock created a hybrid style of rock that incorporated Caribbean and Pan-Latino musical styles such as *salsa*. Panama's rock music scene, based largely in the nation's capital, has produced many successful rock groups who have gone on to receive international acclaim.

Panamanian singer and songwriter Pedro Altamirada is an important popular cultural figure whose music defies generic categorization. Starting in the late 1970s, Altamirada created songs that commingled *calypso* rhythms with musical elements from salsa creating a sound that attracts a multigenerational, as well as ethnically and racially diverse fan base. Altamiranda's music is also strongly influenced by the Panamanian murga, a brass and percussion ensemble that performs a repertoire of Panamanian traditional musics and Caribbean popular, especially during the Carnival season. Altimirada is also recognized for his songwriting, which contains politically charged lyrics and social commentary, often expressed with Panamanian colloquialisms. In fact, several of his songs were censored by the Panamanian government during the 1980s.

Further Reading

Buckley, Francisco. *La Música Salsa En Panamá Y Algo Mas*. Panama: Editorial Universitaria "Carlos Manuel Gasteazoro," 2004.

Guerrón-Montero, Carla. "Can't Beat Me Own Drum in Me Own Native Land: Calypso Music and Tourism in the Panamanian Atlantic Coast." *Anthropological Quarterly* 79, no. 4 (2006): 633–63.

Rivera, R.Z., Marshall, M., and Hernandez, D.P, eds. *Reggaetón*. Durham, NC: Duke University Press, 2009.

Steward, Noel Foster. *Las Expresiones Musicales en Panamé: Una Aproximación*. Panama: Editorial Universitaria, 1997.

Melissa González

Pandeiro

The *pandeiro,* a type of tambourine (a single-headed frame drum with metal jingles), is a versatile Brazilian percussion instrument played with the thumb, fingers, and palm of the hand. Used in hundreds of local and regional musical traditions in **Brazil** during the mid-20th century, the *pandeiro* became the country's de facto national percussion instrument through its associations with *choro* and *samba* in Rio de Janeiro. Contemporary performers have explored virtuosic techniques and electroacoustic possibilities on the instrument.

Historical records of *pandeiros* in Brazil are rather sketchy, but frame drums with jingles (often called *adufe* in rural areas) were likely introduced into Brazil by Portuguese settlers and missionaries early in the 16th century. During colonial and imperial periods, *pandeiros* became common rhythmic accompaniment instruments in the music traditions of privileged and subaltern populations throughout the country. Numerous Brazilian processional and dramatic music and dance traditions use the *pandeiro* (including *pastoril, folia de reis, congada, cavalo marinho,* and *moçambique*). The instrument is also found in many social dance contexts (*samba de roda, coco, forró*) and as accompaniment to specific song genres (*embolada*). The *pandeiro* also accompanies the Afro-Brazilian martial arts–like game dance of *capoeira.*

During the late 19th and early 20th centuries, *pandeiro* players entered hybrid artistic contexts of urban music-making. In Rio de Janeiro, *pandeiros* were used to accompany parading **Carnival** clubs known as *ranchos* and *blocos* and later in the *escolas de samba* (see *samba*) forming in the hillside slums where the majority of the black population was located. In Recife, Pernambuco, the *pandeiro* was used in the Carnival blocos of middle-class Italian immigrants as well as in the pedestrian *frevo* clubs of urban laborers comprising working-class black and *mestiço* populations.

In Rio de Janeiro, the *pandeiro* became an essential component of **choro** ensembles in the 1910s and was included in Brazil's first important popular music group: Pixinguinha's Oito Batutas. In the 1930s, the *pandeiro* became the primary percussion instrument of the *conjuntos regionais* (professional *choro* ensembles used in the broadcast and recording industry). Simultaneously, the *pandeiro* was a key percussion instrument in the emerging urban *samba* music of Rio de Janeiro, a complex field of artistic activity that included the nascent Brazilian music industry and spanned racial and class divisions. Important *pandeiro* players from the early era of Brazilian popular music included Jacó Palmieri and João da Baiana (Ernesto Joaquim Maria dos Santos).

In contemporary Brazil, a variety of regional and national styles of *pandeiro* playing can be found. In the Northeast, unique forms of *pandeiro* are associated with the *coco, cavalo marinho,* and the *frevo*. In Rio de Janeiro, distinct styles include those used in the *escola de samba, pagode,* and in *choro*. Some contemporary percussionists such as Marcos Suzano and Bernardo Aguiar specialize in the *pandeiro* and have incorporated electroacoustic innovations into their playing and have developed new virtuosic techniques. Such innovations have helped establish the Brazilian *pandeiro* as an important global percussion instrument.

Further Reading

Bolão, Oscar. *Batuque é um privilégio: A percussão da música do Rio de Janeiro/ Batuque Is a Privilege: Percussion in Rio de Janeiro's Music.* Rio de Janeiro, Brazil: Lumiar Editora, 2003.

Feiner, Scott. *Pandeiristas: Player Bios.* Pandeiro, www.pandeiro.com/players.php

Larry Crook

Paraguay

Paraguay is one of the only landlocked countries in South America, bordered by **Brazil, Argentina**, and **Bolivia**. Of the population, 95 percent is *mestizo* and the country has two official languages, Spanish and Guaraní, as a large percentage of the population is bilingual. A hybrid language, Jopará, has developed as a result of the combination of the two languages. Paraguayan folk music is closely related to national identity. In 1944, the Paraguayan government designated "Campamento Cerro Léon" by Giménez and Fernández and "India" by Flores and Ortíz Guerrero as Canciones Populares Nacionales. In 1959, the government passed a law mandating that 50 percent of all music played on the radio be composed by Paraguayans, a law which still exists today, although it is not enforced.

The most iconic Paraguayan instrument is the **arpa** *paraguaya*. It was adapted from the European harp brought by the Spanish in the 17th or 18th century. The *arpa*

Some 50 Paraguayan harpists perform at the presidential house in Asuncion to celebrate the World Harp Festival in 2009. (Noberto Duarte/AFP/Getty Images)

is particularly prominent in music from the Guairá region and may be played by a soloist or in a *conjunto*. Two of the most famous *arpistas* from Paraguay include Luis Bordón and Félix Pérez Cardozo, who wrote the well-known **polka** "Pájaro Campana."

The polka is considered the national genre. It differs significantly from the European dance style of the same name. The dance music of the *polca paraguaya* is comprised of a duple rhythm. The different variations of the dance are known by adjectives describing the dance, such as *polca popó* (jumping polka), *polca syryrý* (slippery or smooth), and *polca valseado* (like a waltz, or **vals**). José Asunción Flores is credited with the creation of *guaránia*, a musical genre derived from polka, usually played in a minor mode.

Another important traditional genre in Paraguay is the *galopa*, which contains two parts, the first of which is similar to *polca*. The *galopa* is danced by a woman, who improvises the steps while balancing a pitcher or bottle on top of her head. Paraguayan folk music is frequently played in steakhouses, called *parrilladas*, which remain popular tourist attractions, as they serve traditional meals while *conjuntos* perform live music, sometimes including the *danza de las botellas*. During the *danza de las botellas*, which is performed to polka music, the woman balances bottles on her head, and more are added throughout the dance.

While polka and *guaránia* are still popular in Paraguay today, rock has found an increasingly large following within the country. Rock bands often play both their own music and covers of American rock as entertainment for parties. Under the dictatorship of Alfredo Stroessner (1954–1989), freedom of expression was limited, but in the 1990s, rock flourished in Paraguay. Contemporary popular rock bands include Flou, Revolber and Slow Agony. Paraguayan *Creole* music such as the *polca* may be adapted to popular urban styles. There is also some evidence compiled by Paraguayan musician Luis Szarán of a ***nueva canción*** movement similar to that of **Chile** and **Nicaragua**.

Agustín Barrios (1885–1944) was a famous Paraguayan guitarist and composer. He began his career playing popular music like polkas and *valses*. His music remains influential today, as famous musicians like John Williams acknowledge that Barrios was an influential, talented composer and guitarist.

In 1947, Florentín Giménez (1925–) created his first orchestra, Ritmos de América. In 1950, he formed "Florentín Giménez y su típica moderna," which included singers Oscar Escobar, Juan Carlos Miranda, Carlos Centurión, and Jorge Alonso. His "Symphony No. 6" was dedicated to Agustín Barrios. Luis Alberto del Paraná (1926–1974) is probably the best-selling Paraguayan artist of the 20th century. El Trío Los Paraguayos, comprised of Paraná, Digno García, and Agustín Barboza, performed around the world in the 1950s and 1960s, including a show in which they shared the stage with the Beatles in November 1963. He also directed the *Conjunto Los Paraguayos*. After his death, he was awarded the Ordén Nacional del Mérito by the government of Paraguay.

Further Reading

Colman, Alfredo. "El arpa diatónica paraguaya en la búsqueda del tekora: representaciones de paraguayidad." *Latin American Music Review*. 28, no. 1 (2007): 125–49.

Garcete Salvídar, Bernardo. "Luis Alberto del Paraná: Perfil de un Triunfador." June 2, 2012. http://www.musicaparaguaya.org.py/parana.html.

González Páez, César. "Florentín Giménez: La música como bandera." *LANIC*. January 20, 2010. http://www.musicaparaguaya.org.py/florentin.html.

Jeong, Johnna. "Agustín Barrios Mangoré: The Folkloric, Imitative, and the Religious Influence Behind His Compositions." June 2, 2012. http://www.cybozone.com/fg/jeong.html.

Caitlin Lowery

Pasillo

The *pasillo* is a Latin American variant of the *vals* that is especially popular in **Colombia** and **Ecuador**, though the genre has enjoyed success throughout the years from **Mexico** to **Argentina**. It was cultivated during the colonial period among elite groups as an embraced couple dance in a moderate triple meter. There are two distinct varieties of *pasillo* practiced in Colombia: the *pasillo lento* and the *pasillo instrumental*. The former is usually sung as a solo or a duet, and in moderate time, accompanied either by piano (salon performance), **guitar** and *tiple* with percussion, or by an *estudiantina*. The texts reference an idealized or unrequited love, thus having poetic themes related to the **bolero**. The *pasillo instrumental* is, as its name implies, an instrumental genre for guitar and *tiple* and is much faster in performance than the sung variety, and there is frequent **sesquialtera** between the melody and the accompanying rhythms.

In Ecuador, the *pasillo* is a national song and dance, which during the end of the colonial period was associated with Ecuadorian nationalism. The genre continued to be popular throughout the 20th century, reaching the height of its popularity in the 1950s and 1960s in the career of Julio Jaramillo (1935–1978), an Ecuadorian *pasillo* singer. So closely was Jaramillo's career bound to the *pasillo,* that in 1993, President Sixto Duran Baellén declared September 27 (Juramillo's birthday) as *Día del Pasillo Ecuatoriano* (Day of the Ecuadorian *Pasillo*).

Further Reading

Schechter, John Mendell. *Music in Latin American Culture: Regional Traditions.* New York: Schirmer Books, 1999.

George Torres

Payada

The *payada* is an improvised poetic and musical genre practiced in the Southern Cone regions of **Argentina, Uruguay, Chile**, and southern **Brazil**. It can either be sung as a solo or as a duo accompanied by one or two **guitars**. Its origins go back to 19th century *gaucho* culture and thus was, and has mostly remained, a rural tradition though some successful *payadores* (*payada* singers) have enjoyed success beyond their regions. In Argentina and Uruguay, the *payada* is often sung as a duel between two singers. This type of improvised musical challenge has counterparts throughout Latin America, including **Mexico, Cuba, Puerto Rico**, and **Colombia**. A preferred poetic form for the *payada* is the **décima** to which singers alternate verses with one another, often to rural themes relating to *gaucho* life and countryside. A preferred musical form is the **milonga**, where singers may alternate the same melody, or the singers may each choose their own melody that they will alternate for the performance. The treatment of the melody tends to be more restricted in these *milongas* than traditional ones. The winner of the *payada* contest is determined by either a jury or the audience's applause. The urbanization of traditional rural repertories has brought the *payada* out from the countryside to the cities, which has led to the professionalism of some performers to seek an urban audience and mass media opportunities, such as large-scale concerts and recordings. The influence of the *payada* was evident in the ***nueva canción*** movement; artists from this movement, such as **Atahualpa Yupanqui**, included *payadas* in their repertoire.

Further Reading

Moreno Chá, Ercilia. "Music in the Southern Cone: Chile, Argentina, and Uruguay," in *Music in Latin American Culture: Regional Traditions,* edited by John Mendell Schechter, 236–301. New York: Schirmer Books, 1999.

George Torres

Peru

Peru is a country located in Western South America between **Chile** and **Ecuador** that also borders the South Pacific Ocean. Its population is a diverse combination of Amerindians (45%), *mestizos* (37%), and whites (15%), as well as blacks, Japanese, Chinese, and other (3%). Distinctive social and ethnic groups emerged in Peru as a result of its geography. The country is divided into three distinct geographical and as a result cultural regions: the Andes region, the coastal region, and the Amazonian region.

Geography has been especially important to the development of popular music in Peru. Because Peru contains a low per capita amount of arable land, rural migrants have moved toward urban centers in search of work. As a result, many of the folkloric cultural and musical traditions from the Andes, coastal, and Amazonian regions have become an important part of Peruvian popular music as migrants have tried to reconcile their rural traditions with their urban lifestyles. Musicians such as Victor Alberto Gil Malma, Florencio Coronado, and Yma Sumac that modified folkloric music to fit urban tastes have become successful recording artists in Peru. The popularity of formerly folkloric music gained worldwide recognition when Simon and Garfunkle recorded a cover of the traditional Peruvian song "El Condor Pasa."

In the Andes region, music is rooted in a combination of traditional indigenous music coupled with European influences. ***Huayno*** is the most widespread popular song and dance genre of the Peruvian Andes. While it has an autonomous form (duple meter, AABB musical phrases, and usually features a closing section), it has many regional varieties to reflect the musical tastes of different social and ethnic groups. The *huayno* has changed over time as a result of the adaption of European instruments and esthetic priorities. In the 1950s, it began to gain recognition as a popular music form spreading into coastal and urban centers and even beyond the borders of Peru to influence the neighboring nations such as **Bolivia**,

Garcia Zárate, Raúl

Guitarist Raúl García Zárate (b. 1935) is among Peru's most famous and internationally renowned musicians today. The foremost practitioner of Ayacucho's formidable *mestizo* folk **guitar** tradition since the 1960s, García Zárate has drawn upon classical guitar technique and the esthetics of formal art music to arrange, expand, and promote the repertoire and reputation of Peruvian guitar music.

Less known in international circles are the series of ten LPs recorded by García Zárate with his brother, the vocalist Nery García Zárate, between 1966 and 1980. Containing more than 100 tracks of Ayacuchan *mestizo* folk music, primarily *waynos*, this series of recordings constituted a self-conscious archival project by the brothers to document the music that had accompanied their formative years growing up in the highland city. Released at the height of the golden era of the *wayno* in Peru, the "Hermanos García Zárate" recordings set a standard for performance style and repertoire that came to define Ayacuchan *mestizo* music as a whole. The LPs remain treasured possessions among Ayacuchanos today, with pirate editions still for sale at music markets throughout the country.

Further Reading

Arguedas, José María. 1977. *Nuestra Music Popular y sus Interpretes.* Lima: Mosca Azul and Horizonte.

Jonathan Ritter

Argentina, and Chile. More recently, in the 1970s and 1980s, the *huayno* fused with other musical styles such as *cumbia* and **rock** as Peruvian musicians wrestled with their ethnic identity divided between European, North American, and Amerindian influences.

It is on the Peruvian coasts that the traditional Peruvian music styles (such as *huayno*) have been exposed to the musical tastes of other parts of the world and fused to create uniquely Peruvian styles of popular music. The music of the coasts, known as *musica criolla,* combines indigenous, North American, European, African, and Gypsy influences. In Peru, *cumbia* is a well-known example of a musical style that was imported from another country and adjusted to fit Peruvian tastes. *Cumbia,* imported from **Colombia**, grew in popularity in Peru among indigenous migrants in the late 1960s that began to move to urban centers such as Lima. They combined *cumbia* and *música tropical* with the Andean *huayno* rhythm, and garage-band style **guitars** to create a new musical style that became known as *cumbia amazónica* or **chicha**. For Peruvians, *chicha* became a symbol of cultural hybridity and the working class. In the late 1990s, *cumbia* once again came to the forefront of popular music in Peru with the rise of techno-*cumbia,* which combined elements of *cumbia* music with electronic instruments. Developed in a time of political unrest in Peru, techno-*cumbia* was seen as the spontaneous expression of the people and became a favorite musical genre among Peruvians from all different backgrounds.

Much like the rest of Latin America, Peru was strongly influenced by the rock 'n' roll movement as a result of the growing popularity of the radio in the 1950s and 1960s. Peruvians developed their own interpretation of **rock en español** but, unlike Argentinean rock bands, Peruvian rock artists only had limited international distribution. Big names in Peruvian rock in the 1960s and 1970s included Los Destellos, Los Mirlos, and Los Diablos Rojos. Today, while rock continues to be popular, Latin pop dominates the Peruvian music market and is still distributed to even remote parts of the country with the radio.

Further Reading

Romero, Raul. *Debating the Past: Music, Memory, and Identity in the Andes.* New York: Oxford University Press, 2001.

Romero, Raul. "Popular Music and the Global City." In *From Tejano to Tango*, edited by Walter Aaron Clark, 217–39. New York: Routledge, 2002.

Tracy McFarlan

Plena

Plena, a dance music genre with pan-Caribbean commonalities, is considered to be **Puerto Rico's** foremost synthetic folk and popular expression.

Beginnings

Most sources agree that in the beginning of the 20th century, *plena,* as a dance and song, emerged simultaneously in the marginal urban and rural *barrios* of the southern municipality of Ponce a few years after immigrant workers from the British Caribbean imported some of their own musical traditions and introduced them to local sugarcane laborers. Catherine George, her husband, John Clark, and daughter, Carola, are tied to *plena's* immediate antecedents. They are said to have arrived from Barbados with the *pandero* (a tambourine-shaped instrument with no cymbals), and songs they helped disseminate with the assistance of fellow immigrants from St. Kitts and Nevis.

Their rhythms soon called the attention of a local sugarcane worker and plowman Joselino "Bumbún" Oppenheimer (1884–1929), a descendant of African slaves whose Spanish-based *quatrains,* or *coplas,* were improvised during his work hours at a plantation nearby. They featured the joys and vicissitudes of his community and were rehearsed *a capella* in a song-and-refrain, mostly in A-A, or A-B melodic form with the assistance of young coworkers in charge of the refrain (invariably the introductory melodic theme A), while they guided the ox and cleared the land ahead of Bumbún's plowing. In the evenings, back home in La Joya del Castillo (a marginal neighborhood or *arrabal,* in the urban area of Ponce), Oppenheimer introduced the new *plena* compositions to a growing number of fellow performers (known popularly as *pleneros*).

Afterwards, *plena* quickly became commonplace in the south and southwestern regions of Puerto Rico; first with tambourine and **guitar**, and later (in the 1920s) with the addition of double-keyboard **accordion** and ***güiro***, the latter an indigenous component of Hispanic rural ensembles. Lesser commercial but still popular groups had ensembles of three *panderos.* In order of size from the largest to the smallest, these *panderos* were: the *seguidor* (providing the fundamental pulse), the *segundo* (showing *plena*'s characteristic pattern), and the ***requinto***, for high-pitched improvisation. These groups played to dancing couples, displacing their bodies alternately to the sides, mutually approaching and moving away in an endless parallel motion. In its beginnings, *plena* was to be found in ill-reputed dance parties of *arrabales,* with at least one *plena* **conjunto** for each neighborhood. Three of the early *barrio* groups were led respectively by Chivo Román, Mario Rivera, and the Aranzamendi brothers.

Stylistic Sources

Given its specific association with working class and alien groups, *plena* is often compared with the ***tango*** that was emerging around the same time in similar marginalized enclaves of Buenos Aires, **Argentina**. More significant, however, rural workers of white ancestry (known as *jíbaros*), laborers born of slaves like Bumbún, and immigrants from the English-speaking Caribbean converged in Puerto Rico at the time, to give *plena* a musical and poetic profile that attests to its kinship with forms like the Spanish-Caribbean ***guaracha*** and several Dominican rural forms based on the *copla.* An expression also known as *plena* with similar sociohistorical interests and poetic structure is also reported in the **Dominican Republic** around the 1890s, although no clear musical or choreographic relationship with its Puerto Rican namesake has been found, so far. In **Panama**, *plena* is a term used to refer to ***reggae***. The stress by *pleneros* on the fourth (and last) beat makes it a close relative of some versions of Trinitarian *quadrilles,* of ***calypso***, and Jamaican *mento.* Related basic and near-improvisatory rhythms are registered in recordings of Trinitarian *quadrilles* as well in early 20th century recordings of Puerto Rican *danzas* in Ponce.

Evolution

The Great Depression, Migration, and Canario's Ensemble

Given Puerto Rico's condition as a colony of the **United States**, years of exploitation and social turbulence during the 1910s and 1920s were compounded by the period of Great Depression. Unemployment and misery had compelled rural laborers to establish settlements in the swamps and mangrove areas of San Juan. Along with them followed the rapid dissemination of *plenas* through the main sugarcane centers. In San Juan, *plena* secured its place among the artisan groups of Puerta de Tierra, one of the island's oldest working-class *barrios.*

Around 1927, local musicians moved en masse to New York City and, that year, Manuel Jiménez ("Canario") made the first *plena* recordings in a compromise with major American recording companies that entailed *plena's* first successful international exposure, but one that required the subordination of the *plena* ensemble and its iconic *pandero* to a Cuban-***conjunto*** format. His group, Canario y su Conjunto, embraced the use of a solo voice with **guitar** and **accordion** accompaniment, yet giving the trumpet, ***bongó***, and ***clave*** an outstanding role. The required three-minute standard duration of recordings came to be in stark contrast to *plena's* long-lasting live dance performances. Other groups like Los Reyes de la Plena, the Grupo Ponceño, Los Borinqueños, and Sexteto Flores also made strides by including *plena* in major recordings. But if their repertoire was tied to the saga of the Great Depression, the central theme was nostalgia for the Puerto Rican homeland.

Big Band and Elegant Plena

In Puerto Rico during the second half of the 1940s, industrialization, development, and urbanization brought in flairs of musical elegance akin to those of the major urban centers in the United States. Once an expression consisting of lively sounds of *arrabales* and rural *barrios,* now, in the hands of the Orquesta de César Concepción, *plena* suppressed the emblematic *pandero* and acquiesced to soft-percussion styles presented a few years before by a visiting Cuban orchestra. Standardized big-band musical arrangements and simple dance steps were introduced to local upper- and middle-class couples in major hotel ballrooms.

Back to Its Working-Class Roots

But the musical conformism of Cesar Concepción and his orchestra was overwhelmed by the more active stance of poor neighborhood *plenas:* as the agricultural economy declined and flocks of rural laborers settled in San Juan, conflicts between the rural (slave-related) past and the industrial present fueled *barrio plenas* with faster and satiric stories like "Déjalo que suba," by **Rafael Cortijo** y su Combo. A local Afro-Caribbean synthesis of big-band, **Afro-Cuban**, and *jíbaro* sounds, this group featured the unique, improvisatory *soneos* by singer Ismael Rivera to the accompaniment of piano, the raw and raucuous suburban *barrio* sounds of saxophone, trumpets, and a percussion section of bass (or **marímbula**), *bongós, timbals,* and **güiro**. Although Cortijo's repertoire embraced a Caribbean mélange of **guarachas**, **rumbas**, **congas**, *oriza* rhythms, **montunos**, **merengues**, **boleros**, what is most significant is that *plena* became a rubric intimately tied with the Afro-Puerto Rican **bomba**. After Cortijo, some ensembles are labeled as *bomba y plena* groups. His appearance on television in 1954 earned the acceptance of a widespread audience that years later enjoyed the humorous scat-singings of Efraín "Mon" Rivera, whose *plena* "Aló, ¿quién ñama?," narrates a labor conflict in his native city of Mayagüez to his trombone-and-percussion ensemble.

A developmental gap is noticed until the 1970s, when a new group, Los Pleneros del Quinto Olivo entered the local mass media by embracing an instrumental format similar to the then-in-vogue **salsa** ensembles. By this enhancement, not only did they reintroduce the *pandero,* but adopted for commercial purposes the three-pandero set of *seguidor, segundo,* and *requinto* (as described above), and applied for them techniques from the *conga* drum. Other changes included the elimination of the antiphonal soloist-choir structure in order to give the chorus the leading role along the entire piece. Less commercial were the recollections of *jíbaro* music by Los Pleneros de la 23 abajo, whose 10-line octosyllabic **décimas** shifted *plena* from the nostalgic and pleasurable complacency into matters of harsh social situations. Diverse routes for *plena's* validity and adaptability were taken since 1977 by artists such as Irvin García, Jorge Arce, Tony Croatto, and Andrés Jiménez; and groups such as Atabal, Paracumbé, and Los Guayacanes de San Antón. And once more, a period of international exposure began in the mid-1990s, when Plena Libre entered the American Latino airwaves through their blends of *plena* with world music sounds of the time. Around the time of Plena Libre's breakthrough, Bumbún's "Temporal" was the main theme of an album by Arab-Andalusian group Radio Tarifa, in 1998. More recent trends stretch *plena's* resourcefulness into more elaborate works (as is the case of the Viento de Agua experimental ensemble, or William Cepeda's Afro-Rican **jazz**), and into rap and *reggaetón* styles contained in *plenas* by New York-based groups Yerbabuena, Pleneros de la 21, and Bombayó.

Along the evolutionary line from Bumbún to the present, *plena* has endured formal and stylistic changes while maintaining a core set of elements, comprising Spanish poetic forms of strong social or historical content that are sung to varying styles of instrumental accompaniment on simple chords, and with a distinctive combination of danceable rhythms rooted on pan-Caribbean sources. Perhaps the principal stream explaining these musical changes is traced along recurring socioeconomic cycles of local unemployment, community displacement, and disintegration (as it happened with the neighborhood of La Joya del

Castillo), migration to major economic centers, and the reconstitution of new communities, as it is ultimately observed in major urban centers since the 1930s. As to this day, *pleneros* are known to compensate such vicissitudes with a sense of solidarity symbolized through their adoption and readaptation of rhythms, forms, and styles emblematic of peoples with similar issues in other parts of the Caribbean and the world. Their ability in adjusting to mass media requirements explains why *plena* constitutes a vital musical force whenever it is required, being it in times of economic crisis, or in times of celebration. In the video "Lo que pasó pasó" by **Daddy Yankee**, the sounds of *plena* are hardly felt, but the visual representation of *panderos* in a scene attests to the powerful symbolism this expression still propels.

Further Reading

Echevarria Alvarado, Felix. *La Plena: Origen, Sentido y Derarrollo en el Folklore Puertorriqueño*. Ponce, 1984.

Flores, Juan. "Bumbún and the Beginnings of La Plena." *Centro: Bulletin of the Centro de Estudios Puerterriqueños* 2, no. 3 (1988): 16–25.

López, Ramón. "Breve y ajorada historia de la Plena Enrojecida," *Claridad* (*En Rojo* cultural section), May 10–16, 2007, 21–25.

López, Ramón. *Los bembeteos de la plena puertorriquena*. San Juan: Ediciones Huracán, 2008.

Edgardo Díaz Díaz

Polca. *See* Polka.

Polka

The polka is a dance of Bohemian origin, popular in much of Latin America since it was imported by Central European immigrants in the 19th century. It is performed in a moderately fast tempo in binary 2/4 rhythm, often employing an inverted anapest rhythm of two 16ths followed by an 8th note (short-short-long). Along with other imported dances such as the **waltz,** *shottische*, and *mazurka,* the polka became a mainstay in the salon repertoire among elite social groups, especially in those countries with strong German, Polish, and Bohemian immigrant populations. Those countries include **Argentina, Brazil, Paraguay**, and **Mexico**. Despite the strong European influence, much of the polka appropriation that has occurred in Latin America has resulted in a mixture of European and national styles resulting in a creolization of the polka. In Mexico, the polka was brought in through northern Mexico where it became very popular and maintained its popularity as a social dance into the 20th century. Perhaps the most famous Latin American polka comes from the period of the Mexican Revolution (1910–1917) with the 1916 composition "Jesusita en Chihuahua," by Quirino Mendoza y Cortés, who also composed "Cielito Lindo" (1859–1957). It has become a standard in the *mariachi* repertoire, as well as experiencing popularity in the **United States** where it was marketed as both Jesse polka and cactus polka. In the **tex-mex** *conjunto* repertoire, most of the music is based primarily on polka rhythm.

Further Reading

Peña, Manuel H. *The Texas-Mexican Conjunto: History of a Working-Class Music.* Austin: University of Texas Press, 1985.

George Torres

Porro

Porro is a Colombian musical genre that was the country's most popular and important musical expression throughout the 1940s and 1950s. The genre originated as a folkloric rhythm from La Costa, **Colombia's** northern Caribbean coastal region, and in its urbanized form became the first non-Andean genre to gain national popularity within Colombia. *Porro's* duple meter rhythm, in which both the first and the slightly anticipated second beats are stressed, is rhythmically similar to, and shares a common folkloric musical antecedent with *cumbia*. While Colombian folklorists posit a Colombian origin, others, mainly writers from outside Colombia, refer to it as a local variation on either the Spanish *fandango* or Cuban *danzón*.

A number of theories regarding the genre's provenance have emerged, all following similar narratives wherein the folkloric rhythm was adapted by rural municipal wind bands, with El Carmen del Bolívar and San Pelayo being the most widely supported potential birthplaces. These wind bands—consisting of trumpets, clarinets, *bombardinos* (similar to a euphonium), *bomba* (bass drum), *redoblante* (snare), and cymbals—first became popular throughout the country in the 1840s, playing European rhythms, including marches, waltzes, **polkas**, and *fandangos,* as well as *danzones* and Colombian *bambucos* and *pasillos* at public and private functions sponsored by local elites. Speculation over the genre's birthplace notwithstanding, it is documented that by the beginning of the 20th century wind bands in La Costa featured *porros* within their repertoires.

In the 1920s, as the emerging international recording and film industries formed in Barranquilla and Cartagena, dance orchestras that specialized in North American and Cuban styles disseminated music from **Cuba, Argentina, Mexico**, and the **United States**. These groups played mainly in clubs and hotels for upper- and middle-class audiences and gradually began incorporating urbanized versions of *costeño* folkloric styles such as *porro* and *fandango* alongside **sones**, **boleros**, fox-trots, and Charlestons. Orchestra members from rural backgrounds familiar with wind band repertoires were said to be responsible for this innovation.

A watershed moment for the genre was the 1938 release of the *porro* "Marbella," by Orquesta del Caribe, composed by group director and clarinetist Lucho Bermúdez. The record was released on Discos Fuentes, Colombia's first record label, founded in Cartagena in 1934, and was a hit. While Bermúdez was neither the first to adapt *porro* for dance orchestras nor the first to record *porro* (recordings by pianist Ángel María Camacho y Cano in New York between 1929 and 1931 included *porros*), he is considered an innovator of the style, its foremost exemplar, and essential to its popularization. He helped bring *porro* to a wider Colombian audience through his artistic directorships at Radio Cartagena and Emisora Fuentes, and his extensive recording. He also introduced *porro* to a more affluent audience by being among the first to bring *porro* and other *costeño* rhythms into social clubs and hotels in La Costa and Bogotá, Cali, and Medellín.

In Bermúdez's hands, *porro* was *"se vistió de frac"* ("dressed up in tails"), and the sophisticated presentation of his orchestra and his modern, **jazz**-influenced arrangements aided in the genre's acceptance within elite circles, although its popularity was not limited to these audiences. The orchestras of Bermúdez and others were modeled on American big bands or Cuban *conjuntos,* consisting of piano, bass, drum set, **conga**, **maracas**, large horn sections consisting of three to five saxophones (some doubling on clarinet), two or three trumpets, and in some cases one or two trombones (or a *bombardino*), and a variable number of singers. Arrangements were characterized by the alternation of melodic lines between the woodwinds—commonly played in three octaves—and the brass, the prominence of the clarinet, the drum set adapting (and increasingly standardizing and simplifying) *bomba* and *redoblante* patterns, and a smooth vocal style. Lyrics tended toward romantic themes, rural subjects, extolling the virtues of specific places, and imagery inspired by La Costa.

Dance orchestras that specialized in *porro* also played other urbanized *costeño* rhythms, including **cumbia**, *gaita,* and *mapalé* (referred to collectively by the umbrella terms *música costeña, música tropical,* or even simply *porro*) as well as **boleros**, *pasodobles,* and a variety of Cuban rhythms. Throughout the 1940s and into the 1950s, the *porro* of Bermúdez and others, including Pacho Galán and Antonio María Peñaloza, cemented its broad-based popularity through dissemination on the radio and records, the recording industry being based in La Costa and favoring the music of the region. In time, the genre would transcend its regional beginnings to become an emblem of Colombian identity at both the national and international levels. Bermúdez, and to a much lesser extent Galán, aided this perception through touring, interacting with prominent musicians, and even recording throughout the Americas beginning in the mid-1940s.

The 1950s was dubbed la Epoca Dorada (the golden age) of *costeño* music, and the genre was such a prominent national symbol that in 1954, the first Colombian television broadcast was a performance by Bermúdez's orchestra. The decade also saw significant changes in the recording industry and consumption patterns. The center of the recording industry shifted from La Costa to Medellín and began to utilize more musicians from the area. While some, most notably Edmundo Arias, led large dance orchestras playing *porro,* many groups moved away from this model. Smaller bands utilizing a less refined sound, a distinctly simpler rhythmic esthetic and electric instruments, such as bass, guitar and keyboards, became more common. This new sound was given the title *cumbia,* which would became a new umbrella term for *costeño* rhythms, the label even increasingly utilized by established musicians, including Bermúdez.

By the early 1960s, with *cumbia* being marketed internationally and youth markets increasingly attracted to rock 'n' roll, **pachanga**, and **boogaloo**, big band *porro* had become passé, seen as having elitist connotations. Nevertheless, both Bermúdez and Galán would remain active into the 1980s and their orchestras would continue after their deaths. In the 21st century, *porro* was still strongly associated with the Christmas season and continued to be repackaged and resold by record companies. Additionally, it was among the rhythms that artists in the 2000s explored to create musical hybrids of North American and Colombian genres, the most notable example being singer Adriana Lucia's 2008 album *Porro Nuevo.*

Further Reading

Abadia Morales, Guillermo. 1983. *Compendio General de Folklore Colombiano,* cuarta edición. Bogotá: Biblioteca Banco Popular.

Luis Eduardo "Lucho" Bermúdez (1912–1994). Compositor Colombiano, accessed December 2, 2010, http://www.colarte.com/colarte/conspintores.asp?idartista=13151

Wade, Peter. 2000. *Music, Race, and Nation: Música Tropical in Colombia.* Chicago and London: University of Chicago Press.

Ramón Versage Agudelo

Pregonero

The term *pregonero* is used in Latin American popular music to refer to a lead singer or caller in a group. The term is used regularly in the genre of the **son jarocho** from Veracruz, **Mexico**, and occasionally in Cuban popular music to refer to the lead singer in a **montuno** section of a **son cubano**. In the **son jarocho**, the verses are often sung in some form of leader–group alternation, or call and response. It is believed that the *jarocho* style of music contains strong African influences, and so the leader–group alternation supports that idea. The leader–group alternation between the *pregonero* and the **coro** (chorus) allows the lead singer an opportunity to perform improvised *versos* for the entertainment of the audience while the *coro* responds to the *versos* with a repeated refrain. Often the improvisation will take into account who is in the audience, and the *pregonero* will craft the improvised texts to reflect that. The term *pregonero* is also used in the performance of **montunos** in Cuban **son** performances. After performing the main song, the group goes into a short repeated *montuno* section where the *coro* sings a repeated refrain in alternation with the improvised lead of the *pregonero*. In instrumental *son* performances, the *pregonero* role will be taken by a lead instrument, such as saxophone, which improvises between statements of the *coro's* refrain, as in the Charlie Parker/**Machito** performance of "Manguito Mangüe."

Further Reading

Sheehy, Daniel, "Popular Mexican Musical Traditions," *Music in Latin American Culture: Regional Traditions,* edited by John Schechter, 34–79. New York: Schirmer Books, 1999.

George Torres

Protest Song in Latin America

The protest song in Latin American popular music is a type of musical response or commentary on a particular event, movement, and/or social or political condition that is meant to bring awareness to the audience of the event or situation. Unlike protest songs in the **United States**, which are few by comparison to other parts of the world, the protest song in Latin America has played an important part in forming a collective view toward activism. Protest song examples and movements can be found all over Latin America, but the ways in which the individual movements are carried out are based on the particular set of social conditions of that culture, which result in traditions that vary according to circumstances. Through, for example, the works of artists such as Victor Jara, **Silvio Rodríguez**, and Manno Charlemagne, it is possible to see how music was used as a form of social activism that supports, decries, or questions the sociopolitical norms of a culture, in an effort to bring about a change among the population. In order to see the diversity of Latin American protest song, the following discussion, which is by no means exhaustive, examines some of the larger and more far-reaching examples of outcries and commentaries in Latin American popular music.

The Mexican *corrido*, a narrative balladry tradition that flourished in the 19th and early 20th centuries, used poetry and song to convey socially relevant subjects to listeners. Among the many themes in *corrido* singing are the subject of current events and local political situations. The *corrido,* like the broadsheets of artist José Guadalupe Posada (1852–1913), became an important vehicle to publicize a political cause, immortalize a leader, or conversely, to satirize or mock targeted leaders. For a large part of the population that was unable to read, the oral transmission of the *corrido* became a vital means of communication for current events. The period between Mexican independence (1810–1821) and the Mexican Revolution (1910–1917) marks the period when the genre flourished the most, with songs from the revolution being among Mexico's best known songs. "La Cucaracha" (the cockroach), as a revolutionary era *corrido,* has many verses that name persons and events from the revolution in hidden, but clearly pointed references to Victoriano Huerta (1850–1916) and Venustiano Carranza (1859–1920), opposing leaders of the revolution. Recent examples of politically themed *corridos* include the *narcorrido,* which are ballads relating to drug trafficking. These songs, exemplified in the works of artists such as Chalino Sanchez and Los Tigres del Norte, speak approvingly about the Robin Hood-like deeds of famous drug traffickers, which also carry an antiimperialist or anti-U.S. sentiment with them. A recent song by Los Tigres del Norte entitled "Las Mujeres de Juarez" laments with shame the violence toward women that exists in the border town Juarez, Chihuahua.

There were several protest song movements from the 1960s that had lasting impact on the protest in Latin America. Besides having an inclination toward providing narrative commentary on political themes, these new song movements sought to distance themselves from American-influenced popular music of the 1960s by embracing, studying, and performing regional folk music styles. Much of the groundwork for these movements was laid by **Atahualpa Yupanqui**, from a generation earlier, who had devoted his life to the collection of regional poetry and music by travelling all over the southern cone in an effort to preserve much of the region's music and folklore. Yupanqui also wrote many poems and songs with themes of the regions nature, people, and social customs.

Inspired by the work of Yupanqui, a younger generation of Argentine musicians met in Mendoza Argentine in 1963 to create the *Manifiesto de fundación del Movimiento del Nuevo Cancionero* (Manifesto on the Establishment of the New Song Movement). The group, which included poet Armando Tejada Gómez and singer Mercedes Sosa, sought to create a national song movement that was based on the regional and popular music and which would make the native folk music of **Argentina** an essential ingredient in this new song style. This appropriation of indigenous music would include instruments and forms borrowed from folkloric traditions, a practice that Yupanqui had started a generation earlier. By honoring the musical and artistic contributions of the Indian and the *mestizo,* the new song movements were aligning themselves with an historically oppressed and disenfranchised portion of the population. This sort of populist orientation would feed into the practitioners of the *nueva canción* movement in **Chile**.

The *nueva canción chilena* (new Chilean song) song movement of the 1960s and early 1970s produced socially committed singers and performers who used folkloric instruments and styles that would appeal to middle-class audiences, especially students. Like the Argentine song movement, by using music from rural traditions, the artists were honoring the *mestizo* traditions of their culture's past. Artists such as **Violeta Parra** and Victor Jara would make frequent use of rural dance rhythms such as *cueca*, *zamba*, and *chacarera* to infuse their music with a native sound, which had been previously looked down upon by elite social groups, who generally turned to European models of musical styles in their listening. In spite of their using folkloric dances as the musical basis for many of their compositions, the *nueva canción* repertoire was a listener's genre and did not have a dance function. Perhaps the most influential aspect of the repertoire is the connection with leftist sentiments, especially those denouncing poverty and political injustices. By 1965, Parra, with the aid of her two children Angel and Isabel Parra, had laid the foundation for the *nueva canción* by founding two venues for *nueva canción* performance in Santiago, La Peña and la Carpa de la Reina, which became important meeting places for urban intellectuals and university students. Important songs by Violeta Parra include "Si Somos Americanos" ("If We Are Americans") and "Gracias a la Vida" ("Thanks to Life"); the latter, which was written just before her death in 1967, has become an internationally popular song. After Parra's death, the most notable spokesperson for *nueva canción* was Victor Jara, who through his outspoken commentaries in support of Chile's oppressed (Jara was a member of the Chile's Communist Party) and against human rights violations in Chile, became a highly outspoken champion of the *nueva canción* movement. His song "Plegaria a un labrador" ("Prayer to a Worker") is a call to the *campesinos* (peasant workers) to come together and unite to work for a better future through brotherhood of the common people. One of his most daring songs, "Preguntas por Puerto Montt" ("Questions about Puerto Montt") not only decries the perpetrators who ambushed and killed innocent peasant squatters in that port city, but also names the person responsible, Edmundo Pérez Zujovic, in the text of his song.

Because of the populist sentiments of *nueva canción* songs and performers, the movement was important in supporting the Popular Unity Coalition, and some of the songs used during the 1970 campaign that eventually put Salvador Allende in power became important staples of the repertoire. The Pinochet coup, which effectively ended the Allende regime, resulted in bad times for practitioners of the genre. Many were imprisoned for their part in speaking against the government (Victor Jara was eventually tortured and executed), while others were forced to exile abroad. As a result the *nueva canción* became an underground movement that reemerged later as *canto nuevo,* a somewhat understated version of *nueva canción* which, because of the threatening political environment, resorted to a more metaphorically cautious means of expressing political sentiments.

During the 1960s in **Cuba**, much influenced by the *nueva canción* movement, a new form of Cuban song with a politically conscious expression began to form. Inspired by the American folk movement, these young singers were inspired by

American folk singers like Bob Dylan and used the guitar playing balladeer model, combining it with Cuban-inspired musical genres such as *son* and *bolero* to create a postrevolution style of Cuban song. As a result, this new version of politically enlightened folk singing, which aligned itself with an older tradition of Cuban troubadours, Cuban *trova*, became a strong voice in the social consciousness of Latin America. Singers such as Pablo Milanes and Silvio Rodriguez came together at venues such as the now famous La Casa de Trova and Casa de las Americas to perform their music for other Havana students and intellectuals who supported the ideals of the revolution. In spite of some early resistance to the movement on the part of the Cuban government, *nueva trova* eventually became a government-supported art form, and as the movement became more defined, performers became government employees who travelled around the world as Cuba's cultural and social ambassadors. Rodriguez, in particular, has become extremely popular throughout the Americas and in Europe, selling out large concert venues, and many of his songs, such as "Ojala," "Playa giron," and "Unicornio," have become best sellers. Much inspired by Bob Dylan, Rodriguez's lyrics are considered to be the Latin American counterpart to the former, because of the way he expresses themes ranging from nationalism, to love, to anti-imperialism, often using sophisticated metaphors to convey poignant criticism. Whereas the music of the *nueva canción chilena* exhibited strong musical ties to Andean folkloric tradition, the music of artists such as Rodriguez shows more of a cosmopolitan influence than having an overtly Cuban sound. Nevertheless, artists such as Milanes, who is a more versatile musician than Rodriguez, uses influences from popular genres from Latin America, as in the song "Son Para Despertar A Una Negrita," which is in the *clave* rhythm of the Cuban *son.* A more recent exponent version of *nueva trova,* sometimes called *novisima trova,* is Carlos Varela, whose 1989 album *Jalisco Park* at once supports socialist ideals but is also critical of his own country and the difficulties of Cuban life. Varela's music is important from a post-Soviet era perspective, which resonates strongly with a younger Cuban audience.

Because of the volatile political conditions that existed throughout different parts of Latin America from the 1960s to the present, there have been many examples of protest song throughout the region. While many of the subgenres owe much to the earlier *nueva canción chilena,* its influence can be seen in the formation of similar, yet locally relevant song repertoires in **Mexico, Nicaragua, Costa Rica, Puerto Rico**, and **Haiti**. Inspired by the revolution against the Samoza regime in Nicaragua (1979), there evolved a particularly unique style of protest song that became associated with the support of the Sandinista movement. In particular, the folkloric sounds of brothers Carlos and Luis Enrique Mejía Godoy represented a timely, albeit dated, example of the unique social relevance of this music directed toward workers and revolutionaries. One of Carlos's songs, "El garand,"

El Gran Combo de Puerto Rico

The legendary Puerto Rican *salsa* orchestra, El Gran Combo de Puerto Rico (EGC), formed in 1962. Its original members included Rafaél Ithier and Eddie Perez, both of whom had performed with the band of **Rafael Cortijo**. Ithier and company developed a new repertoire and format, playing *salsa* music with a percussion-centered orchestral ensemble featuring two pianos, two saxophones, two trumpeters, three vocalists and later, trombone. EGC performances are typically large, carefully choreographed stage shows, featuring a solo singer or dancer. Although they have dipped into other Latin styles such as **boogaloo**, **tangos**, and **timba**, they have always returned to *salsa*.

EGC's song lyrics encompass themes from Puerto Rican folklore as well as love, food, drinking, and partying. EGC, always based in **Puerto Rico**, has maintained a consistent *tipico* sound ensuring them a loyal Puerto Rican following. EGC has had significant personnel changes over the past 40 years and the band members' ages span the generations as does their fan base. EGC has toured internationally and received awards and recognition.

Further Reading

Randel, Don Michael. "Crossing over with Rubén Blades." *Journal of the American Musicological Society* 44, no. 2 (Summer, 1991): 301–23.

Rebecca Stuhr

gives detailed instructions on how to assemble a rifle, thus providing valuable information for the unschooled revolutionary. In Haiti, Manno Charlemagne and his style of protest song known as *mizik angaje* ([politically] engaged music) sang about the injustice of Haiti's poor and oppressed population. His music so outraged the Duvalier regime in the 1980s that he was forced to exile to the United States. Nevertheless, his popularity was supported by a large diaspora population, and after the ouster of Duvalier in 1986, he returned to Haiti, where his politically engaged music played an important role in the support and election of Jean-Bertrand Aristide in 1990.

Further Reading

Luft, Murray. "Latin American Protest Music: What Happened to The New Songs?" *Canadian Folk Music Bulletin (Bulletin de musique folklorique canadienne)* 30, no. 3 (September 1, 1996): 10.

Manuel, Peter. *Popular Musics of the Non-Western World: An Introductory Survey.* New York: Oxford University Press, 1988.

Moore, Robin. *Music and Revolution: Cultural Change in Socialist Cuba.* Berkeley: University of California Press, 2006.

Reyes Matta, Fernando. " 'New Song' and Its Confrontation in Latin America." In *Marxism and the Interpretation of Culture,* edited by Cary Nelson and Lawrence Grossberg. Urbana: University of Illinois Press, 1988.

Schechter, John Mendell. *Music in Latin American Culture: Regional Traditions.* New York: Schirmer Books, 1999.

George Torres

Puerto Rico

Puerto Rico is a Spanish-speaking U.S. territory (4,448 sq. mi.; pop. 3,725,789 in 2010) located about 90 miles east of the Dominican Republic. In the United States, the number of Puerto Ricans is estimated at nearly 4.2 million. A product of ceaseless migrations—traced back to its pre-colonial times—Puerto Rico's distinctive musical genres include the early *portorrico de los negros* and *coquis* notated by Mexican scholars and, in the recent era, the popular **bomba** (in its various styles), **danza, plena**, and **reggaetón**. Especially with the New York-based **salsa**, Puerto Rican musicians are known for their versatility and adaptability in fields like **jazz** performance, arrangements, stylistic fusion, and mass production.

Manuel G. Tavárez (1843–1883) and Juan Morel Campos (1857–1896) are the first known composers to have developed the *danza* as an export commodity enjoying popularity and prestige throughout the Caribbean and the United States. The countless of local *danzas* disseminated in the region by local publishing houses, tour orchestras, Spanish regimental bands, and world-ranked concert pianists since the 1870s heralded the period of copious musical production Puerto Rican musicians and composers have achieved from 1900 to the present.

After the United States acquired Puerto Rico as a colony in 1898, their policy of Americanization was imposed to conform the island's culture and society to national standards.

But national papers wrote about Puerto Rican music as "an amiable trait of character that needs no Americanization" with emphasis on the *danza*, "a music of a distinctly high order." Local *danza* recordings made in 1910 and 1917 called much of the national attention due in part to their renditions of clarinet and baritone horn improvisation that were, until then, rarely heard on cylinders. With the U.S. involvement in World War I in 1917, various Puerto Rican musicians were recruited in James Reese Europe's 369th Regiment Hellfighters to create one of the best *jazz* bands of all times. At their return, the *New York Times* referred specifically to "the clarinet section, recruited from the Porto Rican Constabulary Band" as the special feature at a Hellfighters's 1919 fund-raising concert in Carnegie Hall.

Puerto Rican musicians enjoyed a reputation as sight readers. Envisioning new sounds for the upcoming postwar period, African American bandleaders in the 1920s hired many of them, including jazz pioneer Ralph Escudero, Juan Tizol, and the well-known Rafael Hernández. The stylistic input these musicians exerted was felt in Negro musicals, Broadway pit ensembles, musical extravaganzas, in musical genres like the *danza*-related ragtime, and what was then known as hot jazz.

After 1900, as *plena* voiced the precarious conditions of working-class Puerto Ricans, many of them moved in increasing numbers to areas like Arizona, Connecticut, Hawaii, and New York. With it, the center of musical production shifted from the island's principal cities to the mainland.

A study of Richard K. Spottswood's near-exhaustive discography of recordings in the United States from 1898 to 1942 reveals that out of 119 major recording artists from Puerto Rico, 30 of them remained in the island contributing one-tenth of all record matrices produced by the other 89, who settled in the United States. After the 1927 introduction of sound cinema, local musicians employed in local silent film productions soon intensified their migration to exodus proportions. For a group of artists representing an island population one-100th that of Ibero-America and less than one-1000th of the world's, it is staggering that at the time, this latter migratory group from Puerto Rico produced in the United States over 15 percent of the estimated number of record matrices by all Spanish and Latin Americans, and nearly 3.5 percent of production among all worldwide ethnic groups covered in the study.

Modern Latin American popular music is mostly a product of the U.S.-based recording industry with a considerable influence from Puerto Rican musicians, especially after the mass production of electric records began around 1927. This new period was likely initiated by Rafael Hernández, whose career as one of Latin America's prominent composers intensified after he formed the Trío Borinquen, a group that assumed various instrumental formats to explore on hybrid or hyphenated genres like the *bolero-capricho, bolero-son,* and even on moved forms like *merengue, jaleo,* and *son;* to promote a diversity of styles from various composers; and to help devise a new romantic genre, quite distinct from the old Cuban *bolero,* but structurally closer to the *danza* than previously assessed. This new kind of song is also known as *bolero.* Composer Pedro Flores, second in prominence among the Island's composers, with an abundant number of boleros, often referred to them as *danzas modernas,* acknowledging the role of *danza* as forerunner of this modern ballad.

Between the late 1920s to the early 1940s, other major Puerto Rican recording artists included Pedro Flores, Canario y Su Grupo, Rafael Hernández's Grupo Victoria, Pedro "Piquito" Marcano, Johnny Rodríguez, and Cuarteto Mayarí. Most of them remained active after 1942, as did bandleaders Julio Roqué, Noro Morales, Rafael Font, Augusto Coen, and Juanito Sanabria. Mayarí founder Plácido

Acevedo and Felipe Rivera Goyco ("Don Felo") add to the list of major composers as well as Johnny Rodríguez, whose repertory adds to the nearly 2,000 works by Capó. Juan Tizol's 1936 "Caravan" is a song considered to mark the beginnings of **Latin jazz**. Among the singers, Pedro Ortiz Dávila ("Davilita") is considered as Puerto Rico's top iconic voice of all times.

A host of young singers, bandleaders, and composers who displayed their versatility in performing in a range of styles from the slow *bolero* genres to the faster *guarachas* included Daniel Santos and, later on the eve of the *salsa* era, Pablo "Tito" Rodriguez (Johnny's little brother). Santos became a Latin American legendary singer as was Tito Rodríguez, Myrta Silva, and Bobby Capó, all of which are highly revered in Latin America and among the U.S. Latino communities between the 1940s and 1950s.

The New York–founded Trio Los Panchos specialized in *bolero* and invariably featured Puerto Rican solo singers whose incumbencies established the three main eras for this Mexican trío: the periods of Hernando Avilés (1944–1952), Julito Rodríguez (1952–1958), and Johnny Albino (1958–1968). After them, similar trios proliferated in Puerto Rico, Mexico, and elsewhere, and popularized Noel Estrada's "En Mi Viejo San Juan," a song that voiced among Puerto Rican migrants their profound longing for their homeland.

As U.S. big bands left their imprint on local dance orchestras like Orquesta de Rafael Munoz and Cesar Concepción y Su Orquesta in venues like el Escambrón Beach Club, the dramatic exodus of 540,000 Puerto Ricans to the United States favored the sudden reemergence of dance clubs in New York City. With it came the popularity of ***mambo***, a dance reaching its climax in the 1950s at the Palladium Ballroom with the so-called Big Three, composed of Cuban veteran Machito and younger Puerto Rican bandleaders, Tito Rodríguez, and the abovementioned Tito Puente. Their developments infused *mambo* with stylistic innovations, thus tracing a path toward the eventual transfiguration of anything understood as typically Cuban in their music, into a distinctive and true New York Latino music: *salsa*.

Although *salsa* was coined in 1966 as a music-related rubric and later made official, some of its designated sounds were at work in Puerto Rico since 1954 with Rafael Cortijo's fusion of various Caribbean genres—including *bomba, plena,* and ***calypso***—and the vocal improvisations by *sonero* Ismael Rivera. By the early 1960s, pianist Eddie Palmieri explored with jazzy developments on the *montuno* sections and replaced the trumpet section for trombones to create a harsh and aggressive sound. The contributions by Cortijo, Rivera, and Palmieri were eventually adopted as core ingredients of *salsa*, although this rubric was still to be acknowledged by Fania, jointly founded in 1964 by Dominican flutist and bandleader Johnny Pacheco, and Italian American lawyer Jerry Masucci, who envisioned a style imbued with a substantial degree of barrio-street inspiration in recycled Cuban forms. Around that time, an interim period of Latino crossovers into the African American realm of *soul* and **boogaloo** culminated in the Latin *boogaloo* craze (1965–1967), inspired by Joe Cuba, and Cheo Feliciano, among others. *Boogaloo* became an ephemeral style, but many of its performers formed a lineup known as Fania All Starts with the addition of other Puerto Ricans and Nuyoricans (New York–born Puerto Ricans). The artful arrangements, and the compositions of *salsa's* most prolific source of songs, Tite Curet Alonso, made a formidable force steering *salsa*—in various ways—to an intensifying process of sound and rhythmic fusions. Eventually, *salsa* artists waned in popularity at home, or moved on to fields like Latin jazz and *salsa romántica* in the early 1980s, as the genre gained steam in various countries.

Since the mid-1970s, young Nuyoricans formed a prominent group among the top DJs and stage artists in **hip-hop** and related forms like **rap** and freestyle. Charlie Chase, a *salsa* bassist—turned DJ in 1975—is considered a forerunner in the art of DJing, a hip-hop realm known for its considerable Nuyorican representation, with names like Disco Wiz, The Mighty Force, and "Little" Louie Vega; followed in the mid-1980s and early 1990s by Kenny "Dope" González, Ruben, and Vico C. On stage, singer La India's ability to navigate in the urban sounds of freestyle, soul, hip-hop, R&B, electro-funk, and *salsa* is proverbial and exemplary among her fellow Nuyoricans, rather than exceptional.

The boom led by Ricky Martin and Marc Anthony in the late 1990s paralleled the emergence in Puerto Rico of **reggaetón**, a genre influenced by various styles, especially the island-based underground rap/reggae, U.S. hip-hop, Panama's *reggae en espanol,* and Jamaica's *dancehall* **reggae**. Nuyorican Vico C is considered to be the pioneer of the form later popularized by Tego Calderón, Daddy Yankee, and Calle 13.

Further Reading

Conzo, Joe and David A. Pérez. *Mambo Diablo: My Journey with Tito Puente.* Bloomington, IN: AuthorHouse, 2010.

Díaz Díaz, Edgardo. "Danza antillana, conjuntos militares, nacionalismo musical e identidad dominicana: retomando los pasos perdidos del merengue." *Latin American Music Review* 29, no. 2, Fall-Winter (2008): 232–62.

Glasser, Ruth. *My Music Is My Flag.* Los Angeles: University of California Press, 1994.

Long, Pamela. " 'Ruidos con la Inquisición': Los Villancicos de Sor Juana Inés de la Cruz." *Destiempos* (Mexico City) 3/14 March-April (2008): 566–78.

"Native Porto Ricans Are Born Music Lovers; An Amiable Trait of Character That Needs No Americanization—The Music of the Country," *The New York Times*, May 22, 1904, accessed August 29, 2011, http://query.nytimes.com/mem/archive-free/pdf?res=FA0815F8355F13718DDDAB0A94DD405B848CF1D3.

Spottswoods, Richard K. 1990. *Ethnic Music on Records: A Discography of Ethnic Recordings Produced in the United States, 1893–1942.* Champaign, IL: University of Illinois Press.

"369th Band at Carnegie," *The New York Times,* July 27, 1919, accessed August 29, 2011, http://query.nytimes.com/gst/abstract.html?res=F10713F93D5C147A93C5AB178 CD85F4D8185F9&scp=1&sq=porto%20rico%20music%20369th&st=cse.

Edgardo Díaz Díaz

Punto

The Cuban *punto,* also know as *punto guajiro* or *punto cubano,* is a sung musical genre that appeared from the rural countryside in 17th century from Spain via the Canary Islands. The traditional *punto* is a kind of musical duel between two singers or teams of singers that alternate improvised verses in **décima** form. There are two basic styles: *Punto libre* (free *punto*) and *punto fijo* (fixed *punto*). *Punto libre,* common in the Western part of the country, alternates verses in a free meter with instrumental interludes in a fixed 3/4 meter. Fixed *punto,* as its name implies, maintains a fixed meter throughout the performance. Because of the emphasis on the text, the vocal melody tends to play a subordinate roll with singers employing a fixed melody drawn from a finite number of stock tunes. An accompanying instrumentation for a typical *punto* ensemble may consist of a **guitar**, a Cuban *tres*, and/or *laúd* with *clave*, *güiro*, and/or *guayo* (scraper). While *punto* is a rural style of folkloric music, the genre and its practitioners have at times in its history enjoyed popular success. In the 1930s and 1940s, *punto guajiro* musicans performed their improvisations over Cuban Radio, which by 1940 had 12 weekly programs devoted to *punto.* From this repertoire, several musicians have crossed over into the popular sphere, including Antonio "Ñico Saquito" Fernandez, Guillermo Portabales, and **Josetito Fernandez**, the latter whose improvisations over his composition "Guantanamera" earned him an international reputation during and beyond his own lifetime.

Further Reading

Linares, Maria Teresa. "The *Décima* and *Punto* in Cuban Folklore." In *Essays on Cuban Music: North American and Cuban Perspectives,* edited by Peter Lamarche Manuel, 87–111. Lanham, MD: University Press of America, 1991.

Sublette, Ned. *Cuba and Its Music: From the First Drums to the Mambo.* 1st ed. Chicago: Chicago Review Press, 2004.

George Torres

Quena

The *quena* is a vertical notched **flute** mainly used in South American Andean musical traditions from **Bolivia, Peru, Ecuador**, northern **Chile**, and northern **Argentina**. It is considered the traditional flute of the Andes. Modern *quenas* are mostly made of reed, wood, or cane, although different materials such as bone, gold, clay, silver, and gourd have been used in the past. In fact, some ancient *quenas* found in Peru date back to 3000 BC. The *quena* consists of a tube between 25 and 50 centimeters long that generally has six equidistant finger holes in front and one thumb hole in the back of the pipe. The tube is open on both ends. It has a quadrangular notch about 8 millimeters deep at the top end of the pipe. The sound is obtained by directing the air into the notch, blowing downward along the pipe.

When playing pre-Colombian music genres, *quenas* generally are played in consort with a drum, using different sizes of *quenas* tuned in different registers. When playing *mestizo* musical styles such as *huaynos*, *bailecitos, carnavalitos,* etc., one or two *quenas* are played along with *sikus*, **guitars,** *charango*, and *bombo* or some other percussion instrument.

Quenas may have different names (e.g., *kena, kena-kena, kiena, kkhena, qina,* etc.) depending on the musical tradition or the region where the instrument is played. There are numerous *quena* local and regional variants such as *phusipias* or *quenas* that have four finger holes; *quena-quena,* which has six finger holes and is used to play a dance that holds the same name; *quena kharhuani,* which is the *quena* used by lama drivers; and *quena lichihuayus,* which is used in the Bolivian region of Oruro.

Further Reading

Cavour, Ernesto. *Instrumentos musicales de Bolivia.* La Paz, Bolivia: Producciones Cima, 2001.

Olsen, Dale A. *Music of El Dorado: The Ethnomusicology of Ancient South American Cultures.* Jacksonville: University Press of Florida, 2001.

Raquel Paraíso

R

Race Relations

Race relations are the ways that people of different races living together in the same community behave toward one another. Latin America is one of the geographic areas of the world where over different periods of time there have been complex types of relationships among European, indigenous, and African cultures that produced a *mestizo* (mixed) tricultural heritage and diverse communities. In Latin America, these communal relationships and interactions are also important in comprehending how people of different racial backgrounds, heritages, and experiences have influenced the development and mixtures of the popular music.

In Latin American history, European contacts with indigenous and African cultures that stemmed from extensive periods of colonialism enmeshed in types of hegemonic—dominant (European) and subdominant (indigenous and African cultures), social, cultural, and political relationships resulted in a blending and innovation of different musical traditions, popular styles, instruments, esthetics, and techniques that people in the area have often reinvented as symbols of racial, ethnic, and national identity. For example, in **Bolivia**, the Spanish invasion of the southern Andes in the 1530s brought from Europe new musical instruments that profoundly influenced indigenous music. Race relationships of the Spanish were often biased against the indigenous community. The Spanish often used music instruction to Christianize and colonize the indigenous into European customs and traditions.

Also, in Bolivia, the Spanish invaders often viewed indigenous traditional musical instruments with suspicion. They associated panpipes with those played back home in Spain by lowly castrators of pigs and grinders of knives. As a result, the Spanish constantly made efforts to repress the use of indigenous musical instruments and often encouraged the use of instruments such as violins and transverse **flutes**. But, the indigenous sometimes adapted their traditional instruments to play European-style music. In addition, with innovations in more popular music styles, the introduction of the *vihuela* and **guitars** resulted in the creation of hybrid instruments such as the *charango*. Also, over periods of time, many European forms, styles, and rhythms were adopted; and even musical concepts such as that of the siren (Spanish *sirena*) were blended with pre-Hispanic musical practices.

In **Mexico's** colonial history (1521–1810), the indigenous communities experienced many types of religious and musical training, biases, and prejudices by the Spanish. By the late 1700s, among the locals, there was a Mexican racial identity distinct from Spain that represented a discontent of continued Spanish control of Mexican communal life. When Mexican independence arose in 1810, popular music played an important role in the creation of a new Mexican national identity, especially with the popularization of styles such as the *sones* and *jarabes*. However, many Mexicans, particularly those of a growing middle class, continued to look to Europe for their musical models. The waltz, one of Europe's most popular dance forms at the time, quickly became a mainstay among Mexican social dances. In addition, the **polka**, also popular in Europe particularly during the latter years of the 19th century, had a major impact on *música norteña* (northern music) with the arrival of German and other central European migrant mining workers for whom the polka had a special attachment.

During the late 1800s and early 1900s, German immigrant communities also arose especially in **Argentina, Brazil, Chile**, and **Paraguay**. In particular, many German Jews immigrated to escape Nazi-sponsored persecution, and many Volkdeutsche (German-speaking Protestants living in Russia) immigrated into Argentina. The obvious musical instrument legacy of the immigrant German people is the **accordion**, of which two forms are found in parts of Latin America: the button accordion (*acordeón de botones*) and the piano (*acordeón de teclas*). In Argentina, a variant of the first type is known as the *bandoneón*, invented by Heinrich Band after whom it was named became a popular instrument used in the Argentinean *tango*.

European contacts with the massive ethnic groups that were transported as slave labor from West and Central Africa to countries such as Mexico, Brazil, **Puerto Rico, Colombia, Cuba, Peru**, and so forth influenced African cultural traditions into Latin America's social and racial fabric. This historical experience is also one of the prime examples of the complex relationships between Europeans, Africans, and the denial of human rights based on race. Colonizers often attempted to pass legislation that banned African music, drumming, and dance in public settings. But in spite of many biases, restrictions, harsh treatments, and slave practices, Africans attempted to maintain aspects of certain musical traditions. Such traditions often provided tools for developing a sense of ethnic and racial identity outside of Africa. As a result, many different African-influenced rhythms, sounds, textures, dances, genres, performance practices, musical instruments, and distinct playing styles were integrated with European and indigenous traditions. This integration of diverse traditions greatly spurned the creation of new popular music traditions such as *rumba* (Cuba), *samba* (Brazil), *plena*, *bomba* (Puerto Rico), *cumbia* (Colombia), and many others.

In some instances, African-influenced religions such as Cuban *Santeriá* not only influenced expressions of racial heritage but also the development of some Latin American popular music styles and genres. Musically, this religious tradition integrates elements of extensive singing done in call-and-response patterns, polyrhythmic drumming, and dancing. But in a secular sense, this religion often provided local musicians with musical training and skills in which some later applied to innovative popular music. The religious practices of *Santeriá* and the association with fraternal organizations known as Abakwa became interconnected with African American **jazz** and the innovation of **Afro-Cuban** and **Latin jazz**.

During the 1940s, trumpeter Dizzy Gillespie (1917–1993) and Afro-Cuban drummer Chano Pozo (1915–1948) attempted to blend new styles and rhythms that were more rooted in African religious heritage that would be treated with respect rather than a floor show of exoticism. In addition, Pozo's background in the Afro-Cuban *Santeriá* religion and Abakwa drumming traditions presented a type of knowledge that Gillespie was seeking and a connection with African heritage. These musicians later collaborated on *Manteca* (1947), one of the most popular compositions, and created a new musical vocabulary in Afro-Cuban/Latin jazz history.

Sentiments about race relations in Latin America have often been expressed through popular music. Particularly, in the mid-1970s after the popularization of *reggae* music, some communities in Latin America became more active in expressing concerns about race relations and equality in their local communities through their association with ideologies of Pan-Africanism, negritude, civil rights, and black pride. This includes the participation in different social movements as a way of engaging in community activism for expressing class, identity, and social and political sentiments about race relations. For example, in Brazil, many young Afro-Brazilians began to participate in drumming ensembles and became affiliated with social organizations such as the Movimento Negro Unificado (Unified Black Movement [MNU]), an organization that was formed to advocate against racism and unite the struggles of Afro-Brazilians throughout the country. During the mid-1970s in urban cities such as Salvador, Bahia, Brazil, the epicenter of Afro-Brazilian culture, there was a rapid growth of what was known as *blocos afros* (community block drumming groups) that was comprised of lower- and working-class young Afro-Brazilians.

One of the most prominent *blocos afros* organizations is Ilê Aiyê, a community organization that was founded in 1974 as an important vehicle for expressing black pride in an open forum especially during the **Carnival** season when new popular music styles such as *samba-reggae* and *axé* **music** are premiered. Ilê Aiyê presented a positive image of the black Afro-Brazilian with popular songs such as "Que Bloco É Esse" ("What Carnival group is that") where the lyrical content makes reference to "Somos [we are] black power," and an ideology of black is beautiful, as symbols of racial/ethnic identity and connections with blacks outside of Brazil. This song also influenced many other racially centered popular songs of the 1980s and 1990s such as "Kizomba, Festa da Raça" ("Kizomba, Celebration of the Race"), and "Canto do Cor" ("Song of Color") by Banda Reflexu's, another popular *blocos afro* group in Brazil.

In some areas of Latin America as in Brazil, Cuba, and Colombia, poetic rapping and **Hip-Hop** have become popular styles and genres for establishing alliances with local and international communities, professional and cultural activities, and as symbols of positive race relations that are centered on equality.

Further Reading

Clark, Walter. *From Tejano to Tango: Latin Popular Music.* New York and London: Routledge, 2002.

Crook, Larry N. *Brazilian Music: Northeastern Traditions and the Heartbeat of a Modern Nation.* Santa Barbara, CA: ABC-CLIO, 2005.

Olsen, Dale A. "Music of Immigrant Groups." In *The Garland Handbook of Latin American Music,* edited by Dale A. Olsen and Daniel E. Sheehy, 83–91. New York and London: Garland, 2000.

Roberts, John Storm. *Black Music of Two Worlds: Africa, Caribbean, Latin, and African-American Traditions.* 2nd ed. New York: Schirmer Books, 1998.

Sheehy, Daniel E. "Popular Mexican Musical Traditions." In *Music in Latin American Culture: Regional Traditions,* edited by John M. Schechter, 34–79. New York: Schirmer Books, 1999.

Sobart, Henry. "Bolivia." In *The Garland Handbook of Latin American Music,* edited by Dale A. Olsen and Daniel E. Sheehy, 326–43. New York and London: Garland, 2000.

Clarence Henry

Ranchera

The *ranchera,* or more precisely the *canción ranchera* (country song), is regarded as **Mexico's** quintessential popular music genre. It is characterized by its lyrical and often sentimental qualities in both song text and melody. Although usually associated with *mariachi*, an ensemble type from Jalisco, which evolved into Mexico's national music style in the 1930s, *rancheras* are performed by most regional Mexican music ensembles, including *bandas*, *conjuntos*, *norteños*, and *duranguense* groups. More recently, *música ranchera* (ranchera/country music) emerged as a popular umbrella term to designate all kinds of rural-rooted Mexican music genres and styles.

Mexico's repertory of popular musics, from its very beginnings in the 19th century, cannot always be sharply distinguished from those of folk music traditions and art music because these categories overlap substantially. In fact, popular music genres in Mexico were often urban renditions of folk genres, whereas the most popular folk songs were influenced by 19th-century European salon music. Indeed both European romanticism and Italian opera have influenced the *canción,* which reached a high level of popularity by the midcentury when it was heard in the opera house, the salons of the aristocracy and the middle class, as well as throughout the rural village and urban neighborhood. Various musicologists have termed the second half of the 19th century the golden age of Mexican song, however, the Mexican *canción* developed its modern characteristics during the post-1910 revolution period when it was transformed into a simpler and more rural-based song type. These now-called *canciones rancheras,* or peasant/country songs, appealed to the recently urbanized rural masses as well as to the middle-class city dwellers in postrevolutionary Mexico. As momentary recreations of a simpler and romanticized folk heritage, *rancheras* were able to evoke feelings of nostalgia and patriotism, and for that, Mexicanness. The postrevolutionary period in general was characterized by the rise of a strong national identity. The *mestizos* came to form a part of the longed-for national spirit and through them popular music experienced a renewed vigor.

The musical characteristics of the modern *canción ranchera* include the use of tonic and dominant harmonies, a preference for the major mode, 2/4 and 3/4 meters, a melodic style that showcases a strong vocal technique, affected falsetto, *gritos* (yells), wide leaps, and elements such as portamento, sforzando, and ritardando at the end of the phrase. Male singers typically sing in a high register (preferably tenor), while women sing in alto with a hoarse voice (*voz ronca*). The songs are mostly of melodramatic content (unrequited love, abandonment, torment, etc.), eulogize the nation and the region, and romanticize the kind-hearted *hacienda* owners, gallant macho lovers, decent women, and happy peons.

Emerging in the 1930s, the *comedia ranchera* (ranch comedy), the most enduring genre of Mexican cinema, facilitated the establishment of the *canción ranchera,* interpreted by the folk-derived **mariachi** ensemble and the singing *charro* (horseman). The new media also helped to expand the initial realm of popularity of the genre, transitioning from the working class to the middle and upper classes. In the 1940s, the heydays of this genre, *mariachi* had fully incorporated the *canción ranchera.* The ensemble served perfectly to accompany both *canción ranchera* styles, the *estilo bravío* (fierce style) dominated by trumpets, and the *estilo sentimental* (sentimental style) dominated by string instruments. Singer-actors such as Jorge Negrete, Pedro Infante, and José Alfredo Jiménez turned into superstars during the golden era of Mexican cinema. The prominent female *ranchera* singer Lucha Reyes paved the way for a number of *ranchera* queens, such as Lola Beltrán, Amalia Mendoza, and Lucha Villa.

After World War II, the **canción romántica** (romantic song), a more refined version of the *canción ranchera,* arose and gained in popularity, particularly among middle-class urbanites. Popularized by the romantic, **guitar**-based trios, the **bolero** and the *canción-bolero* flourished for more than a decade until they had to give way to new musical developments. Because of the lasting appeal of *mariachi* and other regional ensemble types, the *ranchera* is still widely popular. With a new generation of young *ranchera* singers like Alejandro Fernández, Pepe Aguilar, Pablo Montero, Ezequiel Peña, Ana Gabriel, Graciela Beltrán, and Nydia Rojas, the genre experienced a revival in the late 1990s.

Further Reading

Mendoza, Vicente T. *La canción mexicana: ensayo de clasificación y antología.* Mexico City: Universidad Nacional Autónoma de México, 1961.

Velázquez, Marco, and Mary Kay Vaughan. "Mestizaje and Musical Nationalism in Mexico." In *The Eagle and the Virgin: Nation and Cultural Revolution in Mexico, 1920–1940,* edited by Mary Kay Vaughan and Stephen E. Lewis, 95–118. Durham, NC: Duke University Press, 2006.

Helena Simonett

Rap. *See* Hip-Hop.

Rasgueado

Rasgueado is a right-hand strumming technique. Derived from techniques on the Spanish **guitar** (especially *flamenco* music), the use of *rasgueado* in Latin American music gives much flavor and color to the music. There are many different varieties of *rasgueado* in Latin American music, much of which has worked its way into the popular music sphere, and different strumming techniques may be associated with particular regional varieties of music and genres. Sometimes the strummed *rasgueado* technique may be combined with a plucked, *punteo,* style of playing, where the player plucks out individual notes rather than strumming chords. *Rasgueado* techniques may employ motions generated from the fingers or the twisting of the wrist. The particular effect that is derived from a particular *rasgueado* is determined by several factors including which fingers are used, which direction they are strummed (upstrokes or downstrokes), and the strings to be strummed in the pattern (some concentrate on the treble side while others concentrate on the bass). It is the ordering of the individual strokes that provides accents to the *rasgueado* resulting in a characteristic rhythmic pattern. Notable patterns that utilize *rasgueado* techniques include the Argentine *zamba* and *chacarera*, the Mexican *son huasteco* and *son jalisciense*. One of the distinctive features of Latin American *rasgueado* is the frequent use of a muting technique called *quedo* or *chasquido,* which provides a rhythmic effect.

Further Reading
Stover, Rico. *Latin American Guitar Guide.* Pacific, MO: Mel Bay Publications, 1995.

George Torres

Reco-Reco

The *reco-reco* is a Brazilian percussion instrument made of an open cylinder of wood, metal, or bamboo with grooves notched into the shell over which a stick is scraped. The *reco-reco* can be used to provide rhythmic accompaniment to various folk and popular musical traditions in **Brazil** including *samba*, *coco*, *baião*, *marcha*, and *forró*. A specialized variety, the *reco-reco de mola* (*reco-reco* with a metal spring), is used in the *escola de samba*. A variety of sounds (closed and open, staccato and legato) are achieved on the *reco-reco* by means of hand and finger pressure, the speed and intensity of scraping, and by opening and closing the ends of the cylinder. **Pixinguinha's** group Oito Batutas was one of the earliest groups in Brazil to use the *reco-reco* in a recording (1921).

Further Reading

Bolão, Oscar. *Batuque é um privilégio: A percussão da música do Rio de Janeiro/ Batuque is a privilege: Percussion in Rio de Janeiro's music.* Rio de Janeiro, Brazil: Lumiar Editora, 2003.

Larry Crook

Daddy Yankee

Daddy Yankee (b. 1977) is a successful Latin Grammy Award–winning Puerto Rican–based *reggaetón* recording artist who helped popularize the genre in the United States. Daddy Yankee began his recording career appearing on DJ Playero's 1993 album *Playero 37*. His youthful aspirations of playing Major League baseball ended when he was hit in the leg by a stray bullet at age 16. Nonetheless, he turned adversity into inspiration when he teamed up with Playero. Yankee's skills on the microphone earned him the nickname "king of improvisation" and his rise to international fame parallels the increasing popularity of the *reggaetón* style. The albums *Los Homerunes, El Cangri.com, El Cartel de Yankee,* and *El Cartel de Yankee 2* exemplify Daddy Yankee's brand of *reggaetón,* a Spanish language hybrid of Jamaican dancehall and American **hip-hop**. Further amplifying Daddy Yankee's popularity was the live album *Barrio Fino en Directo,* certified platinum in the United States. His popularity in the United States has increased since the highly successful 2004 single "Gasolina." He has worked with American hip-hop luminaries including N.O.R.E. His increasing accolades include a nomination for the MTV Video Music Awards, the Latin Billboard Awards Reggaetón Album of the Year, and a Latin Grammy.

Further Reading

http://www.reggaetónline.net/daddy-yankee_reggaetón, accessed June 6, 2012.

David Moskowitz

Reggae (reggaespañol, reggae resistencia, reggaetón)

The term *reggae* began as the style descriptor for Jamaican popular music in the late 1960s. The *reggae* style was a combination of Jamaican and international influences; however, the term has now come to denote any Jamaican popular music style including ska, rocksteady, roots *reggae,* and dancehall. At its peak, Jamaican *reggae* was categorized by the use of ska horns, the moderately slow beat of rocksteady, the shuffle rhythm influence of New Orleans rhythm and blues, and the African *burru* drumming tradition filled with syncopation. The standard instrumentation was acquired from American popular music and included electric **guitar**, electric bass, drum set, vocals, and optional keyboards and horn line. The characteristic *reggae* beat pattern is called the one drop rhythm and is achieved when the drum set player only emphasizes the third beat of a four beat measure and the guitar plays off beat choked chords. This brand of *reggae* was best exemplified by the music of Bob Marley and the Wailers (who wrote a song about the beat pattern called "One Drop"). As the use of the term *reggae* evolved it began to describe all of the Jamaican popular music styles generically, just as rock 'n' roll has become a catch all term for American popular music. Additional artists that fit under the *reggae* umbrella include Black Uhuru, Burning Spear, Jimmy Cliff, Desmond Dekker, Inner Circle, Gregory Isaacs, Freddie McGregor, Augustus Pablo, Peter Tosh, and Bunny Wailer.

The Jamaican popular music style that came after *reggae* was called dancehall. This style was ushered in the wake of Bob Marley's death in 1981. The style involves a DJ singing or toasting new lyrics over a repetitive beat. Dancehall takes its name from the venues in which it developed. The lyrics of dancehall songs run the gamut from conscious uplifting of the oppressed Jamaican underclass to discussions of sexual encounters, drug use, or criminal activity (called slackness lyrics). Stylistically, dancehall has more in common with American **hip-hop** than standard Jamaican *reggae.* As dancehall style grew in popularity in Jamaica, it also caught on in other parts of the Caribbean and beyond. Important Jamaican dancehall stars are Buju Banton, Capleton, Eek-A-Mouse, Maxi Preist, Shabba Ranks, and Yellowman. Both Jamaican *reggae* and dancehall had significant influence on popular music styles outside the island.

The *reggae* and dancehall styles migrated from Jamaica and spread to the Caribbean at large, the United Kingdom, the **United States**, and various parts of Latin America. As these styles moved further from their home, they mixed with the regional styles of the diaspora. Thus, a host of *reggae* or dancehall-based style derivations came into existence in the 1990s and beyond. Examples of these new styles include *reggaespanol, reggaetón,* and *reggae resistencia.* Each of these derivations on the original Jamaican styles added regional elements to create musical hybrids. However, the principal difference between standard Jamaican *reggae* and these derivations is that Jamaican *reggae* is performed in English (or the thick Jamaican patois that is based in English) and the other styles are all performed in Spanish or Portuguese.

Reggaespañol (or *reggae en español*) is a style that has strongholds in Latin and Central America, as well as in Spain. Stylistically, *reggaespañol* sounds like Spanish-language Jamaican dancehall. Like dancehall, *reggaespañol* comes in the conscious and slackness lyrical varieties. This type of music is largely created by Black Latinos and rose to popularity in the early 1990s. Columbia Records released the first collection of *reggaespañol* songs in 1991. This compilation included tracks from El General, La Diva, Nardo Boom, La Atrevida, and others. *Reggaespañol* that contains more conscious lyrics is produced by artists such as Chando, Jah Nattoh, Bocer, and Guanche. A stronghold of the conscious variety is Barcelona, Spain.

Reggae resistencia is a term coined by Brazilian *reggae* singer Edson Gomes in the late 1980s. The style is a combination of roots *reggae* and Portuguese language lyrics. Based in Sao Paulo, Gomes writes protest lyrics that discuss politics and religion. EMI released Gomes' album in this style in 1988 under the title *Reggae resistencia*. Since then, Gomes has continued on the road paved by Bob Marley and Jimmy Cliff. He remains active and has released six albums since 2000, including a two-CD live album in 2006.

Reggaetón is the most popular of the Jamaican dancehall derivatives. The style is also known as *regueton* and is a specifically urban style of Spanish-language dancehall that became popular in Latin America in the early 1990s. The style has subsequently become popular internationally and now hosts several superstars, such as **Daddy Yankee**. More accurately, *reggaetón* blends elements of Jamaican dancehall, American hip-hop, and Latin ***bomba***, ***merengue***, and ***bachata***. Singers perform in Spanish and often switch mid-song between Spanish and English. Just as Jamaican dancehall songs take their beats from preexisting songs, the characteristic *reggaetón* beat came from the Shabba Ranks tune "Dem Bow." The unofficial home of *reggaetón* is Puerto Rico, but the style is popular across the Caribbean, Latin America, and the United States. Also, like dancehall, the lyrics of *reggaetón* tend to emphasize discussions of sex and the exploitation of women (standard slackness topics).

Born in **Panama**, *reggaetón* quickly moved to **Puerto Rico** and was described in the 1980s as Spanish-language dancehall. Popular early artists included Chicho Man, Renato, and Black Apache. Once the style moved from Panama to Puerto Rico, it acquired a hip-hop flavor from rapper Vico C and also gained greater distribution. In the 1990s, Puerto Rican *reggaetón* producers were moving away from the reuse of existing backing tracks and began creating their own beats. With this, *reggaetón* gained its true personality by blending dancehall toasting, hip-hop posturing, and Caribbean musical styles.

The mature *reggaetón* style has several musically distinctive qualities. Most recognizable is the heavy emphasis on drum machine produced beats that are focused on snare drum use. The musical backdrop to a *reggaetón* song is largely electronically produced with the synthesizer as a main instrument. The beats employed in *reggaetón* songs are often based on other popular Latin American styles such as **salsa**, *bachata,* and *merengue.*

Throughout the mid-1990s, *reggaetón* was picking up an international audience. Through the work of artists such as DJ Playero and DJ Nelson, the style spread outside the Caribbean and, by the end of the decade, *reggaetón* was an internationally marketable style. Puerto Rican-based Daddy Yankee and **Dominican Republic** products Don Chezina and Luny Tunes have pushed the style into the new millennium and expanded the audience into the United States. The popularity of the style continues to grow. In 2004, American hip-hop artist N.O.R.E. created crossover appeal for the style when he dueted with Daddy Yankee on *"Oye Mi Canto."* This success was amplified by Don Omar's 2006 album *King of Kings,* which climbed into the top ten on the American charts and moved to number one on the Billboard Latin Rhythm Radio Charts.

Reggaetón's popularity continues to grow with artists in the style, making inroads in American hip-hop and in the American film industry. In fact, *reggaetón* is popular enough that hip-hop artists are remixing select tunes to include *reggaetón* beats. Snoop Dogg and Usher have both made *reggaetón* remixes and the trend will likely continue. The crossover between American hip-hop and *reggaetón* is now significant. Daddy Yankee works with hip-hop producers Sean "Diddy" Combs and Pharrell Williams from the Neptunes. *Reggaetón* is now considered a viable international music style and continues to attract new listeners.

Further Reading

Manuel, Peter, Kenneth M. Bilby, and Michael D. Largey. *Caribbean Currents: Caribbean Music from Rumba to Reggae.* Philadelphia, PA: Temple University Press, 2006.

Rivera, Raquel Z., Wayne Marshall, and Deborah Pacini Hernandez, eds. *Reggaetón.* Durham, NC: Duke University Press, 2009.

Samponaro, Philip. "'Oye mi canto' ('Listen to My Song'): The History and Politics of Reggaetón." *Popular Music & Society* 32, no. 4 (2009): 489–506.

David Moskowitz

Reggaetón. *See* Reggae.

Regional (Choro)

The *regional* is a Brazilian music ensemble associated with ***choro***, the urban popular instrumental music genre that dominated the musical scene in Rio de Janeiro in the early part of the 20th century. Very few professional musicians were associated with the early *choro,* which was strongly associated with amateur musicians of the lower middle sector of society. With the development of new entertainment technologies—film, recordings, and radio—a new demand for popular music led to changes in the very nature of the *choro.* With the rise of these new media, *choro* musicians quickly found that their skills were in demand by a larger audience, leading to the evolution of *choro* from a style of playing European dance music performed at parties and other social functions by amateur musicians, to a separate genre of music performed by increasingly larger professional groups. From these early groups came the *regional* (plural, *regionais*), the professional ensemble that became the workhorse of the entertainment industry through the 1940s.

Popular music in **Brazil** came to be influenced by the nascent consumer industries that developed in conjunction with new communication technologies. The budding silent film industry in the early 1900s began to employ musicians to accompany films, to occupy the audience between reel changes, and to entertain the public in the lobby before showings; *choro* ensembles were hired to play at these cinemas, which used the quality and size of the groups as part of their advertising. The result was that *choro* moved from an amateur event to an increasingly professional endeavor. *Choro* ensembles during this transitional period increased steadily in size and complexity as the new media put higher demands on the musicians. The result was greater technical precision and a stylistic change favoring faster, more intricate music, and more professional musicians. As these musicians became part of these new media, their primary audience shifted to the middle and upper classes (in effect, those who could afford to participate in the new types of entertainment).

It is uncertain how these ensembles came to be known as *conjuntos regionais,* or regional ensembles, but it is generally believed that the name came from groups associated with the northeast region of Brazil. Before **samba** predominated as the preferred **Carnival** genre, *choro* ensembles playing **maxixes** were commonly part of the festivities. During the 1910s, it became fashionable for these groups to dress in the manner of rural northeasterners and assume northeastern names such as Turunas Pernambucanos (The Fearless Ones from Pernambuco, a state in northeastern Brazil). Even though they played in a thoroughly Rio de Janeiro style, they were known as regional ensembles since these ensembles evoked the northeast region. Over time, the northeastern associations were lost, and the name was assumed by professional radio and recording ensembles.

The introduction and proliferation of radio also had an enormous impact on the course of popular music as broadcasters scrambled for high-quality music to play on the air, resulting in the formation of a large number of ensembles. By the 1930s, the recording industry employed large numbers of solo singers and instrumentalists, many of whom were featured on radio broadcasts as well. Radio stations and record companies found it convenient to maintain their own *regionais* of 12–15 players, rather than hire freelance musicians piecemeal. These groups were usually named after the lead player and were strongly identified with their parent station or company (such as Rádio Clube with Waldir Azevedo and his Regional, Rádio Tupi with Benedeto Lacerda and his Regional). They functioned as in-house orchestras, and the high demands put on the *regionals* for stylistic versatility and high-quality performances did much to raise the general level of musical skill to even greater heights. New, difficult *choros* were composed to showcase *regionais*. In addition to *choros,* these groups accompanied singers and instrumentalists in a wide array of genres and styles, played dance music, provided background music, and filled in between acts on live radio shows. Radio *regionals* often performed live in front of studio audiences, and some groups even inspired the formation of fan clubs. Through radio, the sound of the *regional* penetrated even the most remote parts of the nation, where it became associated not only with the culture of Rio de Janeiro, but as music representative of the entire nation.

Further Reading

Garcia, Thomas George Caracas. "The Brazilian Choro: Music, Politics and Performance." Ph.D. diss., Duke University, 1997.

Livingston-Isenhour, Tamara Elena, and Thomas George Caracas Garcia. *Choro: A Social History of a Brazilian Popular Music.* Bloomington: Indiana University Press, 2005.

Thomas George Caracas Garcia

Religion and Music

Though Latin America has long been identified with the rites and rituals of Roman Catholicism, numerous challenges to this dominance in the region have emerged since the beginning of the 12th century. In response to the highly ritualized style of Roman Catholic worship, the intermediary clergy, and the emphasis on a centralized, hierarchical governance system, more egalitarian, unbound forms of worship are under consideration. Furthermore, the post-Vatican II groundswell of interest in the plight of the poor and disenfranchised in Latin America was in many respects the orphaned child of the acrimony over the past 30 years between liberation theologians in Latin America and the Vatican. Though Protestant denominations in the region do not seem to have faired better in defending the dispossessed in the region, the historical associations between the Catholic Church, colonial governance, and the land-owning elite, as well as state endorsements of Catholicism as the official religion (often from corrupt or brutally repressive governing regimes) has placed a historical burden on the Catholic Church that has not encumbered the Protestant denominations. In the end, Pentecostalism in particular has provided "a democratic congregationalist experience for the socially disinherited" (Gordon Lewis in Stewart 2004, 588), while circumventing the need to connect social issues to its ecclesiastical mission, given its near total emphasis on individual, spiritual salvation.

Religious Alternatives

Religious plurality is not entirely new to Latin America. Catholicism has, for example, always accommodated elements of folk religion in the region. However, the upsurge in religious alternatives is directly connected to increased globalization after 1950 and an attendant rural-to-urban shift. Though urbanization is often associated in the public imagination with a shift to more secular values, religious zeal actually tends to rise, not decline: as cities find themselves unable to meet the material and social needs of the population boom, new urban dwellers look more fervently to religion in response to their state of dispossession.

Though the growth of evangelical and Pentecostal congregations has been fueled by this demographic shift, these communities vary greatly in their size and affiliation to larger governing bodies. For example, numerous independent, storefront churches can be found in urban centers where congregants can engage in exuberant forms of Christian worship without alliance to larger federations. Yet, other Protestant churches align with transnational Christian conglomerates, remaining conspicuously market-oriented in their presentation: televised religious services with charismatic evangelists; advertised healing hours; donation campaigns; broadcasts from self-owned radio stations, reaching the most remote areas of Latin America; huge arena-style churches that jut out from the colonial cityscapes. These varied types of congregations can also be found among Latin American communities throughout North America as is likely in Houston or Toronto.

Afro-Latin Religion

Afro-Latin religious communities are both significant in size and global in scope. All of them exhibit, to varying degrees, multiple baselines from which their religious fusions arose, in spite of claims of religious singularity. That is, Afro-Latin religions in the Americas are as likely to be influenced by multiple European and Amerindian sources (e.g., Kardecism, Catholic iconography, Coboclos) as they are by multiple African origins. The prominent transnational Afro-Latin religions (e.g., Arará, Candomblé, Garifuna, Palo Monte, Santería, Umbanda, and Vodou) all exhibit eclectic ritual compositions; however, the incorporation of drumming, song and dance, often leading to trance-possession states, tends to be a common and conspicuous feature. And, these religious practices have all migrated from their primary sites and reestablished themselves abroad (e.g., Garifuna in New York City, Vodou in Montréal, *Santería* in Caracas, Umbanda in Paris), giving rise to contestations of authentic practice among the various communities worldwide. Furthermore, the religious musics of these communities have become as transnational as the communities themselves, making these repertoires more accessible to and adaptable by popular music artists.

Religion and Popular Music

The enigmatic ways in which music is able to captivate listeners—particularly effective in engaging the emotions and the body—is undoubtedly why it is such a widespread feature of religious life. However, the entrance of religious matters into the realm of popular culture tends to be of a different order. Religious themes in popular music are as likely to contest prevailing religious practices and ideologies as they are to promote them in the public sphere, making their appearance an inherently political act, blurring any clear separation between music, religion, and politics in popular culture.

In a general sense, the musics of African-derived ritual traditions "have defined Latin American music as well as greatly influenced world music" (Stewart 2004, 569), irrespective of any *direct* link between African and Latin popular musics. Those popular Afro-Latin musical styles that have enjoyed commercial success beyond the geography of Latin America (e.g., *salsa, samba, merengue*) routinely come to stand in for what constitutes Latin music abroad, in spite of the true diversity of musical production in Latin America.

The sensibilities formed by the region's long-standing Catholic heritage have had a lasting influence on all aspects of social life and music making, often yielding resistance in the world of popular music to received notions of moral and ethical propriety. The widespread hypersexualization of commercial *salsa,* for example, is not simply a result of *machismo* or the submission to sexual objectification. Aside from an obvious chauvinism in such an opinion, this facile analysis looks past the ideological positions that such behaviors can, and often do, articulate: the sexualization of *salsa* can be seen in opposition to Catholic patriarchal and sexual mores, particularly the glorification of chastity. Many Latin **hip-hop** artists, particularly women, are tackling these and similar themes, including sexual orientation, in much more overt manners (e.g., Las Krudas, Tina).

References in popular music to Afro-Latin religion tend to be more unambiguous, given the importance of these practices as markers of African heritage and resistance to the vestiges of European colonialism. For example, the mention of **Afro-Cuban** deities and religious life are recurring features in the lyrics of the Cuban-derived popular dance musics of *son*, *salsa*, and *timba* (e.g., Willie Colon, Polo Montañez, Eddie Palmieri, Los Van Van, et al.). References to Afro-Brazilian religions are ostensibly more prevalent: the largest and most renowned *blocos Afros* of Brazilian **Carnival** including **Olodum**, Ilê Aiyê, and Ara Ketu have all taken names of (West African) Yoruba derivation, from where the *orisha* religions of Latin America originated, and have earned marked commercial success. Brazilian *afoxé* music and its principal rhythm *ijexá* (both names are also of Yoruba derivation) are based on *Candomblé* religious music, though recontextualized in secular settings such as Carnival and made adaptable to various sociopolitical agenda such as the celebration of Afro-Brazilian religion or challenges to notions of racial conciliation. Similar musical and political subjects are recurring in the lyrics and the beats of Latin **rap** and *reggaetón* (e.g., Orishas, RZO). Many ensembles have also successfully combined popular dance forms with Afro-Latin religious musics and/or **Latin jazz**, often emphasizing sacred repertoires (songs, drumming, dance) and instruments (e.g., Batacumbele, **Boukman Eksperyans**, Fort Apache Band, Irakere, Síntesis).

The foregrounding of religion as a marketplace in the globalized economy has prompted a growing economy for contemporary Christian music throughout Latin America. Like the affiliated Christian media networks, the Christian music industry exhibits all of the production and marketing savvy of its mainstream counterparts, successfully establishing itself as a transnational force throughout the Americas. Because the musical tastes of the Latin American Christian music market are no less varied than those of the mainstream, Christian music is produced in any of the mainstream popular genres found throughout the Americas, from Christian *ranchera* to *zouk* or *reggaetón* gospel. Any popular musical style can be imbued with an overt Christian message, and many are made available to the Latin American Christian market in French, Portuguese, and Spanish: artists who play Brazilian Praise Punk or imbue Haitian *mizik evanjelik* (evangelical music) with the dance rhythms of *konpa* are finding airplay and markets for their recordings in a rapidly expanding transnational Christian music industry.

Further Reading

Birman, Patricia, and David Lehmann. "Religion and the Media in a Battle for Ideological Hegemony: The Universal Church of the Kingdom of God and TV Globo in Brazil." *Bulletin of Latin American Research* 18, no. 2 (1999): 145–64.

Brown, Diana. *Umbanda: Religion and Politics in Urban Brazil.* 2nd ed. New York: Columbia University Press, 1994.

Butler, M.L. "'Nou Kwe nan Sentespri' (We Believe in the Holy Spirit): Music, Ecstasy, and Identity in Haitian Pentecostal Worship." *Black Music Research Journal* 22, no. 1 (2002): 85–125.

Feldman, Heidi. *Black Rhythms of Peru: Reviving African Musical Heritage in the Black Pacific.* Middletown, CT: Wesleyan University Press, 2006.

Fernandes, Sujatha and Jason Stanyek. "Hip-Hop and the Black Public Spheres in Cuba, Venezuela and Brazil." In *Beyond Slavery: The Multilayered Legacy of Africans in Latin America and the Caribbean,* edited by Darién Davis, 199–222. Maryland: Rowman and Littlefield, 2007.

Matory, J. Lorand. *Black Atlantic Religion: Tradition, Transnationalism, and Matriarchy in the Afro-Brazilian Candomblé.* Princeton: Princeton University Press, 2005.

Perna, Vincenzo. 2004. *Timba: The Sound of the Cuban Crisis.* Burlington, VT: Ashgate.

Smith, Christian. *Latin American Religion in Motion.* Hoboken: Taylor & Francis, 1999.

Stewart, Robert J. "Religion, Myths and Beliefs: Their Sociopolitical Roles." In *General History of the Caribbean, Vol. V: The Caribbean in the Twentieth Century,* edited by B. Brereton, 559–605. Paris-London: UNESCO Publishing-Macmillian Caribbean, 2004.

Michael D. Marcuzzi

Requinto

Requinto is a term used in both Spanish and Portuguese to refer to a small instrument that is tuned to a higher range. The most common usage for *requinto* is for **guitar**-type instruments, although there exists a high drum used in Puerto Rican folk drumming that is known as a *requinto* drum. The name *requinto* has no relationship to the interval of a fifth (as *quinto* might suggest), but comes from the word to tighten or to make taut. Because the word *requinto* is also used as a generic term to designate a type of small, acoustic guitar-like instrument used to play melodic lead in various folk genres, the following will discuss those uses most commonly associated with popular music in Latin America.

Requinto Jarocho

The *requinto jarocho* is a four-string lead guitar used in the **son jarocho** ensemble. It is also known locally as the *guitarra de son* or the *javalina*. It comes in a variety of sizes ranging from about 50 centimeters to just under 100 centimeters. It is tuned primarily in fourths, using thick nylon strings. The instrument is played standing with the strap being slung over the right shoulder, and it is plucked with a pick crafted from an animal horn or made out of plastic. Traditionally, the instrument was carved out of a solid block of red cedar, though nowadays one finds fine crafted instruments that resemble a more traditional Spanish guitar construction. Related to this type of innovation is the use of tuning keys, which traditionally employed friction pegs, like traditional *flamenco* guitars, but more recently, *requinto* makers have been using mechanical tuning machines in their headstocks. With the **arpa** *jarocha,* it plays the melody within the ensemble. Lino Chávez and Rutilo Parroquín are considered to be exemplary *requinto jarocho* players.

Requinto Romántico

The *requinto* (*romántico*) is a small classical guitar tuned a fourth higher than the standard guitar. It can be plucked with either a pick or with the fingers of the right hand, and very often, a thumb pick. The instrument was invented in 1945 by Alfredo Gil of Trio Los Panchos so that he could play introductions and interludes on a guitar without losing any of the sustain from placing a capo too high on the neck. Since Gil's invention of the *requinto* and use of it as the melodic lead instrument, it has become standard in **trío romántico** performance practice. The scale of the instrument is shorter than the standard Spanish guitar, ranging about 53 to 55 centimeters. Because of this, the shortness of its string length allows a greater rapidity in the movements of the left hand, as well as also granting the instrument a sharper timbre than that of the standard guitar. As noted above, the instrument is tuned a fourth higher than the guitar, A-D-G-c-e-a, and a capo is often used in performance to transpose idiomatically to other keys.

Requinto (drum)

The *requinto* drum is a handheld, single-headed frame drum, and it is the smallest of the drums (*panderetas*) used in Puerto Rican **plena** ensembles. The tuning of the *requinto* head is relatively high for hand drums, and it is usually played with two tones, an open tone and a slap tone. Within the drum ensemble, the *requinto* drummer usually plays an improvisation over the holding patterns of the other two drums. In the older tradition, *requinto* players used their fingers in their playing style. More recently, *requinto* performance practice favors use of the entire hand, as in **conga** playing.

Further Reading

Marin, Nidia. "Los Panchos." *Guitarra fácil* 13. Mexico City: Ediciones Libra, n.d.

Torres, George. "The *Bolero Romántico:* From Cuban Dance to International Popular Song," in *From Tejano to Tango: Essays on Latin American Popular Music,* edited by Walter A. Clark, 151–71. New York: Garland, 2002.

George Torres

Rhumba

Rhumba is an English spelling variant of the term *rumba,* which in the non-Spanish-speaking world became the generic coverall term for Latin American popular music compositions. Unfortunately, this was an incorrect use of the term as the true Cuban **rumba** is a folkloric song and dance genre that has nothing in common with the popularized American *rhumbas.* The history of the misnomer has been well documented, and can be traced back to a performance by Justo "Don" Azpiazu of a *son-pregón* by Moisés Simons, "El manicero" ("The Peanut Vendor"), which on the same program included a stylized *rumba.* Since then, American journalists, musicians, and publishers used the term *rhumba* (the presence of the *h* signifying the rolled *r* in Spanish). By the mid-1930s, publishers were profiting by marketing and selling collections of *rhumbas* even though the majority of what they were labeling as a *rhumba* was really a ***son***, ***guaracha***, ***cha-cha-chá***, etc. In spite of the correctly termed popular sheet music from publishers in Havana and Mexico City that sold in this country in the 1940s and 1950s, the term continued to be marketed in the **United States** by those same publishers as *rhumba*. Peer Southern, which published in Havana and the United States, would market their repertoire using the terms *son* and *guaracha* in Havana, while those same tunes sold in the United States as part of the series *Rumba* rhythms. As long as this music remains under copyright, the wrong terminology will continue to be passed on to musicians. A recent publication of the Mexican ***vals*** "La Cucaracha" is labeled "*tempo di rumba*."

Further Reading

Roberts, John Storm. *The Latin Tinge: The Impact of Latin American Music on the United States.* 2nd ed. New York: Oxford University Press, 1999.

George Torres

Rock Brasileiro (Brazilian Rock)

Rock performed by people from **Brazil** dates to Nora Ney's 1955 cover of "Rock around the Clock" and Celly Campelo's 1959 "Estúpido Cupido," a translation of "Stupid Cupid" presented on the national television show *Chacrinha*. Brazilian rock, however, began in the early 1960s, with a generation eventually called the "Jovem Guarda," after a television show of the same name. The most successful of these singers would be Roberto Carlos, Erasmo Carlos, and Wanderléa. Influenced by the likes of Elvis Presley, Little Richard, and the Beatles, they, and bands like the Brazilian Bitles, popularized the "iê-iê-iê" sound.

As Tim Maia explored soul and Jorge Ben shaped *samba*-rock, the 1960s gave birth to a distinctly Brazilian sound. In 1967, a psychedelic trio from São Paulo directed by Rogério Duprat called Os Mutantes placed second while backing **Gilberto Gil** during the 3rd Festival of Música Popular Brasileira (MPB). The next year Gil and fellow Bahian **Caetano Veloso** headed a cast including Os Mutantes and Tom Zé and released *Tropicalia ou Panis et Circencis,* heralding the pan-artistic ***tropicália*** **movement**.

Previously the domain of MPB, the flag of social protest was hoisted by many rockers. Bands under the dictatorship had their songs censored, and artists were tortured and exiled. One was Raul Seixas, who developed his brand of irreverent rock in the early 1970s and, with writer Paulo Coelho, founded the Alternative Society. In São Paulo, Secos & Molhados mixed glam and progressive rock with folklore and politics in complex vocal arrangements. In 1975 Rita Lee & Tutti-Frutti recorded "Fruto Proibido." The diversity of the decade is illustrated in the progressive rock of Vímana (with Lulu Santos, Lobão, and Ritchie) and Terço, the hard rock of Made in Brazil and Casa das Máquinas, the regional rock of Novos Baianos, the rural rock of Sá, Rodrix & Guarabyra, and the fusion rock of Azymuth.

CBS, EMI, Som Livre, and Warner took rock seriously in the 1980s. Numerous compilations were released: *Os Intocáveis, Rock Voador, Rock Wave, Rumores,* and *Rock do Sul* presented diverse flavors; some groups, like Banda 69, Escola de Escândalo, and Eletrodomésticos ("Choveu no meu chip"), were one-hit wonders, while others, like Kid Abelha and Capital Inicial, became giants in "BRock" history. Assisted by President Sarney's Plano Cruzado, which froze prices and exchange rates, the group RPM sold 2,200,000 copies of the 1986 "Rádio Pirata ao vivo." Rio's Barão Vermelho, São Paulo's Titãs, and Brasília's Paralamas do Sucesso and Legião Urbana had gold and platinum disks through the 1990s and, with FM stations like Rádio Fluminense, Rádio Rock, and Transamérica behind them, silenced the decades-old epithets of rockers as alienated, Americanized, and colonized. Noteworthy 1980s groups included Camisa de Vênus, Engenheiros de Hawaii, Blitz, Plebe Rude, Ira! and Ultraje a Rigor, among myriad others.

The compilations *Grito Suburbano* and *O Começo do Fim do Mundo* manifested *rock brasileiro's* other, harder face. Punk and hardcore took root in the twilight of the 1970s with São Paulo's Joelho de Porco, Restos de Nada, and Inocentes, and Brasília's Aborto Elétrico, and in the 1980s with São Paulo's Olho Seco, Garotos Podres, Ratos de Porão, and Cólera, Brasília's ARD and Detrito Federal, Rio's Desordeiros, Porto Alegre's Replicantes, and Belém's Delinqüentes. Dorsal Atlântica (Rio) and Sepultura, Chakal, Sarcófago, and, later, Angra (all from Minas Gerais) cemented metal's presence. Female bands, including Bulimia, Valhalla, Kaos Klitoriano, and No Class, appeared in the underground. Handmade fanzines and home-dubbed cassettes travelled the country over, mapping enduring networks.

President Collor reduced import tariffs in 1990, making equipment and recordings accessible to more aspiring rockers, just as the majors shifted resources away from rock. Established names migrated to MPB or romantic music. New bands opted for pop or regionalized rock, like Chico Science & Nação Zumbi, who propogated *mangue* bit, and Raimundos, creators of *forrócore*. Multicultural bands like Obina Shock and X-GRANITO borrowed from African and Anglo traditions, further hybridizing *rock brasileiro*. Indie labels, like Monstro Discos and Sílvia Records, community organizations like the Cearense Cultural Association of Rock, and festivals like Porão do Rock fortified local scenes. Rappa, Skank, CPM 22, and Mundo Livre S/A are among few major-label national names, while bands like Ação Direta, Mukeka di Rato, DFC, Death Slam, and Besthöven utilize virtual networks to reach large publics at home and abroad. Since 2000, the Latin Grammys have awarded a Best Brazilian Rock Album.

Further Reading

Alexandre, Ricardo. *Dias de luta: o rock e o Brasil dos anos 80.* São Paulo: DBA, 2002.

Dapieve, Artur. *Brock: o rock brasileiro dos anos 80.* São Paulo: Editora 34, 1995.

Galinsky, Philip. *"Maracatu Atômico": Tradition, Modernity, and Postmodernity in the* Mangue *Movement of Recife, Brazil.* New York: Routledge, 2002.

Veloso, Caetano. *Tropical Truth: A Story of Music and Revolution in Brazil.* Trans. Isabel de Sena. New York: Knopf, 2002.

Wheeler, Jesse Samba. "Dark Matter: Towards an Architectonics of Rock, Place, and Identity in Brasília's Utopian Underground." PhD diss., University of California, Los Angeles, 2007.

Jesse Wheeler

Rock en Español

Rock en español is the term used to describe the cultural practice of rock music in Spanish. Given the variety of styles encompassed by this term, it would be difficult to define it in terms of instrumentation or genres, though the electric **guitar** figures highly as a component. Thus, it is best understood as an umbrella-like label, covering a vast array of music associated with contemporary practice in countries all over the Americas.

Generally speaking, *rock en español* is associated with the 1980s and 1990s. As a cultural practice, however, it is much older. The 1980s and 1990s signal only a period of mainstream visibility, but actual practice goes as far back as the late 1950s. It is hard to pinpoint a single location as the actual origin of *rock en español*. Rather, events in **Mexico**, **Cuba**, and **Argentina** point to circumstances contributing to its materialization in an almost simultaneous fashion. Radio stations broadcasting rock music were very popular across the border between the **United States** and Mexico as well as Cuba. In Argentina, familiarity with fashionable music trends sparked initial attempts at local production of rock 'n' roll, however, throughout the hemisphere, a significant event was the incorporation of rock 'n' roll songs in the repertoire of bands at dance halls and clubs of Latin American capitals. Early recordings date as far back as the mid to late 1950s in Mexico and Argentina, with acts like Gloria Ríos in 1957 and Billy Cafaro in 1958. Around the same time, a Cuban group called Los Hot Rockers was, arguably, the first band singing rock and roll in Spanish, though they left no recordings. Eventually, Los Llopis recorded what could be regarded as the first rock 'n' roll-tinged songs for the Cuban music industry.

Though rock in English was widely available thanks to local distribution, record companies soon discovered that, for the music to succeed, Spanish versions would be necessary. The Mexican industry thus focused on recorded covers of American or British hits known as *refritos,* with bands like Los Locos del Ritmo (aka Los Rebeldes del Rock), Los Teen Tops, Los Black Jeans (a.k.a. Los Camisas Negras), Los Apson, Los Loud Jets, and Los Hooligans. Cuba produced Los Zafiros, a legendary doo-wop and rhythm and blues ensemble with a short-lived career, which epitomizes the devastating effect of revolutionary cultural policies.

With teen stars like César Costa and Enrique Guzmán, Mexico was primarily responsible for popularizing this new music through a movement called *La Nueva Ola* (The New Wave). For the most part, *Nueva Ola* was the Spanish version of early rock in English, though its class appeal was limited to privileged sectors of society. It soon became a Latin American constant. In Mexico, magazines like *POP* celebrated singers like Angélica María and Julissa, and bands like Los Yaki, Los Belmonts, and The Rockin' Devils. Television contributed greatly to *Nueva Ola's* popularity. Argentine programs like *El Club del Clan* and *Ritmo y juventud* were adapted in other countries eager to join. In Mexico, the equivalents were programs like *Yeah Yeah* and *Discotheque a gogó.* By the mid-1960s, stars like Guzmán and Costa, and the Argentines Leo Dan, Sandro, and Palito Ortega were quite popular all over Latin America.

In Argentina, rock progressed along two main routes: the rich favored Anglo rock, while, at the lower-class level, a Spanish language version of rock emerged, quite apart from covers. The emergence of a rock in Spanish tradition allowed for a different orientation. Imitating British acts, bands like The Shakers and The Mockers arrived from **Uruguay**, while singers like Mauricio Birabent (a.k.a. Moris) and José Alberto Iglesias (a.k.a. Tanguito) sang original material in Spanish, contributing to the rise of bands like Los Gatos Salvajes and Los Beatniks, some of which arrived to Buenos Aires from the interior of the country. By 1968, two main bands, Almendra and Manal, were considered staples. In addition, by the early 1970s, magazines like *Pinap* and *Pelo* catered to their followers.

Andean/Caribbean nations followed a similar pattern, largely related to Anglo culture and a certain degree of consumerism. In **Colombia**, cities like Bogotá and Medellín witnessed bands like Los Speakers, Los Flippers, Los Danger Twist, and Los Yetis, with the usual Spanish covers. In **Venezuela**, groups like Los Dangers and Los Impalas generated widespread interest. In **Peru**, Los Saicos proposed a different sound, more in line with alternative American and British bands. In **Chile**, bands like Los Rockets and Los Ramblers became household names.

Concerts were another key conduit for the popularization of rock. Though some bands performed in English, the overall effect was the endorsement of local language. Across the Americas, many versions of Woodstock were celebrated: in Argentina, it was Buenos Aires Rock (1971); in Mexico, Avándaro (1971); in Colombia, Ancón (1971). Amid widespread conservatism, concerts were portrayed as inconvenient events with enormous potential for societal instability.

The 1970s were problematic for *rock en español*. Few new stars managed to emerge, chiefly, Argentines like Charly García and Luis Alberto Spinetta, and the presence of authoritarian regimes across the hemisphere didn't help. Conversely, there was a working-class newcomer; punk arrived from abroad and posited itself as the alternative to lighthearted disco and *salsa*. In Peru, bands like Leusemia, Narcosis, and Zcuela Crrada joined a first wave of emulators. Most importantly, Argentina saw the arrival of Luca Prodan, the leader and founder of Sumo (1981), a seminal punk band of the Spanish-speaking Americas.

To a certain extent, repression acted as motivation for the revival of rock. Before the military, it was easy to conceive of rock as cultural resistance. A central case in point is the Guatemalan band Alux Nahual, born in 1979. Composed of classically trained musicians, it engaged in progressive rock and developed lyrics alluding to Mesoamerican conflicts. It also combined elements from Central America's native music heritage, gaining considerable popularity throughout the region. The band remained relevant until the late 1990s, when many political processes concluded with peaceful resolutions.

Amid military oppression, a particular circumstance proved highly influential: during the Malvinas/Falkland conflict, Argentine authorities outlawed the airplay of music in English, jumpstarting the resurgence of a nationally rooted rock. To comply with the ruling, many radio stations dusted off old copies of national recordings in Spanish, showing that society was willing to invest in nationally produced rock music in Spanish and support its integration into the mainstream. This brought about a change in the considerations of Argentine recording studios, which now recognized an economic opportunity.

In 1983, after Argentina's return to democracy, the trend intensified. The death of Franco in Spain brought about a rebirth of Spanish culture, with a tangible rock component. Groups like El Último de la Fila, Siniestro Total, Nacha Pop, Mecano, Alaska y Dinarama, and Los Toreros Muertos, many of which were marketed to the Americas, embodied the diversity of Spain's rock music. Even Chile, which struggled with Pinochet's legacy, managed to produce a groundbreaking band: Los Prisioneros.

By the mid to late 1980s, bands like Soda Stereo (Argentina), Enanitos Verdes (Argentina), and Hombres G (Spain) had toured much of the hemisphere with evangelizing fervor. In Mexico, record companies went to work immediately, coming up with acts like Caifanes and Botellita de Jerez. In most Latin American capitals, bands surfaced: in Venezuela, there was Sentimiento Muerto; in Colombia, Compañía Ilimitada, Pasaporte, and Hora Local; in Peru, Río and Miki Gonzales. Pent-up demand assisted groups that had toiled in the background for a number of years. In Mexico, Alex Lora's El Tri developed a faithful, solid following.

Music of this period reflects changing times: the end of the decade, with its dour monetary implications, and the opening of many economies. In the same open manner, labels supported a wide assortment of styles; hybridity became the norm. Though rooted in punk or ska, bands fused the backbeat with Latin music, from *huapangos* to *cumbia.* In many instances, *rock en español* defied description, with groups like Café Tacuba and Maldita Vecindad (Mexico), Aterciopelados (Colombia), Los Fabulosos Cadillacs and Divididos (Argentina), and Los Amigos Invisibles (Venezuela). In due course, record labels favored acts with successful pop appeal, like Maná, a band from Guadalajara. In addition, hip-hop and rap flourished through the subcontinent: in some cases, in places with little Afro visibility, such as Argentina, with Bersuit Vergarabat and Illya Kuryaki and The Valderramas, or Mexico, with Molotov and Control Machete; in other cases, in places with a strong African tradition, such as Cuba, with the group Orishas.

In the United States, a young Latino population represented a tempting market. With acts like Ricky Martin, Latinos gained presence in the media. Bands like **Puerto Rico's** Puya, with its mix of **salsa** and rap metal; California's Los Lobos, with its lengthy heritage; or even Carlos Santana, the guitar virtuoso of the 1960s, benefited from this new awareness of the Latin music market. In contrast, mainstream production in English reported dismal figures. In the early 2000s, there was a migration to independent labels. In Mexico, indie bands like Noiselab and Nuevos Ricos released innovative work. Electronic music, based on sampling techniques, is a determining factor for this development. The rise of the Internet influenced many bands, which learned to market their music without access to big multinationals. Bands like Sidestepper or the Instituto Mexicano del Sonido reflect the growing relevance of lounge music. The 2000s also saw the rise of a new kind of Latin American rock superstar, evidenced in global figures like Shakira and Juanes. Bands along the border between the United States and Mexico, like Ozomatli and El Gran Silencio, also continued to experiment and produce inter-generic recordings, catering to both the Latin American and U.S. market. In general, a better measure of the acceptance of music is the founding of a tradition of rock festivals like Vive Latino (1998–2010, in Mexico City), Rock al Parque (1995–2010, in Bogotá), Cosquín Rock (2001–2010, in Cosquín, Argentina), and Quilmes Rock (2002–2004, 2007–2010, in Buenos Aires). In this sense, *rock en español* has come of age. It is now fashionably acceptable and does not have to fight for a space. As means of cultural resistance, though, it has lost efficacy.

Further Reading

Arévalo Mateus, Jorge. "Rock en español." *Encyclopedia of Latinos and Latinas in the United States,* edited by Deena J. González and Suzanne Oboler, 29–31. Oxford: Oxford University Press, 2005.

Pacini-Hernandez, Deborah, Héctor Fernández L'Hoeste, and Eric Zolov. *Rockin' Las Americas: The Global Politics of Rock in the Americas.* Pittsburgh, PA: University of Pittsburgh Press, 2004.

Vila, Pablo. "Argentina's Rock Nacional: The Struggle for Meaning." *Latin American Music Review* 10, no. 1 (1989): 1–28.

Zolov, Eric. *Refried Elvis: The Rise of the Mexican Counterculture*. Berkeley: University of California Press, 1999.

Hector Fernández L'Hoeste

Romance

The *romance* is a Spanish narrative ballad that emerged from Spain in the 15th century and was brought to the Americas during the colonial period. The *romance* became one of the most popular song varieties in Spanish-speaking countries, and the genre has produced a lineage of indigenous and regional varieties throughout Latin America. The musical form of a *romance* is usually a strophic repetition of a series of verses (*coplas*) that tell of a legend, event, or a depiction of homeland as a topic. Throughout its history, the *romance* used a variety of verse forms, with the octosyllabic quatrain being the most common and widespread. Framing the series of verses that make up the *romance* are usually an introductory stanza that declares the topic of the narrative, and a closing stanza that bids farewell to the listener (*despedida*). Musically, the melodies and harmonies are relatively uncomplicated, and the accompaniment, usually played on the **guitar**, is also straightforward. The legacy of the *romance* can be found in **Mexico**, where it is known as the *corrido*, in **Colombia**, where it is known as the *copla,* in **Chile**, where it is known as the *tonada*, as well as **Venezuela**, **Argentina**, and **Uruguay**. Though largely a folkloric genre, some traditions have been successful in performing their repertoire of *romance*-based compositions to wider, and sometimes international audiences. In Mexico, the *corrido* also forms part of the *mariachi* repertoire, which has an international audience. Through the popularity of the folkloric movement beginning in the 1960s, Chilean *tonada* became a staple of successful performing groups like Los de Ramon. Similarly, *nueva canción* artists, such as **Violeta Parra**, wrote and performed *tonadas* as part of their repertoire.

Further Reading

Herrera-Sobek, María. *Northward Bound: The Mexican Immigrant Experience in Ballad and Song*. Bloomington: Indiana University Press, 1993.

George Torres

Rondador

The *rondador* is a member of the family of Andean Panpipes, primarily found in **Ecuador** (where it is considered the national instrument) and Northern **Peru**. The design of the *rondador* is a single-rowed, rafted series of pipes of differing lengths. The instrument, unlike the *siku* or the *antara,* whose pipes or tubes ascend in size across the instrument, the *rondador* pipes are laid out in an almost zig-zag with a seemingly irregular pattern. The tuning is pentatonic, but the tubes are laid out in such a way to allow the solo player to blow simultaneous intervals of thirds and fourths. The most common *rondador* has between 8 to around 30 tubes, but some larger varieties have as many as 44. Although Andean panpipes predate Columbus, it is believed that its tuning and preference for thirds developed with Spanish influence, and for that reason, it may be considered a colonial instrument. Unlike the *siku* and its ensemble, which often plays in groups, the *rondador,* like the *antara,* is played as a solo instrument. It is often accompanied by a chordal producing harmony instrument such as the **guitar**, **harp**, or **accordion**.

Further Reading

Schechter, John M. "Ecuador." *The Garland Encyclopedia of World Music, Volume 2: South America, Mexico, Central America, and the Caribbean,* 413–33. New York: Garland Publishing, 1998.

George Torres

Rondalla

The *rondalla* is a Latin American ensemble for voices and plucked strings and is a variant of the **estudiantina**, also known as *La Tuna,* which originated and is still largely popular in Spain. Like the *estudiantina,* the *rondalla* has its roots in fraternal student organizations, known for their perambulatory performances. The origins of these groups go back to the earliest formations of the university in Medieval Spain when wandering students would sing in the streets. Hence, the word *rondalla* is synonymous with street musicians. An additional association with *rondallas* is that they participate in *rondas,* or nocturnal *serenatas*. The instrumentation of *rondallas* varies among countries in Latin America. Some may include a mixture of plucked strings as in the traditional and regional Spanish *estudiantinas* that use **guitar**, *laúds*, and *bandurrias,* while more urban *estudiantinas* like those found in larger cities in **Mexico** may use an instrumentation of guitars, *requintos*, and double bass (when strolling, someone may be asked to carry the end pin of the double bass while the groups walk about). All of the instrumentalists are expected to sing, with the size of the group varying from half a dozen to as many as two dozen musicians. In concert, the *rondallistas* may stroll out on stage, and they may even have some choreography of dance steps prepared for their selections. The repertoire of the modern urban *rondalla* includes favorite regional songs as well as popular love ballads drawn from the *bolero* repertoire.

Further Reading

Morán Saus, Antonio Luis, José Manuel García Lagos, and Emigdio Cano Gómez. *Cancionero de estudiantes de la tuna: el cantar estudiantil de la Edad Media al siglo XX.* 1st. ed. Salamanca: Ediciones Universidad de Salamanca: Diputación Provincial de Cuenca, 2003.

George Torres

Rumba

Rumba is a folkloric percussive dance music originating mostly in Havana and Matanzas, though it is now practiced throughout **Cuba** and abroad. In English-speaking countries, it has historically been confused with Cuban *son* and anglicized by adding an *h* to the spelling (see *rhumba*). Since its beginnings during the end of the 19th century, *rumba* has had a great influence in popular Latin American music and has been carried worldwide by Cuban immigrants, especially to North America where it has been taken up by other nationalities. Originally for spontaneous community entertainment, it is now also performed by groups of professional *rumberos* and heard on studio recordings.

The word *rumba* does not necessarily carry one specific musical connotation. It could be used to refer to any jubilant music making, though it is usually associated with working-class **Afro-Cubans** and drumming. Early popular uses of the term can be found in mid-1800s performances of *zarzuelas* (light operas), though these probably sounded unlike what is now called *rumba*.

Today's *rumba* was mostly influenced by African drumming traditions and *coros de clave,* large popular choral groups accompanied by Cuban instruments. These came from similar Spanish groups but, by the end of the 19th century, they often used Afro-Cuban instruments and became known as *coros de guaguancó.* These groups included two song leaders, a large chorus, tacked-head drums or *cajónes* (box drums), *viola* (a stringless American banjo), occasionally *marimbula*, and small percussion such as *claves*. As the popularity of these groups declined during the early 20th century, smaller groups with fewer singers emerged resembling today's *rumba* groups.

Today, a number of drumming and dance styles exist that can be considered *rumba.* These include secular styles such as *guaguancó, yambú, columbia, jiribilla,* and newer forms such as *batarumba* and *guarapachangeo.* During the last half of the 20th century, *rumba* esthetics have also contributed to emerging religious practices such as *rumba de santo* and *cajón pa' los muertos.* All of these styles have grown out of the multiethnic and multireligious Afro-Cuban experience of postslavery Cuba, especially in predominantly poor, black neighborhoods.

Musically, all *rumba* styles share a nasal vocal quality, call-and-response singing, and the presence of at least three distinct drum parts. There are commonly three *tumbadoras*, given various names based on their role in the ensemble. The largest and lowest-pitched drum, called *salidor* or *llamador,* plays a specific rhythm and converses with the medium-sized drum called *tres dos, tres golpes,* or *segundo.* There is also a small, high-pitch solo drum usually known as *quinto.* Other percussion instruments include *claves*, *chekeré,* and *guagua* (two sticks that embellish the *clave* rhythm on a woodblock, piece of bamboo, or the side of a drum).

Rumba, especially in studio recordings, is usually in three sections. The first section, known as the *diana,* is an improvised syllabic exploration of the scale. The second section, known as the *inspiración* or *canto,* is a text sometimes based on the poetic ***décima*** structure. The third section, called the ***estribillo***, ***montuno***, or ***coro***, uses leader group alternation between the lead singer and chorus. It is during this section that the dancers are usually featured.

The three most common styles of *rumba* today all appeared by the final decades of the 1800s. The *yambú,* considered to be the oldest of these three main styles, is usually played on ***cajónes*** and has a slow tempo that allows the dancers to mimic the movements of the elderly. The fastest of these main styles is the *columbia,* which was likely influenced by the music of the Abakuá society due to its 12/8 meter and solo male dancing. By far, the most popular type of *rumba* is the *guaguancó.* It has a medium to fast tempo and its dance, unlike the other two forms, is characterized by the *vacunao* (vaccination), a symbolic gesture of sexual pursuit from the male dancer towards his female partner.

Folkloric *rumba* was first recorded during the mid-20th century and grew in popularity until reaching a plateau during the 1990s. This helped the success of groups such as Los Muñequitos, Grupo Afrocuba, Yoruba Andabo, Los Papines, and Clave y Guaguancó. It also increasingly influenced other popular Cuban and Latin American musical genres. Artists such as Ignacio Piñeiro, Beny Moré, Orquesta Aragón, **Machito**, **Tito Puente**, Mongo Santamaria, Los Van Van, and Irakere, among others, have based pieces on *rumba.*

Further Reading

Esquenazi Pérez, Martha. *Del Areito y Otros Sones.* Havana: Editorial Letras Cubana, 2001.

Moore, Robin. "The Commercial Rumba: Afrocuban Arts as International Popular Culture." *Latin American Music Review* 16, no. 2 (1995): 165–98.

Nolan Warden

S

Saint Lucia

Saint Lucia is an island in the Caribbean between the Caribbean Sea and North Atlantic Ocean, north of Trinidad and Tobago. The population of Saint Lucia is 82.5 percent black, 11.9 percent mixed, and 2.4 percent East Indian. Throughout its history, Saint Lucia has changed hands at least seven times between the English and the French resulting in a mixture of cultural influences on Saint Lucian music from both England and France, as well as the West African slave population. The popular music of Saint Lucia is also strongly affected by the neighboring countries in the Caribbean due to the shared French *Creole* language.

While there are many different types of folkloric music in Saint Lucia performed for all different religious practices and cultural events, *calypso* is at the forefront of Saint Lucian popular music. It has been popular throughout the country since the 1940s and it is through *calypso* (and later *soca*) that Saint Lucians make their social commentary. New *calypsos* are composed for **Carnival** each year and, as a result, *calypso* represents an ongoing narrative on the lifestyle in Saint Lucia. While American rock, **jazz**, *reggae*, and *zouk* are heard throughout Saint Lucia, *calypso* and *soca* are still by far the most popular genres of music spread throughout the country by local radio stations.

Further Reading

Guilbault, Jocelyn. "St. Lucia." In *The Garland Encyclopedia of World Music Volume 2: South America, Mexico, Central America, and the Caribbean*, edited by Dale A. Olsen and Daniel E. Sheehy, 942–51. New York: Garland Publishing, 1998.

Tracy McFarlan

Salsa

Salsa is a popular Latin dance music, which blends a wide variety of Latin American popular and folkloric forms (the music of **Cuba** being the most pronounced) with influences from **jazz** and American popular music. The accompanying dance is highly stylized and features couples executing fluid and intricate steps. *Salsa* developed in the Latino *barrios* (inner city neighborhoods) of New York City in the 1960s and 1970s, cultivated and performed mostly by Nuyoricans (Puerto Ricans born and raised in New York City). However, its international appeal spread

Salsa music star Ruben Blades plays the *maracas* with his band "Los Seis del Solar" in San Juan, Puerto Rico, in 2009. (AP/Wide World Photos)

quickly spawning a number of vibrant local scenes, most notably in **Puerto Rico, Colombia, Panama**, and **Venezuela**, and later in, Japan, in parts of Africa, and throughout Europe. *Salsa* (literally meaning sauce in Spanish) was a marketing label popularized by Fania Records in the 1970s, serving as an umbrella term for a diverse set of musical practices. This culinary metaphor was not foreign to Latin music performance and had played a role as a performative exclamation and esthetic trope for quite some time. Cuban musicians in the first half of the 20th century used the phrase *toca con salsa!* as a bandstand interjection, meaning "swing it." The title of Cuban composer Ignacio Piñeiro's famous *son* "Echale Salsita" ("put a little sauce in it"), written in 1933, aptly captures this type of usage. Most likely, *salsa* as a generic label stems from Venezuelan disc jockey Phidias Danilo Escalona, who launched a show in 1966 entitled "La hora del sabor, la salsa y el bembé" ("the hour of flavor, salsa and party") playing a variety of modern Latin dance musics.

Salsa, as a musical style, is rather easy to delineate since its performance practice is fairly standardized and has been rather stable since the 1970s. The instrumentation is derived from earlier Cuban ensembles and typically includes three to four percussionists (playing **congas**, **bongos**, *timbals*, a variety of **cowbells**, and hand percussion, such as **maracas**, **güiro**, and/or **claves**), a bass player, a pianist/keyboardist, two to six brass and wind instrumentalists, and a number of vocalists. With a few notable exceptions, *salsa* songs are sung in Spanish and the lyrics include a wide range of topics, such as love and romance, incitations of cultural pride, social commentary, and allegoric stories. There is no typical vocal type or quality preferred in *salsa*. However, stemming from older Cuban styles, high, tenor-ranged male voices with a nasal timbre still predominate. With the growing influence of popular music styles among younger *salsa* singers in the 1990s, many have emerged with a smoother, less nasal, pop-oriented crooning style. The basic formal structure of *salsa* arrangements is most often based on the bipartite form used in *son*, a Cuban genre popular throughout the middle of the 20th century where a main theme, which has a predetermined length, is followed by an open-ended improvisatory section known as the ***montuno***. *Montunos* employ call and response structures in which a lead singer improvises and alternates with a precomposed chorus. The *montuno's* most identifiable feature is a repetitive harmonic and rhythmic vamp. Several contrasting instrumental sections will interrupt this open-ended section. The first, derived from one of *salsa's* stylistic antecedents, is a precomposed section called the ***mambo***. The *mambo* is often characterized by heightened intensity and sound, where intricate and virtuosic horn writing is featured. Additional instrumental sections, called ***monas*** (literally meaning hair curl), follow and are collectively improvised by the horn section.

All musical and dance components in *salsa* performance are rhythmically organized by ***clave*** (literally meaning key, clef, or keystone), a rhythmic concept and organizing principle associated with **Afro-Cuban** musical traditions. In Latin music terminology, the word *clave* refers not only to an instrument (two wooden sticks), but also to the specific rhythmic patterns played on them and the underlying rules that govern these patterns. In performance, the *clave* may be overtly played or

Cruz, Celia

Known as "The Queen of *Salsa*," Celia Cruz (1925–2003) was one of the greatest female singers in the history of **Afro-Cuban** music. Cruz, a versatile artist, mastered many Afro-Caribbean music genres, drawing fans of all ages. Cruz recorded more than 60 albums, 23 of which sold more than half a million copies. All of her music was performed in Spanish. Growing up in Havana, **Cuba**, Cruz enjoyed singing and decided to pursue a singing career after winning a radio contest. In 1950 Cruz became lead singer of the orchestra La Sonora Matancera, performed with the group for 15 years, and toured around the world. In 1965, she launched a solo career with a band formed by **Tito Puente**. Although she recorded many albums during the late 1960s, Cruz did not garner large audiences in the United States until the *salsa* boom that emerged in the 1970s. During her career she collaborated with famous musicians like Johnny Pacheco, Willie Colón, Sonora Ponceña, and the Fania All Stars. Cruz won seven Grammys, a Smithsonian Lifetime Achievement Award, and two honorary doctorate degrees.

Further Reading

Márceles Daconte, Eduardo. *Azúcar!: The Biography of Celia Cruz*. New York: Reed Press, 2004.

Erin Stapleton-Corcoran

simply implied by the other instrumental parts. If adhered to in a competent fashion and felt collectively by all participants, the *clave* provides the rhythmic momentum, drive, and swing in *salsa*.

The emergence of *salsa* stemmed from the vibrant Latino communities that settled in East Harlem and by the effects the civil rights movement of the 1960s had on those communities. Many Latinos adopted similar modes of protest and organization spawning an unprecedented political fervor. A collective of young and innovative musicians began experimenting by combining traditional and folk musics with popular music and jazz, aiming to produce a uniquely Latino mode of musical expression that captured the sentiment of the times. The founding of Fania Records in 1964 by Johnny Pacheco and Jerry Masucci was key in transforming this new music into a commercially viable commodity. Their efforts resulted in *salsa* becoming an international phenomenon with the music being widely associated, especially with respect to *barrio* culture in New York City, with Latino essence in a way that is analogous to the word "soul" as a description for black American essence. The groups they produced included Bobby Valentín, Larry Harlow, Willie Colón, Hector Lavoe, **Ruben Blades**, Ismael Miranda, among others, and their productions featured a raw and driving urban street sound that later became known as *salsa dura* (hard *salsa*). The establishment of the Fania All-Stars in 1971, a collection of musicians consisting of bandleaders signed to Fania and highly regarded musicians, enabled the label to showcase all of their talent internationally while portraying a unified family of *salseros*. This notion of family extended beyond the musicians and was marketed to the communities to which they targeted their sales. This strategy capitalized on the newfound cultural pride being incited within Latino neighborhoods, as well as the calls for a unified Latino consciousness by these new political movements. Fania deliberately constructed *salsa* as an exclusively Latino cultural expression, a discourse that reverberated through the *barrios* swiftly transforming the fledgling company into an economic powerhouse.

In 1979 Fania closed, setting the stage for the emergence of a new *salsa* sound that would predominate through the end of the 20th century. In 1982 and 1983, Louie Ramírez teamed up with Isidro Infante to coproduce two recordings for K-tel Records, known as *Noche Caliente* that featured four up-and-coming *salsa* singers (José Alberto, Tito Allen, Johnny Rivera, and Ray De La Paz) singing popular Latin ballads in a *salsa* format. The arrangements toned down the hard-driving sounds associated with Fania and instead, featured milder and more tranquil sounds with highly polished, pop-influenced studio productions. The lyrics centered on topics of love and avoided images of *barrio* life and political issues. Moreover, borrowing from pop music, an artist's visual and sexual image became increasingly more important than his/her musical prowess. Record companies sought young, predominantly white or light-skinned, male singers with sex appeal. The words used to distinguish this style, *salsa-sensual, salsa-erótica*, and *salsa-romántica* reflected both the content of lyrics as well as images used to market these artists. A group of Puerto Rican singers, including Tito Rojas, Frankie Ruíz, Eddie Santiago, and Lalo Rodríguez, were also important in popularizing this new sound.

The proliferation of *salsa-romántica* was facilitated by the start of RMM Records in 1987, founded by Ralph Mercado. The turning point for his company came in 1989 when a young Nuyorican pianist named Sergio George took over a production for Tito Nieves, inflecting it with a unique blend of *salsa-romántica*, pop, and soul. The overwhelming popularity of that release, *The Classic,* propelled the team of Mercado and George to a dominant position in the New York *salsa* scene. By the early 1990s, RMM Records had effectively filled the void left by the closing of Fania records and was the largest and most influential Latin music record company in the *salsa* business. In 1994, they started the RMM All-Stars, modeled off the Fania All-Stars, which included the singers Jose "El Canario" Alberto, Tito Nieves, Tony Vega, Ray Sepulveda, Domingo Quiñones, Johnny Rivera, Oscar D'Leon, Ray De La Paz, La India and Marc Anthony.

George left RMM in 1996 to form his own record and production company, Sir George Records, and began experimenting further with **hip-hop**, rap, *reggae*, and *salsa* mixtures. DLG (Dark Latin Grooves) was his first project that proved highly influential. In 2000, RMM lost a copyright infringement suit and was forced to close. The absence of RMM records created another vacuum in the *salsa* scene, the effects of which still remain. Regardless, *salsa* dance competitions, studios, and dancing festivals continue to thrive worldwide and a number of bands from New York, the Caribbean, Latin America, Europe, Japan, and Africa continue to tour and perform.

Further Reading

Aparicio, Frances R. *Listening to Salsa: Gender, Latin Popular Music, and Puerto Rican Culture.* Hanover, NH: Wesleyan University Press, 1998.

Duany, Jorge. "Popular Music in Puerto Rico: Toward an Anthropology of Salsa." *Ethnomusicology* 5, no. 2 (1984): 186–216.

Gerard, Charley with Marty Sheller. *Salsa: The Rhythm of Latin Music.* Crown Point, Indiana: White Cliffs Media Company, 1989.

Manuel, Peter. *Caribbean Currents: Caribbean Music from Rumba to Reggae.* Philadelphia: Temple University Press, 1995.

Mauleón, Rebeca. 1993. *Salsa Guidebook for Piano and Ensemble.* Petaluma, CA: Sher Music Co.

Washburne, Christopher. *Sounding Salsa: Performing Latin Music in New York City.* Philadelphia, PA: Temple University Press, 2008.

Waxer, Lise. *Situating Salsa: Global Markets and Local Meanings in Latin Popular Music.* New York: Routledge, 2002.

Chris Washburne

Samba

Samba is a Brazilian music and dance genre with origins in Western European song forms and Central/West African rhythm. Though its roots can be traced to musical styles of the 18th and 19th centuries, *samba* was not recognized as a specific genre until the recording of "Pelo Telefone" in 1917. Though there has since been significant debate on the subject, it is generally agreed that the history of modern urban *samba* begins around this time. Today *samba* remains enormously popular throughout **Brazil**, especially in the largest cities of Rio de Janeiro and São Paulo, and is widely considered to be the country's national music.

As a musical genre *samba* is a very broad term, encompassing several subgenres that have emerged in Brazil since the beginning of the 20th century. Though *samba* has maintained its essential elements throughout its existence, numerous musical and instrumental innovations have been incorporated into the genre. From its roots in the music of enslaved Africans, to its hybridization in contemporary rock and **hip-hop**, *samba* continues to be hailed as the ultimate Brazilian musical expression.

The term *samba* is likely a variation of *semba,* the belly-bump dance of Congo-Angolan origin. The music's most fundamental rhythmic characteristics and its accompanying dance can also be traced directly to the Congo-Angola region of Central Africa, though it also borrows from the musical legacy of Yoruban West Africans. *Samba* is typically played in duple meter with a characteristic heavy emphasis on the second beat, usually played by the bass drum, *surdo.* Numerous other instruments, both percussive and melodic, play syncopated rhythmic variations. There are no absolute standard instrumental configurations in *samba,* as the music is played with a variety of instruments in different contexts. Certain instruments, however, like the Portuguese four-stringed ***cavaquinho*** (related to the ukulele), and the ***pandeiro*** (tambourine), are considered indispensable for *samba* to be played in its most popular format.

In small groups, the *cavaco* and ***pandeiro*** are usually accompanied by six- or seven-string ***violão*** (**guitar**), the ***surdo*** (bass drum), the *ganzá* (shaker), and the ***tamborim*** (a very small drum with no jingles, played with a stick—not to be confused with a tambourine). During the pre-Lenten **Carnival** parades, *baterias* (large drum ensembles) can consist of hundreds of percussionists that play a thunderous *sibatucada*. Additional instruments of African origin used in *samba* include the friction drum *cuíca,* and the *agogô* (a double bell of Yoruban origin). European instruments that are also commonly used in *samba* include the mandolin and various woodwinds and brass instruments.

The aforementioned first recorded *samba* was purportedly written at one of the musical gatherings that regularly occurred at the houses of the *tias baianas* (Bahian aunts, matriarchs of the Afro-Brazilian community) in the port district of Rio de Janeiro around the turn of the 20th century. The Little Africa district (as it is today called by historians) was centered in the growing shantytowns that began to mushroom as the result of migrants pouring in from throughout the country seeking work in the developing city. Though the migrants came from various parts of Brazil bringing with them their regional musical styles, a good majority came from the northeastern state of Bahia. For this reason, it is generally believed that urban *samba* has a significantly Bahian musical heritage, though it was born and raised in the city of Rio de Janeiro.

With the advent of radio in the 1930s, and Rio's primacy as the capital and cultural center of Brazil, *samba* emerged as the national music. In line with the government's nationalist agenda, *samba* provided a musical basis for the construction of a Brazilian national identity. Though dictator (later elected president) Getúlio Vargas's motives seemed to embrace the African heritage that *samba* embodied, Afro-Brazilian musicians remained largely in the shadow of dominant society. Radio stars, predominantly of European descent, sought original compositions from relatively unknown composers, paying meager sums for songs that became extremely successful commercially. By purchasing the songs, the singers were able to credit themselves as composers, only occasionally sharing the writer's credit with the actual composer of the songs. While their songs played successfully on the radio, many composers lived in relative poverty.

The predominance of Euro-Brazilian singers and self-proclaimed composers continued until the 1960s, when more Afro-Brazilian musicians began to emerge as artists and composers in their own right. Throughout this period, *escolas de samba* (*samba* schools) were increasingly emerging from the hillside squatter communities known as *favelas,* or more politely as *morros. Samba* schools are large community ensembles from the *morros* that parade during the yearly pre-Lenten celebrations of Carnaval. Many of Brazil's most revered *samba* composers, who were sought after by the radio stars looking to purchase their next radio hit, emerged from such community *samba* schools.

In the 1970s, *samba* experienced a golden age of commercial recording success with young artists like Paulinho da Viola, Beth Carvalho, Alcione, Clara Nunes, and Martinho da Vila achieving phenomenal record sales. Older artists such as Nelson Cavaquinho and Cartola, who had been previously known only by their famous compositions, recorded their debut albums in the 1960s. Conversely, with the increasing commercialization of the yearly Carnaval pageant, *samba* schools became increasingly gentrified, alienating community members. As the price of participating in a *samba* school's float came at a premium, the coveted spots were being taken by celebrities and wealthy patrons who otherwise had no connection to the communities that had nurtured the *samba* schools for decades.

By the end of the decade, a new generation of *sambistas* (samba practitioners) had left their beloved *samba* schools to form their own **blocos** (smaller, community *samba* schools, or blocks). Young musicians also began sharing new *samba* compositions in small gatherings that typically occurred in backyards or in small bars, reminiscent of the gatherings at the houses of the *tias baianas* at the turn of the century. One particular group from the Ramos suburb in Rio de Janeiro had created a new sound, with aggressive percussion and introducing several new instruments. Among the instrumental innovations was a banjo version of the *cavaquinho,* as well as handheld versions of *samba* school drums previously played with mallets and sticks. The new instrumentation revitalized *samba* as a fresh new sound deeply rooted in tradition. The Ramos musicians caught the attention of well-known recording artist Beth Carvalho, who then recorded with them on several of her albums. They eventually formed the collective Grupo Fundo de Quintal (The Backyard Band), initiating a successful recording career for the group as well as for several for the movement's original members.

After several highly successful albums by musicians from Ramos, the new sound was informally labeled *pagode,* named after the musical gatherings (*pagodes*) that gave birth to the movement. Soon after, the recording industry usurped the term, releasing hundreds of pop *pagode* bands, most with little or no connection to the original movement, fueling criticism from traditionalists. Today, there are hundreds of traditional *pagodes* throughout Rio and other major cities in Brazil. Participants gather around a table with musicians at the center singing an incredible repertory of *sambas* that date back to the beginnings of the genre nearly one hundred years ago.

Further Reading

Browning, Barbara. *Samba: Resistance in Motion.* Bloomington: Indiana University Press, 1995.

Galinsky, Philip. "Co-Option, Cultural Resistance, and Afro-Brazilian Identity: A History of the 'Pagode' Samba Movement in Rio de Janeiro." *Latin American Music Review* 17, no. 2 (1996): 120–49.

McGowan, Chris, and Ricardo Pessanha. *The Brazilian Sound: Samba, Bossa Nova, and the Popular Music of Brazil.* New edition. Philadelphia: Temple University Press, 2009.

Raphael, Alison. "From Popular Culture to Microenterprise: The History of Brazilian Samba Schools." *Latin American Music Review* 11, no. 1 (1990): 73–83.

Vianna, Hermano. *The Mystery of Samba: Popular Music and National Identity in Brazil.* Translated by John Charles Chasteen. Chapel Hill, NC: University of North Carolina Press, 1999.

Beto González

Sanfona (Acordeão)

Sanfona is the popular name in **Brazil** for the musical instrument known as **accordion** (*acordeão* in Brazilian Portuguese). *Sanfona* refers to either a piano accordion or a button accordion. The adjective *sanfonado,* meaning in the shape of a *sanfona,* has to do with the shape of the bellows: layers of folds that are responsive to squeezed air, as the word concertina in English. The bellows are known as *fole,* a male noun that can also designate any of the instruments in the accordion family. European immigrants introduced accordions in Brazil around 1836. By the time of the Paraguay War (1864–1870), they were diffused throughout the country. The first types were button accordions, also known as *pé-de-bode* (goat's foot) or *fole de oito baixos* (eight-bass accordion); they were customarily used to play instrumental music. This version of the instrument was very popular among lower class people, mainly in the Northeast region where it is in the roots of what is called the authentic ***forró*** music, the *forró pé-de-serra* (bottom-of-the-hill, hill's foot *forró*). In the 1950s, the piano accordion became the central instrument in the trio formation called ***trio nordestino***, created by Luiz Gonzaga (1912–1989). Gonzaga used the instrument to accompany vocal music with lyrics. Today, the university *forró* movement that began in São Paulo city, new groups searching for the roots of the genre, turned their attention to button accordions. One such group is the Mestre Ambrósia group, who feature one of their younger members, Hélder Vasconcelos, on the button accordion. Despite this, most young musicians are wary of the instrument, considering it to be old-fashioned, folkloric, difficult to play, and associated with old, unfashionable performers.

Some of the well-known accordion players in Brazil, past and present, are: Sivuca, Hermeto Paschoal, Oswaldinho do Acordeon, Waldonys, Camarão, Arlindo dos Oito Baixos, Renato Borghetti, Dominguinhos, Genaro, Flávio José, Targino Gondim, Raimundinho do Acordeon, Jorge Lunguinho (or Jorginho do Acordeon), Mário Zan, Pedro Sertanejo, Chiquinho do Acordeon, Enok Virgulino, Joca, Zé Gonzaga, Valdir do Acordeon, Luiz Gonzaga, and others.

Further Reading

Schreiner, Claus. *Música Brasileira: A History of Popular Music and the People of Brazil.* New York: M. Boyars, 2002.

Adriana Fernandes

Saya

Saya is the best known Afro-Bolivian music and dance genre and it is performed by singers and percussionists. In call-and-response style, solo vocalists alternate with a group, whose chorus is also referred to as *saya*. The percussionists play three types of drums. The *tambor mayor,* the largest and most prestigious drum, is used to play the basic duple pulse. Interlocking with this part, the *tambor menor* player adds triplets while the *gangingo* (also spelled *gangengo*) performer contributes with quick rolls on the smallest drum. A typical *saya* ensemble also includes a bamboo scraper (*guancha* or *cuancha*) and two types of bells (male and female *cáscabeles*), which the dance leaders wear on each leg.

Afro-Bolivians revived the almost extinct *saya* tradition sometime in the late 1970s or early 1980s. The genre became the main identity emblem for black Bolivians, largely through the efforts of the politically active Movimiento Negro (black movement). Around the same time, Bolivian youths of non-African descent began dancing the *caporal* in highland festivals wearing flashy outfits and accompanied by brass bands. *Saya* is often confused with *caporal,* a *mestizo* genre based loosely on Afro-Bolivian traditions. Bolivian musicians such as the superstar group Los Kjarkas have added to the confusion by labeling *caporales* as *sayas* (or *caporal-sayas*) on hit recordings. Afro-Bolivians have countered with their own recordings of the real *saya.*

Further Reading

Templeman, Robert Whitney. "We are People of the Yungas, We are the Saya Race." In *Blackness in the Americas,* edited by Norman Whitten and Arlene Torres, 426–44. Bloomington: Indiana University Press, 1998.

Fernando Rios

Schottische

Although the *schottische* derives its name from the German word for Scottish, its ultimate origins are contested; what is clear is that this quick, duple-meter dance form gave rise to a vibrant set of Latin American variants. While some scholars identify the *schottische* as rooted in 19th-century German and Bohemian round dances, others link it to the French *ecossaise,* a *contradanse* (country dance) dating back to the 1700s. All agree that by the mid-19th century versions of the *schottische* for couple dancers entered the repertory of the international ballroom dance fashion radiating from Paris. Like other ballroom dances, it was adopted around the world and acquired regional names.

In Spain, the *schottische* became the *chotis* (also *chotís, schotís, chote*), a signature dance representing cosmopolitan Madrid and a featured number in countless *zarzuelas*. In the 19th century, the *chotís* also circulated throughout Spanish-speaking regions of Latin America and the **United States** where it entered the repertory of popular instrumental ensembles performing social dance music and also became associated with rural popular music. In **Mexico** the *schottische* (*chote*) gained popularity during the reign of Maximilian. Reflecting this legacy, the *chote* enjoys continued popularity in ***mariachi*** repertory, in *música* ***norteña***, as well as in the folk music of Hispanic instrumentalists in New Mexico and southern California. Popular Mexican titles, such as *chote vaquero* and *chote zapatilla*, reflect the genre's regional and folk heritage.

In Portugal, the *schottische* became the *xote* (also *xótis, choutiça, xotiça,* or *scotish*), a name by which it was also cultivated in **Brazil**. In the mid-20th century in northeastern Brazil, the *xote* developed alongside the popular style known as ***baião*** and acquired elements of Afro-Brazilian syncopation. Although the rhythms of both dance types feature a characteristic dotted-8th, 16th-note motive, in the *xote* the 16th-note groups are typically swung or performed unevenly as in **jazz**, and the accompaniment parts enter on the upbeat. The *xote* is typically lighter and more romantic in character than the *baião*. Both are associated with the popular contemporary musical style known as ***forró***, played on electric **guitar**, bass, **accordion**, keyboards, and drums. Famous composers of Brazilian *xote* include the popular singer, composer, and accordion player Luiz Gonzaga (1912–1989), as well as his colleague Humberto Teixera (1915–1979). Since the 1980s, singer-composers Alceu Valença (b. 1946) and Geraldo Azevedo (b. 1945) have created rock-inflected *xote.*

In the United States, the *schottische* was also a popular genre for military band music and as such was included in instrumental music instruction in schools. Partly as a result of boarding school music training, Tohono O'odham American Indians living in Arizona and northern Mexico include *chotis* in their repertory of social dances collectively known as *waila:* instrumental dance music influenced by American band practices, northern Mexican fiddle bands, and by the accordion-driven *conjunto* music of northern Mexico.

Further Reading

Loeffler, Jack. *La Música de los Viejitos: Hispano Folk Music of the Rio Grande del Norte.* Albuquerque: University of New Mexico Press, 1999.

Medeiros, Flávio Henrique and Carlos Almada. *Brazilian Rhythms for Solo Guitar.* Pacific, MO: Mel Bay Publications, 1999.

Raices Latinas: *Smithsonian Folkways Latin Roots Collection* (compact disc audio recording). Smithsonian Folkways Recordings, SFW4070, 2002.

Sachs, Curt. *World History of Dance.* New York: Norton, 1965.

Stark, Richard. Liner notes for *Dark and Light in Spanish New Mexico,* compact disc sound recording of 1978 original. New World Records, 1995.

Sturman, Janet. "Movement Analysis as a Tool for Understanding Identity: Retentions, Borrowings, and Transformations in Native American Waila." *The World of Music* 39/3 (1997): 51–70.

Janet L. Sturman

Seis

The *seis* is a song and dance genre from **Puerto Rico**, and it represents the most important and largest body of *Creole* or *jibaro* music from the island. There are two broad categories of *seis:* one of dancing that is fast and lively, and a slower one for singing. The latter category is sometimes referred to as the *seis décima*. There are over 100 types of *seises,* and each one has its own distinct melody and may be named after the region from where it originated, the person who performed or popularized it, or the kind of music or choreography that it was modeled after. A typical *seis* ensemble will consist of one or two singers, two ***cuatros***, a **guitar, bongós**, and ***güiro***. The texts may be either memorized or improvised. In modern *seis* performance, the *cuatros* play an opening melody-harmonic sequence twice, played once in between the verses or stanzas, and twice again at the end as a concluding statement. Since the 1960s, the Instituto de Cultura Puertorriqueña has supported native musics, and this has resulted in a revival of ***jíbaro*** music. Groups such as Ecos de Borriquen, founded and directed by Miguel Santiago Diáz, have recorded and performed the *seis* repertoire throughout Puerto Rico and abroad.

Further Reading

López Cruz, Francisco. *La música folklórica de Puerto Rico.* Sharon, CT: Troutman Press, 1967.

"Seis Chorreao." *Puerto Rican Folkloric Dance.* Puerto Rican Folkloric Dance, Inc. 2009, last modified July 21, 2009, http://www.prfdance.org/chorreao.htm

Sheehy, Daniel. "*Jíbaro Hasta El Hueso Mountain Music of Puerto Rico by Ecos de Borriquen.*" *Jíbaro Hasta El Hueso Mountain Music of Puerto Rico.* Smithsonian Folkways Recordings, 2003, 3–30.

George Torres

Septeto

The *septeto* is a quintessential Cuban ensemble used to perform traditional ***son*** in urban areas. It developed in the second decade of the 20th century, as the result of the addition of a cornet or trumpet to the *sexteto*, an instrument widely used in **jazz** bands and a favorite for its timbre and improvisatory tendencies. The *septeto* formed a transition in the performance of *son* because, at its peak, certain instruments were added, which came to be considered traditional combinations and patterns in the performance of this musical genre. The musical repertoire of *septetos* comes largely from ***guaracha*** and other types of *son* that were popular during its peak. Some *septetos* assumed ***bolero*** as a key element; its dance style was expressed in the *bolero son* and *bolero soneado*.

From the *sexteto*, the *septeto* borrowed the *son* language's outline and basic form. The *septeto* was initially composed of a **guitar**, ***tres***, **bongós**, ***maracas***, sticks and a ***marimbula***, *botija* or counter bass (*contrabajo*). At a certain point in its development, the substitution of the *marimbula* for the counter bass was definitively established in septets, and this change, along with the addition of the aforementioned trumpet, contributed to the increase of its expressive and sonorous possibilities.

The *tres* is the defining feature of the ***tumbao*** of each piece and at the same time provides the melodic function that can be improvisatory and free while the *tres* performs a melodic and harmonic function. The *marimbula* or the *botija* support and give color rather than contribute to the harmonic function, which is later performed by the counter bass. In terms of the percussion, the *maracas* and the sticks provide stability for the tempo while the *bongo* plays a steady **marcha**, which is at times enhanced by enriched patterns and improvisatory moments within the form. In this way, the typical timbre levels of the *son* genre were established.

The first *septeto* to include a trumpet was recorded in 1927 by the Sexteto Habanero but it may have been used in other situations, such as at balls. In fact, evidence of its presence in *sextetos* can be found prior to 1927, as in the case of the Matanzas-based orchestra Botón de Oro, and the Sexteto Oriente, both of which had used the additional trumpet since 1924. Another orchestra, the Enrizo, used the clarinet in recordings as early as 1926. Other later additions to the genre include the piano and **conga**. The first record with a piano was made by the *son sexteto* Gloria Cubana in 1925. The first recording with *congas* dates back to 1936, when **rumba** player Santos Ramirez included percussionist Vidal Bolado in his **Afro-Cuban** *sexteto*. Other *sextetos,* such as the Mikito, added both the piano and the *congas,* together or independently, and continued their own evolution within the style in the 1930s. All this would later contribute to the creation of the orchestra in the 1940s.

The *septeto* ensemble still exists today and has brought recognition to several key players in Cuban popular music, such as the Septeto Habanero and the Septeto Nacional Ignacio Piñeiro, among others. Many modern orchestras have resumed and re-created the septet. These include Sierra Maestra and Jóvenes clásicos del son in Havana, and the Septeto Turquino in Santiago de Cuba. It is important to note that the *septeto* helped to define the urban *son* typical of the western region through the work of the Septeto Nacional Ignacio Piñeiro, directed by Ignacio Piñeiro. The performance of this group epitomizes the synthesis and interaction of the *son* with other genres of Cuban music. Their first pieces brought together *rumba, son, guajira,* and elements of **trova** to set the standard for future *septetos* and ensembles.

Further Reading

Davies, Rick. *Trompeta: Chappottín, Chocolate, and the Afro-Cuban Trumpet Style.* Lanham, MD: Scarecrow Press, 2003.

Gerard, Charley. *Music from Cuba: Mongo Santamaria, Chocolate Armenteros, and Cuban Musicians in the United States.* Westport, CT: Praeger, 2001.

Robbins, James. "The Cuban 'Son' as Form, Genre, and Symbol." *Latin American Music Review (Revista de Música Latinoamericana)* 11, no. 2 (Autumn–Winter 1990): 182–200.

Neris González and Liliana Casanella

Septeto de Son. *See* Septeto.

Serenata

Serenata is a type of musical performance popular in parts of Latin America, notably **Mexico, Guatemala**, and **Colombia**, that is intended as a gift or offering to one's beloved. Traditionally it is done when a man hires a small group of musicians to perform at night or early morning outside of his sweetheart's residence, preferably under her bedroom window.

In places where the genre of performance is popular, the man will hire musicians in advance and arrange the details of time and location, as well as which selections the group is to perform. In some cases the man will sing while the group accompanies him.

The purpose of the event is to wake the partner up with music that is special to her and symbolic of the couple's romance, or songs that they have enjoyed together in their courtship. The woman wakes up and listens from inside her room, and if it pleases her, she will open the window and look out at her loved one, thus showing her approval.

Musically, this type of performance often uses the genre of *boleros*, with their themes of romantic love, and a common instrumentation is the *trío romántico* consisting of two guitars and a *requinto*. Some songs from the repertoire that have the *serenata* as their theme, and are thus favorites for this type of musical event, include "Despierta" by Luis Luna, "Serenata sin luna" by Jose Alfredo Jimenez, and for birthdays, "Las Manianitas."

Further Reading

Sheehy, Daniel E. *Mariachi Music in America: Experiencing Music, Expressing Culture.* New York: Oxford University Press, 2006.

George Torres

Seresta

The *seresta* is a Brazilian romantic love song that is closely related to the **modinha** and attained prominence during the 19th century. So synonymous is the *seresta* with the *modinha* that composers have used the term interchangeably so that the musical differences between the two are indistinguishable. The word *seresta* means serenade in Portuguese, and so the *seresta* has an association with music for outdoor activities, or performances. The instrumental accompaniment at the turn of the 20th century, which was the core accompanying ensemble for popular *serestas*, was the same as for the *modinha* and consisted of **guitar**, wooden **flute**, and *cavaquinho*, a combination referred to as either a *terno* (trio) or *pau e corda* (wood and string). While the *modinha* was a favored genre among elite social groups, the *seresta* was looked upon with some degree of scorn, probably because of its associations with street musicians. Nevertheless, the *seresta* was an important part of love song

Anotonio Carlos Jobim playing his guitar. Jobim recorded a popular version of Heitor Villa-Lobos's "Seresta #5: Modinha" on his 1987 album *Inédito*. (AP/Wide World Photos)

performance in late 19th and early 20th century performance, and composers today still use the term as a nostalgic tribute to a tradition of sentimental song from the past, for example, Baden Powell's *Seresta Brasileira* album from 1988. **Antonio Carlos Jobim** recorded a popular version of Heitor Villa-Lobos's "Seresta #5: Modinha" on his 1987 album *Inédito,* and more recently, on his *UFO Tofu* album from 1992, Bela Fleck recorded "Seresta," composed by fellow bandmate, Howard Levy.

Further Reading

Livingston-Isenhour, Tamara Elena, and Thomas George Caracas Garcia. *Choro: A Social History of a Brazilian Popular Music.* Bloomington: Indiana University Press, 2005.

George Torres

Sesquiáltera

From the Latín *sesquialter, sesquiáltera* refers to the ratio of three and two. In music, the *sesquiáltera* or *hemiola*, literally *seis que altera* (six that alternate), is a combination of groupings of two or three pulses played by the same instrument within melodic lines, or simultaneously by different instruments within an ensemble as if a melodic instrument plays in 3/4 meter and a rhythmic instrument in

6/8 meter. Both meters have the same number of beats although they are arranged differently due to the accents in those beats within a measure (accents in a 6/8 measure subdivide in two and accents in a 3/4 measure subdivide in three). It alternates between duple and triple meter as if musicians were combining 6/8 and 3/4 meter.

According to Arturo Chamorro, the *sesquiáltera* rhythmic feature was present in the old Spanish dances called *zaranbandas* or *sarabandes* that were introduced into Spain by the Moors. According to Rolando Pérez Fernández, the *sesquiáltera* is the result of the binarization process of some African ternary rhythmic patterns.

Sesquiáltera occurs frequently in many folkloric Latin American musical styles that use a triple meter organization or time signature, such as the Argentinean *chacarera*, Bolivian and Chilean *cueca*, Venezuelan *joropo*, etc. It is especially present in the overall rhythmic organization of Mexican *sones* and it contributes to their rhythmic intricacies.

Further Reading

Chamorro, Arturo. *La herencia africana en la música tradicional de las costas y las tierras calientes.* Zamora, Michoacán: El Colegio de Michoacán, 1951.

Pérez Fernández, Rolando. *La música afromestiza mexicana.* Xalapa, Veracruz, México: Editorial UV, 1990.

Stanford, Thomas. "The Mexican Son." *Yearbook of the International Folk Music Council* 4 (1972): 66–86.

Raquel Paraíso

Sexteto. *See* Septeto.

Sexuality in Latin American Music

Two important characteristics of Latin American music are dance and sexuality, which together represent the importance of expressive rituals in Latin American culture. Though it has no prechoreographed movements, dance in Latin America is a combination of decentralized moves, and dense, polyrhythmic figures to act out the roles that each gender plays. It is sensual, expressive, and in some cases erotic. The dance floor is where flirting takes place, and sexuality comes to life in dances such as the **bachata**, *champeta*, **reggaetón**, **cumbia**, **axé**, *punta*, **mambo**, and **tango**. Music is the companion to these Latin American dances and is the medium through which the dancers communicate. Intertwined syncopated rhythm flow together with fast spins, footwork, and ula-ula-hips based to create a combined interpretation of the social role that each dancer plays. Sexuality is not understood as a one-dimensional dialogue, but as a multidirectional communication between a partner, a role, and rhythm, which is why music is such an important part of Latin

American social events. The stylish and thematic elements of music are fundamental to dance. The conception of timbre and tone unfold in rhythm, modes, and pitch, creating different movements that allow the dancer to innovate his or her own choreography.

Such an assemble, in which each gender repeats motives whose constancy circumscribes to a specific space, shapes the traditional standard of simultaneously combine repetition and change, which elaborates diverse rhythmic patterns performed by pairs. Consequently, rhythmic patterns create variations in the body movements that intensify in order to reach a climax, where the compatibility reached by the couple will increase the sensuality and eroticism of the dance.

Individuals identify with the stories that are sung as they dance, which creates a connection between listening and moving that is a unique cultural distinction. As a result, the subject matter of songs is very important. They often describe elements of everyday life such as social classes, feelings, and emotions between men and women. Some tell the story of important people such as, "Pedro Navaja," "Micaela," and "Vivir lo nuestro." Others relate to relationships like "Ironía," "Me faltas tú," "Así es la vida," and "Contra la Corriente." In this context, dance and music are an escape valve for repressed emotions that cannot be freely expressed in daily life because of the confines of society. The body expresses the yearning to escape in the form of steps, gestures, visages, and uncountable dance figures that are often sexual, sensual, and erotic. Lyrics express themes that turn to music as means of recounting essential aspects of society.

Dancing in Latin America is provocative and sensual because it is meant to show interest as a form of greeting and flirting. Such games of seduction can be seen in *reggaetón, champeta, mapalé,* and **soca** where the couple looks for a connection with their bodies. In *bachata, tango,* and *cumbia,* the woman uses displacement to test the perseverance of the man in pursuit of conquest. This conquest develops a struggle between both sexes that seek to establish equality.

As a result of these themes, music and dance are also symbols of national identities that play an ideological function as a struggle that belies the illusion of national consciousness of equality. The body is the object used to transmit sensations, much like a group of people that yearns for liberty through the recollection of tradition. This socialized form recalls the superiority of collectivity over individuality where the national identity is heterogenous. The rhythmic movement rests on the acknowledgment of others on the dance floor, and the capacity of the musicians to follow the art of dancing with the way of playing. Improvisation is the integration of society in this game, ignoring completely the implicit division between the conceptual dichotomy of body and mind. Sexuality in music, under the influence of cultural parameters, is a natural aspect of the human condition that has a tight connection with nature and its processes of birth, growth, and reproduction. Music is the way used by musicians to set rules that accompany the act of dancing as matters of recreation.

Dance simply reveals the sexuality that is already a part of Latin American music. The music was not composed to be only heard; movement is also demanded as the body cannot help but respond to the beats and rhythms.

Further Reading

Beezle, William H. and Curcio-Nagy, and Linda Ann. *Latin American Popular Culture: An Introduction*. Lanham, MD: Scholarly Resources, 2004.

Chasteen, John Charles. *National Rhythms, African Roots: the Deep History of Latin American Popular Dance*. Albuquerque: University of New Mexico Press, 2004.

Fraser, Celeste, José Delgado, and Muñoz, Esteban. *Every Night Life: Culture and Dance in Latin/o America*. Durham, NC: Duke University Press, 2004.

Moreno Fraginals, Manuel. *Africa en América Latina*. México D.F.: Siglo veintiuno editores, S.A. de C.V., 1996.

Rivera, Quintero. *Ángel G. Cuerpo y cultura: las músicas 'mulatás y la subversión del baile*. Mexico, DF: Bonilla Artigas editores, S.A. de C.V., 2009.

Walker, Sheila S. *African Roots/American Cultures: Africa in the Creation of the Americas*. Lanham, MD: Rowman & Littlefield Publishers, Inc., 2001.

Tatiana Flórez-Pérez

Siku

Siku is the Aymara term for a panflute made of multiple vertical reed pipes. Tubes are closed at the distal end and they are held together by one or two thin strips of cane or other materials. The instrument has two rows of pipes, each with a variable number of tubes that can range from two or three to eight or nine. Tubes have different lengths and diameters, placed from small to large in a row. The sound is obtained by blowing air across one of the open ends of the pipe. Traditionally, the *siku* is played in interlocking or alternating fashion, literally sharing a melody between two players. The two rows of the *siku* are called *ira* or male, the one that leads, and *arca* or female, the one that follows.

Siku or *zampoña,* the Spanish term for the instrument, receives different names according to the musical style or the geographical location where it is utilized. Among the various types of *sikus,* we can mention the *sicus de italaque,* which have an extra row of pipes that acts as resonators; *ayarichis,* which only have one row of pipes with resonators; *tabla sicus,* made of pipes that continue after the closed end finishes, the *moroa* or panflute used by the Moré people in the Beni region of Bolivia, and so on.

Traditionally, *sikus* are played collectively in large groups or tropes of 30 or more players who use *sikus* of different sizes. Panpipes are very common throughout the Andean regions in South America, although different variants of panpipes can be found in other parts of South America, Africa, and Australia.

Further Reading

Baumann, Maz Peter. "Music and Worldview of Indian Societies in the Bolivian Andes." In *Music in Latin America and the Caribbean: An Encyclopedic History.* Volume 1: *Performing Beliefs: Indigenous Peoples of South America, Central America, and Mexico,* edited by Malena Kuss, 101–121. Austin: University of Texas Press, 2004.

Turino, Thomas. "Local Practices among the Aymara and Kechua in Conima and Canas, Southern Peru." In *Music in Latin America and the Caribean: An Encyclopedic History.* Volume 1: *Performing Beliefs: Indigenous Peoples of South America, Central America, and Mexico,* edited by Malena Kuss, 123–43. Austin: University of Texas Press, 2004.

Valencia Chacón, Americo. *El Siku o Zampoña. The Altiplano Bipolar Siku: Study and Projection of Peruvian Panpipe Orchestras.* Lima: Centro de Investigación y Desarrollo de la Música Peruana: Artex Editores, 1989.

Raquel Paraíso

Soca

Soca is a style of popular music that emerged in Trinidad and Tobago in the early 1970s. It represents the latest phase in the development of **calypso** music, a song form that has two primary roles in Caribbean culture: as musical accompaniment for **Carnival** and other festivals, and to provide a platform for sociopolitical commentary and critique. During the past 40 years, *soca* has become the dominant form of dance music during Trinidad and Tobago's annual Carnival. *Soca* is crucial to the annual Crop Over Festival in Barbados, and Carnival celebrations throughout the West Indies. The Caribbean diaspora in North America and the United Kingdom also embraces *soca* as a key symbol of homeland and there are many Carnival celebrations around the world in which *soca* music is a prominent feature.

The development of the *soca* sound, and the name of genre, is frequently attributed to the calypsonian Lord Shorty (Garfield Blackman, later Ras Shorty I) and his musical arranger, Ed Watson. Shorty expressed the desire to blend East Indian and African rhythms, suggesting to Ed Watson that he add East Indian percussion instruments, particularly the *dholak* and *dhantal* of Hindu folk and popular music, to his musical arrangements. Shorty called his new style *sokah* in order to emphasize the East Indian contribution. Responding to negative criticism, Shorty asked Watson to transfer the East Indian rhythmic patterns to the drum set, iron, and *congas* of the calypso rhythm section. Watson also foregrounded the bass **guitar**, Hammond B3 organ, and electric **guitar** in musical arrangements, which gave the music a sound and energy similar to 1970s funk and *reggae*. The result was the album *Endless Vibrations,* which was released in 1974. Journalists changed Shorty's spelling from *sokah* to *soca,* further making a connection between soul and calypso, and the new spelling became standard.

Although initially resistant to Shorty's innovations, older calypsonians such as The Mighty Sparrow (Slinger Francisco) and Lord Kitchener (Aldwin Roberts) realized the popularity of the *soca* sound, and wrote compositions in the new style. One of the most successful *soca* songs during this early period was Lord Kitchener's "Sugar Bum Bum," arranged by Ed Watson, and released in 1978. Thanks to the large populations of West Indians in North American cities such as Toronto and New York, and in the British Isles, *soca* quickly came to international attention. The best-known *soca* song of the 1980s was "Hot Hot Hot," recorded by the singer Arrow (Alphonsus Cassell), who was from Montserrat. The song was later brought to the attention of American audiences by the novelty singer Buster Pointdexter (David Johansen). This success opened the way for other artists in foreign markets, and encouraged the emergence of *soca* music scenes in various countries in the Caribbean, North America, and the United Kingdom. Notable performers who became popular during the 1980s include David Rudder, the Mighty Shadow (Winston Bailey), Baron (Timothy Watkins), and Super Blue (Austin Lyons).

By the early 1990s, *soca* had become the most common form of music in Carnival fetes and the preferred form of music to accompany masquerade bands on Carnival Monday and Tuesday. A turning point occurred when Super Blue (Austin Lyons) developed an energized form of *soca* featuring faster tempos, instructions to dancers, shorter call-and-response vocal phrases, and melodic hooks. This is the jump and wave music that came to dominate Carnival dance music. Throughout the 1990s, further experimentation created new variations on *soca* music. Jamaican dancehall had gained enormous popularity among Trinidadian youth during this time. This led to the development of *ragga soca,* which is characterized by a slower tempo and vocal delivery that is similar to dancehall *reggae.* Among the primary proponents of *ragga soca* have been Ghetto Flex (Hilton Dalzell), Denise Belfon, Maximus Dan (Edghill Thomas), Bunji Garlin (Ian Alvarez), and KMC (Ken Marlon Charles). *Chutney soca* also emerged during the same decade and has paved the way for greater visibility of Indo-Trinidadian musical artists. These include Rikki Jai, Sundar Popo, Drupatee Ramgoonai, and Ravi B. (Ravi Bissambhar).

Along with Trinidad and Tobago, *soca* music plays a significant role in Carnival-like celebrations in most English-speaking Caribbean islands, including Barbados, Grenada, St. Vincent and the Grenandines, Antigua, and Barbuda. *Soca* music is popular in the French Antilles, particularly **St. Lucia** and **Dominica**, and was an influence on the development of *zouk* in **Martinique** and **Guadeloupe**. Since the 1980s, *soca* music has also found success outside the West Indian market in North America and the United Kingdom. Some hit songs include the aforementioned "Hot Hot Hot," "Tiney Winey" by Byron Lee and the Dragonaires, "Dollar Wine" by Colin Lucas, "Follow the Leader" by Soca Boys (originally recorded by Nigel and Marvin Lewis), and "Who Let the Dogs Out" by Baha Men (originally sung by Anselm Douglas). In general, *soca* has become a dominant form of dance and party music in the Caribbean and is an important symbol of identity for West Indians today.

Further Reading

Dudley, Shannon. *Carnival Music in Trinidad.* New York: Oxford University Press, 2004.

Guilbault, Jocelyne. *Governing Sound: The Cultural Politics of Trinidad's Carnival Musics.* Chicago: University of Chicago Press, 2007.

Rohlehr, Gordon. "Calypso Reinvents Itself." *Culture in Action: The Trinidad Experience,* ed. Milla Cozart Riggio, 213–27. New York, Routledge, 2004.

Hope Smith

Son (Cuba)

Son cubano is the most important of the many popular music genres that originated and developed in **Cuba** during the 20th century because of its deep penetration into nearly every aspect of musical culture within Cuba, its vast international dissemination and popularization, and its immense impact on Latino popular dance music. The genre, which gave birth to or heavily influenced a multitude of genres, including *mambo*, *rhumba*, *charanga*, **boogaloo**, *salsa, songo, timba*, and **Latin jazz**, is often described as the first invented by Cubans and as the common denominator in almost all of Cuban music. Emerging from the rural areas of *el Oriente,* Cuba's eastern provinces, particularly around Santiago de Cuba and Guantanamo, during the late 19th century, the original manifestations of *son* (the qualifier *cubano* is added only to distinguish the genre from Mexican *sones,* such as *son jalisciense* or *son huasteco*) consisted of a constant alternation between the improvisations of a solo singer and a short composed refrain sung by a small group. As the genre became increasingly urbanized, an additional structural element, an initial closed song section, was added, thereby solidifying the binary form that it retains to this day, the *tema* or *son,* a 32-bar song—usually in AABA form—followed by the *montuno*, which is usually much longer than the *tema* and consists of extended instrumental solos (called the *descarga*) and short precomposed horn sections (the *mambo* or *yambú*) as well as call and response vocals (called the *guajeo* and the *coro* or *estribillo*, respectively).

This binary structure is an example of the *son* representing a mix of European- and African-derived elements, the *tema* being derived from the European song tradition while the call-and-response *montuno* has strong African antecedents. This combination exhibits itself in other elements of the genre, including the instrumental ensemble, where European-based plucked stringed instruments, such as the **guitar** and the *tres* (a Cuban invention consisting of three sets of double strings), play alongside African-based percussion, such as the *bongó* (also a Cuban-invented instrument), and the ***marimbula***, a bass instrument derived from the African thumb piano, the *mbira.* The singing, predominantly black and mulatto musicians singing about Afro-Cuban *barrio* life in a smooth European-based *bel canto* style, and the dance, a combination of a European-derived couples dance with African-derived rhythmic steps and movements, also exemplify this mixture of influences.

The confluence of cultures embodied by *son* would lead to its adoption as an important marker of an emerging Cuban national identity that began developing in the decades following Cuba's independence from Spain in 1902 and that sought to unite the entire country, black, white and *mulatto.* This process began with the genre's introduction in the capital city of Havana around 1909, brought by immigrants from *el Oriente* serving obligatory terms as soldiers of the permanent army, a practice that led to mass urbanization during this time. The early *son* ensembles were ***tríos***, consisting of **guitar**, ***tres***, and ***maracas***, with at least two of the musicians singing, exemplified by Trío Matamoros, which was founded in Santiago in 1912 by Miguel Matamoros and would reach its height of popularity in the 1920s and 1930s, and Trío Oriente, a group formed within the army before 1910, which would, once its members moved to Havana, add a *bongocero,* effectively transforming itself into a ***cuarteto***. While the practice of *tríos* and ***cuartetos*** performing at dances and parties was brought from *el Oriente,* other performance practices emerged in Havana after *son*'s introduction. These include the publication, in the form of sheet music, and recording of *sones* and the development of *coros de son,* choral groups of 18 to 20 singers, in Havana *barrios,* the groups often being associated with a particular *barrio.*

The development of *son* as a marker of national identity continued in the early 1920s when the genre became popular throughout Cuba, spurred in part by the increasing availability of record players, more affordable records, and the introduction of regular radio broadcasts on the island in 1922. *Tríos* and *cuartetos* were playing at parties thrown by some of the richest white families in Santiago by around 1920, but the elite in Havana was slower to embrace the genre. In 1924 "you couldn't play *son* in Havana yet," according to Matamoros. In fact, with the exception of their hugely popular "El son de la loma," Trío Matamoros was playing exclusively ***danzónes*** in their performances in the capital. The genre's general acceptance by Havana's largely white upper class would not be solidified until the 1926 appearance of Sexteto Habanero, a *son* group consisting of black musicians, at the presidential palace in Havana at the invitation of *mulatto* President Machado.

Son's continued popularity in Havana in the 1920s also led to increased urbanization and sophistication within the genre to accommodate for larger, more cosmopolitan audiences. The *son cuarteto* was soon eclipsed by the *sexteto,* which added ***claves*** and ***marímbula*** (later replaced by the stringed bass), and the ***septeto de son,*** which added a trumpet. Recordings by the leading exemplar of this format, Ignacio Piñeiro's Septeto Nacional, and Sexteto Habanera became popular throughout Cuba and abroad. This international dissemination eventually led to the emergence of New York and Paris as important centers for performance and recording by Cuban musicians and to contact between *son* and **jazz** musicians, which would affect both genres greatly over the ensuing decades. The immediate effect on *son* was the integration of more complex, jazz-influenced harmonies, faster tempos, and the development of a more percussive, rhythmic sound.

The event that served as a catalyst for the popularity of Cuban music worldwide was the 1931 release of Don Azpiazú's ground-breaking recording of "The Peanut Vendor," an arrangement of the Moisés Simón-penned *son-pregón* "El manicero" (derived from the calls of street vendors in Havana), which, while it had no connection or similarity to the Cuban genre *rumba*, was given the name *rhumba*. The record was a massive nationwide hit in the United States and triggered a *rhumba* craze on Tin Pan Alley, on Broadway, and in Hollywood, where in the hands of American songwriters and musicians it became diluted and Americanized, even though its exoticism was one of the main reasons for its popularity. The most prominent figure in popularizing *rhumba* was the Spanish-born and Cuban-bred Xavier Cugat. Cugat, who, in addition to recording and touring appeared in a number of Hollywood films, made no claims to the authenticity of the music he was playing, preferring to point to it as a way of introducing Americans to Latin music.

In Cuba, *son* continued to develop and exert great influence throughout the 1930s and 1940s. Its capacity for hybridization led to the development of genres such as *bolero-son, son-guaguancó,* and even *blue-son* and its popularity and influence permeated Cuban music to the extent that **charanga** bands—flute and violin orchestras that had, to that point, mainly been playing *danzónes* and *boleros*—began including *sones* in their repertoire and, in accordance, incorporating more rhythmic elements into their music. The *son* ensemble continued to grow, with *tres* player, arranger and composer **Arsenio Rodríguez** taking the step of adding **congas** to his band in 1938. Rodríguez, along with Conjunto Casino, would be a guiding force in the development of the genre. The inclusion of *congas* was followed by the addition of piano and a second trumpet, forming a new ensemble, dubbed a *conjunto sonero*. In addition to, and perhaps because of the expanded format, arrangements became increasingly regulated, including the incorporation of precomposed trumpet parts and a standardization of the accompaniment patterns played by the rhythm section. In the process, the *son* gave up some of its informal, collective looseness.

The 1940s also saw the development of *mambo,* a combination of Afro-Cuban rhythms and big band jazz, the development of which is alternately attributed to Rodríguez in Cuba, **Pérez Prado** in **México**, the West Coast of the **United States**, and **Machito** and Mario Bauzá in New York. The genre began as an expansion of the *mambo* section, the horn-driven section of the *montuno* in *son* and incorporated elements of *son,* including the common use of ostinato patterns in the saxophones adapted from the *tres* patterns of *son.* The subsequent *mambo* craze in the United States during the early 1950s was paralleled in Cuba by *conjunto sonero*'s period of greatest popularity, attributable in part to the introduction of television to the island. This popularity was led by artists such as Beny Moré—a singer who, after working with many groups including Trío Matamoros and Prado's orchestra, led his own group, Banda Gigante, which incorporated *mambo* elements into *son*—and La Sonora Matancera, which featured a four-trumpet horn line and a succession of singers that included Daniel Santos and a young **Celia Cruz**.

Son fell out of official favor after the 1959 revolution, being derided by the Castro government as a vestige of the decadent Batista regime. However, variants on the genre, including the ***changüí*** from Guantanamo, remained popular in the rural areas of the Oriente. Meanwhile in New York, bands that had been playing *charanga* and *bugalú* (a mix of Afro-Cuban rhythms with rock 'n' roll that served as a survival technique for *mambo* groups in the wake of the latter genre's vast popularity) turned to the *conjunto sonero,* spurring what was called a *típico* revival in the mid-1960s. This revival was partially the result of the influence that **Arsenio Rodríguez**, who had relocated there from Cuba in 1950, was having on the local music scene, and of appearances in the city by La Sonora Matancera.

Around this same time, a brasher, rawer version of *son,* dubbed *salsa* in order to obscure its Cuban origins, was being embraced by Nuyoricans as a musical expression of their ethnic identity in light of the new social consciousness that was seizing the racially volatile urban areas of the United States. This new style was exemplified by Willie Colón, a Nuyorican teenager who led a band featuring a trombone section in the place of the standard trumpets and represented himself as *el malo* (the bad boy), the image reflecting the alienated energy of the barrio. ***Salsa*** would go on to attain popularity in many parts of Latin America and be seen by many as the foremost expression of Latino music in the 1970s, becoming a symbol of pan-Latino identity in the process.

During the 1970s, the dual trends of experimentalism and traditionalism typified *son* in Cuba. The decade's experimental movement was preceded by the formation of Los Van Van in 1969, led by Juan Formell, bass player and former musical director of Orquesta Revé, a *charanga* that specialized in *changüí* and incorporated experimental elements, such as the inclusion of an expanded set of *timbals*, trombones, and *batá* drums. Los Van Van, also a *charanga,* infused *son* with elements from rock, rhythm and blues, jazz and Brazilian music, including the addition of electric guitars, synthesizers, and a drum set, and abandoned traditional standardized rhythmic patterns in the bass and piano, naming the new hybrid ***songo***. Following in this same vein was singer-songwriter Adalberto Alvarez's group, Son 14. The leaders of the movement toward traditionalism were *tres* player and former rock guitarist Juan de Marcos González, who formed Sierra Maestra along with future ¡Cubanismo! founder Jesús Alemañy in 1976 with the goal of keeping the torch of the great *septetos* alive for a younger generation, and guitarist and singer Eliades

Ochoa, who took over the leadership of Cuarteto Patria, a group that had existed since the 1940s, in 1978.

In 1988, former Los Van Van and Irakere flutist José Luis "El Tosco" Cortés formed NG (Nueva Generación) La Banda, a group that combined *songo* with funk and rap influences, spawning the new genre ***timba***. With NG La Banda, El Tosco's aim was to combine the flavor of Los Van Van with the musical aggressiveness of the Latin jazz giants Irakere. *Timba* continued its popularity into the mid-1990s, when the *son* of the *conjuntos soneros* of the 1950s was given unexpected and unprecedented exposure and popularity at an international level with the 1997 release of *Buena Vista Social Club*. Begun by musical director and organizer Juan de Marcos González and producer Ry Cooder, the American guitarist, as a tribute to the artists of the past, the album went on to sell four million copies, win a Grammy Award, and spawn international tours, a host of solo albums by musicians featured on the original recording, and an Academy Award–nominated documentary.

While Cooder insists in his liner notes to *Buena Vista Social Club* that "this music is alive in Cuba, not some remnant in a museum that we stumbled into," director Wim Wenders's documentary posits the endeavor as a salvation project, not merely of the careers of singer Ibrahim Ferrer and pianist Rubén González, both of whom had retired from performing, but of the genre. Wenders focused the attention of the film on the older musicians, such as Ferrer, González, Pio Leyva, and Compay Segundo (whose participation was secured only after he returned to Cuba from an international tour) and gave much screen time to the white American Cooder—who has always downplayed his role in the recordings—while almost completely ignoring the original impetus of the project, the black Cuban Juan de Marcos González. *Buena Vista Social Club* and its many offspring served to fuel a roots movement among musicians in Cuba and nostalgia for an imagined pre–Castro Cuba in the United States that dovetailed with the retro-lounge trend of the late 1990s and with a more sympathetic and open attitude toward Cuba on the part of both the Clinton government and a good portion of the American public.

Further Reading

Cooder, Ry, Nick Gold and Nigel Williamson. Liner notes, *Buena Vista Social Club*. Nonesuch Records 79478-2, 1997.

Manuel, Peter with Kenneth Bilby and Michael Largely. *Caribbean Currents: Caribbean Music from Rumba to Reggae*. Philadelphia: Temple University Press, 1995.

Olsen, Dale A, and Daniel E. Sheehy. *The Garland Encyclopedia of World Music: Volume 2*. New York: Garland Publishers, 1998.

Public Broadcasting System. "Interview with Juan de Marcos González," last modified August 17, 2003, http://www.pbs.org/buenavista/musicians/bios/demarcos_edited_int_eng.html.

Public Broadcasting System. "PBS presents Buena Vista Social Club," last modified August 17, 2003, http://www.pbs.org/buenavista/film/index.html.

Robbins, James. "The Cuban *son* as Form, Genre, and Symbol." *Latin American Music Review,* 11, no. 2 (December 1990): 182–200.

Roberts, John Storm. *The Latin Tinge: The Impact of Latin American Music on the United States.* 2nd ed. New York: Oxford University Press, 1999.

Rodríguez, Olavo Alén. "Cuba." *The Garland Encyclopedia of World Music, vol. 2— South America, Mexico, Central America, Central America and the Caribbean.* New York: Garland Publishers, 1998.

Rondón, Cesar Miguel. *El Libro de la Salsa.* Caracas: Impreso por Editorial Arte, 1980.

Steward, Sue. *¡Musica! Salsa, Rumba, Merengue, and More.* San Francisco: Chronicle Books, 1999.

Ramón Versage Agudelo

Son (Mexico)

Son is a secular folkloric music genre that originated in rural **Mexico** from a fusion of Spanish, African, and indigenous music. The term *son* (Spanish for tune or sound) usually refers to a string-dominated genre of *mestizo* music, but can also be applied to certain indigenous and folk melodies.

Regional Styles

The use of the word *son* for rural folk music comes from a colonial distinction made between *música* (formal, harmonically complex music of the church and court) and the more derogatory *son* (tunes passed by oral transmission). Since the late 18th century, most *sones* have a compound meter and a rhythmic drive appropriate for social dancing; audiences and professional dancers often contribute foot-stomping *zapateado* patterns to emphasize rhythmic shifts. This music is performed by groups of 3 to 12 instrumentalists, many of whom sing *décimas* (verses of ten lines) arranged in *coplas* (couplets).

The modern *son* has developed into several regional styles, differentiated by instrumentation, singing style, repertoire, and use of language. *Mestizo son* traditions include the **son jalisciense** (from the lowlands of Jalisco and Colima), the brisk **son jarocho** (from Veracruz), *son arribeño* (from the Sierra Gorda), **son calentano** (from the Balsas River basin in southern Mexico), *son de arpa grande* (from western Mexico), and the popular trio-based **son huasteco** (adapted from the Huastec people). *Mestizo sones* are usually structured around partly improvised *versos* (sung poetic stanzas) alternating with instrumental interludes.

In contrast, Indian or indigenous *sones* tend to consist of one or two short melodic phrases, performed instrumentally and repeated at length. Indigenous Mexican *son* traditions include the *son abajeño* (from the Purépecha people in Michoacán) and the bilingual **son istmeño** (from the Zapotecs in Oaxaca).

African Influence

By 1580, the African population in New Spain outnumbered the European population, and African Americans played a major role in *mestizaje* (Spanish for the cultural amalgam resulting from the mixing of races). They were active in the official musical activities of the colony; the choir of the Oaxaca Cathedral included professional African American singers throughout the 17th century, and even an African American choir director (by 1648). In spite of laws designed to limit cross-cultural interaction, syncretic religious festivals existed as early as 1669, including African Americans and indigenous people playing local percussion instruments like the *huehuetl* and singing songs for dances accompanied by harps, guitars, and drums; these were precursors to later *son* and *jarabe* gatherings. Modern *sones jarochos* still show discernible African influence through complex polyrhythms and responsorial singing style. **Harp** trios in Veracruz often feature African American musicians.

Castas and Banned *Sones*

During the Spanish colonial period, Spaniards developed complex *castas* (a system of castes based on race). Both the *Peninsular* (Spaniard born in Spain) and the *Indio/India* (indigenous person) could be a recognized member of an aristocracy, but *Indios* were legally treated as minors. The term *Negro/Negra* referred to people of sub-Saharan African descent, but quickly divided into groupings that recognized mixed ancestry (including *Zambos*—African/indigenous; *Mullatos*—Spanish/African; *Mestizos*—Spanish/indigenous; and *Pardos*—Spanish/African/Indian). *The* term *Criollo/Criolla* referred to a person of Spanish descent born in the New World and was historically applied to both white and black nonindigenous persons born in the Americas.

The first written records of the *son* in Mexico were documented by the Inquisition and have been collected in the *Ramo de Inquisición.* In 1766, an early example of *son jarocho* named Chuchumbé became the first Mexican song to be banned (it depicts soldiers and friars fighting to seduce women). Particularly popular among the *mestizos* and *pardos,* many of whom served in the Spanish army, Chuchumbé was performed in the port of Veracruz by vulgar people and sailors, and to young ladies in Mexico City with illustrative obscene gestures. The rhymed text for the *tonadilla* (folk melody) ridiculed the authorities; they issued an edict banning its "lascivious *sones* and obscene *coplas.*" The dance encouraged physical proximity of bodies (*abrazos y dar barriga con barriga*/touching belly to belly) and of racial groups (*de gente de color quebrado . . . soldados, marineros . . .*/of people of broken color . . . soldiers, sailors . . .). Four trials resulted in excommunications for performing or witnessing the *son*. It was not legal to destroy copies of the text, as the inquisitors collected them for use as evidence.

By 1787, the organist of Xalapa Cathedral had been denounced for playing the Chuchumbé tune during mass, and many people were reprimanded for singing new (less offensive) *coplas* to the original *tonadilla*. A 1779 document from Zacatlán preserves 40 early verses, beginning with the following two *coplas: En la esquina está parado/ Un fraile de la Merced/ Con los abitos alzados/ Enceñado el chuchumbé* (On the corner is standing/ A friar from the Merced/ With his habit raised up/ Showing his chuchumbé) and *Esta vieja santularia/ Que va ibiene a San Franco/ Toma el Padre, daca el Padre/ Y es el Padre desus hijos* (This saintly woman/ Who comes and goes to St. Francis/ The Father gives, the Father takes/ And he is the father of her children).

While the spirited, humorous tone of the *son* was muted as it entered the musical mainstream, many *coplas* with *doble sentido* (double meaning) have been preserved. In modern times, *son* texts might draw from oral tradition, be improvised, or be published by professional song composers. Contemporary texts show self-conscious expressions of pride in a city, state, or region. Older *coplas* include archaic word usage*, poetic rural imagery+, and folk wisdom^. An example is the following, from the *son* "El Pasajero":

> Yo vide* pelear un oso+/ Con una garza morena+
> Que siendo el hombre vicioso/ Aunque la suya esté buena
> No hay bocado más sabroso/ Como el de la casa ajena^.

> I saw a bear fighting/ With a dark heron
> For a man who is licentious/ Even though what he has is good
> There is no morsel more delicious/ Than that from another house.

Bandas *populares* (civilian brass bands) were introduced to northwestern Mexico in the 1800s; they maintained a repertoire of folk *sones*. Independence from Spain and the decline of ecclesiastical influence brought Mexican secular music to greater prominence. *Sones* associated with political insurgence were honored as symbols of national identity, and the early 20th century brought the first recording of the Mexican *son* (Chicago, 1908).

As *mariachi* groups began to record and tour, the introduction of the modern guitar replaced traditional instruments such as harps. By the 1930s, traditional repertoire featuring *son jalisciense* expanded to include *son jarocho* and *son huasteco* (requiring more violins and replacing the harp with the **guitarrón**, a large, deep-bodied, six-string bass), identifiable by nostalgic migrants. At that time, *banda* (woodwind and brass) musicians in Sinaloa played a similar repertory of popular tunes and regional *sones*.

Musical Style

Most *sones* have a competitive aspect, with improvised rhyming *coplas*. *Son arribeño* is particularly known for textual innovation. Many of the tunes come from 16th-century Spain, and new improvised texts follow the typical octosyllabic form. Indigenous forms of *son* incorporate, alternate, or replace Spanish texts (*sones istemeños* are sung in both Zapotec and Spanish). Some *canciones* interpolate a section of *son* structure. *Sones abajeños* are often played in alternation with *pirekaus*, a form of native love song from Michoacán.

Son is typified by a complex triple or compound meter, with a chordal string instrument (guitar or harp) playing one distinct rhythm while the bass stringed instrument (*guitarrón* or harp) emphasizes a contrasting pattern.

Instrumentation

The guitar and violin are present in most varieties of Mexican *son*. *Son arribeño* and *son hausteco* retain small trios. Indigenous *son* performers often include traditional instruments such as *ocarina, caracol*, and *flauta de tres hoyes*. *Son huasteco* and *huapango* employ falsetto singing and focus on vocal and textual improvisation.

Some *sones* employ percussion, such as those from Tixtla, which require a *tapeador* tapping on a board in a wooden box; the *son jarocho,* which employs a *quijada* (donkey jaw) and *pandero* (wood frame tambourine); and the *son calentano Balsas,* which combines one or two violins, one or more guitars, a *tamborito* (small double drum), and competitive dancing performed on a wooden *tarima* (platform). *Son calentano* also has the most complex violin music, and *son de arpa grande* is dominated by a harp.

The *son jarocho* shares the rhythm and high vocal timbre (but not falsetto) of the *huapango;* typical instruments include the percussive harp and *jarana*, a small, deep-bodied rhythm guitar. In southern Veracruz, there is still a discernible indigenous presence, and the *sones* of that region are played more slowly and employ different sizes and tunings of *requinto* and *jarana* guitars. The *son calentano* from the Tepalcatepec river basin is notable for a 36-string harp struck with the palm of the hand, accompanied by two violins, a *vihuela*, and a guitar with two courses of strings. As *mariachi* groups evolved, this instrumentation was transformed by replacing the harp with a *guitarrón*, enlarging the number of violins and guitars, and including trumpets.

Conjunto groups who perform *sones* have a wider variety of plucked strings, including *bajo quinto* (*mixteco*), ***bajo sexto*** and double bass (***norteño***), *leona* (*jarocho*), and *huapanguera* (*huasteco*). Modern *mariachi* groups and *banda* groups include brass instruments, clarinets, saxophones, **accordians**, and even electric instruments.

Further Reading

Llerenas, Eduardo, Enrique Ramírez de Arellano, and Baruj Lieberman, producers. "The Son," in liner notes to Antología del Son de Mexico. 3 Compact Discs. Mexico: Corason, 1985.

Sheehy, Daniel. "Mexico." *The Garland Handbook of Latin American Music.* New York: Garland, 2000.

Sheehy, Daniel. "The Son Jarocho: The History, Style, and Repertory of a Changing Mexican Musical Tradition." Ph.D diss., UCLA, 1979.

Stanford, E. Thomas. *El Son Mexicano.* Mexico: Fondo de Cultura Económica, 1984.

Laura Stanfield Prichard

Son Calentano

The *son calentano* is a type of Mexican *son* from the geographic area in south central **Mexico** known as Tierra Caliente. The region includes some areas through the states of Michoacán, Guerrero, and Mexico (Estado de Mexico). The *sones* from this region can be broadly distinguished as two types: the *son calentano* from Balsas, and the *son calentano* from Tepalcatepec.

The *sones* from Balsas come from the basin of the River Balsas and include parts of Michoacán and Guerrero. The repertoire, consisting mostly of *sones,* is performed on one or two violins, one or more **guitars**, and a little double-headed drum called a *tamborito*. Occasionally one sees a ***guitarrón*** playing the bass function in the ensemble. One of the great interpreters of this style was Juan Reynoso Portillo (1912–2007) from Altamirano Guerrero, who late in his life performed extensively throughout the country and became a national treasure. Prior to Reynoso, the repertoire from this area seldom left the region.

The *sones* from the Tepalcatepec region come from the basin of the Tepalcatepec river in Michoacán. The repertoire, also consisting mostly of *sones,* is performed on one or two violins, an ***arpa***, and a selection of guitars, including *guitarra de golpe* and *vihuela*. The percussion role that was provided by the *tamborito* in the *sones* from Balsas, is, in Tepalcatepec *sones,* provided by the harp's soundboard, usually played by another player or tamborero. Several groups from this area have gone on to make recordings that have circulated beyond the region. Notable among these groups is Los Campesinos de Michoacán, which now resides and performs in the **United States**.

Further Reading

Llerenas, Eduardo, Enrique Ramírez de Arellano, and Baruj Lieberman, producers. "The *son,*" in liner notes to *Antología del Son de Mexico.* 3 Compact Discs. Mexico City: Corason, 1985.

George Torres

Son cubano. *See* Son (Cuba).

Son Guatemalteco (Son Chapín)

The *son guatemalteco* is a dance and music genre of **Guatemala**. It has its origins in the Hispanic cultures, and it is performed and celebrated among the Ladino population. It is also known as the *son chapín* (*chapín* is a nickname for a Guatemalan). The *son guatemalteco* is the national dance of Guatemala, and is usually accompanied by Guatemala's national instrument, the ***marimba***, or by a group of vocalists with guitars known as a *zarabanda*. The repertoire of *sones* represents a vast complex of regional varieties, resulting in a variety of performance practices. For example, a performance of the *son guatemalteco* in remote rural areas would likely use the earthy sounding *marimba de tecomates* (gourd *marimba*), while an urban performance in Guatemala City might make use of the *marimba doble* (double *marimba*) ensemble (usually four players on two *marimbas*), with an added bass and drum set. Like the Mexican ***son***, the majority of *sones guatemaltecos* make use of ***sesquiáltera***, though some examples of the *son guatemalteco* use duple or irregular meters. It is a couples dance where the performers use much ***zapateado*** (foot stomping), and it is performed in a moderate to rapid tempo.

Further Reading

Navarrete Pellicer, Sergio. *Los Significados De La Música: La Marimba Maya Achí De Guatemala.* 1st ed. México: CIESAS, 2005.

George Torres

Son Huasteco

The *son huasteco* is a ***son***-based, traditional Mexican musical genre that comes from the Huasteca region of Northeast **Mexico**, usually performed in a trio format, with the ***huapango*** as its primary form. Although traditionally a folkloric form, the *son huasteco* has become internationally popular through the touring groups of the *ballet folklórico* and also through the recordings and performances of professional groups such as Los Camperos del Valle.

The Huasteca region comprises portions of the states of Tamaulipas, Hidalgo, Veracruz, San Luis Potosí, Querétaro, and Puebla. The urban *son huasteco* is a stylization of the folk *huapango* and was among the mix of musical styles that arrived with the enormous migration of people to Mexico City in the 1940s to 1950s.

Unlike their rustic predecessors, commercial *huapangos* are written by known composers and sung in a slow tempo, often in bel canto style wherein the falsetto breaks are exaggerated into extended solo or group passages. Moreover, the additive, strophic form of the traditional *huapango* is modified or forsaken to incorporate sectional song form with a clear dramatic climax and definitive sense of closure. The *huapangos* of urban trios were widely disseminated by and inextricably associated with the mass media: a few Huastecan musician-composers, Nicandro Castilo in particular, were successful in creating a style of *son huasteco* that appealed to urban audiences. José Alfredo Jiménez, who in the 1950–1960s wrote hundreds of successful songs, composed many modern *sones huastecos* that have become standards in the *mariachi* repertoire. This early trio repertory enjoyed market popularity until the 1960s, when they were overwhelmed by the sentimental *balada romántica*.

Son huasteco is marked by three traits: the use of falsetto leaps to adorn the vocal melodies, a focus on ornate violin playing as the lead melodic instrument, and distinctive 6/8–3/4 **sesquiáltera** (hemiola) rhythm, in which the downbeats are consistently muted and unstressed. This rhythmic shifting can also be found in the **son jalisciense**, but the *huasteco* style incorporates both major and minor keys. Traditional versions were performed by a trio of musicians playing a violin, a **jarana** *huasteca* (small five-stringed Mexican guitar), and a *huapanguera* (*guitarra quinta*, a deep-bodied Mexican guitar with a larger resonator and eight strings (five courses of two single and three double strings), and the form has been expanded by *mariachi* groups.

The violinist adapts the role of the harp in *son jarocho*, playing flamboyant, highly syncopated melodies, improvising during interludes between the sung verses, and striking the golpe, a staccato downbow strike at the frog of the bow, usually followed by a crisp strum pattern on the guitars.

One or two guitars accompany in a strumming (*rasgueado*) style, with the *huapanguera* player occasionally adding single-string countermelodies. This style is usually based in triple meter with a *mánico* extended over six beats. The *mánico* incorporates ornamentation sometimes referred to as *redoble* with an 8th-16th-16th figure, with two down-strums and a third up-strum, on the first beat of the second measure. In effect, the 16th notes have doubled a space where the eighth note might have been executed. One of the better known *son huastecos* to highlight this strumming style is "La Malagueña" ("The Woman from Málaga").

The vocal style includes brief, ornamental breaks into falsetto. *Quintillas* and *sextillas* (five- and six-line *coplas*, respectively) are favored. Singers often improvise texts appropriate to the performance situation. The singing of the *copla* typically involves certain patterns of repeating lines of the *copla* that allow fuller vocal treatment of the text and time for the singer to compose improvised *coplas*. Typical *sones huastecos* featuring falsetto breaks include "Cielito lindo," "La Rosa," "La Azucena," "El Llorar," "El Toro Sacamandú," "El Gusto," and "La Huasanga."

The *son huasteco* shares several elements with the *son jarocho*: the leading melodic role of the violin or **harp**, the incorporation of rhythmic dancing (**zapateado**) on a hard floor (*tarima*), and roots in the Spanish *fandango*. These elements blend to make the forms poignant expressions of regional *mestizo* identity. During the revolution, political *sones huastecos* such as "El Soldado de Levita" were composed and adapted for radio plays.

Further Reading

Azuara, C. *Huapango: el son huasteco y sus instrumentos en los siglos XIX y XX.* Mexico, 2003.

Carter Muñoz, K. "Que siga el huapango! Reclaiming the Décima and Political Commentary in Son Huasteca and Arribeño and 'La Leva's' Re-Signification in Mexican Rock." MA Thesis, University of Washington, 2006.

Florencia, Pulido, and Patricia del Carmen. *Crónica histórica del huapango huasteco veracruzano: trovas, musica, danza y tradiciones.* Xalapa, Equiz: Gobierno del Estado de Veracruz, Secretaria de Educación y Cultura, 1991.

Geijerstam, Claes. *Popular Music in Mexico.* Albuquerque: University of New Mexico, 1976.

Manuel, Peter. "Formal Structure in Popular Music as a Reflection of Socio-Economic Change." *International Review of the Aesthetics and Sociology of Music* 16/2 (1985) 163–80.

Martínez Hernández, R. *Fiesta en la Huasteca: una Mirada a la huapangueada, los sones, la poesía y las danzes tradicionales de mi tierra.* México, 2005.

Nevin, Jeff. *Virtuoso mariachi.* Lanham, MD: University Press of America, 2002.

Saunders, Lawrence. "The Son Huasteco: A Historical, Social, and Analytical Study of a Mexican Regional Folk Genre." MA Thesis, UCLA, 1976.

Strachwitz, Chris. *Music of Mexico, Vol. 3: La Huasteca; Huapangos y Sones Huastecos; Los Caimanes y Los Caporales de Panuco.* El Cerrito, CA: Arhoolie Records CD431, 1995.

Laura Stanfield Prichard

Son Istmeño

Son istmeño is a variety of the Mexican **son**. It is heard throughout the entire region of Tehuantepec in the southeast state of Oaxaca, although it is also cultivated in the bordering communities of Chiapas. The traditional instrumentation is generally **guitar**-based, with one or two guitars, a **requinto**, and sometimes a *bajo quinto*. In some regions, it is not uncommon to use the **marimba** and an electric bass and drum set. The repertoire is in triple meter, more akin to the Mexican **vals** than to other more syncopated *sones*. Nevertheless, one still hears elements of cross rhythms between 3/4 and 6/8, reflecting the traditional **sesquialtera** so typical of the Mexican *son*. Melodically and harmonically, the repertoire exhibits more tonal than modal composition, having more tonic dominant cadences. The vocal style is also more lyrical than the traditional, more rural examples of *son*. The vocal part is often performed as a **duo** with vocal harmonies in thirds and sixths. Occasionally the texts of the *istmeño* repertoire will be in the Zapotec idiom, with some versions being translated in performance to Spanish. The genre is the principal type of the region, and the Oaxacan people claim it as their own. Important songs from the repertoire include "La Zandunga" and "La Llorona."

Further Reading

Llerenas, Eduardo, Enrique Ramírez de Arellano, and Baruj Lieberman, producers. "The *son,*" in liner notes to *Antología del Son de Mexico*. 3 Compact Discs. Mexico City: Cora-son, 1985, 5–7.

George Torres

Son Jalisciense

The *son jalisciense* is a *son*-based, traditional Mexican instrumental and vocal genre that comes from the subtropical lowlands in the states of Jalisco and Co-lima. Although traditionally a folkloric form, the *son jalisciense* is the most widely known of Mexican *sones* through its performance by *mariachis*.

The *son jasciliense* has a typical major mode harmonic structure. It is character-ized by a 12/8 rhythmic pattern with *contratiempos* (fluctuations of stress) in the melody and *maniocs* (strumming patterns). Some of the oldest *sones* of this type are very difficult to play and depart from the 12/8 meter: they are rhythmically com-plex, with ornate *manico* patterns for the stringed instruments and 3/4–6/8 musi-cal ambiguities. One important *manico* of this type is the *caballito* (little horse): it creates a distinctive galloping sound by grouping strums into threes (two down and one up), with a harsh accent on the second of three beats. This emphasizes a 6/8 feeling, whereas the simpler *manico pajero* or simple up-and-down strumming brings out a 3/4 rhythm. Vihuela players sometimes reverse the *pajero* stroke by starting to strum up on a strong beat, so this variation can be referred to as *manico pa'rriba* (up) or *manico pa'bajo* (down).

Mariachi holds the unique status of the national music of Mexico and is an ur-banized genre that originated in the regional *son jalisciense* string ensembles of the western states of Colima and Jalisco. From the earliest *mariachi* recordings in 1908 in Chicago, the accompaniment to this *son* was one or two violins, a *vihuela,* perhaps a *guitarra de golpe* and a **harp** (later replaced by the **guitarrón**). Around this time, the devastating introduction of the six-stringed guitar began to drown out more subtle traditional instruments such as the harp and caused the violins to at-rophy. After the Mexican Revolution of 1910, the *son jalisciense* was featured by Mexican presidents for official and political functions. Trumpets were introduced into the *son jalisciense* in the 1920s and became standard by the late 1930s. This genre of *son* dominates Mexican sound films of the 1930–1940s and established the traditional core of the *mariachi* repertoire.

Most *sones jaliciensces* are strophic songs, beginning with an *entrada, verso,* and **coro**. Witty and flirtatious four-line *coplas* alternate with a simple chorus (*Ay sí sí, ay no no*) or with melodically fixed instrumental interludes. The *coro* section may be presented responsorially (between a soloist and group) or as a separate refrain. The final section reprises a shortened version of the *entrada*. Melodic lines are usually doubled at the major third, and **sesquiáltera** (fluctuations in the way a 6/8 pattern is accented) provides restless unpredictability to the beat. "La Negra" is a familiar example of this style, and other *mariachi sones* in this style include "La Culebra," "El Carretero," "Camino Real de Comina," and "El Triste."

The lyrics of *sones jaliscienses* frequently focus on country life: in particular, the plants, animals, and people of the region. These lyrics are highly suggestive, often using imagery of the courtship of farm animals to describe the relations of women and men. The traditional dance technique associated with both the *son jalisciense* and the *son jarocho* is the **zapateado**, a distinctive style of footwork that originated in Spain. The rhythms created by the dancers' heels are often syncopated against the main melody of the *son,* and upper body movements often represent the images and farmyard courtships described in the *coplas* for each verse.

The *son jalisciense* is closely related to the *son michoacano* (which often adds percussion instruments such as wooden log drums made of the ceiba tree) and to a lesser extent to other Mixtec *sones* throughout the territory stretching from southern Sinaloa to Guerrero.

Further Readings

Fogelquist, Mark. "Rhythm and Form in the Contemporary Son Jalisciense." M.A. thesis, UCLA, 1975.

Nevin, Jeff. *Virtuoso mariachi.* Lanham, MD: University Press of America, 2002.

Sonnichsen, Philip. *Mexico's Pioneer Mariachis, Vol. 1: Mariachi Coculense de Cirilo Marmolejo, plus Several Sones by Cuarteto Coculense: the Very First Mariachi Recordings from 1908.* El Cerrito, CA: Arhoolie Records CD7011, 1993.

Vázquz Valle, Irene, series director. *El Son del Sur de Jalisco.* Vols. 1, 2, 18, and 9. Mexico: Instituto Nacional de Antropología e Historia, 1976.

Laura Stanfield Prichard

Son Jarocho

The *son jarocho* is a variety of the Mexican **son**, as it is practiced and performed in the *jarocho* region of southern Veracruz, **Mexico**. It is a song and dance tradition that is easily recognizable by both its sound and its visual manifestation of regional material culture. Although the music originated from a folkloric tradition, *sones* from the *jarocho* repertoire have migrated beyond the region to enjoy widespread popularity.

As a folkloric idiom that eventually crossed over to the popular sphere, the performance practice among ensembles was established in the middle of the 20th century when notable *jarocho* musicians Lino Chavez and Andres Huesca began making commercial recordings. It was their ensembles in particular, Conjunto Medellin and Los Costeños, that were responsible for the professionalization of the *jarocho* sound; both made recordings for the RCA Camden label in the 1940s and 1950s. The ensembles hence became an emblem of regional identity and their inclusion in major cultural festivals in Mexico and abroad, as well as a prominent place in the programs of Mexican ballet *folklorico* performances, did much to introduce the repertoire to areas outside the *jarocho* region.

The sound of the ensemble is string based, and because of the combination of regional instruments, produces a distinct and easily recognizable sound. The standard professional ensembles today consist of ***arpa** jarocho*, ***jarana*** (a rhythm guitar that is strummed), a ***requinto*** *jarocho* that plays a lead melody), and **guitars**. Instrumentalists sing the vocal parts, often alternating between a ***pregonero***, or lead singer, and a chorus. The songs are usually short, around three minutes in length.

A typical *son* may begin with an instrumental introduction followed by verses in strophic form, usually alternating between verses and a repeated chorus. Toward the end of the *son,* there will be a break where the harp plays alone, after which the *requinto* will solo along with the harp, and the latter of the two will be joined by the remaining instruments for the remainder of the instrumental. Like most Mexican *sones,* the concluding verse, or *despedida,* will bid farewell to the listener. The main verses of the *sones* are often improvised with the texts of the chorus being fixed, and the latter often carrying the name of the song. Popular units from the repertoire include "Maria Chuchena," "La Bamba," "El Tilingo Lingo," and "La Bruja." The music is lively and bright, often in a major key with rudimentary harmonic progressions (e.g., I-IV-V). The verse melody is in a relatively narrow range, and the choruses are often harmonized in thirds.

Commercial recording of *jarocho* ensembles are readily available in Mexico and the **United States**, especially in the latter's southwest where there is a large Mexican American population. The commercialization of the *son jarocho* through the recording of "La Bamba" by the Mexican American Ritchie Valens did much to popularize the genre. The Valens version was an individual rock 'n' roll innovation on a traditional style of music from Mexico. It neither changed the performance tradition in Veracruz directly, nor did it immediately bring about a rock 'n' roll movement to singing folkloric Mexican repertoire in the mainstream. Nevertheless, the influence of the *son jarocho* and Valen's recording of "La Bamba" had an impact on subsequent generations of Chicano musicians and their own musical identities. The East Los Angeles-based Chicano band Los Lobos used traditional *jarocho* instruments for their performances of some traditional *jarocho* songs on their first album, *Los Lobos Del Este De Los Angeles,* an album sung entirely in Spanish. These songs included "El Canelo" and "Maria Chuchena." When Luis Valdez's 1987 Ritchie Valens biopic "La Bamba" released a music video with the title track performed by Los Lobos, the latter concluded their rock 'n' roll version with an instrumental interpretation of the traditional *son* using *jarocho* instruments.

Further Reading

Fernández, Pérez, and Rolando Antonio. "El son jarocho como expresión musical afro-mestiza." *Musical Cultures of Latin America. Global Effects, Past and Present* (Proceedings of an International Conference), in *UCLA Selected Reports in Ethnomusicology,* XI, edited by Steven Loza, 39–56.

Loza, Steven. "From Veracruz to Los Angeles: The Reinterpretation of the Son Jarocho." *Latin American Music Review* 13.2 (1992): 179-94.

Sheehy, Daniel. "Popular Mexican Musical Traditions: The Mariachi of West Mexico and the Conjunto Jarocho of Veracruz." *Music in Latin American Culture,* edited by John Schechter. New York: Schirmer, 1999.

George Torres

Son Montuno

Son montuno is a generic type of ***son*** for singing and dancing of Cuban origin. It has a festive character and is widely present in the popular environment of Latin America and the Caribbean.

There are few musicological references to *son montuno,* which together with the historical information, also use the word *montuno* to occasionally differentiate two different species, when they are actually referring to the same typology. Nonetheless, it must be said that the word *montuno* also names a section of the *son* pieces; its main objective is to fuel the enjoyment of the dancers and the climactic moments of the piece.

Musically speaking, the *son montuno* is recognized by having a binary character and a rhythmic pattern supported by the denominated Cuban stick. In its performance can be noticed the existence of four characteristic timbric levels: the strummed string, rhythmic figures of independent character, constant and regular rhythmic figures and the harmonic tone bass, each of them with a clearly defined function: improvisation, accompaniment, harmonic support and stabilizing guide. The bass performs a regular design that distinguishes the *son sintaxis* from the syncopated anticipation of time.

The structure of *son montuno* is the only difference from canonical *son.* While the *son* follows a classic structure organized in three main sections–introduction (almost always instrumental), presentation or body of the piece (in which the topic of the piece is presented by the soloist), and *montuno* (based in the alternancy soloist-chorus)—the *son montuno* is organized in a round way from beginning to end since it is conceived in the alternancy soloists-chorus in the segment in which the presentation takes place. At the same time, when the section corresponding to the *montuno* appears, the alternation is established with improvisations sung by the soloists or by instrument passages that are generally performed on the piano, the tres and the trumpet, depending on the performing format. Therefore, the functions of introduction, presentation and *montuno* can be defined in this genre as macro sections.

Concretely speaking, in the canonical pieces of *son montuno* or *son*, a regular and stable structure can be appreciated, made up of an introduction and a *montuno*, the latter being understood as the part of the piece in which the above-mentioned alternation soloist-chorus occurs. The introduction is generally brief and its thematic material, which is poorly developed, keeps a relative independence from the rest of the number.

Several modifications can be seen within this general conception, which comprises a larger or shorter extension of the introduction (from a motif or a phrase); the absence of a presentation section with narration, which appears rarely and in the cases it does is very reduced and with poor text and music, unlike *son*; and the presence or absence of a final *montuno* as a section.

From the point of view of the dramaturgical conception, the introductory segment, which is almost always instrumental, is followed by the *montuno*, which is notable for its marked slow, cadential, and weighty character, underlined by the peculiar stressing of the rhythm. It has only one chorus repeated through the piece, although another can appear but it is just a modification of the main chorus by reducing the text to look for semantic synthesis. This process can take place in a more or less segmented way and overlapped with the improvisations by the soloist or the instruments, and it is more noticeable in modern pieces.

Lyrics are composed in traditional eight-syllable structures like ***décima*** or quatrains. The stanzas, in some cases, have relative autonomy from the point of view of the content, while the chorus can be in stanzas of two or four verses. It has a popular character similar to that of *son* in terms of tone, devices, and language used. The themes can be rural or urban depending on the musical references of the performers and the composers. Thus, several types of *montunos* exist with different styles derived from country music, New Orleans **jazz**, pop, or other genres existing at the moment of the creation of the piece.

As to its origin, it is supposed that *son montuno* began in the early stages of the evolutionary process of *son* as musical genre, since it keeps the alternating principal characteristic of the first pieces of *son*, together with other traditional species with shared common roots such as ***changüí*** and *nengon*, which contain structure developed prior to the incorporation of the presentation section of narrative character that is common in later pieces. Although rural roots and references can be clearly recognized, the most canonical type of *son montuno* is mostly located in the city, since a large number of relevant musicians who established the guidelines of this genre developed their careers intensively in the cities (in spite of their rural origin or deep contact with rural expressions).

Son montuno is performed by various instrument groups associated with diverse environments. It is very common in the song listing of ensembles, septets and sextets that perform *son,* jazz bands, *son* **duos**, and trios, as well as country music ensembles. It has also been assumed by other types of groups such as the vocal group Vocal Sampling, together with others who have followed and have given a new meaning to its musical discourse, which is why it is performed by wind instrument quartets or choirs, which have added it to their repertoire as a way of appealing to different kinds of audiences.

Some important names in the evolution of *son* include **Arsenio Rodríguez**, Lilí Martínez, Niño Rivera, Benny Moré, Chano Pozo, Celina González, Compay Segundo, Los Compadres duet, and Pío Leyva among other important creators and interpreters who, although they were born in cities, villages, or suburbs, have deep contact with rural expressions at the same time their musical careers developed in the cities.

Representative pieces of *son montuno* are "Sazonando" by Lilí Martínez; "Yo como candela" by Félix Chapottín; "La ternera" by Pío Leyva; "Caña quemá" by Lorenzo Hierrezuelo; "Chan chan" by Compay Segundo; "Cómetelo to," "Serende," and "Seven seven" by Chano Pozo; and "Yo soy el punto cubano," "Oye mi leloley," and "El guarapo y la melcocha" made popular by Celina González, among others.

In modern times, the legacy of *son montuno* is present in other genres such as *salsa*, *songo*, and *timba* that use the rondal principle and add new structural variants such as the incorporation of new choruses, for example, especially in the final segments. Although there is no doubt of its Cuban origin, the international transcendency of *son montuno* cannot be denied, as it has been taken up by countless musical groups in Latin America and the Caribbean, not only in cover versions but also original pieces. This is largely due to the impact of the groups and composers from Cuba.

Further Reading

Garciá, David F. *Arsenio Rodríguez and the Transnational Flows of Latin Popular Music.* Studies in Latin American and Caribbean Music. Philadelphia, PA: Temple University Press, 2006.

González, Neris, Grizel Hernández y Liliana Casanella. 2002. "La encuesta del siglo XX. Música cubana." Multimedia (Inédito) La Habana.

Sublette, Ned. *Cuba and Its Music: From the First Drums to the Mambo.* Chicago: Chicago Press Review, 2004.

Waxer, Lise. *The City of Musical Memory: Salsa, Record Grooves, and Popular Culture in Cali, Colombia.* Middletown, CT: Wesleyan University Press, 2002.

Neris González and Liliana Casanella

Songo

The *songo* is a Cuban musical genre created by Juan Formell in 1969. It represents a major legacy and is a predecessor to the ***son*** in contemporary Cuban popular music. It has also inspired the repertoire of several orchestras such as Los Van Van, Pupy y los que son son, and other orchestras inside and outside of **Cuba**. According to Formell, the term *songo* comes from the combination of *son* as a genre and go, from go-go. The last word was also a play on words mirroring the name of the orchestra Los Van Van, Formell's orchestra, since the word go is the English equivalent of the Spanish word *van*.

Songo is distinctive for its integration of different elements and styles and has become one of the most representative forms of dance music. It combines ***rumba***, **jazz, rock**, beat, pop, ***bossa nova***, and even rap, ***reggaetón***, and funk, somehow finding a way to integrate all of these styles and rhythms into the *son* tradition.

Cuban Orchestra leader Juan Formell performs at the North Sea Jazz Festival in the Congresgebouw in The Hague, Netherlands, 1986. (Redferns/Getty Images)

This fusion of musical genre has been expressed in many different ways throughout the evolution of *songo*. Its progression can be followed through the song repertoire of Los Van Van orchestra. The *rumba* and *son* remain the foundation of this eclectic and international fusion of popular styles. Of all the variations, the most developed is *merensongo*.

Formell's creativity is evident in the everchanging nature of *songo*. *Songo* is distinguished by the peculiar off-beat stress matching the pattern of the **congas**. This is mixed with the solo breaks performed on the Cuban *timbals* and the drum forming a strong foundation. *Songo* is also characterized by the melodic-rhythmic formulas, cadences and phrase closures; the unique combination of violins and **flutes**, as well as the design, mobility and rhythmic richness of the bass, the performance of which goes beyond the traditional harmonic support. Another feature of *songo* is the convergence of the strong tradition on **montunos**, and the occasional use of the stresses associated with **changüí** and *reggae;* the mixture of **tumbao** with slow *conga* and especially a particular and paradigmatic arrangement of the chorus.

Although *songo* is the result of the inspiration of Juan Formell, as realized in the orchestra Los Van Van together with drummer Blas Egües in 1969, it owes its evolution largely to Cuban percussionist José Luis Quintana Changuito who took *songo* through many transformations, using a variety of instrumentation, which resulted in the overall timbre of the orchestra. Cesar Pupy Pedroso, the director of the orchestra Pupy y los que son son, pioneered the use of the piano *tumbaos* and this also contributed to the formation of *songo*.

The repertoire of this genre shows a variety of themes primarily focused on love, women, Cuba and its regions, dance, the orchestra itself, food, friendship, Afro-Cuban religion, and popular philosophy, together with topics of a general nature. The lyrics of Formell and Pupy, the two main composers, fall within the custom of historical narratives and are notable for telling a story and commenting on social issues at the same time. Frequently, their songs feature characters from daily life who embody the moral quality associated with Cuban identity. Humor is also a common quality in four decades of *songo* lyrics.

Morphologically, *songo* makes use of the principle of rondal found in other Cuban musical genres, especially in *son montuno*. *Son montuno* features an alternating solo-chorus throughout a piece. This structure coexists with the different varieties of the classical architecture of *son:* introduction, body of the piece and *montuno*.

Representative pieces of this genre include "Por encima del nivel," "La titimanía," "Hoy se cumplen seis semanas," and "Esto te pone la cabeza mala" (in the boundaries of *timba*).

Further Reading

Gerard, Charley. *Music from Cuba: Mongo Santamaria, Chocolate Armenteros, and Cuban Musicians in the United States.* Westport, CT: Praeger, 2001.

Moore, Robin. *Music and Revolution: Cultural Change in Socialist Cuba.* Music of the African Diaspora, 9. Berkeley: University of California Press, 2006.

Perna, Vincenzo. *Timba: The Sound of the Cuban Crisis.* Burlington, VT: Ashgate, 2005.

Prince, Rob. "Afro-Cuban." *Folk Roots* 67 (1989): 17.

Neris González and Liliana Casanella

Surdo

The *surdo* is a deep, double-headed bass drum in various sizes (from about 16 to 24 inches in diameter and about 20 inches in length) used in many Brazilian styles of **samba**. It is typically played with a soft mallet in the right hand while the left hand controls the open or dampened vibrations of the nylon or goat skin head. In the **baterias** (percussion sections) of the *escolas de samba,* three sizes of *surdo* (*primeira, segunda,* and *corte*) are used. The *primeira* and *segunda surdos* serve the function of marking the basic pulse of the *samba* (alternating beats one and two of each measure) and hence are sometimes called *surdos de maracação.* The *corte* (cutting) *surdo,* also called *terceira,* plays syncopated rhythmic variations that cut across the regular pulses of the marking *surdos.* Bide (Alcebíades Maia Barcelos), a legendary percussionist and composer who helped found Rio de Janeiro's first *escola de samba,* Deixa Falar (1928), is often credited with introducing the *surdo* into the *escola de samba* tradition. Brazilian percussionists use a single *surdo* when playing *sambas* in smaller groups and in informal gatherings. In the Bahian tradition of the **blocos afro**, four sizes of *surdo* are used to create interlocking patterns.

Further Reading

Bolão, Oscar. *Batuque é um privilégio: A percussão da música do Rio de Janeiro/ Batuque is a privilege: Percussion in Rio de Janeiro's music.* Rio de Janeiro, Brazil: Lumiar Editora, 2003.

Crook, Larry. *Brazilian Music: Northeastern Traditions and the Heartbeat of a Modern Nation.* Santa Barbara, CA: ABC-CLIO, 2005.

Larry Crook

T

Tamborím

The *tamborím* is a small (five to six inches in diameter), single-headed drum of wood or metal used in various folk and popular musical traditions in **Brazil**, especially those associated with *samba*. Technically a frame drum, the instrument is used extensively in the *baterias* (percussion sections) of the *escolas de samba* (*samba* schools) of Rio de Janeiro's **Carnival**. In the *escola de samba,* the *tamborím* is played with a flexible plastic stick (usually comprising a bundle of three to six thin plastic rods) in the right hand while the left hand holds and controls the rotating movement of the

---

Gardel, Carlos

Singer, composer, and guitarist, Carlos Gardel (1887?–1935) began his professional career singing duets with Uruguayan José Razzano in 1913. They performed together until 1925 with a repertoire of Argentinean folklore music, including *zamba*, *chacarera*, and *queca tonada*. Gardel signed with Columbia Records in 1913, but his career was made in 1917 with his recording of "Mi Noche Triste." It sold 100,000 copies, making Gardel the icon of the *tango* to the present day. As he became a star in New York and Paris, the upper classes of **Argentina** began to embrace Gardel and his melancholy, seductive interpretation of *tango* song. Gardel recorded over 1,000 songs and made 11 major films. He died in a plane crash in 1935.

The rise of Gardel's career coincides with the birth of the recording, film, and radio industries. Gardel's fame and the popularity of *tango* spread quickly because of these new media, but in turn, his popularity was instrumental in creating an audience for these new industries.

Further Reading

Castro, Donald. S. "Massification of the Tango: The Electronic Media, the Popular Theatre and the Cabaret from Contursi to Perón, 1917–1955." *Studies in Latin American Popular Culture* 18 (1999): 93–114.

Rebecca Stuhr

drum. This technique allows single and bounced strokes to be executed rapidly on the drum and its rim. In the *escola de samba* context, multiple *tamborím* players execute tightly coordinated and syncopated unison patterns (*desenhos*) that serve as creative markers of individual schools. In softer contexts of musical performance, Brazilian percussionists often use a single wooden stick or even the fingers to perform syncopated *clave*-like figures (repeating rhythms). Bide (Alcebíades Maia Barcelos), a legendary percussionist and composer who helped found Rio de Janeiro's first *escola de samba,* Deixa Falar (1928), is frequently credited as one of the first musicians to introduce the *tamborím* into the *bateria* of the *escola de samba.*

Further Reading

Bolão, Oscar. *Batuque é um privilégio: A percussão da música do Rio de Janeiro* (Batuque Is a Privilege: Percussion in Rio de Janeiro's Music). Rio de Janeiro, Brazil: Lumiar Editora, 2003.

Larry Crook

Tango

Tango is a dance, song, and musical form that emerged in the poor suburbs of the Uruguayan capital of Montevideo and the Argentine capital of Buenos Aires starting in the late 19th century. By 1913, it had gained popularity in Paris and London as a salon dance, and as a result eventually gained acceptance by middle- and upper-class Argentine society. It was the most prominent urban popular music and dance of the Argentine capital from the 1920s through the 1940s, and is often identified as the musical national symbol of **Argentina**.

Origins

The term *tango* came into Spanish from the West African Bantu languages spoken by African populations brought to the River Plate region. By the late 19th century, it was used here to describe three interrelated concepts, all derived from cultural practices relating to this population of African descendants: *tango* referred to a drum, a particular form of dance, and a place or event where Afro-Argentines and Afro-Uruguayans would gather to dance. The word also took on a more general meaning in the Spanish-speaking world, as a form of music played or sung by blacks. It was this latter meaning that led to the development of the *tango andaluz,* a *flamenco* genre that is otherwise musically unrelated to the *tango* of the River Plate region.

The *tango* emerged first as a unique dance and only later as a specific genre of music. One of the first chroniclers of the genre, known as "*El Viejo Tanguero*" ("The old tangoer"), claims that the term was used to identify a new dance that borrowed choreography from the *candombe* as early as 1877.

La Guardia Vieja (The Old Guard)

The *tango* as a distinct musical style began to consolidate in the last two decades of the 19th century. Demonstrating the influences of European popular song and a prevalent rhythmic pattern derived from the Cuban ***habanera***, *tangos* in this period were typically written in three contrasting sections with the last marked as a **trio**. In performance, these *tangos* would feature one or more instruments playing a simple melody in unison with a simple chordal accompaniment in *habanera* rhythm. This oral tradition form of playing, where distribution of melodic and accompanimental roles is resolved spontaneously and without reference to a prewritten arrangement, was known as *a la parrilla* and remains in use among traditional *tango* musicians to this day. The most typical instrumental ensemble consisted of a trio of **flute, guitar**, and violin, but the music and the social sphere it occupied were loosely structured enough to permit variants. It was not until the turn of the century that the instrument that would come to play the most prominent role as sonic and visual icon of the *tango,* the German-made ***bandoneón***, began to appear in *tango* ensembles. This instrument, a free-reed *concertina,* entered *tango* ensembles as a replacement or supplement to the flute, playing simple unadorned melodies, but its role and the associated technique would develop significantly in the coming decades. Many of these early *tango* musicians were not formally trained in music, and generally pieces were learned and transmitted orally. Retroactively, this generation of musicians would become known as *la guardia vieja* (the old guard), distinguishing them from the next generation and their stylistic innovations starting around 1920.

From 1897 onward, local publishing houses began printing scores of *tangos* for piano, suggesting both a growing interest by formally trained musicians and at least some part of the middle and upper classes. Rosendo Mendizábal's "El entrerriano" ("the man from Entre Ríos province") was the first published *tango,* which was printed under the pseudonym A. Rosendo. Mendizábal was a pianist, and an Argentine of African descent. In fact, a significant number of *guardia vieja* musicians were Afro-Argentine, including the violinist known as El Negro Casimiro and the first exponent of a local style of *bandoneón* playing, Sebastián Ramos Mejía. Other prominent composers of the period included Angel Villoldo ("El choclo"), *bandoneonist* Eduardo Arolas, and Vicente Greco. *Tango* music during this period reached an increasingly wider public. No longer was it heard only in the *academias* (public dance halls in the poor outer suburbs of Buenos Aires that were closely associated with prostitution) but in other spaces as well. Composers of the *sainetes,* popular theater productions aimed at a principally bourgeois audience, began to include *tangos* in their productions, and organ-grinders playing on the street began to play popular *tangos* as well.

From 1910 to 1920, the most important musical innovations in the *tango* came in the form of new instrumentation: the piano began to replace the guitar as the most common harmonic and rhythmic instrument, and the *bandoneón* gained prominence. *Bandoneonist* Vicente Greco coined the term *orquesta típica criolla*, later shortened to **orquesta típica,** to describe the ensemble he formed in 1911. Greco's group included a flute, an instrument that would soon fall out of favor, but his basic configuration of sections of *bandoneones* and bowed strings, with a piano and contrabass providing rhythmic and harmonic support, would become the standard instrumentation for the coming decades.

International Diffusion

The year 1913 marked the explosion of the *tango* craze in Paris where, introduced by wealthy Argentine elites, a more buttoned-down and restrained version of the dance caught on in ballrooms, society teas, and among dance teachers. London, Germany, and major cities in the **United States** soon followed, and bands and dancers in those locales had generated local versions of *tango* dance and music by the mid-1910s. While often this *tango* bore little musical or choreographic resemblance to what was being played and danced in Argentina at the time, the growing global enthusiasm for the dance among a cosmopolitan elite certainly influenced *tango*'s growing acceptance back in Argentina. Furthermore, the growing international market led to interest by both local and foreign record companies and film producers. By 1920 *tango* was being mass-produced and sold on a global scale, both on record and in film.

Tango Song and Lyrics

While the earliest *tangos* may have had lyrics, few of them survive, and accounts of the period suggest that they may have been improvised and frequently were lighthearted and bawdy in character. This practice was to change radically with the introduction of *tango canción,* or *tango* song, and the worldwide success of its best-known exponent, **Carlos Gardel**. Gardel had already attained a modest degree of success performing as a singer in a folk **duo** when he began to incorporate *tangos* into his repertoire. His 1917 recording of Pascual Contursi's lyric "*Mi noche triste*" marked the emergence of a new style of singing and a new genre of *tango* music. *Tango* lyrics took on a melancholy, cynical worldview, often describing failed love affairs through a philosophical style of complaint known as *la mufa*. Local slang, or *lunfardo,* originally associated with the criminal class, began to be incorporated into these lyrics. Through the contributions of poets such as Enrique Santos Discépolo and Homero Manzi, the *tango* lyrics of the golden age of *tango* remain some of the most important contributions to Argentine literature of the 20th century and are a frequent topic of serious literary analysis.

The Golden Age

With the growing national and international interest in *tango* music, song, and dance, the period between roughly 1920 and 1940 witnessed a proliferation in all aspects of *tango* art. *Orquestas típicas* grew in size with the greater degree of financial opportunity, including sometimes up to five *bandoneones* and violins. Some bandleaders experimented with other instruments, such as Osvaldo Fresedo's use of the drum set and Horacio Salgán's incorporation of the bass clarinet. Bandleaders and arrangers worked to develop distinctive styles, and dancers would often develop strong loyalties to a particular *orquesta's* style. Historians generally divide the *orquestas* of this period into two broad categories: traditionalist leaders (e.g., Francisco Canaro, Juan d'Arienzo) had a more conservative approach to arranging and emphasized clear, danceable rhythmic arrangements, while revolutionary directors (e.g., Fresedo, Aníbal Troilo, Osvaldo Pugliese) made more radical changes and elaborations upon musical form, harmony, and melody.

Tango Nuevo

Public interest in *tango* waned in the late 1940s and 1950s due to economic crises, increasingly militarized and authoritarian governments, and other social changes. Some *tango* musicians developed smaller ensemble sounds that were meant for the concert hall rather than for the dancer. The best-known and most polemic of these was *bandoneonist* **Astor Pantaleón Piazzolla** (1921–1992), who combined classical training and an interest in **jazz** with his background in *tango* to create a self-consciously revolutionary style he termed *tango nuevo* or new *tango*. Piazzolla's music initially met with derision by the traditional *tango* community, while reaching new audiences among **jazz** and classical music fans internationally. He has since become the best-known and best-selling Argentine composer and performer of any genre of music internationally.

Resurgence

Following the massive political and economic crisis of late 2001, there has been a resurgence of interest in *tango* among young Argentines. A sense of mistrust in foreign musical and cultural influence, coupled with an identification with the deeply cynical lyrics of early *tango,* has led new groups ranging from traditional *orquesta típica* formation (e.g., Orquesta Típica Fernandez Fierro) to smaller electric ensembles influenced by rock (e.g., La Biyuya, Buenos Aires Negro) to develop new forms of *tango*. Internationally, groups using *tango* instruments, either live or sampled, in electronic dance music (e.g., Gotán Project, Bajofondo Tango Club) have formed a genre called *electrotango* that has generated significant commercial and critical interest.

Piazzolla, Astor Pantaleón

Astor Piazzolla (1921–1992) was an Argentinean composer and **bandoneon** player. He developed the new *tango* from the traditional *tango*. His new approach incited bitter controversies among orthodox *tangueros* in his native land. Piazzolla lived in New York City from 1925 to 1936. In 1941 he began his composition studies with Alberto Ginastera. In 1946 Piazzolla formed his own orchestra and started developing his musical ideas. From 1954, he studied in Paris with Nadia Boulanger, the illustrious French composition pedagogue. By that time Piazzolla had decided to become a classical composer, but Boulanger urged him to develop his own style through *tango*. On his return to **Argentina** in 1955, Piazzolla began performing his original *tango* compositions with various chamber ensembles, incorporating elements of classical music and jazz such as counterpoint and improvisation, as well as nontraditional instruments like the electric guitar and saxophone. From the 1970s, he performed extensively in South America, the United States, Europe, and Japan. Some of Piazzolla's best known pieces are "Libertango," "Adiós Nonino," and "Balada para un loco."

Further Reading

Azzi, María Susana, and Simon Collier. *Le Grand Tango: The Life and Music of Astor Piazzolla.* New York: Oxford University Press, 2000.

Katia Chornik

Further Reading

Azzi, María Susana and Simon Collier. *Le Grand Tango: A Biography of Astor Piazzolla.* Oxford: Oxford University Press, 2000.

Collier, Simon, et al. *¡Tango! The Dance, the Song, the Story.* New York: Thames and Hudson. 1995.

García Blaya, Ricardo, et al., eds., last modified September 14, 2007, http://www.todo tango.com/english/main.html.

Savigliano, Marta. *Tango and the Political Economy of Passion.* Boulder, CO: Westview Press, 1995.

Michael O'Brien

Taquirari

Taquirari is a duple meter, *mestizo* dance, and music genre from **Bolivia's** Eastern lowlands. In AABB or AABBCC form, the *taquirari* is derived from the rural indigenous *takirari*. Urban Bolivian musicians began to record this genre in the

1940s. The first to do so were *orquestas de jazz* (swing bands with saxophones and trumpets) and vocalists accompanied by **guitars** or piano. The La Paz vocal **duos** Las Kantutas and Los Indios Latinos, though not from Eastern Bolivia, performed on nationally broadcast radio programs (e.g., La Paz's Radio Illimani), helping to popularize the *taquirari* across the country. The genre entered the national music repertory of Bolivian brass bands and folkloric ensembles far away from the lowland tropics. Since the 1960s, Bolivian folkloric-popular groups mainly dedicated to Andean music (e.g., **huaynos**) have played the *taquirari* with highland instruments such as the *kena* (bamboo flute) and *zampoña* (pan-pipe). In contrast, eastern Bolivian musicians typically perform the *taquirari* with guitars, mandolins, and/or violins, not with Andean instruments, and call the genre *música oriental* (Eastern music) rather than national music, which reflects regional divisions. The *taquirari* is an important *camba* (eastern Bolivian) identity emblem. Classic *taquiraris* include "Viva Santa Cruz" by Gilberto Rojas, "Sombrero de Sao" by Pedro Shimose, and "Lunita Camba" by Percy Ávila. Singer Gladys Moreno and the group Los Cambitas are among the most famous interpreters of the *taquirari*.

Further Reading

Terceros Rojas, Armando. *Libro de Oro de los Interpretes de la Musica Cruceña.* Santa Cruz, Bolivia: AP Industrias Gráficas, 1989.

Fernando Rios

Tejano. *See* Tex-Mex.

Tex-Mex

Tex-Mex is a style of **accordion** music associated with the *tejanos* of south Texas. The formation of this *tejano* music dates back to the 1930s when the style was first commercially recorded. These people of Mexican descent, born and living in Texas, have fused Northern Mexican folk and popular music and American popular music to create their own genre.

Tex-Mex clearly resembles Northern Mexican **norteño** music. Before World War II, the music of southern Texas and northern **Mexico** were practically the same. This is the reason Mexican Americans refer to Tex-Mex music as *musica norteña*. Many dances were performed in northern Mexico during the late 19th century such as the **polka**, *mazurka, redova,* **vals**, and *chotis*, and then the *paso doble* and **corrido** in the 20th century. The main instruments used to back these dance forms were the accordion and **bajo sexto**, a 12-string bass **guitar**. It is these forms and instruments that would shape the first recorded Tex-Mex music of the 20th century.

While Tex-Mex is a genre of popular music, its sound, at least in early recordings, resembles Mexican folk music. The *corrido* form, for example, is a folk ballad or narrative backed by guitar commonly expressing the raw emotions and everyday life experienced by Mexicans. For this reason there has been a conflict between the various forms of Tex-Mex that eventually came into the recording scene. The conflict is rooted in differing beliefs as to how deeply a *tejano* should assimilate into American culture. One will find the Mexican American musicians that have distanced themselves from the rural folk traditions of northern Mexico creating a sound that is more like American rock 'n' roll or **jazz**. Still, through immigration, the polka, *schottische*, waltz, and accordion use in late 20th-century Mexico came from Europe, namely the Czech Republic and Germany, and so Tex-Mex music can ultimately be looked at as a European, Mexican, and American form.

Tex-Mex music officially began in 1935 when accordionist Narciso Martínez, nicknamed El Hurucan del Valle, made his first commercial recording. In the 1920s American record companies began looking for international music and found success with the African and Caribbean roots of jazz. In southern Texas, the accordion had been used since 1850 and by the 1900s *tejanos* were dancing to accordion music at *funciones* such as weddings. By the 1930s American record companies found a vibrant dance music north of the Rio Grande that combined rural Mexican music with European melodies. Martínez would become the father of **conjunto** music after recording for IDEAL records, a small record company, which focused exclusively on the regional music of south Texas. The *conjunto* music of South Texas was made up of a two-row, diatonic button accordion along with a *bajo sexto,* a bass guitar with six pairs of strings tuned in fourths at F, C, G, D, A, and E. There were also the *tololóche* (double bass), a drum set, and later the electric bass. Martínez and his *bajista*, Santiago Almeida, revolutionized the Tex-Mex *conjunto* sound. Instead of playing bass notes on the accordion, Martínez emphasized the treble buttons with strong articulations. He created his own bright sound and left the bass and chordal accompaniments to Almeida. This *conjunto* along with the **mariachi** would reign as the most popular musics of the Tex-Mex region. Importantly, the *conjunto* sound was reminiscent of *norteño* music, especially being based off of polkas and *corridos* and Martínez, though a popular recording artist, considered himself a folk musician playing regional folk music. This image would persist in the Tex-Mex *conjunto* as a music for the lower, working class, which also had not assimilated into American society as much as other *tejanos*.

Numerous *Tejanos* would follow in Martínez's footsteps while adding elements to the basic *conjunto* structure. Santiago Jiménez Sr., also an accordionist, famous for his legato technique, added the *tololóche* to the ensemble in the 1940s. Valerio Longoria played accordion but more importantly incorporated vocals, specifically *canciónes* **rancheras** (ranch songs). These vocals evoke the romantic nationalism found in Mexico since the revolution of 1910 and remain an element of *conjunto* music that cannot be separated from Mexico. Longoria also sang **boleros**, experimented with the accordion reeds to create different sounds, and introduced drums into the ensemble. The *conjunto* ensemble standard of accordion, *bajo sexto,* bass, and drums therefore owes much of its structure to Longoria and later Tony De La Rosa, an accordionist of the 1950s who kept the drum set and replaced the *tololóche* with the electric bass. The 1960s saw more innovations from artists like Paulino Bernal who used three-part vocals, two chromatic accordions, and advanced harmonies, and Esteban Jordan who incorporated jazz. This incorporation has influenced decades of modern *conjunto* groups that have used saxophones, keyboards, and synthesizers.

The *conjunto* is not the only popular exponent of *Tejano* musicians. **Orquestas** (orchestras), featuring at least six members but usually over ten due to a large reed section, were very popular in south Texas from 1945 to 1980. These big bands attracted a middle-class audience, an audience more eager to assimilate with American culture. Beto Villa would first popularize the *orquesta* sound by playing **rancheras** and American big band music for IDEAL records. Isidro "El Indio" López played saxophone and sang, becoming popular in the late 1950s. He played

---

Selena

Selena Quintanilla Pérez (1971–1995), the queen of **tejano** music, had been performing for 15 years, and was a multiaward-winning vocalist, before her death at the age of 23. Selena began singing with her father's band Los Dinos at the age of eight. Los Dinos featured Selena on vocals, her sister Suzette, brother A.B., and, later her husband Chris Pérez. At 15, Selena was named Female Vocalist of the Year and Performer of the Year at the Tejano Music Awards, a title she maintained until her death. Selena's distinctive *tejano* style joined traditional Mexican music, pop, country, **jazz**, **rock**, and rap to the standard *tejano* **polka** rhythm, which Selena made popular in **Puerto Rico**, **Mexico**, and Central America.

Selena's career included two gold albums, *Ven Conmigo,* and *Entre a Mi Mundo,* a first for a female *tejano* artist, a Grammy award for *Selena Live,* and platinum status for her posthumously released *Dreaming of You.*

Further Reading

Koegel, John. "Crossing Borders: Mexicana, Tejana, and Chicana Musicians in the United States and Mexico." *From Tejano to Tango: Latin American Popular Music,* 97–125. New York: Routledge, 2002.

Rebecca Stuhr

with Narciso Martínez and his *orquesta* had seventeen members at times. *Orquestas* featured more American than Mexican aesthetics, moving away from the *norteño* folk sound, but still included *rancheras*. Also, because of artists like Jordan, the distinction between *orquestas* and *conjuntos* was blurred. By the 1980s the popularity of synthesizers reduced the number of players necessary in a band, ending many *orquestas*. The impact of *orquesta* music is still felt with the 1980s *polquita* (little polka) *conjunto,* which featured horn and accordion alternations. Also, solos in *conjunto* groups by artists Roberto Pulido and David Lee Garza were inspired by *orquestas*.

The recent decades have seen the popularity of Tex-Mex music spread throughout America and the rest of the world. Jiménez's son, Flaco, has played in Europe and fused American rock 'n' roll and country music with the Grammy-award winning group The Texas Tornadoes. While some of the lyrics are still sung in Spanish, groups like The Tornadoes have edited the *conjunto* ensemble to include an electric guitar, played by Freddy Fender, and a piano, while still keeping the classic accordion sound. *Conjuntos* have sprouted in Japan (Los Gatos) and France (Los Gallos). In the 1990s, featuring entirely electronic instrumention, **Selena** y los Dinos achieved huge success in the **United States** with the backing of large American record companies. Tierra Tejana has fused *conjunto* with rap and **hip-hop** in much the same way *orquestas* had incorporated popular African American genres years before them. Still an annual event, the *Tejano Conjunto* Music Festival began in 1982 in San Antonio, sponsored by the radio station KEDA. The lineup in 2007 included Joel Guzmán, Flaco Jiménez y su Conjunto, and accordionist Eva Ybarra, one of the first popular female Tex-Mex musicians who is not a singer.

Further Reading

Flores, Gomez, and Carlos Jesus. "The Accordion on Both Sides of the Border." In *Puro Conjunto: An Album in Words and Pictures: Writings, Posters, and Photographs from the Tejano Conjunto Festival En San Antonio, 1982–1998,* edited by Juan Tejeda and Avelardo Valdez, 71–80. Austin, TX: CMAS Books, 2001.

Guadalupe, San Miguel. *Tejano Proud: Tex-Mex Music in the Twentieth Century.* Fronteras Series 1. Austin: Texas A&M University Press, 2002.

Peña, Manuel. *The Texas-Mexican Conjunto: History of a Working-Class Music.* Austin: University of Texas Press, 1985.

Raymond Epstein

Timba

Timba is a style of contemporary black Cuban dance music, sometimes called *salsa cubana,* that emerged in Havana in the early 1990s. Popularized by bands such as NG La Banda, La Charanga Habanera, Los Van Van, and Bamboleo, and once dubbed by Puerto Rican jazzman David Sanchez as "the smartest pop music I've ever heard" (Watrous), *timba* is an eclectic fusion of *son* and *rumba* with elements of U.S. **jazz**, funk, and rap.

The term *timba* has long been used in **Cuba** as a synonym for ***rumba***, and today it describes a type of music that sounds loosely similar to ***salsa*** in its bipartite form (ballad-like first part with a driving call-and-response as a second part), prominent horns, and choreographic elements (as in the Cuban couple dancing variant called *casino*). Important differences, however, include content and language (*timba* frequently contains **Afro-Cuban** slang terms) and instrumentation (where *salsa* generally employs the acoustic/baby bass, trombones, and no drum-kit, *timba* uses the electric bass, trumpets/saxes, and a drum-kit). *Timba* also differs from *salsa* in its structure (with a minimal narrative section and an extended second part replete with *coros*, i.e., anthemic choral refrains), intricate rhythmic texture (played by percussive and melodic instruments and often dominated by *rumba guaguancó clave*), and vocal style (resonant with *rumba* but also, often, Latin Soul).

Extremely popular among black audiences, *timba* is typically played by a 12-piece or more big band and relies much on the technical virtuosity of an almost all-black line up, thus expressing both the esthetic ambitions of Cuban musicians and their loyalty to Afro-Cuban popular culture. Its origins can be traced in the process of re-Africanization of Cuban popular music visible in the work of seminal dance bands in the 1970s and 1980s such as Irakere, Los Van Van, and Ritmo Oriental, who experimented with fusions including Afro-Cuban folklore, jazz, and rock.

The emergence and success of *timba* in the 1990s was inextricably tied to the special period (*período especial*): the abysmal economic crisis caused by the collapse of the Soviet Union that prompted the Cuban government to legalize the circulation of foreign currency, open up to tourism, and attract foreign investment. With the arrival of masses of foreigners and the opening of new hotels and clubs, the early 1990s saw a revitalization of Havana nightlife and a boom of live dance music (and, sadly, of sex tourism). In that context, the challenging attitude and flashy lifestyle of *timberos,* together with the controversial content and the perceived closeness to the street of their songs, gave musicians the status of popular heroes among increasingly disaffected *barrio* youth.

Economic reforms encouraged the arrival of foreign record companies in Cuba (not from the **United States**) and extensive touring by Cuban dance bands (including in the United States), leading them to rule the Latin live circuit in various European countries and elsewhere. By the mid-1990s, *timba* had become the most popular style in Cuba, dominating radio programs and live shows and granting bandleaders such as José Luis Cortés of NG La Banda, David Calzado of La Charanga Habanera, and Juan Formell of Los Van Van significant symbolic and financial power.

In addition to its more rhythmically charged version, *timba* developed also a romantic, *salsa*-leaning variant embodied by singers such as Manolín Gonzalez

("*El Médico de la Salsa*"), Paulito FG, and Issac Delgado. In terms of content, the style thus was able to navigate between escapism and social chronicle, with lyrics dealing with topics such as love and everyday life in the *barrio,* but also producing (often ambiguous and sexist) comments on tourism and prostitution (NG La Banda's song "La bruja"; La Charanga Habanera's "Superturística"), materialism (Los Van Van's "La Chopimaniaca"; NG La Banda's "La apretadora"), official attitudes (NG La Banda's "Picadillo de soya" and "Cara de guante"), black identity, and Santería (e.g., Adalberto Alvarez, Los Van Van, NG La Banda), often touching on issues of gender, class, and race (La Charanga Habanera's song "El temba," for example, started as a love ballad and ended with a refrain that parodized a revolutionary poem).

Composers generally avoided censorship by using slang and metaphors and promoting an image of *timba* as good-time, tropical dance music, which in a sense was true. By the mid-1990s, however, the style had given a new visibility to Afro-Cuban popular culture (which the revolution had previously celebrated, but also sanitized and sometimes repressed), hinting at a process of crystallization of a new black Cuban and possibly separate social identity (in 1994, for the first time after 1959, black people were seen rioting in Havana against the government). As the soundtrack of Havana's new *dolce vita, timba* also appeared dangerously close to rampant black economy and sex tourism. In many ways, *timberos* challenged mainstream values even without singing challenging lyrics: by consciously confronting dominant codes of music (hedonistic versus engaged music, foreign versus national music, working class versus elitist expression), language (black slang versus articulated language), content (life in the barrio versus abstract love), clothing (by wearing Santería necklaces, golden chains and American symbols), and dance (sexy individual dancing as practiced by *jineteras* (prostitutes) versus couple dancing, in a social context where young women were becoming the new breadwinners).

The very reasons that made *timberos* successful with their audiences, therefore, made them increasingly unwelcome in official circles, leading the state-controlled press to portray them as new rich and scapegoats for the social inequalities of the special period. In the second half of the 1990s, the mild recovery of the Cuban economy brought about restrictions in economic freedom, crackdowns on crime and political dissent, and a repression of the perceived excesses of *timba,* thus marking the end of institutional tolerance. After their allegedly offensive performance during a televised mass concert in 1997, La Charanga Habanera were banned from playing, broadcasting, and travelling for six months (they later disbanded and re-formed with only two original components, including leader Calzado). The repressive wave made popular artists more cautious, and later persuaded some to leave the island in search of better artistic chances in the United States such as singers Manolín, Carlos Manuel Pruneda, and Issac Delgado.

Another important factor in the taming of *timba* was the phenomenal success of Buena Vista Social Club, the record project and loosely formed band of elderly

Cuban artists conceived in 1996 by American guitarist and producer Ry Cooder. Since then the Buena Vista Social Club has become enormously popular with millions of albums sold and countless tours. They have promoted, on a global scale, an unchallenged image of Cuban traditional music that has further marginalized contemporary music. Not surprisingly, the Buena Vista Social Club album was hailed by Cuban critics of *timba* as the authentic image of national music and opposed to the overindulgence and vulgarity of dance music.

In the 2000s, *timba* has faced limited success abroad and a relative artistic stalemate, partially explained by its lost of novelty, tendency to increasing commercialization, and difficulty in distributing their recordings outside Cuba (due both to the U.S. trade embargo and to its own specific features: Hispanic audiences find *timba* much more arduous than *salsa* in terms of lyrics, rhythm, and dance style). With bandleaders on the defensive and a musical scene now remarkably diversified, *timba* has thus entered a settle-down process at home but it continues to be the most popular form of recreational music among adult blacks. *Timba* has represented an important moment of rearticulation of black Caribbean identity through music and dance, and a crucial, if deeply controversial, response to the material and moral crisis of contemporary Cuba. It has played a key role in the process of revitalization of black Cuban culture now visible not only in music (with the revival of black folkore, the popularity of *rumba* and **son**, the international success of Cuban jazz; the local popularity of rap and **reggaetón**), but also in the growing role played by Afro-Cuban performing arts and religion both locally and internationally.

Further Reading

Moore, Robin D. *Music & Revolution. Cultural Change in Socialist Cuba.* Berkeley: University of California Press, 2006.

Perna, Vincenzo Timba. *The Sound of the Cuban Crisis.* Aldershot: Ashgate, 2005.

Timba, http://timba.com (The Home of Cuban Music on the Web).

Watrous, Peter. "Havana Jazz Festival: International Dissonance Aside, Harmony in Cuba." *The New York Times,* December 24, 1997.

Vincenzo Perna

Timbal

Commonly known as *timbals* in English, the *timbal* is a set of two drums, usually with metallic shells. It developed in **Cuba** where it is also known as *paila* or *timbals criollos.* The larger drum, known as *hembra* (female), is commonly 15 inches in diameter, while the smaller drum, called *macho* (male), is often 14 inches in diameter. The drumheads are usually made of plastic, though they were historically made of goat hide. It is standard practice to attach at least one **cencerro** (cowbell), though two is more common, and they are often accompanied by a woodblock, cymbal, and even a bass or snare drum. The *timbal* is mostly played with sticks and is usually responsible for playing *cascara* (literally shell, referring to the part of the *timbal* where the rhythm is played) and *abanico* (fan), a rhythmic segue consisting of a rimshot, roll, and another rimshot landing on beat one.

In Cuba, *timbal* and *paila* are mostly synonymous, a carry-over from the Colonial Era when the terms were used to refer to the kettle-shaped orchestral tympani brought from Europe. *Timbals* (from the French word for tympani) or *paila* (kettle) appeared in Cuba by the mid-1700s and saw use in theaters and military bands, eventually making their way into the dance music of high society. Those who performed on *timbal* (*timbaleros*), however, were usually at least partly of African descent. It is no surprise, then, that the musical performance of the *timbal* is heavily based on an African esthetic.

The popularity of the spherical *timbal* increased with styles such as the **danzón** until the early 1900s when the modern shell construction appeared. The

---

Puente, Tito

Ernest Anthony Puente (1923–2000) was born to Puerto Rican immigrant parents in Spanish Harlem. He was later to become known as the king of Latin music or simply El Rey. As a prolific output as a bandleader, percussionist, arranger, and composer, he was key to the development of various Latin styles during the second half of the 20th century. In addition to Cuban music, Puente was influenced by the popular music of his youth, especially big-band **jazz**. With influences from **Machito** and Mario Bauzá, Puente became a leading force in the **mambo** revival of the 1950s.

Puente was influential in the development of **Latin jazz** and may be considered a forefather of *salsa*, a term he never embraced. He was the first to move the **timbal** to the front of an orchestra and introduced the vibraphone into Latin music. He recorded well over 100 albums but is most widely known for the song "Oye Como Va," which was popularized by Carlos Santana. Throughout his career, Puente earned many honors, including six Grammy Awards, a National Medal of the Arts, and a star on the Hollywood Walk of Fame.

Further Reading

Loza, Steven. *Tito Puente and the Making of Latin Music.* Chicago: University of Illinois Press, 1999.

Nolan Warden

catalyst for this change is unclear, but there are two plausible explanations. The most common oral history of this process is that at some point the kettle versions had their bottom halves removed, possibly for economic or other practical reasons. Another theory is that the modern construction was influenced by early **jazz** drumsets that were making their way to Cuba. Cuban dance bands began to play both jazz and Cuban music, thus the drumset's early tom-toms (which were often single headed like the modern *timbal*) might have been used as musical substitutes for the larger kettles, eventually being separated from the drumset itself.

In the 1940s and 1950s, the *timbal* began to be known worldwide as it was central to the **mambo** style popularized during those decades. The most influential *timbalero* yet has been Tito Puente, often known as *El Rey del Timbal* (King of the Timbal). As a bandleader, Puente brought the *timbal* out from behind the horn section and stood while performing, both innovations that are now standard practice. His skill and showmanship on the instrument helped make the *timbal* the well-known instrument that it is today.

Further Reading

Quintana, José Luis, and Chuck Silverman. *Changuito, a Master's Approach to Timbals.* New York: Manhattan Music Publications, 1998.

Nolan Warden

Timbalada

Timbalada is a Brazilian **bloco afro** established in the 1990s, based in the Candeal neighborhood of Salvador, Bahia, **Brazil**. The group is known for their innovative, percussion-dominated pop songs, and upbeat music that mixes Afro-Brazilian styles with Caribbean and American dance rhythms. They have integrated two percussion instruments into Brazilian popular music, the *timbau* and the *tres surdos*. The latter is a set of three differently sized *surdos* (bass drums) set on a rack, played by one percussionist. They won the Prêmio Sharp award and Troféu Bahia Folia **Carnival** awards.

The group is named after the *timbau*, an Afro-Brazilian drum the group's director, percussionist and composer Carlinhos Brown adopted from the streets of Candeal. Brown established an outreach organization to engage local youths and train them in percussion. In 1990, he began running weekly public rehearsals and the top percussionists from these sessions formed the group Vai Quem Vem, which subsequently participated in the Grammy-winning recording *Brasileiro*. Brown changed the name to Timbalada and in 1993 the group released their first recording, *Timbalada*. Since the group's inception, they have inspired Brazilians to dedicate themselves to percussion and Afro-Brazilian culture and have contributed to the development of Candeal.

Further Reading

Perrone, Charles A. and Christopher Dunn. *Brazilian Popular Music and Globalization.* New York: Routledge, 2001.

Thomas Rohde

Timbau

The *timbau* (also spelled *timbal*) is a long, conically shaped drum commonly used in *axé* music and a variety of other Afro-Brazilian music styles from Bahia, **Brazil**. It is usually made of wood and has one, tightly tuned, plastic head that produces its characteristic high-pitched popping sound. The instrument is loud and lightweight and can be mounted on a stand or easily carried using a strap. It is usually played with the hands, in the same fashion as the *djembe* and *atabaque* (*conga*-like drum used in the Afro-Brazilian religion *candomblé*), but sticks are sometimes used. The *timbau* produces a variety of sounds and is often used as a lead instrument to call breaks and mark transitions. Its basic tones are open, high-pitched slap, and low bass.

There are many theories about the origin of the *timbau.* The instrument's roots and playing style were established and continue to be developed in the Brazilian folkloric genre *samba de roda* (circle *samba*), and in the neighborhoods and streets of Bahia. During the late 1980s, the percussionist Carlinhos Brown adopted the instrument from the streets of Candeal, Bahia, and began integrating it into Brazilian popular music. It soon became a prominent feature of Brown's group **Timbalada**, whose name was derived from the instrument. For their 1992 **Carnival** debut, the group used 200 *timbaus.* The success of Timbalada quickly popularized the instrument, making its use standard in *blocos afro* and *axé* music. It is currently being slowly integrated into many other Brazilian styles.

Further Reading

Crook, Larry. *Brazilian Music: Northeastern Traditions and the Heartbeat of a Modern Nation.* ABC-CLIO World Music Series. Santa Barbara, CA: ABC-CLIO, 2005.

Thomas Rohde

Tiple

The *tiple* is a small **guitar** that appears in several countries such as Spain, **Colombia, Guatemala, Argentina, Venezuela, Puerto Rico, Cuba**, and the **Dominican**

Republic. *Tiple* is the Spanish word for treble or soprano, which applies to the *tiple* itself since this instrument is a smaller version of a guitar and it has a higher pitched voice. The *tiple's* sizes and tunings are not standard and vary from region to region.

Scholars agree that the *tiple* from the Canary Islands was the predecessor to the Colombian and Puerto Rican *tiples*. The instrument has four or five strings like the first Colombian and Puerto Rican *tiples*. It was probably brought to the Caribbean during the early colonial time, changing the number of strings and tunings over the centuries. In Puerto Rico, the *tiple* was used in orchestras that played European dances such as waltzes and minuets. Its shape is similar to the Puerto Rican *cuatro*. The Colombian *tiple* is very similar in shape to a guitar. It has 12 metal strings arranged in four triple courses. It is tuned d-g-b-e like the first four strings of the guitar. It is used in Andean Colombian music as well as in other Latin American folkloric musical styles (see *bambuco*). The Venezuelan *tiple* is a little different. It has either four of five strings arranged in double or triple courses. Other *tiples* have a variable number of metallic strings that range from four single strings like the Peruvian *tiple* to ten strings arranged in five double courses like the Cuban one. All of them look like small guitars.

Further Reading

Cuatro Project. The Tiples of Puerto Rico [Online]. The Cuatro Project Web site, www.cuatro-pr.org/Home/Eng/Instrmus/Tiples/tiples.htm.

Raquel Paraíso

Tonada

Tonada is the name given to different modalities of traditional music, which varies based on the country. In **Cuba**, *tonada* designates the melody with which the *punto cubano* is sung. It is named after the choruses, authors, musical referents, or devices that are used and aimed at different purposes, situations, and themes. In **Ecuador**, *tonada* is a type of music and dance derived from the dancing genre. It is written in a minor pitch and in a 6/8 beat measure. The titles of these *tonadas* suggest their textual content, which is written in quatrains with one verse used as the chorus. In Ecuador *tonada* is typical of the Creole **Carnival** in the province of Chimborazo. In **Chile**, *tonada* is the name of a mono-rhythmic folk singing, which may or may not have chorus. It is characterized by its alternation and metric superposition of the melody (6/8 and 3/4 beat measure). It is accompanied by **guitars** and **harps** and its verses are different forms of eight-syllable verses. They are classified according to the situation in which they are sung: serenade, praise, or blessing for the grooms, **romance, corrido**, or Christmas carol. In **Argentina**, *tonada* designates a *Creole* rural song sung by one or two voices in parallel thirds. It juxtaposes 3/4 and 6/8 compasses for the accompaniment and the singing. It is always performed by string instruments in different combinations and is one of the most representative musics of the region of Cuyo. In **Venezuela**, *tonada* is a genre of song inspired in the traditional plain chants from which it takes its basic melodic twists. Although the tertiary metric is very frequent, it is performed with a great freedom of metric and tempo. It is usually about love and it is accompanied by the **cuatro**. Finally, in the **Dominican Republic**, *tonada* is a type of rural song sung a capella or with accompaniment. Unlike other regions, in the Dominican Republic the *tonada* does not have particular characteristics; instead it is the performer who identifies it as a *tonada*.

Further Reading

Schechter, John M. *Music in Latin American Culture: Regional Traditions.* New York: Schirmer Books, 1999.

Neris González and Liliana Casanella

Tres

Arsenio Rodríguez plays the *tres* in a recording studio in the 1950s. (Frank Driggs Collection/Getty Images)

The *tres* is a six-string **guitar**-like instrument, which, due to its rich history, is considered the national string instrument of **Cuba**. The *tres* is frequently used in *punto **guajiro*** and ***son***. The modern *tres* developed from two distinct sources. The first was from Spanish double-strung instruments that performed a harmonic function. The other was from (with a reinterpretation) types of indigenous African chordophones. In Cuba, these single-strung African chordophones were turned into three double courses, for which the *tres* was named. From a morphologic point of view, the instrument possesses diverse variants according to the form and shape of the body.

Its transmission and performance practices developed both orally and experimentally. The *tres* is sometimes plucked with a tortoise shell pick and at times with the fingers of the right hand. Its technique is based on three fundamental movements: *punteado* (finger picking), *rayado* (strumming), and *alza-púa* (alternate picking). The rhythmic and accented patterns are associated with the Bantu and Dahomeyan peoples, which has reinforced the *alza-púa* technique. Records show that the *tres* developed simultaneously in eastern, western, and central regions of Cuba but there is one legendary figure, Nené Manfugás, who supposedly brought the *tres* from the village of Baracoa to Santiago de Cuba around 1892.

The **son** and *punto guajiro* have emerged as the genres best suited for the *tres*. It is used especially in smaller ensembles, such as *sexteto* and **septeto**, where it acts as a lead instrument and is responsible for introductions and transitions, similar to a **tumbao**. It can be a solo or an accompanying instrument, but it is mainly used in *son* to establish patterns that fade then reappear within the context of the piece, which gives it a unique character. At times, it assumes an improvisational role, which requires a virtuosic execution, and alternates with the guitar. It is also a key element in guiding the way the other instruments of the ensemble interact and compliment each other.

In addition to the *son*, the *tres* is regularly used in the performance of other traditional genres such as **changüí**, *sucu sucu*, and **guaracha**. In *changüí*, the *tres* functions as a kind of lead instrument used to articulate melodic rhythmic patterns and emphasize accents. It has many roles within the *changüí*: it provides introductions, accompanies other instruments, creates melodies, facilitates the climaxes of the piece, and it performs additional phrases that act as instrumental fill-ins at the end of each verse. In *sucu sucu*, it performs a plucking pattern that is maintained throughout a piece, while in *guaracha* it generally has a harmonic function. In the *punto guajiro*, it takes on an improvisatory and harmonic role while also performing virtuosic passages in the interludes between verses.

Notable performers include **Arsenio Rodríguez**, Niño Rivera, Isaac Oviedo, Luis Lija, Chito Latamblet, Pancho Amat, and Juan de la Cruz Antomarchi Cotó. These *treseros* were among the first to establish a definitive style for the *tres* that was carried on by subsequent generations of players. By the 1940s, the *tres* became well known within other genres of popular music such as the **conjunto**, as well as those previously mentioned. Also, since the end of the 1980s works have been composed, both solo and chamber, for the *tres* and symphony orchestra. Since 1990, the study of the *tres* has been institutionalized and included in schools of music. *Tres* methods in Cuba developed such as the one by Félix Guerrero in 1927 and more recently, a method by Efrain Amador and Doris Oropesa. Although it is considered a native instrument of Cuba, it has a well-known presence in Puerto Rico where it is strung as three triple courses especially in their interpretation of traditional **salsa** music.

Rodríguez, Arsenio

Blind since childhood, Ignacio Jacinto Loyola Rodríguez, also known as *El ciego maravilloso* (1911–1970), played the **marimbula**, *botija, tingo talango,* and **tres**. He created a unique style of **guitar** playing notable for its sonority and virtuosity, its improvisatory capacity and its rhythmic and percussive use of the strings.

Around 1930, he joined the *son* performers of Havana, **Cuba**, and started performing with the *Sexteto Boston,* which he would later direct. His work with the **son** septet led to its redefinition as **conjunto**. Rodríguez added accompanying instruments to the *son* including the piano, a set of **congas**, and three trumpets. In 1940 Rodriguez created his own orchestra, which was called Conjunto de Arsenio Rodríguez. Rodríguez influenced the development of *son* by creating a new pattern within the genre, and additionally, he widened and developed the rhythm section. Rodríguez is the composer of famous pieces such as "Bruca maniguá," "La vida es un sueño," and "Dile a Catalina." Latin musicians such as Willie Colón and Johnny Pacheco cited him as the originator of the main school of **salsa**.

Further Reading

García, David F. *Arsenio Rodríguez and the Transnational Flows of Latin Popular Music.* Philadelphia: Temple University Press. 2006.

Neris González and Liliana Casanella

Further Reading

González, Nelson. *Tres Guitar Method.* Pacific, MO: Mel Bay Publications, 2006.

González Bello, Neris, Liliana Casanella y Grizel Hernández. La Encuesta del Siglo XX. Música Cubana. Multimedia. (Inédito).

Sublette, Ned. *Cuba and Its Music: From the First Drums to the Mambo.* Chicago: Chicago Review Press, 2004.

Neris González and Liliana Casanella

Tresillo

Tresillo is a rhythmic group used abundantly in Cuban and **salsa** music. It consists of a three-note measure and therefore becomes the first measure of a 3–2 *clave* or the second measure of a 2–3 *clave.* The rhythm of these three notes is described as *fuerte* (strong) and begins the tension that is relaxed in the two-note measure of the *clave.* The *tresillo's* presence in Cuban music can be traced back to African musical practices, one example being Yoruban music featuring 6/8 measures containing one eighth-note every other beat. In 2/4, such a measure can be written as a dotted 8th, 16th, 8th rest, and 8th note. With a slight duration change, the 2/4 measure becomes two-dotted eighth notes plus an eighth note, yielding the first measure of a 3–2 *son clave,* signature of the Cuban **son**. *Tresillo* also occurs in the **rumba** *clave* with slight duration alterations, and the **cinquillo** rhythm becomes *tresillo* with the removal of the second and forth notes. This three-note grouping not only occurs in Cuban popular music and **Latin jazz**, but in all forms of **jazz**, even those forms most would assume have no Latin elements. Breaks before solos, composing patterns, horn backgrounds, lead melodies, and phrasings during a solo are all based on the *tresillo.*

Claves

An example of *tresillo* rhythm on *claves* over two measures. (George Torres)

Further Reading

Floyd, Samuel A., Jr. "Black Music in the Circum-Caribbean." *American Music* 17, no. 1 (Spring 1999): 1–37.

Raymond Epstein

Trío Nordestino

Trío nordestino means Northeastern **trio**, but it can designate two distinct elements in the realm of Brazilian music. It can refer to the trio created by Luiz Gonzaga (1912–1989) around the 1950s to play mainly Northeastern dance music, such as *forró* music. The trio is made up of *zabumba* (a medium-size double-headed drum), piano **accordion**, and triangle. Trío Nordestino is also the name of a famous *forró* group that appeared in the 1960s playing in the Northeastern trio formation. The first members of the group were: Lindu (Lindolfo Barbosa), singing, playing piano accordion, and composing many of their hits; Coroné on *zabumba*; and Cobrinha on triangle (these last two members are known by their nicknames).

With regard to the first meaning, according to recent research this type of trio did not exist before Gonzaga and, hence, he was the creator of *trío nordestino.* He wanted to perform with a group of instruments that were known and familiar to Northeasterners. Gonzaga also placed the instruments on stage thinking about sound balance: *zabumba* on the left, accordion in the middle, and triangle on the right (as seen by the audience). Another advantage of this particular instrument formation was the ease of finding players for the group. Considering that Gonzaga used to travel through the interior setting up performances on the way, this formation was an easy way to deal with his need to find musicians in different locations (three musicians, readily available) and the rough playing conditions (no amplification). This trio can also be called *regional nordestino* (Northeastern regional ensemble).

With regard to the second meaning, Trío Nordestino represents, in the trajectory of *forró* music, a transition between Luiz Gonzaga's and Jackson do Pandeiro's (1919–1982) styles. In the recordings, Gonzaga's trio experimented with going beyond the three instruments adding the electric bass, drumset, **cavaquinho** (small four-string guitar), **flutes, pandeiro** (a sort of large tambourine with little jingles around the side), *agogô* (double cowbell), shakers, and **guitars** (six, seven and ten strings). Trío Nordestino's lyrics were characteristically hot and good humored. Some songs used double entendre, while others were more subtle, but most of them drew upon Northeastern issues and themes.

The group had one of their first hits, "Procurando Tu" ("Searching You") in 1970, which was composed by Antonio Barros and had double entendre lyrics. Other hits came in 1974 including "Chililique," "Conversa de Motorista" ("Driver's Conversation"), 1975 with "Forró Pesado" ("Heavy Forró"), and 1978 with "Chinelo de Rosinha" ("Rosinha's flip-flop"), "Forró no Claro" ("Forró at Daylight"), and "Petrolina/Juazeiro."

Trío Nordestino was claimed to be the best Northeastern music group during the dictatorship (1964–1984). Despite the fact that their members changed over the years, Trío Nordestino continuously released recordings including seven disks in the 1960s, nine in the 1970s, ten in the 1980s, seven in the 1990s, and since 2000 two CDs have been released. Nowadays, prompted by the university *forró* movement, the trio has Luís Mário, son of Lindu on triangle and vocals, Bebeto, godson of Lindu on accordion, and Carlinhos Coroneto, grandson of Coroné on *zabumba*.

Further Reading

Fernandes, Adriana. "Music, Migrancy, and Modernity: A Study of Brazilian Forró." Ph.D. diss., University of Illinois at Urbana-Champaign, 2005.

Adriana Fernandes

Trío Romántico

The *trío romántico* is a vocal and instrumental ensemble that consists of three singers, usually male, sometimes accompanied by **guitar** and percussion. The musical repertoire is dominated by the ***bolero***, though most trios include other genres such as *vals*, *son*, *cha-cha-chá* as well as regional varieties like the *vals peruano* and *huapangos*. The height of the *trio romántico's* popularity was in the 1940s and 1950s, with the most internationally famous *trío romántico,* **Trío Los Panchos**, which defined the standard for *trío romántico* performance practice. The popularity of the *tríos romantícos* largely coincided with the career of Los Panchos and their emulators. Some of these groups continued to have success into the 1970s. Today's *trios* have reverted to the style represented by Los Panchos, and they can be found performing in urban centers in Latin America and abroad. Their repertoire looks back to the classic *Época de oro* (golden age of the 1940s and 1950s) songs made famous by Los Panchos.

Trios románticos developed their performance style from a mix of different influences. The music consists of voices, chordal instruments, a lead instrument, and layered percussion: an instrumentation found in many Latin American popular music ensembles. By the 1930s other important groups had influenced the generation of *trio* performers. These included Los Hermanos Martínez Gil (1928) and Trio Calaveras (1938). By the time Los Panchos debuted in 1944, there were signs that the performance of the urban *bolero* was returning to a guitar-based instrumentation with a higher, sweeter-sounding contratenor as the lead voice.

The standard *trío* ensemble now consists of vocals, guitars, and rhythm section. The vocals are usually three independent vocal lines with a lead tenor (*primera voz*) and two lower harmonizing vocals (*segunda* and *tercera voz*). Often, the upper voice sings the melody while the bottom voices move along stepwise to fit the harmony. In a typical performance, the three voices may sing the song together in rhythmic unison the first time through, and the second time through the lead sings the melody with words while the two lower voices hum a background harmony in longer note values. One of the distinguishing features of the ensemble is the use of the guitars as the principal accompaniment. The early innovators of the style developed a type of guitar virtuosity that has remained unparalleled in Latin American popular music. Generally speaking, there are two guitars and a *requinto*, which is a type of small lead guitar. With regard to texture, the two standard guitars perform an accompaniment, often in different registers, while the *requinto* either supplies a melodic lead, or embellishes the sections between the sung verses. This is demonstrated in Los Panchos recordings of "Caminemos," "Contigo," and "Sin ti." Another option is for the *requinto* player to play a melodic duet with the first guitarist while the second guitarist plays a *bolero* rhythm underneath.

While it is not unusual for trios to perform without percussion, on recordings and live performances a small Latin American rhythm section often accompanies the group. The rhythm section evolved out of the **Afro-Cuban** practice of layered percussion, which provides a composite dance rhythm (e.g., *bolero, son,* etc.). Most often the rhythm instruments consist of *maracas*, *bongos/timbals*, and upright bass. The maracas generally play a common timeline pattern of steady eighth notes, while the *timbal* (if used) plays rhythmic variations of the other timeline patterns. Sometimes the *timbal* player will strike the side of the drum frame with the sticks, a technique known as *paila* or *cascara*. The identity of the percussionists is generally unknown to us; the focus is on the three members of the trio, and the rhythm section only serves as an anonymous backup. Nevertheless, the rhythm section of the *tríos* was important in maintaining a steady dance rhythm, and their inclusion in recordings and in live performance was crucial for the success of the sound.

Although the commercial success of the *trío romántico* largely ended by the 1960s, the *trío romántico* remains a popular ensemble for a variety of social occasions including, *serenatas,* weddings, and restaurant engagements, where they perform *al talon* (that is, they take requests and charge by the song). The relative ease of performance, due to the portability of the group, along with a shared repertoire that was firmly established by 1960, makes it easy for trios to perform in a variety of contexts. There are *tríos románticos* all over Latin America and in cities in the **United States** that have a Latin American population. One can safely say that they remain the most popular of all Latin American ensembles.

Further Reading

Ortíz, Ramos P. M. *A Tres Voces Y Guitarras: Los Tríos En Puerto Rico.* San Juan, P.R: s.n., 1991.

Ortíz, Ramos P. M. *El Trío Los Panchos: Historia Y Crónica.* San Juan, P.R: P.M. Ortíz Ramos, 2004.

Torres, George. "The *Bolero Romántico:* From Cuban Dance to International Popular Song." In *From Tejano to Tango: Essays on Latin American Popular Music,* edited by Walter A. Clark, 151–71. New York: Garland, 2002.

George Torres

Tropicália

Tropicália was a Brazilian musical movement in the late 1960s that was formed mainly by Bahian composers and interpreters, such as leaders **Caetano Veloso** and **Gilberto Gil**, composer Tom Zé, singers Gal Costa and Nara Leão, lyricists Torquato Neto and Capinam, the group Mutantes, and arrangers Rogério Duprat, Damiano Cozzella, and Júlio Medalha. The collective album-manifesto that these artists collaborated on, *Tropicália, ou panis et circensis* (1968), is the ultimate *Tropicalista* musical reference. *Tropicália* represented a major rupture in Brazilian esthetics due to its behavioral, cultural and political implications, which is at a point of convergence of several radical artistic vanguards (like the modernist anthropophagy of the 1920s, and concrete poetry of the 1950s) and other turning points like *bossa* *nova*. Despite its short life, *Tropicália* remained influential to many artists who were in tune with its counter-cultural, ironic, rebellious, and antinationalistic sentiments. After its antiestablishment start, *Tropicália* quickly became highly prestigious and commercially successful, attaining a ubiquitous status in the media. It commemorated 30 years in 1998, enjoying mainstream acclaim.

Tropicália emerged during a revolutionary moment when **Brazil** was being traversed by several contradictory forces. While many Brazilians wanted to join the transnational community that was enjoying the Beatles's **rock** music, antiwar protests, and the counterculture movement, they also considered it necessary to actively oppose the rightwing military dictatorship imposed by the 1964 coup. This contradiction is illustrated in a prevalent oversimplified opposition between **MPB** and *Tropicália*. According to this narrative, MPB songs represented an ideal of resistance against the dictatorship and the international political and economic powers associated with it. As a consequence, in the esthetic field, MPB drew mainly from Brazilian genres, which stood for the Brazilian masses. Rock music and other Anglo-American styles, even musical instruments such as the electric **guitar**, were associated with imperialism and the dictatorship, and consequently banned from 1960s MPB. The artists of this movement were suspicious of consumerism and the mass media, which they saw as a necessary evil. They wore everyday clothes in their performances and tried to behave not as superstars, but as average middle-class people. Due to censorship, their song lyrics relied heavily on metaphor to convey hidden leftist oppositional messages, encouraging the masses to resist the dictatorship.

Gilberto Gil, a central figure in Brazilian *Tropicália*, performs on stage during a concert in 2007. (AP/Wide World Photos)

Conversely, the *Tropicalista* composers made use of all of MPB's forbidden icons with the very aim of provoking scandal among the leftist nationalists. Their music juxtaposed national and transnational genres (in which the electric guitar played a prominent role) and their lyrics were not leftist but surreal and anarchic (for example, those of "It is Forbidden to Forbid"). Juxtaposition was central to *Tropicália,* which merged contradictions such as the modern/archaic, the national/foreign, and high/mass culture; artists used star appeal, fashion, and the mass media to challenge MPB's populist ideals of authenticity. In comparison to the didactic approach of protest songs, *Tropicalista* production seemed chaotic, nihilistic, and aimless when the genre emerged. The actual impact of this music's critique was only appreciated when its major innovators Caetano Veloso and Gilberto Gil were arrested and exiled by the military in 1968 in the midst of the release of Institutional Act 5 (AI-5), which opened the way for the most violent period of the dictatorship.

Tropicália was not merely a rupture emanating from a small group of middle-class musicians, but an organic movement embracing the entirety of Brazilian society. In 1967, film director and writer Glauber Rocha launched his masterpiece *Terra em Transe,* which became highly influential as a vision of Brazil for all those who would propose *Tropicália*-like movements in the visual arts, theater, literature, fashion, and music. Though similar in many ways, none of these movements was consciously interrelated, and in the words of influential *Tropicalista* theater director José Celso Martinez Corrêa, instead of a *Tropicalista* movement, there was a confluence of anxieties brought by social movements that were being formed. This draws the attention to the intense change of mentality that was happening among the common people as opposed to the conservative romantic leftist idealism of the intellectual leaders criticized by Rocha in his film. To agree with Corrêa adding to a deeper understanding of the cultural struggles of the 1960s, new evidence shows that MPB audiences were attracted by the genre and movement called *Jovem Guarda,* which existed before *Tropicália* and was a Brazilian version of the 1960s British neorock, complete with the accompanying generational criticism brought by the new adolescent behaviors. As such, *Jovem Guarda* was harshly criticized by nationalist-leftist ideologues, as *Tropicália* would be. When *Tropicália* came to light, many listeners identified both with MPB and *Tropicália,* which relativizes dichotomies, oppositions and neat categorizations, and establishes both denominations as two faces of the same process.

Tropicália's music relies on a frenetic carnivalization of musical genres, fusing the urban **samba** to Frank Sinatra's "My Way," rural **baião** to Jimi Hendrix, martial marches to **bolero** (regarded as kitsch by the middle classes), and *bossa nova* to outdated styles from 1930s radio. Rejecting protest song's epic, heroic activism, *Tropicália* adopted a cynical attitude through the mixture of discrepant elements. Instead of proposing concrete answers for the end of the dream of economic development of the 1950s, the *Tropicalistas* expressed hopelessness through ironic laughter. In this vein, one of the icons appropriated by *Tropicália* from the start was **Carmen Miranda**, who was generally taken by middle-class Brazilians to be an exotic and incongruous mixture of Brazilian clichés for tourists and American colonialism.

A literary influence that was soon appropriated by the nascent *Tropicalista* movement was modernist writer and critic Oswald de Andrade's concept of anthropophagy, which consisted in a critical appropriation of developed countries' technology and culture as a means to lessen the cultural and economic discrepancies between those countries and Brazil. Thus, the *Tropicalistas* assimilated international pop music ironically, and that appropriation took hold in the national imaginary, raising public awareness of imperialism. The *Tropicalistas* denounced Brazilian underdevelopment and social injustice by juxtaposing, not opposing, the country's archaic and modern stages of development, including its transnational fluxes, thus denying the possibility of any synthesis arising from the contradiction between thesis and antithesis, as the Marxist intellectuals would have it.

Escaping definitions, the *Tropicalistas* produced an allegory of Brazil that was very much attuned to posterior postmodern theorizations like indeterminacy, a challenge to the stable categories of reason. A look into one of the songs from the *Tropicália* album, "Lindonéia," illustrates these indeterminacy effects. Lindonéia, the song's protagonist, was inspired by a serigraphy by Rubens Gerchman, "Lindonéia, a Gioconda do Subúrbio," which was, in turn, inspired by the life and disappearance of an actual person, a 20-something girl from the lower classes, who lived in a working-class neighborhood of Rio de Janeiro. As a missing person, the real-life Lindonéia hit the headlines and achieved notoriety after a life of obscurity, which is, in itself, ironic, and prompted comments on mass media by Gerchman's work. The lyrics of "Lindonéia" juxtapose images of tropical violence ("Torn into pieces/ Hit by cars/Dogs dead in the streets/Policemen watching/The sun hitting the fruits/Bleeding") with the insignificance of Lindonéia's life (commenting on prosaic, quotidian issues of her life). The juxtaposition of images of development with images of death and mutilation make fail all attempts to a synthesis, exploding the text into a multitude of significations. However, the music itself conveys indeterminacy. The song plays with the conventions of the sentimental and outdated *bolero* genre, opposing it to both **bossa nova** and iê-iê-iê styles (yeah yeah yeah a reference to popular songs by the Beatles such as "She Loves You"), associated with modernization. Iê-iê-iê is a Brazilian genre produced by the *Jovem Guarda* movement mentioned above that was inspired by 1960s Anglo-American rock, and was taken to be an uncritical emulation of the colonizers' music, which implies irony. The ironic use of iê-iê-iê by the *Tropicalistas* also conveys "Lindonéia's" indeterminacy: the irony was a challenge to nationalist discourses and implied the contradictions of Brazilian society, in which some people could be attuned to First World culture and technology while others like Lindonéia would barely survive. However, the meanings of the song's text (both music and lyrics) were indeterminate. In "Lindonéia," there was no explicit political statement, nor any attempt to construe a direct relationship between dictatorship and violence. Nara Leão's absolutely colloquial and *bossa nova*–like rendition broke away from dramatic styles associated with unambiguous denunciation. The same can be said of the musical sounds as a whole, which remind the listener of the protagonist's alienation and social condition through an antiquated *bolero*. The *bolero,* one of the genres used in "Lindonéia," is appropriate for connoting sentimentality and a lack of middle-class sophistication. The critical intention only emerges from the decoding of the song, which depends on each listener's critical and cultural literacy in the conventions of the genres utilized by the song; ultimately, however, the song's discourse is indeterminate—as is that of *Tropicália*.

Further Reading

Dunn, Christopher. *Brutality Garden: Tropicália and the Emergence of a Brazilian Counterculture*. Chapel Hill, NC: University of North Carolina Press, 2001.

Veloso, Caetano, and Barbara Einzig. *Tropical Truth: A Story of Music and Revolution in Brazil*. New York: A.A. Knopf, 2002.

Alvaro Neder

Trova Tradicional (Vieja Trova)

Trova tradicional is an old-style song genre that grew popular in **Cuba** at the end of the 19th century. It takes its place within the history of Cuba's tradition of poetic songs that express the feelings of their time. Song genres of the 20th century that emanate from *trova tradicional* include **nueva trova** from the 1960s, *novisima trova,* performed by the generation of song artists from the 1980s referred to as *generacion de los topos,* and, from later in the decade, the younger *trovadores* who met with poets at events such as live acoustic music series known as Guitarra Limpia and Puntal Alto. *Trova tradicional's* own antecedents are in the nationalist song genre *cancion cubana,* exhibiting both patriotic and lyrical aspects. With its birthplace in Santiago de Cuba, *trova tradicional* spread throughout Cuba with important centers in the cities of Sancti Spiritus and Havana. Its popularity was at its height between 1900 and 1925.

The Sancti Spiritus *trova* had its earliest origins in the choruses of **claves** and **tonadas**. In Havana, the *trovadores* of the island popularized their work through live concerts, radio, and recording performances. The Cuban comic theater troupes took the *trova* into Central America and **Mexico** where it also grew in popularity. Many types of *trova* songbooks, serving diverse aims, were published following the turn of the century. These publications were commercially successful and enjoyed wide distribution.

Trova singers were characteristically bohemian and festive in spirit. They tended to come from the working classes, especially trades that were both social and practical such as barbers, tobaccanists, and tailors. The music also developed in social settings as the singers performed **serenatas** for lovers and birthdays or for celebrations of saints' days. *Trova* did much to promote the figure of the singer with a **guitar**, although it was common for two singers be accompanied by guitars. The practice of performing ***boleros*** with two voices (*prima* and *segunda voz*) is a genre that arose from this regional context of Spirit Sanctus *trova*.

Trova tradicional made use of an ample variety of musical expressions and the *trova* singers incorporated into the core of their repertoire such important styles as ***habaneras***, *criollas,* **guarachas**, *canciones, claves,* **sones**, and ***bambucos.*** *Trovadores* have also been central to the practice of **Carnival**. Since the end of the 19th century, *trova* singers had as their charge the words and music of district *comparsas.* These Carnival songs became popular beyond the Carnival festival, and *trova* flourished in the Santiago districts of El Tivoli, San Augustin, and Los Hoyos.

In the first decades of the 20th century, **duos, trios**, and other groupings emerged that interpreted the *trovadoresco* style. Trio Matamoros, pioneers of the *bolero-son,* duos like those of Maria Teresa Vera and Rafael Zequeira, and also the famous duo of Los Compadres, are some examples. Groups such as these assured the continuity of the *trova* repertoire as the *son* became the prominent genre. The topics addressed in the repertoire of *trova tradicional* are idyllic and unrequited love, praising a woman using a poetic language that is linked to nature, and sensual love. There are also frequent occurrences of metaphor, humor, and irony. Within the metrical structure of stanzas, octosyllablic verses, quatrains, and ***décimas*** predominate, among others, which can be combined within the same subject.

Shorter songs with binary nonrepetitive structures predominate. The musical phrasing seeks the development of great melodic lyricism. The relationship between antecedent and consequent musical phrases in correlation with the literary discourse predominate, with cadences that resolve within a diatonic harmony. *Trova* also uses ascending and descending melodic movements, chromaticism, altered chords, the repeated use of neighboring tones, and other ornamental turns, as well as frequent contrasts between minor and major modes in sections.

The accompaniment style is the defining characteristic for each rhythmic genre within the *trovas.* The ***rasgueado***, or strumming of the guitar, is one of the techniques used in traditional *trova*. The style of strumming was unique to each *trovador.* For example, Alberto Villalón did not strum, but played upon the bass strings creating a melodic-harmonic movement, whereas Eusebio Delfin chose a semiarpeggiated style of accompanying. Singing to this guitar accompaniment has become a symbol of *trovadoresca* identity and of patriotic sentiment.

The songs of contestation or self-contestation in the form of a dispute were a creative style among the *trovadores* of the time, and very famous themed pairs of songs emerged such as the song "Aurora" in response to the song "Longina"; "La Habanera" to "La Bayamesa"; "Animada" to "Timidez"; and "Amparo" to "Alfonsa."

Pepe Sánchez (Santiago de Cuba, 1856–1920) is considered the precursor of the Cuban *trovador* movement. The Big Five of *trovas* include Sindo Garay, Manuel Corona, Alberto Villalón, Rosendo Ruiz, and Patricio Ballagas. In addition, many anonymous guitarist accompanists have contributed to the accompanimental style of the Cuban *trova*.

Important *Trovadores* come from across the island. Juan de Dios Echavarria, Fermin Castillo, Eusebio Premión, Paquito Portela, Pepe Banderas, Rufino and Ramon Marquez, and Emiliano Blez are from Santiago de Cuba; Graciano Gomez and Oscar Hernández are from Matanzas; Miguel Companioni, Rafael Teofilito Gomez, Manuel Gallo, Carlos Alfredo Varona Díaz de Tata Villegas, Sigifredo Mora Palma, and Rafael Rodriguez are from Sancti Spiritus; Alfredo Sanchez is from Villa Clara; and *trovadores* María Teresa Vera, among others, is from Havana. Among the relevant duos are Hermanas Marti, Hilda Santana y Luz Mustelieer, Hermanas Junco, Alfredo Gonzalez "Sirique"-Miguel Doyble, Hermanas Castro, Guarionex y Sindo Garay; representative *tríos* include Azul, Apolo, Matamoros; and among quartets are included Villalón, Cuba and Cancioneros de Oriente.

In 1908, *trova* competitions were held in front of Acera del Louvre. Performances and musical soirees were carried out in the Havana neighborhoods of Jesús del Monte, El Pilar, and Luyanó, and the most popular singers and guitarists of the era could be found performing in Barbaria Guayo. Many theaters and cinemas in the capital served as locations for the movement, including el Politeama grande, y Politeama chico, el recreo de Belascoain, and, the location considered to be the Mecca of Cuban *trova,* Cine Variedades y Cine Esmeralda.

Further Reading

Betancourt Molina, Lino. *La trova en Santiago de Cuba. Apuntes históricos.* La Habana: Andante Editora musical de Cuba, 2005.

Cañizares, Dulcila. *La trova tradicional cubana.* La Habana: Editorial Letras cubanas, 1992.

De León, Carmela. *Sindo Garay: memorias de un trovador.* Le Habana: Editorial Letras cubanas, 1990.

Díaz Pérez, Clara. *Sobre la guitarra la voz.* Le Habana: Editorial Letras cubanas, 1994.

Loyola, Fernández J. En Ritmo De Bolero: El Bolero En La Música Bailable Cubana. Ciudad de la Habana: Ediciones Unión, 1997.

Rodríguez, Ezequiel (recop. y coord.) *Iconografía de la Trova. Creadores e intérpretes.* Ediciones de la coordinación Provincial Habana del C.N.C.

Roy, Maya. *Músicas Cubanas.* Tres Cantos, Madrid: Akal, 2003.

Ruiz Elcoro, José. "Sindo Garay, el trovador supremo," en Revista *Clave,* año 3, no. 1, La Habana.

Valdés, Marta. *Donde vive la música.* Ediciones Unión, 2004.

Zamora Céspedes, Bladimir y Fidel Díaz Castro (comp.) *Cualquier flor. . . De la trova tradicional cubana.* Casa Editora Abril, 2006.

Liliana González

Tumbadora

The *tumbadora* is a Cuban barrel-shaped drum, usually made of wood with cow- or mule-skin heads. In English, it is usually called a ***conga*** drum, though this is somewhat mistaken. *Tumbadoras* come in different sizes, though they are usually around 30 to 32 inches tall, allowing them to be played while seated. Their heads commonly range from 10 to 12 inches in diameter, though smaller and larger sizes also exist. Early versions were based on African antecedents, having the skins tacked to the drum itself. Today, however, they are tuned by metal tensioning rods or lugs. They were originally associated with the secular ***rumba*** music of the early 20th century, but have become known worldwide through their use in genres such as ***mambo***, **Latin jazz**, ***salsa***, and even non-Latin popular music.

The root word of *tumbadora, tumba,* is of Bantu linguistic provenance, due to the large numbers of Cuban slaves brought from Bantu-speaking ethnic groups. Depending on the dialect, though, it could have different meanings, including a drum, but also a dance, ceremony, or herbalist. It could also simply be onomatopoeic. The word *conga,* the common word for the same drum in English, was originally only used to refer to drums used during **Carnival** for the rhythm called *la conga.* Tourists to Cuba during the early 20th century likely heard *tambores de conga* and translated it as *conga* drums. The word was then applied to any drum of similar construction.

The *tumbadora* was created in **Cuba** but had many African antecedents, the most obvious being associated with Central and West African ethnic groups. The word *ngoma* is often invoked in telling the history of the *tumbadora,* but this is an imprecise term that simply means drum in Bantu languages. Of the Bantu-speaking ethnic groups in Cuba, the drums most influencing the *tumbadora* were the *makúta* and *yuka.* Additionally, it is likely that Lucumí (Yoruba) drums, known as *bembé,* had some influence on early *tumbadora* construction. The *tumbadora* did not originally have a religious purpose. Instead, it was developed for secular entertainment in postslavery Cuba, especially in the *solares* (multifamily buildings with a shared common area). The *solares* were a meeting place of various African ethnic lineages and religious groups. It was these living situations that gave rise to the *tumbadora* and the music known as *rumba. Tumbadoras* were so connected to *rumba* that in the 1950s the Cuban scholar Fernando Ortiz referred to them simply as *tambores de rumba.*

The sonic capabilities of the *tumbadora* gave it a musical advantage that became an economic one as well. They increasingly entered religious practices since it was more financially practical to have one drum with multiple uses than many drums, each with only one purpose. Their construction—of staves rather than carved from a single log—was also advantageous. It was an easier method of construction that served to distinguish the *tumbadora* from its highly persecuted African antecedents.

The popularity of the *tumbadora* grew among Afro-Cubans and, during the mid-20th century, began a path toward worldwide recognition. **Arsenio Rodríguez** was probably the first to add a *tumbadora* as a standard instrument in the Cuban *conjunto,* doing so by 1940. In the **United States**, bandleader **Machito** embraced the *tumbadora* in the early 1940s. It also entered **jazz** music through the famous pairing of percussionist Chano Pozo and trumpeter Dizzy Gillespie, beginning what became known as Latin jazz. Its fame spread worldwide through *mambo* and, later, *salsa,* but also entered styles such as **rock** and rhythm and blues.

The musical popularity of the *tumbadora* was aided by changes in its construction. By the 1950s, the tacked-on animal skins which had to be tuned by heat were replaced with metal tuning lugs (thus greatly increasing its pitch range). By the 1960s, fiberglass shells had become common and, over the past decade, synthetic heads have seen more use due to their imperviousness to changing humidity. American manufacturers also began to mass-produce the *tumbadora,* bringing it to a wider audience. This commercialization resulted in the three main sizes referred to as *quinto* (small), *conga* (medium), and *tumbadora* (large). However, there was never a traditional ensemble that combined these names in such a way.

There have been many influential *tumbadora* players such as Tata Güines, Giovanni Hidalgo, Miguel "Angá" Díaz, and Carlos "Patato" Valdez. Candido Camero was one of the first to play multiple *tumbadoras* at once, while Ramón "Mongo" Santamaria was one of the most successful musicians to lead a band from behind the *tumbadoras.*

Further Reading

Warden, Nolan. "A History of the Conga Drum." *Percussive Notes* 43, no. 1 (2005): 8–15.

Nolan Warden

Tumbao

In Cuban music, *tumbao* encompasses the basic meter and rhythm pattern, harmony, and melody of a variety of major Cuban popular music genres although its character is defined and it is most importantly associated with the different **sons**.

Tumbao is generally executed by the **tres** bass or the piano or keyboard, although other instruments can be used depending on the type of orchestra. References to this musical form are found in the patterns of popular 19th-century *contradanses,* as well as in the left hand of certain keyboard pieces by Manuel Saumell, Ignacio

Cervantes, and others. In fact, composers viewed the *tumbao* as a synthesis of the stress patterns found in works such as the **habanera**, especially in the second section of the pieces. Such use of the *tumbao* has turned it into one of the national elements of Cuban music.

There are different models of *tumbao* that appear in a variety of Cuban dance music such as *son,* **cha-cha-chá**, **danzon**, and **timba**. Together with its characteristic rhythm and melody, the *tumbao* is also identified by specific qualities of articulation, interval relations, and stresses. Depending on the creativity of the instrumentalist, these features allow *tumbao* to interact stylistically with diverse musical genres.

Tumbao is central to Cuban musical identity and one of the most enjoyable elements of Cuban dance music.

Further Reading

Leymarie, Isabelle. *Cuban Fire: The Story of Salsa and Latin Jazz.* New York: Continuum, 2002.

Neris González and Liliana Casanella

United States

The United States has welcomed Latin American musical styles, performers, and listeners, and been the site of the genesis of new artists, styles, forms, and networks of support that have in turn influenced music making in Latin America. Patterns of residency, emigration, and regular contact across borders have contributed to the vibrant cultivation of Latin music. American record labels were instrumental in the rise to international popularity of various Latin musical genres such as *mambo*, *tango*, *bolero*, and *salsa*, while Hollywood delivered styles such as *mariachi* and *samba* to American audiences and beyond. At the same time that the media and commercial networks of exchange have helped establish shared tastes and trends across regions, diverse local histories and geographic settlement patterns reinforce persisting regional differences and musical identities. Major urban centers such as New York, Miami, San Antonio, and Los Angeles all boast vibrant but different Latino music cultures.

Historical Overview of Shared Trends

A quick review of major historical trends offers a useful template for a more detailed review of regional patterns of production and taste. The importation of Iberian musical tastes began in the 16th century with the first Spanish settlements in what is now the United States. Music that reflects this colonial influence survives in the form of religious festivities, dance dramas, instrumental practices, and song forms including *estribillos* and *coplas* (verses and refrains) cultivated across the American southwest.

The 19th-century stage provided a popular venue for new forms of entertainment, so in the 1850s, Mexican and Latin American theatrical companies were touring the United States continuously, bringing musical revues, *zarzuelas*, and dramas including popular songs and dances. Residents along the shifting United States and Mexican border favored *canciones* and *corridos* and *bailes* developed from country and ballroom dance styles such as the *chótis, mazurka,* **polka**, and *varvosienne*. These forms would later surface in the traditions of **Tex-Mex,** *tejano*, and *norteño* music.

The development of **jazz** in the United States, beginning in 1895, provided an important integrative esthetic that embraced musical influences from Latin America.

Mendoza, Lydia

Lydia Mendoza (1916–2007), known to her fans as *La Alondra de la Frontera* (The Meadowlark of the Border), was the first female performer of Mexican American vernacular music to gain stardom in the fledgling commercial music industry of the 1930s. Mendoza is most commonly lauded for her solo singing and her unique playing style on 12-string **guitar**, however, she was also a skilled ensemble performer of *conjunto norteño*, **mariachi**, and **orquestra** music. In the early 1930s, Mendoza had a regular spot on radio host Manuel J. Cortez Mendoza's weekly program, *La Voz Latina*. She released her first solo recording, "Mal Hombre," a song she learned from a bubblegum wrapper, which garnered her national attention and a 10-year recording contract. Mendoza had a career of recording and performing that spanned nearly 60 years. Highlights include Mendoza's performance at the Smithsonian Festival of American Folklife in Canada (1971) and a performance for President Carter at the John F. Kennedy Center in Washington, D.C. (1975). She was inducted into the *Tejano* Music Hall of Fame in 1984 and the *Conjunto* Music Hall of Fame in 1991.

Further Reading

Broyles-González, *Yolanda Lydia Mendoza's Life in Music: La Historia de Lydia Mendoza*. New York: Oxford University Press, 2001.

Erin Stapleton-Corcoran

In New Orleans, Spanish and French *Creole* culture, invigorated by Caribbean influences, gave rise to musical developments such as Jelly Roll Morton's use of the Cuban *habanera* rhythm in "St. Louis Blues."

The emergence of an international ballroom dance movement provided another avenue for contact with Latin American music and dance. Vernon and Irene Castle helped popularize ballroom-style versions of the Argentine *tango* and the Brazilian *maxixe* in the United States via their appearances on stage, their dance manual, and at their dance academy. The nascent recording industry courted American interest in international music traditions, including Latin American styles. New York City, Camden, and later San Antonio and Los Angeles emerged as early recording centers for Latin American music.

Mambo and **Latin jazz** ruled the 1940s and 1950s. Dizzy Gillespie, with Afro-Cuban *bongó* player Chano Pozo, composed the influential "Manteca" in 1947. The orchestras of Frank "**Machito**" Grillo, **Tito Puente**, and others thrilled audiences with their Cuban and Puerto Rican-inflected jazz and dance bands. Beto

Villa's *tejano* orchestra and the band Conjunto Bernal offered contrasting blends of Mexican dance music and swing jazz. The era also saw the rise of the ***bolero romantico*** with the formation of the Mexican **Trio Los Panchos** in New York. American composers, including George Gershwin, Aaron Copland, and Leonard Bernstein, incorporated Cuban and other Latin rhythms into their symphonic and stage works.

The rock era of the 1960s was one of revolution in society and music. Fidel Castro's Cuban Revolution and the civil rights movement helped inspire Latino and Chicano identity movements. ***Nueva canción*** and ***nueva trova*** voiced the views of intellectuals and socially conscious musicians. American folk-rock musicians Joan Baez, Bob Dylan, and Pete Seeger were connecting with Latin American singer songwriters including **Violeta Parra** and Victor Jara of **Chile**, Mercedes Sosa of **Argentina**, and **Silvio Rodríguez** of **Cuba**. The emphasis on poetic social commentary and a principled resistance to commercial esthetics set ***nueva canción*** apart from the **rock** movement, despite mutually acknowledged inspirations. Latin American artists also contributed directly to rock 'n' roll with influential superstars Richie Valens, Freddy Fender, and Carlos Santana leading the list.

The emergence of ***salsa*** in the 1970s in New York ultimately transformed the international music scene. The decade was an era of religious transformation as Catholic liberation theology emerged in Central America and competed with a new wave of evangelical and Pentecostal Protestantism. The Latino gospel music emerging from this practice is popular throughout the United States, particularly in contemporary Latino congregations in Chicago and the American south.

New York and the Northeast

The center of Latin music performance and production is New York City, which has not only promoted the consumption and exchange of Latin American music, but is also the birthplace of *salsa,* **boogaloo**, and Latin Soul. However, Caribbean perspectives, principally Puerto Rican, Cuban, Dominican, and Colombian dominate New York and much of the northeast.

Many of the biggest names in Latin jazz called New York their home and it was New York musicians that helped lead the nation in connecting the black pride of the civil rights movement to Latin American heritage and to music that reflected that pride. The Latino umbrella promoted new interest in Afro-Latin practices including the drums of Santeria and the *berimbau* music associated with Brazilian *capoeira*. A generation of New York-born-and-raised Puerto Ricans called themselves Nuyorican, and celebrated the confluence of Latin American and African roots in newly defined styles such as *salsa,* Latin soul, and boogaloo.

New York's Fania Records, founded in 1964 by singer and pianist Johnny Pacheco and attorney Jerry Masucciled, brought *salsa* to an international audience.

Fania Records helped build the careers of Nuyorican *salsa* singer Hector LaVoe, as well as *conga* virtuoso Ray Barretto. Other artists represented by Fania included superstars **Celia Cruz**, Luis Perico Ortiz, Bobby Valentin, and **Ruben Blades**. In the late 1970s, *salsa* drew increasing competition from *merengue* in the city's dance clubs, credited in part to *merengue's* simpler dance steps and the growing Dominican population.

Cuban **hip-hop** and Puerto Rican *reggaetón* are among the most recent Latin contributions to New York's music scene.

The Southeast

Early Latin American settlement in Tampa and New Orleans represented contrasting poles of southeastern practice, with Spanish-language theater in Tampa, and the integration of Cuban, Haitian, and other Caribbean influences by Spanish and *Creole* musicians in the development of jazz in New Orleans. Established Hispanic communities in 19th-century Florida and Louisiana gave rise to rural musical traditions shaped by family life and community celebrations. In Louisiana, for example, the *Isleños* of New Iberia, a rural community supported by commercial fishing and agriculture, still continue to sing *décimas* in the tradition of their great-grandparents, many of whom hailed from the Canary Islands. In recent years they have incorporated *corridos* and *rancheras* popular with their Texas-Mexican neighbors.

Spanish-speaking people have lived in Miami since the city's founding in 1896, but the city gained its reputation for promoting Latin music following the wave of postrevolution Cuban immigration in the 1960s. Subsequent waves brought large numbers of immigrants from **Venezuela, Haiti, Colombia, Peru**, the **Dominican Republic**, and **Brazil**, resulting in an increased emphasis on dance styles, particularly *salsa*, *timba*, *merengue,* hip-hop and new DJ styles. Beginning in the 1970s, Miami recording studios became known for promoting Latin pop. Less glossy versions of *vallenato, cumbia,* and other genres from Colombia such as *musica llanera* (from the plains performed with *arpa*, *cuatro* and *maracas*) and *bambuco* can also be heard in contexts supporting popular folkloric music.

The Cuban exile community continues to dominate Miami's scene, and it includes legendary *mambo*-era bassist Israel Cachao Lopez, Latin jazz clarinetist and saxophone player Paquito D'Rivera, Israel Kantor, formerly of the *timba* group Los Van Van, and trumpeter Arturo Sandoval. Miami leads the still emerging *timba* scene in the United States with performers such as *Timba Libre,* the Cuban *Timba* All-Stars, and N'talla. The city's nightspots and party circuit offer Cuban Casino *salsa,* and *salsa rueda,* both club-based dance styles. Miami-based Cuban rapper Pitbull is a current favorite on the hip-hop scene. Caribbean dance music, including *bachata*, *merengue, soca, konpa, zouk*, as well as the increased popularity of *calypso* and steelband pan music, reflect both the beach culture of the region and the growing population from French, English, and Spanish Caribbean nations in Miami.

The Southwest

Spanish speakers resided in the Southwest and California long before English-speaking Americans. Tensions and exchanges across the U.S.-Mexican border, past and present, produced and continue to produce a rich body of music. Popular songs known as *corridos* are sung by Mexican *balladeers* usually to the accompaniment of solo guitar or a small acoustic ensemble; the poetic lyrics regularly address the conflict between non-Spanish-speaking settlers and Mexican residents. Many *corridos* have passed from generation to generation, documenting both the ordinary and the heroic activities of Mexican Americans and their neighbors.

New *corridos* in the folkloric style continue to be composed today. A more controversial form of the *corrido,* the *narco-corrido,* can be heard on contemporary Spanish-language radio stations, typically performed by the modern electric **conjuntos** (bands with **accordion**, 12-string bass **guitar** or *bajo sexto*, drum set, saxophone, and synthesizer) or *banda* (a brass, woodwind and percussion group, originally influenced by German polka bands). The *narco-corrido* style emerged from Sinaloa in northern Mexico, but the most famous representatives of this style, such as Los Tigres del Norte, perform throughout the Southwest.

Multiple Grammy Award winner and virtuoso accordionist, Flaco Jimenez popularized the *conjunto* sound with non-Hispanic audiences. He blended rhythm and blues with rock sensibilities in his performances of classic *rancheras, boleros,* and polkas. Competing with this original *conjunto* style was the new *tejano orquesta* sound developed in the 1930s and 1940s by Texas-born bandleader Beto Villa, a founder of the *jaitón* (high tone) jazz dance band format favored by middle-class patrons. Famous singers of this new genre include **Selena** and the West Texas rock band Los Lonely Boys.

The *mariachi* tradition is firmly, and proudly, ensconced throughout the Southwest, extending across the country. Tucson, Arizona, home to the annual international *Mariachi* festival, and San Antonio, Texas, are two of the cities known for their youth *mariachi* programs in schools as well as for supporting a larger number of professional *mariachis.* Popular *mariachi* singer Pepe Aguilar hails from San Antonio.

In New Mexico, Spanish speakers often identify themselves as *hispanos*, stressing their ties to old Spain. Many musical genres, including *alabados* (songs of praise) and *despedimientos* (funeral hymns), are primarily associated with religious occasions and festivals. Popular musical forms associated with entertainment include **romances** (ballads), *coplas* (couplets), *bailes* (dances), and *canciones* (songs in any verse form). *Inditas* and *comanches* are song types illustrating the interaction between Hispano and American Indian populations.

Los Angeles, Southern California, and the West Coast

The cosmopolitan milieu of Los Angeles showcases Mexican and Chicano music. Its vibrant street culture and alternative theater circuit counters romanticized or stereotypical images promoted by Hollywood. Los Angeles emerged in the 1960s as a center for development of the assertive Chicano identity movement. It was the home of Richie Valens, whose cross-over success with "La Bamba" brought **Chicano rock** to mainstream audiences. In the 1970s, East Los Angeles gained attention for a new and distinctive *Angeleno* sound perfectly suited to the new Chicano consciousness. In 1973, the band *Los Lobos* began performing the signature blend of Mexican traditional music with blues, rockabilly, and jazz that has earned them international acclaim. Other Chicano rockers linked to this decade include the band Tierra, El Chicano, and Marc Guerrero.

A Chicano perspective pervades Latino hip-hop in Los Angeles. Born Arturo Molina Jr., in East LA, Kid Frost began rapping in the 1980s. Frost's song "La Raza," and the album *Hispanic Causing Panic,* became hits in 1990. Mellow Man Ace, one of the first to employ Spanglish in his rap (born Upiano Sergio Reyes, in Havana) worked with the hip-hop legends of Cyprus Hill. The oppositional politics and art-world sensibilities fuel Ozomatli's mix of Spanish and English rap framed by a mix fusing *salsa,* funk, *cumbia,* and hip-hop.

The strength of regional habits and character constantly compete with the representation of Latin artists by the major record labels and the ubiquitous presence of international Spanish-language television stations such as *Televisa, Univision,* and *Telemundo.* Across the United States, Latin America, and the world, fans listen Latin American artists, which illustrate the continued influence of Spanish music on the Americas. The music of these Spaniards reflects the returning influence of sounds and practices shaped by a long history of American interaction.

Further Reading

Austerlitz, Paul. *Merengue: Dominican Music and Dominican Identity.* Philadelphia: Temple University Press, 1997.

Behague, Gerard. "Bossa and Bossas: Recent Changes in Brazilian Urban Popular Music." *Ethnomusicology* 17 (1973): 209–33.

Bensusan, Guy and Charles R. Carlisle. "Raices y Ritmos/Roots and Rhythms: Our Heritage of Latin American Music." *Latin American Research Review* 13/3 (1978): 155–60.

Broyles, Yolanda. *Lydia Mendoza's Life in Music.* New York: Oxford University Press, 2001.

Burr, Ramiro. *The Billboard Guide to Tejano and Mexican Music.* New York: Billboard Books, 1999.

Campo-Flores, Arian. "The Battle for Latino Souls." *Newsweek,* March 21, 2006. Online, September 2007, www.msnbc.msn.com/id/7168826/site/newsweek.

Clark, Walter Aaron. *From Tejano to Tango: Latin American Popular Music.* New York: Routledge, 2002.

Fernandez, Raul A. *From Afro-Cuban Rhythms to Latin Jazz.* Berkeley: University of California Press, 2006.

Glasser, Ruth. *My Music Is My Flag: Puerto Rican Musicians and Their New York Communities, 1917–1940.* Berkeley: University of California Press, 1995.

Gutierrez, Felix F. and Jorge Reina Schement. *Spanish-Language Radio in the Southwestern United States.* Austin: University of Texas at Austin, Center for Mexican American Studies, 1979.

Hernandez, Edwin. *Emerging Voices, Urgent Choices: Essays on Latino/a Religious Leadership.* Boston: Brill, 2006.

Herrera-Sobek, Maria. *Northward Bound: The Mexican Immigrant Experience in Ballad and Song.* Bloomington: Indiana University Press, 1993.

Koegel, John. "Canciones del país: Mexican Musical Life in California after the Gold Rush." *California History,* 78, no. 3 (1999): 160–87.

Koegel, John. "Mexican Musicians in the United States, 1910–1950." *California History,* 84, no. 1(2006): 6–24.

Koegel, John. "Village Musical Life Along the Rio Grande." *Latin American Research Review,* 18, no. 2 (1997): 173–251.

Leoffler, Jack. *La Música de los Viejitos: Hispano Folk Music of the Río Grande del Norte.* Albuquerque: University of New Mexico Press, 1999.

Lipsitz, George. "Cruising Around the Historical Bloc: Postmodernism and Popular Music in East Los Angeles." *Cultural Critique,* 5 (1987): 157–77.

Loza, Steven. *Barrio Rhythm: Mexican American Music in Los Angeles.* Urbana: University of Illinois Press, 1993.

Loza, Steven. *Tito Puente and the Making of Latin Music.* Urbana: University of Illinois Press, 1999.

Manuel, Peter. "Latin Music in the United States: Salsa and the Mass Media." *Journal of Communication* 41, no. 1 (1991): 104–16.

Mendoza de Arce, Daniel. *Music in Ibero-America to 1850: A Historical Survey.* Lanham, MD: Scarecrow Press, 2001.

Paredes, Américo. *A Texas-Mexican Cancionero.* Urbana: University of Illinois Press, 1976.

Paredes, Américo. *"With His Pistol in His Hand": A Border Ballad and Its Hero.* Austin: University of Texas Press, 1958.

Reyes, David and Tom Waldman. *Land of a Thousand Dances: Chicano Rock 'n' Roll from Southern California.* Albuquerque: University of New Mexico Press, 1998.

Roberts, John Storm. *The Latin Tinge,* second edition. New York: Oxford University Press, 1999a.

Roberts, John Storm. *Latin Jazz—The First of the Fusions, 1880s to Today.* New York: Schirmer Books, 1999b.

Romero, Brenda. "Cultural Interaction in the Matachines Dance." In *Musics in Multicultural America,* edited by Kip Lornell and Anne Rassmussen. New York: Macmillan, 1997.

Savino, Giovanni. *Bachata Musica del Pueblo* (video). New York: Arte Magnetica Productions, 2002.

Smith, Heather A. and Owen J. Furuseth. *Latinos in the New South: Transformations of Place.* Burlington, VT: Ashgate, 2006.

Spottswood, Richard. *Ethnic Music on Records: A Discography of Ethnic Recordings Produced in the United States.* Urbana: University of Illinois Press, 1990.

Strachwitz, Chris. *Arhoolie Records, Tejano Roots,* liner notes and webpage, accessed June 3, 2012, http://www.lib.utexas.edu/benson/border/arhoolie2/raices.html.

Sturman, Janet. "Iberian Music in the United States." In *Garland Encyclopedia of World Music, Vol. 3, The United States & Canada,* edited by Ellen Koskoff, 847–53. New York: Garland Press, 2000.

Wald, Elijah. *Narco-corrido: A Journey into the Music of Drugs, Guns, and Guerrillas.* New York: Harper Collins, 2002.

Websites

Arhoolie Records—Tejano Collection, Online, accessed June 3, 2012, http://www.arhoolie.com/mexican-regional-tejano

Frontera Collection of Mexican American Music, Online, accessed June 3, 2012, http://frontera.library.ucla.edu

Hutchinson, Sydney. *Merenge Típico,* Online, accessed June 3, 2012, http://merengue-ripiao.com/

Janet L. Sturman

Uruguay

Uruguay is located in South America, between **Argentina** and **Brazil**. The capital, Montevideo, is located on Uruguay's southern coast and is a major port city. Of the population, 88 percent is white, as compared to minority groups, such as the *mestizo* (8%), black (4%), and Amerindian (less than 1%) populations. As a result, in Uruguay, many popular musical styles are *Creole* forms that evolved from European dances, such as the **polka, *vals, danza*** (or *habanera*), and *mazurka*. These forms are still found in rural festivals and in family gatherings. Also in rural areas, the Colombian ***cumbia*** is very common. Tropical music (*música tropical*) as well as Caribbean styles like ***salsa, merengue***, and ***plena*** are enjoyed throughout the country.

The traditional figure of the *payador* sings improvised poetry, usually in 8-syllable, 10-line stanzas known as ***décimas***. In a *payada de contrapunto,* two singers face off in order to showcase their talent. A slow version of the *milonga,* a popular genre in Uruguay, accompanies ***payadas***. Faster versions are usually considered dance music and often do not contain lyrics. *Milonga* is also popular in the southern regions of Argentina, Brazil, and **Chile**.

The *tango* developed in both Argentina and **Uruguay** around the same time, on both sides of the *Río Uruguay.* The earliest traces of the *tango* date back to the 1880s. The most famous Uruguayan *tango* is "La cumparsita" ("The Little Parade"), which is well known internationally as well. *Estilo* (also called *triste*) was popular in Uruguay until the 1930s and had a significant impact on the development of *tango* singing. The birthplace of **Carlos Gardel**, arguably the most well-known *tango* musician, is disputed between France and Uruguay.

The *tamboril* is a key instrument in *candombe,* an Afro-Uruguayan genre. The *candombe* is typically played by *conjuntos lubolos*, in black communities around Montevideo, and is sometimes associated with **Carnival** celebrations. *Candombe* is often accompanied by *llamada* drumming. The genre experienced a popular revival in the second half of the 20th century.

In the 1960s, rock entered the global music, beginning in Britain and North America. The Beatles were popular in Uruguay as in the rest of the world, and served as the catalyst for the Argentine rock movement. Other international styles like **jazz** also gained popularity at this time. Cover bands of major British rock groups like the Beatles and the Rolling Stones were in demand, until the military coup of 1973, which toppled the unstable government of President Bordaberry and defeated the guerrilla group *Movimiento de Liberación Nacional,* also known as the *Tupamaros* (National Liberation Movement). Free elections did not occur again until 1984.

Murga is a type of dance theater performed during Carnival season, which consists of more than 80 days of celebration and is the longest in the world. *Murga* is related to the Spanish **zarzuela** and to *teatro callejero* (street theater). The *murga* is of Spanish origin, but has undergone many transformations since its conception. In the 1990s, *murga* gained acceptance as part of the sphere of Uruguayan popular music.

Canto popular uruguayo is a musical style comparable to **nueva canción** and **nueva trova** that developed in the 1970s. *Canto popular uruguayo* was the most dominant genre in Uruguayan music until the 1990s. *Canto popular uruguayo* is sung in Spanish, as opposed to most rock music, which is performed in English. *Los Olimareños* was a **duo** comprised of Pepe Guerra and Braulio López in the early 1960s. They criticized the restrictive government and pushed for economic and social change, with the result that their music was banned during the military dictatorship.

Other famous Uruguayan artists include Daniel Viglietti, Alfredo Zitarroja, and Eduardo Fabini. Daniel Viglietti, a singer, guitarist and composer, was influential in the *canto popular uruguayo* movement. Zitarrosa also sung and composed songs that formed part of the *canto popular uruguayo* repertoire. Their music was banned in 1976, and did not receive air time on the radio until 1984, at which time Zitarrosa returned from exile.

Further Reading

Beattie, John W. and Louis Woodson Curtis. "South American Music Pilgrimage. IV. Argentina and Uruguay." *Music Educators Journal* 28, no. 5 (1942): 22–27.

Béhague, Gerard. *Music in Latin America: An Introduction.* Englewood Cliffs, NJ: Prentice Hall, 1979.

Martins, Carlos Alberto, Catherine Boyle, and Mike Gonzalez. "Popular Music as Alternative Communication: Uruguay, 1973–82." *Popular Music* 7, no. 1 (1988): 77–94.

Schechter, John Mendell. *Music in Latin American Culture: Regional Traditions.* New York: Schirmer Books, 1999.

Caitlin Lowery

V–W

Vallenato

Vallenato is a music and dance genre from northern **Colombia** found in the coastal Caribbean region. Originally a rural tradition that came out in the early 20th century, *vallenato* emerged within the popular music sphere in the 1950s through the efforts of pioneers like Rafel Escalón. The original ***conjunto*** *de vallenato* ensemble consisted of an **accordion, *caja***, and ***guaracha***, and it would play genres like ***merengues*** and *paseos*. During the 1960s and 1970s, *vallenato* spread from the rural areas to city centers, at which time the electric bass, **guitar**, and **Afro-Cuban** percussion (e.g., ***conga*** and cowbell) were added to the original trio instrumentation, and thus acquired a more modern sound that reflected urban tastes for music such as *salsa*. During the 1980s, the popular modernized *vallenato* became one of Colombia's most popular music genres. In the 1990s Colombian pop star Carlos Vives began recording traditional *vallenato* that used a mixture of some old-guard folkloric musicians and younger professional musicians from Bogotá. His 1994 album *Clásicos de la Provincia* was a great success for Vives, and it helped to spread the success of urban *vallenato* beyond Colombia to international popularity among Spanish speaking regions in Latin America, Spain, and the **United States**.

Further Reading

Marre, Jeremy and Hannah Charlton. "Shotguns and Accordions: Music of the Marijuana Regions of Colombia." *Beats of the Heart: Popular Music of the World.* London: Pluto Press in Association with Channel Four Television Company, Ltd., 1985.

Sturman, Janet L. "Technology and Identity in Colombian Popular Music: Techno-Macondismo in Carlos Vives's Approach to Vallenato." In *Music and Technoculture,* edited by René T. A. Lysloff and Leslie C. Gay, Jr., 153–81. Middletown, CT: Wesleyan University Press, 2003.

George Torres

Vals/Valse

Widespread throughout Latin America, the *vals* or *valse* developed from the triple-meter European waltz, eventually evolving into numerous national genres. The *vals* appears in multiple forms: dance, vocal music, and instrumental music. As with dances such as the *mazurka,* **polka,** *schottische,* and *contredanse,* colonial aristocracy in Latin America retained the *vals* as a formal dance, and during the 19th century the *vals* also flourished within the *salón* tradition as solo piano music. By the middle of the 19th century, the *vals* diverged significantly from the European waltz, employing freer choreography and greater movement of the hip and arms. In particular regions, the *vals* went through advanced processes of creolization and the genre served as a national music derived from urban popular music. Traditionally, the performance of a *vals* includes such musical instruments as the **guitar,** *tiple,* **cuatro**, *bandúrria,* violin, and **harp**.

A social dance encountered in many parts of Latin America, the *vals* appears in diverse settings such as Andean festivals and Argentinean equestrian spectacles known as *jineteadas.* Best known as the *pasillo* or *vals del país* in the countries of **Colombia** and **Ecuador**, the music remains in triple meter. Often in the minor mode, the nostalgic music frequently portrays melancholic emotions. In **Peru**, the *vals criollo* emerged as an urban genre; however, in the 20th century, as the genre eventually waned within urban populations, the *vals criollo* flourished as popular music in rural areas of the country. The *vals criollo* serves as the most important genre of *música criolla*—a classification implying that the music displays features of both Iberian and Peruvian heritage. In Peru, the *vals*—influenced by the *jota* and *mazurka*—first appeared and gained popularity in the urban centers situated on the coast. At the beginning of the 20th century, Peruvians associated the *vals* with the working class. Principally a vocal genre, the text of songs regularly dealt with the struggles of daily life. The rising popularity of foreign genres (fox trot, *tango*, and *ranchera*) led to the decline of the *vals* in the late 1920s. Frequent use of syncopation takes place in the melodies of *vals criollo,* employing occasional rubato. Early instrumentation included the guitar, *laúd*, and *bandúrria;* however, the guitar—the requisite instrument of the *vals criollo*—ultimately replaced both the *laúd* and *bandúrria.* By 1950, the Afro-Peruvian inclusion of the *cajón*, spoons, and *quijada* (donkey jawbone) became commonplace for the genre, with two guitars and *cajón* serving as the standard.

Further Reading

Olsen, Dale, and Daniel Sheehy, eds. *The Garland Encyclopedia of World Music,* Vol. 2. New York: Garland Publishing, 1998.

Santa Cruz Gamarra, César. *El waltz y el valse criollo.* Lima: Instituto Nacional de Cultura, 1989.

Mark E. Perry

Vals Criolla. *See* Vals/Valse.

Venezuela

The Bolivarian republic of Venezuela is a country in the north of South America. It is bordered by the Caribbean Sea to the north, **Brazil** to the south, Guyana to the east, and **Colombia** to the west. The music from Venezuela is relatively unknown outside of the country but the newer generation of musicians now attracts international attention. Its musical life is diverse and vibrant.

Being located on the southern part of the Caribbean, and a Spanish speaking country, it is not surprising that popular musical forms from Spanish-speaking Caribbean islands as *son, salsa, merengue, bachata, bolero*, and the more recent *reggaetón* are much appreciated in Venezuelan urban centers. *Reggaetón* originates from **Puerto Rico** and **Panama** and contains elements of **hip-hop** music mingled with Dominican *merengue* and *salsa;* it is popular among the youth and is very danceable. One of the first orchestras that started to perform in Caracas since the early 1940s was the Billo's Caracas Boys by the bandleader Billo Frómeta, originally from the Dominican Republic but establishing himself in Venezuela since 1937; this band is still active and they play *merengues, boleros* and *son* with their own unique style. Other orchestras were the Porfi Jimenez Orquestra and Los Melódicos. Since the 1960s, singer and bass player Oscar de Leon gained national and international fame as one of the best *soneros* (vocal salsa improvising) in *salsa.* Besides these Caribbean forms, the Venezuela *gaita* (*zuliana*) is also a popular dance form, played generally during Christmas, and is originally from the Zulia state. Venezuelan pop musicians have gained popularity in other Latin American countries besides Venezuela, as Ricardo Montaner (very popular in Chile), José Luis Rodríguez "El Puma," Ilan Chester, and Franco DeVita. Since the end of the 1980s, young musicians created the Venezuelan Ska movement, and the most well-known group was Desorden Publico.

Since the 1940s, popular urban music influenced by traditional Hispano-Venezuelan and Afro-Venezuelan music attained a dynamic and vibrant character. The precursor of the rich variety of groups and outstanding musicians was the choral group Quinteto Contrapunto who made elaborate choral arrangements of traditional rural musical traditions, and the composer and bandleader Aldemaro Romero in the 1950s, 1960s, and 1970s based his musical compositions and performances on rural musical traditions mixed with **jazz** and Brazilian *bossa nova.* Thereafter, several groups were formed such as Serenata Guayanesa, El Cuarteto, Ensamble Gurrufio, Onkora, Recoveco, and many others. These groups include the *joropo*, the national dance of the country, the Venezuelan *merengue,* the *vals*, the *pasaje,* the *gaita,* the *alguinaldo* and other musical expressions from the hinterlands and the capital Caracas in their repertoire, and elaborate these musical forms in a more academic manner in chamber ensemble formats and jazz-like arrangements

Anibal Castillo, center, and his sons play traditional Venezuelan music outside of the Congress in Caracas, Venezuela, in 2003. (AP/Wide World Photos)

and performance style. In aftermath of these groups, a younger generation of musicians baptized a musical scene called the urban acoustic movement (the so-called MAU), with the main characteristic of mingling traditional musical expressions with other non-Venezuelan influences such as jazz and the Brazilian *choro* (chamber music). The musical movement is characterized by the dynamism of musical creation, by virtuoso and playful performances on professional handmade instruments, improvisation, and the interchanges of musicians in different groups and recordings. Some of the musical groups forming part of this movement are C4 Trio, Encayapa, Kapicua and Los Sinverguenzas,

The main musical instruments from Hispano-Venezuelan music are: the ***cuatro***, the *llanera* and central **harp**, the ***maraca***, the ***bandola***, the mandoline, and the **guitar**. The *cuatro* is considered the national instrument of Venezuela, and a new generation of instrumentalists brought this instrument to the concert halls in popular, chamber, and jazz group formats.

Further Reading

Agerkop, Yukio. "La Bandola de Venezuela: El Lugar y la Innovación Musical." *Revista Musica e Investigación* 9, no. 17 (2011).

Gerard Béhague, et al. "Venezuela." *The New Grove Dictionary of Music and Musicians,* edited by S. Sadie and J. Tyrrell. London: Macmillan, 2001.

Salazar, Rafael. "Música y Tradición en la Región Capital." *Revista Musical de Venezuela* 18 (1986).

Yukio Agerkop

Vihuela

The *vihuela* is an old Spanish **guitar** that was very fashionable during the late 15th and 16th centuries before it was replaced by the guitar. In fact, it is considered the precursor of the modern guitar. Similar to the **lute** in Europe, it placed an important role in Spanish music of the time. Important Spanish composers who wrote music for the *vihuela* include Luis de Narváez, Luis de Millán, Alonso Mudarra, Antonio Cabezón, and Diego Pisador, among others.

The instrument was fretted with movable, wrapped-around, and tied-on gut frets. It had 12 gut strings arranged in six double courses. Even though there were several tunings for the *vihuela,* it was common to use a tuning that was very similar to the modern guitar, except that the third string was tuned a half step lower (e-a-d-f#-b-e).

Vihuela music was commonly written in tablature, a system that uses horizontal lines to represent the strings and numbers, letters or symbols to indicate the fret where the note is supposed to be played. The rhythm is indicated using traditional solfeggio notation.

Apart from this *vihuela,* which was plucked with the fingers, there were other *vihuelas* such as the *vihuela de penola* that was played with a plectrum, and a bowed *vihuela* called *vihuela de arco,* the predecessor of the *viola da gamba. Vihuelas* faded as the polyphonic music lost its importance at the end of the 16th century and the *vihuela's* place was taken by the Baroque guitar.

The Mexican *vihuela* is a five-string, deep-bodied, bellied guitar that resembles the shape of the *guitarrón,* the bass guitar used by the ***mariachi*** ensembles. It is tuned like the first five strings of a guitar and its fourth and fifth strings are tuned an octave higher than the guitar. It is used in *mariachi* ensembles as well as in other ensembles that play *sones abajeños* and *sones arribeños* (see ***sones***) from the states of Michoacan and Jalisco. Some *vihuelas* are fretted and some that do not have inlaid frets use gut frets for the lower half of the neck, the upper half being fretless. *Vihuela* is usually strummed and has a chordal function within the ensemble.

Further Reading

Cano Tamayo, Manuel. *La guitarra: historia, estudios y aportaciones al arte flamenco.* Granada: Ediciones ANEL, 1986.

Raquel Paraíso

Villancico

Villancico is a musical and poetic form. The *villancico's* antecedents were in medieval song and dance forms. It first appeared in Spain in the 15th century and in time became the most important secular genre in both Spain and colonial Latin America. Exempt from the formal and stylistic rigidity that applied to other genres, early *villancicos* evolved freely, allowing for loose structures and diverse compositional styles. A *villancico* could be a freestyle folkish composition or a solemn work strictly in accordance with Renaissance rules of counterpoint. By the 17th century, however, the *villancico* had evolved into a well-established form, with an opening *estribillo* (refrain) sung by the choir, alternating with several **coplas** (stanzas) sung by a soloist or group of soloists, ending with a final *estribillo*. *Villancicos* often make use of the *sesquiáltera* (hemiola) inherited from its Spanish medieval roots, as well as octosyllabic lines, typical of Spanish poetry.

Literally peasant songs (from the Spanish *villano* meaning peasant), *villancicos* emerged in rural areas as simple monophonic folk songs, reflecting the rustic lifestyle, with humorous and satirical themes. They often made use of stock characters from Spanish popular culture, with theatrical stories that represented regional and ethnic stereotypes. They became widespread in Spain in the 15th century, and in time became mannered expressions of courtly love, usually performed a capella, or accompanied by vihuela, harp, or other instruments. Many *villancicos* were also semireligious songs of faith and praise, but they were always in vernacular languages such as Spanish, Portuguese or ethnic dialects, never in Latin. In the 16th century, they were adopted by the polyphonists of the golden age, and gained a level of polyphonic sophistication, increased expressivity, and rhythmic diversity, including syncopations and frequent meter changes. During this period, and particularly after the counterreformation, *villancicos* were performed liturgically on specific feast days, notably Christmas, Epiphany, and Corpus Christi. Because the more popular *villancicos* were those associated with the Christmas season, the term itself became synonymous with Christmas carols. By the 18th century, *villancicos* adopted elements of Italian opera, often reflecting the structure of da capo arias, with recitatives and concertato accompaniment. The popularity of the *villancico* declined in the second half of the 18th century.

Villancicos often appeared in sets of 7 to 10 poems in different meters, sung in church during the service to entertain the public after each responsorial. Because a religious service that included a complete *villancico* cycle was often quite long, the last song usually had a light, joyful, and cheerful character, achieved by comical situations and stories, and the imitation of Spanish accents. These works came to be identified with those groups, with names such as *gallegos* and *gitanos*. Aspects of black culture had also appeared in Spanish *villancicos* as early as the 15th century, owing to the important slave population in Spain and Portugal, most of whom came from Guinea and Angola. As a result, these *villancicos* came to be called *negros*, *negrillos*, or *guineos*. They were usually in 6/8 meter, and often sought to parody African accents and pronunciation. By the 17th century, the practice of including a *guineo* in a *villancico* cycle was common, and had become a convention, no longer necessarily imitating African languages. Many *guineos* were composed simply out of custom in places where no blacks had ever lived.

The *villancico* came to the Americas in the first half of the 16th century, and it quickly reached a measure of richness and originality that, in retrospect, placed it at the pinnacle of New World composition, though at the time it was viewed as a secondary genre. As in Spain, Latin American *villancicos* came to occupy an important position in the great cathedrals such as Mexico City, Puebla and Lima, composed by notable chapelmasters and other church musicians such as Gaspar Fernandes, Juan Gutiérrez de Padilla, Juan de Araujo, and Manuel de Sumaya. The *villancico's* flexibility and broad stylistic background served the genre well in the Spanish and Portuguese colonies. Many composers continued to write *gitanos* and *gallegos* in the old European style, but for the most part the genre quickly developed past its Iberian counterpart, able to absorb the vast, though often subtle, stylistic influences of the different ethnic groups. The most prominent of these was the *mestizo* e indio, which purported to imitate various native languages, with complex syncopations meant to represent the exotic cultures. *Negros* and *guineos* also took on a new life and intensity, due to the increased racial and cultural diversity in the New World. Texts were a mixture of Spanish, Portuguese, native dialects, and African (especially Yoruba) languages, usually deliberately distorted in a humorous and disparaging way, often offensive to modern sensibilities. With little relation to actual native or African cultures, these mannered *villancicos* are more revealing about the composers and their audiences than about the ethnic groups themselves. In spite of this, the *villancico* became at once a means for colonial artistic expression and a symbol for social and ethnic syncretism.

Many *villancicos* began to evolve into more popular genres. Some were so infused with dance rhythms that they in turn were called by the names of the dances, such as the *tocotín* of Náhuatl origin, which was performed in churches during the colonial period, and the *paya*, which combined elements from mulatto, black and *mestizo* culture. These genres were infused with popular characteristics, sung in African or native languages and accompanied by native instruments, but still answering to the harmonic and even formal demands of the Spanish homeland. European dances such as *sarabandes*, *chaconnes*, *canarios*, and *folías* also began to change, infused with *guineo* and native elements. All of this music had an important influence on the development of popular and folk styles such as **romances**, **décimas**, *aguinaldos*, *alabados*, **corridos**, and countless other genres, from **Mexico** to **Cuba** and **Puerto Rico**, from **Colombia** and **Venezuela** to **Chile** and **Argentina**.

Further Reading

González-Quiñones, J. "The Orchestrally Accompanied villancico in Mexico in the Eighteenth Century." Ph.D. diss., City University of New York, 1990.

Grebe, M. E. "Introducción al estudio del villancico en Latinoamerica," *RMC*, no. 107 (1969), 7–31.

Melis, A. *Poesia e musica nell'America Coloniale: il caso si sor Juana Inés de la Cruz,* Florence, 1994.

Ramón y Rivera, L. F. "Del villancico al corrido mexicano," *Heterofonía* vii (1974): 10–13.

Stanford, E. T. *El villancico y el corrido mexicano.* Mexico City, 1974.

Mark Brill

Violão de Sete Cordas

The *violão de sete cordas* is a Brazilian seven-string, classical-style **guitar**, typically used in traditional *choro* and *samba* groups. The instrument was first adapted for use in popular Brazilian music in the early 1900s. Valued for its extended bass range, it is known for providing melodic bass lines, called *baixarias*. Over the past century, several players have developed the techniques and vocabulary of playing the instrument. The early pioneers, "Tute" and "Dino Sete Cordas," used it in popular ensembles and more recently, Raphael Rabello and Yamandú Costa have popularized it as a solo instrument.

The seventh (lowest) string of the *violão de sete cordas* is tuned to C or B followed by the standard six-string guitar tuning E, A, D, G, B, and E. It is played using classical guitar finger-picking techniques and has become an ideal accompaniment instrument due to its full sound and ability to play low bass notes and chords simultaneously. When playing *baixarias,* the thumb plays repeated rest strokes, primarily on the lower strings, facilitated by the frequent use of legatos. A thumb pick, usually made of pliable metal, is typically used as it adds volume and protects the thumb, but some players use natural or acrylic fingernails.

History

The vocabulary of the *baixaria* style was first established on the *violão* (six-string guitar) during the late 1800s in the popular *terno* ensembles which were comprised of **flute**, **cavaquinho**, and **guitar**. The origins of the *violão de sete cordas* are uncertain, but the instrument has roots in Europe and Russia dating back to the Renaissance. It began to appear in **Brazil** during the beginning of the 20th century and Russian immigrants that settled in Catumbi, a neighborhood in Rio de Janeiro, are believed to have brought it to Brazil. As a result of interactions with gypsies from Catumbi, the guitarists "China" (Otávio Viana) and "Tute" (Artur de Souza Nascimento) both associated with Pixinguinha's famous group, Os Oito Batutas (1919–27), adopted the instrument and are credited with integrating it into Brazilian popular music.

By the mid-1920s, the *violão de sete cordas* and **pandeiro** were added to the *ternos* and became standard components of the *conjunto regional* or regional group. Throughout the 1930s and 1940s, these groups were hired by recording companies and radio stations to provide music for a variety of formats. They specialized in **choro**, **samba**, and other popular music and thus defined the sound and instrumentation of traditional Brazilian music. During the 1950s and 1960s, most of the *regional* groups disbanded and use of the *violão de sete cordas* declined as traditional Brazilian music was replaced by **bossa nova** and American music.

The techniques and musical language of the *violão de sete cordas* continued to be developed through the innovations of guitarist Horondino José da Silva (1918–2006) or "Dino Sete Cordas." Dino played the six-string guitar for many years in *regional* groups, but after the guitarist Tute retired in 1950, he began playing the seven-string and was invited to join Benedito Lacerda's *regional* in 1952. During the 1960s, Dino joined Jacob do Bandolim's group Época de Ouro and recorded definitive versions of *choro* standards. Throughout his career, Dino played a De Souto seven-string built in 1953 by Sylvestre Domingos.

Before the invention of nylon strings after World War II, steel strings were used instead of gut because they were stronger, stayed in tune longer, and could withstand tropical heat and humidity. Dino used a combination of strings. A low C cello string for the seventh string, flat wound steel strings for the E, A, D, and G, and nylon for the B and high E. Steel strings were used on seven-string guitars until 1983 when Luiz Otávio Braga, guitarist for Camerata Carioca, was the first to use an all-nylon string instrument that since has become the standard for most players.

The *choro* revival of the 1970s created renewed interest in traditional music and instruments. This led to the establishment of regular *rodas de choro* (informal *choro* jam sessions) and *choro* clubs in several Brazilian cities. It was during this time that the *violão de sete cordas* began to be integrated into the *escola de samba*. The revival reached its peak with the arrival of guitarist Raphael Rabello (1962–1995) who quickly became one of the world's greatest guitarists with his brilliant *baixarias,* virtuosic solo work, and duets with a variety of artists. His recordings and collaborations helped solidify the role and popularity of the instrument.

Further Reading

Cazes, H. *Choro: Do Quintal ao Municipal.* Rio de Janeiro: Editora 34, 1998.

Diniz, A. *Almanaque do Choro: A história do chorinho, o que ouvir, o queler, onde curtir.* Rio de Janeiro: Jorge Zahar Ed., 2003.

Livingston-Isenhour, T. and Garcia, T. *Choro: A Social History of a Brazilian Popular Music.* Bloomington: Indiana University Press, 2005.

Taborda, M.E. *Dino Sete Cordas e o Acompanhamento de Violãona Musica Popular Brasileira.* Dissertação de Mestrado, Universidade Federal do Rio de Janeiro, 1995.

Thomas Rohde

Volcanto (Nicaragua)

The term *Volcanto* refers to protest song in Central America and is derived from the fusion of the two words, *volcán* (volcano) and *canto* (song), a term inspired by the many volcanoes that distinguish the natural landscape of western Central America. Of the several terms available to denote protest music in Latin America (***nueva canción, nueva trova***, *música testimonial*), *volcanto* was created specifically as a new handle for music of the region, yet it appears to only have become a fixed term in **Nicaragua**. It began to be used after the revolution in 1979, becoming prevalent in the 1980s, long after *nueva cancion* had established itself as the preeminent genre of protest song in Latin America. One of the best-known *volcanto* artists from Nicaragua is Luis Enrique Mejia Godoy. While the music of *volcanto* may not be discernibly Nicaraguan, the texts are what mark this repertoire's point of origin, with many songs making direct references to the local struggles of the Nicaraguan people. *Volcanto* music, rather than forging a decisive path for protest song in Central America, became one of many different types of *música testimonial*.

Further Reading

Scruggs, Thomas M. "Socially Conscious Music Forming the Social Conscience: Nicaraguan *Música Testimonial* and the Creation of a Revolutionary Moment." In *From Tejano to Tango: Essays on Latin American Popular Music,* edited by Walter A. Clark, 41–69. New York: Garland, 2002.

George Torres

Waltz. *See* Vals.

Wayno. *See* Huayno.

Z

Zabumba

Zabumba is a Brazilian term that refers to both a musical instrument as well as a type of musical ensemble. Both the instrument and the ensemble are primarily associated with the Northeast region of **Brazil**. The musical instrument known as *zabumba* is a type of deep military-style side drum with rope-tensioned counterhoops that was introduced into Brazil during colonial days by the Portuguese. *Zabumbas* of this type are still present in many Brazilian processional traditions and may also be called *bumbo, ze-pereira, bumba, tambor grande,* and *caixa grande.* In the *maracatu carnival* tradition from Recife, multiple *zabumbas* (commonly called *alfaia*) are played with thick wooden sticks.

The *zabumba's* most typical association today is with northeastern *baião*, *forró*, and *banda de pífano* music. In these contexts, the instrument developed into a rather shallow bass drum carried at chest level (rather than at the side) by a neck strap and is played with a short soft mallet on one head of the drum while the hand or a thin stick plays counter rhythms on the bottom head. Luiz Gonzaga popularized this instrument nationally in the 1950s as part of a northeastern trio format involving **accordion**, triangle, and *zabumba* drum.

The term *zabumba* also refers to a type of instrumental folk ensemble of the fife-and-drum variety typical in rural areas of northeastern Brazil, especially in the hinterland zone called the *sertão*. Also generically known as *banda de pífanos* (band of fifes), these ensembles are the preferred musical accompaniment for a range of religious rituals of folk Catholicism and social festivities among the *caboclo* (*mestizo*) populations. *Zabumba* musical ensembles, also called *banda cabaçal, terno de zabumba,* and *esquenta mulher,* comprise two cane **flutes**, a snare drum, and the *zabumba* bass drum. The musical repertory of the *zabumba* ensembles includes marches, religious hymns and praise songs, waltzes, *baiões, frevos, forrós, cocos, choros,* and many other styles. In the early 1970s, the Banda de Pífano Zabumba Caruaru (from Caruaru, Pernambuco) made a national impact via collaborations with **Gilberto Gil** and **Caetano Veloso**.

Further Reading

Crook, Larry. *Brazilian Music: Northeastern Traditions and the Heartbeat of a Modern Nation.* Santa Barbara, CA: ABC-CLIO, 2005.

Crook, Larry. "Northeast Brazil." In *Music in Latin America: Regional Traditions,* edited by John M. Schechter, 192–235. New York: Schirmer Books, 1999.

Larry Crook

Zamba

A folkloric dance and song form most closely associated with the Tucumán and Santiago del Estero provinces in northwest **Argentina**, the *zamba* is a derivative of the 18th-century *zamacueca.* While the *zamacueca* was originally a *salon* dance popular in the urban centers of **Peru**, its popularity quickly spread across class and national boundaries. By the mid-19th century, it had generated local variants, both urban and rural, across South America, including the *zamba* as well as Chilean, Argentine, and Bolivian versions of the *cueca,* and the Peruvian *marinera.*

While each of these genres currently can be differentiated by differences in form, tempo, or instrumentation, they share musical and choreographic commonalities. They are flirtatious courtship dances, danced by nonembracing couples, and classified as *danzas de pañuelo,* or handkerchief dances, referring to the obligatory kerchief that each partner carries and uses to enact flirtatious gestures. Unlike many folkloric dances of the region, the *zamba* does not have a fixed choreography; instead, dancers are free to improvise, drawing from a number of established movements in a spontaneous fashion.

Musically, the *zamba* shares with the other *zamacueca* derivatives a bimetric rhythmic organization. That is, triple meter (3/4) and compound duple meter (6/8) are simultaneously present. Modern *zambas* are generally slower than other members of the *zamacueca* family, with the exception of the *zamba carpera,* or tent *zamba,* a lively dance associated primarily with **Carnival** festivities.

The earliest references to *zamba* as a dance distinct from the *zamacueca* date to the 1820s in **Chile**, and suggest that it was popularly known and danced by that name as early as 1813. Nonetheless, according to Argentine folklorist Carlos Vega, until the mid-19th century there was no discernible musical or choreographic difference between the *cueca* and *zamba* in the region, and in fact requesting the two genres one after another as if there was a difference became a popular joke.

By the mid-19th century, however, musicians in the Santiago del Estero and Tucumán regions of Argentina began to slow the dance down. This trend became even more exaggerated in the 1930s, when guitarist-composer Atahualpa Yupanqui (1908–1992) recorded a series of *zambas* that were noticeably slower, and composed not for dancing. Many of these pieces, such as "Viene clareando," "Zamba del grillo," and "Luna tucumana," became well-known standards recorded by succeeding generations of folk and popular musicians in Argentina, including notable recordings by Mercedes Sosa (b. 1935). In the mass-mediated folklore boom that followed, the *zamba* became, along with the **chacarera**, one of the most widely performed and recorded folkloric genres at the national level. Besides Yupanqui, important composers who have contributed well-known *zambas* during the mid-20th century include Los Hermanos Ábalos, Gustavo "Cuchi" Leguizamón (1917–2000), Eduardo Falú (b. 1923), and Juan Falú (b. 1948); landmark performing and recording artists whose recordings led in part to these composers' popularity have included the vocal groups Los Fronterizos, Los Chalchaleros, Horacio Guarany (b. 1925), Mercedes Sosa, and in many cases the composers themselves.

Further Reading

Aretz, Isabel. *El folklore musical argentino,* 183–92. Buenos Aires: Ricordi, 1952.

Pérez Bugallo, Rubén. "Zamacueca;" "Zamba." *Diccionario de la música española e hispanoamericana.* Ed. Emilio *Casares Rodicio,* 1082–83. Madrid: Sociedad General de Autores y Editores, 2002.

Vega, Carlos. *La zamacueca (cueca, zamba, chilena, marinera). La zamba antigua.* Buenos Aires: Editorial Julio Korn. 1952.

Michael O'Brien

Zampoña. *See* Siku.

Zapateado. *See* Zapateo.

Zapateo

Zapateo or *zapateado* literally means footwork, the alternating of rhythmical patterns of feet movement and stampings of the floor. Lively rhythm punctuation is attained by striking the dancer's shoes against a hard wooden surface or against the floor. The *zapateado* was transplanted to the Americas during colonial times from the different traditions of *flamenco* dancing. It is the core in the Mexican **sones**' dance and it has different styles according to the type of *son* in which it is used. Dancers use hard shoes to obtain the sound of the tapping, which functions as another percussion instrument within the ensemble. Generally, *zapateado* takes place over a *tarima* or wooden platform that accentuates the percussive sounds of the dance.

The *zapateado* takes place during the instrumental sections in Mexican *sones* leaving the sung verses to be danced with a *valseado,* slower pace steps that allow the verses to be heard and the dancers to take a break from the intense *zapateado.* It incorporates specific steps for each *son* tradition. In Calentano *sones* from the state of Guerrero, those steps are called *pespunteo, banqueado,* and *redoble* or *repique-teo.* The *zapateo,* vigorous in nature, incorporates highly rhythmic ornaments that can be done with one or both feet.

Further Reading

Stanford, E. Thomas. "The Mexican Son." *Yearbook of the International Folk Music Council* 4 (1972): 66–86.

Raquel Paraíso

Zarzuela

The *zarzuela,* a category of Spanish play with music and dance, arrived in Latin America during the conquest where it was immediately embraced and subsequently adapted. As a signature national genre with a 500-year history, the *zarzuela* developed a repertory and practice that straddled the worlds of classical and popular music. Operatically conceived arias, mostly for solo and **duo** singers, adorn plays with spoken dialogue. Most *zarzuelas* depend on ensemble interaction highlighted by key musical scenes that feature chorus and popular dances accompanied by a small orchestra or instrumental ensemble. In Latin America, and elsewhere in the Iberian diaspora, this semiclassic, and widely popular, genre provided a rich source of appealing music, and an ideal model for new composition and performance addressing local circumstances and identities.

American variants date from the 18th century. In 1701 in Lima, the Spanish-born Peruvian composer Tomás Torrejón y Velasco wrote new music for Calderón de la Barca's courtly *zarzuela La Purpura de la Rosa.* The famous Mexican-born chapelmaster Manuel de Sumaya composed *La Parténope,* credited as one of the first operas of New Spain, 11 years later. The *zarzuela* inspired shorter popular Spanish song dramas such as the *tonadilla* and *sainete* in the 1770s which were better suited for the growing audiences at theaters and salons and which also inspired composers in the Americas to create musical theater reflecting local customs. Argentine composers, for example, created short music dramas addressing the life of the *guacho* cowboys of the *pampas* (prairies) called *sainetes gauchescos.*

Parallel with the development of local approaches in the New World, the Spanish *zarzuela* repertory blossomed in the late 19th and early 20th centuries, resulting in thousands of works, a hundred or so becoming classics. Professional touring companies from Spain brought *zarzuelas* that would become favorites with Latin American performers and with Spanish-speaking audiences throughout the Americas. Tunes and spoken lines from these dramas entered the popular vocabulary and even today Latin Americans born before 1960 might ask in everyday conversation *"Dónde vás con manton de Manila?"* ("Where are you going with that shawl from

Manila?") quoting a line from *La Verbena de la Paloma* by Tomás Bretón (1894), perhaps the most famous of all Spanish *zarzuelas,* as a means of inquiring, "Where are you going, looking so fine?"

While the *zarzuela* was developed widely in the Americas, it found a special place in the hearts of Cubans. Cuban composers such as Ernesto Lecuona (1896–1963), Gonzalo Roig (1890–1970), Jorge Anckerman (1877–1941), and Eliseo Grenet (1863–1950) borrowed the structure of the Spanish *zarzuela* but created distinctively Cuban music, adding Afro-Cuban instruments to the orchestra and setting the melodies to the rhythms of the *habanera, contradanza, danzón, conga* and **rumba**. The stories of these *zarzuelas cubanas* also reflected local concerns. Roig's *Cecilia Valdes,* for example, is a musical setting of the famous 1882 novel of the same name by Cirilo Villaverde. Its tragic tale of a *mulatta,* mixed race woman, who bears a child with an aristocratic lover that she does not realize is her half brother, exemplifies the treatment of race relations, miscegenation, and class divisions that made the *zarzuela* so compelling to audiences in the emerging Cuban republic.

Only a few contemporary composers create new *zarzuelas*. A notable example is Puerto-Rican-born composer Manuel B. Gonzalez. His *Los Jíbaros Progresistas* (1981), based on the story by Ramón Méndea Quiñones, is still performed in New York City where the composer resides. Although *zarzuela* is no longer as popular as it was in previous centuries, the influence of the genre persists in Latin American popular music. Many individual songs, now performed in completely different styles, live on in the repertories of contemporary popular performers, although many people may no longer recall their original titles or provenance. The song "El Condor Pasa," popularized in the United States by Simon and Garfunkel and performed as an Andean folksong by singers and instrumentalists around the world, is the title song from the 1913 *zarzuela* by Peruvian composer Daniel Alomía Robles. Similarly the popular **mariachi** show number colloquially known as "Las Bodas" comes from the overture of the *zarzuela La Boda de Luis Alonso* composed in 1897 by Spaniard Gerónimo Giménez.

Further Reading

Stein, Louis. *Songs of Mortals, Dialogues of the Gods: Music and Theatre in Seventeenth-Century Spain.* Oxford: Clarendon, 1993.

Sturman, Janet. Zaruzela: *Spanish Operetta, American Stage.* Urbana and Chicago: University of Illinois Press, 2000.

Thomas, Susan. *Cuban Zarzuela: Performing Race and Gender on Havana's Lyric Stage.* Urbana and Chicago: University of Illinois Press, 2008.

Webber, Christopher. *The Zarzuela Companion.* Lanham, MD: Scarecrow Press, 2002.

Webber, Christopher. *Zarzuela.net,* Online September 2007, www.zarzuela.net.

Janet L. Sturman

Zouk

Zouk is a style of popular music that emerged in the French Caribbean in the 1980s. The term *zouk* originated in **Martinique** where it is a generic term for dance party or festival. However, *zouk* music is a transnational genre that blends aspects of popular dance music from throughout the Caribbean and other parts of the African diaspora. It is the first style of popular music sung in *Creole* to be successful internationally. Its popularity is strongest in the islands of Martinique, **Guadeloupe**, St. Lucia, and **Dominica**, but the genres that have influenced *zouk* musicians extend beyond these four islands to include other parts of the French- and English-speaking Caribbean, as well as the African subcontinent. Over the past three decades, *zouk* has spread to many parts of the world, particularly Quebec and France, where there are large communities of Antillean émigrés, as well as various countries in South America, Africa, and Asia.

The development of *zouk* as a musical genre is attributed to the brothers Pierre-Edouard Décimus and Georges Décimus, and Jacob F. Desvarieux, respected musicians from Guadeloupe who had played in Paris throughout the 1970s. At the time, foreign musical styles had come to dominate in their home country, overshadowing local forms such as *biguine* and *mazouk*. These foreign styles included Haitian *cadence-rampa* and *compas direct* (brought by Haitian refugees fleeing political unrest in their home country), *cadence-lypso* from Dominica, as well as *salsa* and other popular dance styles from the Spanish Caribbean, and **calypso** and *soca* from Trinidad and Tobago. With the intent of creating a modernized version of the **Carnival** music of Guadeloupe, the Décimus brothers and Desvarieux joined with other Parisian studio musicians to create the band Kassav' in 1979. Experimenting with various combinations of popular styles, incorporating rhythms from Guadeloupean *gwo ka* drumming, and most importantly, using *Creole* lyrics, Kassav' eventually created a signature sound that could be understood by an international audience yet still sound specifically Antillean. In 1984, their song "Zouk-La Sé Sèl Médikaman Nou Ni" ("Zouk Is the Only Medicine We Have") became a worldwide hit, stirring audiences in the Caribbean, Europe, and Africa, and earning Kassav' the first Disque d'Or to be awarded to an Antillean group.

Zouk quickly became a dominant form of party music in the French Antilles and won over non-Antillean audiences in France and Quebec. Established bands were quick to take advantage of the new sound. Expérience 7 from Guadeloupe hired Joëlle Ursull, Christiane Obydol, and Dominique Zorobabe to front their band and record under the name Zouk Machine. Malavoi from Martinique, a string-based dance band that specialized in a range of styles from Martinican *biguine* and *quadrille* to *rumba*, *bossa nova*, and *merengue*, quickly added *zouk* to their repertoire.

In her book-length study of *zouk* music, Jocelyne Guilbault estimates that more than 130 *zouk* albums were made annually in the Antilles from 1986 to 1989, launching the careers of new singers such as Joelle Ursuli, Edith Lefel, and Tanya St. Val, as well as redefining older ones such as Frankie Vincent and Ralph Thamar as *zouk* artists.

As Guilbault notes, the original rhythm of *zouk* was played at a fast tempo, (between 120 and 145 beats per minute), with a driving percussive line and horn section playing at full volume. Eventually, a style called *zouk*-love emerged, featuring slower tempos (95–100 beats per minute), and a smoother and quieter accompaniment. *Zouk* lyrics may address a wide range of topics. The joie de vivre of dancing at Carnival and other holidays is a popular topic, as is romantic love and related feelings and sensations. Other songs express respect for ancestors, profess national pride, explore the African roots of Antillean culture, or address issues of world interest such as HIV/AIDS. In general, songwriters tend to avoid topics that are controversial or that express concerns that cannot be understood beyond their local communities, and this has facilitated the appeal of *zouk* worldwide.

The rhythmic vitality of *zouk,* and the sensual choreography that it accompanies, has made it a popular style of dance music in many parts of the world. *Zouk* was particularly popular in the Francophone and Lusophone countries of West and Central Africa, and today it continues to be an important musical influence in Angola and Cape Verde on the musical genres *kizomba* and *cola-zouk* respectively. The *zouk-lambada* emerged in the late 1980s, and over time various dance teachers in Brazil developed regional styles based on the choreography of *zouk,* although in practice dancers may move to any music that has the proper syncopation and tempo. Dance crews and DJs have taken *zouk,* or at least the name and the choreography, to nearly every part of Western and Eastern Europe as well as Israel, Australia, Japan, and Singapore. Generally, *zouk* has joined the lexicon of electronic dance music, and the name *zouk* seems to have enough currency to generate interest among a very varied community of clubbers worldwide.

Meanwhile, Antillean musicians have created new innovations on the *zouk* sound. Current trends include *Zouk* R&B or *Zouk Nouvelle Génération,* a variation on *zouk*-love that incorporates aspects of rhythm and blues, and is expressed by Guadeloupean artists such as Slaï (Patrice Sylvestre), Thierry Cham, and Jane Fostin (who replaced Joelle Ursull in Zouk Machine in 1988). There are also fusions of dancehall **reggae** and *zouk* called *ragga-zouk* or simply *ragga.* Lord Kossity (Thierry Moutoussamy) from Martinique and Colonel Reyel (Rémy Ranguin) from Guadeloupe are current purveyors of this style. Although it has gone through many changes, *zouk* remains an important influence on French Caribbean music both at home and abroad.

Further Reading

Berrian, Brenda. *Awakening Spaces: French Caribbean Popular Songs, Music, and Culture*. Chicago: University of Chicago Press, 2000.

Guilbault, Jocelyne with Gage Averill, Édouard Benoit, and Gregory Rabes. *Zouk: World Music in the West Indies*. Chicago: University of Chicago Press, 1993.

Manuel, Peter. *Caribbean Currents: Caribbean Music from Rumba to Reggae*. Revised and expanded edition. Philadelphia: Temple University Press, 2006.

Hope Smith

Bibliography

Websites

All Music Guide, Latin America, accessed June 9, 2012, http://www.allmusic.com/explore/genre/latin-d4300

Caribbean Radio Stations, accessed June 9, 2012, http://www.caribbeannews.com/radio.html

Center for Music of the Americas, Florida State University, accessed June 9, 2012, http://www.music.fsu.edu/Music-Research-Centers/Center-for-Music-of-the-Americas

Glossary of Latin American Music Terms, accessed June 9, 2012, http://www.salsaholic.de/glossary.htm

Klemetz, Henrik. Latin American Music Styles, accessed June 9, 2012, http://www.longitude13degreeseast.com/LAMusicStyles.html

Latin American Music Review, accessed June 9, 2012, http://www.utexas.edu/utpress/journals/jlamr.html

Latin Grammy Awards, accessed June 9, 2012, http://www.latingrammy.com/

Books and Articles

Aparicio, Frances R. *Listening to Salsa: Gender, Latin Popular Music, and Puerto Rican Cultures.* Hanover, NH: University Press of New England, 1998.

Appleby, David. "Folk, Popular, and Art Music." *The Music of Brazil,* 94–115. Austin: University of Texas Press, 1989.

Austerlitz, Paul. *Merengue: Dominican Music and Dominican Identity.* Philadelphia: Temple University Press, 1997.

Behague, Gerard. "Music, c. 1920–c. 1980." In *A Cultural History of Latin America: Literature, Music and the Visual Arts in the 19th and 20th Centuries,* edited by Leslie Bethell. 311–67. New York: Cambridge University Press, 1998.

Behague, Gerard. "Popular Music." In *Handbook of Latin American Popular Culture,* edited by Harold E. Hinds and Charles M. Tatum, 2–38. Westport, CT: Greenwood Press, 1985.

Bilby, Kenneth M, Michael D. Largey, and Peter Manuel. *Caribbean Currents: Caribbean Music from Rumba to Reggae.* Philadelphia: Temple University Press, 2006.

Booth, Gregory, and Terry Lee Kuhn. "Economic and Transmission Factors as Essential Element in the Definition of Folk, Art, and Pop Music." *The Musical Quarterly* 74 (1990): 411–38.

Clark, Walter Aaron. *From Tejano to Tango: Latin American Popular Music.* New York: Routledge, 2002.

Colburn, Forrest D. *Latin America at the End of Politics.* Princeton: Princeton University Press, 2002.

Hamm, Charles. "Popular Music." *The New Harvard Dictionary of Music,* edited by Don Michael Randel, 646–49. Cambridge: Belknap Press, 1986.

Kuss, Malena. *Music in Latin America and the Caribbean: An Encyclopedic History.* Austin: University of Texas Press, 2004. Currently, only the first two volumes are available: Volume 1: *Performing Beliefs: Indigenous Peoples of South America, Central America, and Mexico* (2004) and Volume 2: *Performing the Caribbean Experience.*

Loza, Steven Joseph. *Tito Puente and the Making of Latin Music.* Urbana: University of Illinois Press, 1999.

Manuel, Peter. "Perspectives on the Study of Non-Western Popular Musics." *Popular Musics of the Non-Western World: An Introductory Survey.* New York: Oxford University Press, 1998.

Moore, Robin. *Nationalizing Blackness: Afrocubanismo and Artistic Revolution in Havana, 1920–1940.* Pittsburgh, PA: University of Pittsburgh Press, 1997.

Nettl, Bruno. "Folk Music." *The New Harvard Dictionary of Music,* edited by Don Michael Randel, 315–19. Cambridge: Belknap Press, 1986.

Olsen, Dale A. and Daniel E. Sheehy, eds. *The Garland Encyclopedia of World Music, Volume 2: South America, Mexico, Central America, and the Caribbean.* New York and London: Garland, 1998.

Pacini Hernandez, Deborah, Héctor D. Fernández l'Hoeste, and Eric Zolov. *Rockin' Las Américas: The Global Politics of Rock in Latin/O America.* Pittsburgh, PA: University of Pittsburgh Press, 2004.

Perrone, Charles A. and Christopher Dunn, eds. *Brazilian Popular Music and Globalization.* New York: Routledge, 2002.

Roberts, John Storm. *The Latin Tinge: The Impact of Latin American Music on the United States.* 2nd ed. New York: Oxford University Press, 1999.

Schechter, John Mendell. *Music in Latin American Culture: Regional Traditions.* New York: Schirmer Books, 1999.

Shaw, Lisa, and Stephanie Dennison. "Introduction: Defining the Popular in the Latin American Context." *Pop Culture Latin America!: Media, Arts, And Lifestyle,* 1–7. Santa Barbara: ABC-CLIO, 2005.

Sublette, Ned. *Cuba and Its Music: From the First Drums to the Mambo.* Chicago: Chicago Review Press, 2004.

Whitehead, Laurence. *Latin America: A New Interpretation.* New York: Palgrave Macmillan, 2006.

About the Editor

George Torres received his PhD in musicology from Cornell University. His research examines 17th-century French lute performance, the Latin American *bolero romántico,* and primary sources for Latin American big band music. His publications have appeared in the *Journal of the Lute Society of America, American Music, Notes, Yearbook for Traditional Music,* and *Symposium.* As a performer, he has published the recording *Flute and Guitar Music* for Centaur Records, and Trillenium Publications and Clear Note Publications have published his musical editions for guitar. His article on the *bolero romántico* is included in the collection *From Tejano to Tango: Latin American Popular Music* (2002). He has taught at St. Lawrence University and Grinnell College, and he is currently associate professor of music at Lafayette College, where he teaches courses in music history and world music. He also directs the Marquis Consort, an ensemble dedicated to the performance of early music.

Contributors

Yukio Agerkop, Amsterdam, Netherlands (Venezuela)

Juan C. Agudelo, Austin, Texas

Ramón Versage Agudelo, Cali, Colombia

Paul Austerlitz, Gettysburg College, Gettysburg, Pennsylvania

Mark Brill, University of Texas, San Antonio, Texas

Thomas George Caracas Garcia, Miami University, Oxford, Ohio

Liliana Casanella, Havana, Cuba

Katia Chornik, University of Manchester, United Kingdom

Larry Crook, University of Florida, Gainsville, Florida

Alexander Sebastian Dent, George Washington University, Washington, D.C.

Edgardo Díaz Díaz, City University of New York

Raymond Epstein, Hillsborough, New Jersey

Michael Farley, St. Lawrence University, Canton, New York

Adriana Fernandes, Goiania, Brazil

Hector Fernández L'Hoeste, Georgia State University, Atlanta, Georgia

Tatiana Flórez-Pérez, Berlin, Germany

Beto González, Los Angeles, California

Liliana González, Havana, Cuba

Melissa González, Columbia University, New York

Neris González, Havana, Cuba

Lars Helgert, Shenandoah University, Winchester, Virginia

Clarence Henry, Columbia University, New York

Grizel Hernández, Havana, Cuba

J. Jesús Jáuregui Jimenez, Mexico City, Mexico

Caitlin Lowery, Lafayette College, Easton, Pennsylvania

Noriko Manabe, Princeton University, Princeton, New Jersey

Michael D. Marcuzzi, York University, Toronto, Ontario, Canada

Tracy McFarlan, Lafayette College, Easton, Pennsylvania

David Moskowitz, University of South Dakota, Vermillion, South Dakota

Alvaro Neder, Rio de Janeiro, Brazil

Michael O'Brien, Buenos Aires, Argentina

Carlos Odria, Tallahassee, Florida

Francisco Orozco, University of Washington, Seattle, Washington

Bernardo Padrón, Toronto, Canada

Raquel Paraíso, Madison, Wisconsin

Rolando Antonio Pérez Fernández, Mexico City, Mexico

Vincenzo Perna, Torino, Italy

Mark E. Perry, North Georgia College & State University, Dahlonega, Georgia

Laura Stanfield Prichard, Carlisle, Massachusetts

José Raffaelli, Rio de Janiero, Brazil

Thomas Rohde, Attleboro, Massachusetts

Fernando Rios, Poughkeepsie, New York

Jonathan Ritter, George Washington University, Washington, D.C.

Thomas Rohde, Attleboro, Massachusetts

Helena Simonett, Vanderbilt University, Nashville, Tennessee

Hope Smith, California State University, Chico

Erin Stapleton-Corcoran, University of Chicago, Chicago, Illinois

Rebecca Stuhr, University of Pennsylvania, Philadelphia, Pennsylvania

Janet L. Sturman, University of Arizona, Tucson, Arizona

Angelina Tallaj, Brooklyn, New York

George Torres, Lafayette College, Easton, Pennsylvania

Ramón Versage Agudelo, Cali, Colombia

Nolan Warden, Chicago, Illinois

Chris Washburne, Columbia University, New York

Jesse Wheeler, Brasilia, Brazil

Talia Wooldridge, York University, Toronto, Ontario, Canada

Index

Note: Page numbers in **bold** indicate main entries and sidebars in the Encyclopedia.